THE BRICS-LAWYERS' GUIDE TO BRICS TEXTS AND MATERIALS

I0127163

ROSTAM J. NEUWIRTH

University of Macau

ALEXANDR SVETLICINII

University of Macau

BRICS
LAWYERS

⚖ **B R I C S**
L A W Y E R S

University of Macau
Faculty of Law E32
Avenida da Universidade
Macau (CHINA)

© BRICS-LAWYERS 2019

First published June 2019

Cataloging-in-Publication

Names: Neuwirth, Rostam J., author | Svetlicinii, Alexandr, author.
Title: The BRICS-Lawyers' guide to BRICS texts and materials.
Description: First edition | Macau: BRICS-Lawyers, 2019 |
602 pages | Includes bibliographical references and index.
Subjects: LCSH: 1. Comparative law 2. BRIC countries – Foreign
economic relations 3. Law – BRIC countries 4. International economic
relations 5. Foreign trade regulation.
Classification: LCC: K3823

ISBN 978-99965-1-117-2 (paperback)

THE BRICS-LAWYERS' GUIDE TO
BRICS TEXTS AND MATERIALS

In the arena of global law and policymaking, the emerging economies – Brazil, Russia, India, China and South Africa have created a dialogue and cooperation platform that is known as "BRICS". Initially conceived to drive global change through economic growth, the global financial crisis and an occasional reversal of fortunes of the BRICS countries domestically have raised questions about their ability to have an impact on the governance of global affairs. Following ten successful BRICS Summits in the years from 2009 until 2018, it is now time to examine the legal foundations for their future cooperation in greater detail. Over the last decade, BRICS have produced a considerable amount of official texts and materials that – for the purpose of their future analysis and application – requires more systematic organisation. This book first presents a chronology of the evolution of BRICS cooperation. It then proceeds with a discussion about the sources of (international) law from a comparative perspective so as to facilitate attempts to classify the various BRICS documents in terms of "sources of BRICS law". The appendix includes the most important texts and materials produced by the BRICS cooperation platform, such as the BRICS Summit Declarations by Heads of States, the BRICS Ministerial Declarations, the Declarations adopted by the BRICS Legal Forums and the binding agreements establishing the Contingent Reserve Arrangement, the New Development Bank (NDB) and the BRICS Agreement on Culture. These documents are organised in chronological and thematic orders, which makes them easy to use by government officials, practicing lawyers and arbitrators, journalists, scholars and students of international relations, business, economics and law.

Rostam J. Neuwirth is Professor of Law and Coordinator of the Master's Programme in International Business Law (IBL) at the Faculty of Law of the University of Macau (China). He holds law degrees obtained from the European University Institute in Florence (Ph.D.), McGill University in Montreal (LL.M.) and the Karl-Franzens University of Graz (Mag. iur.). Before joining the University of Macau, he taught at the Hidayatullah National Law University (HNLU) in Raipur and the National University of Juridical Sciences (NUJS) in Kolkata (India), and worked in the *Völkerrechtsbüro* (International Law Bureau) of the Austrian Federal Ministry for Foreign Affairs.

Alexandr Svetlicinii is Assistant Professor of Law at the University of Macau (China). Dr Svetlicinii received his law degree at the Free International University of Moldova, his LL.M in International Business Law at the Central European University in Budapest, and Master's of Research in Law and his Ph.D. in Law at the European University Institute in Florence. His primary fields of expertise are competition law, international trade and investment law, and alternative dispute resolution. Dr Svetlicinii has served as a nongovernmental advisor to the International Competition Network and as a legal expert on a number of research projects conducted by the EU Commission.

CONTENTS

ABBREVIATIONS

ABGF	Brazilian Guarantees and Fund Managements Agency
ACFC	Agreement between the Governments of the BRICS States on Cooperation in the Field of Culture
ACIRC	African Capacity for Immediate Responses to Crises
ACWG	Agricultural Cooperation Working Group
AEOI	Automatic Exchange of Tax Information
AfCFTA	African Continental Free Trade Area
AFTA	ASEAN Free Trade Area
AI	Artificial Intelligence
AMIS	Agricultural Marketing Information System
AMISOM	African Union Mission in Somalia
AML/CFT	Anti-Money Laundering and Countering Financing of Terrorism
AMR	Anti-Microbial Resistance
ANSF	Afghan National Security Forces
AO	Appellations of Origin
ARC	Africa Regional Centre
ARG	Argentina
ARP	Agricultural Research Platform
ART	Antiretroviral Therapy
ASEAN	Association of Southeast Asian Nations
ASF	African Standby Force
AU	African Union
BAIES	Basic Agriculture Information Exchange System
BARC	BRICS Agriculture Research Centre
BBC	BRICS Business Council
BBF	BRICS Bond Fund
BEPS	Base Erosion and Profit Shifting
BEST	BRICS Environmentally Sound Technology
BEWG	BRICS Employment Working Group
BIPM	International Bureau of Weights and Measures
BNDES	Brazilian Development Bank (Banco Nacional de Desenvolvimento Econômico e Social)
BRA	Brazil
BRICS	Brazil, Russia, India, China, South Africa
BRICS NU	BRICS Network University
BRICS RINP	BRICS Research and Innovation Networking Platform
BRICS-GRAIN	BRICS Global Research Advanced Infrastructure Network

BRICSUL	BRICS University League
BTTC	BRICS Think-Tank Council
CAC	Codex Alimentarius Commission
CACs	Collective Action Clauses
CADE	Administrative Council for Economic Defence (*Conselho Administrativo de Defesa Econômica* (BRA))
CAPES	Brazilian Federal Agency for Support and Evaluation of Higher Education
CAR	Central African Republic
CBD COP11	11th Conference of the Parties to the United Nations Conference on Biological Diversity
CBDR	Common But Differentiated Responsibilities
CBDR&RC	Common But Differentiated Responsibilities and Respective Capabilities
CCI	Competition Commission of India
CCIT	Comprehensive Convention on International Terrorism
CCM	Common Market Council
CCSA	Competition Commission of South Africa
CDB	China Development Bank Corporation
CEWG	Consultative Expert Working Group
CFS	Committee on World Food Security
CGETI	Contact Group on Economic and Trade Issues
CGIAR	Consultative Group on International Agricultural Research
CHE	Switzerland
CHN	China
CIS	Commonwealth of Independent States
CISG	Convention on Contracts for the International Sales of Goods
CITES	Convention on International Trade in Endangered Species of Wild Fauna and Flora
CJEU	Court of Justice of the EU
CMG	Common Market Group
COP	Conference
COP18/CMP8	18th yearly session of the Conference of the Parties (COP) to the 1992 United Nations Framework Convention on Climate Change (UNFCCC) / 8th session of the Meeting of the Parties (CMP) to the 1997 Kyoto Protocol
CPLP	Community of Portuguese-Speaking Countries (*Comunidade dos Países de Língua Portuguesa*)
CRA	Contingent Reserve Arrangement
CSF	Committee on World Food Security
CSIRT	Computer Security Incident Response Team
CSOs	Civil Society Organizations
CTWG	Counter-Terrorism Working Group

DBSA	Development Bank of Southern Africa
DDA	Doha Development Agenda
DDR	Disarmament, Demobilization and Reintegration
DPAs	Development Partnership Administrations
DPRK	Democratic People's Republic of Korea
DRC	Democratic Republic of the Congo
DRI	Director of International Relations
DSB	Dispute Settlement Body
DSSs	Decision Support Systems
DST	Department of Science and Technology
EAEU [or EEU]	Eurasian Economic Union
ECAs	Export Credit Agencies
ECGC	Export Credit Guarantee Corporation of India
ECIC SA	Export Credit Insurance Corporation of South Africa
ECOSOC	United Nations Economic and Social Council
ECOWAS	Economic Community of West African States
EFA	Education for All
EIAs	Economic Integration Agreements
EMDCs	Emerging Market and Developing Countries
EPIC	Equal Pay International Coalition
EU	European Union
EurAsEC	Eurasian Economic Community
EVD	Ebola Virus Disease
EWG	Employment Working Group
EWS	Early Warning Systems
EXIAR	Export Insurance Agency of Russia
EXIM	Export-Import Banks
FAO	Food and Agriculture Organization
FAS	Federal Antimonopoly Service
FATF	Financial Actions Task Force
FCTC	Framework Convention on Tobacco Control
FDLR	Democratic Forces for the Liberation of Rwanda
FIDC	Forum for Indian Development Cooperation
FRA	France
FSRBs	FATF-Style Regional Bodies
FTAs	Free Trade Agreements
FTSE	Financial Times Stock Exchange
G20	Group of Twenty
G8	Group of Eight

GATS	General Agreement on Trade in Services
GATT	General Agreement on Tariffs and Trade
GAVI	Vaccine Alliance
GCC	Gulf Cooperation Council
GCF	Green Climate Fund
GDP	Gross Domestic Product
GEOLAW	Global Electronically Operated Law Administration Web
GESDPE	Sustainable Development and Poverty Eradication
GI	Geographical Indications
GLONASS	Global Navigation Satellite System
GOARIN	Global Outbreak Alert and Response Network
GR	Genetic Resources
GRPs	Good Regulatory Practices
GSPA-PHI	Global Strategy and Plan of Action on Public Health, Innovation and Intellectual Property
HIPO	Heads of Intellectual Property Office
HIV/AIDS	Human immunodeficiency virus infection and acquired immune deficiency syndrome
HLPF	High Level Political Forum on Sustainable Development
IAEA	International Atomic Energy Agency
IAF	International Accreditation Forum
IBA	International Bar Association
IBL	International Business Law
ICARRD	International Conference on Agrarian Reform and Rural Development
ICJ	International Court of Justice
ICPD	International Conference on Population and Development
ICTs	Information and Communication Technologies
IDA	International Development Association
IEC	International Electrotechnical Commission
IFAD	International Fund for Agricultural Development
IFIs	International and Financial Institutions
IFSD	Institutional Framework for Sustainable Development
IGAD	Intergovernmental Authority on Development
IGB	International Governing Board
IHR	International Health Regulations
IIT	Indian Institute of Technology
ILAC	International Laboratory Accreditation Cooperation
ILC	International Law Commission
ILO	International Labour Organization
IMF	International Monetary Fund

IND	India
IOs	International Organizations
IP	Intellectual Property
IPPC	International Plant Protection Convention
IPR	Intellectual Property Right
IPRCM	Implementation Framework for Intellectual Property Rights Cooperation Mechanism
IPU	Inter-Parliamentary Union
IR	International Relations
ISCED	International Standard Classification of Education
ISIL	Islamic State of Iraq and the Levant
ISIS	Islamic State of Iraq and Syria
ISO	International Organization for Standardization
ISSA	International Social Security Association
ITC	International Trade Centre
ITeS	Information Technology Enabled Services
ITGs	International Thematic Groups
ITO	International Trade Organization
ITU	International Telecommunication Union
IWC	International Whaling Commission
IYFF	International Year of Family Farming
JCPOA	Joint Comprehensive Plan of Action
JPOI	Johannesburg plan of Implementation
L/C	Letter of Credit
LDCs	Least Developed Countries
LEMM	Meeting for BRICS Ministers for Labour & Employment
LICs	Low Income Countries
MC10	10th WTO Ministerial Conference
MC9	9th WTO Ministerial Conference
MCM	Ministerial Conference Meeting
MCTI	Ministry of Science, Technology and Innovation
MDBs	Multilateral Development Banks
MDGs	Millennium Development Goals
MDR-TB	Multi-drug-resistant tuberculosis
MEC	Ministry of Education
MENA	Middle East and North Africa
MERCOSUR	Southern Common Market
MES	Ministry of Education and Science
MEX	Mexico
MINUSCA	UN Multidimensional Integrated Stabilization Mission in the CAR

MINUSMA	United Nations Multidimensional Integrated Stabilization Mission in Mali
MISCA	African-led International Support Mission to the CAR
MOFCOM	Ministry of Commerce of the People's Republic of China
MONUSCO	United Nations Organization Stabilization Mission in the Democratic Republic of the Congo
MOOCs	Massive Open Online Courses
MOST	Ministry of Science and Technology
MoU	Memorandum of Understanding
MSME	Micro Small and Medium Enterprises
MTC	MERCOSUR Trade Commission
MTS	Multilateral Trading System
NAMA	Non-Agricultural Market Access
NCC	National Coordination Committee
NCDs	Non-Communicable Diseases
NDB	New Development Bank
NDCs	Nationally Determined Contributions
NDRC	National Development and Reform Commission
NEPAD	New Partnership for Africa's Development
NGO	Non-Governmental Organization
NLD	The Netherlands
NPT	Treaty on the Non-Proliferation of Nuclear Weapons
NTD	Neglected Tropical Diseases
NTMs	Non-Tariff Measures
OAB	Brazil Bar Association (Ordem dos Advogados do Brasil)
ODA	Official Development Assistance
OIE	World Organisation for Animal Health
OIML	International Organization of Legal Metrology
OPCW	Organisation for the Prohibition of Chemical Weapons
OWG-SDG	Open Working Group on Sustainable Development Goals
PA	Paris Agreement
PartNIR	Partnership on New Industrial Revolution
PICI	Presidential Infrastructure Championing Initiative
PIDA	Programme for Infrastructure Development in Africa
PLO	Palestinian Liberation Organization
PPP	Public Private Partnerships
PRC	People's Republic of China
R&D	Research and Development
RDBs	Regional Development Banks

RI	Research Infrastructure
Rio+20	United Nations Conference on Sustainable Development
RTAs	Regional Trade Agreements
RUS	Russian Federation
S&T	Science and Technology
SA	South Africa
SADC	Southern African Development Community
SAIC	State Administration for Industry and Commerce
SCO	Shanghai Cooperation Organization
SCP	Sustainable Consumption and Production
SDGs	Sustainable Development Goals
SDR	Special Drawing Rights
SEMI	CRA System of Exchange in Macroeconomic Information
SINOSURE	China Export & Credit Insurance Corporation
SME	Small and Medium Enterprises
SMTA	Standard Material Transfer Agreement
SOCs	State Owned Companies
SOM	Senior Officials Meeting
SPS	Sanitary and Phytosanitary
SRM	Standard Review Mechanism
SSFFC	Substandard, Spurious, Falsely Labelled, Falsified and Counterfeit
SSL	Solid-State Lightning
STI	Science, Technology and Innovation
STIEP	Science Technology Innovation and Entrepreneurship Partnership
TBT	Technical Barriers to Trade
TCEs	Traditional Cultural Expressions
TEEB	The Economy of Ecosystems and Biodiversity
TFA	Trade Facilitation Agreement
TFEU	Treaty on the Functioning of the European Union
TIWG	Trade and Investment Working Group
TK	Traditional Knowledge
ToR	Terms of Reference
TRIMS	Agreement on Trade-Related Investment Measures
TRIPS	Agreement on Trade-Related Aspects of Intellectual Property Rights
TVET	Technical and Vocational Education and Training
UFPE	Federal University of Pernambuco
UHC	Universal Health Coverage
UNAIDS	Joint United Nations Programme on HIV and AIDS
UNASUR	Union of South American Nations
UNCAC	United Nations Convention against Corruption

UNCCD   United Nations Convention to Combat Desertification
UNCITRAL   United Nations Commission on International Trade Law
UNCOPUOS   UN Committee on the Peaceful Uses of Outer Space
UNCRD   United Nations Centre for Regional Development
UNCTAD   United Nations Conference on Trade and Development
UNDP   United Nations Development Programme
UNEA   United Nations Environment Assembly
UNESCO   United Nations Educational, Scientific and Cultural Organization
UNFCCC   United Nations Framework Convention on Climate Change
UNGA   United Nations General Assembly
UNGASS   UN General Assembly Special Session
UNIDO   United Nations Industrial Development Organization
UNISPACE+50   50th Anniversary of the first United Nations Conference on the
                      Exploration and Peaceful Uses of Outer Space
UNMEER   UN Mission For Ebola Emergency Response
UNMIS   United Nations Mission in South Sudan
UNRWA   United Nations Relief and Works Agency
UNSC   United Nations Security Council
USA   United States of America (the)
USSR   Union of Soviet Socialist Republics

VAT   Value Added Tax
VGGT   Voluntary Guidelines on the Responsible Governance of Tenure of
                      Land, Fisheries and Forests in the Context of National Food Security
VIP   Virtual Institute of Photonics

WBG   World Bank Group
WBL   Workplace-Based Learning
WFC   World Forestry Congress
WFP   World Food Programme
WG Biomed   Working Group on Biotechnology and Biomedicine including Human
                      Health and Neuroscience
WHA   World Health Assembly
WHO   World Health Organization
WIPO   World Intellectual Property Organization
WMD   Weapon of Mass Destruction
WTO   World Trade Organization

YSF   Young Scientist Forum

ZAF   South Africa

PREFACE

When we began working on the *BRICS-Lawyers' Guide to Global Cooperation* (Cambridge University Press, 2017) in 2016, the principal question in scholarly and political debate at that time was whether the cooperation of the BRICS countries would continue, or had already failed. Internationally, numerous commentators on BRICS cooperation questioned whether the differences between the countries in the sense of diversity, from political, economic, historical, cultural and legal perspectives, posed an insurmountable obstacle that was preventing a deeper and more continuous form of cooperation, and, consequently, preventing them from having a serious impact on the future governance of global affairs. When the *BRICS-Lawyers' Guide to Global Cooperation* was published in autumn 2017, the sixteen chapters written by experts in their representative legal fields showed that there was already a significant number of examples that concretised the output of their cooperation. As "BRICS-Lawyers" ourselves, and based on these findings, we thus considered the role that law played in the future of BRICS cooperation to be functioning as "the mortar holding the bricks of different layers of life, particularly politics and economics, together, especially in turbulent times characterized by rapid and drastic change".[1]

In fact, the book covered very different fields of legal cooperation, ranging from international trade, competition and investment law, to arbitration, contract law, intellectual property rights, outer space activities, cooperation in culture and legal education. It thus provided strong evidence that the differences between the BRICS countries, which were initially considered the main obstacle to their success, had now proved to be the maxim, and perhaps the benchmark for future collaboration. We believe we have shown that what really matters is not their own differences, but instead the difference that BRICS can make in the process of establishing the foundations for the future of global governance.

---

[1] See Rostam J. Neuwirth, Alexandr Svetlicinii, and Denis De Castro Halis (eds.), *The BRICS-Lawyers' Guide to Global Cooperation* (Cambridge: Cambridge University Press, 2017) at 376.

Around the same time, the 2017 Xiamen Declaration was adopted, and re-newed hope in BRICS cooperation, providing important and perhaps essen-tial input into the debate about the governance of global affairs in the future, and notably the contours of a future global legal order.[2] The 2018 Johannes-burg Declaration confirmed the former trend. In fact, a number of interna-tional agreements adopted by the BRICS countries had entered into force, and the New Development Bank (NDB) or so-called "BRICS Bank", as the first permanent institution of the BRICS, has now notably become operational.

In other words, the focus appears now to have shifted from the question of *whether* BRICS can realise their many objectives, such as "a more just, equi-table, fair, democratic and representative international political and eco-nomic order",[3] to *how* they can best achieve the objectives set in a sustainable way. This principal question can be taken as the overarching goal of the present book, to provide the starting point for a deepening and widening of legal cooperation while still maintaining the current levels of openness and flexibility. The widening of the scope of cooperation also faces the serious danger of centrifugal forces to win the upper hand, which may result in a lack of coherence, unnecessary duplication or even the emergence of conflicts between the different policy objectives pursued. A systematic consolidation and compilation of the core documents will help to avoid the dangers related to a widening of fields of cooperation. This, in particular, is where the role of law assumes great significance. To cut a long and complex story short, the time has come to search for novel forms of legal sources and instruments to adapt to the rapidly changing context, not only in the BRICS countries but in the global community as a whole.

The search for, and research into, novel forms of legal sources and instru-ments is a massive task in BRICS and in the global context. This is because, so far, the official documents about the scope of BRICS cooperation are scat-tered across a multitude of national institutions and lack systematic compi-lation and organisation. A growing number of BRICS documents is also added on a regular basis, produced by a number of stakeholders. It is noteworthy that, even though the idea of a virtual e-BRICS Secretariat has been aired sev-eral times, it has not been realised so far. The creation of a Joint BRICS Web-site was also suggested, but only partly realised. We therefore undertake this

---

[2] See also Alexandr Svetlicinii, "Five Economic Highlights of the 2017 BRICS Summit Xiamen Declaration" (7 November 2017); available at: https://davastrat.org/2017/11/07/five-economic-highlights-of-the-2017-brics-summit-xiamen-declarations/.

[3] Xiamen Declaration 2017; Appendix II.2 A.

effort to compile the most important BRICS texts and materials, in order to facilitate research undertaken by policymakers, practitioners and scholars interested in BRICS affairs from the perspectives of different scientific disciplines (e.g. international relations, economics, business and law). We also deem it necessary in order to highlight the need for the systematic organisation of BRICS documents, with a view to fostering the establishment of a virtual e-BRICS Secretariat, including a well-organised BRICS website featuring the core documents.

In view of the many difficult tasks, we would like to note that we have received a great deal of assistance, support and inspiration from many other "BRICS-Lawyers" and wish to express our sincere appreciation to all the individuals and institutions who contributed to the present book project in various ways. First of all, we acknowledge the continuous support for our collaborative research efforts that was granted by the University of Macau and the Faculty of Law. We also benefited from the support accorded by the Research Services and Knowledge Transfer Office and the Centre for Teaching and Learning Enhancement.

This project originated in our friendship and collegiality, but was strengthened by discussions and feedback during several academic conferences where we had an opportunity to present our BRICS-related research. Among these, the following deserve special mention:

A seminar entitled "BRICS-Lawyers" at the University of the Western Cape (UWC) in Cape Town, South Africa (19 April 2019), with special thanks to Riekie Wandrag and Patricia Lenaghan as well as Lisa Ingrid Thompson, Pamela Tsolekile-De Wet and Gregory Ruiters; The Juris Diversitas 6th General Conference "Law, Roots and Space" in Potchefstroom, South Africa (April 15-17, 2019) with special thanks to Christa Rautenbach; the Comparative Law Symposium "Legal Pluralism in the Twenty-First Century", hosted by the University of Canterbury in Christchurch, New Zealand (February 7, 2019) with special thanks to W. John Hopkins and Jennifer Corrin; the Law and Society Association (LSA), which hosted its Annual Meeting on Law and Society "Law at Crossroads: Le droit à la croisée des Chemins" in Toronto, Canada (June 6-10, 2018) with special thanks to Fernanda Duarte, Rafael Mario Iorio Filho, Asya Ostroukh, and Kay-Wah Chan; the Institute for Global Law and Policy (IGLP), which hosted the "Law in Global Political Economy: Heterodoxy Now" conference at Harvard Law School in Boston, United States (June 2-3, 2018) with special thanks to Mihaela Papa and Fabio de Sá e Silva; the Institute of Rule of Law for Innovation and Development of the Shenzhen University, School of Law, which hosted an open lecture on competition law cooperation of the BRICS countries in Shenzhen, China (April 20, 2018) with special thanks to Ye Weiping; the O.P. Jindal Global University, which hosted the 15th International Conference on Alternative Perspectives and Global Concerns with the Special Theme *Spirituality, Mysticism and Politics in the Age of Globality*" in Sonipat, India (January 23–24, 2018) with special thanks to Sanjeev P. Sahni, Pankaj Gupta, Mahmoud Masaeli, and Rico Sneller; the Association of Lawyers of Russia, which hosted the IV BRICS Legal Forum in Moscow, Russia (November 30, 2017); Fudan University, School of International Relations and Public Affairs, which hosted the Second International Symposium on Development and Governance in BRICS *International Development Aid in the BRICS*" (September 23, 2017) with special thanks to Yijia Jing and Jose A. Puppim de Oliveira; EM Lyon Business School, which hosted International Workshop *BRICS & Anticompetitive Practices: The Key Issues*" in Lyon, France (July 7, 2017) with special thanks to Anne Tercinet, Cyril Nourissat, Georges De Nemeskeri-Kiss, and Avinash Dadhich; the Law and Society Association, which hosted its Annual Meeting on Law and Society *Walls, Borders, and Bridges: Law and Society in an Inter-Connected World*" in Mexico City, Mexico (June 19-23, 2017); Universidad del Azuay, which hosted *II Congreso de Comercio Exterior y Negociación Internacional* in Cuenca, Ecuador (June 15, 2017) with special thanks to Cecilia Ugalde Sánchez and Daniel Gudiño; Universidad Andina Simón Bolívar, which hosted panel *An Overview of BRICS from Global Governance, Cooperation in Trade and Competition & Governance of Investments*" in Quito, Ecuador (June 13, 2017) with special thanks to Michel Levi Coral, Wolf Grabendorff, and Esteban Nicholls; the Southwest University of Science and Technology, Faculty of Law, which hosted Seminar on the BRICS Legal Global Cooperation in Mianyang, China (May 12, 2017) with special thanks to Zhai Rui; and the Chinese University of Hong Kong, which hosted 7th Annual International Research Exchange & Faculty Development Conference *Social Innovation and Social Media*" in Hong Kong SAR, China (April 9, 2017).

At various stages of this project we also received research and technical assistance from our postgraduate students Guo Jingrong, Li Chen, Li Yimo, Long Linyun, Ilidia Mazuze, Niu Jiaxin, Riccardo Vecellio Segate, Ina Virtosu, Yan Jieqiong, Sun Yifan, and Zhang Juanjuan. We also acknowledge the inspiration drawn from all the participants in the postgraduate course "Advanced Issues of International Trade Law: *Business Law in the BRICS*

Countries" offered since 2017 by the International Business Law (IBL) programme in English language of the Faculty of Law of the University of Macau.

We are also grateful to the following individuals who have supported our BRICS-related research by writing reviews and offering other types of publicity: Horia Ciurtin, Tim W. Dornis, Mateja Durovic, Iris Eisenberger, Andre Janssen, Danielle Menz, Alexander Molotnikov, Bogdan Mochula, Maria Novoselova, Rafael Mario Iorio Filho, Fabio Morosini, Lilian Richieri Hanania, Fabio de Sá e Silva, Lucia Scaffardi, Franziska Sucker, Gonzalo Villalta Puig, Paris West, Lutz-Christian Wolff, Chen Zhijie, and Zhang Han.

Many thanks are given to our University of Macau Wu Yee Sun Library colleagues, Lillian Tam and Priscilla Pun, for guiding us through the publishing process.

Many other individuals deserve a note of appreciation for their friendship and collaboration in this and other projects that were instrumental in promoting the collaborative and interdisciplinary research that preceded the present work. They are Denis De Castro Halis, Valentin Jeutner, Umakrishnan Kollamparabil, Michel Levi Coral, Muruga Perumal Ramaswamy, Salvatore Mancuso, Vera Lúcia Raposo, Christopher Allen Fulton, Zhao Yun, Akira Saito, and Mahendra P. Singh.

For their continuous support we also express special thanks to our family members, Su and Pui Mang, as well as Elam J. and Lea J.

Rostam J. Neuwirth and Alexandr Svetlicinii

Macao S.A.R. (China), May 2019

INTRODUCTION

Constant change, and the pace of change apparently accelerating further, is a common characteristic of the present period of globalisation, and in the growing awareness of a global information society. The accelerating pace of change can be felt in all areas of life, but is mostly hailed and driven by efforts in the context of technology and innovation. In law, by contrast, the accelerated pace of change runs parallel with more data and increasing complexity, which are said to threaten and possibly "undermine law and especially the rule of law as an instrument providing legal certainty and predictability".[1] In the context of a proliferation of legal instruments and institutions that potentially and actually undermine the rule of law, however, it is paradoxically often forgotten that law can itself be the remedy for the very malaise it causes.

The crucial and constructive role that law can play shall be exemplified by reference to the BRICS cooperation, which now spans a little over a decade, from 2009 until 2019. Currently, BRICS cooperation is organised more like a "dialogue and cooperation platform" rather than a supra- or transnational organisation in a strictly legal sense, yet, BRICS have made considerable progress and widened as well as deepened their cooperation in a great many fields. This expansion is generally laudable, as it increases the opportunity for a more holistic approach to global law and policy making. At the same time, it also increases the danger of a lack of coherence, or overlapping and even conflicting mandates capable of undermining the overall effectiveness of the system, as was found to have affected the United Nations system.[2] Today, however, problems related to lack of coherence, possible conflicts between different policies and increasing legal uncertainty and legal

---

[1] Rostam J. Neuwirth, *Law in Times of Oxymora: A Synaesthesia of Language, Logic and Law* (London: Routledge, 2018) at xiii.

[2] United Nations High Level Panel on Coherence, *Delivering as One: Report of the High-level Panel on United Nations System-wide Coherence in the Areas of Development, Humanitarian Assistance and the Environment*, G.A. A/61/583 (9 November 2006).

predictability can be found to exist at all levels of governance and law making: the local, national, regional and global level.

Seen from a different angle, the law can, and is called upon to, also play the role of a guarantor of stability and continuity, as well as greater consistency. Most of all, it can help to handle "big data", the deluge of documents, texts and materials. For instance, *pro futuro* a BRICS Charter or BRICS Declaration of Fundamental Principles, supported by a virtual BRICS Secretariat featuring a comprehensive and interactive internet-based legal database, can help to avoid the unnecessary duplication of, or conflicts between, the principal (policy) goals enshrined in the many documents and materials. These are among the principal aims pursued by this book: compiling the principal documents produced by the BRICS countries and presenting them in a comprehensive, and yet easily accessible way, so as to facilitate research related to BRICS and reinforce their cooperation in the future.

To achieve these goals, and to contribute to a fruitful and constructive debate about the future of BRICS cooperation in particular and global governance in general, the present book is structured into three chapters, plus a comprehensive appendix containing the most important BRICS texts and materials produced so far. **Chapter 1** traces the present state of BRICS affairs to the origins in order to inform our readers about the scope, depth and time frame of the cooperation between the BRICS countries. It not only follows the chronological order of the major events in the history of BRICS cooperation, but also presents and discusses the cornerstones of the different meetings that have helped to set off the dynamic process of BRICS cooperation.

As the existing BRICS texts and materials are scattered around many webpages, set up and maintained by a multitude of national institutions, and therefore generally lack systematic compilation and organisation, there is also considerable doubt about each document's precise legal status or relevance. The precise legal classification of the cooperation between the BRICS countries as an international or regional organisation is also not (yet) possible. **Chapter 2** therefore offers a broad discussion of the question of "BRICS sources of law" from a comparative perspective. The comparison includes sources of international law, regional law, and law in general, whereby the emphasis is placed on the urgent necessity of finding and agreeing about perhaps novel sources of law, in times of fast technological and scientific progress with unprecedented consequences for societies around the world.

Following the comparative analysis of various sources of law, **Chapter 3** attempts to cast light on the future by synthesising the findings of the previous chapters. The dynamics begun via BRICS cooperation, with their first summit held in 2009, can now perhaps be used to invite a broader discussion of the question of whether their cooperation should at any time in the near future lead to a greater consolidation of existing, and the emergence of a category of "BRICS Law", as has emerged from other regional cooperation projects, such as the European Union (EU) or the Association of Southeast Asian Nations (ASEAN). Alternatively, whether BRICS should continue in their current format as a "dialogue and cooperation platform" may be considered. To help answer these fundamental questions, **Chapter 3** concludes with a short section providing guidance for the user of the book.

These questions are deemed useful not only for the BRICS countries themselves, but for all members of the global community. To invite everyone to participate in the debate, and help to find novel legal instruments capable of providing solutions to the most serious problems of the present, the final section of the book is a comprehensive **Appendix**, which lists the most significant BRICS texts and materials adopted so far.

CHAPTER 1

BRICS Cooperation: A Brief 'History of the Future'

A Chronology of Events

As for the future of the BRICS countries, the best way of predicting it is to create it.[1]

The term "BRIC" was coined by Goldman Sachs Chief Economist Jim O'Neill in 2001, in the context of predicting the economic growth of these large emerging economies,[2] but it took several years for the BRIC countries (Brazil, Russia, India and China) to appear in this format in the international arena. The leaders of China, India, and Russia met in 2006 on the margins of the G8 Outreach Summit in St Petersburg.[3] The same year saw the gathering of the BRIC foreign ministers on the sidelines of the UN General Assembly's session in New York City.[4] The first meeting of the BRIC leaders in this format was organised at the G8 Summit in 2008, which was hosted by Japan on the island of Hokkaido. The meeting was attended by Russian President Dmitry Medvedev, Chinese President Hu Jintao, Indian Prime Minister Manmohan Singh and Brazilian President Luis Inácio Lula da Silva. From 2009 the leaders of BRIC, and then (from 2011 onwards) BRICS (including South Africa), have met annually.

---

[1] Rostam J. Neuwirth, "The Enantiosis of BRICS: BRICS La[w]yers and the Difference that They Can Make", in Rostam J. Neuwirth, Alexandr Svetlicinii, and Denis De Castro Halis (eds.), *The BRICS-Lawyers' Guide to Global Cooperation* (Cambridge: Cambridge University Press, 2017) 8 at 23.

[2] See also Dominic Wilson and Roopa Purushothaman, *Dreaming with BRICs: The Path to 2050*, Goldman Sachs Global Economic Paper No. 99 (1 October 2003); available at: https://www.goldmansachs.com/insights/archive/archive-pdfs/brics-dream.pdf.

[3] See "China, Russia, India Hold 1st Trilateral Summit", *Xinhua News Agency* (18 July 2006); available at: http://www.china.org.cn/english/2006/Jul/175028.htm.

[4] See also Bas Hooijmaaijers and Stephan Keukeleire, "Voting Cohesion of the BRICS Countries in the UN General Assembly, 2006-2014: A BRICS Too Far?" (2016) 22 *Global Governance* 389.

A decade (2009-2019) of BRICS cooperation in the international arena has produced a multitude of views as to the nature and substance of this heterogeneous grouping. For example, in 2015 John Kirton identified at least ten diverging perceptions on the motivation and performance results of the BRICS summits as follows: (1) the BRICS group is of little relevance to its members and those beyond; (2) BRICS is experiencing a boom-to-bust decline; (3) BRICS features a "facade of unity"; (4) BRICS is a short-term, single-issue, successful response to the financial crisis that created it; (5) the BRICS group is becoming increasingly influential, but is still far from being a unified geopolitical bloc or alliance; (6) BRICS is Russia's counter-hegemonic coalition; (7) BRICS is a broader developing country coalition seeking to shift the balance of global political influence from the West toward the developing world as a whole; (8) BRICS is a stand-alone success in international cooperation; (9) BRICS is a successful competitor to the G8 and G20; (10) BRICS is a successful cooperator with the G20 and the G8.[5]

More useful and critical observations on the different motivations and expectations voiced in the context of BRICS cooperation and the changing perception of the BRICS were presented in the edited volume *BRICS – An Anti-Capitalist Critique* in 2015.[6] Here especially the importance of the multilevel involvement in BRICS cooperation needs to be highlighted, which was classified as follows:

> BRICS from above – heads of state, corporates and elite allies;
> BRICS from the middle – BRICS Academic Forum, intellectuals, trade unions, NGOs;
> BRICS from below – grassroots activists whose visions run local to global.[7]

This multitude of different perceptions is best contrasted with the evolving scope and depth of their cooperation, as visible in the central documents, namely the annual BRICS Summit Declarations.

---

[5] See John Kirton, "BRICS Evolving Institutional Identity: Explaining the BRICS Summit's Solid, Strengthening Success" (2015) 10(2) *International Organisations Research Journal* 9 at 10-12.

[6] Patrick Bond and Ana Garcia (eds.), *BRICS: An Anti-Capitalist Critique* (London: Pluto Press, 2015).

[7] Ana Garcia and Patrick Bond, "Introduction", in Patrick Bond and Ana Garcia (eds.), *BRICS: An Anti-Capitalist Critique* (London: Pluto Press, 2015) 1 at 6-7.

I.   BRICS HEADS OF STATE

I.1.   The Annual BRICS Summits

The annual BRICS Summits can be seen as the central high-level forum setting the agenda of the BRICS cooperation. The first BRIC Summit in 2009, which transformed BRIC "from a financial category to a political grouping"[8] was hosted by Russia in the city of Yekaterinburg. The ensuing 2009 BRIC Summit Declaration, adopted in the aftermath of the global financial crisis, contained numerous references to the long-awaited reform of the global financial system. The text is relatively short, and contains only 16 paragraphs. It restates the BRIC countries' support for the G20, the World Trade Organization (WTO), the Millennium Development Goals (MDGs), and the fight against terrorism, and pledges to advance BRIC cooperation in a wide variety of other domains. Principally, the declaration states that the "dialogue and cooperation of the BRIC countries is conducive not only to serving common interests of emerging market economies and developing countries, but also to building a harmonious world of lasting peace and common prosperity".[9]

In 2010, the annual summit of the BRIC leaders was held in Brasília. The resulting declaration of the BRIC leaders almost doubled in length, reaching a total of 32 paragraphs. The major theme of economics and finance dominated the agenda, such as the reform of the Bretton Woods institutions, an appeal to the G20 to accelerate this reform, and an expression of support for the WTO and the MDGs. The joint statement contained references to the sectoral dialogues that had started to appear among the BRIC nations, covering *inter alia* agriculture, security, development banks, courts, competition authorities,[10] business community, and think-tanks.[11] The BRIC countries

[8] See Oliver Stuenkel, "Emerging Powers and Status: The Case of the First BRICS Summit" (2014) 38 *Asian Perspective* 1.

[9] 2009 BRIC Summit Declaration, para 15, Appendix II.10 A.

[10] See also Alexandr Svetlicinii, "BRICS Countries and Their Cooperation in the Field of Competition Law and Policy: A New Voice in International Antitrust?" (2017) 64 *Revue Lamy de la concurrence* 20 and Alexandr Svetlicinii and Juanjuan Zhang, "The Competition Law Institutions in the BRICS Countries: Developing Better Institutional Models for the Protection of Market Competition" (2017) 2 *Chinese Political Science Review* 85.

[11] 2010 BRIC Summit Declaration, para 27, Appendix II.9 A.

equally endeavoured to produce a joint statistical publication[12] and to study the feasibility of developing a joint BRIC encyclopaedia.[13]

In 2011, at their annual summit hosted by China on the island of Hainan, the BRIC countries were for the first time joined by South Africa, which effectively transformed BRIC into the BRICS. The Sanya Declaration is 32 paragraphs long, describing BRICS as a "forum", a "major platform for dialogue and cooperation", a "partnership for common development", and its members were termed "emerging countries".[14] As the year was marked by the Libyan civil war, the Sanya Declaration contains numerous expressions of support for the United Nations and the African Union in contributing to the peace dialogue, and a resolute condemnation of terrorist activities.[15] The support for the G20-led reform of international financial institutions, the WTO's Doha Round negotiations, and the United Nations' MDG agenda were among the "traditional" points of the BRICS consensus. The agenda for BRICS cooperation became more structured and detailed, this time consolidated into the Sanya Action Plan, which was attached to the Sanya Declaration. The said action plan introduced, among other things, the following new areas of BRICS cooperation: cities and local administrations, health care, joint research on economic and trade issues, a bibliography of the BRICS countries, sports, and culture (including a proposal to establish a BRICS-UNESCO Group).[16]

Hosted by India in 2012, the BRICS New Delhi Summit was held under the general theme "BRICS Partnership for Global Stability, Security and Prosperity", and produced a 50-paragraph long declaration. This document reiterated BRICS' support for the WTO, which after Russia's accession in 2012 eventually included all BRICS countries. The membership of BRICS in the WTO not only provided a great opportunity to better coordinate their trade policies, but also considerably added to the value of the WTO as a universal international organisation.[17] Marked by the events in the Middle East at the

---

[12] The first Joint Statistical Publication by BRIC countries appeared in 2010 and was published by the Brazilian Institute of Geography and Statistics; available at: http://www.gks.ru/free_doc/new_site/m-sotrudn/eng_site/brics_2010.pdf.

[13] 2010 BRIC Summit Declaration, para 28, Appendix II.9 A.

[14] 2011 BRICS Summit Declaration, paras 2, 5, and 6, Appendix II.8 A.

[15] Notably, in 2011 all BRICS countries were holding sets at the UN Security Council. See Oliver Stuenkel, "The BRICS and the Future of R2P: Was Syria or Libya the Exception?" (2014) 6 *Global Responsibility to Protect* 3.

[16] 2011 Sanya Action Plan, paras II and III, Appendix II.8 B.

[17] See also Lisa Toohey, "Barriers to Universal Membership of the World Trade Organization" (2012) 19 *Australian Journal of International Law* 97.

time, the declaration expressed concern regarding the situation in Syria, the Israeli-Palestinian conflict, the provision of development assistance to Afghanistan, and the talks with Iran about its nuclear programme. Climate change, sustainable development, the green economy, and renewable energy were among the topics covered in the 2012 BRICS Summit Declaration. The Delhi Action Plan attached to the declaration listed numerous sectoral meetings of various ministries and authorities from the BRICS countries. It further suggested new areas for BRICS cooperation, such as multilateral energy cooperation,[18] general academic evaluation, a BRICS youth policy dialogue, and cooperation in population related issues.[19]

In 2013, South Africa hosted the annual BRICS Summit in Durban under the general theme "BRICS and Africa: Partnership for Development, Integration and Industrialisation". The resulting eThekwini Declaration contained 47 paragraphs. In addition to Africa-specific subjects, the 2013 BRICS Summit Declaration concluded that the establishment of the New Development (BRICS) Bank and the Contingent Reserve Arrangement (CRA) were both feasible and viable.[20] BRICS continued to express their support for the G20-led reform of the global financial institutions, the UN's MDG agenda, the development agenda driven by the United Nations Conference on Trade and Development (UNCTAD), and the WTO's Doha Round negotiations. The related events in Syria, Palestine, Iran, Mali, Central African Republic, Democratic Republic of the Congo, and Afghanistan were also considered, with BRICS expressing their support for peaceful negotiations and the political inclusiveness of the peace processes.[21] It is worth noting that, for the first time, the BRICS Summit Declaration contained references to cyberspace cooperation and security.[22] The eThekwini Action Plan summarised various sectoral dialogues and outlined the fields of future BRICS cooperation, mentioning public diplomacy, anti-corruption, state owned enterprises, drug

---

[18] See also Jenya Grigorova and Julia Motte Baumvol, "BRICS in the Energy Trade Debate", in Rostam J Neuwirth, Alexandr Svetlicinii, and Denis De Castro Halis (eds.), *The BRICS-Lawyers' Guide to Global Cooperation* (Cambridge: Cambridge University Press, 2017) 180.

[19] 2012 New Delhi Action Plan, para 17, Appendix II.7 B.

[20] 2013 BRICS Summit Declaration, paras 9-10, Appendix II.6 A.

[21] See also Oliver P. Richmond and Ioannis Tellidis, *The BRICS and International Peacebuilding and Statebuilding* (Norwegian Peacebuilding Resource Centre, January 2013), available at: https://www.files.ethz.ch/isn/160996/5f8c6a3d43ec8fff5692d7b596af2491.pdf.

[22] 2012 BRICS Summit Declaration, para 34, Appendix II.7 A.

control, youth policy, tourism, and sports.[23] In a brief note, it also mentioned the possibility of establishing a BRICS virtual secretariat.

In 2014, Brazil welcomed BRICS leaders to their annual summit in Fortaleza, held under the general theme "Inclusive Growth: Sustainable Solutions". A 72-paragraph long Fortaleza Declaration summarised the milestones of BRICS cooperation during the first five-year cycle, and outlined directions for further actions. Most importantly, BRICS announced the signing of the Agreement establishing the New Development Bank, a new multilateral development bank with an initial authorised capital of USD 100 billion, and the signing of the Treaty for the Establishment of the BRICS Contingent Reserve Arrangement, with an initial size of USD 100 billion.[24] BRICS also decided to further formalise their cooperation by developing the BRICS Economic Cooperation Strategy, and the Framework of BRICS Closer Economic Partnership, two roadmaps aimed at the promotion of intra-BRICS economic cooperation.[25] Concern about events in Mali, South Sudan, the Central African Republic, the Democratic Republic of the Congo, Syria, Palestine, Iran, Afghanistan and Ukraine, as well as condemnation of all forms of terrorism and piracy, occupied a substantial part of the declaration. The topic of cyberspace and cooperation in information and communication technologies (ICT) appeared again, with BRICS calling for the negotiation of a universal, legally binding instrument for combatting cybercrimes.[26] The Fortaleza Action Plan added the following fields to the impressive list of BRICS exchanges: mutual recognition of higher education degrees and diplomas, labour and social policies, insurance and reinsurance, and, last but not least, e-commerce.[27]

The 2015 Ufa Declaration is a 77-paragraph long document, adopted under the theme "BRICS Partnership – a Powerful Factor of Global Development", which reflected the expanding scope of BRICS cooperation, and of topics of international affairs addressed by the BRICS countries. The Russian BRICS chairpersonship[28] affected the contents of the Ufa Declaration. Accordingly, it featured meetings with leaders of the Eurasian Economic Union and the

---

[23] 2013 eThekwini Action Plan, para 18, Appendix II.6 B.

[24] 2014 BRICS Summit Declaration, paras 11-13, Appendix II.5 A.

[25] *Ibid*, para 20.

[26] *Ibid*, para 50.

[27] Fortaleza Action Plan, para 23, Appendix II.5 B.

[28] See also Marina Larionova, "Russia's 2015 BRICS Presidency: Models of Engagement with International Organizations" (2016) 11(2) *International Organisations Research Journal* 113. The Concept of participation of the Russian Federation in BRICS was approved by the President in 2013; available at: http://static.kremlin.ru/media/events/eng/files/41d452b13d9c2624d228.pdf.

Shanghai Cooperation Organisation, a commemoration of the 70th anniversary of World War II and the founding of the UN, a rejection of "double standards" in international law, "placing interests of some countries above others",[29] a condemnation of military interventions and economic sanctions, support for Russian efforts "aimed at promoting a political settlement in Syria", [30] and the expression of deep concerns about the situation in Ukraine.[31] The BRICS leaders also welcomed the next step in the establishment of the NDB, the signing of the Memorandum of Understanding on Cooperation with the New Development Bank by the national development banks.[32] The following issues in international affairs remained the subject of BRICS' attention: the Israeli-Palestine conflict, the Syrian and Libyan civil wars, the security situation in Iraq, Iran's nuclear programme, the security situation in Afghanistan, the humanitarian crises in South Sudan and the Democratic Republic of the Congo, the political crises in Mali and Burundi, and the refugee crisis in Europe. The Ufa Declaration also noted the establishment of the BRICS Network University, a BRICS University League and BRICS cooperation in the fields of science, technology and innovation.[33] 2015 also marked the signing of the Agreement between the Governments of the BRICS Member States on Cooperation in the Field of Culture. The declaration also dealt with the "traditional issues", such as the UN's MDGs, development assistance, climate change, and renewable energies. The Ufa Action Plan further explored new areas for BRICS cooperation, such as a dialogue on peacekeeping, the establishment of the BRICS Council of Regions, and an exchange of media professionals.[34]

The 2015 BRICS Summit also celebrated the adoption of the Strategy for the BRICS Economic Partnership. The strategy was based on the following principles: (1) full respect for the sovereignty of the Member States; (2) commitment to international law and recognition of the central role of the United Nations in peace, security and development; (3) taking into account national interests, priorities, growth and development strategies of the Member States; (4) openness, sharing of information and consensus in decision-making; (5) commitment to the rules and principles of the multilateral trading

---

[29] 2015 BRICS Summit Declaration, para 6, Appendix II.4 A.
[30] *Ibid*, para 36.
[31] *Ibid*, para 43.
[32] *Ibid*, para 14.
[33] *Ibid*, para 62.
[34] See also Victoria Panova, "The BRICS Security Agenda and Prospects for the BRICS Ufa Summit" (2015) 10(2) *International Organisations Research Journal* 90.

system as embodied in the World Trade Organization (WTO); (6) recognition of the multipolar nature of the global economic and financial system; (7) support for greater exchanges of best practices in enhancing the business environment; (8) transparency and predictability in the investment environment in line with national policies and priorities; (9) commitment to supporting sustainable development, strong, balanced and inclusive growth, financial stability, and a balanced combination of measures ensuring social and economic development and protection of the environment; (10) commitment to mutually beneficial cooperation with other countries; and (11) the inadmissibility of unilateral economic sanctions in violation of universally recognised norms of international relations.[35] It laid out a number of objectives for BRICS cooperation in trade and investment, manufacturing and minerals processing, energy, agriculture, science, technology, and innovation, finances, connectivity, and ICT cooperation. While the objectives of the BRICS Economic Partnership are not binding, the strategy established an implementation monitoring mechanism, with a sherpas' review every five years and annual progress reports.[36]

In 2016, the annual BRICS Summit was convened in the Indian seaside state of Goa, under the theme "Building Responsive, Inclusive and Collective Solutions". The resulting declaration reached a record length of 110 paragraphs. This length was achieved partly due to the detailed enumeration and description of various BRICS sectoral dialogues and meetings. The declaration accorded special attention to the issues of peace and security under the auspices of the UN and the UN Security Council. It included "traditional BRICS issues" such as global financial governance, development assistance, the role of multilateral development banks (MDBs), the WTO Doha Round, cooperation with G20, climate change, and the fight against terrorism. The Goa Action Plan is also very detailed, and includes more than 100 BRICS-related meetings held during India's BRICS chairpersonship in 2016.

In 2017, China chaired the annual BRICS Summit in the coastal city of Xiamen under the general theme "BRICS: Stronger Partnership for a Brighter Future". Chinese pragmatism left its mark on the contents of the 71-paragraph long

---

[35] Strategy for the BRICS Economic Partnership, para I.2, Appendix II.4 C.

[36] *Ibid*, Section IV. See e.g. Progress Report on the Implementation of the Strategy for BRICS Economic Partnership (August 2017); available at: https://www.ranepa.ru/images/media/brics/2017/BRICS%20Strategy%20Progress%20Report_25.08.2017.pdf.

Xiamen Declaration,[37] which focused on particular issues of the BRICS economic partnership, including but not limited to ICT, trade, public private partnerships, national currency bonds,[38] science, technology and innovation, industrial cooperation, and the work of the NDB and its cooperation with other international financial institutions. The annex to the declaration lists 40 BRICS cooperation outcome documents adopted during the year of the Chinese BRICS chairpersonship. The "traditional BRICS issues" were also included, such as support for the WTO, energy cooperation, sustainable development, climate change, G20 cooperation, and the fight against terrorism, to name but a few. Contemporary international affairs were also commented on, particularly the Syrian civil war, the Israeli-Palestinian conflict, the fight against ISIL in Iraq, nuclear tests by the Democratic People's Republic of Korea (DPRK), and violence in Afghanistan. Special attention was accorded to the intra-BRICS people-to-people exchanges in the fields of culture, education, sports, and youth policies. The Xiamen Action Plan enumerated the various sectoral meetings and events held in 2017. It also explored the possible areas for future cooperation, centred around the oceans, public private partnership, an energy cooperation platform, customs training, tourism, the establishment of the BRICS Cultural Council, the BRICS Council of Regions, and the BRICS Working Group on Regional Aviation.

In 2018, the BRICS Summit was back in South Africa, marked by the centenary of the birth of Nelson Mandela and featuring a theme that was both regional and global: "BRICS in Africa: Collaboration for Inclusive Growth and Shared Prosperity in the 4th Industrial Revolution". The lengthy, 102-paragraph long Johannesburg Declaration covered a range of contemporary topics on which BRICS leaders had managed to find a consensus: multilateralism (support for UN institutions, with a simultaneous call for the reform of the UN Security Council), sustainable development and climate change, peace and security cooperation [39] (the Israeli-Palestinian conflict, civil war in Yemen, diplomatic crisis in the Gulf region, peace building in Afghanistan,

---

[37] See also Alexandr Svetlicinii, "Five Economic Highlights of the 2017 BRICS Summit Xiamen Declaration" (7 November 2017); available at: https://davastrat.org/2017/11/07/five-econo mic-highlights-of-the-2017-brics-summit-xiamen-declarations/.

[38] See also Russian Institute for Strategic Studies, *Use of National Currencies in International Settlements. Experience of the BRICS Countries* (2017); available at: https://en.riss.ru/wp-cont ent/uploads/sites/5/2017/12/Joint-Research-Paper-2017-1.pdf.

[39] See also Adriana Erthal Abdenur, "Can BRICS Cooperate in International Security?" (2017) 12(3) *International Organisations Research Journal* 73.

conflict in Syria, the denuclearisation of the Korean Peninsula, etc.). The eco-nomic component of the declaration focused on the features of the fourth in-dustrial revolution, namely inclusive growth, the role of the internet, and the protection of IP rights. BRICS again expressed their continuous support for the WTO by stating, as follows:

> We note with concern the impasse in the selection process for new Appellate Body Members that can paralyse the dispute settlement system and under-mine the rights and obligations of all Members. We, therefore, urge all Members to engage constructively to address this challenge as a matter of priority.[40]

At the same time, for the most part, the Johannesburg Declaration merely acknowledges the wide range of areas where BRICS countries had initiated various forms of cooperation and reiterated the leaders' support for those initiatives. For example, Section V on People-to-People Cooperation simply enumerated various events and initiatives launched in the preceding period, without laying down any concrete directions for further cooperation in this domain.[41] Despite its theme being "BRICS in Africa",[42] the Johannesburg Declaration contained relatively few Africa-related subjects. The BRICS coun-tries expressed their support for the efforts of the African Union aimed at industrialisation, economic growth, infrastructure and connectivity, without, however, providing any specific directions for the BRICS role in these pro-cesses except noting the Africa Regional Centre of the New Development Bank and the bank's role "in catalysing private sector financing for public infrastructure and investment".[43]

The annual BRICS Summits also offered a platform for the broader so-called "South-South dialogue". The evolution of BRICS cooperation can be seen through the common positions announced in the annual summit declarations.

---

[40] 2018 Johannesburg Declaration, para 64, Appendix II.1 A.

[41] *Ibid*, paras 86-102.

[42] See also Alioune Badara Thiam, "China-Africa and the BRICS: An Insight into the Development Cooperation and Investment Policies", in Rostam J Neuwirth, Alexandr Svetlicinii, and Denis De Castro Halis (eds.), *The BRICS-Lawyers' Guide to Global Cooperation* (Cambridge: Cambridge University Press, 2017) 106.

[43] 2018 Johannesburg Declaration, para 75, Appendix II.1 A. See also Catherine Elkemann and Oliver C. Ruppel, "Chinese Foreign Direct Investment into Africa in the Context of BRICS and Sino-African Bilateral Investment Treaties" (2015) 13(4) *Richmond Journal of Global Law and Business* 593. The authors argue that BRICS cooperation with African countries provides an enormous potential for the development due to China's ever increasing attention to BRICS in its Africa relations.

To date, ten annual BRICS summits have been successfully held between 2009 and 2018 as can be seen from the following list:

BRICS Annual Summits

Year	Location	Theme	BRICS Leaders
2009	Yekaterinburg (RUS)	BRIC Summit	Luiz Inácio Lula da Silva, Dmitry Medvedev (host), Manmohan Singh, Hu Jintao
2010	Brasília (BRAI)	BRIC Summit	Luiz Inácio Lula da Silva (host), Dmitry Medvedev, Manmohan Singh, Hu Jintao
2011	Sanya (CHN)	BRICS Summit	Dilma Rousseff, Dmitry Medvedev, Manmohan Singh, Hu Jintao (host), Jacob Zuma
2012	New Delhi (IND)	BRICS Partnership for Global Stability, Security and Prosperity	Dilma Rousseff, Dmitry Medvedev, Manmohan Singh (host), Hu Jintao, Jacob Zuma
2013	Durban (ZAR)	BRICS and Africa: Partnership for Development, Integration and Industrialisation	Dilma Rousseff, Vladimir Putin, Manmohan Singh, Xi Jinping, Jacob Zuma (host)
2014	Fortaleza (BRA)	Inclusive Growth: Sustainable Solutions	Dilma Rousseff (host), Vladimir Putin, Narendra Modi, Xi Jinping, Jacob Zuma
2015	Ufa (RUS)	BRICS Partnership – a Powerful Factor of Global Development	Dilma Rousseff, Vladimir Putin (host), Narendra Modi, Xi Jinping, Jacob Zuma
2016	Goa (RUS)	Building Responsive, Inclusive and Collective Solutions	Michel Temer, Vladimir Putin, Narendra Modi (host), Xi Jinping, Jacob Zuma
2017	Xiamen (CHN)	BRICS: Stronger Partnership for a Brighter Future	Michel Temer, Vladimir Putin, Narendra Modi, Xi Jinping (host), Jacob Zuma
2018	Johannesburg (ZAR)	BRICS in Africa: Collaboration for Inclusive Growth and Shared Prosperity in the 4th Industrial Revolution	Michel Temer, Vladimir Putin, Narendra Modi, Xi Jinping, Cyril Ramaphosa (host)
2019	Brasília (BRA)	TBD	TBD
2020	Chelyabinsk (RUS)	TBD	TBD

In 2014, following their annual meeting in Fortaleza (Brazil), the BRICS leaders held a joint summit with the leaders of the Union of South American Nations.[44]

---

[44] The Union of South American Nations (UNASUR) includes Argentina, Bolivia, Chile, Colombia, Ecuador, Guyana, Paraguay, Peru, Suriname, Uruguay, and Venezuela; see the UNASUR Homepage; available at: https://www.unasursg.org/.

The 2015 BRICS Summit in Ufa (Russia) was followed by a joint summit with the leaders of the Shanghai Cooperation Organisation[45] and the Eurasian Economic Union.[46]

In 2016, India, as a host of the BRICS Summit in Goa, invited the leaders of the Bay of Bengal Initiative for Multi-Sectoral Technical and Economic Cooperation[47] to hold a joint summit with BRICS.

In 2017, China introduced a BRICS+ format,[48] which provided for the summit attendance of the foreign leaders invited by the host state. At China's invitation, the leaders of Egypt, Guinea, Mexico, Tajikistan and Thailand attended the BRICS Summit in Xiamen.

In 2018, South Africa followed suit, and the BRICS Summit in Johannesburg was joined by the heads of the following countries: Angola, Botswana, Ethiopia, Gabon, Lesotho, Madagascar, Mauritius, Malawi, Mozambique, Namibia, Rwanda, Senegal, the Seychelles, Tanzania, Togo, Uganda, Zambia, Zimbabwe, Argentina, Turkey, and Jamaica.

The annual summit declarations show certain trends that are likely to inform the development of BRICS cooperation in the future. At the inception of their cooperation, the annual declarations contained a number of common positions adopted on various subjects of global political and economic governance: the reform of the UN system, including the Security Council, support for and reform of the WTO, calls for the reform of the global financial system, including the IMF and the World Bank, the condemnation of terrorist activities and armed conflicts, and so on. As the fields of BRICS cooperation grew by subject and scope, and the contact between the BRICS states was increasingly shifted to the level of ministries, specialised agencies and other public institutions, the annual declarations have been largely transformed into summaries of these multilateral meetings and initiatives, and broad plans to

---

[45] The Shanghai Cooperation Organisation (SCO) includes Kazakhstan, Kyrgyzstan, Pakistan, Tajikistan and Uzbekistan; see the SCO Homepage; available at: http://eng.sectsco.org/.

[46] The Eurasian Economic Union includes Afghanistan, Armenia, Belarus, Iran, Kazakhstan, Kyrgyzstan, Mongolia, Pakistan, Tajikistan, and Uzbekistan; see the EAEU Homepage; available at: http://www.eaeunion.org/.

[47] The Bay of Bengal Initiative for Multi-Sectoral Technical and Economic Cooperation (BIMSTEC) includes Bangladesh, Bhutan, Myanmar, Nepal, Sri Lanka and Thailand; see the BIMSTEC Homepage; available at: https://bimstec.org/.

[48] See also Yaroslav Lissovolik and Evgeny Vinokurov, "Extending BRICS to BRICS+: the potential for development finance, connectivity and financial stability" (2019) *Area Development and Policy*; available at: https://doi.org/10.1080/23792949.2018.1535246.

expand the cooperation into the new areas.[49] While serving as important basic documents tracing the progress of BRICS cooperation, and outlining the directions for its further development, the contents of the annual declarations and the progress of the implementation of the announced initiatives and measures should therefore be followed by a study of the "secondary BRICS documents", the ministerial and other sector-specific statements, communiques, and declarations.

II.   BRICS MINISTERIAL MEETINGS

II.1.   Meetings of BRICS Foreign Ministers

The dialogue between foreign ministers was established at the outset of the consolidation of the BRICS group.[50] Within BRICS, foreign ministers are responsible for the organisation of the annual BRICS summits of the Heads of State and coordination of the rotating BRICS chairpersonship. Externally, the foreign ministers play an important role in coordinating the BRICS' countries positions on the various issues of global governance that are discussed in numerous international fora, such as the UN, WTO and other international organisations. These coordinating and representative roles mean that the documents produced by the BRICS foreign ministers for the most part reiterate the BRICS countries' position on various current international issues. These positions are also reproduced in the annual BRICS summit declarations, as discussed above.

The first meeting of the BRIC foreign ministers in 2008 addressed the reform of the UN system (according greater roles to Brazil and India), peace and

---

[49] See Ming Liu, "BRICS Development: A Long Way to a Powerful Economic Club and New International Organization" (2016) 29(3) *The Pacific Review* 443 at 449. The author identifies the following categories of the BRICS meetings: (1) working groups on CRA and NDB, and on strategy of BRICS economic partnership and non-politics cooperation; (2) experts groups for functioning coordination or professional dialogue; (3) ministers and governors regular meetings; (4) network conference for responsible officials; (5) foreign policy and defense-related issues consultation; (6) academic conference; (7) parliamentary and business forums.

[50] It should not be confused with other formats of multilateral dialogue with participation of the BRICS. For example, long before the consolidation of the BRICS group, the foreign ministers of Russia, India, and China have been meeting in this trilateral RIC format. In 2019 they held 16th such meeting in Wuzhen, China. Another platform for RIC exchanges is the Shanghai Cooperation Organization (SCO), which besides RIC countries brings together Kazakhstan, the Kyrgyz Republic, Pakistan, Tajikistan, and Uzbekistan. The SCO Homepage; available at http://eng.sectsco.org/.

security (including the condemnation of terrorism), poverty and food short-ages, environmental protection and climate change. Support for various UN-led projects and initiatives is a common topic at BRICS foreign minister meet-ings, and includes among other things, the 2030 Agenda for Sustainable Development, the High Level Political Forum on Sustainable Development, a Comprehensive Convention on International Terrorism at the United Nations, the United Nations Framework Convention on Climate Change, and the United Nations Relief and Works Agency for Palestine Refugees in the Near East, to mention but a few.[51]

In 2011, with the Arab Spring revolts unfolding in the Middle East and North Africa (MENA), the BRICS high level diplomats convened in Moscow to reit-erate their common position concerning these events. BRICS had rejected unilateral sanctions and military interventions by some states, insisting that the political conflicts in the MENA region (including Libya, Syria, Yemen) must be settled through peaceful negotiations under the supervision of the UN Security Council. In relation to the Israeli-Palestinian conflict, BRICS have called for the "establishment of an independent, viable and territorially con-tiguous Palestinian State with full sovereignty within the 1967 borders, with agreed-upon territorial swaps and with East Jerusalem as its capital".[52] As the events in the MENA continued to escalate, the BRICS countries repeatedly called on the warring sides in Libya, Syria, and Yemen to negotiate, offering strong support for the UNSC resolutions and rejecting unilateral sanctions and military interventions. In 2015, BRICS' position remained unchanged in relation to the Israeli-Palestinian conflict: "establishing an independent, viable and territorially contiguous Palestinian State within the borders based on June 4, 1967 lines and with East Jerusalem as its capital".[53] When meeting on the sidelines of the 68th UN General Assembly on 26 September 2013 in New York, the BRICS foreign ministers reaffirmed their support for a peace-ful resolution of the Syrian conflict with the participation of the UN, and reit-erated their support for Palestinian statehood: "a two state solution with a

---

[51] See e.g. Meeting of BRICS Ministers of Foreign Affairs/International Relations, 21 September 2017, New York (United States), Appendix III.1 B; Meeting of BRICS Ministers of Foreign Affairs/International Relations, 4 June 2018, Pretoria (South Africa), Appendix III.1 A.

[52] Joint Statement of the occasion of the Meeting of the BRICS Deputy Ministers of Foreign Affairs on the situation in the Middle East and North Africa, 24 November 2011, Moscow (Russia), Appendix III.1 I.

[53] Joint Communiqué on the Outcome of the Meeting of BRICS Deputy Foreign Ministers on the Situation in the Middle East (West Asia) and North Africa, 22 May 2015, Moscow (Russia), Appendix III.1 F.

contiguous and economically viable Palestinian state, existing side by side in peace with Israel, within internationally recognized borders, based on those existing on 4 June 1967, with East Jerusalem as its capital".[54]

In 2014, the BRICS foreign ministers met on the margins of the Nuclear Security Summit in The Hague, Netherlands. This meeting was preceded by the events in Crimea, which escalated Russia-West confrontation. Without supporting either side, the BRICS foreign ministers concluded that "BRICS countries agreed that the challenges that exist within the regions of the BRICS countries must be addressed within the fold of the United Nations in a calm and level-headed manner. The escalation of hostile language, sanctions and counter-sanctions, and force does not contribute to a sustainable and peaceful solution, according to international law, including the principles and purposes of the United Nations Charter."[55] The same approach was confirmed by the BRICS foreign ministers in 2015 on the margins of the annual session of the UNGA: "The Ministers reiterated their deep concern about the situation in Ukraine. They emphasized that there is no military solution to the conflict and that the only way to reconciliation is through inclusive political dialogue. The Ministers called on all parties to comply with all provisions of the Minsk Agreements adopted in February 2015."[56]

It should be noted that BRICS foreign ministers normally did not discuss bilateral issues in the BRICS format, always emphasising the principle of non-interference in the domestic affairs of sovereign states. When addressing the conflicts that plagued other countries, BRICS always adopted a careful approach, emphasising that domestic political conflicts have to be solved without foreign interference. The solution to the Syrian conflict must thus be "Syrian-led, Syrian-owned" and the political reconciliation in Afghanistan, "Afghan-led and Afghan-owned".[57] When addressing other issues of global concern, the BRICS foreign ministers continued to reinforce the positions voiced by their respective leaders in various international fora. One such position has been continuous support for the UN, which BRICS regarded "as

---

[54] Joint Statement issued on the occasion of the BRICS Foreign Ministers Meeting on the sidelines of the 68th UN General Assembly, 26 September 2013, New York (United States), Appendix III.1 H.

[55] Meeting of BRICS Ministers on the Sidelines of the Nuclear Security Summit, 24 March 2014, The Hague (Netherlands), Appendix III.1 G.

[56] Meeting of BRICS Ministers of Foreign Affairs, 29 September 2015, New York (United States), Appendix III.1 E.

[57] Meeting of the BRICS Ministers of Foreign Affairs/International Relations: 18-19 June 2017, Beijing (China), paras 12-13, Appendix III.1 C.

the universal multilateral organisation entrusted with the mandate for maintaining international peace and security, advancing global development and to promoting and protecting human rights so as to build a brighter shared future for the global community".[58] As a result, the joint statements and communiques produced by the BRICS foreign ministers mainly express the common position of BRICS countries on issues of global concern, without addressing the details of intra-BRICS cooperation. The latter task is fulfilled by the ministerial dialogue and cooperation in specific fields, as exemplified in the next sections of this chapter.

II.2.   Meetings of BRICS Trade Ministers

Each of the BRICS countries has played a leading role in their respective regional economic integration projects: Brazil in the Southern Common Market (MERCOSUR);[59] Russia in the Eurasian Economic Union (EAEU)[60] and the Commonwealth of Independent States (CIS) Free Trade Area;[61] India in the South Asian Free Trade Area with the South Asian Association for Regional Cooperation;[62] China in China-ASEAN Free Trade Area,[63] and South Africa in the Southern African Customs Union.[64] At the same time, BRICS cooperation in the field of trade has been always connected to the WTO as a single multilateral trade governance mechanism, where all BRICS countries have been

---

[58] Meeting of BRICS Ministers of Foreign Affairs/International Relations, 4 June 2018, Pretoria (South Africa), para 5, Appendix III.1 A.

[59] The Southern Common Market (MERCOSUR) also includes Argentina, Paraguay, Uruguay, and Venezuela; see the MERCOSUR Homepage; available at: https://www.mercosur.int/.

[60] The Eurasian Economic Union (EEAU) also includes Armenia, Belarus, Kazakhstan, Kyrgyzstan; see the EAEU Homepage; available at: http://www.eaeunion.org/. See also Alexandr Svetlicinii, "China's Belt and Road Initiative and the Eurasian Economic Union: "Integrating the Integrations" (2018) 5 *Public Administration Issues* 7.

[61] The Commonwealth of Independent States (CIS) also includes Armenia, Belarus, Kazakhstan, Kyrgyzstan, Moldova, Tajikistan, Ukraine, and Uzbekistan; see the CIS Homepage; available at: http://www.cis.minsk.by/.

[62] The South Asian Association for Regional Cooperation (SAARC) also includes Afghanistan, Bangladesh, Bhutan, Maldives, Nepal, Pakistan and Sri Lanka; see the SAARC Homepage; available at: http://www.saarc-sec.org/.

[63] The China-ASEAN Free Trade Area Homepage; available at: http://www.asean-cn.org/; The ASEAN member states are: Brunei, Cambodia, Indonesia, Laos, Malaysia, Myanmar, Philippines, Singapore, Thailand, and Vietnam.

[64] The Southern African Customs Union includes Botswana, Lesotho, Namibia, and Swaziland; see the Southern African Customs Union's Homepage; available at: http://www.sacu.int/.

members since 2012.[65] Notably, the first meeting of the BRICS trade ministers took place in Geneva on the sidelines of the Eighth WTO Ministerial Conference, which marked Russia's accession to this organisation. The BRICS trade ministers extended their congratulations to "Russia, the largest economy outside the multilateral trading system, on the successful conclusion of the accession process to the WTO, and look forward to the forthcoming Ministerial Conference to formally endorse Russia as a new member".[66]

At their second meeting in New Delhi in 2012, the BRICS trade ministers were primarily concerned with the impasse of the WTO's Doha Development Agenda, and called for identification of specific areas where progress could be achieved.[67] The same year, 2012, saw the BRICS trade ministers reuniting at the G20 summit hosted by Mexico in Puerto Vallarta. On this occasion, the BRICS trade ministers expressed their concern about the specific development needs of the "developing countries", which should be taken into account when considering the liberalisation of trade in services, the supervision of financial markets, the trade facilitation measures and other trade-related issues.[68]

At their 2013 meeting in Durban, the BRICS trade ministers endorsed the BRICS Trade and Investment Cooperation Framework, which was developed by the Contact Group on Economic and Trade Issues (CGETI). The framework set out the following fields for cooperation: multilateral cooperation and coordination, promotion and facilitation of trade and investment, innovation cooperation, SME cooperation, IP rights protection, infrastructure and industrial development.[69] It should be noted that the framework did not envisage the establishment of any new multilateral organisations, or the conclusion of any treaties or other binding agreements. Instead, BRICS directed their cooperation towards an increase in transparency and information exchanges, and

---

[65] Brazil, India and South Africa have been WTO members since its establishment in 1995. China joined the organization on 11 December 2001. Russia's accession was completed on 22 August 2012.

[66] Declaration of the BRICS Trade Ministers, 14 December 2011, Geneva (Switzerland), para 6, Appendix III.2 J.

[67] Declaration of the BRICS Trade Ministers, 28 March 2012, New Delhi (India), paras 2-4, Appendix III.2 I.

[68] Declaration of the BRICS Trade Ministers, 19 April 2012, Puerto Vallarta (Mexico), Appendix III.2 H.

[69] See also Denis De Castro Halis and Guilherme Vargas Castilhos, "The BRICS Investment Framework: Catching Up with Trade", in Rostam J Neuwirth, Alexandr Svetlicinii, and Denis De Castro Halis (eds.), *The BRICS-Lawyers' Guide to Global Cooperation* (Cambridge: Cambridge University Press, 2017) 78.

cooperation within existing international organisations like the WTO.[70] In 2014, the BRICS trade ministers received the CGETI's Joint Trade Study, which made "important recommendations for promoting value-added exports among our countries and ensuring that intra-BRICS trade is more sustainable".[71]

BRICS have continually followed the path of intra-BRICS trade and investment facilitation. At their 2015 meeting in Moscow the BRICS trade ministers considered the exchange of best practices on investment climate improvement, and suggested that BRICS export credit agencies exchange experiences on risk analysis.[72] They also noted that "investment facilitation as well as strengthening cooperation in the areas of standards, technical regulation and conformity assessment procedures would create favourable conditions for enhancing intra-BRICS trade".[73] The range of topics discussed was expanded to include ICT solutions, e-commerce, SMEs, protection of IP rights, and "green economy".[74]

At their 2016 meeting in New Delhi, the BRICS trade ministers endorsed several thematic cooperation frameworks: the BRICS Micro Small and Medium Enterprises (MSME) Cooperation Framework, the BRICS Roadmap for Trade, Economic and Investment Cooperation, the BRICS Mechanism for Non-Tariff Measures Resolution, the Framework for Cooperation on Standardisation, the Framework for Cooperation on Trade in Services, the Framework for BRICS Single Window Cooperation, and the BRICS IPR Cooperation Mechanism, the Framework for BRICS E-Commerce Cooperation.

In 2017, the BRICS trade ministers produced several documents covering various aspects of economic cooperation. One was the Terms of Reference of

---

[70] See also Kristen Hopewell, "Different Paths to Power: The Rise of Brazil, India and China at the World Trade Organization" (2015) 22(2) *Review of International Political Economy* 311.

[71] Declaration of the BRICS Trade Ministers, 14 July 2013, Fortaleza (Brazil), para 7, Appendix III.2 E. See also Umakrishnan Kollamparambil, "Diversity and Intra-BRICS Trade: Patterns, Risks and Potential", in Rostam Neuwirth, Alexandr Svetlicinii, and Denis De Castro Halis (eds.),*The BRICS-Lawyers' Guide to Global Cooperation* (Cambridge: Cambridge University Press, 2017) 31.

[72] Declaration of the BRICS Trade Ministers, 7 July 2015, Moscow (Russia), para 16, Appendix III.2 D.

[73] *Ibid*, para 19.

[74] See also Lesley Wentworth and Chijioke Oji, "The Green Economy and the BRICS Countries: Bringing Them Together", *South African Institute of International Affairs*, Occasional paper No. 170 (Dec. 2013); available at: https://saiia.org.za/wp-content/uploads/2014/02/saiia_sop_170-_-wentworth-oji_20140213.pdf.

BRICS Model E-Port Network.[75] The e-port is a "particular form of an integrated electronic platform to process and monitor cross-border movement of merchandise and transportation vessels at a port level".[76] Other documents produced at the 2017 meeting include: the Outlines for BRICS Investment Facilitation, the BRICS Trade in Services Cooperation Roadmap, the BRICS E-Commerce Cooperation Initiative, the BRICS IPR Cooperation Guidelines,[77] and the Framework on Strengthening the Economic and Technical Cooperation for BRICS Countries.[78]

In 2018, the meeting of the BRICS trade ministers was hosted in Magaliesburg (South Africa). One of the focal issues was the deadlock in the confirmation of the WTO Appellate Body's members and the rise of protectionist measures. In their joint statement the BRICS trade ministers emphasised "the importance of a functional and effective dispute settlement mechanism in supporting a rules-based multilateral trading system and in promoting transparent and predictable trade relations among WTO Members".[79] By regarding the WTO dispute settlement system as a "cornerstone of the MTS [multilateral trading system] and is designed to enhance security and predictability in international trade" the trade ministers expressed their concerns about "the impasse in the selection process for new Appellate Body Members that can paralyze the dispute settlement system and undermine the rights and obligations of all Members".[80] At the same time, BRICS continued working towards the further facilitation of trade and investment among its members. The trade ministers endorsed the Working Mechanism on Technical Regulations, Standards, Metrology and Conformity

---

[75] Terms of Reference of BRICS Model E-Port Network; available at: https://www.brics2017. org/wdfj/201708/t20170831_1830.html.

[76] Declaration of the BRICS Trade Ministers, 31 August 2017, Shanghai (China), Annex I, Appendix III.2 B.

[77] See also Peter K. Yu, "Intellectual Property Negotiations, the BRICS Factor and the Changing North-South Debate", in Rostam J Neuwirth, Alexandr Svetlicinii, and Denis De Castro Halis (eds.), *The BRICS-Lawyers' Guide to Global Cooperation* (Cambridge: Cambridge University Press, 2017) 148.

[78] Declaration of the BRICS Trade Ministers, 31 August 2017, Shanghai (China), Annexes II-VI, Appendix III.2 B.

[79] Declaration of the BRICS Trade Ministers, 5 July 2018, Magaliesburg (South Africa), Annex A, Appendix III.2 A.

[80] *Ibid*, Annex B. See also Alexandr Svetlicinii and Zhang Juan, "Defending Trade Multilateralism: The BRICS Countries in the World Trade Organization's Dispute Settlement Mechanism", in Rostam J Neuwirth, Alexandr Svetlicinii, and Denis De Castro Halis (eds.), *The BRICS-Lawyers' Guide to Global Cooperation* (Cambridge: Cambridge University Press, 2017) 54.

Assessment Procedures for Cooperation to Facilitate Trade, [81] the Implementation Framework and Action Plan for BRICS Intellectual Property Rights Cooperation Mechanism,[82] the Outline for the Guidebook on IP Rights in BRICS Countries,[83] the BRICS Cooperation Framework on Inclusive E-Commerce Development, [84] and the Terms of Reference to Strengthen Institutional Arrangements on MSME Cooperation.[85]

The specified activities of the trade ministers from the BRICS countries have evolved continually, and expanded into various trade-related topics such as IP rights protection, investment facilitation, and support for e-commerce and SMEs. The work of the CGETI has been carried out in coordination with the BRICS Business Council, which allowed for the involvement of the private sector. At the same time, the BRICS nations have continued to rely on the WTO trade governance system as the basis for the development of intra-BRICS trade and economic relations with other countries.

II.3.   BRICS Cooperation in the Fields of Science, Technology and Innovation

In line with the mandate of the 2013 eThekwini Declaration, the BRICS ministers for science, technology and innovation convened their first meeting in Cape Town in 2014 in order to discuss and coordinate positions of mutual interest, and to identify future directions for institutionalising cooperation in these fields. They outlined five thematic areas for cooperation: (1) climate change and natural disaster mitigation (led by Brazil); (2) water resources and pollution treatment (led by Russia); (3) geospatial technology and its applications (led by India); (4) new and renewable energy, and energy efficiency (led by China); and (5) astronomy[86] (led by South Africa).[87] At their second meeting, held in 2015 in Brasília, the BRICS ministers of science, technology and innovation pledged to develop a Work Plan 2015-2018.[88]

---

[81] Declaration of the BRICS Trade Ministers, 5 July 2018, Magaliesburg (South Africa), Annex D, Appendix III.2.

[82] *Ibid*, Annexes E and F.

[83] *Ibid*, Annex G.

[84] *Ibid*, Annex H.

[85] *Ibid*, Annex I.

[86] BRICS Astronomy Working Group; available at: https://www.bricsastronomy.org/.

[87] Declaration of BRICS Science, Technology and Innovation Ministerial Meeting, 10 February 2014, Cape Town (South Africa), para 8, Appendix III.4 I.

[88] Declaration of BRICS Science, Technology and Innovation Ministerial Meeting, 18 March 2015, Brasilia (Brazil), para 6, Appendix III.4 H.

At their 2014 summit in Fortaleza, the BRICS countries concluded a memo-randum of understanding (MoU) on cooperation in science, technology and innovation, which designated their respective national authorities for the im-plementation of this MoU: for Brazil - the Ministry of Science, Technology and Innovation (MCTI);[89] for Russia - the Ministry of Education and Science (MES);[90] for India - the Department of Science and Technology (DST, India);[91] for China - the Ministry of Science and Technology (MOST);[92] and for South Africa - the Department of Science and Technology (DST, South Africa).[93] The Memorandum of Understanding includes a wide range of areas for possible cooperation.[94] The institutional structure for such cooperation consists of the Ministerial Meeting,[95] the Senior Officials Meeting,[96] and the Working Group.[97]

In 2015, at their third meeting, the BRICS ministers of science, technology and innovation adopted Work Plan 2015-2018, which added the following initiatives to the five focus areas, as specified above: (1) creation of BRICS Young Scientists Forum[98] (India as coordinating country); (2) cooperation on biotechnology and biomedicine, including human health and neurosci-ence (Russia and Brazil as coordinating countries); (3) cooperation on infor-mation technologies and high performance computing (China and South Africa as coordinating countries); (4) cooperation on ocean and polar science and technology (Brazil and Russia as coordinating countries); (5) coop-eration on material science, including nanotechnology (India and Russia as coordinating countries); and (6) cooperation on photonics (India and Russia as coordinating countries).[99] The Work Plan provided for the development

---

[89] Ministry of Science, Technology and Innovation; available at: http://www.mctic.gov.br/.

[90] Ministry of Education and Science; available at: https://www.minobrnauki.gov.ru/.

[91] Department of Science and Technology; available at: http://www.dst.gov.in/.

[92] Ministry of Science and Technology; available at: http://www.most.gov.cn/.

[93] Department of Science and Technology; available at: https://www.dst.gov.za/.

[94] BRICS MoU on Cooperation in Science, Technology and Innovation, Article 3, Appendix III.4 G.

[95] The Ministerial Meeting should convene on the yearly basis in order to provide common vision, set priorities for cooperation and facilitate linkages between working groups and other national institutions.

[96] The Senior Officials Meeting should convene on the yearly basis in order to exchange information, approve programmes and initiatives, review progress and provide recommendations.

[97] The Working Group consisting of national coordinators is expected to serve as a secretariat to organize meetings, develop their agendas and record their proceedings.

[98] BRICS Young Scientist Forum; available at: http://www.brics-ysf.org/.

[99] BRICS Science, Technology and Innovation Work Plan 2015-2018, 27 October 2015, Moscow (Russia), para 3.1, Appendix III.4 F.

of the BRICS Framework Programme [100] for funding multilateral joint projects for research, technology commercialisation and innovation. The BRICS ministers also called for the establishment of the BRICS Research and Innovation Networking Platform.[101]

The fourth BRICS ministerial meeting on science, technology and innovation was hosted in Jaipur (India) on 8 October 2016.[102] The ministers noted the progress of the BRICS STI Framework Programme, which had successfully carried out the first BRICS Pilot Call for projects in 2016[103] and agreed to launch the next call for jointly funded projects in 2017.[104] At their fifth meeting in 2017, the BRICS ministers for science, technology and innovation adopted the BRICS Action Plan for Innovation Cooperation.[105] The implementation of the action plan was entrusted to the BRICS Science Technology Innovation and Entrepreneurship Partnership (STIEP) Working Group, which was supposed to focus on the creation of science parks and technology business incubators.

In 2018, the sixth BRICS ministerial meeting on science, technology and innovation took place in Durban.[106] The ministers agreed on a series of new initiatives including, among others: the BRICS Vaccine Research and Development Centre,[107] a web portal to facilitate cooperation between the BRICS countries in the domain of research infrastructure and mega-science projects, the BRICS Network Centre for Material Sciences and Nanotechnologies, the BRICS Virtual Institute of Photonics, and the BRICS Technology Transfer Center.

---

[100] BRICS Science, Technology and Innovation Framework Programme; available at: http://brics-sti.org/.

[101] Declaration of BRICS Science, Technology and Innovation Ministerial Meeting, 28 October 2015, Moscow (Russia), para 10, Appendix III.4 E.

[102] Declaration of BRICS Science, Technology and Innovation Ministerial Meeting, 8 October 2016, Jaipur (India), Appendix III.4 D.

[103] BRICS 1st Pilot Call for Projects; available at: http://brics-sti.org/index.php?p=projects/BRICS+STI+FP+Pilot+Call+2016.

[104] BRICS 2nd Call for Projects; available at: http://brics-sti.org/index.php?p=projects/BRICS+STI+FP+2nd+Call+2017.

[105] Declaration of BRICS Science, Technology and Innovation Ministerial Meeting, 18 July 2017, Hangzhou (China), Appendix III.4 B.

[106] Declaration of BRICS Science, Technology and Innovation Ministerial Meeting, 3 July 2018, Durban (South Africa), III.4 A.

[107] See also Miloud Kaddar, Julie Milstien, and Sarah Schmitt, "Impact of BRICS' Investment in Vaccine Development on the Global Vaccine Market" (2014) 92(6) *Bulletin of the World Health Organization* 436.

II.4.   BRICS Cooperation in the Field of Agriculture and Food Supply

The 2009 BRIC Joint Statement on Global Food Safety called for both developed and developing countries to address food shortages based on the principle of common but differentiated responsibility.[108] It enumerated various causes of the recurrent food security problems: climate change, trade-distorting agricultural subsidies, production of biofuels, and so on. The range of possible policy responses included upgrading the agricultural infra-structure, food aid and other forms of assistance for developing countries, and international cooperation to introduce technological innovations in the agricultural sector.

At the 2010 BRIC Summit, the agriculture ministers of the four nations concentrated their attention on mapping the directions for BRIC cooperation in this sector: the creation of an agricultural information base system for the BRIC countries, development of a general strategy for ensuring access to food for the most vulnerable population, a reduction in the negative impact of climate change on food security and adaptation of agriculture to climatic changes, agricultural technology cooperation and innovation.[109]

In 2011, at their meeting in Chengdu (China), the BRICS agriculture ministers approved a more detailed Action Plan 2012-2016 for the Agricultural Cooperation of BRICS Countries[110] with the following priorities: (1) creation of basic agricultural information exchange system of BRICS countries (coordinated by China);[111] (2) development of a general strategy for ensuring access to food for the most vulnerable population (coordinated by Brazil); (3) a re-

---

[108] BRIC Joint Statement of Global Food Safety, 16 June 2009, Yekaterinburg (Russia), para 2, Appendix III.3 K.

[109] Declaration of the First Meeting of BRIC Ministers of Agriculture and Agrarian Development, 26 March 2010, Moscow (Russia), Appendix III.3 J.

[110] Declaration of the Second Meeting of BRICS Ministers of Agriculture and Agrarian Development, 30 October 2011, Chengdu (China), para 24, Appendix III.3 H.

[111] This information to be exchanged includes: (a) agricultural development policies, including agricultural price support policies, rural finance and insurance policies and agricultural management systems; (b) agricultural trade data and policies; (c) market prices of major agricultural products; (d) dynamic information, such as the latest development in agricultural science and technology; (e) Legislation, policies and management strategies related to fisheries and aquaculture. The BRICS countries noted that the envisaged platform should not duplicate the Agriculture Marketing Information System (AMIS) created under the G20 and administered by the Food and Agriculture Organisation (FAO).

duction in the negative impact of climate change on food security and the adaptation of agriculture to climate change (coordinated by South Africa);[112] (4) agricultural technology cooperation and innovation (coordinated by India); and (5) trade and investment promotion (coordinated by Russia). In order to coordinate their work in a continuous manner, the BRICS countries established the Agricultural Cooperation Working Group and approved its working procedures.

The third meeting of BRICS ministers of agriculture and agrarian development was held in 2013 under the theme "The Negative Effect of Climate Change on World Food Security". It did not result in the establishment of any new cooperation initiatives and the BRICS agriculture ministers reaffirmed their support for the existing exchanges and cooperation in their field.

In 2015, at their fourth meeting, held in Brasília, the BRICS ministers of agriculture "agreed to establish cooperation agreements and arrangements among BRICS countries, with a view to facilitate greater access to their agricultural markets".[113] Their joint declaration was characterised by numerous references to the existing international organisations, fora and standards in the field of agriculture: World Trade Organization (WTO), Food and Agriculture Organisation (FAO), Agricultural Marketing Information System (AMIS), UN Sustainable Development Goals, FAO/WHO Codex Alimentarius Commission and the World Organisation for Animal Health.

At their fifth meeting, the BRICS agriculture ministers noted the "established mechanism of consultations among Permanent Representatives of the BRICS nations to the Food and Agriculture Organisation"[114] and supported an initiative to establish the BRICS Agriculture Research Centre (BARC) proposed by India.[115]

The sixth meeting of the BRICS ministers of agriculture took place in New Delhi on 23 September 2016. The resulting declaration reflected the specific concerns of the hosting country, supported by other BRICS members: access

---

[112] This would include joint R&D activities, technological cooperation, and the organization of educational and training activities (seminars).

[113] Declaration of the Fourth Meeting of the BRICS Ministers of Agriculture and Agrarian Development, 13 March 2015, Brasilia (Brazil), para 11, Appendix III.3 F.

[114] Declaration of the Fifth Meeting of the BRICS Ministers of Agriculture and Agrarian Development, 9 October 2015, Moscow (Russia), para 6, Appendix III.3 E.

[115] *Ibid*, para 21.

to food for the most vulnerable populations, the need to raise the productivity of smallholders and the purchasing power of the poor, the need to strengthen support for family farming and small agricultural holdings.[116]

At their seventh meeting, held under the theme of "BRICS: Innovating and Sharing to Power Agriculture", the BRICS ministers of agriculture approved the Action Plan 2017-2020 for Agricultural Cooperation of BRICS Countries.[117] The plan highlighted the following priorities: accelerating agricultural development to enhance food security and nutrition, promoting cooperation and exchange on climate change for stronger agricultural resilience to natural risks, strengthening technology innovation and demonstration for greater agricultural sustainability, improving safe agricultural trade and expanding agricultural investment, and strengthening, sharing and the exchange of information for better ICT application in BRICS agriculture. The eighth meeting of the BRICS agriculture ministers took place in Skukuza (South Africa) in 2018 under the theme "Promoting Climate Smart Approaches and Actions to Enhance Resilience of Agriculture and Food Production Systems". The resulting declaration included the following topics: agricultural development to enhance food security and nutrition, climate change and agricultural resilience to its adverse impacts, research and innovation for improved agricultural sustainability, and ICT applications in agriculture, trade and agricultural investment.[118] The ministers expressed their support for the establishment of the BRICS Agricultural Research Platform (ARP) initiated by India in 2016[119] and called upon the NDB to finance sustainable development projects in agriculture.[120]

II.5.   Meetings of BRICS Health Ministers

The first meeting of the BRICS health ministers took place in Beijing on 11 July 2011. The BRICS countries pledged "to promote BRICS as a forum of coordination, cooperation and consultation on relevant matters related to

---

[116] Declaration of the Sixth Meeting of BRICS Ministers of Agriculture, 23 September, New Delhi (India), Appendix III.3 D.

[117] Declaration of the Seventh Meeting of BRICS Ministers of Agriculture, 16 June 2017, Nanjing (China), para 26, Appendix III.3 B.

[118] Joint Declaration of the Eighth Meeting of BRICS Ministers of Agriculture, 22 June 2018, Skukuza (South Africa), Appendix III.3 A.

[119] *Ibid*, para 14.

[120] *Ibid*, para 22.

global public health".[121] Acknowledging that public health is a complex subject, which is affected by a multitude of factors that enter into the regulatory ambit of multiple international organisations, the BRICS countries expressed their support for the World Health Organisation in order to strengthen its role in global health governance.[122]

In 2012, the BRICS health ministers met on the sidelines of the 65th session of the World Health Assembly in Geneva. In their declaration BRICS expressed their continuous support for the WHO and urged the organisation to refrain from involvement in issues related to intellectual property rights enforcement.[123] Support for the WHO and its leading role in global health governance was reiterated by the BRICS health ministers at the 66th World Health Assembly in 2013.[124] Another theme in their discussion was access to health technologies and generic medicines. The BRICS countries reaffirmed the right of WTO members to protect public health and promote access to medicines for all, as agreed in the 2001 Doha Declaration.[125] In 2014, the BRICS health ministers again "underlined the importance of ensuring access to affordable, quality, efficacious and safe medical products, including generic medicines, biological products, and diagnostics, through the use of TRIPS flexibilities, for the realization of the right to health."[126]

At their second meeting in New Delhi in 2013, the BRICS health ministers addressed a range of health-related subjects: non-communicable diseases, mental disorders, tobacco use and control, tuberculosis, [127] HIV/AIDS, malaria, infant mortality, universal health coverage, the use of ICT in health services, and traditional medicine, among others.[128] Later that year, at their third meeting in Cape Town, the BRICS health ministers endorsed the BRICS Framework for Collaboration on Strategic Projects in Health.[129] The framework laid down the following focus areas for cooperation: public health,

---

[121] BRICS Health Ministers Declaration, 11 July 2011, Beijing (China), para 9, Appendix III.5 N.

[122] *Ibid*, para 5.

[123] BRICS Health Ministers Declaration, 22 May 2012, Geneva (Switzerland), para 14, Appendix III.5 M.

[124] BRICS Health Ministers Declaration, 22 May 2013, Geneva (Switzerland), Appendix III.5 K.

[125] BRICS Health Ministers Declaration, 22 May 2012, Geneva (Switzerland), para 22, Appendix III.5 M.

[126] BRICS Health Ministers Declaration, 20 May 2014, Geneva (Switzerland), para 5, Appendix III.5 I.

[127] See also Jacob Creswell et al., "Tuberculosis in BRICS: Challenges and Opportunities for Leadership within the Post-2015 Agenda" (2014) 92(6) *Bulletin of the World Health Organization* 459.

[128] BRICS Health Ministers Declaration, 11 January 2013, New Delhi (India), Appendix III.5 L.

[129] BRICS Health Ministers Declaration, 7 November 2013, Cape Town (South Africa), para 17, Appendix III.5 J.

health care systems, and biomedical sciences.[130] In 2014 and 2015, the range of topics discussed by the BRICS health ministers expanded, now including: tuberculosis, the Ebola outbreak, HIV/AIDS, neglected tropical diseases, antimicrobial resistance, chronic non-communicable diseases, obesity and malnutrition-related chronic diseases, tobacco-related diseases, and road safety.[131]

With the increase of health-related issues on the BRICS cooperation agenda, the BRICS countries organised a number of specialised events dedicated to their discussion. At their 2016 meeting in New Delhi the BRICS health ministers thus noted the following such examples: the BRICS workshop on drugs and medical devices in Goa, India in November 2016; the BRICS workshop on HIV and Tuberculosis, held in Ahmedabad, India in November 2016; the BRICS Workshop "Strengthening Health Surveillance: System and Best Practices" in Bengaluru, India in August 2016; the BRICS Wellness Workshop in Bengaluru, India in September 2016; and the BRICS Senior Health Officials meeting in New Delhi, India in December 2016.[132]

The 2017 meeting of the BRICS health ministers in Tianjin celebrated two specific initiatives: the TB Cooperation Plan and the Declaration of BRICS Countries on Strengthening Cooperation in Traditional Medicine, which acknowledges that BRICS countries "have rich heritage, wide experience and application of traditional medicine as precious treasure of health, culture, science and technology resources".[133] BRICS cooperation in this field was linked to the WHO Traditional Medicine Strategy (2014-2023).[134] The health ministers also expressed their support for "the collaboration among BRICS regulatory authorities with a view to improving the regulatory standards, and certification systems for medical products".[135]

In 2018 the BRICS health ministers met in Durban (South Africa) and expressed their support for various international health-related initiatives led by the WHO: universal health coverage, ending tuberculosis, the prevention

---

[130] See also Jarbas Barbosa da Silva et al., "BRICS Cooperation in Strategic Health Projects" (2014) 92(6) *Bulletin of the World Health Organization* 388.

[131] BRICS Health Ministers Declaration, 5 December 2014, Brasília (Brazil); BRICS Health Ministers Declaration, 30 October 2015, Moscow (Russia), Appendix III.5 H and III.5 F.

[132] BRICS Health Ministers Declaration, 16 December 2016, New Delhi (India), Appendix III.5 D.

[133] BRICS Countries on Strengthening Cooperation in Traditional Medicine, 6 July 2017, Tianjin (China), para 7; Appendix III.5 C.

[134] WHO Traditional Medicine Strategy (2014-2023); available at: https://www.who.int/medicines/publications/traditional/trm_strategy14_23/en/.

[135] BRICS Health Ministers Declaration, 6 July 2017, Tianjin (China), para 11, Appendix III.5 B.

and control of non-communicable diseases, efforts to combat anti-microbial resistance, the implementation of the WHO International Health Regulations and the WHO Framework Convention on Tobacco Control.[136]

Overall, BRICS cooperation in the field of health care has had a tendency to shift from deliberation to institutionalisation and decision-making. At the same time, unlike the economic objectives (trade, investment, finances), the health agenda remained relatively low among the BRICS cooperation priorities. In this regard it was suggested that "the BRICS should elevate health agenda to the leaders' level, strengthen decision making and delivery, and change the pattern of members' cooperation with relevant institutions from the expression of a collective stance to productive cooperation that involves relevant institutions such as the UN and WHO in the full chain of global governance functions."[137]

II.6.   Meetings of BRICS Ministers of Education and the BRICS Network University

The BRICS ministers of education had their first meeting in 2013, on the sidelines of the 37th session of the UNESCO General Conference in Paris. At their second meeting in 2015, the BRICS education ministers declared higher education and research a priority.[138] They supported the initiative of the BRICS University League and the establishment of a working group to determine the modalities of a BRICS Network University.[139] The BRICS Network University, as a network of higher education institutions from the BRICS countries, was established on 18 November 2015 at the third meeting of BRICS education ministers in Moscow,[140] and held its first forum in 2016 at the Ural Federal University in Yekaterinburg.[141] At the stage of establishment each BRICS

---

[136] BRICS Health Ministers Declaration, 20 July 2018, Durban (South Africa), Appendix III.5 A.

[137] Marina Larionova et al., "BRICS: Emergence of Health Agenda" (2014) 9(4) *International Organisations Research Journal* 73 at 86.

[138] Declaration of the II Meeting of BRICS Ministers of Education, 2 March 2015, Brasília (Brazil), para 8, Appendix III.8 E.

[139] *Ibid*, para 9.

[140] MoU on Establishment of the BRICS Network University (18 November 2015); available at: https://nu-brics.ru/media/uploads/filestorage/documents/MoU_SU_BRICS.pdf; Appendix IV.4.

[141] See Iana Smagina, "The First Forum of the BRICS Network University" (2016) 3(1) *BRICS Law Journal* 144.

country could nominate no more than 12 institutions participating in the BRICS NU.[142] In 2018, the BRICS NU included the following universities:[143]

Country	Institutions
BRAZIL	• Federal University of Minas Gerais (https://ufmg.br/) • Federal University of Rio de Janeiro (https://ufrj.br/) • Federal University of Rio Grande do Sul (http://www.ufrgs.br/) • Federal University of Santa Catarina (https://ufsc.br/) • Federal University of Viçosa (https://www.ufv.br/) • Fluminense Federal University (http://www.uff.br/) • National Institute of Amazonian Research (https://www.inpa.gov.br/) • Pontifical Catholic University of Rio de Janeiro (http://www.puc-rio.br/) • University of Campinas (https://www.unicamp.br/)
RUSSIA	• Higher School of Economics (https://www.hse.ru/) • ITMO University (http://en.ifmo.ru/) • MGIMO University (http://english.mgimo.ru/) • Moscow Institute of Physics and Technology (https://mipt.ru/) • National University of Science and Technology (http://en.misis.ru/) • Moscow Power Engineering Institute (https://mpei.ru/) • Moscow State University (https://www.msu.ru/) • Peoples' Friendship University of Russia (http://eng.rudn.ru/) • St Petersburg State University (http://english.spbu.ru/) • Tomsk Polytechnic University (https://tpu.ru/) • Tomsk State University (http://en.tsu.ru/) • Ural Federal University (https://urfu.ru/)
INDIA	• Banaras Hindu University Varanasi (http://www.bhu.ac.in/) • Indian Institute of Technology Bombay (http://www.iitb.ac.in/) • Indian Institute of Technology Kanpur (https://iitk.ac.in/) • Indian Institute of Technology Kharagpur (http://www.iitkgp.ac.in/) • Indira Gandhi Institute of Development Research (http://www.igidr.ac.in/) • Jamia Millia Islamia University (https://www.jmi.ac.in/) • National Institute of Technology Durgapur (https://www.nitdgp.ac.in/) • National Institute of Technology Warangal (https://www.nitw.ac.in/) • Tata Institute of Social Sciences (http://www.tiss.edu/) • TERI University (http://www.terisas.ac.in/) • University of Delhi (http://www.du.ac.in/du/) • Visvesvaraya National Institute of Technology Nagpur (http://www.vnit.ac.in/)
CHINA	• Beijing Normal University (http://english.bnu.edu.cn/) • Fudan University (http://www.fudan.edu.cn/en/) • Hohai University (http://en.hhu.edu.cn/) • Huazhong University of Science and Technology (http://english.hust.edu.cn/) • Hunan University (http://www-en.hnu.edu.cn/) • Jilin University (http://global.jlu.edu.cn/) • North China University of Water Resources and Electric Power (http://www5.ncwu.edu.cn/ncwuenglish/) • Northeast Forestry University (http://en.nefu.edu.cn/) • Sichuan University (http://www.scu.edu.cn/) • Southwest University (http://www.swu.edu.cn/) • Zhejiang University (https://www.zju.edu.cn/)
SOUTH AFRICA	• Central University of Technology (https://www.cut.ac.za/) • Durban University of Technology (http://www.dut.ac.za/) • North West University (http://www.nwu.ac.za/) • Rhodes University (https://www.ru.ac.za/) • Stellenbosch University (https://www.sun.ac.za/) • Tshwane University of Technology (https://www.tut.ac.za/) • University of Cape Town (http://www.uct.ac.za/) • University of Johannesburg (https://www.uj.ac.za/) • University of Limpopo (https://www.ul.ac.za/) • University of Pretoria (https://www.up.ac.za/) • University of Venda (http://www.univen.ac.za/) • University of Witwatersrand (https://www.wits.ac.za/)

---

[142] BRICS NU MoU, Article 5, Appendix IV.4.
[143] BRICS NU, Participant Universities; available at: https://nu-brics.ru/universities/.

The BRICS NU was established to organise the following activities: (1) offer Master's and PhD programmes, short-term training and modular courses; (2) to develop and implement joint research projects; and (3) to organise academic mobility programmes for students and university staff.[144] When it was established, the BRICS NU outlined the following priority areas: (1) energy, (2) computer science and information technology, (3) BRICS studies, (4) ecology and climate change, (5) water resources and pollution treatment, and (6) economics.

These areas of priorities conditioned the establishment of the six international thematic groups (ITGs). The ITGs are tasked with the following functions: (1) appraisal of the educational programmes proposed by the participants of the BRICS NU; (2) elaboration of common approaches towards the content and structures of the BRICS NU educational programmes; (3) analysis of academic mobility among BRICS NU participants in the six priority fields; and (4) the drafting and submission of annual reports to the International Governing Board.[145] The ITGs meet at least twice per year, adopt their decisions by consensus and use English as their working language.[146]

The International Governing Board is the principal body responsible for coordinating the work of the BRICS NU.[147] The IGB brings together three representatives from each BRICS country, including the representatives of the respective ministries of education and representatives of the BRICS NU member institutions. In 2016, the composition of the BRICS NU IGB was as follows: for Brazil (Mrs Connie McManus Pimentel, Director of International Relations (DRI), Brazilian Federal Agency for Support and Evaluation of Higher Education (CAPES), Mr Leandro Gomes Cardoso, Head of the International Affairs Office, Ministry of Education (MEC), Mr Anísio Brasileiro de Freitas Dourado, Rector of the Federal University of Pernambuco (UFPE), National Association of Presidents of Federal Institutions for Higher Education (Andifes); for Russia (Mr Alexander Sobolev, Head of the Department of the State Policy in the Sphere of Higher Education of the Ministry of Education and Science, Mr Vladimir Timonin, Deputy Head of the Department of the State Policy in the Sphere of Higher Education of the Ministry of Education and Science, Mr Maxim Khomyakov, Vice-Rector for International

---

[144] BRICS NU MoU, Article 4.
[145] BRICS NU, Statute for the BRICS NU ITGs (2 July 2017), para 4.2.
[146] *Ibid*, para 7.
[147] BRICS NU MoU, Article 10, Appendix IV.4.

Relations of Ural Federal University and a Head of Russian National Coordinating Committee); for India (Mr Vinay Sheel Oberoi, Secretary (Higher Education), Ministry of Human Resource Development, Government of India, Mr Devang Khakhar, Director of the Indian Institute of Technology (IIT), Bombey, Mr Ved Prakash, Chairman of the University Grants Commission); for China (to be appointed); for South Africa (Ms Diane Parker, Deputy Director-General, University Branch, Department of Higher education and Training, Ministry of Higher Education, Dr Sizwe Mabizela, Vice Chancellor, Rhodes University, Prof. Ahmed Bawa, Vice-Chancellor of the Durban University of Technology, Prof. Cheryl de la Rey, Vice Chancellor, University of Pretoria).[148]

The IGB has the following functions: (1) consolidation and approval of the annual action plan for the BRICS NU; (2) approval of educational programmes proposed by ITGs; (3) approval of changes in structure, composition and focus areas of the BRICS NU; (4) approval of the statutes of the ITGs; (5) coordination and review of the implementation of the annual action plans; (6) development of strategic directions for the BRICS NU; and (7) articulation of joint initiatives with other bodies and institutions of the BRICS.[149] At their 2017 meeting in Zhengzhou, the members of the IGB declared: "We believe that participating in the BRICS NU will play an important role in enhancing cooperation and exchanges among all member universities, strengthening their visibility, impact and competitiveness".[150]

In their 2016 New Delhi Declaration on Education, the BRICS ministers of education encouraged the active involvement of the universities participating in the BRICS NU and called on the BRICS NU to facilitate the mobility of students and scholars, especially those working in the six priority fields of the BRICS NU.[151] At their fifth meeting in Beijing on 5 July 2017, the BRICS ministers of education reiterated their support for the BRICS NU.[152] At their 2018 meeting in Cape Town, the BRICS ministers of education urged the BRICS NU to strengthen its coordination process, to develop a proposal for a BRICS NU doctoral programme, to work on the harmonisation of educational quality standards, to develop a draft-referencing framework on quality

---

[148] BRICS NU IGB; available at: https://nu-brics.ru/pages/igb/.
[149] BRICS NU, Regulations of the International Governing Board of the BRICS NU (2 July 2017), para 4.2
[150] BRICS NU Annual Conference, Zhengzhou Consensus (2 July 2017).
[151] New Delhi Declaration on Education (30 September 2016), paras 12 and 14, Appendix III.8.C.
[152] Beijing Declaration on Education (5 July 2017), para 1, Appendix III.8 B.

assurance, the accreditation and recognition of qualifications, to actively pursue research collaboration on the fourth industrial revolution, and to develop proposals on instructor and student mobility.[153]

The QS University Rankings have introduced the a BRICS group ranking, developed with the Russian news agency Interfax in 2013.[154] In 2014, the Times Higher Education followed the suit and introduced the BRICS and Emerging Economies Rankings, which included BRICS countries and other emerging economies as classified by the FTSE.[155] In 2018, however, the agency abandoned the BRICS acronym and re-named the respective rankings as the Emerging Economies University Rankings, which includes countries regarded as "advanced emerging", "secondary emerging", and "frontier".[156] The Spain-based Webometrics Ranking of World Universities also maintains a distinct ranking group for the BRICS countries.[157]

III.   BRICS TREATIES AND AGREEMENTS

III.1.   The New Development Bank (NDB)

The New Development Bank (NDB) was the first permanent international organisation established by the BRICS countries, and represents a stark departure from the traditional "BRICS way" of cooperation through non-binding declarations, sectoral meetings and information exchanges.[158] The idea of establishing their own multilateral development bank was included in the 2012 New Delhi Declaration: "We have considered the possibility of setting up a new Development Bank for mobilizing resources for infra-

---

[153] Cape Town Declaration on Education and Training (10 July 2018), paras 3-9, Appendix III.8 A.

[154] QS University Rankings: BRICS 2013; available at: https://www.topuniversities.com/university-rankings/brics-rankings/2013.

[155] BRICS & Emerging Economies Rankings 2014; available at: https://www.timeshighereducation.com/world-university-rankings/2014/brics-and-emerging-economies#!/page/0/length/25/sort_by/rank/sort_order/asc/cols/undefined.

[156] Emerging Economies University Rankings 2018; available at: https://www.timeshighereducation.com/world-university-rankings/2018/emerging-economies-university-rankings#survey-answer.

[157] Webometrics Ranking of World Universities; available at: http://www.webometrics.info/en/World/Brics.

[158] See Mzukisi Qobo and Mills Soko, "The Rise of Emerging Powers in the Global Development Finance Architecture: The Case of the BRICS and the New Development Bank" (2015) 22(3) *South African Journal of International Affairs* 277.

structure and sustainable development projects in BRICS and other emerging economies and developing countries, to supplement the existing efforts of multilateral and regional financial institutions for global growth and development."[159] The NDB was unveiled two years later at the BRICS annual summit in Fortaleza (Brazil): "We are pleased to announce the signing of the Agreement establishing the New Development Bank (NDB), with the purpose of mobilising resources for infrastructure and sustainable development projects in BRICS and other emerging and developing economies." [160] The inaugural meeting of the NDB Board of Governors took place in Moscow on 7 July 2015. On 9 July 2015, the national development banks of the BRICS states concluded a Memorandum of Understanding on cooperation with the NDB.[161] The first meeting of the NDB Board of Directors was convened in Shanghai on 21 July 2015. In February 2016, the NDB signed a host agreement with China, which provided the premises of the NDB headquarters in Shanghai. In 2016, the NDB approved the first set of projects involving all BRICS countries. One year later, in 2017, the NDB opened its first regional office in Johannesburg.

The NDB Agreement stipulates that "Membership of the Bank shall be open to members of the United Nations in accordance with the provisions of the Articles of Agreement of the New Development Bank".[162] The BRICS countries (founding members) have safeguarded their control over the bank by introducing the following restrictions on the increase in membership: (1) not to reduce the voting power of the founding members below 55% of the total voting power; (2) not to increase the voting power of the non-borrowing member countries above 20% of the total voting power; and (3) not to increase the voting power of a non-founding member country above 7% of total voting power.[163] The NDB Agreement also stipulates that the President of the NDB is elected from one of the founding members on a rotational basis, and that there shall be at least one Vice-President from each of the other founding members.

---

[159] 4th BRICS Summit, New Delhi Declaration, March 29, 2012, para 13, Appendix II.7 A.
[160] 6th BRICS Summit, Fortaleza Declaration, July 15, 2014, para 11, Appendix II.5 A.
[161] The Memorandum of Understanding on Cooperation with the New Development Bank (Appendix I.1 D) was concluded by Banco Nacional de Desenvolvimento Econômico e Social (Brazil), Bank for Development and Foreign Economic Affairs (Russia), Export-Import Bank of India, China Development Bank Corporation, and Development Bank of Southern Africa.
[162] NDB Agreement, Article 2, Appendix I.1 E.
[163] NDB Agreement, Article 8, Appendix I.1 E.

In financial terms, the NDB organizational and shareholding structure can be illustrated by the following table:

Country	Number of Shares	Shareholding (%)	Voting Rights (%)	Authorised Capital (USD billion)
Brazil	100,000	20	20	10
Russia	100,000	20	20	10
India	100,000	20	20	10
China	100,000	20	20	10
South Africa	100,000	20	20	10
Unallocated shares	500,000	N/A	N/A	50
TOTAL	1,000,000	100	100	100

The governance of the NDB is carried out by the Board of Governors and the Board of Directors. The Board of Governors comprises the Ministers of Finance of the BRICS countries and meets on an annual basis. The members of the Board of Directors are appointed on two-year terms and meet on a quarterly basis. The senior management of the NDB currently consists of five executives: the President and four Vice-Presidents (Chief Risk Officer, Chief Administrative Officer, Chief Operations Officer, and Chief Financial Officer).

The NDB has already concluded various cooperation agreements with the following institutions: the Brazilian Development Bank (BNDES),[164] the China Development Bank, the Development Bank of Latin America,[165] the members of the BRICS Interbank Cooperation Mechanism,[166] the Asian Development Bank,[167] the World Bank Group,[168] the Asian Infrastructure

---

[164] MoU between BNDES and New Development Bank, 8 September 2015; available at: https://www.ndb.int/wp-content/uploads/2017/02/MOU-NDB-BNDES.pdf.

[165] MoU between New Development Bank and Corporacion Andina de Fomento on Strategic Cooperation, 9 September 2016; available at: https://www.ndb.int/wp-content/uploads/2017/01/MOU-NDB-CAF.pdf.

[166] MoU amongst BNDES, Vneshekonombank, Export-Import Bank of India, China Development Bank, Development Bank of Southern Africa and New Development Bank on General Cooperation, 15 October 2016; available at: https://www.ndb.int/wp-content/uploads/2017/01/MOU-NDB-BRICS-Development-Banks.pdf.

[167] MoU between Asian Development Bank and New Development Bank on General Cooperation, 4 July 2016; available at: https://www.adb.org/sites/default/files/institutional-document/219871/mou-adb-ndb.pdf.

[168] MoU between International Bank for Reconstruction and Development, International Development Association, International Finance Corporation, Multilateral Investment Guarantee Agency and New Development Bank, 9 September 2016; available at: https://www.ndb.int/wp-content/uploads/2017/01/MOU-NDB-WBG.pdf.

Development Bank,[169] the European Bank for Reconstruction and Development, [170] the European Investment Bank, [171] the Eurasian Development Bank,[172] the International Investment Bank,[173] the Inter-American Development Bank,[174] the Inter-American Investment Corporation, the Development Bank of Southern Africa,[175] the Plata Basin Financial Development Fund,[176] the State Bank of India, Banco Santander (Brazil), the Industrial and Commercial Bank of China, the Agricultural Bank of China, the Bank of Communications (China), the Standard Bank of South Africa, the China Construction Bank, the Industrial Credit and Investment Corporation of India, the Bank of China, the BRICS Business Council, BRICS Export Credit Agencies, Russian Railways, and the Shanghai University of Finance and Economics.[177]

From the commencement of its operations, the NDB has consistently focused on sustainable development through green infrastructure, and the majority of its investment projects involved renewable energy: "We note with appreciation the approval of the first set of loans by the New Development Bank (NDB), particularly in the renewable energy projects in BRICS countries. We express satisfaction with NDB's issuance of the first set of green bonds in

---

[169] MoU between New Development Bank and Asian Infrastructure Investment Bank, 1 April 2017; available at: https://www.aiib.org/en/news-events/news/2017/_download/201705 02101038900.pdf.

[170] MoU between the New Development Bank and the European Bank for Reconstruction and Development, 1 April 2107; available at: https://www.ndb.int/wp-content/uploads/2017/ 04/MOU-with-EBRDApril-2017.pdf.

[171] MoU between New Development Bank and European Investment Bank, 1 April 2017; available at: https://www.ndb.int/wp-content/uploads/2017/04/MOU-with-EIBApril-2017.pdf.

[172] MoU between the New Development Bank and the Eurasian Development Bank on General Cooperation, 1 April 2017; available at: https://www.ndb.int/wp-content/uploads/2017/04/ MOU-with-EDBApril-2017.pdf.

[173] MoU between New Development Bank and International Investment Bank on Strategic Cooperation, 1 April 2017; available at: https://www.ndb.int/wp-content/uploads/2017/04/ MOU-with-IIBArpil-2017.pdf.

[174] MoU between the Inter-American Development Bank and the Inter-American Investment Corporation and the New Development Bank on General Cooperation, 19 April 2018; available at: https://www.ndb.int/wp-content/uploads/2018/09/MOU-with-IDB-IDB-Invest-signed.pdf.

[175] MoU between the New Development Bank and the Development Bank of Southern Africa on General Cooperation, 28 May 2018; available at: https://www.ndb.int/wp-content/uploads/ 2018/09/MOU-with-DBSA-signed-1.pdf.

[176] MoU between New Development Bank and Fondo Financiero para el Desarrollo de los Países de la Cuenca del Plata on Strategic Cooperation; available at: https://www.ndb.int/wp-content/uploads/2017/05/MOU-with-FONPLATAApril-2017.pdf.

[177] The full list of NDB partnerships is available at: https://www.ndb.int/partnerships/list-of-partnerships/.

RMB".[178] The first batch of renewable energy projects approved by the NDB in 2016 included: renewable energy projects in India through a loan extended to Canara Bank,[179] solar panels[180] and offshore wind turbines[181] projects in China, loans to BNDES to support renewables in Brazil,[182] transmission project in South Africa connecting the producers of renewable energy to the central grid managed by Eskom,[183] and the construction of hydro power plants in Russia in cooperation with the Eurasian Development Bank and International Investment Bank.[184]

In its development strategy for 2017-2021, the NDB pledged "to become an important player in helping BRICS and other EMDCs achieve the UN's 2030 Sustainable Development Goals, and those of the Addis Ababa Action Agenda on Financing for Development and the 2015 Paris Agreement on Climate Change."[185] Starting from 2017, the NDB allocated significant resources for the financing of infrastructure projects such as upgrading district roads in India,[186] building highway exits in Russia,[187] expanding a container seaport terminal in South Africa,[188] and building subways[189] and airports[190] in China. Several projects financed by the NDB support the improvement of the water supply and sanitation systems in Hunan (China),[191] Rajasthan (India),[192] Volga River Basin (Russia),[193] and Lesotho Highlands (South Africa).[194]

---

[178] 8th BRICS Summit, Goa Declaration, 16 October 2016, para 4, Appendix II.3 A.
[179] NDB, Canara renewable energy financing scheme (https://www.ndb.int/canara-india/).
[180] NDB, Lingang distributed solar power project (https://www.ndb.int/lingang-china/).
[181] NDB, Putian Pinghai Bay offshore wind power project (https://www.ndb.int/pinghai-china/).
[182] NDB, Financing of renewable energy projects and associated transmission (https://www.ndb.int/bndes-brazil/).
[183] NDB, Project finance facility for Eskom (https://www.ndb.int/eskom-south-africa/).
[184] NDB, Two loans to EDB and IIB for Nord-Hydro (https://www.ndb.int/edbiib-russia/).
[185] NDB's General Strategy: 2017-2021, 30 June 2017, pp. 12-13.
[186] NDB, Madhya Pradesh major district roads project (https://www.ndb.int/madhya-pradesh-india/).
[187] NDB, Ufa Eastern Exit project (https://www.ndb.int/ufa-road-russia/).
[188] NDB, Durban container terminal berth reconstruction project (https://www.ndb.int/transnet-south-africa/).
[189] NDB, Luoyang metro project (https://www.ndb.int/luoyang-china/).
[190] NDB, Hohhot new airport project (https://www.ndb.int/hohhot-new-airport-project/).
[191] NDB, Hunan ecological development project (https://www.ndb.int/hunan-china/).
[192] NDB, Rajasthan water sector restructuring project (https://www.ndb.int/rajasthan-water-india/).
[193] NDB, Development of water supply and sanitation systems project (https://www.ndb.int/projects-volgarussia/).
[194] NDB, Lesotho highlands water project phase II (https://www.ndb.int/lesotho-highlands-water-project-phase-ii/).

The NDB's policy documents place special emphasis on the "environmental and social soundness and sustainability of projects."[195] The proposed projects are ranked into three categories based on their potential environmental impacts: Category A (significant adverse environmental and social impacts); Category B (potential adverse environmental and social impacts which are less adverse than Category A); and Category C (minimal or no adverse environmental impacts).[196] For category A and B projects, the client is required to conduct an environmental and social impact assessment and to develop specific management plans to address these impacts. In the management of social and environmental risks the NDB relies on the existing country and corporate systems, provided they are consistent with the key requirements of the NDB's Environment and Social Policy as well as Environmental and Social Standards.[197]

Being so far the only international organisation established by the BRICS group, "[the NDB's] success or failure as an institution will perhaps be the most important litmus test for BRICS in terms of their willingness and ability to contribute to development elsewhere and improve global governance".[198] It remains to be seen whether the NDB will become a driving force in formulating the "BRICS approach" to "sustainable development" that could encourage more South-South cooperation and supplement the efforts of various international organisations and development banks.[199]

III.2. BRICS Finance Ministers and the Contingent Reserve Arrangement (CRA)

The first meeting of the BRIC ministers of finance took place in 2008 on the sidelines of the Meeting of Finance Ministers and Central Bank Governors of the G20 in São Paulo (Brazil), in the midst of the global financial crisis. Echoing the official positions of their respective governments, the BRIC ministers of finance "called for the reform of multilateral institutions in order that they

---

[195] NDB. 2016. "NDB Environment and Social Framework." March 11, pp. 3-4.

[196] *Ibid* at 7-8.

[197] *Ibid* at 6.

[198] Deepak Nayyar, "BRICS, Developing Countries and Global Governance" (2016) 37(4) *Third World Quarterly* 575 at 588.

[199] See Alexandr Svetlicinii, "Sustainable Development and the New Development (BRICS) Bank: The Contribution of the BRICS Countries", in Jose A. Puppim de Oliveira and Yijia Jing (eds.), *International Development Assistance, China and the BRICS* (New York: Palgrave, 2019).

reflect the structural changes in the world economy and the increasingly central role that emerging markets now play".[200]

In 2009, the BRIC finance ministers attended the Meeting of Finance Ministers and Central Bank Governors of the G20 in Horsham (United Kingdom). In their joint communique the BRIC finance ministers outlined the major directions for the reforming of the IMF: general increase of permanent quotas, more equitable representation of the membership, substantial SDR allocation, developing new credit facilities, and strengthening IMF's surveillance capability.[201] BRICs also called for the increased representation of the emerging economies and developing countries in the World Bank, the Financial Stability Forum, the Basel Committee on Banking Supervision, and the International Accounting Standards Board.[202] It was proposed to "shift of the order of 7% in the IMF and 6% in the World Bank Group so as to reach an equitable distribution of voting power between advanced and developing countries".[203] The same messages, supplemented by the calls for the increased attention of the multilateral development banks on emerging economies, were voiced in 2011 at the BRICS finance ministers' meeting in Washington.[204]

In 2014, at the BRICS annual summit in Fortaleza, the BRICS countries established a Contingent Reserve Arrangement (CRA), which should serve as a mechanism of support through liquidity and precautionary instruments in response to the actual or potential short-term balance of payments.

The CRA governance comprises a Governing Council and a Standing Committee. The Governing Council decides on all major constitutive issues, such as the amount of contributions, admission of new members, preconditions for drawings and renewals, provisions on default and sanctions, and on its own procedural rules. The Governing Council takes all decisions by consensus. The operations of the CRA are entrusted to the Standing Committee, which makes decisions concerning requests for support through the liquidity or precautionary instruments, requests for renewals of support through the

---

[200] Joint communique of the BRIC finance ministers, 7 November 2008, São Paulo (Brazil), para 7.
[201] Joint communique of the BRIC finance ministers, 14 March 2009, Horsham (United Kingdom), para 9.
[202] *Ibid*, paras 10-11.
[203] BRIC finance ministers and central bank governors' communiqué, 4 September 2009, London (United Kingdom).
[204] Joint communiqué of the BRIC finance ministers, 22 September 2011, Washington (USA), para 7.

liquidity or precautionary instruments, encashment requests, and the imposition of sanctions for the breach of the treaty. The treaty also provides for the possibility of establishing a permanent secretariat or a dedicated surveillance unit. [205] The requests for support and requests for renewal are approved by a simple majority vote. Each party is attributed 5% of the voting rights plus voting rights calculated based on the amount of its contribution.

BRICS Participation in the CRA

Country	Contribution (USD billion)[206]	Access to Funds[207]	Voting Rights[208]
Brazil	18	18	18.10
Russia	18	18	18.10
India	18	18	18.10
China	41	21	39.95
South Africa	5	10	5.75
TOTAL	100	85	100.00

Although the CRA has been called a potential alternative to IMF financing,[209] access to CRA funds has been linked to IMF assistance. For instance, 70% of the funds available to each party are conditioned by the existence of an on-track arrangement between the IMF and the Requesting Party which involves a commitment by the IMF to provide financing to the Requesting Party and the compliance of the Requesting Party with the terms and conditions of the arrangement with the IMF.[210] The remaining 30% are de-linked from the IMF and can be accessed whenever the Requesting Party meets the conditions of the CRA. The support funds are denominated in USD and provided through currency swaps carried out between the central banks of the BRICS countries: [211] the Requesting Party purchases USD from the Providing Party's central bank in exchange for the Requesting Party currency, and repurchases the Requesting Party currency on a later date in exchange for USD. The IMF-linked drawings have a maturity period of one year and may be renewed on

---

[205] CRA, Article 3(b)(ix), Appendix I.2.

[206] CRA, Article 2(a), Appendix I.2.

[207] CRA, Article 5, Appendix I.2.

[208] CRA, Article 3(e), Appendix I.2 .

[209] See Raj M. Desai and James Raymond Vreeland, "What the New Bank of BRICS is All About", *Washington Post* (17 July 2014); available at: https://www.washingtonpost.com/news/monkey-cage/wp/2014/07/17/what-the-new-bank-of-brics-is-all-about/?noredirect=on&utm_term=.4b7b8e913a16.

[210] CRA, Article 5(d), Appendix I.2.

[211] CRA, Article 7, Appendix I.2.

no more than two occasions.[212] The IMF de-linked drawings are issued for a six months period, with the possibility of three renewals.[213]

Unlike the NDB, the CRA does not have an independent legal personality and cannot enter into agreement or be sued.[214] Where there are disagreements related to the CRA Treaty, unless the Governing Council can find an amicable solution, the parties can resort to arbitration under UNCTRAL Arbitration Rules.[215]

III.3.   The BRICS Agreement on Cooperation in the Field of Culture

The Agreement between the Governments of the BRICS States on Coop-eration in the Field of Culture (ACFC) was concluded on 9 July 2015.[216] It lays out in broad terms the framework for cooperation and exchanges "in the spirit of openness, inclusiveness, equality, respect for cultural diversity, and mutual respect and learning".[217]

The ACFC provides for cooperation between the BRICS countries in the fol-lowing fields: the training and skills upgrading of culture and art professionals and heritage practitioners; exchanges of scientific and research workers, academics, experts and students; the protection, preservation, res-toration, return and utilisation of cultural heritage objects; popular and traditional expressions of culture, including organisation of exhibitions, festivals, national culture days, traditional festivities and performances of traditional cultural groups; traditional knowledge and cultural expressions; exhibitions, between libraries and museums; printing and publishing, participation in international book fairs; and the exchange of experiences between agencies of cultural and education sectors working in the field of creative industries.

The BRICS countries have explicitly recognised "the contribution of cultural heritage to the sustainable development agenda" and agreed to cooperate on programmes in this regard.[218] It should be also noted that all BRICS states

---

[212] CRA, Article 12(b), Appendix I.2.
[213] CRA, Article 12(a), Appendix I.2.
[214] CRA, Article 19, Appendix I.2.
[215] CRA, Article 20(b), Appendix I.2.
[216] Agreement between the Governments of the BRICS States on Cooperation in the Field of Culture, 9 July 2015, Ufa (Russia), Appendix I.3.
[217] ACFC, Preamble, Appendix I.3.
[218] ACFC, Article 4, Appendix I.3.

except Russia have ratified[219] the 2005 UNESCO Convention on the Protection and Promotion of the Diversity of Cultural Expressions. As a result, it was suggested that the convention could become the core instrument of the BRICS future agenda on the creative economy.[220]

IV. ADDITIONAL BRICS SOURCES

As demonstrated in the selective review of the most representative formats of BRICS cooperation, this process has evolved from a more centralised, top-down format to decentralised, horizontal, multi-sectoral cooperation. Certainly, the annual BRICS Summits of the Heads of State remain the most authoritative gatherings, summarising the achievements of the BRICS platform and setting the goals and policy priorities for the future. This approach is reflected in the current structure of the BRICS summit declarations, which in addition to summarising the BRICS position on various issues of global concern and intra-BRICS cooperation, include action plans for the next year.

The sectoral cooperation is coordinated by the specific ministries: foreign affairs; finance; environmental; agriculture and agrarian development; science, technology and innovation; energy; industry; trade; education; finance; health; and disaster management. As far as was possible, the most relevant documents produced by these ministerial meetings are listed in the Appendix to this volume. At the lower levels of the executive hierarchy, BRICS cooperation is carried forward by the specialised agencies and state bodies such as national competition authorities, national statistics offices, or customs and revenue agencies. An example of such cooperation is the BRICS dialogue in the field of competition law and policy, which is discussed in the next section.

In order to coordinate the cooperation on specific issues and ensure the wider participation of various stakeholders, the BRICS countries have established a number of working groups with distinct mandates in their respective sectors. These include, *inter alia*: the Anti-Corruption Working Group, the

---

[219] The list of state parties to the UNESCO Convention on the Protection and Promotion of the Diversity of Cultural Expressions is available at: http://portal.unesco.org/en/ev.php-URL_ID=31038&URL_DO=DO_TOPIC&URL_SECTION=201.html#STATE_PARTIES.

[220] See Lilian Richieri Hanania and Antonios Vlassis, "For a BRICS Agenda on Culture and the Creative Economy", in Rostam J Neuwirth, Alexandr Svetlicinii, and Denis De Castro Halis (eds.), *The BRICS-Lawyers Guide to Global Cooperation* (Cambridge: Cambridge University Press, 2017) 333 at 335.

Contact Group on Economic and Trade Issues, the BRICS Bond Fund Working Group, the Counter-Terrorism Working Group, the Labour & Employment Working Group, the E-commerce Working Group, the Trade Promotion Working Group, the Environmental Affairs Working Group, the Energy Efficiency & Energy Saving Working Group, the Agriculture Cooperation Working Group, and the Working Group on ICT Cooperation. These working groups meet on a regular basis (at least yearly) and, depending on their mandates, propose various policies, evaluate the feasibility of various initiatives, or simply engage in experience sharing and discussions.

BRICS cooperation has also expanded beyond the public bodies of the BRICS states, and includes participants from the private sector, academia, civil society and other interest groups. The most prominent example is the BRICS Business Council, established in 2013, which brings together business communities from the BRICS countries with the aim of promoting business, trade and investment ties and ensuring regular dialogue with the BRICS governments. Following the chamber of commerce model, the BRICS Business Council has set up national chapters and specialised working groups involving the diverse fields of infrastructure, manufacturing, financial services, energy and green economy, skills development, agribusiness, deregulation, regional aviation and digital economy.

Other examples of BRICS communities are: the BRICS Think-Tank Council, the BRICS Academic Forum, the Young Diplomats Forum, and the Young Scientists Forum. The specifics of this book mean that we have accorded special attention to the cooperation of the BRICS legal communities, which has been carried out through the annual BRICS Legal Forums, which has led to several important initiatives in the field of law, including the establishment of the BRICS Dispute Resolution Centre in Shanghai. The declarations of the BRICS Legal Forum are included in the Appendix and we provide a brief summary of the BRICS Legal Forum experiences below.

Another BRICS community that has been covered in detail is the BRICS Network University, which is an initiative bringing together the higher education communities of the BRICS countries through the development of common study programmes and other forms of academic exchanges. BRICS cooperation has also evolved through the organisation of regular thematic events, which allow further dialogue and stimulates people-to-people exchanges: the

BRICS Youth Summit,[221] the BRICS Games, the BRICS Film Festival,[222] the BRICS Business Forum,[223] the BRICS Friendship Cities and Local Government Cooperation Forum,[224] the BRICS Media Forum, the BRICS SoE Forum on Governance and Reform, and others.

IV.1. National Competition Authorities of the BRICS Countries

In their 2015 Ufa Declaration, BRICS expressed their support for "an inclusive and open world economy characterized by efficient resource distribution, free movement of capital, labor and goods, and fair and efficiently regulated competition".[225] In the field of competition law and policy, cooperation between the BRICS countries has involved specialised agencies, the national competition authorities (NCAs):[226] for Brazil – the Administrative Council for Economic Defense (known by its Portuguese acronym CADE (*Conselho Administrativo de Defesa Econômica*);[227] for Russia – the Federal Anti-Monopoly Service (known by its Russian acronym FAS (*Federal'naya Antimonopol'naya Sluzhba*);[228] for India - the Competition Commission of India (CCI);[229] for China - the Ministry of Commerce (MOFCOM),[230] the National Development and Reform Commission (NDRC), [231] and the State Administration for Industry and Commerce (SAIC),[232] and from 2018 – the State Administration for Market Regulation (SAMR);[233] for South Africa - the Competition Commission.[234]

---

[221] The 2018 BRICS Youth Summit was hosted by the National Youth Development Agency of South Africa in Bela Bela, Limpopo (South Africa) on 16-18 July 2018.

[222] The 3rd BRICS Film Festival took place in Durban (South Africa) on 22-27 July 2018 along with the International Durban Film Festival.

[223] The 2018 BRICS Business Forum was held on 21-23 May 2018 in New Delhi (India), http://bricsbusiness.org/.

[224] The BRICS Friendship Cities and Local Government Cooperation Urbanisation Forum took place on 28-29 June 2018 in East London (South Africa).

[225] 7th BRICS Summit (9 July 2015) Ufa (Russia), para. 12, Appendix II.4 A.

[226] See Alexandr Svetlicinii and Juanjuan Zhang, "The Competition Law Institutions in the BRICS Countries: Developing Better Institutional Models for the Protection of Market Competition" (2017) 2 *Chinese Political Science Review* 85.

[227] Administrative Council for Economic Defense; available at: http://www.cade.gov.br/.

[228] Federal Anti-Monopoly Service; available at: https://fas.gov.ru/.

[229] Competition Commission of India; available at: https://www.cci.gov.in/.

[230] Ministry of Commerce; available at: http://english.mofcom.gov.cn/.

[231] National Development and Reform Commission; available at: http://en.ndrc.gov.cn/.

[232] State Administration for Industry and Commerce; available at: http://www.saic.gov.cn/.

[233] State Administration for Market Regulation; available at: http://www.samr.gov.cn/.

[234] Competition Commission; available at: http://www.compcom.co.za/.

The BRICS NCAs have carried out their dialogue in the form of biennial international competition conferences.[235] At the 2013 conference in New Delhi the heads of the BRICS NCAs considered "the need of establishing good communication between the BRICS Competition Authorities on competition law and policy to further improving and strengthening the relationship between the BRICS Competition Authorities".[236] This regular communication and experience exchange has led to the establishment of the BRICS Working Group for the Research of Competition Issues on the BRICS Markets of Social Importance, which involved telecommunications, pharmaceuticals and health care, construction, energy, and the food industry.[237] At their 2017 conference, the BRICS NCAs agreed "to address the challenges of global economic development including growing inequality and technological transformation through strengthening cooperation in analysis of global markets and innovation landscape for improving merger review and antitrust enforcement in the BRICS countries".[238]

In 2015, the BRICS NCAs recognised the importance of a "strengthening of the cooperation and coordination between the BRICS competition authorities" and agreed "to conclude the Memorandum of Understanding in the field of competition policy in order to strengthen the cooperation and coordination between the BRICS competition authorities".[239] The respective memorandum was concluded on 19 May 2016 in St Petersburg, Russia. The MoU provides for the following forms of cooperation: (1) exchanging policies, laws, and rules, as well as the progress of legislation and enforcement in the competition field; (2) organising joint studies for the purpose of providing common knowledge on competition issues; (3) promoting participation in international conferences, seminars and other relevant events on competition issues organised by the Parties, in particular the BRICS International

---

[235] 1st BRIC International Competition Conference,1 September 2009, Kazan (Russia); 2nd BRICS International Competition Conference, 20-22 September 2011, Beijing (China); 3rd BRICS International Competition Conference, 21-22 November 2013, New Delhi (India); 4th BRICS International Competition Conference, 10-13 November 2015, Durban (South Africa); 5th BRICS International Competition Conference, 8-10 November 2017, Brasilia (Brazil).

[236] Joint Statement of the Heads of BRICS Competition Authorities, 21 November 2013, New Delhi (India), Appendix IV.2 D.

[237] See Alexandr Svetlicinii, "BRICS Countries and Their Cooperation in the Field of Competition Law and Policy: A New Voice in International Antitrust?" (2017) 64 *Revue Lamy de la concurrence* 20.

[238] Joint Statement of the Heads of BRICS Competition Authorities, 10 November 2017, Brasilia (Brazil), Appendix IV.2 A.

[239] Joint Statement of the Heads of BRICS Competition Authorities, 13 November 2015, Durban (South Africa), Appendix IV.2 C.

Competition Conference held once every two years; and (4) cooperating and coordinating with each other if necessary and under reasonable circumstances, subject to their respective laws, in investigations or enforcement proceedings pertaining to violation of competition laws.[240] The full texts of the 2016 MoU and the biennial joint statements of the BRICS NCAs are included in the Appendix to this volume.

IV.2.   The BRICS Legal Forum

Another important initiative resulting from the BRICS cooperation is found in the BRICS Legal Forum, which has been described by the BRICS Law Institute as follows:

> The BRICS Legal Forum is a high-level dialogue platform to promote communication and cooperation among government officials, legal professionals and entrepreneurs of the BRICS countries, which aims at enhancing mutual understanding and communication among legal circles, promoting practical legal cooperation, and advancing rule of law progress of the BRICS member states, practicing legal diplomacy, improving discourse and decision-making power of the developing countries, pushing the establishment of a more justified international order and system, and providing legal support for political, economic and cultural development of the BRICS member countries and the BRICS cooperation mechanism.[241]

The BRICS Legal Forum was founded in Brasília on 12 December 2014 by the following organisations: the Bar Association of Brazil,[242] the Association of Lawyers of Russia,[243] the Bar Association of India,[244] the China Law Society,[245] the Law Society of South Africa,[246] the University of Cape Town,[247] and the East China University of Political Science and Law.[248] The representatives of the forum have noted their awareness that "law and the legal community have a role to play in developing a legal framework and normative structure

---

[240] Memorandum of Understanding between the competition authorities of the Federative Republic of Brazil, the Russian Federation, the Republic of India, the People's Republic of China and the Republic of South Africa on cooperation in the field of competition law and policy, 19 May 2016, St Petersburg (Russia), para 2.1, Appendix IV.2 B.
[241] BRICS Law Institute, "BRICS Legal Forum"; available at: http://bricslawinstitute.com/en/brics-forum.html.
[242] Bar Association of Brazil; available at: https://www.oab.org.br/.
[243] Association of Lawyers of Russia; available at: http://alrf.ru/.
[244] Bar Association of India; available at: http://www.barindia.in/.
[245] China Law Society; available at: https://www.chinalaw.org.cn/.
[246] Law Society of South Africa; available at: http://www.lssa.org.za/.
[247] University of Cape Town; available at: http://www.uct.ac.za/.
[248] East China University of Political Science and Law; available at: http://www.ecupl.edu.cn/.

for a new world economic order that caters to the needs of more than half the population of the world".[249] The forum has set out the following objectives: (1) to provide a platform for high-level interactions between legal professionals; (2) to promote mutual understanding of diverse BRICS legal systems; (3) to assist in the development of a conducive legal and policy framework for the growth of business and trade in the BRICS; and (4) to promote excellence in the legal profession, encourage legal research on issues of common importance and provide legal-intellectual support for the development of policy and legislative frameworks.[250] The forum has outlined the following priority areas for independent and collaborative research activities: legal research, financial cooperation, alternative dispute resolution, legal services and legal professional training.[251] The establishment of the BRICS Legal Forum was led jointly by legal professionals and the legal academic community, which has left its distinct imprint on the objectives and priorities of the forum activities.

The second BRICS Legal Forum was held in Shanghai on 15 October 2015. In addition to the founding members, the forum was marked by the participation of state institutions and law firms, including the Bureau of International Cooperation of the Supreme People's Procuratorate of the PRC, the Beijing Law Society, the Shanghai Law Society, the Chongqing Law Society, the Guangxi Law Society, the Yunnan Law Society, the Shanghai International Arbitration Centre,[252] the Arbitration Foundation of Southern Africa,[253] the Africa Dispute Resolution, [254] the Association of Arbitrators (Southern Africa),[255] the Grandall Law Firm,[256] and the Shanghai Junyue Law Firm. The new academic participants of the BRICS Legal Forum included: the University of São Paulo, [257] the Shanghai University of Finance and Economics,[258] the

---

[249] BRICS Legal Forum, Brasilia Declaration (12 December 2014), Preamble, Appendix V.5.

[250] *Ibid*, Section II Vision, Mission and Strategy.

[251] *Ibid*.

[252] Shanghai International Arbitration Centre; available at: http://www.shiac.org/.

[253] Arbitration Foundation of Southern Africa; available at: http://arbitration.co.za/.

[254] Africa Dispute Resolution; available at: http://adr.co.za/.

[255] Association of Arbitrators (Southern Africa); available at: http://www.arbitrators.co.za/.

[256] Grandall Law Firm; available at: http://www.grandall.com.cn/.

[257] University of São Paulo; available at: https://www5.usp.br/.

[258] Shanghai University of Finance and Economics; available at: https://zs.shufe.edu.cn/.

Ural State Law University,[259] the India Law Institute,[260] the Yunnan University,[261] the Amity University,[262] the Liaoning University,[263] and the Pontifical Catholic University of São Paulo.[264] The theme of the forum, "Legal Cooperation: Towards a BRICS Community of Shared Destiny", was obviously inspired by the term "community of common destiny", which is used widely by China in its foreign policy discourse.[265] The 2015 forum established the Steering Committee, which should meet at least once a year, called by the host association of the BRICS Legal Forum in the respective year. The forum participants have noted the establishment of BRICS-related legal research centres: the BRICS Legal Research Institute at the East China University of Political Science and Law, the BRICS Law Institute at the Ural State Law University,[266] and the research unit within the Centre for Comparative Law in Africa at the University of Cape Town.[267] The Pontifical Catholic University of São Paulo, the Ural State Law University, the Kutafin Moscow State Law University,[268] the Amity Law School,[269] the Indian Law Institute, the East China University of Political Science and Law, and the University of Cape Town put forward an initiative to establish the Alliance of BRICS Law Universities as a multilateral legal cooperation platform for the universities of the BRICS countries.[270] The forum has accorded special attention to the field of dispute

---

[259] Ural State Law University; available at: http://en.usla.ru/.

[260] India Law Institute; available at: http://ili.ac.in/.

[261] Yunnan University; available at: http://www.ynu.edu.cn/.

[262] Amity University; available at: http://www.amity.edu/.

[263] Liaoning University; available at: http://enweb.lnu.edu.cn/.

[264] Pontifical Catholic University of São Paulo; available at: https://www4.pucsp.br/.

[265] See Build a Community of Shared Destiny for Common Progress (18 July 2014), keynote speech by Xi Jinping, the President of the PRC at China-Latin American and Caribbean Countries Leaders Meeting in Brasilia; available at: https://www.fmprc.gov.cn/mfa_eng/wjdt_665385/zyjh_665391/t1184869.shtml. See also Denghua Zhang, "The Concept of 'Community of Common Destiny' in China's Diplomacy: Meaning, Motives and Implications" (2018) 5(2) *Asia & The Pacific Policy Studies* 196 and Jun Ding and Hongjin Cheng, "China's Proposition to Build a Community of Shared Future for Mankind and the Middle East Governance" (2017) 11(4) *Asian Journal of Middle Eastern and Islamic Studies* 1.

[266] BRICS Law Institute at the Ural State Law University; available at: http://bricslawinstitute.com/.

[267] Centre for Comparative Law in Africa at the University of Cape Town; available at: http://www.comparativelaw.uct.ac.za/.

[268] Kutafin Moscow State Law University; available at: https://msal.ru/.

[269] Amity Law School; available at: http://www.amity.edu/als/.

[270] BRICS Legal Forum, Shanghai Declaration (15 October 2015), para 7, Appendix V.4.

resolution, marked by the inauguration of the BRICS Dispute resolution Center in Shanghai.[271]

The third BRICS Legal Forum took place in New Delhi on 12 September 2016 under the theme "Developing Legal Frameworks for Building Responsive, Inclusive and Collective Solutions". The forum noted the establishment of two more BRICS-related dispute resolution institutions: the International Dispute Resolution Centre for BRICS and Emerging Economies in New Delhi[272] and the Mediation Centre for BRICS and Developing Countries in Ekaterinburg.

In their New Delhi Declaration the participants of the forum criticised the current trends in international investment law, arguing that "global regimes being pushed for acceptance and recognition as preconditions for investment in the form of labour standards, environment and intellectual property regimes, may have restrictive propensity, and tend to become discriminatory in operation and can work as devices to pare down cost advantage and render manufacturing uncompetitive".[273] As a response, to these emerging trends, the BRICS lawyers noted their "resolve to create within BRICS the standards and principles regarding labour standards, environmental standards, intellectual property regimes which are in harmony with the needs and requirements of BRICS countries to serve their vast populations".[274] A more controversial statement included in the New Delhi declaration stipulates that "any investor entity, foreign or domestic, which makes investment, as a business proposition, to profit from exploitation of natural resources or access to local markets, is solely responsible for being diligent to safeguard its commercial interests, and cannot claim reparation of losses through treaty arbitration or other such devices, from sovereign governments, at the cost of local populations, to serve whom such investment proposals brought in the first place".[275]

The fourth BRICS Legal Forum was held in Moscow on 1 December 2017 with the theme "Interaction Between the Legal Systems of the BRICS Member

---

[271] BRICS Dispute resolution Center in Shanghai; available at: http://www.shiac.org/BRICS/index_E.aspx.

[272] See Fernando Dias Simões, "A Dispute Resolution Centre for the BRICS?", in Rostam Neuwirth, Alexandr Svetlicinii, and Denis De Castro Halis (eds.), *The BRICS-Lawyers Guide to Global Cooperation* (Cambridge: Cambridge University Press, 2017) 270.

[273] BRICS Legal Forum, New Delhi Declaration (12 September 2016) at 4, Appendix V.3.

[274] *Ibid.*

[275] *Ibid* at 5.

States: Towards an Equitable Global Order".[276] The Moscow Declaration contains numerous objectives of legal cooperation within BRICS: (1) the exchange of experience; (2) exchange of knowledge; (3) establishment of a BRICS Legal Forum think-tank as a Centre for Legal Policy for BRICS; (4) establishment of a board of governors and a panel of arbitrators for the already established BRICS dispute resolution centres in Shanghai and New Delhi; (5) preparation of analytic reviews of legislation of the BRICS countries; (6) publication of a research journal on the development of the BRICS legislation; and (7) the formation of working groups with the focus on tax law, digital economy and governance, business and contract law.[277] The participants of the forum agreed that the development of uniform legal approaches and standards would be beneficial not only for BRICS, but also for international cooperation per se.[278] They pledged to work towards the unification of national substantive and conflict-of-law rules, mutual recognition and enforcement of foreign judgments and arbitral awards. Influenced by the doping scandals involving Russian athletes, the participants of the forum agreed that "preventing and combating doping and corruption in sports are an important area of legal cooperation of the BRICS member states. With particular interest, we explore the possibility of forming an international legal mechanism of realisation and protection of intellectual property (IP) rights of the sportspersons."[279]

The fifth BRICS Legal Forum was hosted by the Law Society of South Africa in Cape Town on 24 August 2018. In 2018 the BRICS Legal Forum was included in the official and sectoral meetings noted in the BRICS Summit Johannesburg Declaration. The forum featured three key themes: arbitration, contracts and company law, and financial and tax law.[280] Instead of formulating new topics for their cooperation, the participants of the forum established the Evaluation and Coordination Committee of the BRICS Legal Forum to monitor the implementation of the declarations adopted at their annual forums.[281] It was decided to establish two more working groups: on the implementation and enforcement of laws related to drug trafficking and drug induced crimes, and on legal cooperation related to the custody of children

---

[276] Fourth BRICS Legal Forum, Appendix V.2; available at: http://brics-legal.com/eng/.
[277] BRICS Legal Forum, Moscow Declaration (1 December 2017) at 2-3, Appendix V.2.
[278] *Ibid* at 4.
[279] *Ibid* at 5.
[280] Fifth BRICS Legal Forum, Appendix V.1; available at: http://bricslegalforum2018.org/speakers/.
[281] BRICS Legal Forum, Cape Town Declaration (24 August 2018), para 11, Appendix V.1.

in cross-border family disputes.[282] In order to strengthen the links between the BRICS Legal Forum and the official BRICS Summits, the forum participants decided to strengthen their collaboration in the fields noted in the Johannesburg Declaration: artificial intelligence and information technology, and the UN 2030 Agenda of Sustainable Development and Sustainable Development Goals.[283]

The next BRICS Legal Forum is scheduled to be hosted by the Order of Attorneys of Brazil (AOB), in Rio de Janeiro on 14, 15 and 16 October 2019.[284] Generally, it is hoped that the BRICS Legal Forum will assume a greater role in the legal aspects of the global governance debate in general, and the process of the consolidation and systematisation of BRICS materials in particular.

V.   INTERIM REMARKS

The process of BRICS cooperation has evolved through multiple channels of the executive hierarchies, as well as through non-state activities and various other private initiatives. In this way, it has produced a growing number of treaties, agreements, memoranda of understanding, declarations, joint statements and communiques, action plans, sector-specific cooperation agendas and roadmaps, terms of reference and other types of documents. This steadily growing body of norms, rules, principles, plans and common positions shapes the dynamics of intra-BRICS cooperation, and the involvement of BRICS countries in various international organisations and other global governance regimes. Understanding BRICS cooperation, with its internal and external dimensions, urgently requires a process of consolidation and systematisation of the abovementioned documents, which could be broadly termed as emerging "sources of BRICS law".

In order to inform the public about their cooperation, the BRICS countries agreed in 2015 to set up a joint BRICS website, which would include the module of the BRICS Official Documents Archive. [285] The successful implementation of this project, however, requires the systematic organization of the BRICS official documents, which would greatly facilitate BRICS-

---

[282] *Ibid*, para 14.

[283] *Ibid*, para 15.

[284] BRICS Legal Forum 2018, Appendix V.1; available at: http://bricslegalforum2018.org/brazil-2019/.

[285] MoU on the Creation of the Joint BRICS Website, 9 July 2015, Ufa (Russia), Appendix IV.3.

related research and also contribute to the greater coherence of the existing BRICS policies and objectives. Such systematisation cannot be achieved without considering the possible hierarchies and relationships between various "BRICS sources of law". Our contribution to this task appears in the following chapter, where the concept of sources of law drawing from the experience of various regional integration groupings is discussed, as they are considered to be instructive for the future of BRICS cooperation.

VI.   REFERENCES

Abdenur, Adriana Erthal, "Can BRICS Cooperate in International Security?" (2017) 12(3) *International Organisations Research Journal* 73.

Barbosa da Silva, Jarbas et al., "BRICS Cooperation in Strategic Health Projects" (2014) 92(6) *Bulletin of the World Health Organization* 388.

Bond, Patrick and Garcia, Ana (eds.), *BRICS: An Anti-Capitalist Critique* (London: Pluto Press, 2015).

Creswell, Jacob et al., "Tuberculosis in BRICS: Challenges and Opportunities for Leadership within the Post-2015 Agenda" (2014) 92(6) *Bulletin of the World Health Organization* 459.

De Castro Halis, Denis and Vargas Castilhos, Guilherme, "The BRICS Investment Framework: Catching Up with Trade", in Rostam J Neuwirth, Alexandr Svetlicinii, and Denis De Castro Halis (eds.) *The BRICS-Lawyers' Guide to Global Cooperation* (Cambridge: Cambridge University Press, 2017) 78.

Desai, Raj M. and Vreeland, James Raymond, "What the new bank of BRICS is all about", *Washington Post* 17 July 2014); available at: https://www.washington post.com/news/monkey-cage/wp/2014/07/17/what-the-new-bank-of-brics-is-all-about/?noredirect=on&utm_term=.4b7b8e913a16.

Dias Simões, Fernando, "A Dispute Resolution Centre for the BRICS?", in Rostam Neuwirth, Alexandr Svetlicinii, and Denis De Castro Halis (eds.), *The BRICS-Lawyers Guide to Global Cooperation* (Cambridge: Cambridge University Press, 2017) 270.

Ding, Jun and Cheng, Hongjin, "China's Proposition to Build a Community of Shared Future for Mankind and the Middle East Governance" (2017) 11(4) *Asian Journal of Middle Eastern and Islamic Studies* 1.

Elkemann, Catherine and Ruppel, Oliver C., "Chinese Foreign Direct Investment into Africa in the Context of BRICS and Sino-African Bilateral Investment Treaties" (2015) 13(4) *Richmond Journal of Global Law and Business* 593.

Garcia, Ana and Bond, Patrick, "Introduction", in Patrick Bond and Ana Garcia (eds.), *BRICS: An Anti-Capitalist Critique* (London: Pluto Press, 2015) 1.

Grigorova, Jenya and Motte Baumvol, Julia, "BRICS in the Energy Trade Debate", in Rostam J Neuwirth, Alexandr Svetlicinii, and Denis De Castro Halis (eds.), *The BRICS-Lawyers' Guide to Global Cooperation* (Cambridge: Cambridge University Press, 2017) 180.

Hooijmaaijers, Bas and Keukeleire, Stephan, "Voting Cohesion of the BRICS Countries in the UN General Assembly, 2006-2014: A BRICS Too Far?" (2016) 22 *Global Governance* 389.

Hopewell, Kristen, "Different Paths to Power: The Rise of Brazil, India and China at the World Trade Organization" (2015) 22(2) *Review of International Political Economy* 311.

Kaddar, Miloud, Milstien, Julie, and Schmitt, Sarah, "Impact of BRICS' Investment in Vaccine Development on the Global Vaccine Market" (2014) 92(6) *Bulletin of the World Health Organization* 436.

Kirton, John, "BRICS Evolving Institutional Identity: Explaining the BRICS Summit's Solid, Strengthening Success" (2015) 10(2) *International Organisations Research Journal* 9.

Kollamparambil, Umakrishnan, "Diversity and Intra-BRICS Trade: Patterns, Risks and Potential", in Rostam Neuwirth, Alexandr Svetlicinii, and Denis De Castro Halis (eds.), *The BRICS-Lawyers' Guide to Global Cooperation* (Cambridge: Cambridge University Press, 2017) 31.

Larionova, Marina et al., "BRICS: Emergence of Health Agenda" (2014) 9(4) *International Organisations Research Journal* 73.

Larionova, Marina, "Russia's 2015 BRICS Presidency: Models of Engagement with International Organizations" (2016) 11(2) *International Organisations Research Journal* 113.

Lissovolik, Yaroslav and Vinokurov, Evgeny, "Extending BRICS to BRICS+: the potential for development finance, connectivity and financial stability" (2019) *Area Development and Policy*; available at: https://doi.org/10.1080/23792949.2018.1535246.

Liu, Ming, "BRICS Development: A Long Way to a Powerful Economic Club and New International Organization" (2016) 29(3) *The Pacific Review* 443.

Nayyar, Deepak, "BRICS, Developing Countries and Global Governance" (2016) 37(4) *Third World Quarterly* 575.

Neuwirth, Rostam J., "The Enantiosis of BRICS: BRICS La[w]yers and the Difference that They Can Make", in Rostam J. Neuwirth, Alexandr Svetlicinii, and Denis De Castro Halis (eds), *The BRICS-Lawyers' Guide to Global Cooperation* (Cambridge: Cambridge University Press, 2017) 8.

Panova, Victoria, "The BRICS Security Agenda and Prospects for the BRICS Ufa Summit" (2015) 10(2) *International Organisations Research Journal* 90.

Qobo, Mzukisi and Soko, Mills, "The Rise of Emerging Powers in the Global Development Finance Architecture: The Case of the BRICS and the New Development Bank" (2015) 22(3) *South African Journal of International Affairs* 277.

Richieri Hanania, Lilian and Vlassis, Antonios, "For a BRICS Agenda on Culture and the Creative Economy", in Rostam J Neuwirth, Alexandr Svetlicinii, and Denis De Castro Halis (eds.), *The BRICS-Lawyers Guide to Global Cooperation* (Cambridge: Cambridge University Press, 2017) 333.

Richmond, Oliver P. and Tellidis, Ioannis, *The BRICS and International Peacebuilding and Statebuilding* (Norwegian Peacebuilding Resource Centre, January 2013), available at: https://www.files.ethz.ch/isn/160996/ 5f8c6a3d43ec8fff5692d7b596af2491.pdf.

Russian Institute for Strategic Studies, *Use of National Currencies in International Settlements. Experience of the BRICS Countries* (2017); available at: https://en.riss.ru/wp-content/uploads/sites/5/2017/12/Joint-Research-Paper-2017-1.pdf.

Smagina, Iana, "The First Forum of the BRICS Network University" (2016) 3(1) *BRICS Law Journal* 144.

Stuenkel, Oliver, "Emerging Powers and Status: The Case of the First BRICS Summit" (2014) 38 *Asian Perspective* 1.

Stuenkel, Oliver, "The BRICS and the Future of R2P: Was Syria or Libya the Exception?" (2014) 6 *Global Responsibility to Protect* 3.

Svetlicinii, Alexandr and Zhang, Juan, "Defending Trade Multilateralism: The BRICS Countries in the World Trade Organization's Dispute Settlement Mechanism", in Rostam J Neuwirth, Alexandr Svetlicinii, and Denis De Castro Halis (eds.), *The BRICS-Lawyers' Guide to Global Cooperation* (Cambridge: Cambridge University Press, 2017) 54.

Svetlicinii, Alexandr and Zhang, Juanjuan, "The Competition Law Institutions in the BRICS Countries: Developing Better Institutional Models for the Protection of Market Competition" (2017) 2 *Chinese Political Science Review* 85.

Svetlicinii, Alexandr, "BRICS Countries and Their Cooperation in the Field of Competition Law and Policy: A New Voice in International Antitrust?" (2017) 64 *Revue Lamy de la concurrence* 20.

Svetlicinii, Alexandr, "Five Economic Highlights of the 2017 BRICS Summit Xiamen Declaration" (7 November 2017); available at: https://davastrat.org/2017/11/07/five-economic-highlights-of-the-2017-brics-summit-xiamen-declarations/.

Svetlicinii, Alexandr, "Sustainable Development and the New Development (BRICS) Bank: The Contribution of the BRICS Countries", in Jose A. Puppim de

Oliveira and Yijia Jing (eds.), *International Development Assistance, China and the BRICS* (New York: Palgrave, 2019).

Thiam, Alioune Badara, "China-Africa and the BRICS: An Insight into the Development Cooperation and Investment Policies", in Rostam J Neuwirth, Alexandr Svetlicinii, and Denis De Castro Halis (eds.), *The BRICS-Lawyers' Guide to Global Cooperation* (Cambridge: Cambridge University Press, 2017) 106.

Toohey, Lisa, "Barriers to Universal Membership of the World Trade Organization" (2012) 19 *Australian Journal of International Law* 97.

Wentworth, Lesley and Oji, Chijioke, "The Green Economy and the BRICS Countries: Bringing Them Together", *South African Institute of International Affairs*, Occasional paper No. 170 (December 2013); available at: https://saiia.org.za/wp-content/uploads/2014/02/saia_sop_170-_-wentworth-oji_20140213.pdf.

Wilson, Dominic and Purushothaman, Roopa, *Dreaming with BRICs: The Path to 2050*, Goldman Sachs Global Economic Paper No. 99 (1 October 2003); available at: https://www.goldmansachs.com/insights/archive/archive-pdfs/brics-dream.pdf.

Yu, Peter K., "Intellectual Property Negotiations, the BRICS Factor and the Changing North-South Debate", in Rostam J Neuwirth, Alexandr Svetlicinii, and Denis De Castro Halis (eds.), *The BRICS-Lawyers' Guide to Global Cooperation* (Cambridge: Cambridge University Press, 2017) 148.

Zhang, Denghua, "The Concept of 'Community of Common Destiny' in China's Diplomacy: Meaning, Motives and Implications" (2018) 5(2) *Asia & The Pacific Policy Studies* 196.

CHAPTER 2

Sources of Law in Light of BRICS

A Comparative Overview

For a long time there was much confusion in the use of the term "source of law." Indeed, the term is still used in a number of senses, often without distinguishing the different things called by the same name.[1]

One of the most pertinent but equally difficult questions in law, and about the nature of law, is about its "sources". Given that law itself is a dynamic and contested concept,[2] the question about sources is equally contested. In fact, a long time ago the warning was issued that "the term *sources of law* has many uses and it is a frequent cause of error".[3] It is therefore necessary to examine the use and context of this term with care. However, the quest for sources of law is aggravated by a range of factors, such as changes in context, in criteria, and in theoretical or philosophical views. Therefore, the question about sources of law pertains to both legal theory and practice, so far as this distinction has ever made or still continues to make sense today. More concretely, the question of sources of law was considered the "evergreen" question in the evolution of international law, and its relevance for both practitioners and scholars has been outlined as follows:

> For practitioners, the sources of law are not so much a point of reflection and study as they are for scholars. However, they constitute the foundations of the profession. Because the most basic piece of knowledge that a lawyer must have is that which allows him or her to identify legal norms, all modern manuals on international law deal with this issue.[4]

---

[1] Roscoe Pound, "Sources and Forms of Law" (1946) 21 *Notre Dame Lawyer* 247 at 247.

[2] George Whitecross Paton, *A Textbook of Jurisprudence* (Oxford: Clarendon Press, 1946) at 2.

[3] *Ibid* at 52.

[4] See Carlos Iván Fuentes, *Normative Plurality in International Law: A Theory of the Determination of Applicable Rules* (Springer International Publishing, 2016) at 27.

In a time of ever faster change that affects the law as much as anything else and even threatens to undermine the rule of law, the quest for legal sources must therefore also accelerate. Much like the taxonomies of legal traditions, the classification of law frequently changes over time, in its territorial or temporal scope or the doctrinal definition of a field of law, as new legal systems are constantly being formed while old ones become transformed or fall into oblivion.

Yet, despite the laws and the context constantly changing, the quest for the relevant sources of law remains the most important foundation for anyone seeking to identify a relevant law and apply as well as enforce it. This is especially true in an age of rapid change, when laws and their sources are in constant flux. It is even more relevant in the context of the BRICS countries individually and the BRICS cooperation collectively, given that the existence of the BRICS as a cooperation and dialogue platform is being questioned, from both the *de lege lata* and the *de lege ferenda* perspectives. This means that opinions, in terms both of the law as it is and the law as it should be, diverge as to the rationale, need and prospects for the BRICS countries to coordinate their actions collectively and, if they are to do so, in what form and through what legal instruments and related institutions they do it. These questions alone are of immense relevance, given that the BRICS countries individually are important drivers of faster change, irrespective of whether this change is caused by an active effort (like policy change or foreign investment) or mere default (like demographic growth and environmental degradation).

Against the background of the existing structures and action plans adopted by the BRICS countries, the need for the identification of the relevant sources of law for a legal system is real and is likely to grow with every meeting and every agreement and summit declaration. So far, the legal state of BRICS cooperation has merely been described as follows:

> As a global legal actor, the BRICS is effectively "under construction," which means that innovation in the legal sphere at either the BRICS level or the global level depends on putting the right processes in place.[5]

Moreover, the body of BRICS law has emerged in soft forms, and it is surprising "how little attention is given to the cooperation in the field of law in functional cooperation".[6] However, the question about the existence of

---

[5] See Mihaela Papa, "BRICS as a Global Legal Actor: From Regulatory Innovation to BRICS Law?" (2014) 20 *federalismi.it* 2 at 44.

[6] *Ibid.*

BRICS law is closely and paradoxically tied to the one of whether there should be BRICS law at all. If the answer to the latter question is positive, namely that there is need for a body of BRICS law to develop, then there is also a matter of identifying its legal sources. Herein lies another paradox, which consists of the problem of how to identify the legal sources of a law or legal system if the existence of the legal system itself is contested and questionable. Put differently, it entails the question of what comes first, the creation of formal sources of law or the body of law. These preliminary questions also help to explain the main rationale for this book and the following sections, which try not only to solve this paradox but also to transcend this purely binary thinking by accepting the possibility that a legal system and its sources may develop simultaneously. Equally, it also entails a new cognitive mind-set that is open to the existence, formulation or creation of novel forms of legal sources as a foundation for novel kinds of legal systems or regional and global governance models.

In order to assess the actual and potential existence of sources of law as the foundation for a sui generis body of BRICS law, it is deemed useful first to look at some principal questions related to the issue of sources of law, and second to provide a brief survey of existing legal regimes and their sources.

To begin with, the existence of law presupposes a community or society; this is reflected in the Latin maxim *ubi societas, ibi ius*,[7] meaning that "wherever there is society, there is law".[8] If this maxim is accepted, there is no need to inquire further which element was first, the society or the law. Like the chicken and the egg dilemma, it is safe to assume that, in the same way that every chicken is born from another chicken (namely its egg), law is born from society and, by logical extension, from all the humans constituting it.[9] Similarly, it can be assumed that wherever there is law, there are also various sources of law. Again, it should matter little whether the sources or the law appeared first as, generally, their existence is assessed at a later stage. What matters is a pragmatic question of what law a society plans to formulate, adopt and enforce and, related to that, what form or forms this law should take. This interrelated set of questions is of particular relevance in the global

---

[7] On the origin of the maxim, see also Giorgio Del Vecchio, *Justice: An Historical and Philosophical Essay* (New York: Philosophical Library, 1953) at 124.

[8] See Aaron X. Fellmeth and Maurice Horwitz, *Guide to Latin in International Law* (Oxford: Oxford University Press, 2009) at 281 and George Whitecross Paton, *A Textbook of Jurisprudence* (Oxford: Clarendon Press, 1946) at 82.

[9] See Roger Teichmann, "The Chicken and the Egg" (1991) 100(3) *Mind* 371.

governance debate, which is concerned with the twofold problem of understanding how we are governed and how we want to govern the world in the decades to come.[10]

In the process of linking our understanding of how we are governed with the vision of how we want to govern the world, the issue of sources of law is especially important. This is because a single legal act initiates the lengthy process towards the establishment of a new legal order, just like a long journey begins with a single step. For this reason, a single source of law may mark a crucial element in the birth of a new legal system. Therefore, it is also helpful to consider, briefly, the main criteria applied to the general classification of legal sources.

It was said at the outset that the term "sources of law" often gives rise to confusion. Roscoe Pound, for instance, identifies five different meanings attributed to the term "sources of law". First, he mentions the sense of "fountain of law, that is, the immediate practical source of the authority of legal precepts".[11] The second sense is in the meaning of "authoritative texts which are the basis of juristic and doctrinal development of the traditional element of a legal system".[12] Thirdly, it is understood as "raw material, as it were, both statutory and traditional, from which the judges derive the grounds of deciding the cases brought before them".[13] Fourth, it may be used to describe the "formulating agencies by which rules or principles or conceptions are shaped so that legislation and judicial decision may give them authority".[14] Fifth and finally, it can refer to "literary shapes, as it were, in which legal precepts are found; the forms in which we find them expressed".[15]

In more simplified terms and by using a largely dualist reasoning, the large bandwidth of meanings is reduced by moulding them into dichotomies or opposites, such as that of formal versus material sources. The difference between formal and material sources has been outlined as follows:

> A formal source is that from which a rule of law derives its force and validity. It is that from which the authority of the law proceeds. The material sources,

---

[10] See also David Kennedy, "The Mystery of Global Governance" (2008) 34(3) *Ohio Northern University Law Review* 827 at 827, 832-6, and 859.

[11] Roscoe Pound, "Sources and Forms of Law" (1946) 21 *Notre Dame Lawyer* 247 at 247.

[12] *Ibid* at 247-8.

[13] *Ibid* at 248.

[14] *Ibid*.

[15] *Ibid*.

on the other hand, are those from which is derived the matter, not the validity of the law. The material source supplies the substance of the rule to which the formal source gives the force and nature of law.[16]

Overall, the exact classification of formal and material sources is difficult and is met with uncertainty, particularly in the case of international law.[17] Adding to the uncertainty is the fact that several other dichotomies are used, as is explained by Gerald Fitzmaurice in the following paragraph:

> Accepting this classification, it is of course possible to use other terms to describe the formal and material sources. Thus they may be described as, respectively, the legal sources and the historical sources, as direct and indirect, as proximate or immediate, and remote or ultimate, and so on. Or, as has been suggested, the material sources might better be described as the 'origins' of law.[18]

It is even questioned whether different classifications are needed for the sources of law.[19] It could be asked whether, instead, a source of law should, as Hart put it, be seen as "simply the causal or historical influences which account for the existence of a given rule of law at a given time and place".[20]

Another principal dichotomy would be the classification of sources of law as being of domestic or internal versus foreign or external origin. In other words, even in our common conception of law as territorial, there are instances where legal sources from outside, that is, foreign law, are cited in the judgments of domestic courts, mainly because of their "persuasive authority".[21] However, the issue remains controversial and often divides judges in the same court.[22] Similarly, the same question arises in the context of the existence of so-called "sui generis legal regimes" or "special regimes",

---

[16] See John W. Salmond, *Jurisprudence or the Theory of the Law*, 2nd ed (London: Steven and Haynes, 1907) at 117.

[17] See e.g. Jörg Kammerhofer, "Uncertainty in the Formal Sources of International Law: Customary International Law and Some of Its Problems" (2004) 15(3) *European Journal of International Law* 523 and Wolfgang Friedmann, "The Uses of "General Principles" in the Development of International Law" (1963) 57(2) *The American Journal of International Law* 279 at 279 (Fn 2).

[18] See Gerald G. Fitzmaurice, "Some Problems Regarding the Formal Sources of International Law" (1958) *Symbolae Verzijl* 153, reprinted in Martin Dixon, Robert McCorquodale and Sarah Williams, *Cases & Materials on International Law*, 6th ed (Oxford: Oxford University Press, 2016) 23 at 23.

[19] *Ibid* at 24 (Note 3).

[20] Herbert L. A. Hart, *The Concept of Law*, 2nd ed. (Ocford: Clarendon Press, 1994) at 294.

[21] See also H. Patrick Glenn, "Persuasive Authority" (1987) 32(2) *McGill Law Journal* 261.

[22] See e.g. Steven G. Calabresi and Stephanie Dotson Zimdahl, "The Supreme Court and Foreign Sources of Law: Two Hundred Years of Practice and the Juvenile Death Penalty Decision" (2005) 47(3) *William and Mary Law Review* 743.

when it is asked whether sources other than the regime's own sources can be used in the process of rendering a judgment or legal decision; an example is whether the WTO dispute settlement mechanism is "willing to accept general international law as a consideration in its decisions".[23] The term "domestic sources of law" is also discussed in the context of the relevance of these sources for international law. This proves that dichotomies are usually related, as they originate from the same kind of mind-set.[24]

In parallel to the controversy about the origins of law, which is often framed in the dichotomy of natural law versus positivism,[25] there is also a distinction between natural and positive sources of law.[26] This opens the debate about who can be the source for sources of law, or, to put it better, what can provide the original source for law: is law perhaps of divine origin, or is the human nature or the human mind or spirit the first source of law?[27]

This also raises the possibility of a distinction between human and non-human sources of law. For instance, there are records of the "land" (rather than humans and their customs) constituting a source of law, even though this was said not to "fit into the formulaic jurisprudential scholarly papers, let alone reference the Western or Eastern jurisprudential greats".[28] In an age of rapid technological innovation, such non-human sources of law could also originate from machines or robots, relying on artificial intelligence (AI), algorithms or blockchain technology. Or, perhaps, can new media, and social media in particular, be sources of law, or are they this already? Such a dichotomy between humans and technology would also relate to the dichotomy between old and new sources or that between past and future

---

[23] See e.g. Anja Lindroos and Michael Mehling, "Dispelling the Chimera of 'Self-Contained Regimes' International Law and the WTO" (2006) 16(5) *The European Journal of International Law* 857 at 858.

[24] See Earl Weisbaum, "Domestic Sources of International Law" (1983) 76(3) *Law Library Journal* 436.

[25] See e.g. Barney Reynolds, "Natural Law versus Positivism: The Fundamental Conflict" (1993) 13(4) *Oxford Journal of Legal Studies* 441.

[26] See e.g. Helen Silving, "The Twilight Zone of Positive and Natural Law" (1955) 43(3) *California Law Review* 477 at 480.

[27] See e.g. Carlos Iván Fuentes, *Normative Plurality in International Law: A Theory of the Determination of Applicable Rules* (Springer International Publishing, 2016) at 32-41, Giorgio Del Vecchio, "The Problem of the Sources of Positive Law" (1935) 47(3) *Juridical Review* 253 at 253 and 257 and Rostam J. Neuwirth, "Law as Mnemonics: The Mind as the Prime Source of Normativity" (2008) 2(1) *European Journal of Legal Studies* 143 at 144.

[28] See C.F. Black, *The Land is the Source of the Law: A Dialogic Encounter with Indigenous Jurisprudence* (Oxon: Routledge, 2011) at 24.

sources.[29] In the end, it must be accepted that the times are changing and that change has always accompanied the discussion about sources, as was well summarized as follows:

> From divine or natural law in the classics of our discipline to the general principles of law, principles of justice, jus cogens or soft law in more recent constructions of the law of nations, there has always been a variable in the equation, an external element which did not fit an objective and ordered set of sources.[30]

In view of these changes, it is also argued that "our legal classifications must be revised from time to time to keep them as close as possible to a changing social reality".[31] This must also apply to the classification of sources of law, and even address deeper layers of our legal thinking and legal logic. This is particularly important when an era of rapid and possibly accelerating change is combined with the proliferation of new regional cooperation and integration projects that have a role in the quest for a more coherent and truly global legal order.

The fundamental question in the context of an inquiry into the existence of a coherent legal system is dependent on the ability to identify a set of underlying legal sources, and vice versa. Both questions about legal sources and those about a legal system are usually mirrored against the taxonomy of the existing legal traditions of the world. However, the taxonomy of legal traditions is constantly undergoing change and has visibly changed through-out recent decades, with certain categories of law disappearing altogether (e.g. Soviet law)[32] and new ones being recognized (e.g. chthonic law).[33] Equally, one can observe a trend towards a greater distinction and specifica-tion of existing legal traditions: for example, the generic term "Asian Law" has been broken down into different Asian legal traditions, including Hindu

---

[29] See also Max Radin, "Sources of Law – New and Old" (1928) 1(5) *Southern California Law Review* 411.

[30] See Carlos Iván Fuentes, *Normative Plurality in International Law: A Theory of the Determination of Applicable Rules* (Springer International Publishing, 2016) at viii.

[31] See Mary Ann Glendon, "The Sources of Law in a Changing Legal Order" (1983) 17(3) *Creighton Law Review* 663 at 698.

[32] See e.g. René David and John E.C. Brierley, *Major Legal Systems in the World Today: Introduction to the Comparative Study of Law*, 3rd ed (London: Stevens & Sons, 1985) at 181-224.

[33] Cf. H. Patrick Glenn, *Legal Traditions of the World: Sustainable Diversity in Law*, 3rd ed (Oxford: Oxford University Press, 2007) at 60 ("There was no point of origin of a chthonic legal tradition. There was no recorded revelation; no dramatic rupture from other traditions; no single, literally unforgettable achievement. A chthonic legal tradition simply emerged, as experience grew and orality and memory did their work").

Law, Japanese Law and Chinese Law.[34] Even domestically, the interest in identifying the sources of a national or municipal legal system is increasing, leading towards the increasingly common qualification of "hybrid", "mixed" or "polyjural" legal systems, that is, "systems that are built on several different legal traditions whose contribution to the recipient legal system is individually discernible".[35] Moreover, it is possible even to discern a trend towards the classification of unique or so-called "sui generis" legal systems (e.g. those of the WTO,[36] the EU[37] or India[38]). Unique approaches using the "sui generis" connotation have also been applied to single treaties (e.g. treaties between the Crown and Indian nations)[39] or specific laws governing novel fields (e.g. the protection of computer software).[40]

It is therefore possible to observe a paradoxical trend towards, on the one hand, a greater divergence of legal systems, while, on the other, there is a need for greater regulatory convergence because of the progress of economic globalization and international trade relations and business transactions. Within these apparently opposite forces, of law and of its context, the BRICS cooperation, as well as the cooperation of other regional cooperation or integration organizations, is to be placed. For the BRICS in particular, this means untying the knot of a set of intrinsically related questions. These questions include, first, one about the exact legal nature of the cooperation, namely whether the countries are pursuing the goals of regional integration or cooperation. The second question is about the legal status of the BRICS

---

[34] See e.g. René David and John E.C. Brierley, *Major Legal Systems in the World Today: Introduction to the Comparative Study of Law*, 3rd ed (London: Stevens & Sons, 1985) at 484-546.

[35] See Biagio Andò, "'As Slippery as an Eel'? Comparative Law and Polyjural Systems", in Vernon Valentine Palmer, Mohamed Y. Mattar and Anna Koppel (eds.), *Mixed Legal Systems, East and West* (Surrey: Ashgate, 2015) 3 at 3; see also Vernon Valentine Palmer, "Mixed Legal Systems... and the Myth of Pure Laws" (2007) 67(4) *Louisiana Law Review* 1205.

[36] See *Decision of the General Council on Conditions of Service applicable to the Staff of the WTO Secretariat of 7, 8 and 13 November 1996*, WTO Doc. WT/L/197 (18 November 1996).

[37] Robert Schütze, "On "Federal Ground: The European Union as an (Inter)National Phenomenon" (2009) 46(4) *Common Market Law Review* 1069 at 1091.

[38] See e.g. Mahendra P. Singh and Surya Deva, "The Constitution of India: Symbol of Unity in Diversity" (2005) 53 *Jahrbuch des Öffentlichen Rechts der Gegenwart/Yearbook of Public Law (Germany)* 649.

[39] James (Sakej) Youngblood Henderson, "Interpreting Sui Generis Treaties" (1997) 36(1) *Alberta Law Review* 46 at 76.

[40] See John C. Phillips, "Sui Generis Intellectual Property Protection for Computer Software" (1992) 60 (4) *George Washington Law Review* 997.

cooperation, namely whether it constitutes a mere "dialogue and cooper-ation platform",[41] a "multi-centre legal network",[42] a "coalition or alliance",[43] or something else, possibly entirely new.

Against the backdrop of the legal uncertainty surrounding the form of coop-eration between the BRICS countries, especially from a legal perspective, as well as the generally rapidly changing global regulatory environment, it is deemed useful to provide a brief overview of the issue of sources of law within different legal systems, globally, regionally, and locally.

I.   GLOBAL LAW AND ITS SOURCES

After decades of rapid globalization since the creation of the United Nations in 1945, it is time to reconsider the foundations of the existing international legal order and ponder on the establishment of a future global legal order. In fact, it has been said that the "task of international legal reform is no longer merely a morally permissible option, something to be pursued only so far as it promotes the 'national interest'; it is a moral necessity".[44] Perhaps this is too weak an argument, as this reform may even already be not a moral obligation but a matter of the survival of humanity and the planet in the long term. The reason is that humanity probably entered the Anthropocene age at the time of the industrial revolution and, at present, the impact of humans on the earth's system has become a recognizable and perhaps even decisive force for the survival of both humanity and the planet.[45] Apart from climate change or the threat of the instant destruction of the planet through nuclear weapons, other existential threats in our world are visible in numerous military conflicts and humanitarian crises as well as generally in numerous anomalies recorded in politics, the economy, science, the environment,

---

[41] See Strategy for BRICS Economic Partnership (Ufa, Russia, 2015); see Appendix II.4C.
[42] See Lucia Scaffardi, "BRICS, a Multi-Centre 'Legal Network'?" (2014) 5 *Beijing Law Review* 140 at 140.
[43] See e.g. Peter K. Yu, "Intellectual Property Negotiations, the BRICS Factor and the Changing North–South Debate", in Rostam J. Neuwirth, Svetlicinii, Alexandr, and Denis De Castro Halis, (eds.), *The BRICS-Lawyers' Guide to Global Cooperation* (Cambridge: Cambridge University Press, 2017) 148 at 150.
[44] See Allen Buchanan, *Justice, Legitimacy, and Self-Determination: Moral Foundations for International Law* (Oxford: Oxford University Press, 2007) at 432.
[45] See Wolfram Mauser, "Global Change Research in the Anthropocene: Introductory Remarks", in Eckart Ehlers and Thomas Krafft (eds.), *Earth System Science in the Anthropocene* (Berlin: Springer, 2006) 3 at 3.

global health epidemics, widespread poverty and widening inequality, to mention but a few.[46]

To put it briefly, it has therefore been stated that "globalization commands a reformulation of the law, an appropriate legal response to changing times to avoid becoming hostage to outmoded, transient paragons", and that the time has come for "a global law just as earlier, the time was ripe for the law of nations and what later became 'international law'."[47] This statement also suggests that before proper reform can materialize, a change in the terminology, or the underlying language, must take place. At present, there is no consistent body of global law. "Global law" has even been described as an oxymoron, "because the conditions it portrays do not exist in reality".[48] At best, there only exists a global governance debate, which, in trying to solve the "mystery of global governance",[49] aims to "anticipate the prospects for global governance in the decades ahead"; global governance is said to lie in the solution of "powerful tensions, profound contradictions, and perplexing paradoxes".[50] In view of these contradictions, it has also been suggested that the term "glocal law" should perhaps be preferred to "global law", because the term "glocalization" has been found to be more appropriate than the term "globalization".[51]

In the search for a global law, however, there is one major obstacle, which has been termed the paradox of global governance and characterized as follows:

> The dilemma encountered at the global level can itself be traced back to a paradox, namely the so-called "global governance paradox", which, put briefly, consists in a problem similar to the chicken-and-egg paradox, namely that in order to create a global legal order, the world community needs a global governance platform which is absent so far.[52]

---

[46] See also United Nations, *Transforming Our World: The 2030 Agenda for Sustainable Development*, General Assembly A/RES/70/1 (21 October 2015) at 5-6.

[47] See Rafael Domingo, *The New Global Law* (Cambridge: Cambridge University Press, 2010) at xiv.

[48] See Rostam J. Neuwirth, *Law in Times of Oxymora: A Synaesthesia of Language, Logic and Law* (London: Routledge, 2018) at 87.

[49] See David Kennedy, "The Mystery of Global Governance" (2008) 34(3) *Ohio Northern University Law Review* 827.

[50] See James N. Rosenau, "Governance in the 21st Century" (1995) 1(1) *Global Governance* 13 at 13.

[51] See Rostam J. Neuwirth, *Law in Times of Oxymora: A Synaesthesia of Language, Logic and Law* (London: Routledge, 2018) at 87 and Habibul H. Khondker, "Globalisation to Glocalisation: A Conceptual Exploration" (2005) 13(2) *Intellectual Discourse* 181 at 187–188.

[52] See Rostam J. Neuwirth, *Law in Times of Oxymora: A Synaesthesia of Language, Logic and Law* (London: Routledge, 2018) at 87.

Given that, to date, such a global legal order, or an adequate platform for deliberations to this end, is absent and purely theoretical, it has been suggested that at least a "common language for global law" should be developed.[53] The notion of a "common language" is to be taken not literally but as an accord regarding the use of the concept of global law and as a means "to discuss greater convergence and to argue over present discord, among the different legal provisions and perspectives found within the societies of the world".[54] Such a discussion will also have to take into account the question of the sources of law. In this regard, it was in an article published in 1964 that a former judge of the International Court of Justice, Robert Yewdall Jennings, suggested the need for a fresh look at the whole question of sources of international law.[55]

I.1.   The United Nations Charter and Public International Law

A brief inquiry into the foundations of the present international legal system usually starts with the United Nations Charter, which established the United Nations Organization in 1945. The UN Charter is certainly one of the most important sources of international law in itself, but its status as a "constitution of the international community" is still contested. [56] Idealistically, it looks very much like a constitution, but realistically it is not one. Perhaps it is merely a treaty and not a constitution, or it is merely a dream about a constitution,[57] or it is a treaty but a special one, namely one vested with supremacy over other treaties (Art. 103 UN Charter). These questions themselves depend on the theoretical approach taken or the assumptions one has about a constitution or a treaty. They also depend on what are considered to be the origins of modern international law. For instance, the birth of international law at the time of the Treaty of Westphalia has been contested, and its state-centric or Eurocentric origins questioned,

---

[53] See Andrew Halpin and Volker Roeben (eds.), *Theorising the Global Legal Order* (Oxford: Hart, 2009) at 6.

[54] *Ibid.*

[55] Robert Y. Jennings, "Recent Developments in the International Law Commission: Its Relation to the Sources of International Law" (1964) 13(2) *International and Comparative Law Quarterly* 385 at 387.

[56] See generally W. Michael Reisman, "The Constitutional Crisis in the United Nations" (1993) 87(1) *American Journal of International Law* 83; see also Pierre-Marie Dupuy, "The Constitutional Dimension of the Charter of the United Nations Revisited" (1997) 1 *Max Planck Yearbook of United Nations Law* 1 at 2-3 and Bardo Fassbender, *The United Nations Charter as the Constitution of the International Community* (Leiden: Martinus Nijhoff, 2009).

[57] See e.g. Thomas M. Franck, *Nation Against Nation: What Happened to the U.N. Dream and What the U.S. Can Do About It* (New York: Oxford University Press, 1985).

which shows that different historical views may also alter the definition and the concept of international law today. [58] Even the concept given to a particular legal system has wide implications, as is shown in the replacement of the term "law of nations" by the neologism "international law", which was most likely made for the first time by Jeremy Bentham in 1780.[59] By the same token, it has become an urgent necessity, as Philipp Jessup showed in 1956, that a complex interrelated world community that he described as "beginning with the individual and reaching up to the so-called 'family of nations'" required a novel concept, namely that of transnational law.[60] That was in 1956 and today it is possible that even transnational law appears too narrow, and that an even more inclusive concept, like the one of "global law", is called for.

Leaving aside the conceptual question, the UN Charter is also the origin of the statute of the International Court of Justice (ICJ), which lists the most important sources of international law as follows:

Article 38 ICJ Statute

1. The Court, whose function is to decide in accordance with international law such disputes as are submitted to it, shall apply:

international conventions, whether general or particular, establishing rules expressly recognized by the contesting states;

international custom, as evidence of a general practice accepted as law;

the general principles of law recognized by civilized nations;

subject to the provisions of Article 59, judicial decisions and the teachings of the most highly qualified publicists of the various nations, as subsidiary means for the determination of rules of law.

2. This provision shall not prejudice the power of the Court to decide a case *ex aequo et bono*, if the parties agree thereto.[61]

---

[58] See Yasuaki Onuma, "When was the Law of International Society Born? – An Inquiry of the History of International Law from an Intercivilizational Perspective" (2000) 2(1) *Journal of History of international Law* 1 and Stéphane Beaulac, "The Westphalian Model in Defining International Law: Challenging the Myth" (2004) 8(2) *Australian Journal of History of Law* 181.

[59] See Jeremy Bentham, *Introduction to the Principles of Morals and Legislation* (London: T. Payne, 1789) at 324.

[60] See also Christian Tietje and Karsten Nowrot, "Laying Conceptual Ghosts of the Past to Rest: the Rise of Philip C. Jessup's 'Transnational Law' in the Regulatory Governance of the International Economic System", in Christian Tietje, Alan Brouder and Karsten Nowrot (eds.), *Philip C. Jessup's Transnational Law Revisited. On the Occasion of the 50th Anniversary of its Publication* (Halle: Institut für Wirtschaftsrecht, 2006.) 17 at 27.

[61] Statute of the International Court of Justice, June 26, 1945, 33 U.N.T.S. 933.

These five sources certainly provide a useful starting point in the search for the sources of international law. While in the past their interpretation was considered to pose no particular difficulty, this has been held to be no longer true today.[62] For instance, the meaning and scope of each individual source may be ambiguous or contested.[63] Even the single words or phrases used in Article 38 ICJ Statute, such as "subsidiary means for the determination of rules of law", have given rise to debate. [64] Equally, the mutual relation between these sources and, in particular, the distinction of one from another source, may pose difficulties, as can be seen from the treaty/customary law dichotomy.[65] It has also been debated for a long time whether there is a hierarchy among the sources listed in Article 38 ICJ Statute.[66] This question is again tied to different philosophical approaches to law, such as natural law or positive law theories, as well as to the existence of sources of law such as peremptory norms (*jus cogens*).[67] Generally, it has been held that there exists no formal hierarchy between the sources of international law, but that there may be an informal one, in the sense that treaties generally enjoy priority over custom, local customs have primacy over general customary law, and customary law has primacy over the general principles of law.[68] In this respect, the question of the sources of international law is closely related to

---

[62] See Mohamed Shahabuddeen, *Precedent in the World Court* (Cambridge: Cambridge University Press, 1997) at 7.

[63] See generally Martin Dixon, Robert McCorquodale and Sarah Williams, *Cases & Materials on International Law*, 6th ed (Oxford: Oxford University Press, 2016) 18-54; see also David J. Bederman, *Custom as a Source of Law* (Cambridge: Cambridge University Press, 2010) at 144-51 and 155-9 and Fábio P. Shecaira, *Legal Scholarship as a Source of Law* (Cham: Springer, 2013).

[64] See e.g. Aldo Zammit Borda, "A Formal Approach to Article 38(1)(d) of the ICJ Statute from the Perspective of the International Criminal Courts and Tribunals" (2013) 24(2) *European Journal of International Law* 649.

[65] See e.g. Gary L. Scott and Craig L. Carr, "The International Court of Justice and the Treaty/Custom Dichotomy" (1981)16(3) *Texas International law Journal* 347.

[66] See e.g. Mario Prost, "Hierarchy and the Sources of International Law: A Critique" (2017) 39(2) *Houston Journal of International Law* 285.

[67] See e.g. Stefan Kadelbach, "Jus Cogens, Obligations Erga Omnes and other Rules – The Identification of Fundamental Norms", in Christian Tomuschat and Jean Marc Thouvenin (eds.), *The Fundamental Rules of the International Legal Order: Jus Cogens and Obligations Erga Omnes* (Leiden: Martinus Nijhoff, 2006) 21 at 28-35; see also Art. 53 Vienna Convention on the Law of Treaties (VCLT), 1155 U.N.T.S. 331.

[68] See Martti Koskenniemi, *Fragmentation of International Law: Difficulties Arising from the Diversification and Expansion of International Law (Report of the Study Group of the International Law Commission)*, UNGA A/CN.4/L.682 (13 April 2006) at 47.

the rules for the interpretation of treaties (Articles 31-33 Vienna Convention on the Law of Treaties).

What is even less clear, and maybe of greater significance for the future given the rapid development of the global community, is whether the list provided in Article 38 ICJ Statute is exhaustive or is open (meaning that more sources exist or can be created). In this respect, a general trend towards a multiplication of sources has been noted, particularly in the inclusion in domestic legal systems of "factual, political and even cultural sources".[69] By analogy, in the international legal system, the emergence of the following source was noted, namely "the creation of rules by international organizations", which was said to have "given rise to the problem of determining the place of the resolutions and declarations of principles adopted by international organizations in the system of sources".[70]

The rising significance of the rules created by international organizations is again closely related to the overall trend known as the fragmentation of international law.[71] This trend has been said to create several conflicts, for instance among different law-making treaties. The reasons for the fragmentation have been outlined as follows:

- The proliferation of international regulations;
- Increasing political fragmentation (juxtaposed with growing regional and global interdependence in such areas as economics, the environment, energy, resources, health, and the proliferation of weapons of mass destruction);
- The regionalization of international law due to a rise in the number of regional fora engaged in the formulation of international regulations;
- The emancipation of individuals from States; and
- The specialization of international regulations.[72]

In what seems to be a paradox, the ensuing fragmentation of international law can have both positive and negative effects. Positive effects may be found in a greater regulatory density and, perhaps, the absence of lacunae. Negative effects, on the other hand, are that the fragmentation may cause conflicts

---

[69] See Riccardo Monaco, "Sources of International Law", in Rudolf Bernhardt (ed.), *Encyclopedia of Public International Law*, vol 7 (Amsterdam: North-Holland, 1984) 424 at 433.

[70] *Ibid.*

[71] See generally Martti Koskenniemi, *Fragmentation of International Law: Difficulties Arising from the Diversification and Expansion of International Law (Report of the Study Group of the International Law Commission)*, UNGA A/CN.4/L.682 (13 April 2006).

[72] See Gerhard Hafner, "Pros and Cons Ensuing from Fragmentation of International Law" (2004) 25(4) *Michigan Journal of International Law* 849 at 849-50 [footnote omitted].

between treaties and "frictions and contradictions between the various legal regulations and imposing on States mutually exclusive obligations".[73] They may thus lead to conflicts between treaties or even a collision of legal regimes.[74]

Generally, it has been stated that we "undoubtedly live in an age of pluralized normativity" and that "both the norm-making processes and the norms produced thereby at the international level have undergone a profound pluralization".[75] This is why it is also necessary to consider potential conflicts that may arise from divergent sources not only of domestic law but increasingly also of international law, or from different specialized regimes of international law. In this respect it has been argued that, while it is good to maintain a certain degree of regulatory competition between different legal systems or regimes, there is also a strong necessity for complementary measures of regulatory cooperation. This was first applied to regulation at the national level in terms of "regulatory coopetition".[76] Later, the concept was extended to the interaction between international regulatory regimes, as follows:

> Translated into the regulatory realm, this means that greater emphasis should be placed on what is termed here "inter-regime regulatory coopetition" or, in other words, a better coordination, through both regulatory competition and regulatory cooperation, between the different national as well as international regulatory regimes of both a public and a private nature.[77]

Fragmentation also exists between, or is aggravated by the ongoing divide between, public and private international law, which has also been said to give rise to the following paradox:

> The separation, as maintained by the public/private distinction, is reproduced by academic and practical lawyers and by governmental and

---

[73] Gerhard Hafner, "Pros and Cons Ensuing from Fragmentation of International Law" (2004) 25(4) *Michigan Journal of International Law* 849 at 850-1; see also C. Wilfred Jenks, "The Conflict of Law-Making Treaties" (1953) *British Yearbook of International Law* 401.

[74] See generally Margaret A. Young (ed.), *Regime Interaction in International Law: Facing Fragmentation* (Cambridge: Cambridge University Press, 2012).

[75] See Jean D'Aspremont, *Formalism and the Sources of International Law: A Theory of the Ascertainment of Legal Rules* (Oxford: Oxford University Press, 2011) at 221.

[76] See Daniel C. Esty and Damien Geradin, "Regulatory Co-opetition" (2000) 3(2) *Journal of International Economic Law* 235 at 237.

[77] See Rostam J. Neuwirth and Alexandr Svetlicinii, "Law as a Social Medicine: Enhancing International Inter-Regime Regulatory Coopetition as a Means for the Establishment of a Global Health Governance Framework" (2015) 36 (3-4) *The Journal of Legal Medicine* 330 at 332 [footnote omitted].

private elites, obscuring the paradoxical result of private actors legitimately exercising public functions.[78]

Overall, there is a need to maintain and even enhance the unity of international law as well as the coherence between different sources of international law.[79] To this end, new approaches may need to be formulated, which will at the same time have to take into account the legal system in question, its sources, and its relationship to other related legal systems or regimes. Put briefly, a more holistic approach will have to be found to address the problems related to the fragmentation of international law. In this respect, even the dominant modes of cognition, such as dualistic thinking and its effect on legal reasoning, as well as the architecture of the international legal system, need to be taken into account.[80] This again also leads back to the initial question about the constitutional nature of the UN Charter, which could contribute to a greater unity of a future global legal order. The need for such considerations was formulated as follows:

> The United Nations Charter is only a part of this ongoing world constitutive process, but a full understanding of what the Charter has been able to achieve and what it is capable of achieving in the future requires clarification of critical international policies and the invention and appraisal of alternatives.[81]

In this respect, Onuma Yasuaki provides an alternative by proposing another perspective, which also takes into account cognitive levels, in what he calls an "emerging multi-polar and multi-civilizational world of the twenty-first century", and which he describes in the following paragraph:

> A transcivilizational perspective is a perspective from which we see, sense, recognize, interpret, assess, and seek to propose solutions to ideas, activities, phenomena and problems transcending national boundaries, by developing a cognitive and evaluative framework based on the recognition of plurality of civilizations and cultures that have long existed in human history.[82]

---

[78] See A. Claire Cutler, *Private Power and Global Authority: Transnational Merchant Law in the Global Political Economy* (Cambridge: Cambridge University Press, 2003) at 54 [footnote omitted].

[79] See generally Mario Prost, *The Concept of Unity in Public International Law* (Oxford: Hart, 2012) and Denis Alland et al. (eds.), *Unité et Diversité du Droit International / Unity and Diversity of International Law: Ecrits en L'honneur du Professeur Pierre-Marie Dupuy / Essays in Honour of Professor Pierre-Marie Dupuy* (Leiden: Martinus Nijhoff, 2014).

[80] See also Rostam J. Neuwirth, *Law in Times of Oxymora: A Synaesthesia of Language, Logic and Law* (London: Routledge, 2018) mainly at 170.

[81] See W. Michael Reisman, "The Constitutional Crisis in the United Nations" (1993) 87(1) *American Journal of International Law* 83 at 100.

[82] See Onuma Yasuaki, *A Transcivilizational Perspective on International Law: Questioning Prevalent Cognitive Frameworks in the Emerging Multi-Polar and Multi-Civilizational World of the Twenty-First Century* (Leiden: Martinus Nijhoff, 2010) at 130-1.

This statement also supports the rationale for the BRICS cooperation as a way of perceiving the diversity of the BRICS countries to be an incentive to make a difference in the global governance debate. Before the role of the BRICS cooperation is further assessed, it is useful to look at how one of the major actors in the creation of such "new sources of international law", namely the World Trade Organization (WTO), affects the unity of international law and also deals internally with the question of its legal sources.

I.2.   The Sources of WTO Law

The Agreement Establishing the World Trade Organization (WTO), succeeding the 1947 General Agreement on Tariffs and Trade (GATT), has been termed the "constitution of international trade law" or, more briefly, the "WTO Constitution". However, like the debate about the UN Charter, the constitutional character of the Marrakesh Agreement Establishing the World Trade Organization (WTO Agreement) is not without controversy. For instance, the Appellate Body of the WTO itself characterized the WTO Agreement as follows:

> The *WTO Agreement* is a treaty – the international equivalent of a contract. It is self-evident that in an exercise of their sovereignty, and in pursuit of their own respective national interests, the Members of the WTO have made a bargain.[83]

For the sake, in particular, of the overall unity of a future global legal order, perhaps what is today more important than the question about the exact qualification of the WTO Agreement as a treaty or a constitution is the question about the WTO's relation to the United Nations Organization and its treaties. Historically, the WTO goes back to the GATT, which itself was planned to be part of the International Trade Organization (ITO). The ITO was intended to be a specialized agency of the United Nations Organization. However, it failed to materialize, and this led to the creation of the GATT, which was described as follows:

> A pragmatic and sometimes groping attitude towards constitutional and legal structures was thus forced upon GATT, which found itself without an adequate legal and constitutional base and required to fill a vacuum created by the failure of the ITO.[84]

---

[83] WTO Appellate Body, *Japan – Taxes on Alcoholic beverages*, WT/DS1/AB/R, WT/DS10/AB/R, WT/DS22/AB/R (4 October 1996) at 14.

[84] See John H. Jackson, *World Trade and the Law of GATT* (Indianapolis: The Bobbs Merril Company, 1969) at 51.

The failure of the ITO and the ensuing establishment of the GATT outside the UN system can be taken as the first serious crack in the unity of the international legal order. It is a systemic flaw, which has been widened by separating the world into so-called "trade problems" and "non-trade problems". It is also the source of many so-called "trade and ..." problems, like those of "trade and security",[85] "trade and culture",[86] "trade and development",[87] and "trade and health",[88] to mention but a few. Many more such pairs exist, and together they form what is called the "trade linkage debate".[89] In sum, the terminology underlying the debate seems to support the calls for greater coherence and unity, particularly between economic and political, social, cultural and other related areas. It is therefore necessary to overcome the present "either/or" thinking in international trade and the separation of trade from non-trade issues. In institutional terms, it would be necessary to streamline and better coordinate the architecture of the UN system with that of the WTO. Finally, it would also be helpful to avoid the potential conflicts between treaties adopted under general international law and agreements covered by the WTO.

In the context of a quest for greater coherence between the UN and the WTO, it is important to highlight that the WTO General Council noted that "the WTO is a sui generis organization established outside the United Nations system". [90] In contrast to this comment by the General Council on the institutional structure, the Appellate Body came to a different assessment of

---

[85] See e.g. Rostam J. Neuwirth, and Alexandr Svetlicinii, "The Economic Sanctions Over the Ukraine Conflict and the WTO: "Catch XXI" and the Revival of the Debate on Security Exceptions" (2015) 49(5) *Journal of World Trade* 891.

[86] See e.g. Rostam J. Neuwirth, "The Future of the Culture and Trade Debate: A Legal Outlook" (2013) 47(2) *Journal of World Trade* 391.

[87] See e.g. V.N. Balasubramanyam (ed.), *Trade and Development: Essays in Honour of Jagdish Bhagwati* (Basingslake: MacMillan, 1996).

[88] See e.g. Rostam J. Neuwirth and Alexandr Svetlicinii, "The Regulation of Trade and Public Health in Asia-Pacific: A Case for 'Inter-Regime Co-opetition'" (2015) 10(2) *Asian Journal of WTO & International Health Law and Policy* 349.

[89] See e.g. Andrew T. F. Lang, "Reflecting on 'Linkage': Cognitive and Institutional Change in the International Trading System" (2007) 70(4) *Modern Law Review* 523, Joel P. Trachtman, "Institutional Linkage: Transcending 'Trade and ...'" (2002) 96(1) *American Journal of International Law* 77; Joel P. Trachtman, "Trade and . . . Problems, Cost-Benefit Analysis and Subsidiarity" (1998) 9(1) *European Journal of International Law* 32 and Frank J. Garcia, "Trade and Justice: Linking the Trade Linkage Debates" (1998) 19(2) *University of Pennsylvania Journal of International Economic Law* 391.

[90] WTO, *Decision of the General Council on Conditions of Service applicable to the Staff of the WTO Secretariat of 7/8 and 13 November 1996*, WTO Doc. WT/L/197 (18 November 1996) [emphasis in original].

the relationship between the agreements of public international law and those of the WTO. By referring to the general rule of interpretation, whereby a "treaty shall be interpreted in good faith in accordance with the ordinary meaning to be given to the terms of the treaty in their context and in the light of its object and purpose", the WTO Appellate Body concluded that the agreements covered by the WTO are "not to be read in clinical isolation from public international law".[91]

This is an important clarification, first for the question of how WTO law relates to other rules of international law and, second, for the question of what constitute the sources of WTO law.

As for the first point, the relation of WTO to other rules of international law, the problem was summarized as follows:

> The interplay of norms in international law is no longer of academic interest only. In today's interdependent world, where states must cooperate in pursuit of common objectives and do so under the auspices of an ever increasing number of distinct international organisations, the potential for conflict between norms is very real, indeed.[92]

These serious conflicts can only be avoided by a careful look at the sources of WTO law. Put briefly, it could be said that while the WTO is institutionally a self-contained regime, separate from the UN system, it is substantively part – as a special branch of public international law – of the wider system of international law.

As for the sources of WTO law, their identification appears fairly easy at first sight and starts from the Final Act Embodying the Results of the Uruguay Round of Multilateral Trade Negotiations, concluded in Marrakesh, Morocco, on 15 April 1994, as well as the WTO Agreement.[93] The WTO Agreement itself states that the "agreements and associated legal instruments included in Annexes 1, 2 and 3 (hereinafter referred to as "Multilateral Trade Agreements") are integral parts of this Agreement, binding on all Members".[94] The so-called "plurilateral trade agreements" included in Annex 4 are equally part of the WTO Agreement but are only binding on those Members that have

---

[91] WTO Appellate Body, *United States – Standards for Reformulated and Conventional Gasoline*, WT/DS2/AB/R (29 April 1996) at 16-7.

[92] See Joost Pauwelyn, *Conflict of Norms in Public International Law: How WTO Law Relates to other Rules of International Law* (Cambridge: Cambridge University Press, 2003) at 487.

[93] Final Act Embodying the Results of the Uruguay Round of Multilateral Trade Negotiations, Apr. 15, 1994, 33 I.L.M. 1143 (1994).

[94] Art. II:2 Marrakesh Agreement Establishing the World Trade Organization, Annex 1A, 1867 U.N.T.S. 410.

accepted them.[95] To put it briefly, the fundamental sources of WTO law are the so-called "WTO covered agreements".[96] Following the overall categories of sources of international law as codified in Article 38 ICJ Statute, when applied to the WTO, one arrives at the following list of WTO sources of law:

- WTO agreements;
- Acts of WTO organs;
- GATT/WTO "custom" and "subsequent practice";
- WTO judicial decisions and doctrine;
- Unilateral acts of WTO members.[97]

In the case of the WTO it is more difficult to establish a system of primary and secondary sources, as the WTO has no explicit legislative powers, and mainly pursues its objectives through methods of negative integration, while powers to adopt measures of positive integration are widely absent or in an early and merely nascent stage.

The key question about sources of WTO law at this point is how we should conceptually deal with the ambiguous situation of the WTO being institutionally separate from the UN at the same time as its covered agreements and related acts form part of the wider or general public international law. This has also been expressed by way of the description of the WTO legal system as being "largely" but "not entirely" self-contained.[98] This ambiguity probably mirrors the overall conceptual problems underlying the current architecture of the international legal order, which is highly fragmented. More specifically, in the case of the WTO legal system, the limitations of a binary mode of thinking surface in the problem of the division into two separate categories of so-called "trade" and "non-trade" concerns.[99] While the debate on the trade linkage is already highlighting these deficiencies, their recognition at the level of treaties is progressing only slowly. In this respect, the changing terminology from "non-trade" to "trade-related

---

[95] Art. II:3 Marrakesh Agreement Establishing the World Trade Organization, Annex 1A, 1867 U.N.T.S. 410.

[96] See also David Palmeter and Petros C. Mavroidis, "The WTO Legal System: Sources of Law" (1998) 92(3) *American Journal of International Law* 398 at 398.

[97] See Joost Pauwelyn, *Conflict of Norms in Public International Law: How WTO Law Relates to other Rules of International Law* (Cambridge: Cambridge University Press, 2003) at 40-52.

[98] See David Palmeter and Petros C. Mavroidis, "The WTO Legal System: Sources of Law" (1998) 92(3) *American Journal of International Law* 398 at 413.

[99] See e.g. Recital 6 of the Preamble of the Agreement on Agriculture, Apr. 15, 1994, Marrakesh Agreement Establishing the World Trade Organization, Annex 1A, 1867 U.N.T.S. 410 ("[...] having regard to non-trade concerns, including food security and the need to protect the environment [...]").

aspects", as used in the case of the Agreement on Trade-Related Aspects of Intellectual Property Rights (TRIPS) and the Agreement on Trade-Related Investment Measures (TRIMS),[100] is a first but modest step in the direction towards greater coherence in international law and policy making. Nevertheless, further action is urgently needed if the global legal community desires to follow the mind-set of the global economy, was and this has been characterized as follows:

> No game is an island. Even so, people draw boundaries and divide the world up into many separate games. It's easy to fall into the trap of analyzing these separate games in isolation—imagining that there's no larger game. The problem is that mental boundaries aren't real boundaries—there are no real boundaries. Every game is linked to other games: a game in one place affects games elsewhere, and a game today influences games tomorrow.[101]

There is still a long way to go before the WTO legal system realizes its optimal compatibility with the UN legal system and vice versa. Moreover, in addition to the fragmentation between public international law and international economic law, there is a new danger being reported, which consists in the fragmentation of WTO law itself. The problem of the fragmentation of WTO law was reported to consist in the following three facts:

- *Fact 1*: The world trade system is marked by a motley assortment of discriminatory trade agreements known as the 'Spaghetti Bowl'.
- *Fact 2*: Regionalism is here to stay. Trade agreements will continue to proliferate even after the current trade round meanders to a conclusion.
- *Fact 3*: This tangle of trade deals is a sub-optimal way to organise world trade. The discrimination inherent in regionalism is economically inefficient and the costs rise as manufacturing becomes ever more internationalised and supply chains grow across national borders.[102]

A solution to the problem of the Spaghetti Bowl and to growing fragmentation within the multilateral trading regime, in addition to the high levels of fragmentation within the international legal system as a whole, was said to

---

[100] Agreement on Trade-Related Investment Measures, Apr. 15, 1994, Marrakesh Agreement Establishing the World Trade Organization, Annex 1A, 1868 U.N.T.S. 186.

[101] Adam M. Brandenburger and Barry J. Nalebuff, *Co-opetition: A Revolution Mindset That Combines Competition and Cooperation: The Game Theory Strategy That's Changing the Game of Business* (New York: Doubleday, 1996) at 234.

[102] Richard Baldwin and Theresa Carpenter, "Regionalism: Moving from Fragmentation towards Coherence", in Thomas Cottier and Panagiotis Delimatsis (eds.), *The Prospects of International Trade Regulation: From Fragmentation to Coherence* (Cambridge: Cambridge University Press 2011) 136 at 136.

lie in the urgent necessity of "multilateralizing regionalism".[103] The fact that the multilateralization of regionalism appears as yet another legal oxymoron can be seen as further evidence that binary thinking is the source of the problem of the fragmentation of laws and different sources of laws.[104]

The argument that the problems related to fragmentation are caused by binary thinking and an exclusive logic can be seen in the recent revival of the question of the national security exceptions of Article XXI GATT and Article XIV[bis] GATS.[105] In the case of national security exceptions, the continuing fragmentation between the WTO and the UN system was caused or aggravated by the failure of the International Trade Organization to materialize. The institutional separation of the WTO and the UN contradicts the logic of the intrinsic ties between international trade norms and norms related to security concerns. This amounts to a so-called legal dilemma, or a catch-22 situation, described as a "Catch-XXI" problem in view of Article XXI GATT.[106] In short, it is a legal paradox or legal dilemma, and has also been defined as a situation in which a "legal actor confronts an irresolvable conflict between legal norms so that the application of one norm necessarily impairs the other".[107]

The fact that these legal dilemmas or paradoxes caused by fragmentation are serious can be seen from the recent developments in the WTO, where several countries have resorted to unilateral measures that are imposed and justified on the basis of national security concerns.[108] If this problem is not addressed at its root, this trend may even further aggravate the crisis surrounding the WTO and, in particular, erode the effective functioning of the WTO dispute settlement mechanism by blocking the appointment of new Appellate Body

---

[103] *Ibid*; see also Richard Baldwin and Patrick Low (eds.), *Multilateralizing Regionalism* (Cambridge: Cambridge University Press, 2008).

[104] See also Rostam J. Neuwirth, *Law in Times of Oxymora: A Synaesthesia of Language, Logic and Law* (London: Routledge, 2018) at 156 and 233.

[105] See e.g. WTO Panel Report, *Russia – Measures Concerning Traffic in Transit*, WT/DS512/R (5 April 2019).

[106] See Rostam J. Neuwirth and Alexandr Svetlicinii, "The Economic Sanctions Over the Ukraine Conflict and the WTO: 'Catch XXI' and the Revival of the Debate on Security Exceptions" (2015) 49(5) *Journal of World Trade* 891, Shin-yi Peng, "Cybersecurity Threats and the WTO National Security Exceptions" 18(2) *Journal of International Economic Law* 449, and Ji Yeong Yoo and Dukgeun Ahn, "Security Exceptions in the WTO System: Bridge or Bottle-Neck for Trade and Security?" (2016) 19(2) *Journal of International Economic Law* 417.

[107] See Valentin Jeutner, *Irresolvable Norm Conflicts in International Law: The Concept of a Legal Dilemma* (Oxford: Oxford University Press, 2017) at 4.

[108] See also Stuart S. Malawer, "Trump's China Trade Policies: Threats and Constraints" (2017) 1 *China and WTO Review* 109.

members by the United States. The reasons for this crisis, which may derail the WTO's future altogether, are said to be rooted in systemic issues (the national security exceptions as well as a judicial overreach) coupled with the creation by the Appellate Body of its own rules.[109] Thus in the present crisis many leftover problems and unsolved issues from the past emerge and await the moment of their resolution in the future. These problems are primarily related to institutional issues as well as the sources of law, which are combined in the debate about the status of the WTO as a self-contained regime. For these reasons, it is important to pursue further, but briefly, the question of sources at the regional level.

II. REGIONAL SOURCES OF LAW

Since the creation of the WTO in 1995, there has been a noticeable rise in the negotiation of regional trade agreements or, more broadly, a strong trend towards economic integration at the regional level. This trend has been said to cause serious challenges to the governance of multilateral trade relations, as explained in the following paragraph:

> This proliferation of regional agreements has created a spaghetti bowl of criss-crossing arrangements, with little attention to coherence among agreements or to the implications of so many regimes for trade costs, efficiency, and the conditions of competition in global markets.[110]

As the large and growing number of regional trade agreements (RTAs) also has a considerable effect on global governance, it is important to consider the sources of law on which these regional orders are built. Their content, scope and even geographical configurations are diverse. In this context, it is important to highlight that the cooperation between the BRICS countries displays several unique features, which is why a brief but closer look at some of the existing regional integration projects is deemed useful.

---

[109] See Tetyana Payosova, Gary Clyde Hufbauer, and Jeffrey J. Schott, *The Dispute Settlement Crisis in the World Trade Organization: Causes and Cures*, Peterson Institute for International Economics Policy Brief (May 2018); available at: https://www.law.berkeley.edu/wp-content/uploads/2018/01/WTO-dispute-settlement.pdf.

[110] See Richard Baldwin and Patrick Low, "Introduction", in Richard Baldwin and Patrick Low (eds.), *Multilateralizing Regionalism* (Cambridge: Cambridge University Press, 2008) 1 at 1.

II.1. The European Union (EU)

To begin with, the European Union (EU),[111] which is one of the most advanced regional integration organizations, provides an excellent point of departure for the study of sources of law in the context of international or regional cooperation.

The reasons are that, first and foremost, it is a sui generis legal order, which was created based on an idea and realized by virtue of law and related legal instruments.[112] Second, the European Union, its institutional framework and its law evolved and expanded very quickly from its humble beginnings as the European Coal and Steel Community in 1952 and the European Economic Community in 1958 until the Lisbon Treaty in 2007. It, therefore, provides a good example for testing the dynamics underlying the theory of economic integration, in which the following stages or varying degrees of integration can be distinguished: (1) international cooperation; (2) free trade area; (3) customs union; (4) common market; (5) economic (and monetary) union; and (6) complete integration.[113]

The EU does this by providing a relatively transparent and accessible system of sources of law, but also shows how the sources of law, their classification and even their hierarchy are subject to frequent changes in line with important changes in the context. At the present, the EU's legal order knows, in principle, the following three categories of sources of law, namely (1) primary law, (2) secondary law and (3) supplementary sources of law, which are outlined as follows:

---

[111] The member states are: Austria, Belgium, Bulgaria, Croatia, Cyprus, Czech Republic, Denmark, Estonia, Finland, France, Germany, Greece, Hungary, Ireland, Italy, Latvia, Lithuania, Luxembourg, Malta, Netherlands, Poland, Portugal, Romania, Slovakia, Slovenia, Spain, Sweden, United Kingdom. For the time being, the UK remains a full member of the EU and rights and obligations continue to fully apply in and to the UK. See European Union Countries; available at: https://europa.eu/european-union/about-eu/countries_en.

[112] See also Case 6-64, *Flaminio Costa v E.N.E.L.*, [1964] E.C.R. 585; see also Derrick Wyatt, "New Legal Order, or Old?" (1982) 7 *European Law Review* 147 and Bruno de Witte, "Retour à « Costa » La primauté du droit communautaire à la lumière du droit international" (1984) 20(3) *Revue trimestrielle de droit européen* 425 mainly at 446-450; see also Case 294/83, *Parti écologiste "Les Verts" v European Parliament*, [1986] E.C.R. 1339 at para. 23, calling the Treaty of the EEC the "basic constitutional charter".

[113] Bela Balassa, *The Theory of Economic Integration* (London: George Allen & Unwin Ltd, 1962) at 2.

European Union Law Sources

Primary law

The main sources of primary law are the treaties establishing the EU: the Treaty on the EU and the Treaty on the Functioning of the EU. These treaties set out the distribution of competences between the EU and the EU countries and describe the powers of the European institutions. They therefore determine the legal framework within which the EU institutions have to work to implement policies.

Primary law also includes:

- the amending EU Treaties;
- the protocols annexed to the founding treaties and to the amending treaties;
- the treaties on the accession of new countries to the EU.

Secondary law

Secondary sources are legal instruments based on the treaties.

Secondary law comprises unilateral acts and agreements.

Unilateral acts can be divided into two categories:

- those listed in Article 288 TFEU: regulations, directives, decisions, opinions and recommendations;
- those not listed in Article 288 TFEU, i.e. 'atypical' acts such as communications and recommendations, and white and green papers.

Conventions and agreements include:

- international agreements, signed by the EU and a country or outside organisation;
- agreements between EU countries; and
- interinstitutional agreements, i.e. agreements between the EU institutions.

Supplementary sources of law

Supplementary sources are elements of law not specifically mentioned in the treaties. This category includes:

- case-law of the Court of Justice of the EU (CJEU);
- international law — often a source of inspiration for the CJEU when developing its case-law. The CJEU cites written law, custom and usage;
- general principles of law — unwritten sources of law developed by the case-law of the CJEU. They have allowed the CJEU to implement rules in various areas that are not mentioned in the treaties.[114]

However, as in the case of public international law, the debate about the sources of EU law is not closed, and questions about additional or novel sources of law continue to arise in the EU context.

---

[114] See e.g. EUR-Lex, "Sources of EU Law"; available at: https://eur-lex.europa.eu/legal-content/EN/ALL/?uri=LEGISSUM:l14534.

A first such source of law that has been mentioned is "unwritten sources of law", which has been said to include but not to be limited to the following sources:

> [...] the general principles of law or the jurisprudence of the Court of Justice; the rules of law whose origin is outside the Union legal order, originating from external liabilities of the Communities, of EU, respectively, and the complementary law derived from conventional acts concluded between the member states, for enforcing the Treaties.[115]

Another example is found in soft law, which is used in different contexts in the EU, such as in competition law,[116] state aid,[117] fiscal governance,[118] tax law[119] or the construction of social Europe.[120] To sum up, the debate about soft law in particular can be seen as evidence of the rapid transformation of law, and perhaps also of the inadequacy of binary thinking in law in terms of the hard versus soft law dichotomy. Paradoxically, the sources of EU law also include atypical acts, such as communications and recommendations, which per se are not legally binding. Additionally, soft law may be legally binding or it may not be binding but at least have legal effect,[121] depending on the overall understanding of (EU) law.[122] What a different view of law means for the meaning and binding nature of soft law has been outlined as follows:

> Some authors clearly adhere to a limited concept of law, equating sources of law to those that have been attributed legally binding force in some way. In their conception, the use of the term soft law is a *contradictio in terminis*; soft law without legal effect is not law and soft law with legal effect is hard law. Others have adopted a far broader view, considering as sources of law all rules,

---

[115] See Roxana-Mariana Popescu, "Features of the Unwritten Sources of European Union Law" (2013) 20 *Lex ET Scientia International Journal* 98 at 98.

[116] See e.g. Zlatina Georgieva, "Soft Law in EU Competition Law and Its Judicial Reception in Member States: A Theoretical Perspective" (2015) 16(2) *German Law Journal* 223.

[117] See e.g. Michelle Cini, "The Soft Law Approach: Commission Rule-Making in the EU's State Aid Regime" (2001) 8(2) *Journal of European Public Policy* 19.

[118] See e.g. Waltraud Schelkle, "EU Fiscal Governance: Hard Law in the Shadow of Soft Law" (2007) 13(3) *Columbia Journal of European Law* 705.

[119] See e.g. Hans Gribnau, "Soft Law and Taxation: EU and International Aspects" (2008) 2(2) *Legisprudence* 67.

[120] See e.g. David M. Trubek and Louise G. Trubek, "Hard and Soft Law in the Construction of Social Europe: the Role of the Open Method of Co-ordination" (2005) 11(3) *European Law Journal* 343.

[121] See e.g. Emilia Korkea-Aho, "EU Soft Law in Domestic Legal Systems: Flexibility and Diversity Guaranteed, (2009) 16(3) *Maastricht Journal of European & Comparative Law* 271 at 272 and Linda Senden, *Soft Law in European Community Law* (Oxford: Hart, 2004) at 3.

[122] See e.g. Fabien Terpan, "Soft Law in the European Union—The Changing Nature of EU Law" (2015) 21(1) *European Law Journal* 68 at 71.

norms and principles that can be invoked in court as standards for review, either as independent standards or as standards for interpretation.[123]

The controversy or paradox is thus evidence that legal science must expand its scope of inquiry and also devote time to the space between the opposite types of norms. This space has also been called "a continuum running from non-legal positions to legally binding and judicially controlled commit-ments".[124] Thus, it is necessary to supplement a theory of a binary view (relative normativity) with a theory of a continuum view (graduated normativity).[125] The theory of graduated normativity was described as the recognition that "law may have various different legal effects and consequences, which may be direct or indirect, weaker or stronger, harder and softer".[126] Considering law as a process, and considering the particularities of the process of law making, a wider understanding of the links between law and its society or, to use a better term, its "community" will surface. In the EU context, further sources of law (or at least sources having legal relevance), such as political and cultural sources, have been mentioned, as follows:

> The political sources of law are the conclusive result of a debate where opposing political forces clashed in order to influence the manifestation of the will of the state represented by the law and its content; the cultural sources are inferred from the experience of the past (customs, judicial precedent) or from the rational analysis of legal phenomena (the role of the scholars for example).[127]

Overall, the EU's legal system – despite its highly sophisticated legalistic character – proves that society, law and legal science must remain open and must also continue the search for novel modes of governance and more efficient legal instruments based on the identification or creation of new legal sources.

---

[123] Linda Senden, *Soft Law in European Community Law* (Oxford: Hart, 2004) at 3.

[124] See e.g. Fabien Terpan, "Soft Law in the European Union—The Changing Nature of EU Law" (2015) 21(1) *European Law Journal* 68 at 70.

[125] See e.g. Verena Rosic Fegus, "The Growing Importance of Soft Law in the EU" (2014) 1(1) *Journal for International and European Law, Economics and Market Integrations* 145 at 147.

[126] *Ibid.*

[127] See Giuseppe Martinico, "Complexity and Cultural Sources of Law in the EU Context: from the Multilevel Constitutionalism to the Constitutional Synallagma" (2007) 8(3) *German Law Journal* 205 at 224.

II.2. The Economic Community of West African States (ECOWAS)

The Economic Community of West African States (ECOWAS) was established in 1975 on the basis of the Treaty of Lagos and includes as member states 15 states located in Western Africa.[128] ECOWAS can be taken as a useful example, in general, of regional integration on the African continent and, in particular, of a setting in a different cultural and geographic context. More than this, it has also been described as "an additional African contribution to universal international economic law". [129] It is of great interest as it combines predominantly French, English and Portuguese speaking members, and includes countries that were influenced more by a civil or a common law legal tradition.

At present, the main goals of ECOWAS are outlined in Article 3(1) of the ECOWAS Revised Treaty as follows:

> Article 3
> AIMS AND OBJECTIVES
> 1. The aims of the Community are to promote co-operation and integration, leading to the establishment of an economic union in West Africa in order to raise the living standards of its peoples, and to maintain and enhance economic stability, foster relations among Member States and contribute to the progress and development of the African Continent.[130]

In addition to the promotion of "co-operation and integration, leading to the establishment of an economic union in West Africa", Article 3(2) ECOWAS Revised Treaty gives further detail on the specific goals to be achieved. As far as the degree of integration is concerned, the goals are rather broad, and point towards complete integration. In concrete terms, ECOWAS has created an institutional framework, including the Authority of Heads of State and Government, the Council of Ministers, the Community Parliament, and the Community Court of Justice, to mention but a few (Article 6 ECOWAS Treaty).

---

[128] The member states are: Benin, Burkina Faso, Cape Verde, Ivory Coast, Gambia, Ghana, Guinea, Guinea-Bissau, Liberia, Mali, Niger, Nigeria, Senegal, Sierra Leone, Togo; see The Economic Community of West African States (ECOWAS); available at: http://www.ecowas.int/member-states/.

[129] See Sunday Babalola Ajulo, "Sources of the Law of the Economic Community of West African States (ECOWAS)" (2001) 45(1) Journal of African Law 73 at 77.

[130] See Article 3(1) ECOWAS Revised Treaty of 24th July, 1993; available at: http://www.ecowas.int/wp-content/uploads/2015/01/Revised-treaty.pdf.

ECOWAS has also established a customs union, which was notified to the WTO in 2005.[131]

In terms of law, the sources of ECOWAS law are said to include the following instruments:

> [T]he Revised Treaty of 1993, protocols, convention, supplementary act, decisions and regulation. They also include subsidiary legal instruments, Article 38 of the Statutes of International Court of Justice, as well as opinions, recommendation and directives of the institutions of ECOWAS.[132]

So far, the system of sources of law is rather conventional and similar to other systems, like the one of the EU. Like the EU, ECOWAS law classifies its sources into primary and secondary (or derived) sources of law. More interesting is the classification between autochthonous and non-autochthonous sources, the former being understood as those sources that are "derived from instruments of the Economic Community of West African States, namely (a) the Revised Treaty, (b) convention, (c) supplementary acts, (d) protocol, (e) regulation, (f) decision, (g) other subsidiary legislation and (h) judgment of the Community Court".[133] Non-autochthonous sources comprise sources that "did not originate from the Economic Community of West African States and its jurisdiction", and refer to laws made applicable through Article 38 of the ICJ Statute and the African Charter on Human and People's Rights, which is a text created by the African Union.[134]

Last but not least, it is also argued that the judgments of the ECOWAS Community Court of Justice can be considered a source of law within the Community legal order, even though there is no explicit establishment of the doctrine of judicial precedent.[135] This position is derived by way of the argument that judicial decisions from external tribunals can command "persuasive authority in the ECOWAS Court of Justice".[136]

However, what remains uncertain is the extent to which various customary or religious laws, like Islamic law, can be considered as a source of ECOWAS law. This argument has largely been denied, based on the secular nature of

---

[131] See World Trade Organization (WTO), "Regional Trade Agreements Information System (RTA-IS)"; available at: http://rtais.wto.org/UI/PublicShowRTAIDCard.aspx?rtaid=36.

[132] See Jerry Ukaigwe, *ECOWAS Law* (Cham: Springer International, 2015) at 33.

[133] *Ibid* at 48.

[134] *Ibid*.

[135] *Ibid* at 50.

[136] See Sunday Babalola Ajulo, "Sources of the Law of the Economic Community of West African States (ECOWAS)" (2001) 45(1) *Journal of African Law* 73 at 89.

ECOWAS.[137] However, like soft law, these local customary or religious laws may not have a binding legal nature per se but may still have legal effect, if only indirectly. In the African context, the limitations of a binary view thus emerge more in temporal terms, i.e. between pre-colonial and colonial sources of law, and also in geographic and cultural terms, namely whether there is a single African legal tradition or African law or even if there could be one.[138] Certainly, answers to these questions will largely depend on need and arise from changes in the context. In the short term, such a need may in fact arise in the economic context of the proliferation of regional trade agreements on the African continent alone.[139] Most of all, in the context of ECOWAS, too, the classification of sources of law in purely binary terms will not suffice to embrace the complexity of the reality.

II.3. The Gulf Cooperation Council (GCC)

In the Middle East, an interesting regional economic integration project is found in the Gulf Cooperation Council (GCC), which was founded in 1981 on the basis of the Charter of the Gulf Cooperation Council.[140] The GCC Charter stipulates the following main objectives of the cooperation:

Article Four
Objectives

To effect coordination, integration and inter-connection between Member States in all fields in order to achieve unity between them.

To deepen and strengthen relations, links and areas of cooperation now prevailing between their peoples in various fields.

To formulate similar regulations in various fields including the following:
Economic and financial affairs
Commerce, customs and communications
Education and culture

To stimulate scientific and technological progress in the fields of industry, mining, agriculture, water and animal resources; to establish scientific research; to establish joint ventures and encourage cooperation by the private sector for the good of their peoples.[141]

---

[137] *Ibid* at 94.

[138] *Ibid* at 76.

[139] See generally James Thuo Gathii, *African Regional Trade Agreements as Legal Regimes* (Cambridge: Cambridge University Press, 2011).

[140] Secretariat General of the Gulf Cooperation Council, available at: http://www.gcc-sg.org/en-us/Pages/default.aspx.

[141] Article 4 of the GCC Charter; Gulf Cooperation Council (GCC); available at: http://www.gcc-sg.org/en-us/AboutGCC/Pages/Primarylaw.aspx.

In 2003, the GCC established a customs union among its members: Bahrain, Kuwait, Oman, Qatar, Saudi Arabia, and the United Arab Emirates.[142] Being primarily of an economic nature but also pursuing broader goals, interesting questions regarding the sources of law of the GCC have been raised. These questions are primarily centred on the applicability of the *Shari'a*, i.e. the sacred law of Islam.[143] It is important to stress that Islamic law, because of its particular character and origin, cannot easily be compared to secular legal systems, because "Shari'a is not strictly speaking, a legal system, for it reaches much deeper into thought, life and conduct than a purely legal system can aspire to do".[144] Yet, the *Shari'a* itself is based on numerous sources similar to secular legal systems, and these have been categorized into primary and secondary sources. The primary sources comprise the *Qur'an* and the *Sunna*, whereas the secondary or dependent sources are said to be not sources stricto sensu but rather to serve as a means for discovering the law by means of interpretation based on *Ijma*, or consensus, and *Ijtihad*, or reasoning.[145] An important controversy regarding Islamic law concerns this last dependent source, *Ijtihad* (reasoning), and is whether the "gate of *Ijtihad*" (or "of independent reasoning") was or was not closed at the end of the ninth century.[146] This is a matter of principal concern, as any legal system faces tensions arising from changes since the time of the original revelation or creation of the law.

For the GCC, it has been said that the *"Shari'a* runs like a golden thread through the jurisprudence of the Gulf States", while the individual legal systems of the GCC member countries differ widely, especially in matters of civil and commercial law.[147] The fact is that the GCC member countries have quite different characteristics, and may follow civil or common law traditions. A comparative study on the sources of law in the GCC member states reveals that the impact that the *Shari'a* may have on a decision on any legal matter may vary "from 'not at all' in a problem falling within the Commercial Code

---

[142] See World Trade Organization (WTO), "Regional Trade Agreements Information System (RTA-IS)"; available at: https://rtais.wto.org/UI/PublicShowRTAIDCard.aspx?rtaid=17.

[143] See Joseph Schacht, *An Introduction to Islamic Law* (Oxford: Clarendon Press, 1982) at 1.

[144] See C. G. Weeramantry, *Islamic Jurisprudence: An International Perspective* (Basingstoke: MacMillan, 1988) at 1.

[145] *Ibid* at 31 and 32-45.

[146] See Wael B. Hallaq, "Was the Gate of Ijtihad Closed?" (1984) 16(1) *International Journal of Middle East Studies* 3 and Joseph Schacht, *An Introduction to Islamic Law* (Oxford: Clarendon Press, 1982) at 69-75.

[147] See W. M. Ballantyne, "The States of the GCC: Sources of Law, the Shari'a and the Extent to Which It Applies" (1985) 1(1) *Arab Law Quarterly* 3 at 3.

of Kuwait to 'basically' in a problem in Saudi Arabia, while in the other jurisdictions, the answer may be somewhere between these extremes".[148] In conclusion, the author of this study suggests that the answer to these questions should be sought first in the constitution of the relevant member, then in the codes and their commentaries and, for those countries with a common law element, in the common law books and precedents.[149]

In the end, the example of the GCC reveals problems in the reconciliation of secular law with religious norms, and of legal systems based more heavily on either civil or common law traditions or even that rely on both. It also highlights the difficulty of separating commercial from other civil matters. Hence, the GCC experience also seems to question the accuracy and utility of a binary theory of sources of law.

II.4. The Association of Southeast Asian Nations (ASEAN)

In Asia, a good example of regional integration is provided by the Association of Southeast Asian Nations (ASEAN), which was established in 1967 in Bangkok.[150] ASEAN has also established a free trade area among its members, the ASEAN Free Trade Area (AFTA), which was notified to the WTO in 1993. Since that date four more free trade agreements (FTAs) and economic integration agreements (EIAs) have been notified and have entered into force, with India (2010/2015), South Korea (2010), Australia–New Zealand (2010) and China (2005/2007), and there is also one free trade agreement for goods only with Japan (2008).[151]

Since 2008, the ASEAN Charter has been a legally binding agreement among the ten ASEAN Member States, and it has established a new legal framework with a number of new organs to pursue its central objectives.

Like the EU Treaties, the ASEAN Charter pursues rather broad objectives, ranging from the maintenance of peace and security and the promotion of greater political, security, economic and socio-cultural cooperation, to the preservation of Southeast Asia as a Nuclear Weapon-Free Zone, the creation of a single market and production base, the alleviation of poverty and

---

[148] *Ibid.*
[149] *Ibid.*
[150] Association of Southeast Asian Nations (ASEAN); available at: http://asean.org/. The members include: Brunei, Cambodia, Indonesia, Laos, Malaysia, Myanmar, Philippines, Singapore, Thailand, and Vietnam.
[151] See World Trade Organization (WTO), "Regional Trade Agreements Information System (RTA-IS)"; available at: https://rtais.wto.org/UI/PublicAllRTAList.aspx.

narrowing of the development gap, the strengthening of democracy, good governance, the rule of law, the promotion of human rights protection and fundamental freedoms, and sustainable development, to mention but a few (Article 1 ASEAN Charter). The main difference from the EU and maybe from other projects is that it aims to realize these objectives in the "ASEAN way". This particular way of cooperation is based on consensus in decision making, which the Charter stipulates as follows:

Article 20

CONSULTATION AND CONSENSUS

1. As a basic principle, decision-making in ASEAN shall be based on consultation and consensus.

2. Where consensus cannot be achieved, the ASEAN Summit may decide how a specific decision can be made.

3. Nothing in paragraphs 1 and 2 of this Article shall affect the modes of decision-making as contained in the relevant ASEAN legal instruments.

4. In the case of a serious breach of the Charter or non-compliance, the matter shall be referred to the ASEAN Summit for decision.[152]

The particular way of ASEAN is said to be rooted in history and culture, and proceeds less "through rules and regulations, but through discussion, consultation and consensus". It consists of a consensus approach, which relies "largely on patient consensus-building to arrive at informal understandings or loose agreements".[153]

In terms of the sources of ASEAN law, there are first and foremost the primary sources, namely treaties like the Bangkok Treaty and the ASEAN Charter, and the various agreements signed by the ASEAN countries themselves (e.g. the 1992 ASEAN Free Trade Agreement (AFTA) or the 2003 Declaration of ASEAN Concord II (Bali Concord II) establishing the ASEAN Community) and those with third countries (e.g. the agreements with India, South Korea, Australia–New Zealand, China and Japan (ASEAN Plus)).

A category of secondary sources of ASEAN law is said to include "all resolutions of inter-state organs which generally take the form of declarations, plans of action, memorandums of agreement, etc., that is to say acts that are legally non-binding".[154] Yet, as with soft law in the EU, these

---

[152] Charter of the Association of Southeast Asian Nations, 20 November 2007 (ASEAN Charter); available at: http://asean.org/storage/images/archive/publications/ASEAN-Charter.pdf.

[153] See Paul J. Davidson, "The ASEAN Way and the Role of Law in ASEAN Economic Cooperation" (2004) 8 *Singapore Yearbook of International Law* 165 at 165-6.

[154] See Laurence Henry, "The ASEAN Way and Community Integration: Two Different Models of Regionalism" (2007) 13(6) *European Law Journal* 857 at 866.

various ASEAN acts, and particularly their declarations, have been found to be not legally binding but to "nonetheless have legal effect".[155] Still, there is a general trend towards the rule of law that is also noticeable in the case of ASEAN.[156] This becomes visible in the case of the so-called "Blueprints". There are three blueprints, namely one for the ASEAN Political-Security Community, one for the ASEAN Economic Community,[157] and a third one for the ASEAN Socio-Cultural Community, and they have been compiled and re-named the Roadmap for an ASEAN Community 2009-2015.[158] The implementation of the Roadmap is further guided by the soft laws created by various working groups. For example, the Blueprint for the ASEAN Economic Community envisaged a "greater harmonization of competition policy and law in ASEAN by developing a regional strategy on convergence".[159] To realize this objective, the ASEAN Experts Group on Competition prepared the 2010 ASEAN Regional Guidelines on Competition Policy,[160] which constitute non-binding guidance for the ASEAN Member States. The non-binding nature of the Guidelines can be exemplified by the fact that the competition laws of the ASEAN Member States adopted after the publication of the Guidelines display a significant degree of divergence in both substantive and procedural rules.[161] Scholars have criticized the "ASEAN way" of dealing with economic integration, and have argued that the building of a common market and the attraction of foreign investment will require the "legalization" of the eco-nomic integration process.[162] Nevertheless, given the low level of integration

---

[155] *Ibid.*

[156] See Michael Ewing-Chow and Tan Hsien-Li, "The Role of the Rule of Law in ASEAN Integration", *EUI Working Paper RSCAS 2013/16* (March 2013) at 11; available at: http://cadmus.eui.eu/bitstream/handle/1814/26452/RSCAS_2013_16.pdf?sequence=1&isAllowed=y.

[157] See Siow Yue Chia and Michael G. Plummer, *ASEAN Economic Cooperation and Integration: Progress, Challenges and Future Directions* (Cambridge: Cambridge University Press, 2015).

[158] See Michael Ewing-Chow and Tan Hsien-Li, "The Role of the Rule of Law in ASEAN Integration", *EUI Working Paper RSCAS 2013/16* (March 2013) at 1 and 3; available at: http://cadmus.eui.eu/bitstream/handle/1814/26452/RSCAS_2013_16.pdf?sequence=1&isAllowed=y.

[159] AEC Blueprint 2025, para 27(v).

[160] ASEAN Regional Guidelines on Competition Policy (Jakarta, 2010), available at: http://www.asean.org/storage/images/2012/publications/ASEAN%20Regional%20Guidelines%20on%20Competition%20Policy.pdf.

[161] See Alexandr Svetlicinii, "Building Regional Competition Policy in ASEAN: Lessons from the European Competition Network" (2017) 15(3) *Asia Europe Journal* 341.

[162] See e.g. Simon Chesterman, *From Community to Compliance?: The Evolution of Monitoring Obligations in ASEAN* (Cambridge: Cambridge University Press, 2015); Michael Ewing-Chow, "Culture Club or Chameleon: Should ASEAN Adopt Legalization for Economic Integration?" (2004) 8 *Singapore Yearbook of International Law* 225; Jean-Claude Piris and Walter Woon,

and the absence of supranational structures or compulsory dispute resolution mechanisms, it has been suggested that the "ASEAN way" is likely to persist.[163]

Finally, there is also great diversity among the legal systems of the ASEAN Member States as each of their individual systems is rooted in different legal contexts and traditions.[164] These domestic laws also have an important impact, albeit only an indirect one, on the overall body of ASEAN law. As with the GCC, there are also members with a greater focus on religious laws, like Islamic law in Indonesia, or Malay, Hindu, and Chinese customary laws in Malaysia, and these exercise a direct or indirect influence on the understanding of the rule of law.

As for the existence of a body termed "ASEAN law", it has been noted that "ASEAN States had already built up a copious body of 'ASEAN Law' – separately negotiated treaties, agreements and other instruments that applied to specific regulatory areas" and that "the Southeast Asian region appears to be evolving towards the consolidation of 'ASEAN Law'".[165]

II.5.   The Southern Common Market (MERCOSUR)

The South American continent, too, participates in the wider trend of a proliferation of regional integration and cooperation projects. Among these projects, MERCOSUR, a trade bloc established by the Treaty of Asunción in 1991 and the Protocol of Ouro Preto in 1994, stands out.[166] Its special status is explained by the fact that MERCOSUR includes Brazil, a member of the BRICS group and the largest South American economy, along with Argentina, Paraguay and Uruguay; Venezuela and Bolivia complete the list of six full members (with Venezuela currently being suspended and Bolivia still completing the accession process). There are also six associate countries: Chile, Colombia, Ecuador, Guyana, Peru, and Surinam.[167] The MERCOSUR

Towards a Rules-Based Community: An ASEAN Legal Service (Cambridge: Cambridge University Press, 2015).

[163] See Huong Ly Luu, "Regional Harmonization of Competition Law and Policy: An ASEAN Approach" (2012) 2(2) *Asian Journal of International Law* 291.

[164] See ASEAN Law Association, "Legal Systems in ASEAN"; available at: https://www.aseanlaw association.org/legal.html.

[165] See Diane A. Desierto, "ASEAN's Constitutionalization of International Law: Challenges to Evolution under the New ASEAN Charter" (2011) 49(2) *Columbia Journal of Transnational Law* 268 at 274 and 285.

[166] MERCOSUR; available at: http://www.mercosur.int/.

[167] See MERCOSUR, "Países del MERCOSUR"; available at: https://www.mercosur.int/quienes-somos/paises-del-mercosur/.

members notified their RTA, in the form of a customs union and economic integration arrangements, to the WTO in 1991 for goods and in 2006 for services.[168] In addition to the MERCOSUR RTA, the MERCOSUR members have also notified free trade agreements to the WTO with India (2010), Mexico (2017), Chile (2017), the South African Customs Union (2017) and Egypt (2018).[169] The MERCOSUR countries have thus also associated themselves with two more BRICS members, India and South Africa. In sum, MERCOSUR has also been said to offer "an interesting model for comparative integration studies, as it by no means aims at becoming a complex integration process such as the European Union, while at the same time aiming at being more than the NAFTA".[170] These qualities also make it an interesting model for a comparison with the BRICS model of cooperation and integration.

In terms of objectives, the Treaty of Asunción lays out the purposes, principles, and instruments as follows:

CHAPTER I – Purposes, Principles and Instruments

Article 1

The States Parties hereby decide to establish a common market, which shall be in place by 31 December 1994 and shall be called the "common market of the southern cone" (MERCOSUR).

This common market shall involve:

The free movement of goods, services and factors of production between countries through, inter alia, the elimination of customs duties and non-tariff restrictions on the movement of goods, and any other equivalent measures;

The establishment of a common external tariff and the adoption of a common trade policy in relation to third States or groups of States, and the co-ordination of positions in regional and international economic and commercial forums;

The co-ordination of macroeconomic and sectoral policies between the States Parties in the areas of foreign trade, agriculture, industry, fiscal and monetary matters, foreign exchange and capital, services, customs, transport and communications and any other areas that may be agreed upon, in order to ensure proper competition between the States Parties;

The commitment by States Parties to harmonize their legislation in the relevant areas in order to strengthen the integration process.[171]

---

[168] See World Trade Organization (WTO), "Regional Trade Agrements Information System"; available at: http://rtais.wto.org/UI/PublicShowRTAIDCard.aspx?rtaid=130.

[169] *Ibid.*

[170] See Marcílio Toscano Franca Filho, Lucas Lixinski, and María Belén Olmos Giupponi, "Introduction to the Law of MERCOSUR", in Marcílio Toscano Franca Filho, Lucas Lixinski, and María Belén Olmos Giupponi (eds.), *The Law of MERCOSUR* (Oxford: Hart, 2010) 1 at 1.

[171] Article 1 of the Treaty Establishing a Common Market between the Argentine Republic, the Federal Republic of Brazil, the Republic of Paraguay and the Eastern Republic of Uruguay, 26

The objectives laid down in the Treaty of Asunción thus contain a strong commitment towards greater economic integration on the South American continent. Since 1991, several additional agreements or instruments have been signed that reinforce the legal framework of MERCOSUR. These include various agreements on different topics, like the "Protocol of Brasilia for the Solution of Controversies", the "Protocol of Colonia for the Promotion and Protection of Investments", the "Customs Code of MERCOSUR", the "Protocol for the Harmonization of Intellectual Property Norms", the "Protocol for the Defense of Competition", [172] the "Legal Framework on the Regulations Regarding Dumping on Imports from non-MERCOSUR Countries", the "International Commercial Arbitration Agreement of MERCOSUR", the "Protocol of Montevideo on Trade in Services" and the "Agreement for International Freight Contracts Jurisdiction between MERCOSUR Countries".[173]

As for MERCOSUR sources of law, a distinction between primary and secondary sources is also drawn. The primary sources are the founding treaties, whereas the secondary sources include the laws produced by MERCOSUR's main bodies. As for primary sources, the Protocol of Ouro Preto, signed on 17 December 1994, lists them as follows:

> Chapter V: Legal Sources of Mercosul
> Article 41
> The legal sources of Mercosul are:
> I. The Treaty of Asuncion, its protocols and the additional or supplementary instruments;
> II. The agreements concluded within the framework of the Treaty of Asuncion and its protocols;
> III. The Decisions of the Council of the Common Market, the Resolutions of the Common Market Group and the Directives of the Mercosul Trade Commission adopted since the entry into force of the Treaty of Asuncion.[174]

March 1991; (Treaty of Asunción); available at: http://www.sice.oas.org/Trade/MRCSR/TreatyAsun_e.asp#CHAPTER_I.

[172] See also Marco Botta, "The Cooperation between the Competition Authorities of the Developing Countries: Why it does not Work? Case Study on Argentina and Brazil" (2009) 5(2) *Competition Law Review* 153; Alexandr Svetlicinii and Juanjuan Zhang, "The Competition Law Institutions in the BRICS Countries: Developing Better Institutional Models for the Protection of Market Competition" (2017) 2(1) *Chinese Political Science Review* 85.

[173] See Organization of American States (OAS), "Legal Framework of the Common Market of the Southern Cone"; available at: http://www.sice.oas.org/Mercosur/instmt_e.asp.

[174] Article 41 of the Additional Protocol to the Treaty of Asunción on the Institutional Structure of MERCOSUR (Protocol of Ouro Preto); available at: http://www.sice.oas.org/trade/mrcsr/ourop/ourop_e.asp.

These primary sources also include a large number of agreements concluded since the entry into force of the Protocol of Ouro Preto, which include agreements of a political, commercial, cultural and educational nature.[175]

Secondary sources of MERCOSUR law are mainly the legislative acts produced by its main bodies, the Common Market Council (CCM), the Common Market Group (CMG), and the MERCOSUR Trade Commission (MTC).[176] In addition to the types of secondary law of Decisions, Resolutions and Directives mentioned in Article 41 of the Protocol of Ouro Preto, agreements with third countries and international organizations are also said to be included in the category of secondary law of MERCOSUR.[177] Last but not least, given also the different constitutional settings of its members, MERCOSUR secondary law norms are said not to possess a self-executing nature, and they therefore need to be incorporated into internal legal orders in accordance with the applicable domestic legal system.[178]

Like the WTO and other regional systems, MERCOSUR struggles with the exact relevance given to doctrine and case law, as well as with its exact place in, and relation to, international law.[179] Most of all, it struggles with the problems relating from an acceleration of the pace of change, and a proliferation of primary and secondary sources of law as an attempt to respond to the needs for legal certainty and predictability as well as greater legal complexity. This shows that – despite the diversity of these projects, both internally and externally, and their uniqueness in manifold ways – the MERCOSUR project faces similar challenges to those faced by cooperation and integration projects elsewhere. In sum, the MERCOSUR model also appears to underscore the universal need for a combined consideration of sources of law and the institutional setting, of domestic and international law, of private and public law, as well as numerous other dichotomies or, in short, it supports the need for a new conceptual and cognitive framework based on a more differentiated approach to dualist thinking as the sole basis for legal reasoning. The reason is that, while dualist thinking may have advantages in the short term, it probably "trades accuracy for simplicity" in the long run.[180]

---

[175] See Belén Olmos Giupponi, "International Law and Sources of Law in MERCOSUR: An Analysis of a 20-Year Relationship" (2012) 25(3) *Leiden Journal of International Law* 707 at 710.

[176] *Ibid* at 711.

[177] *Ibid* at 712 (Fn 34).

[178] *Ibid* at 713.

[179] *Ibid* at 718 and 733.

[180] See Bart Kosko, *Fuzzy Thinking: The New Science of Fuzzy Logic* (New York: Hyperion, 1993) at 21.

For this and other reasons, an extension of cognitive modes and legal logic will be warranted because of the emergence of new challenges that may well produce novel sources of law as well as new concepts and integration models.

II.6.   The Eurasian Economic Union (EAEU)

In the aftermath of the disintegration of the Soviet Union, the newly independent states attempted to preserve the economic ties between the former USSR republics that had been established during the period of the centrally planned economy. In 1999, the Russian Federation and the Republic of Belarus established a union state that abolished immigration and customs controls between the two nations. [181] In 2000, Russia, Belarus, Kazakhstan, the Kyrgyz Republic and Tajikistan formed the Eurasian Economic Community (EurAsEC). [182] In 2007, Russia, Belarus and Kazakhstan proceeded with the creation of a customs union[183] and they implemented a common external tariff by 2010. In 2015, the Eurasian integration of the former Soviet republics culminated in the Eurasian Economic Union (EAEU). [184]

Like the EU, the EAEU has supranational institutions, vested with rule-making powers: the Supreme Eurasian Economic Council, the Eurasian Inter-governmental Council, the Eurasian Economic Commission, and the Court of the EAEU. The decisions of the Supreme Eurasian Economic Council and the Eurasian Intergovernmental Council are transposed into the national legislation of the EAEU Member States, while the decisions of the Eurasian Economic Commission have direct effect and can be enforced without transposition or ratification. [185] Despite the institutional similarities with the EU, the supranational powers of the EAEU institutions (the EAEU Commission

---

[181] Treaty on the Establishment of a Union State between the Russian Federation and the Republic of Belarus of 8 December 1999.

[182] Treaty on the Establishment of the Eurasian Economic Community of 10 October 2000. See also A. I. Zybaylo, "Sources of EurAsEC Law and Methods of their Implementation in the Legislation of the Member States" (2013) *Mezhdunarodnoe publichnoe, mezhdunarodnoe chastnoe i evropeyskoe pravo* 47.

[183] Agreement concerning the creation of the united customs territory and the creation of the customs union of 6 October 2007.

[184] See also A. Ya. Kapustin, "The Treaty of the Eurasian Economic Union – New Page of Legal Development of Eurasian Integration" (2014) 12 *Zhurnal rossiyskogo prava* 98.

[185] The legislative activity of the Eurasian Economic Commission is subject to the prior public consultation and regulatory impact assessment procedures, which were introduced in 2015 as a response to the concerns of the business community burdened by the proliferation of the EAEU regulations. See O.Yu. Bakaeva, "Acts of the Eurasian Economic Commission as a source of law EAEC" (2016) 3(8) *Russian Journal of Legal Studies* 73.

and the EAEU Court) are substantially weaker than their EU counterparts, which also diminishes the role of the EAEU *aquis communautaire*.[186] The harmonization and unification of the trade rules is carried out primarily at the national level by the Member States.[187] The following provision of the EAEU Treaty summarizes the hierarchy of sources of the EAEU law:

Article 6 Law of the Union

1. The Law of the Union shall consist of the following:

this Treaty;

international treaties within the Union;

international treaties of the Union with a third party;

decisions and dispositions of the Supreme Eurasian Economic Council, the Eurasian Intergovernmental Council, and the Eurasian Economic Commission adopted within the powers provided for by this Treaty and international treaties within the Union.

Decisions of the Supreme Eurasian Economic Council and Eurasian Intergovernmental Council shall be enforceable by the Member States in the procedure provided for by their national legislation

International treaties of the Union with a third party shall not contradict the basic objectives, principles and rules of the functioning of the Union.

In case of conflict between international treaties within the Union and this Treaty, this Treaty shall prevail.

Decisions and dispositions of the Union shall not be inconsistent with this Treaty and international treaties within the Union.

In case of conflict between decisions of the Supreme Eurasian Economic Council, the Eurasian Intergovernmental Council, or the Eurasian Economic Commission:

decisions of the Supreme Eurasian Economic Council shall prevail over decisions of the Eurasian Intergovernmental Council and the Eurasian Economic Commission;

decisions of the Eurasian Intergovernmental Council shall prevail over decisions of the Eurasian Economic Commission.

The Court of the EAEU, like the Court of Justice of the European Union, is entrusted with the judicial review of the legislative and administrative acts of the EAEU institutions. The Court is also authorized to issue interpretations concerning the provisions of the EAEU Treaty, upon request of the Member

---

[186] See A. Ya. Kapustin, "The Law of Eurasian Economic Union: International Legal Discourse" (2015) 11 *Zhurnal rossiyskogo prava* 59.

[187] See V. P. Kirilenko and D. G. Demidov, "Principles of Functioning of the Eurasian Economic Union (International Legal Aspects) (2015) 3 *Upravlencheskoe konsultirovanie* 83.

States or the Eurasian Economic Commission.[188] In the administration of justice, the EAEU Court applies:

1)   the generally recognised principles and rules of international law;
2)   the EAEU Treaty, international treaties within the EAEU and other international treaties to which the states that are parties to the dispute are participants;
3)   decisions and directions of the bodies of the EAEU;
4)   international custom as evidence of the general practice accepted as law.[189]

However, unlike the authority of its EU counterpart, the precedent-setting authority of the EAEU Court is expressly restricted by the EAEU Treaty: "A judgment of the Court cannot amend and/or abrogate the existing rules of the law of the Union and the legislation of the Member States, and cannot create new ones."[190] This cautious attitude to the rule-setting role of the EAEU Court expressed by the Member States in the EAEU Treaty can be partly explained by the interpretative practice of its predecessor, the Court of EurAsEC, which engaged in a proactive introduction of *res judicata* to the EAEU legal system.[191] Although the decisions of the EAEU Court are binding on the parties to the dispute, if a Member State fails to comply then the issue is decided at the Supreme Eurasian Economic Council, the political body of the EAEU, which adopts all decisions by consensus.[192] This substantially undermines the enforceability of the Court's judgments and leads companies to settle their disputes against EAEU Member States in the WTO, the European Court of Human Rights, investment arbitration, or the constitutional courts of the EAEU Member States.[193] Since neither the Court nor the Eurasian Economic Commission have been accorded enforcement powers that would ensure the implementation of the EAEU agreements by the Member States, the process of Eurasian economic integration remains

---

[188] See A. V. Kovalev, "The Interpretation of the Eurasian Economic Union Law: the Legal Grounds for the Preparation of Clarification and Evolution of Interpretive Process" (2016) 62 *Aktualnye problemy rossiyskogo prava* 187.

[189] EAEU Treaty, Annex 2 Statute of the Court of the Eurasian Economic Union, para 50.

[190] *Ibid* para 102.

[191] See I. S. Iksanov and I. Yu. Kosirev, "The Problems of Supranational Legal Regulation in the Activities of the Court of the Eurasian Economic Union" (2017) 5 *Gumanitarnye nauki. Vestnik finansovogo universiteta* 6; N. A. Sokolova, "Eurasian Integration: Powers of the Eurasian Union Court" (2015) CVIII(11) *Lex Russica* 96.

[192] EAEU Treaty, Annex 2 Statute of the Court of the Eurasian Economic Union, paras 114-115.

[193] See Alexey Ispolinov, "Statute of EAEU Court as Reflection of EAEU Members Concerns and Doubts" (2016) 4 *Pravo. Zhurnal Vysshey shkoly ekonomiki* 152.

largely dependent on the political will of the participating countries.[194] Being aware of the important role of the Member States and the harmonization of national legislation for the purposes of Eurasian economic integration, legal scholars have examined the possibilities of harmonizing various areas of national law that are pertinent to the enforcement of the EAEU agreements.[195]

As the EAEU Treaty primarily concerns the trade in goods among the Member States, the majority of whom are also members of the WTO,[196] the EAEU Treaty was notified to the WTO.[197] One of the critical issues for the understanding of EAEU law is its relationship with the WTO system. The compatibility of EAEU law with WTO law has been questioned in at least three WTO disputes against Russia: DS479 *Russia – Anti-Dumping Duties on Light Commercial Vehicles from Germany and Italy*;[198] DS485 *Russia – Tariff Treatment of Certain Agricultural and Manufacturing Products*;[199] and DS499 *Russia – Measures affecting the importation of railway equipment and parts thereof.*[200] In DS499, the panel concluded that the application of EAEU tariff duties can be imputed to Russia and can be reviewed as part of Russia's WTO commitments.[201] Hence, one can argue that the WTO Dispute Settlement Body (DSB) has considered the EAEU rules to be Russian measures and not international law norms.[202] On the other hand, the EAEU Court held that WTO agreements cannot be viewed as part of EAEU law, for the mere formal reason that they cannot be considered to be "other international treaties to

---

[194] See N. E. Kotova, "Eurasian Economic Union: Improving the Legal Framework" (2016) 5 *Mirovaya ekonomika. Vestnik finansovogo universiteta* 126.

[195] See e.g. N. A. Nyrkova, "Integration of Criminal Law of the Customs Union: Problem Identification" (2014) XCVI(11) *Lex Russica* 1338; E. Yu. Petrov and E. S. Grinberg, "Anti-Monopoly Policy of European Union and Eurasian Economic Union: View from Inside" (2014) 6 *Vestnik Moskovskogo universiteta MVD Rossii* 244.

[196] The following EAEU Member States are also members of the WTO: Armenia (5 February 2003), Kazakhstan (30 November 2015), the Kyrgyz Republic (20 December 1998) and Russia (22 August 2012). Belarus has initiated accession process, which is still ongoing.

[197] See World Trade Organization (WTO), "Regional Trade Agreements Information System (RTA-IS)", http://rtais.wto.org/UI/PublicShowMemberRTAIDCard.aspx?rtaid=909.

[198] See World Trade Organization (WTO), "Dispute Settlement"; available at: https://www.wto.org/english/tratop_e/dispu_e/cases_e/ds479_e.htm.

[199] *Ibid.*

[200] *Ibid.*

[201] WTO, *Russia – Tariff Treatment of Certain Agricultural and Manufacturing Products*, WT/DS485/R, paras 7.42-7.46.

[202] See Darya Boklan, "Eurasian Economic Union and World Trade Organization: Interrelation of Legal Regimes" (2017) 2 *Pravo. Zhurnal Vysshey shkoly ekonomiki* 223 at 230.

which the states that are parties to the dispute are participants" within the meaning of the Court's statute, since Belarus is not a WTO member.[203] As a result, the EAEU Court, at least for the time being, will not engage in the interpretation of the WTO rules, in line with the ruling of the panel in DS152 *United States – Sections 301-310 of the Trade Act 1974*,[204] which urged WTO members to resort exclusively to the WTO Dispute Settlement Mechanism for the resolution of issues regulated by WTO rules.[205] Hence, despite calls by legal scholars that the WTO DSB should interpret WTO law taking into account the existing international law in force between the WTO members,[206] in the relationship between the WTO and the EAEU, at least, the fragmentation is likely to persist.

Besides being a representative example of regional economic integration, which has unique legal features bearing both resemblances to and differences from other similar projects, the EAEU also has the potential to foster inter-BRICS economic cooperation by directly engaging Russia, India, and China. In 2015, Russia and China issued a joint statement concerning cooperation by the EAEU with the Belt and Road Initiative.[207] In the same year, at the St. Petersburg International Economic Forum, Russia and India set up a Joint Feasibility Study Group on the India–EAEU free trade agreement, while the formal negotiations commenced in 2017.[208] In 2018, the EAEU and China concluded an agreement on trade and economic cooperation.[209]

---

[203] See EAEU Court, Judgment of 21 June 2016 in case No. CE-1-2/2-16-AP.

[204] See World Trade Organization (WTO), "Dispute Settlement"; available at: https://www.wto. org/english/tratop_e/dispu_e/cases_e/ds152_e.htm.

[205] WT/DS152/R, para 7.43: "Article 23.1 [DSU]...imposes on all Members to "have recourse to" the multilateral process set out in the DSU when they seek the redress of a WTO inconsistency."

[206] See Gabrielle Marceau, "Conflicts of Norms of Jurisdictions: The Relationship between the WTO Agreement and MEAs and Other Treaties" (2001) 35(6) *Journal of World Trade* 1081.

[207] See Alexandr Svetlicinii, "China's Belt and Road Initiative and the Eurasian Economic Union: "Integrating the Integrations" (2018) 5 *Public Administration Issues* 7.

[208] See Eurasian Economic Commission, EAEU and India began formal negotiations on a free trade agreement (3 June 2017); available at: http://www.eurasiancommission.org/en/nae/ news/Pages/3-06-2017.aspx.

[209] See Eurasian Economic Commission, Agreement signed on trade and economic cooperation between EAEU and PRC (17 May 2018); available at: http://www.eurasiancommission.org/ en/nae/news/Pages/17-05-2018-5.aspx.

III. NATIONAL AND NOVEL SOURCES OF LAW

The question about global and regional sources of law is set in the context of an overall debate about the future role of the territorial nation state in global regulation and law as well as in policy making. While some commentators see the future of global law to lie outside the state, and the role of the nation state to be in decline,[210] others defend the concept of territorial sovereignty and even argue that states will play an increasingly important role when compared to international organizations.[211] Thus it is again through a dichotomy, namely that between the local and the global, that the answer to the solutions to the regulatory challenges of the future is sought.

As the rise of regionalism has already proved, the situation is again too complex to be addressed by way of dualistic thinking expressed in dichotomies alone. As usual, the reality is more complex, and a more accurate assessment lies somewhere in a twilight zone between the local and the global.[212] Or, to put it better, such an assessment must manage to include them both and to reconcile the antagonism. For instance, the oxymoronic term "glocalization" literally reconciles the "global" and the "local" and is said to have several advantages over that of "globalization".[213] By the same token, a reconciliation of their apparent contradiction can take the form of a paradox, as has been formulated in the following way:

> The dynamics of this globalization are multifaceted and seemingly contradictory. In some respects they undermine the power of states. The power of transnational corporations, the limits imposed on government policy by currency markets, the transborder politics of NGOs, the transfiguring power of global media – all reduce the autonomy of national governments. But in other respects, globalization strengthens the state and extends its influence: in the international protection of human rights or in the cooperation that states undertake to preserve the oceans, eradicate disease,

---

[210] See e.g. Michael Mann (ed.), *The Rise and Decline of the Nation State* (Oxford: Basil Blackwell Ltd, 1990), Masao Miyoshi, "A Borderless World? From Colonialism to Transnationalism and the Decline of the Nation-State" (1993) 19(4) *Critical Inquiry* 726, Jáuregui Bereciartu Gurutz, *Decline of the Nation State* (Reno: University of Nevada Press, 1994), and Gunther Teubner (ed.), *Global Law without a State* (Aldershot: Dartmouth, 1997).

[211] See e.g. Jeremy A. Rabkin, *Law Without Nations? Why Constitutional Government Requires Sovereign States* (Princeton: Princeton University Press, 2005).

[212] See also Prem Shankar Jha, *The Twilight of the Nation State Globalisation, Chaos and War* (London: Pluto Press, 2006).

[213] See Habibul H. Khondker, "Globalisation to Glocalisation: A Conceptual Exploration" (2005) 13(2) *Intellectual Discourse* 181 at 187–188.

subdue the contagion of financial shocks, or stabilize global warming. Sovereignty is not what it used to be. It is more. And it is also less.[214]

Another way is to create a layer in between, which is already happening and can be seen in the rise and increase in number of regional cooperation and integration projects.[215]

However, trying to predict the future with regard to the gravitational centres for legal development is hard, as it poses a kind of "three-body gravitational problem" between forces at the local, the regional and the global levels. Often a complex problem can be solved by seeking alternative solutions, which can mean reconsidering other gravitational centres, such as the one recalled by Eugen Ehrlich:

> The center of gravity of legal development therefore from time immemorial has not lain in the activity of the state, but in society itself, and must be sought there at the present time.[216]

The centres of gravity can also be sought in, or shifted to, new legal universes through novel ideas and concepts. But before that, it is necessary to take a holistic approach to existing sources and materials. Hence, it is safer to expect that none of the current concepts will emerge unaltered from the rapid changes to which they are exposed. It is therefore better to analyse their mutual impact, particularly from a legal angle.[217] This means that each of the levels alone must first be studied, because of the potential danger that Robert Jennings pointed out, as follows:

> But it is not always realised how much the treatment of the very sources of international law rests upon assumptions which emanate from municipal law experience; and may prove in the end to be quite misleading for international law.[218]

The question of sources of law should also include a discussion of novel sources of law, which do not have to be "new" sources (e.g. "land" or "society" as sources of law) but which will definitely have to include sources related to

---

[214] See Gordon Smith and Moisés Naím, *Altered States: Globalization, Sovereignty, and Governance* (Ottawa: International Development Research Centre, 2000) at xiii.

[215] See also Kenichi Ohmae, *The End of the Nation State: The Rise of Regional Economies* (London: HarperCollins, 1995).

[216] Eugen Ehrlich, *Fundamental Principles of the Sociology of Law* (Oxon: Routledge, 2017) at 390.

[217] See e.g. Oscar Schachter, "The Decline of the Nation-State and its Implications for International Law" (1998) 36(1) *Columbia Journal of Transnational Law* 7.

[218] Robert Y. Jennings, "Recent Developments in the International Law Commission: Its Relation to the Sources of International Law" (1964) 13(2) *International and Comparative Law Quarterly* 385 at 388.

new technologies. There is already a vast list of potential candidates for novel sources that should be included in the current system of the classification of sources of law.

A first new technology that potentially constitutes a novel source of law is the Internet, which led to the following question in the context of the harmonization pursued by the Convention on Contracts for the International Sale of Goods (CISG):

> With all this use of the Internet directly in practice, can we deem it a source of law in itself, instead of categorising it solely as a resource of information or a source of sources?[219]

The answer to the question, it was said, depends on the kind of criteria applied to the term "sources of law".[220]

A related but slightly different potential source of law has been identified in the form of mass media in general, or social media in particular. Here too, whether they qualify as sources of law depends on the criteria applied to sources of law and the relevant organizational structure or ownership of the media themselves.[221]

Another technology is that of "blockchain", which has been described as "a distributed database of records, or public ledger of all transactions or digital events that have been executed and shared among participating parties".[222] Blockchain technology also enables the use of cryptocurrencies such as Bitcoin, which – under the heading of "cryptocurrency-based law" – have also already been investigated for their potential use as sources of law.[223] Among cryptocurrencies, Bitcoin, a kind of decentralized peer-to-peer digital currency, is usually given as the most popular example of the use of blockchain technology. The specific problem in this context is whether a peer-to-peer protocol can be understood as an institution that makes normative decisions, and this question has been phrased as follows:

---

[219] See Camilla Baasch Andersen, "From Resource of Law to Source of Law: The Internet as a Source of Law in Unifying the Jurisprudence of the CISG" (2004) *Journal of Information Law & Technology (JILT)*; available at: https://warwick.ac.uk/fac/soc/law/elj/jilt/2004_3/andersen.

[220] *Ibid.*

[221] See e.g. Tahirih V. Lee, "Media Products as Law: The Mass Media as Enforcers and Sources of Law in China" (2011) 39(3) *Denver Journal of International Law and Policy* 437.

[222] See Michael Crosby et al., "Block Chain Technology: Beyond Bitcoin" (2016) 2 *Applied Innovation Review* 7 at 8.

[223] See Michael Abramowicz, "Cryptocurrency-Based Law" (2016) 58(2) *Arizona Law Review* 359.

> But the possibility of peer-to-peer decision-making challenges the conventional assumption that centralized institutions (such as legislatures and courts) are needed to produce law of sufficient clarity to be workable.[224]

Blockchain technologies can be also used for a plethora of other issues, such as smart contracts, which use a blockchain technology and have a capacity that allows "complex contracts to be created and automatically enforced".[225] In this sense, even algorithms, although they are not human agents, can assume the role of a source of law when they help to determine a party's contractual obligation.[226] However, these peer-to-peer networks, matching Eugen Ehrlich's view that the gravitational centre lies in society itself, are said to allow for "dialogue" and not just power to emerge "as a source of law across technology".[227] As a consequence of these novel and rapidly evolving technologies, it will be necessary to follow their impact on law and the legal profession closely. In particular, the development of artificial intelligence (AI) can be expected to carry the process further. AI must therefore be closely monitored, because it is expected to imitate more and more operations of the human mind and is predicted to be "commonplace in legal work within ten years".[228] Just on the basis of the existing peer-to-peer technologies, an open mind with regard to novel sources must be maintained, as was suggested in the following paragraph:

> Peer-to-peer law is likely to emerge slowly and in unpredictable ways, but it has the potential to create authoritative decisions without authoritative decision-makers. There may be decisive arguments against particular peer-to-peer institutions, but legal theorists should at least allow peer-to-peer institutions to join the menu of possible regulatory arrangements.[229]

Finally, the past reminds us that the best way to predict the future is by creating it. It was in the realm of international law that drastic changes based

---

[224] *Ibid* at 367.

[225] See Steve Omohundro, "Cryptocurrencies, Smart Contracts, and Artificial Intelligence" (2014) 1(2) *AI Matters* 19 at 19.

[226] See Lauren Henry Scholz, "Algorithmic Contracts" (2017) 20(2) *Stanford Technology Law Review* 128 at 165.

[227] Pompeu Casanovas, "Conceptualisation of Rights and Meta-Rule of Law for the Web of Data" (2015) 12 *Democracia Digital e Governo Eletrônico* 18 at 25.

[228] See Lauri Donahue, "A Primer on Using Artificial Intelligence in the Legal Profession" (3 January 2018) The Digest of the Harvard Journal of Law & Technology (JOLT); available at: https://jolt.law.harvard.edu/digest/a-primer-on-using-artificial-intelligence-in-the-legal-profession.

[229] See Michael Abramaowicz, "Cryptocurrency-Based Law" (2016) 58(2) *Arizona Law Review* 359 at 420.

on new technologies were already predicted for the turn of the millennium, as follows:

> By the dawn of the new millennium, the "recognized manifestations of international law" will be interconnected in a complex information system accessible from anywhere in the world. Electronic information systems will make a *cyber-Oppenheim* possible. If those systems are managed intelligently by those who appreciate the subject, the international law of the 21st century will be characterized by greater clarity, fuller compliance, and more broadly based appreciation.[230]

In 2019, the global community is already almost two decades behind plan, if it wants to establish a global legal order based on the existing technologies that may fulfil these functions and the goals that the global community has set, for instance in the Sustainable Development Goals (SDGs).[231]

IV. REFERENCES

Abramaowicz, Michael, "Cryptocurrency-Based Law" (2016) 58(2) *Arizona Law Review* 359.

Alland, Denis et al. (eds.), *Unité et Diversité du Droit International / Unity and Diversity of International Law: Ecrits en L'honneur du Professeur Pierre-Marie Dupuy / Essays in Honour of Professor Pierre-Marie Dupuy* (Leiden: Martinus Nijhoff, 2014).

Andò, Biagio, "'As Slippery as an Eel'? Comparative Law and Polyjural Systems", in Vernon Valentine Palmer, Mohamed Y. Mattar and Anna Koppel (eds.), *Mixed Legal Systems, East and West* (Surrey: Ashgate, 2015) 3.

Baasch Andersen, Camilla, "From Resource of Law to Source of Law: The Internet as a Source of Law in Unifying the Jurisprudence of the CISG" (2004) *Journal of Information Law & Technology (JILT)*; available at: https://warwick.ac.uk/ fac/soc/law/elj/jilt/2004_3/andersen.

Babalola Ajulo, Sunday, "Sources of the Law of the Economic Community of West African States (ECOWAS)" (2001) 45(1) *Journal of African Law* 73.

---

[230] See John King Gamble, "New Information Technologies and the Sources of International Law: Convergence, Divergence, Obsolescence and/or Transformation" (1998) 41 *German Yearbook of International Law* 170 at 205.

[231] United Nations, *Transforming our World: The 2030 Agenda for Sustainable Development*, Resolution adopted by the General Assembly on 25 September 2015, Seventieth session, A/RES/70/l, 21 October 2015; available at http://www.un.org/en/development/ desa/population/migration/generalassembly/docs/globalcompact/A_RES_70_1_E.pdf.

Bakaeva, O. Yu., "Acts of the Eurasian Economic Commission as a source of law EAEC" (2016) 3(8) *Russian Journal of Legal Studies* 73.

Balassa, Bela, *The Theory of Economic Integration* (London: George Allen & Unwin Ltd, 1962).

Balasubramanyam, V.N. (ed.), *Trade and Development: Essays in Honour of Jagdish Bhagwati* (Basingslake: MacMillan, 1996).

Baldwin, Richard and Carpenter, Theresa, "Regionalism: Moving from Fragmentation towards Coherence", in Thomas Cottier and Panagiotis Delimatsis (eds.), *The Prospects of International Trade Regulation: From Fragmentation to Coherence* (Cambridge: Cambridge University Press 2011) 136.

Baldwin, Richard and Low, Patrick (eds.), *Multilateralizing Regionalism* (Cambridge: Cambridge University Press, 2008).

Ballantyne, W. M., "The States of the GCC: Sources of Law, the Shari'a and the Extent to Which It Applies" (1985) 1(1) *Arab Law Quarterly* 3.

Beaulac, Stéphane, "The Westphalian Model in Defining International Law: Challenging the Myth" (2004) 8(2) *Australian Journal of History of Law* 181.

Bederman, David J., *Custom as a Source of Law* (Cambridge: Cambridge University Press, 2010).

Bentham, Jeremy, *Introduction to the Principles of Morals and Legislation* (London: T. Payne, 1789).

Black, C.F., *The Land is the Source of the Law: A Dialogic Encounter with Indigenous Jurisprudence* (Oxon: Routledge, 2011).

Boklan, Darya, "Eurasian Economic Union and World Trade Organization: Interrelation of Legal Regimes" (2017) 2 *Pravo. Zhurnal Vysshey shkoly ekonomiki* 223.

Botta, Marco, "The Cooperation between the Competition Authorities of the Developing Countries: Why it does not Work? Case Study on Argentina and Brazil" (2009) 5(2) *Competition Law Review* 153.

Brandenburger, Adam M. and Nalebuff, Barry J., *Co-opetition: A Revolution Mindset That Combines Competition and Cooperation: The Game Theory Strategy That's Changing the Game of Business* (New York: Doubleday, 1996).

Buchanan, Allen, *Justice, Legitimacy, and Self-Determination: Moral Foundations for International Law* (Oxford: Oxford University Press, 2007).

Calabresi, Steven G. and Dotson Zimdahl, Stephanie, "The Supreme Court and Foreign Sources of Law: Two Hundred Years of Practice and the Juvenile Death Penalty Decision" (2005) 47(3) *William and Mary Law Review* 743.

Casanovas, Pompeu, "Conceptualisation of Rights and Meta-Rule of Law for the Web of Data" (2015) 12 *Democracia Digital e Governo Eletrônico* 18.

Chesterman, Simon, *From Community to Compliance?: The Evolution of Monitoring Obligations in ASEAN* (Cambridge: Cambridge University Press, 2015).

Cini, Michelle, "The Soft Law Approach: Commission Rule-Making in the EU's State Aid Regime" (2001) 8(2) *Journal of European Public Policy* 19.

Crosby, Michael et al., "Block Chain Technology: Beyond Bitcoin" (2016) 2 *Applied Innovation Review* 7.

Cutler, A. Claire, *Private Power and Global Authority: Transnational Merchant Law in the Global Political Economy* (Cambridge: Cambridge University Press, 2003).

D'Aspremont, Jean, *Formalism and the Sources of International Law: A Theory of the Ascertainment of Legal Rules* (Oxford: Oxford University Press, 2011).

David, René and Brierley, John E. C., *Major Legal Systems in the World Today: Introduction to the Comparative Study of Law*, 3rd ed (London: Stevens & Sons, 1985).

Davidson, Paul J., "The ASEAN Way and the Role of Law in ASEAN Economic Cooperation" (2004) 8 *Singapore Yearbook of International Law* 165.

de Witte, Bruno, "Retour à « Costa » La primauté du droit communautaire à la lumière du droit international" (1984) 20(3) *Revue trimestrielle de droit européen* 425.

Del Vecchio, Giorgio, "The Problem of the Sources of Positive Law" (1935) 47(3) *Juridical Review* 253.

Del Vecchio, Giorgio, *Justice: An Historical and Philosophical Essay* (New York: Philosophical Library, 1953).

Desierto, Diane A., "ASEAN's Constitutionalization of International Law: Challenges to Evolution under the New ASEAN Charter" (2011) 49(2) *Columbia Journal of Transnational Law* 268.

Dixon, Martin, McCorquodale, Robert, and Williams, Sarah, *Cases & Materials on International Law*, 6th ed (Oxford: Oxford University Press, 2016).

Domingo, Rafael, *The New Global Law* (Cambridge: Cambridge University Press, 2010).

Donahue, Lauri, "A Primer on Using Artificial Intelligence in the Legal Profession" (3 January 2018) The Digest of the Harvard Journal of Law & Technology (JOLT); available at: https://jolt.law.harvard.edu/digest/a-primer-on-using-artificial-intelligence-in-the-legal-profession.

Dupuy, Pierre-Marie, "The Constitutional Dimension of the Charter of the United Nations Revisited" (1997) 1 *Max Planck Yearbook of United Nations Law* 1.

Ehrlich, Eugen, *Fundamental Principles of the Sociology of Law* (Oxon: Routledge, 2017).

Esty, Daniel C. and Geradin, Damien, "Regulatory Co-opetition" (2000) 3(2) *Journal of International Economic Law* 235.

EUR-Lex, "Sources of EU Law"; available at: https://eur-lex.europa.eu/legal-content/ EN/ALL/?uri=LEGISSUM:l14534.

Ewing-Chow, Michael and Hsien-Li, Tan, "The Role of the Rule of Law in ASEAN Integration", *EUI Working Paper RSCAS 2013/16* (March 2013); available at: http://cadmus.eui.eu/bitstream/handle/1814/26452/RSCAS_2013_16.pdf? sequence=1&isAllowed=y.

Ewing-Chow, Michael, "Culture Club or Chameleon: Should ASEAN Adopt Legalization for Economic Integration?" (2004) 8 *Singapore Yearbook of International Law* 225.

Fassbender, Bardo, *The United Nations Charter as the Constitution of the International Community* (Leiden: Martinus Nijhoff, 2009).

Fellmeth, Aaron X. and Horwitz, Maurice, *Guide to Latin in International Law* (Oxford: Oxford University Press, 2009).

Fitzmaurice, Gerald, "Some Problems Regarding the Formal Sources of International Law" (1958) *Symbolae Verzijl* 153, reprinted in Martin Dixon, Robert McCorquodale and Sarah Williams, *Cases & Materials on International Law*, 6th ed (Oxford: Oxford University Press, 2016) 23.

Franck, Thomas M., *Nation Against Nation: What Happened to the U.N. Dream and What the U.S. Can Do About It* (New York: Oxford University Press, 1985).

Friedmann, Wolfgang, "The Uses of "General Principles" in the Development of International Law" (1963) 57(2) *The American Journal of International Law* 279.

Fuentes, Carlos Iván, *Normative Plurality in International Law: A Theory of the Determination of Applicable Rules* (Springer International Publishing, 2016).

Garcia, Frank J., "Trade and Justice: Linking the Trade Linkage Debates" (1998) 19(2) *University of Pennsylvania Journal of International Economic Law* 391.

Georgieva, Zlatina, "Soft Law in EU Competition Law and Its Judicial Reception in Member States: A Theoretical Perspective" (2015) 16(2) *German Law Journal* 223.

Glendon, Mary Ann, "The Sources of Law in a Changing Legal Order" (1983) 17(3) *Creighton Law Review* 663.

Glenn, H. Patrick, "Persuasive Authority" (1987) 32(2) *McGill Law Journal* 261.

Glenn, H. Patrick, *Legal Traditions of the World: Sustainable Diversity in Law*, 3rd ed (Oxford: Oxford University Press, 2007).

Gribnau, Hans, "Soft Law and Taxation: EU and International Aspects" (2008) 2(2) *Legisprudence* 67.

Gurutz, Jáuregui Bereciartu, *Decline of the Nation State* (Reno: University of Nevada Press, 1994).

Hafner, Gerhard, "Pros and Cons Ensuing from Fragmentation of International Law" (2004) 25(4) *Michigan Journal of International Law* 849.

Hallaq, Wael B., "Was the Gate of Ijtihad Closed?" (1984) 16(1) *International Journal of Middle East Studies* 3.

Halpin, Andrew and Roeben, Volker (eds.), *Theorising the Global Legal Order* (Oxford: Hart, 2009).

Hart, Herbert L. A., *The Concept of Law*, 2nd ed. (Ocford: Clarendon Press, 1994).

Henry, Laurence, "The ASEAN Way and Community Integration: Two Different Models of Regionalism" (2007) 13(6) *European Law Journal* 857.

Iksanov, I. S. and Kosirev, I. Yu., "The Problems of Supranational Legal Regulation in the Activities of the Court of the Eurasian Economic Union" (2017) 5 *Gumanitarnye nauki. Vestnik finansovogo universiteta* 6.

Ispolinov, Alexey, "Statute of EAEU Court as Reflection of EAEU Members Concerns and Doubts" (2016) 4 *Pravo. Zhurnal Vysshey shkoly ekonomiki* 152.

Jackson, John H., *World Trade and the Law of GATT* (Indianapolis: The Bobbs Merril Company, 1969).

Jenks, C. Wilfred, "The Conflict of Law-Making Treaties" (1953) *British Yearbook of International Law* 401.

Jennings, Robert Y., "Recent Developments in the International Law Commission: Its Relation to the Sources of International Law" (1964) 13(2) *International and Comparative Law Quarterly* 385.

Jeutner, Valentin, *Irresolvable Norm Conflicts in International Law: The Concept of a Legal Dilemma* (Oxford: Oxford University Press, 2017).

Kadelbach, Stefan, "Jus Cogens, Obligations Erga Omnes and other Rules – The Identification of Fundamental Norms", in Christian Tomuschat and Jean Marc Thouvenin (eds.), *The Fundamental Rules of the International Legal Order: Jus Cogens and Obligations Erga Omnes* (Leiden: Martinus Nijhoff, 2006) 21.

Kammerhofer, Jörg, "Uncertainty in the Formal Sources of International Law: Customary International Law and Some of Its Problems" (2004) 15(3) *European Journal of International Law* 523.

Kapustin, A. Ya., "The Law of Eurasian Economic Union: International Legal Discourse" (2015) 11 *Zhurnal rossiyskogo prava* 59.

Kapustin, A. Ya., "The Treaty of the Eurasian Economic Union – New Page of Legal Development of Eurasian Integration" (2014) 12 *Zhurnal rossiyskogo prava* 98.

Kennedy, David, "The Mystery of Global Governance" (2008) 34(3) *Ohio Northern University Law Review* 827.

Khondker, Habibul H., "Globalisation to Glocalisation: A Conceptual Exploration" (2005) 13(2) *Intellectual Discourse* 181.

King Gamble, John, "New Information Technologies and the Sources of International Law: Convergence, Divergence, Obsolescence and/or Transformation" (1998) 41 *German Yearbook of International Law* 170.

Kirilenko, V. P. and Demidov, D. G., "Principles of Functioning of the Eurasian Economic Union (International Legal Aspects) (2015) 3 *Upravlencheskoe konsultirovanie* 83.

Korkea-Aho, Emilia, "EU Soft Law in Domestic Legal Systems: Flexibility and Diversity Guaranteed, (2009) 16(3) *Maastricht Journal of European & Comparative Law* 271.

Koskenniemi, Martti, *Fragmentation of International Law: Difficulties Arising from the Diversification and Expansion of International Law (Report of the Study Group of the International Law Commission)*, UNGA A/CN.4/L.682 (13 April 2006).

Kosko, Bart, *Fuzzy Thinking: The New Science of Fuzzy Logic* (New York: Hyperion, 1993).

Kotova, N. E., "Eurasian Economic Union: Improving the Legal Framework" (2016) 5 *Mirovaya ekonomika. Vestnik finansovogo universiteta* 126.

Kovalev, A. V., "The Interpretation of the Eurasian Economic Union Law: the Legal Grounds for the Preparation of Clarification and Evolution of Interpretive Process" (2016) 62 *Aktualnye problemy rossiyskogo prava* 187.

Lang, Andrew T. F., "Reflecting on 'Linkage': Cognitive and Institutional Change in the International Trading System" (2007) 70(4) *Modern Law Review* 523.

Lee, Tahirih V., "Media Products as Law: The Mass Media as Enforcers and Sources of Law in China" (2011) 39(3) *Denver Journal of International Law and Policy* 437.

Lindroos, Anja and Mehling, Michael, "Dispelling the Chimera of 'Self-Contained Regimes' International Law and the WTO" (2006) 16(5) *The European Journal of International Law* 857.

Ly Luu, Huong, "Regional Harmonization of Competition Law and Policy: An ASEAN Approach" (2012) 2(2) *Asian Journal of International Law* 291.

Malawer, Stuart S., "Trump's China Trade Policies: Threats and Constraints" (2017) 1 *China and WTO Review* 109.

Mann, Michael (ed.), *The Rise and Decline of the Nation State* (Oxford: Basil Blackwell Ltd, 1990).

Marceau, Gabrielle, "Conflicts of Norms of Jurisdictions: The Relationship between the WTO Agreement and MEAs and Other Treaties" (2001) 35(6) *Journal of World Trade* 1081.

Martinico, Giuseppe, "Complexity and Cultural Sources of Law in the EU Context: from the Multilevel Constitutionalism to the Constitutional Synallagma" (2007) 8(3) *German Law Journal* 205.

Mauser, Wolfram, "Global Change Research in the Anthropocene: Introductory Remarks", in Eckart Ehlers and Thomas Krafft (eds.), *Earth System Science in the Anthropocene* (Berlin: Springer, 2006) 3.

Miyoshi, Masao, "A Borderless World? From Colonialism to Transnationalism and the Decline of the Nation-State" (1993) 19(4) *Critical Inquiry* 726.

Monaco, Riccardo, "Sources of International Law", in Rudolf Bernhardt (ed.), *Encyclopedia of Public International Law*, vol 7 (Amsterdam: North-Holland, 1984) 424.

Neuwirth, Rostam J. and Svetlicinii, Alexandr, "Law as a Social Medicine: Enhancing International Inter-Regime Regulatory Coopetition as a Means for the Establishment of a Global Health Governance Framework" (2015) 36 (3–4) *The Journal of Legal Medicine* 330.

Neuwirth, Rostam J. and Svetlicinii, Alexandr, "The Economic Sanctions Over the Ukraine Conflict and the WTO: 'Catch XXI' and the Revival of the Debate on Security Exceptions" (2015) 49(5) *Journal of World Trade* 891.

Neuwirth, Rostam J. and Svetlicinii, Alexandr, "The Regulation of Trade and Public Health in Asia-Pacific: A Case for 'Inter-Regime Co-opetition'" (2015) 10(2) *Asian Journal of WTO & International Health Law and Policy* 349.

Neuwirth, Rostam J., "Law as Mnemonics: The Mind as the Prime Source of Normativity" (2008) 2(1) *European Journal of Legal Studies* 143.

Neuwirth, Rostam J., "The Future of the Culture and Trade Debate: A Legal Outlook" (2013) 47(2) *Journal of World Trade* 391.

Neuwirth, Rostam J., *Law in Times of Oxymora: A Synaesthesia of Language, Logic and Law* (London: Routledge, 2018).

Nyrkova, N. A., "Integration of Criminal Law of the Customs Union: Problem Identification" (2014) XCVI(11) *Lex Russica* 1338.

Ohmae, Kenichi, *The End of the Nation State: The Rise of Regional Economies* (London: HarperCollins, 1995).

Olmos Giupponi, Belén, "International Law and Sources of Law in MERCOSUR: An Analysis of a 20-Year Relationship" (2012) 25(3) *Leiden Journal of International Law* 707.

Omohundro, Steve, "Cryptocurrencies, Smart Contracts, and Artificial Intelligence" (2014) 1(2) *AI Matters* 19.

Onuma, Yasuaki, "When was the Law of International Society Born? – An Inquiry of the History of International Law from an Intercivilizational Perspective" (2000) 2(1) *Journal of History of international Law* 1.

Organization of American States (OAS), "Legal Framework of the Common Market of the Southern Cone"; available at: http://www.sice.oas.org/Mercosur/instmt_e.asp.

Palmer, Vernon Valentine, "Mixed Legal Systems... and the Myth of Pure Laws" (2007) 67(4) *Louisiana Law Review* 1205.

Palmeter, David and Mavroidis, Petros C., "The WTO Legal System: Sources of Law" (1998) 92(3) *American Journal of International Law* 398.

Papa, Mihaela, "BRICS as a Global Legal Actor: From Regulatory Innovation to BRICS Law?" (2014) 20 *federalismi.it* 2.

Pauwelyn, Joost, *Conflict of Norms in Public International Law: How WTO Law Relates to other Rules of International Law* (Cambridge: Cambridge University Press, 2003).

Payosova, Tetyana, Hufbauer, Gary Clyde, and Schott, Jeffrey J., *The Dispute Settlement Crisis in the World Trade Organization: Causes and Cures*, Peterson Institute for International Economics Policy Brief (May 2018); available at: https://www.law.berkeley.edu/wp-content/uploads/2018/01/WTO-dispute-settlement.pdf.

Peng, Shin-yi, "Cybersecurity Threats and the WTO National Security Exceptions" 18(2) *Journal of International Economic Law* 449.

Petrov, E. Yu. and Grinberg, E. S., "Anti-Monopoly Policy of European Union and Eurasian Economic Union: View from Inside" (2014) 6 *Vestnik Moskovskogo universiteta MVD Rossii* 244.

Phillips, John C., "Sui Generis Intellectual Property Protection for Computer Software" (1992) 60 (4) *George Washington Law Review* 997.

Piris, Jean-Claude and Woon, Walter, *Towards a Rules-Based Community: An ASEAN Legal Service* (Cambridge: Cambridge University Press, 2015).

Popescu, Roxana-Mariana, "Features of the Unwritten Sources of European Union Law" (2013) 20 *Lex ET Scientia International Journal* 98.

Pound, Roscoe, "Sources and Forms of Law" (1946) 21 *Notre Dame Lawyer* 247.

Prost, Mario, "Hierarchy and the Sources of International Law: A Critique" (2017) 39(2) *Houston Journal of International Law* 285.

Prost, Mario, *The Concept of Unity in Public International Law* (Oxford: Hart, 2012).

Rabkin, Jeremy A., *Law Without Nations? Why Constitutional Government Requires Sovereign States* (Princeton: Princeton University Press, 2005).

Radin, Max, "Sources of Law – New and Old" (1928) 1(5) *Southern California Law Review* 411.

Reisman, W. Michael, "The Constitutional Crisis in the United Nations" (1993) 87(1) *American Journal of International Law* 83.

Reynolds, Barney, "Natural Law versus Positivism: The Fundamental Conflict" (1993) 13(4) *Oxford Journal of Legal Studies* 441.

Rosenau, James N., "Governance in the 21st Century" (1995) 1(1) *Global Governance* 13.

Rosic Fegus, Verena, "The Growing Importance of Soft Law in the EU" (2014) 1(1) *Journal for International and European Law, Economics and Market Integrations* 145.

Salmond, John W., *Jurisprudence or the Theory of the Law*, 2nd ed (London: Steven and Haynes, 1907).

Scaffardi, Lucia, "BRICS, a Multi-Centre 'Legal Network'?" (2014) 5 *Beijing Law Review* 140.

Schacht, Joseph, *An Introduction to Islamic Law* (Oxford: Clarendon Press, 1982).

Schachter, Oscar, "The Decline of the Nation-State and its Implications for International Law" (1998) 36(1) *Columbia Journal of Transnational Law* 7.

Schelkle, Waltraud, "EU Fiscal Governance: Hard Law in the Shadow of Soft Law" (2007) 13(3) *Columbia Journal of European Law* 705.

Scholz, Lauren Henry, "Algorithmic Contracts" (2017) 20(2) *Stanford Technology Law Review* 128.

Schütze, Robert, "On "Federal Ground: The European Union as an (Inter)National Phenomenon" (2009) 46(4) *Common Market Law Review* 1069.

Scott, Gary L. and Carr, Craig L., "The International Court of Justice and the Treaty/Custom Dichotomy" (1981)16(3) *Texas International law Journal* 347.

Senden, Linda, *Soft Law in European Community Law* (Oxford: Hart, 2004).

Shahabuddeen, Mohamed, *Precedent in the World Court* (Cambridge: Cambridge University Press, 1997).

Shankar Jha, Prem, *The Twilight of the Nation State Globalisation, Chaos and War* (London: Pluto Press, 2006).

Shecaira, Fábio P., *Legal Scholarship as a Source of Law* (Cham: Springer, 2013).

Silving, Helen, "The Twilight Zone of Positive and Natural Law" (1955) 43(3) *California Law Review* 477.

Singh, Mahendra P. and Deva, Surya, "The Constitution of India: Symbol of Unity in Diversity" (2005) 53 *Jahrbuch des Öffentlichen Rechts der Gegenwart/Yearbook of Public Law (Germany)* 649.

Smith, Gordon and Naím, Moisés, *Altered States: Globalization, Sovereignty, and Governance* (Ottawa: International Development Research Centre, 2000).

Sokolova, N. A., "Eurasian Integration: Powers of the Eurasian Union Court" (2015) CVIII(11) *Lex Russica* 96.

Svetlicinii, Alexandr and Zhang, Juanjuan, "The Competition Law Institutions in the BRICS Countries: Developing Better Institutional Models for the Protection of Market Competition" (2017) 2(1) *Chinese Political Science Review* 85.

Svetlicinii, Alexandr, "Building Regional Competition Policy in ASEAN: Lessons from the European Competition Network" (2017) 15(3) *Asia Europe Journal* 341.

Svetlicinii, Alexandr, "China's Belt and Road Initiative and the Eurasian Economic Union: "Integrating the Integrations" (2018) 5 *Public Administration Issues* 7.

Teichmann, Roger, "The Chicken and the Egg" (1991) 100(3) *Mind* 371.

Terpan, Fabien, "Soft Law in the European Union—The Changing Nature of EU Law" (2015) 21(1) *European Law Journal* 68.

Teubner, Gunther (ed.), *Global Law without a State* (Aldershot: Dartmouth, 1997).

Thuo Gathii, James, *African Regional Trade Agreements as Legal Regimes* (Cambridge: Cambridge University Press, 2011).

Tietje, Christian and Nowrot, Karsten, "Laying Conceptual Ghosts of the Past to Rest: the Rise of Philip C. Jessup's 'Transnational Law' in the Regulatory Governance of the International Economic System", in Christian Tietje, Alan Brouder and Karsten Nowrot (eds.), *Philip C. Jessup's Transnational Law Revisited. On the Occasion of the 50th Anniversary of its Publication* (Halle: Institut für Wirtschaftsrecht, 2006.) 17.

Toscano, Marcílio Filho, Franca, Lixinski, Lucas, and Olmos Giupponi, María Belén, "Introduction to the Law of MERCOSUR", in Marcílio Toscano Franca Filho, Lucas Lixinski and María Belén Olmos Giupponi (eds.), *The Law of MERCOSUR* (Oxford: Hart, 2010) 1.

Trachtman, Joel P., "Institutional Linkage: Transcending 'Trade and ...'" (2002) 96(1) *American Journal of International Law* 77.

Trachtman, Joel P., "Trade and . . . Problems, Cost-Benefit Analysis and Subsidiarity" (1998) 9(1) *European Journal of International Law* 32.

Trubek, David M. and Trubek, Louise G., "Hard and Soft Law in the Construction of Social Europe: the Role of the Open Method of Co-ordination" (2005) 11(3) *European Law Journal* 343.

Ukaigwe, Jerry, *ECOWAS Law* (Cham: Springer International, 2015).

United Nations, *Transforming Our World: The 2030 Agenda for Sustainable Development*, General Assembly A/RES/70/1 (21 October 2015).

United Nations, *Transforming our World: The 2030 Agenda for Sustainable Development*, Resolution adopted by the General Assembly on 25 September 2015, Seventieth session, A/RES/70/l, 21 October 2015.

Weeramantry, C. G., *Islamic Jurisprudence: An International Perspective* (Basingstoke: MacMillan, 1988).

Weisbaum, Earl, "Domestic Sources of International Law" (1983) 76(3) *Law Library Journal* 436.

Whitecross Paton, George, *A Textbook of Jurisprudence* (Oxford: Clarendon Press, 1946).

World Trade Organization (WTO), "Dispute Settlement"; available at: https://www.wto.org/english/tratop_e/dispu_e/cases_e/ds152_e.htm.

Wyatt, Derrick, "New Legal Order, or Old?" (1982) 7 *European Law Review* 147.

Yasuaki, Onuma, *A Transcivilizational Perspective on International Law: Questioning Prevalent Cognitive Frameworks in the Emerging Multi-Polar and Multi-Civilizational World of the Twenty-First Century* (Leiden: Martinus Nijhoff, 2010).

Yoo, Ji Yeong and Ahn, Dukgeun, "Security Exceptions in the WTO System: Bridge or Bottle-Neck for Trade and Security?" (2016) 19(2) *Journal of International Economic Law* 417.

Young, Margaret A. (ed.), *Regime Interaction in International Law: Facing Fragmentation* (Cambridge: Cambridge University Press, 2012).

Youngblood Henderson, James (Sakej), "Interpreting Sui Generis Treaties" (1997) 36(1) *Alberta Law Review* 46.

Yu, Peter K., "Intellectual Property Negotiations, the BRICS Factor and the Changing North–South Debate", in Rostam J. Neuwirth, Svetlicinii, Alexandr, and Denis De Castro Halis, (eds.), *The BRICS-Lawyers' Guide to Global Cooperation* (Cambridge: Cambridge University Press, 2017) 148.

Yue Chia, Siow and Plummer, Michael G., *ASEAN Economic Cooperation and Integration: Progress, Challenges and Future Directions* (Cambridge: Cambridge University Press, 2015).

Zammit Borda, Aldo, "A Formal Approach to Article 38(1)(d) of the ICJ Statute from the Perspective of the International Criminal Courts and Tribunals" (2013) 24(2) *European Journal of International Law* 649.

Zybaylo, A. I., "Sources of EurAsEC Law and Methods of their Implementation in the Legislation of the Member States" (2013) *Mezhdunarodnoe publichnoe, mezhdunarodnoe chastnoe i evropeyskoe pravo* 47.

CHAPTER 3

The Way Forward

Towards a BRICS Law?

> *It is only when a transnational regional organization starts to become a transnational regional polity – i.e., only when it acquires some capacity (however limited) to act on its own by initiating proposals, making decisions, and/or implementing policies – that the process switches from regional cooperation to regional integration.*[1]

The question of sources of law is one of extreme importance for the development and application of law. It has, in fact, rightly been termed the evergreen question in the doctrine of international law. However, there is no exhaustive list of which sources constitute sources of law, either in international law or in the different national legal systems. On the contrary, it has been said that there is no consensus, and Oscar Schachter rightly wrote that "no single theory has received general agreement and sometimes it seems as though there are as many theories or at least formulations as there are scholars".[2] In the same breath, he listed the following sources that do not constitute sources of law but can at least give rise to obligations in international law:

    i.   Consent of states
    ii.   Customary practice
    iii. A sense of "rightness" – the juridical conscience
    iv. Natural law or natural reason
    v.   Social necessity

---

[1] See Philippe C. Schmitter and Sunhyuk Ki, "Comparing Processes of Regional Integration: European 'Lessons' and Northeast Asian Reflections" (2008) 17(1) *Current Politics and Economics of Asia* 11 at 13.

[2] Oscar Schachter, "Towards a Theory of International Obligation" (1968) 8(2) *Virginia Journal of International Law* 300 at 301.

vi. The will ("consensus") of the international community

vii. Direct (or "stigmatic") intuition

viii. Common purposes of the participants

ix. Effectiveness

x. Sanctions

xi. "Systemic" goals

xii. Shared expectations as to authority

xiii. Rules of recognition[3]

This illustrative list merely serves to highlight that even though the core sources of international law, as listed in Article 38 ICJ Statute, are contested, there are still many more sources being mentioned and used.

Indeed, as written by Judge Robert Y. Jennings in 1964, a "fresh approach to this whole question of sources is much needed".[4] In fact, we may need many fresh approaches, one of which may be the BRICS cooperation model, which can contribute to the enhancement and reform of the present international legal order and the establishment of a more efficient, fair and equitable, as well as a more coherent, global legal order. In this respect, the hope is mainly placed on novel cognitive approaches, including holistic and non-binary ones. The reason is that the preceding sections have shown how frequent, but at the same time how limited, dichotomies are. The international legal system as a whole, and every single cooperation and integration project, is struggling with the limitations imposed by dichotomies that are based on dualistic thinking and binary logic. Moreover, the limitations are becoming more visible and tangible, given the frequency and continuing rise of paradoxes or oxymora, like the paradox of global governance or the oxymoron of glocalization.

The solution to these paradoxes can be exemplified by another fundamental dichotomy, namely that between nature and nurture, or whether we are determined by biology or by culture. The reply given from a holistic perspective is that as humans "we are 100% innate, 100% acquired" or else "100% biological, 100% cultural".[5] Applied to the BRICS cooperation, a

---

[3] Oscar Schachter, "Towards a Theory of International Obligation" (1968) 8(2) *Virginia Journal of International Law* 300 at 301 [footnotes omitted].

[4] Robert Y. Jennings, "Recent Developments in the International Law Commission: Its Relation to the Sources of International Law" (1964) 13 *International and Comparative Law Quarterly* 385 at 387.

[5] See Daniel G. Freedman, *Human Sociobiology: A Holistic Approach* (New York: The Free Press, 1979) at 141 and D. O. Hebb, "Heredity and Environment in Mammalian Behaviour" (1953) 1(2) *The British Journal of Animal Behaviour* 43.

possible answer about its place in a multilevel governance system is 100% local, 100% regional and 100% global.

This means that locally, each of the BRICS countries can already make a huge impact, and jointly at the regional and global level they can do more. Their grouping already fills gaps in the equal geographic representation of the peoples on different continents caused by the absence of any African or South American country as a permanent representative on the UN Security Council. It can also be argued that the BRICS cooperation has already yielded a change of thinking in another important but sadly deplorable dichotomy, the one of the so-called "developing versus developed countries". [6] The gradual abandonment of this historically, philosophically and linguistically flawed dichotomy, which, especially from a cultural perspective, is untenable, has to be accelerated, and the dichotomy has to be replaced by a more inclusive and more differentiated terminology.[7] Following critical comments by scholars, a first formal step in this direction was taken in 2016 by the World Bank, when it stated the following in its World Indicators Report:

> Motivated by the universal agenda of the Sustainable Development Goals, this edition of World Development Indicators also introduces a change in the way that global and regional aggregates are presented in tables and figures. Unless otherwise noted, there is no longer a distinction between developing countries (defined in previous editions as low- and middle-income countries) and developed countries (defined in previous editions as high-income countries).[8]

It can be argued that this change in terminology is likely to have also been influenced by the growing role of the BRICS countries separately and jointly

---

[6] See also Rostam J. Neuwirth, "The 'End of 'Development Assistance' and the BRICS", in Jose A. Puppim de Oliveira, and Yijia Jing (eds.), *International Development Assistance, China and the BRICS* (New York: Palgrave, 2019).

[7] See Rostam J. Neuwirth, "Global Law and Sustainable Development: Change and the "Developing-Developed Country" Terminology", (2016) 29(4) *European Journal of Development Research* 911, Rostam J. Neuwirth, "A Constitutional Tribute to Global Governance: Overcoming the Chimera of the Developing-Developed Country Dichotomy", *European University Institute (EUI) Working Paper LAW 2010/20* (2010), available at: http://cadmus.eui.eu/handle/1814/15704, Rostam J. Neuwirth, "Global Governance and the Creative Economy: The Developing versus Developed Country Dichotomy Revisited" (2013) 1(1) *Frontiers of Legal Research* 127, Christiaan De Beukelaer, "Creative Industries in "Developing" Countries: Questioning Country Classifications in the UNCTAD Creative Economy Reports" (2014) 23(4) *Cultural Trends* 232, and Christiaan De Beukelaer, *Developing Cultural Industries: Learning from the Palimpsest of Practice* (Amsterdam: European Cultural Foundation, 2015).

[8] See World Bank, *2016 World Development Indicators* (Washington: The World Bank, 2016) at iii.

in the global arena.[9] Given that law changes when language changes, this can be seen as a meaningful step towards the dissolution of the artificial boundaries drawn between South and North, East and West, or so-called "developing" and "developed" countries. If it is followed up by a more coherent and inclusive spirit, it can also be regarded as a first step towards the more just, equitable, fair and multipolar international political and economic order that is needed to establish a future global legal order.

Such a future global legal order will also require serious analysis and debate about the question of sources of law. In this respect, a more inclusive and holistic approach needs to be taken. One of the preliminary conditions was described by Giorgio Del Vecchio as follows:

> Every distinction, as is well known, implies at the same time connection and union; scientific analysis cannot be, as it were, a tearing into pieces of reality. One who forgets this runs the risk of estranging science from its own object, which is living reality, reducing it to a sterile game of arbitrarily fashioned concepts. Nothing is more harmful than to separate the philosophy of law absolutely from the science of law, as if in the science of law itself there were not implicit (as the Roman jurists well knew) philosophical elements; and as if, in consequence, every true jurist were not, and must not be of necessity, something of a philosopher.[10]

This means an approach that reconciles not only the separation of legal theory from practice but also many more pairs of apparent opposites that were squeezed into dichotomies. Such a paradoxical or holistic approach should also govern the BRICS countries in their quest for an optimal framework or platform for their cooperation. Ideally, this quest should entail a dynamic approach, meaning that it rethinks and adjusts the exact form of cooperation and institutional basis in correspondence to each stage or field of cooperation. Moreover, the BRICS countries should also remain open to occasional cooperation with non-BRICS members, and possibly even to the acceptance of a new member, so as to maintain high levels of flexibility in rapidly evolving times. From a legal perspective, it also means both consolidating the existing texts, materials and instruments and also pondering new ones. For this reason, at this stage, an open-ended, non-hierarchical approach to BRICS legal sources is also recommended.

---

[9] Rostam J. Neuwirth, "The 'End of 'Development Assistance' and the BRICS", in Jose A. Puppim de Oliveira, and Yijia Jing (eds.), *International Development Assistance, China and the BRICS* (New York: Palgrave, 2019).

[10] See Giorgio Del Vecchio, "The Problem of the Sources of Positive Law" (1935) 47(3) *Juridical Review* 253 at 253-4.

I.   "BRICS Law": On Cooperation, Consolidation and Codification

It has been stated that "the ability of the BRICS to influence global regulation as a global legal actor lies in its internal cohesion and the development of its legal cooperation".[11] At the same time, though, the legal aspect in general is ignored, and "cooperation among legal professionals is missing and presents a barrier to reaching the BRICS' regulatory potential".[12] This is an incentive and a mandate to observe the political transformation in each BRICS country together with the related efforts for legal reform. All BRICS countries are under pressure to reform their legal systems, but they are confronted with different constraints, priorities or challenges.[13] This process also entails a constant critical consideration and updating of the legal system's underlying legal sources. For most BRICS countries, writings about the sources of law in their legal systems are either outdated or absent.[14] At the same time, the efforts made towards legal reform and the debate about the relevant sources of law must be combined with a search for the optimal legal instruments and

---

[11] Mihaela Papa, "BRICS as a Global Legal Actor: From Regulatory Innovation to BRICS Law?" (2014) 20 *federalismi.it* 2 at 36; see also Rostam J. Neuwirth, Alexandr Svetlicinii, and Denis De Castro Halis, "Introduction", in Rostam J. Neuwirth, Alexandr Svetlicinii, and Denis De Castro Halis, (eds.), *The BRICS-Lawyers' Guide to Global Cooperation* (Cambridge: Cambridge University Press, 2017) 1 at 2 (Fn 5).

[12] Mihaela Papa, "BRICS as a Global Legal Actor: From Regulatory Innovation to BRICS Law?" (2014) 20 *federalismi.it* 2 at 36.

[13] See e.g. Organisation for Economic Co-operation and Development (OECD), *OECD Reviews of Regulatory Reform: Russia – Building the Rules for the Market* (Paris: OECD, 2005), Organisation for Economic Co-operation and Development (OECD), *OECD Reviews of Regulatory Reform: Brazil – Strengthening Governance for Growth* (Paris: OECD, 2008), Organisation for Economic Co-operation and Development (OECD), *OECD Reviews of Regulatory Reform: China – Defining the Boundary between the Market and the State* (Paris: OECD, 2009), Christopher P. M. Waters, "Defending Rights in Russia: Lawyers, the State and Legal Reform in the Post-Soviet Era" (2006) 13(2) *International Journal of the Legal Profession* 185, Sudhir Krishnaswamy, Sindhu K. Sivakumar and Shishir Bail, "Legal and Judicial Reform in India: A Call for Systemic and Empirical Approaches" (2014) 2 *Journal of National Law University, Delhi* 1, Pitman B. Potter, "Legal Reform in China: Institutions, Culture, and Selective Adaptation" (2004) 29(2) *Law & Social Inquiry* 465, and Christa Rautenbach, "Legal Reform of Traditional Courts in South Africa: Exploring the Links between UBUNTU, Restorative Justice and Therapeutic Jurisprudence" (2015) 2(2) *Journal of International and Comparative Law* 275.

[14] See e.g. Tao-Tai Hsia, "Sources of Law in the People's Republic of China: Recent Developments" (1980) 14(1) *International Lawyer* 25 and C. H. van Zyl, "The Sources of South African Law" (1901) 18(3) *South African Law Journal* 272.

regulatory methods to accomplish the objectives set out in the constitution and other relevant legal texts.

In this respect, the question of sources of law is inextricably linked to comparative law in a threefold way. First, global comparative law is poised "to become the 'science of tomorrow', the tool for understanding laws and cultures in the globalizing world of the twenty-first century" as well as the "twenty-second century" and even beyond.[15] It may also resume greater significance in the light of serious challenges posed by new technologies. Second, global comparative law can help to identify the determining traits of each legal system in accordance with the existing taxonomies of the world's legal traditions. Last but not least, comparative law can also internally help to strengthen and improve the domestic legal system so that it can better meet the particular challenges it faces. It is clear that the legal system of each of the BRICS countries is a kind of hybrid or mixed legal system.[16]

In fact, it seems that, generally, the legal world is undergoing the paradox of an almost simultaneous increase in local, regional and global integration efforts, with greater harmonization of laws being sought at each of these levels, while single legal systems are moving towards a greater differentiation, meaning that each legal system is putting more emphasis on the unique features that establish it as a sui generis system. In this context, it is noteworthy that the appearance of paradoxes and oxymora has been said to indicate the existence of "possible gaps in prevailing theories" [17] or "instances where current knowledge may be deficient".[18] Thus, to fill these gaps and complete the existing knowledge means that each of the countries – next to their existing legal sources – will need to ponder possible novel sources of law, such as those provided by both the challenges and the opportunities arising from new technologies and scientific innovation. They can best do that in combination in a joint effort, such as the one provided by the BRICS dialogue and cooperation platform.

---

[15] See Esin Örücü, *The Enigma of Comparative Law: Variations on a Theme for the Twenty-First Century* (Dordrecht: Springer, 2004) at 1 and Mathias M. Siems, "Comparative Law in the 22nd Century" (2016) 23(2) *Maastricht Journal of European and Comparative Law* 2.

[16] See also Vernon Valentine Palmer, "Mixed Legal Systems... and the Myth of Pure Laws" (2007) 67(4) *Louisiana Law Review* 1205 at 1205.

[17] See Dean I. Radin, *The Noetic Universe: The Scientific Evidence for Psychic Phenomena* (London: Transworld Publishers, 2009) at 3.

[18] See Narinder Kapur et al., "The Paradoxical Nature of Nature", in Narinder Kapur (ed.), *The Paradoxical Brain* (Cambridge: Cambridge University Press, 2011) 1 at 1.

It has to be noted that there are several indicators that the role of law and the legal profession are being strongly affected by the rise of new and possibly disruptive technologies.[19] Bar associations in several different countries have begun to pay attention to the changing technological environment and its impact on law and the legal profession.[20] Following the example of an overview by the International Bar Association (IBA),[21] the BRICS countries' individual bar associations, by virtue of their cooperation in the BRICS Legal Forum, should also address these questions in a joint initiative. As a first concrete step, the idea proposed by the Russian government, first in 2013 and later in 2015 during the Russian BRICS chairpersonship, of establishing a permanent BRICS virtual secretariat, should be further developed beyond a mere website, and should be realized as soon as possible.[22]

The reason for the urgent need for the establishment of a permanent BRICS virtual secretariat is that, at present, BRICS-related information is scattered around on webpages maintained by the individual BRICS countries holding the chairpersonship.[23] Further information is available at various websites maintained by specific BRICS research or information centres.[24] All of these

---

[19] See e.g. Richard E. Susskind, *The Future of Law: Facing the Challenges of Information Technology* (Oxford: Clarendon Press, 1996), Richard E. Susskind, *Tomorrow's Lawyers: An Introduction to Your Future*, 2nd ed (Oxford: Oxford University Press, 2017) and Mark McKamey, "Legal Technology: Artificial Intelligence and the Future of Law Practice" (2017) 22 *Appeal: Review of Current Law and Law Reform* 45.

[20] See e.g. The Canadian Bar Association (CBA), *The Future of Legal Services in Canada: Trends and Issues* (2013) at 27-29; available at: https://www.cba.org/CBAMediaLibrary/cba_na/PDFs/CBA%20Legal%20Futures%20PDFS/trends-isssues-eng.pdf and Kami Haeri, *L'avenir de la profession d'avocat* (February 2017) at 16; available at: http://www.justice.gouv.fr/publication/rapport_kami_haeri.pdf.

[21] See International Bar Association, *IBA Global Regulation and Trade in Legal Services Report 2014* (London: International Bar Association, 2014).

[22] See e.g. Yuri Paniev, "BRICS countries seek 'virtual secretariat'", *Russia Beyond* (18 February 2013); available at: https://www.rbth.com/economics/2013/02/18/brics_countries_seek_virtual_secretariat_22337 and "BRICS countries to create a 'virtual secretariat'", *Russian News Agency TASS* (13 March 2015); available at: https://www.rbth.com/news/2015/03/13/brics_countries_create_a_virtual_secretariatbrics_countries_create_a_vir_41981.

[23] See e.g. 2017 BRICS Chairpersonship (China), https://www.brics2017.org/English/; 2015 BRICS Chairpersonship (Russia), http://en.brics2015.ru/; 2014 BRICS Chairpersonship (Brazil), http://brics.itamaraty.gov.br/media2/press-releases/214-sixth-brics-summit-fortaleza-declaration.

[24] See e.g. South African BRICS Think Tank, http://sabtt.org.za/; University of Toronto, BRICS Information Centre, http://www.brics.utoronto.ca/; Human Sciences Research Council (HSRC), BRICS Research Centre, http://www.hsrc.ac.za/en/departments/brics-research-centre; Pontifical Catholic University of Rio de Janeiro (PUC-Rio), BRICS Policy Center, http://bricspolicycenter.org/; Ural Federal University, BRICS Studies Centre, http://center-brics.urfu.ru/centre/; University of Parma, BRICS Parma, http://www.brics.unipr.it/.

sources provide insufficient reliability with regard to the completeness, accuracy and authenticity, as well as the actuality, of the information provided. Additionally, the BRICS virtual secretariat should host or be supported by a "permanent BRICS steering committee to oversee the coherence of all the areas of cooperation from a legal perspective".[25]

This means that even if BRICS wants to maintain its current status as a mere "cooperation and dialogue platform", or "a soft structure capable of producing legal flows of policy transfer",[26] and not go so far as becoming an efficient "multi-centre legal network"[27], the BRICS countries will need to consolidate the growing quantity of relevant texts and materials and provide a permanent – even if merely "virtual" – minimal institutional structure. In an age of the advancement of electronic (digital) governance (e-governance),[28] a database for BRICS materials should not pose a serious challenge in logistical and financial terms. Therefore, such a virtual BRICS secretariat should also include the creation of an electronic BRICS-LAW database. A database like this would not only help the better coordination of joint BRICS initiatives at the national level, but would also secure optimal levels of policy coherence at the regional and global level. It has also been described as a way to guarantee that "BRICS countries' public authorities and other stakeholders can have instant electronic access to the relevant laws and regulations", which would help to complement, enhance and reinforce the present state of a loose multi-centre legal network.[29] Perhaps parts, at least, of the database could also be made public, which would strengthen the spirit of the BRICS people-to-people exchange and cooperation, and complement the top-down by a bottom-up approach to cooperation, as was again emphasized in the 2017 Xiamen Declaration.[30] Lastly, it would provide

---

[25] Rostam J. Neuwirth, "The Enantiosis of BRICS: BRICS La[w]yers and the Difference that They Can Make", in Rostam J. Neuwirth, Alexandr Svetlicinii, and Denis De Castro Halis (eds.), *The BRICS-Lawyers' Guide to Global Cooperation* (Cambridge: Cambridge University Press, 2017) 8 at 23.

[26] See Mihaela Papa, "BRICS as a Global Legal Actor: From Regulatory Innovation to BRICS Law?" (2014) 20 *federalismi.it* 2 at 7.

[27] See Lucia Scaffardi, "BRICS, a Multi-Centre 'Legal Network'?" (2014) 5 *Beijing Law Review* 140.

[28] See generally Organisation for Economic Co-operation and Development (OECD), *OECD E-Government Studies: E-Government for Better Government* (Paris: OECD, 2005).

[29] Rostam J. Neuwirth, "The Enantiosis of BRICS: BRICS La[w]yers and the Difference that They Can Make", in Rostam J. Neuwirth, Alexandr Svetlicinii, and Denis De Castro Halis (eds.), *The BRICS-Lawyers' Guide to Global Cooperation* (Cambridge: Cambridge University Press, 2017) 8 at 23.

[30] See 2017 Xiamen Declaration ("We will embrace cultural diversity and promote people-to-people exchanges to gamer more popular support for BRICS cooperation through deepened

a unique opportunity for the BRICS countries to make a difference in global (e-)governance and set a pioneering example for greater coherence in law and policy making, which a future global system should also adopt. Such a system could follow the "GEOLAW" model, that is to say a "Glocal Electronically Operated Law Administration Web", which is inspired by Internet search engines and similar related services, and could be put to use for the following purposes:

• To provide access for both civil servants and citizens to the existing legislation in force, both at the international level (e.g. conventions, treaties etc.) and at the regional and national level (e.g. supranational regulations and domestic laws).

• To create an electronic filing system for public administration that allows states and international organizations simultaneously to release information and/or comment on various legislative proposals or similar actions of legal relevance (e.g. such exchange of information could precede the negotiations for international legislative efforts). This has the advantage that all members of the international community are constantly and simultaneously informed about developments and can act when they are affected. This may reduce the need for the great number of preparatory meetings in different formats. Some issues require only a local, national or regional involvement while others require the broadest multilateral formation possible.

• To provide relevant services to individuals and legal persons. The extension of the system to private parties, however, can only be realized following drastic changes in and to the legal structure underlying the present international legal order, through which the role of private parties should be enhanced so that they receive the status of legal subjects under international law. Concrete areas of application can range from simple visa applications to deep sea oil exploration licences and the like. On a more general note, it is necessary to restore the balance between individual rights at the global level and the growing number of obligations deriving from international law that have a direct or indirect effect on individuals.[31]

---

traditional friendships. We will expand people-to-people exchanges in all dimensions, encourage all fabrics of the society to participate in BRICS cooperation, promote mutual learning between our cultures and civilizations, enhance communication and mutual understanding among our peoples and deepen traditional friendships, thus making BRICS partnership closer to our people's hearts"), Appendix II.2 A.

[31] See Rostam J. Neuwirth, "Governar a Glocalização: 'Ter em Mente a Mudança' ou 'Mudar a Mente'?", (2011) 30 *Boletim da Faculdade de Direito* 47 (Jiang Yi Wa, trans.) [in English: "Governing Glocalisation: 'Mind the Change' or 'Change the Mind'?"].

Finally, to nurture the global governance debate with new ideas and to produce further positive synergies for this debate by way of the BRICS cooperation, it is thought to be useful to record and systematize their past cooperation efforts as laid down in numerous declarations, action plans and other texts and materials. It is at a certain point in time that cooperation, when having continued to widen in scope, also needs to deepen, which can be realized through a compilation and later consolidation of its texts and materials. Eventually, the consolidation of texts and materials can also lead to their codification, which may be beneficial for strengthening the rule of law. To contribute to achieving these objectives is the prime goal of the present handbook.

II.   GUIDANCE AS FOR THE USE OF THE HANDBOOK

Before turning to the Appendix listing the core BRICS texts and materials, it is useful to provide some brief information to assist in the use of the present book. It was during their research in general and in particular when working on this comprehensive compilation of the official BRICS texts and materials that the authors found themselves confronted with a number of difficult problems impeding the progress and consistency of the research.

First, there is the continuing problem of the general absence of an official repository of BRICS documents, given in particular that the virtual secretariat is still a "virtual" initiative and its construction is pending.[32]

A second problem lies in the fact that the chairpersonship of the BRICS cooperation platform rotates on an annual basis, and the websites maintained by the respective BRICS countries usually cease to be updated after the chairpersonship moves to the next country.[33] This can mean that, after some time, a specific document that is referenced in a subsequent BRICS declaration of a particular kind can no longer be accessed.

Third, it also frequently happens that the same document can be made available by various sources (e.g. national authorities, annual summit websites,

---

[32] The official BRICS Information Portal (http://infobrics.org/) contains various official BRICS texts adopted in different years, but is in no way a comprehensive repository.

[33] For example, the following websites are maintained without update: http://en.brics2015.ru/ (Russia's 2015 BRICS chairpersonship) or http://brics2016.gov.in/ (India's 2016 BRICS chairpersonship). On the other hand, the South Africa's BRICS 2018 chairpersonship website http://www.brics2018.org.za/ is no longer active.

research centres, or media outlets).[34] Furthermore, any specific document may be made available in different formats (e.g. a signed original, an unsigned copy, a draft, a reprint, etc.), which makes it problematic or impossible to verify its authenticity.[35]

Fourth, the BRICS countries do not follow any particular format, let alone a consistent one, when drafting their cooperation documents, which results in a wide range of formats, styles, numbering and structuring of the documents.[36]

Fifth and last, there is no specific language agreed upon, although all BRICS documents are drafted in the English language. In the absence of a coordinated language format, the BRICS texts therefore exhibit a variety of spelling,[37] punctuation, terminology,[38] and abbreviations.[39]

---

[34] For example, the 2017 BRICS Summit Xiamen Declaration can be accessed from the following sites: 1) China's 2017 BRICS chairpersonship website; available at: https://www.brics 2017.org/english/documents/summit/201709/t20170908_2021.html; 2) The Ministry of External Affairs of India, available at: https://mea.gov.in/bilateral-documents.htm?dtl/28912/ BRICS+Leaders+Xiamen+Declaration+Xiamen+China+September+04+2017; 3) the Indian Prime Minister's Office, available at: http://pib.nic.in/newsite/PrintRelease.aspx?relid= 170485; and 4) China's official media portal Xinhua, available at: http://www.xinhua net.com//english/2017-09/04/c_136583396.htm.

[35] For example, the 2016 BRICS Summit Goa Declaration can be accessed from the India's 2016 BRICS chairpersonship website (http://brics2016.gov.in/upload/Goa%20Declaration%20 and%20Action%20Plan.pdf) in a single paginated document together with the Goa Action Plan. The same declaration, but without action plan and in a different format appears at the website of the Indian Ministry of External Affairs (https://www.mea.gov.in/bilateral-documents.htm? dtl/27491/Goa+Declaration+at+8th+BRICS+Summit).

[36] An illustrative example in this regard is the format of the annual BRICS Legal Forum declarations. The 2014 Brasilia Declarations contains both Roman and Arabic numbering; 2015 Shanghai Declaration contains exclusively Arabic numbers; 2016 New Delhi Declaration does not have any numbering of its paragraphs.

[37] For example, the 2016 BRICS Summit Goa Declaration is using the British spelling of the term "organisation", while the 2015 BRICS Summit Ufa Declaration is following the American spelling "organization".

[38] For example, when designating the rotating BRICS chairpersonship, the 2018 BRICS Summit Johannesburg Declaration uses the term "chairship" (para 101), whereas the 2017 BRICS Summit Xiamen Declaration refers to "chairmanship" (para 67) and the 2018 BRICS trade ministers joint communique uses the term "presidency" (para 12).

[39] For example, the term "small and medium-sized enterprises" or SMEs can be found in the 2018 BRICS Summit Johannesburg Declaration in two distinct formats: Small and Medium-sized Enterprises (para 56) and Micro, Small and Medium Enterprises (para 80). The 2017 BRICS Summit Xiamen Declaration refers to "small, micro and medium-sized enterprises (SMMEs)" (para 13) while 2016 BRICS Summit Goa Declaration mentions "micro, small and medium enterprises (MSMEs)" (para 36).

The above-mentioned problems underscore the urgent need for additional efforts toward a better systematization and standardization, and the authors of the present volume have undertaken this in relation to the selected documents included in the Appendix. Where available and when possible, the authors have verified the authenticity of each document included in the compilation by comparing documents from more than one source.[40] However, it is impossible to guarantee their authenticity and accuracy, given that even some of the documents made available contain typographical errors.

Nonetheless, the Appendix compiled in the present volume marks a first comprehensive (but not a complete) repository of all official BRICS documents. Their large volume means that they cannot be organized in the restricted format of a single handbook. As a result, the authors were confronted with the difficult task of selecting the most pertinent BRICS documents that were available, and these can be found listed in the Appendix. In this regard, however, the present volume and, especially, the electronic version of the book are believed to provide relief and also to point the way for a future joint BRICS website and possible electronic BRICS (Law) Database. This is of particular significance in view of the fact that new relevant documents by the BRICS cooperation are being created on a constant basis.

As a further point, it is important to stress that, while the international agreements related to the establishment and functioning of the New Development Bank (NDB) and its regional offices in Brazil and South Africa were included, because of their binding nature, the declarations of the BRICS Heads of State adopted at the annual BRICS summits have been selected because of their political significance and their general nature of summarizing the development of BRICS cooperation in numerous areas. The selection of the ministerial declarations has been made in a more subjective manner and should in no way minimize the importance of the BRICS cooperation in other fields (e.g. finance, industry or migration) that has not been covered in the present compilation. Thus, the authors have decided to include the declarations of the foreign ministers, trade ministers, ministers of agriculture and rural development, ministers responsible for science, technology and innovation, health ministers, ministers of environmental protection, labour and employment

---

[40] As a first point of call we have used the official websites of the BRICS annual summits and the government websites of the BRICS countries. Where the relevant documents were no longer accessible from such official sources, the authors have referred to the research institutions and/or media outlets reporting on the BRICS cooperation activities.

ministers, and ministers of education. The reason for their selection was, inter alia, that there was at least some historical continuity in their meetings.

As the authors of this volume have a legal background, it is no surprise that they attribute special attention to the development of the legal cooperation among the BRICS countries, which also explains the inclusion of the BRICS Legal Forum declarations. However, this does not mean that this volume is primarily for lawyers or scholars with a legal interest or background. On the contrary, it is designed to serve the wider scientific community, noting that in the past more attention to BRICS has been paid by non-legal scholars, such as economists or political scientists, as well as by the media or business community in general.

In the *BRICS-Lawyers' Guide to Global Cooperation*, it was therefore already stressed that the term "BRICS-Lawyers" was chosen as an invitation to every-one to become a BRICKs-Layer of the foundations on which a future global governance framework is to be established,[41] and it was also stated that "bric(k)s are for building bridges, not walls!",[42] which is not only a reminder for states to cooperate in constructive terms and by using the rule of law but also points to another important legal aspect. This aspect lies in the role of law as a tool that helps to "engineer" bridges between scientific disciplines, i.e. to foster transdisciplinarity, which assumes particular significance in times of greater complexity. The reason is that transdisciplinarity can help to address complexity, when it is interpreted as a means to foster the under-standing of the world through the unity of knowledge.[43] In this respect, the volume is intended to help to tackle the problems resulting from fragmentation and to avoid possible conflicts of laws, supporting the assertion that "[C]omparative law can help to identify the paths traced by norm producers in fragmented spaces".[44]

---

[41] Rostam J. Neuwirth, Alexandr Svetlicinii, and Denis De Castro Halis, "Conclusion: BRICS Lawyers as Bricklayers", in Rostam J. Neuwirth, Alexandr Svetlicinii, and Denis De Castro Halis (eds.), *The BRICS-Lawyers' Guide to Global Cooperation* (Cambridge: Cambridge University Press, 2017) 378.

[42] Rostam J. Neuwirth, "The Enantiosis of BRICS: BRICS La[w]yers and the Difference that They Can Make", in Rostam J. Neuwirth, Alexandr Svetlicinii, and Denis De Castro Halis (eds.), *The BRICS-Lawyers' Guide to Global Cooperation* (Cambridge: Cambridge University Press, 2017) 8 at 23.

[43] See Basarab Nicolescu, "Methodology of Transdisciplinarity – Levels of Reality, Logic of the Included Middle and Complexity" (2010) 1(1) *Transdisciplinary Journal of Engineering & Science* 19 at 22.

[44] Marcelo Dias Varella, *Internationalization of Law Globalization, International Law and Complexity* (Berlin: Springer, 2014) at 116.

Bearing in mind the need for greater transdisciplinarity, and in view of the novel fields of cooperation being explored, the authors have also added to the Appendix several additional, sector-specific BRICS documents, which are intended to serve as examples of BRICS cooperation in certain fields that has not (yet) evolved to the level of regular meetings or a systematized ministerial cooperation framework. For example, one of these sources is the Memorandum of Understanding (MoU) concluded by the national competition authorities from the BRICS countries in 2016. While in the majority of the BRICS states, these authorities are independent from the executive branch,[45] their dialogue and cooperation has evolved through the biennial international conferences.[46] Another peculiar example is the "BRICS Multilateral Cooperation Agreement on Innovation", which may sound like an intergovernmental agreement concluded by the BRICS countries but is in fact an agreement between several state-owned development finance institutions from the BRICS countries: Banco Nacional de Desenvolvimento Econômico e Social, the Bank for Development and Foreign Economic Affairs (Vnesheconombank), the Export-Import Bank of India, the China Development Bank Corporation, and the Development Bank of Southern Africa.

The inclusion of the above mentioned documents in the Appendix provides additional points of reference for BRICS researchers from different backgrounds, even though the present compilation does not and cannot include all existing BRICS texts. It should, however, help to prepare the future of cooperation, particularly as new areas of cooperation have already been mentioned in the various existing documents and could thus be elevated to a more systematized mode of cooperation in the future.

Last but not least, in respect of the present categorization and systematization of the various BRICS texts and materials, two caveats should be made. First, since the debate on the inclusiveness and hierarchy of the sources of law in general is ongoing, the order in which the BRICS documents appear in the compilation does not carry any normative claims, and it primarily follows the objective of functionality that should be expected from a reference handbook. Second, as specified above, the precise legal status of the BRICS

---

[45] See Alexandr Svetlicinii and Juanjuan Zhang, "The Competition Law Institutions in the BRICS Countries: Developing Better Institutional Models for the Protection of Market Competition" (2017) 2 *Chinese Political Science Review* 85.

[46] 6th BRICS Competition Conference will be held on 16-19 September 2019 in Moscow, https://www.bricscompetition.org/.

remains open, as the BRICS countries are still in search of an optimal framework for their cooperation. Therefore, the volume does not intend to impede
the experimentation with various novel models and innovative formats,
which may be top-down or bottom-up, centralized or decentralized, and
public or private, as well as following binding or non-binding approaches.

This is the reason why the present systematization is in no way authoritative
or reflective of the BRICS countries' official position on the hierarchy or legal
status of the official texts governing their multilevel cooperation. Instead, the
priority here lies in fostering the debate about the future of BRICS cooperation and the search for novel and innovative modes of governance at all
levels, national, regional, and global. In brief, it is intended to generate an
open-minded debate on the future of sources of law in particular and on
novel (i.e., more coherent and sustainable) modes of cooperation in the
governance of global affairs.

In greater detail, **Section I** of the Appendix features BRICS texts that have
been adopted in the form of international treaties, namely the Agreement on
the NDB (followed by agreements concerning its headquarters and regional
offices), the BRICS Contingent Reserve Arrangement (CRA), and the BRICS
Agreement on Culture. **Section II** contains the output of the annual BRICS
summit meetings of the Heads of State, which includes the summit
declarations, various action plans for the upcoming year, plus the Strategy
for BRICS Economic Partnership, which was adopted during the 2015 BRICS
Summit in Ufa. In the following **Section III**, documents adopted at the
ministerial meetings in different formations are listed. For the most part,
these meetings are held on an annual basis. Additionally, certain ministers
also meet on the sidelines of sector-specific international fora such as the
World Health Organization's Assembly, for health ministers, or the UN
General Assembly, for foreign ministers. Besides ministerial declarations,
Section III also contains various policies, strategies and action plans adopted
at the ministerial level. These include the BRICS Trade and Investment Cooperation Framework, the Action Plan 2017-2020 for Agricultural Cooperation
of BRICS Countries, the BRICS Action Plan for Innovation Cooperation (2017-
2020), and the Joint Declaration of BRICS countries on strengthening cooperation in traditional medicine, to mention but a few. **Section IV** includes the
declarations adopted by the BRICS Legal Forum, a cooperation venue of
special significance for BRICS-Lawyers. Finally, **Section V** contains samples
of other sector-specific BRICS cooperation documents such as different
Memoranda of Understanding, like the ones on the Establishment of the

BRICS Network University or on the Cooperation among BRICS Export Credit Insurance Agencies.

Generally, all the documents included in the Appendix are reproduced in reverse chronological order for each section, starting from the most recent and ending with the earliest, covering the first decade of BRICS cooperation (2009-2019). For all the BRICS texts included in the Appendix, the original structure and numbering is preserved but the format, font and appearance of the texts has been unified to the extent possible. For instance, while some of the original BRICS texts bear the official logos of the annual meetings, the logos of participating organizations, or the signatures of the parties, most of the time the authors have omitted these items in order to preserve the uniformity in appearance.

Without a claim as to its completeness, the Appendix includes all major BRICS texts in a format that significantly facilitates their referencing in academic works and other types of publication, since the BRICS texts are accessible in different formats from a variety of electronic resources, some of which may have become inactive or inaccessible over time. For example, one of these texts can be referenced in the following way:

> **7th Meeting of the BRICS Trade Ministers, 31 August 2017, Shanghai (China).** Reprinted in Rostam J. Neuwirth and Alexandr Svetlicinii (2019). *The BRICS-Lawyers' Guide to BRICS Texts and Materials*, 375-385. Macau: BRICS-Lawyers.

These references will be especially useful in relation to BRICS texts that do not have any official pagination or numbering, or those with a complex internal structure using numerous headings and sub-headings.

Finally, as a further means to facilitate the use of the book for research into the BRICS texts and materials, the present volume also features an index using a list of the most important keywords. These keywords stem from the various subjects of BRICS cooperation (e.g. agriculture, cybersecurity, peace-keeping, or sustainable development, etc.) as well as major BRICS-specific terms and concepts (e.g. the BRICS Economic Partnership, the BRICS Network University, or Emerging Markets and Developing Countries (EMDCs), etc.). As a means to highlight the BRICS group's position on various issues of global governance, references to specific countries (e.g. Afghanistan, DPRK, and Iraq), issues (e.g. nuclear weapons and South–South cooperation, etc.), and international organizations and fora (e.g. the IMF, the UN, the WTO, WIPO, or the World Bank, etc.) are also included.

When working with the keywords and locating them in the BRICS texts and materials, readers will inevitably notice a certain repetitiveness, which is due to the fact that the bulk of BRICS communication takes place at annual summits and meetings, and these are normally concluded by a joint declaration/statement/communiqué. As a result, the BRICS documents tend to contain frequent repetitions of the BRICS countries' positions or attitudes towards certain issues, positions or attitudes that remain unchanged through the years.[47] As the BRICS cooperation continues to develop in a wide variety of fields, the production of BRICS texts continues to intensify.

For this reason, the present book also expresses the hope that it can make a humble contribution to providing interested readers with an easy reference to the official BRICS texts. In addition, it hopes to serve as a reminder to the officials of the BRICS countries to work to consolidate, harmonize or unify their widely accepted and largely unchanged positions on various matters of inter-BRICS cooperation in the global governance debate by, for instance, including a set of "BRICS principles" in a single document. Such a document could be named the "BRICS Charter" or the "BRICS Declaration of Fundamental Principles", or it could introduce an entirely new (legal) terminology.

It is submitted that this kind of consolidated presentation of the many BRICS objectives and principles could help to reduce the quantity but add to the quality, in terms of weight and importance, of the "BRICS approach" to global cooperation and global governance in the twenty-first century and beyond. On a more practical note, it would alleviate the need to repeat these principles in the emerging BRICS texts at various levels and would considerably shorten the length of these texts. In the long history of law, an important role of the law is to process "big data" collected by all legally relevant stakeholders and to formulate them into the concise and universally applicable format

---

[47] For example, BRICS have continuously supported the WTO dispute settlement system and the relevant declarations are found in numerous BRICS texts: "We recall that the WTO Dispute Settlement System is a cornerstone of the multilateral trading system and is designed to enhance security and predictability in international trade" (2018 BRICS Summit Johannesburg Declaration, para 64, Appendix II.1 A); "We strongly support the WTO dispute settlement system as a cornerstone of the security and predictability of the multilateral trading system" (2014 BRICS Summit Fortaleza Declaration, para 21, Appendix II.5 A); "WTO Dispute Settlement System is a cornerstone of the MTS as it is designed to enhance security and predictability in international trade" (2018 Meeting of BRICS ministers of foreign affairs, para 12, Appendix III.1 A); "WTO dispute settlement system is a cornerstone of the MTS and is designed to enhance security and predictability in international trade" (8th Meeting of BRICS Trade Ministers, 5 July 2018, Annex B Statement on WTO Matters, Appendix III.2 A).

of a code. In this regard, the present volume also hopes to help with the process of consolidating existing as well as future BRICS documents in a systematized way, so as to enhance the coherence, consistency and cooperation in a growing number of different policy fields that have already been identified or that will be explored in the future. As a kind of tenth anniversary edition, the present book thus aims to assist in the process of establishing a joint BRICS website as well as a BRICS virtual secretariat to foster BRICS cooperation during the next decade, beginning with the 11th BRICS Summit of Heads of State to be held in Brazil later this year.

III. REFERENCES

Canadian Bar Association (CBA), *The Future of Legal Services in Canada: Trends and Issues* (2013).

De Beukelaer, Christiaan, "Creative Industries in "Developing" Countries: Questioning Country Classifications in the UNCTAD Creative Economy Reports" (2014) 23(4) *Cultural Trends* 232.

De Beukelaer, Christiaan, *Developing Cultural Industries: Learning from the Palimpsest of Practice* (Amsterdam: European Cultural Foundation, 2015).

Del Vecchio, Giorgio, "The Problem of the Sources of Positive Law" (1935) 47(3) *Juridical Review* 253.

Dias Varella, Marcelo, *Internationalization of Law Globalization, International Law and Complexity* (Berlin: Springer, 2014).

Freedman, Daniel G., *Human Sociobiology: A Holistic Approach* (New York: The Free Press, 1979).

Haeri, Kami, *L'avenir de la profession d'avocat* (February 2017); available at: http://www.justice.gouv.fr/publication/rapport_kami_haeri.pdf.

Hebb, D. O., "Heredity and Environment in Mammalian Behaviour" (1953) 1(2) *The British Journal of Animal Behaviour* 43.

Hsia, Tao-Tai, "Sources of Law in the People's Republic of China: Recent Developments" (1980) 14(1) *International Lawyer* 25.

International Bar Association, *IBA Global Regulation and Trade in Legal Services Report 2014* (London: International Bar Association, 2014).

Jennings, Robert Y., "Recent Developments in the International Law Commission: Its Relation to the Sources of International Law" (1964) 13 *International and Comparative Law Quarterly* 385.

Kapur, Narinder et al., "The Paradoxical Nature of Nature", in Narinder Kapur (ed.), *The Paradoxical Brain* (Cambridge: Cambridge University Press, 2011) 1.

McKamey, Mark, "Legal Technology: Artificial Intelligence and the Future of Law Practice" (2017) 22 *Appeal: Review of Current Law and Law Reform* 45.

Neuwirth, Rostam J., "A Constitutional Tribute to Global Governance: Overcoming the Chimera of the Developing-Developed Country Dichotomy", *European University Institute (EUI) Working Paper LAW 2010/20* (2010).

Neuwirth, Rostam J., "Global Governance and the Creative Economy: The Developing versus Developed Country Dichotomy Revisited" (2013) 1(1) *Frontiers of Legal Research* 127.

Neuwirth, Rostam J., "Global Law and Sustainable Development: Change and the "Developing-Developed Country" Terminology", (2016) 29(4) *European Journal of Development Research* 911.

Neuwirth, Rostam J., "Governar a Glocalização: 'Ter em Mente a Mudança' ou 'Mudar a Mente'?", (2011) 30 *Boletim da Faculdade de Direito* 47.

Neuwirth, Rostam J., "The 'End of 'Development Assistance' and the BRICS", in Jose A. Puppim de Oliveira, and Yijia Jing (eds.), *International Development Assistance, China and the BRICS* (New York: Palgrave, 2019).

Neuwirth, Rostam J., Svetlicinii, Alexandr and De Castro Halis, Denis (eds.), *The BRICS-Lawyers' Guide to Global Cooperation* (Cambridge: Cambridge University Press, 2017).

Nicolescu, Basarab, "Methodology of Transdisciplinarity – Levels of Reality, Logic of the Included Middle and Complexity" (2010) 1(1) *Transdisciplinary Journal of Engineering & Science* 19.

Organisation for Economic Co-operation and Development (OECD), *OECD Reviews of Regulatory Reform: Russia – Building the Rules for the Market* (Paris: OECD, 2005).

Organisation for Economic Co-operation and Development (OECD), *OECD Reviews of Regulatory Reform: Brazil – Strengthening Governance for Growth* (Paris: OECD, 2008).

Organisation for Economic Co-operation and Development (OECD), *OECD Reviews of Regulatory Reform: China – Defining the Boundary between the Market and the State* (Paris: OECD, 2009).

Organisation for Economic Co-operation and Development (OECD), *OECD E-Government Studies: E-Government for Better Government* (Paris: OECD, 2005).

Örücü, Esin, *The Enigma of Comparative Law: Variations on a Theme for the Twenty-First Century* (Dordrecht: Springer, 2004).

Palmer, Vernon Valentine, "Mixed Legal Systems... and the Myth of Pure Laws" (2007) 67(4) *Louisiana Law Review* 1205.

Paníev, Yuri, "BRICS countries seek "virtual secretariat"", *Russia Beyond* (18 February 2013).

Papa, Mihaela, "BRICS as a Global Legal Actor: From Regulatory Innovation to BRICS Law?" (2014) 20 *federalismi.it* 2.

Potter, Pitman B., "Legal Reform in China: Institutions, Culture, and Selective Adaptation" (2004) 29(2) *Law & Social Inquiry* 465.

Radin, Dean I., *The Noetic Universe: The Scientific Evidence for Psychic Phenomena* (London: Transworld Publishers, 2009).

Rautenbach, Christa, "Legal Reform of Traditional Courts in South Africa: Exploring the Links between UBUNTU, Restorative Justice and Therapeutic Jurisprudence" (2015) 2(2) *Journal of International and Comparative Law* 275.

Scaffardi, Lucia, "BRICS, a Multi-Centre 'Legal Network'?" (2014) 5 *Beijing Law Review* 140.

Schachter, Oscar, "Towards a Theory of International Obligation" (1968) 8(2) *Virginia Journal of International Law* 300.

Schmitter, Philippe C. and Ki, Sunhyuk, "Comparing Processes of Regional Integration: European 'Lessons' and Northeast Asian Reflections" (2008) 17(1) *Current Politics and Economics of Asia* 11.

Siems, Mathias M., "Comparative Law in the 22nd Century" (2016) 23(2) *Maastricht Journal of European and Comparative Law* 2.

Sudhir Krishnaswamy, Sindhu K. Sivakumar and Shishir Bail, "Legal and Judicial Reform in India: A Call for Systemic and Empirical Approaches" (2014) 2 *Journal of National Law University, Delhi* 1.

Susskind, Richard E., *The Future of Law: Facing the Challenges of Information Technology* (Oxford: Clarendon Press, 1996).

Susskind, Richard E., *Tomorrow's Lawyers: An Introduction to Your Future*, 2nd ed (Oxford: Oxford University Press, 2017).

Svetlicinii, Alexandr and Zhang, Juanjuan, "The Competition Law Institutions in the BRICS Countries: Developing Better Institutional Models for the Protection of Market Competition" (2017) 2 *Chinese Political Science Review* 85.

van Zyl, C. H., "The Sources of South African Law" (1901) 18(3) *South African Law Journal* 272.

Waters, Christopher P. M., "Defending Rights in Russia: Lawyers, the State and Legal Reform in the Post-Soviet Era" (2006) 13(2) *International Journal of the Legal Profession* 185.

World Bank, *2016 World Development Indicators* (Washington: The World Bank, 2016).

Official BRICS Texts and Materials

The Parties will create a joint website to cover BRICS activities. The website will be a free online public resource.

Memorandum of Understanding
on the Creation of the Joint BRICS
Website
9 Jul. 2015, Ufa (RUS)

I.   BRICS TREATY LAW

I.1.   The Agreements on the New Development Bank (NDB)

A.   Headquarter/Host Country Agreements – Brazil 2018

AGREEMENT BETWEEN THE FEDERATIVE REPUBLIC OF BRAZIL AND THE NEW
DEVELOPMENT BANK ON THE HOSTING OF THE NEW DEVELOPMENT BANK
AMERICAS REGIONAL OFFICE IN THE FEDERATIVE REPUBLIC OF BRAZIL

Preamble

The Federative Republic of Brazil

and

the New Development Bank

(hereinafter jointly referred to as the "Parties" and in the singular as a "Party");

TAKING INTO ACCOUNT the Agreement on the New Development Bank and its Annex on the Articles
of Agreement of the New Development Bank between the Governments of the Federative Republic
of Brazil, the Russian Federation, the Republic of India, the People's Republic of China and the
Republic of South Africa, signed in Fortaleza, on 15 July 2014;

RECALLING Article 4 of the Articles of Agreement of the New Development Bank contained in the
Annex to the Agreement on the New Development Bank, which stipulates that the New Development
Bank may establish offices necessary for the performance of its functions;

FURTHER RECALLING the BRICS Ministerial Meeting held in Fortaleza on 15 July 2014, on which
occasion it was decided that the second regional office of the New Development Bank shall be
established in Brazil;

DESIROUS THEREFORE to conclude an agreement regarding the hosting of the New Development
Bank office in the Federative Republic of Brazil;

HAVE AGREED as follows,

Article 1
Definitions

For the purpose of this Agreement, including all annexes, appendices and all amendments made from)
time to time, the following terms shall have, unless the content otherwise requires, the meanings
ascribed to them as below:

   (a) "Americas Regional Office" means the regional office of the New Development Bank in the
        Federative Republic of Brazil;

   (b) "Agreement on the New Development Bank" means the Agreement on the New
        Development Bank including its Annex between the Governments of the Federative
        Republic of Brazil, the Russian Federation, the Republic of India, the People's Republic of
        China and the Republic of South Africa, signed on 15 July 2014 at the city of Fortaleza, Brazil
        and any amendments thereto;

   (c) "Archives of the Bank" means the records, correspondence, documents, manuscripts, still
        and moving pictures, films, sound recordings, electronic records including email, computer
        programs, written materials, video tapes or discs, discs or tapes containing data, and any
        information contained therein stored In electronic form or any other form whatsoever,
        belonging to, are held by the Bank;

(d) "Bank" means the New Development Bank, including the Americas Regional Office, unless specifically referred to separately;

(e) "Brazil" means the Federative Republic of Brazil and its territory;

(f) "Director-General" means the principal executive officer of the Americas Regional Office, appointed by the Bank, and, during her or his absence or incapacity, the person authorized to act as Director-General;

(g) "Experts and Consultants" means persons who, not being Staff of the Bank, have been contracted by the Bank via global recruitment process in accordance with the provisions of the Human Resources policies of the Bank for the purpose of providing expertise and performing certain tasks for of on behalf of the Bank;

(h) "Government" means the Government of the Federative Republic of Brazil;

(i) "Laws of the Federative Republic of Brazil, or: laws of Brazil" includes the Constitution of the Federative Republic of Brazil and legislative acts, decrees, regulations and orders issued by, or under authority of, the Government or any appropriate authority in the Federative Republic of Brazil;

(j) "Local Staff" means persons who are locally hired to perform administrative and support activities for the Bank in accordance with the provisions of the Human Resources policies of the Bank;

(k) "Member" means a member of the Bank as defined in the Agreement on the New Development Bank;

(l) "Member of the family" means the spouse and dependent children under the age of 18 years, any other dependent family member officially recognized as such by the Bank, and the spouse or life partner of a Staff member officially recognized as such by the Bank, It being understood that the Government may also consider members of the family other persons, In accordance with applicable legislation and practice;

(m) "Premises" means the land, building, parts of building and includes access facilities for the official purposes of the Americas Regional Office;

(n) "President" means the President of the Bank and, during her or his absence or incapacity, the person authorized to act as President; and

(o) "Staff of the Bank" or "Staff means persons employed by the Bank, to work at the Americas Regional Office, in accordance with the provisions of the Human Resources policies of the Bank and other relevant internal regulations in force, and excluding the Local Staff and all other persons assigned on hourly rates.

Article 2
Seat of the Americas Regional Office

1. The seat of the Americas Regional Office shall be in the city of Sao Paulo.

2. The Bank may establish Premises also in Brasilia, and, upon consent by the Government, other cities within Brazil.

Article 3
Functions and activities of the Americas Regional Office

The Americas Regional Office shall undertake such functions and activities pursuant to provisions of the Agreement on the New Development Bank and, in conformity with the said Agreement and this Agreement, other activities as determined by the Bank.

Article 4
Legal personality

1. The Government recognizes the International legal personality and capacity of the Bank for the purposes of exercising its functions in Brazil including to contract, acquire and dispose of movable and immovable property and to institute legal proceedings.

2.   The Americas Regional Office shall have the independence and freedom of action similar to those available to other international organizations operating In Brazil.

3.   The Americas Regional Office shall have the right to display the Bank's flag and its emblem on the Premises and the motor vehicles belonging to or in use by the Bank for the President and the Director-General.

Article 5
Premises and facilities

1.   The Government shall provide or arrange for suitable office accommodation to serve as the seat of the Americas Regional Office in Sao Paulo and its sub-office in Brasilia, as wall as-such other facilities as required for the operations of the Americas Regional Office and Its sub-office. The terms of such support, including its duration, shall be agreed upon by the pertinent authorities of Brazil and the Bank. The Government shall be responsible for maintenance and repairs of a non-recurring nature of the Americas Regional Office and its sub- office, as well as for their accommodation, furniture, equipment and other facilities required for the operation of the Americas Regional Office and its sub-office. The terms of such support, including its duration, shall also be agreed upon by the pertinent authorities of Brazil and the Bank.

2.   The office accommodation, its furniture and equipment and the other facilities referred to in paragraph (1) above shall be determined in consultation with the Bank.

3.   The Bank shall be responsible for the day-to-day maintenance of the Premises, furniture and equipment other than on account of normal wear and tear, and making arrangements for any other services as may be required by it.

4.   As the operations of the Americas Regional Office evolve, the Bank and the Government will consider building and furnishing a suitable office building ta serve a5 permanent seat of the Americas Regional Office. The Government shall provide a suitable plot of land, subject to availability, and facilitate the construction of the building to be undertaken by the Bank, it being understood that the Government will not be required to cover the expenses related to construction.

Article 6
Immunity of property, funds and assets

1.   The Bank and its property, funds and assets, wherever located and by whomsoever held, shall enjoy the status, Immunities and privileges as provided for by Chapter VI of the Annex of the Agreement on the New Development Bank, except:

    (a)   to the extent that the Bank shall have expressly waived such immunity in-any particular case in accordance with the provisions of Article 36 of the Annex of "Articles of Agreement of the New Development Bank";

    (b)   in respect of every form of legal process in Brazil, which, for the purposes of this paragraph, include administrative procedures, arising out a or in connection with its powers to raise funds, through borrowings or other means, to guarantee obligations, or to buy and sell or underwrite the sale of securities;

    (c)   in respect of a civil action brought by a third party for damages arising from an accident caused by a vehicle belonging to the Bank or operated on its behalf;

    (d)   in respect of the enforcement of an arbitration award made against the Bank as a result of an express submission to arbitration by or on behalf of the Bank;

or

    (e)   in respect of any counter-claim directly connected with court proceedings initiated by the Bank.

2.   The property of the Bank shall be immune from all forms of seizure, attachment or execution before the delivery of final judgment against the Bank.

3.   The property, funds and assets of the Bank wherever situated in Brazil and by whomsoever held, shall be immune from seizure, search, requisition, foreclosure, confiscation, expropriation and any other form of interference whether by executive, administrative, judicial or legislative action. To the extent necessary for the operation of the Americas Regional Office in Brazil and subject to the provisions of this Agreement, ail property and other assets of the Bank shall be exempt from restrictions, regulations, controls and moratoria of any nature.

4.   No action shall be brought against the Bank by the Government, or by any of its agencies or instrumentalities or by any entity or person directly or indirectly acting for or deriving claims from the Government or from any of Its agencies or instrumentalities.

Article 7
Inviolability of the premises and archives and immunity of property and assets

1.   The Premises shall be inviolable and under the exclusive control and authority of the Americas Regional Office. The property and assets of the Bank, wherever located and by whomsoever held, shall be immune from search, requisition, confiscation, expropriation and any other form of interference, whether by executive, administrative, Judicial or legislative action.

2.   The Archives of the Bank shall be inviolable, wherever located and by whomsoever held within Brazil.

3.   The authorities of Brazil shall not enter the Premises for any reason, including the performance of any official duties therein or execution of any legal process of to perform any ancillary act such as the seizure of private property, All entries shall be subject to the consent and conditions agreed to by the Director-General.

4.   The Director-General and the Government shall agree on the circumstances under and the manner in which the authorities of Brazil may enter the Premises. In the event of natural disaster, fire or any other emergency, constituting an immediate threat to human life, the consent of the Bank to enter the Premises is presumed. The entry into the Premises under these conditions shall be immediately communicated to the Director-General by the appropriate authorities.

5.   The Bank shall have the power to make rules and regulations operative within the Premises for the full independent exercise of its operations, administration and performance of its activities and functions. Except as otherwise provided in this Agreement, or in the Agreement on the New Development Hank, the laws of Brazil shall apply within the Premises, The Bank, its Staff, Local Staff, Experts and Consultants shall respect the laws of Brazil.

6.   Without prejudice to the terms of this Agreement, the Bank shall prevent the Premises from becoming a refuge for fugitives from justice, of for persons subject to extradition, or persons avoiding service of legal process or judicial proceedings under the laws of Brazil.

Article 8
Protection of the premises

The Government shall exercise due diligence to ensure the safety and tranquillity of the Premises. The Government shall accord to it the same protection and provide security to it on the same basis as is provided to other international organizations and diplomatic missions operating in Brazil in accordance with the Vienna Convention on Diplomatic Relations, 1961.

Article 9
Public utility services

1.   The Government undertakes to assist the Bank for the purposes of the operation of the Americas Regional Office, to the extent necessary, In making available necessary public services, including but not limited to water, electricity, telephone, fax, internet and other facilities at rates or charges not less favorable than those charged to ether comparable international organizations, and in the case of interruption or threatened interruption of service, to give, as far as within its powers, the same priority to the needs of the Bank as to other comparable international organizations and shall take

appropriate measures to ensure to that the operations of the Americas Regional Office are not prejudiced.

2.   The Americas Regional Office shall allow duly authorized representatives of public utilities to inspect, repair, maintain, reconstruct, and relocate utilities, conduits, mains and sewers within the Premises in accordance with the procedures established in consultation with the Bank.

Article 10
Facilities in respect of communications

1.   The Bank shall enjoy, in respect of their official communications and the transfer of documents, treatment no less favorable than that accorded by the Government to other international organizations or any other government, including the latter's diplomatic mission, in the matter of priorities, rates and taxes on mall, cablegrams, telephotos, telephone, telegraph, telex, telefax, internet and other modes of communication.

2.   The official communications and correspondence to, from and between the Bank and/or the Americas Regional Office, in whatever form transmitted, shall be inviolable and shall not be subject to any censorship or any form of interference. For the purposes of this Article, "communications" shall include, but not be limited to, publications, documents, still and moving pictures, films and sound recordings, and electronic and other modes of communication.

3.   The Bank shall have the fight to use codes and to dispatch and receive correspondence and other materials by courier of in sealed bags, which shall have the same privileges and immunities as diplomatic couriers and bags.

Article 11
Exemption from taxation, customs duties, prohibitions or restrictions on imports and exports

1.   With respect to all official activities, operations and transactions, the Bank, its assets, income and property in Brazil shall be:

   (a)   exempt from all forms of direct and, subject to the laws of Brazil, indirect taxation, in a manner not less favorable that the one applicable to other international organizations in Brazil; it being understood, however, that it will not claim exemption from taxes which are, in fact, me more than charges for public utility Services paid by other international organizations in Brazil;

   (b)   exempt from all customs duties, prohibitions and restrictions on goods and articles, including motor vehicles and spare parts, publications, films, still and moving pictures; imported or exported for its official purposes. It is understood, however, that goods Imported under such exemption shall be limited to a reasonable quantity and will only be sold in accordance with the laws of Brazil,

   (c)   While the Bank will not, as a general rule, claim exemption from excise duties and from taxes on the sale of movable and immovable property which form part of the price to be paid, when the Americas Regional Office makes important purchases for official use of property on which such duties and taxes have been charged or are chargeable, the Government will make, in accordance with the laws of Brazil, appropriate administrative arrangements for the remission of return of the amount of duty or tax.

Article 12
Financial transactions

The Bank may hold and use funds of negotiable instruments of any kind. The Government recognizes the right of the Bank to maintain and operate accounts in any currency and convert any currency held by it into any other currency. The Bank may freely transfer its funds into Brazil and, through a non-resident bank account, may also at any time freely transfer all or part of the balance thereof out of Brazil, which for that purpose may be switched into any foreign currency.

Article 13
Immunities and privileges of the Director-General and Staff

1.   The Government shall accord to Director-General and members of his or her family, the same privileges and immunities, exemptions and facilities, including those related to tax exemption, as accorded to heads of diplomatic missions.

2.   The Government shall accord to the Staff, as applicable, the following status, immunities and privileges:

(a)   Immunity from jurisdiction and all forms of legal process in respect of words spoken or written and all acts performed by them In their official capacity, which shall continue after their termination of service;

(b)   immunity from personal arrest or detention for all acts performed by them in their official capacity, which shall continue after their termination of service;

(c)   exemption from taxation in respect of salaries and emoluments paid by the Bank;

(d)   immunity from national service obligations;

(e)   immunity, together with members of their family, from immigration restrictions and alien registration and from formalities for the purposes of immigration control;

(f)   the same privileges in respect of exchange facilities as are accorded to officials of comparable rank of diplomatic missions,

(g)   the same treatment in respect of travelling facilities as it Is generally accorded to officials of comparable rank of diplomatic missions;

(h)   together with members of their family, the same repatriation facilities in time of international crisis.as officials of comparable rank of diplomatic missions,

(i)   freedom of movement, within or from Brazil to the extent necessary for carrying out their activities and functions for and on behalf of the Bank and for the purpose of their official communications, to use codes and receive papers and correspondence by courier or sealed in bags;

(j)   the same immunities and facilities, including Immunity from inspection and seizure of their official baggage, as are accorded to officials in diplomatic Missions;

(k)   refund of indirect taxes on purchase of goods and services procured or chargeable In Brazil, when such possibility Is provided for under the laws of Brazil;

(l)   the right for personal use, free of duty or other levies, prohibitions and restrictions (i) to import at the time of first taking up their post and within a period of 6 (six) months and (ii) to export. upon termination of their services with the Bank, within a period of 1 (one) year:

a.   their furniture and personal effects; and

b.   1 (one) motor vehicle.

3.   Articles imported under such exemptions will not be sold in Brazil except under conditions agreed upon with the Government and in any case not being less favorable than those extended to officials of comparable ranks of other International organizations in Brazil.

4.   Nationals or permanent residents of Brazil who are appointed as the Director: General or employed as Staff shall be entitled only to the immunities set out in paragraph 2 (a), (c) and (j) of this Article.

5.   The Bank shall communicate to the Government the names of Staff and members of their family to whom the provisions of the present Article are applicable.

6.   The Government shall provide the Director-General, Staff and members of the family with a special identity card which shall serve to identify the holder to the authorities of Brazil and to certify that the holder enjoys the privileges and immunities specified in this Agreement. Upon the termination of employment or reassignment from Brazil, the special identity card shall be returned promptly to the Government for cancellation.

7.   The Government shall authorize and facilitate the registration of vehicles utilized by the Director-General and Staff as vehicles of similar status of comparable international organizations accredited in Brazil, and issue them with license plates.

8.   The Director-General and the Staff shall be subject to Brazilian social security legislation, except if covered by another social security system.

Article 14
Immunities and privileges of Governors, Directors and representatives of Members of the bank

All Governors, Directors and representatives of Members of the Bank shall have the following immunities and privileges when travelling to Brazil on official missions:

   (a)   immunity from legal process with respect to acts performed by them in their official capacity, except when the Bank waives this immunity;

   (b)   when not Brazilian nationals, the same immunities from immigration restrictions, alien registration requirements and national service obligations and the same facilities as regards exchange provisions as are accorded by Brazil to the representatives, officials, and employees of comparable rank of other members;

   (c)   the same privileges in respect of traveling facilities as are accorded by Brazil to representatives, officials and employees of comparable rank or other members.

Article 15
Immunities and privileges of Experts and Consultants

1.   Experts and Consultants performing functions for the Bank shall have the following immunities and privileges as are necessary for the independent exercise of their functions during the period of their mission or contract, including time spent on journeys in connection with their functions:

   (a)   Immunity from jurisdiction and legal process, including detention and arrest, even after termination of their mission or service, in respect of acts performed by them in their official capacity, including words written or spoken by them;

   (b)   the same facilities in respect of currency or exchange restrictions as are accorded to representatives of foreign governments on temporary official missions;

   (c)   the same protection and repatriation facilities with respect to themselves, and members of their families, as are accorded in time of international crisis: to persons of comparable rank of diplomatic missions;

   (d)   for the purpose of their communication with the Bank, the right to use codes and to receive papers or correspondence by courier or in sealed bags,

   (e)   exemption from taxation in respect of salaries and emoluments paid by the Bank; and

   (f)   the right for personal use, free of duty or other levies, prohibitions and restrictions (i) to import at the time of first taking up their pest and within a period of 6 (six) months and (Ii) to export, Upon termination of their services with the Bank, within a period of 1 (one) year, their furniture and personal effects.

2.   Experts and Consultants who are Brazilian nationals shall be afforded the immunities and privileges referred to in paragraph (1), except immunity from detention and arrest, provided that they do not permanently reside in Brazil at the time that they are hired and that they are sent to Brazil to perform a temporary mission for or on behalf of the Bank.

3.   Experts and Consultants who, being either Brazilian or foreign nationals, permanently reside in Brazil at the time that they are hired shall be afforded only the immunities and privileges referred to in paragraphs 1a), except immunity from detention and arrest, and 1(d).

Article 16
Local staff

1.   Members of the local staff of the Bank in Brazil shall be hired under the Brazilian labor legislation and shall not be exempted from tax or social security payments on the salaries paid to them by the Bank, as well as from any other legal obligation arising from their employment.

2.   The Bank shall net be exempted from collecting the applicable taxes, as well as social security or any other payments in accordance with Brazilian legislation, in respect of the salaries paid to the local staff. Such obligation may be fulfilled through a service provider retained by the Bank for this purpose.

Article 17
Employment of spouses

Employment of spouses of Staff shall be regulated in a separate agreement.

Article 18
Waiver of Immunity

1.   Privileges and immunities are conferred under this Agreement in the interest of the Bank and not for the personal benefit of the individuals themselves.

2.   The Bank may waive to such extent, and upon such conditions as it may determine, any of the privileges, immunities and exemptions conferred under this Agreement in cases where such action would, in its opinion, be appropriate and in the best interests of the Bank. The President shall have the right and duty to waive any privilege, immunity or exemption in respect of any Staff of the Bank or any Expert or Consultant performing services for the Bank, other than the President or a Vice-President, where, in her or his opinion, the privilege, immunity of exemption would Impede the course of justice and can be waived without prejudice to the interests of the Bank. In similar circumstances and under the same conditions, the Board of Directors shall have the right and duty to waive any privilege, immunity or exemption in respect of the President and a Vice-President.

3.   The Bank shall co-operate at all times with the Government to facilitate the proper administration of justice, secure the observance of the laws of Brazil and prevent the occurrence of any abuse In connection with the Immunities and privileges granted in this Agreement.

Article 19
Settlement of disputes

Any dispute between the Bank and the Government arising out of or relating to this Agreement, including tax-related matters, shall be settled amicably by negotiation or other mode of settlement as may be agreed.

Article 20
Interpretation

This Agreement shall be interpreted in accordance with the rules of interpretation provided for in the 1969 Vienna Convention on the Law of Treaties. This Agreement shall not modify or derogate from the provisions of the Agreement on the New Development Bank.

Article 21
Entry into force, amendment and termination

1.   This Agreement may be amended by mutual consent of the Parties. Amendments shall take the form of a written agreement which shall enter into force in the same manner as this Agreement.

2.   The Parties may enter into such supplementary agreements as may be necessary within the scope of this Agreement.

3.   This Agreement shall enter into force on the date of receipt by the Bank of written notice by which the Federative Republic of Brazil informs the fulfilment of its internal legal procedures required for the entry into force of this Agreement, which shall remain in force until it is terminated pursuant to paragraph 5 of this Article.

4.   In case of conflict between this Agreement and the Agreement on the New Development Bank, the Agreement on the New Development Bank shall prevail.

5.   The Agreement may be terminated by either Party, termination shall have effect 1 (one) year after the receipt, through diplomatic channels, of a note indicating such intent, or after any other extended period as may be agreed to by the Parties.

6.   In the event of the termination of this Agreement, all relevant provisions shall continue to be applicable for a reasonable period, as agreed to by the Parties, required for settlement of the affairs of the Bank and disposal of its property in Brazil.

IN WITNESS WHEREOF the undersigned, being duly authorized thereto, have on

behalf of the Parties signed and sealed this Agreement in duplicate in the Portuguese and English languages, both the texts being equally authentic.

Done at Johannesburg on this day of July of 2018.

FOR THE FEDERATIVE REPUBLIC OF BRAZIL   FOR THE NEW DEVELOPMENT BANK

Aloysio Nunes Ferreira   **K.V. Kamath**
Minister of Foreign Affairs   President

Eduarde Guardia
Minister of Finance

B.   Headquarter/Host Country Agreements – South Africa 2017

AGREEMENT BETWEEN THE NEW DEVELOPMENT BANK AND THE GOVERNMENT OF THE REPUBLIC OF SOUTH AFRICA ON THE HOSTING OF THE NEW DEVELOPMENT BANK AFRICA REGIONAL CENTRE IN THE REPUBLIC OF SOUTH AFRICA

Preamble

The New Development Bank and the Government of the Republic of South Africa (hereinafter jointly referred to as the "Parties" and in the singular as a "Party");

TAKING INTO ACCOUNT the Agreement on the New Development Bank and its Annex on the Articles of Agreement of the New Development Bank between the Governments of the Federative Republic of Brazil, the Russian Federation, the Republic of India, the People's Republic of China and the Republic of South Africa, signed on 15 July 2014;

RECALLING the Fortaleza Declaration adopted at the Sixth BRICS Summit held in Fortaleza, Brazil, on 15 July 2014, that provided that the New Development Bank, Africa Regional Centre shall be established in the Republic of South Africa;

FURTHER RECALLING Article 4 of the Articles of Agreement of the New Development Bank contained in the Annex to the Agreement on the New Development Bank, stipulates that the first regional office of the New Development Bank shall be in Johannesburg;

DESIROUS THEREFORE to conclude an agreement regarding the hosting of the New Development Bank, Africa Regional Centre in Johannesburg in the Republic of South Africa;

HAVE AGREED as follows:

Article 1
Definitions

For the purpose of this Agreement, including all annexures, appendices and all amendments made from time to time, the following terms shall have, unless the context otherwise requires, the meanings ascribed to them as below:

(a) **"Africa Regional Centre"** means the regional office of the New Development Bank in Johannesburg in the Republic of South Africa;

(b) **"Agreement on the New Development Bank"** means the Agreement on the New Development Bank including its Annex between the Governments of the Federative Republic of Brazil, the Russian Federation, the Republic of India, the People's Republic of China and the Republic of South Africa, signed on 15 July 2014 at the city of Fortaleza, Brazil and any amendments thereto;

(c) **"Archives of the Bank"** means the records, correspondence, documents, manuscripts, still and moving pictures, films, sound recordings, electronic records including email, computer programs, written materials, video tapes or discs, discs or tapes containing data, and, any information contained therein stored in electronic form or any other form whatsoever, belonging to, or held by the Bank;

(d) **"Bank"** means the New Development Bank, including the Africa Regional Centre, unless specifically referred to separately;

(e) **"Director-General: Africa Regional Centre"** means the principal executive officer of the Africa Regional Centre, appointed by the Bank, and, during her or his absence or incapacity, the person authorised to act as Director-General: Africa Regional Centre;

(f) **"Experts and Consultants"** means persons who, not being Staff of the Bank, have been contracted by the Bank for the purpose of providing expertise and performing certain tasks for or on behalf of the Bank;

(g) **"Government"** means the Government of the Republic of South Africa;

(h) **"Laws of South Africa"** includes the Constitution of South Africa, 1996 and legislative acts, decrees, regulations and orders issued by, or under authority of, the Government or any appropriate authority in South Africa;

(i) **"Local terms"** means recruitment made by the Bank or the Africa Regional Centre for the employment of personnel in terms of South African Law;

(j) **"Member"** means a member of the Bank as defined in the Agreement on the New Development Bank;

(k) **"Member of a family"** means the spouse and dependent children under the age of 18 years, any other dependent family member officially recognised as such by the Bank, and the spouse or life partner officially recognised as such by the Bank of a Staff member.

(l) **"Premises"** means the land, building, parts of building and includes access facilities for the official purposes of the Africa Regional Centre;

(m) **"President"** means the President of the Bank and, during her or his absence or incapacity, the person authorised to act as President;

(n) **"South Africa"** means the Republic of South Africa and its territory; and

(o) **"Staff of the Bank"** or **"Staff"** means persons employed by the Bank, to work at the Africa Regional Centre, in accordance with the provisions of the Human Resources policies of the Bank and other relevant internal regulations in force, and excluding all other persons recruited on local terms and assigned to hourly rates.

Article 2
Seat of the Africa Regional Centre

The seat of the Africa Regional Centre shall be in Johannesburg, South Africa.

Article 3
Functions and Activities of the Africa Regional Centre

The Africa Regional Centre shall undertake such functions and activities pursuant to provisions of the Agreement on the New Development Bank and as determined by the Bank.

Article 4
Legal Personality

1.   The Government recognizes the international legal personality and capacity of the Bank for the purposes of exercising its functions in South Africa including to contract, acquire and dispose of movable and immovable property and to institute legal proceedings.

2.   The Africa Regional Centre shall have the independence and freedom of action similar to those available to other international organisations operating in South Africa.

3.   The Africa Regional Centre shall have the right to display the Bank's flag and its emblem on the Premises and the motor vehicles belonging to or in use by the Bank for the President and Director-General: Africa Regional Centre.

Article 5
Premises and Facilities

1.   The Government shall, free of charge, provide and furnish suitable office accommodation to serve as the Premises in Johannesburg, and shall provide such other facilities as required for the operations of the Africa Regional Centre, and be responsible, at its own cost, for maintenance and

repairs of a non-recurring nature for a period of one (1) year, whereafter the Bank shall be responsible for the office accommodation, furniture, equipment and other facilities required for the operation of the Africa Regional Centre in South Africa.

2.   The office accommodation, its furniture and equipment and the other facilities referred to in sub-Article (1) above shall be determined in consultation with the Bank and as detailed in Annexure A hereto, which shall form an integral part of this Agreement.

3.   Any requirement by the Bank for the operation of its Africa Regional Centre that falls outside the specifications of Annexure A or that would have additional financial implications beyond that amount, shall be for the account of the Bank.

4.   The Bank shall be responsible for the day to day maintenance of the Premises, furniture and equipment other than on account of normal wear and tear, and making arrangements for any other services as may be required by it.

5.   As the operations of the Africa Regional Centre evolve, the Government may consider providing suitable office accommodation to serve as the permanent seat of the Africa Regional Centre.

Article 6
Immunity of Property, Funds and Assets

1.   The Bank and its property, funds and assets, wherever located and by whomsoever held, shall be immune from every form of legal process, except as provided for under the Agreement on the New Development Bank:

    (a) to the extent that the Bank shall have expressly waived such immunity in any particular case in accordance with the provisions of Article 36 of the Articles of Agreement of the New Development Bank;

    (b) in respect of a civil action in South Africa arising out of or in connection with its powers to raise funds, through borrowings or other means, to guarantee obligations, or to buy and sell or underwrite the sale of securities;

    (c) in respect of a civil action brought by a third party for damages arising from an accident caused by a vehicle belonging to the Bank or operated on its behalf:

    (d) in respect of the enforcement of an arbitration award made against the Bank as a result of an express submission to arbitration by or on behalf of the Bank; or

    (e) in respect of any counter-claim directly connected with court proceedings initiated by the Bank.

2.   Notwithstanding anything contained herein above, the property of the Bank shall be immune from all forms of seizure, attachment or execution before the delivery of final judgment against the Bank.

3.   The property, funds and assets of the Bank wherever situated in South Africa and by whomsoever held, shall be immune from seizure, search, requisition, foreclosure, confiscation, expropriation and any other form of interference whether by executive, administrative, judicial or legislative action. To the extent necessary for the operation of the Africa Regional Centre in South Africa and subject to the provisions of this Agreement, all property and other assets of the Bank shall be exempt from restrictions, regulations, controls and moratoria of any nature.

4.   Notwithstanding the provisions of sub-Articles (1) and (2), no action shall be brought against the Bank by the Government, or by any of its agencies or instrumentalities or 'by any entity or person directly or indirectly acting for or deriving claims from the Government or from any of its agencies or instrumentalities.

Article 7
Inviolability of the Premises and Archives and Immunity of Property and Assets

1.   The Premises shall be inviolable and under the exclusive control and authority of the Africa Regional Centre. The property and assets of the Bank, wherever located and by | whomsoever held,

shall be immune from search, requisition, confiscation, expropriation and any other form of interference, whether by executive, administrative, judicial or legislative action.

2.   The Archives of the Bank shall be inviolable, wherever located and by whomsoever held within South Africa.

3.   The authorities of South Africa shall not enter the Premises for any reason, including the performance of any official duties therein or execution of any legal process or perform any ancillary act such as the seizure of private property. All entries shall be subject to the consent and conditions agreed to by the Director-General: Africa Regional Centre.

4.   The Director-General: Africa Regional Centre and the Government shall agree on the circumstances under and the manner in which the authorities of South Africa may enter the Premises. In the event of natural disaster, fire or any other emergency, constituting an immediate threat to human life, the consent of the Bank to enter the Premises is presumed, if the Director-General: Africa Regional Centre cannot be reached in time and in the manner agreed upon.

5.   The Bank shall have the power to make rules and regulations operative within the Premises for the full independent exercise of its operations, administration and performance of its activities and functions. Except as otherwise provided in this Agreement, or in the Agreement on the New Development Bank, the laws applicable in South Africa shall apply within the Premises. The Bank, its Staff, Experts and Consultants shall respect the laws of South Africa.

6.   Without prejudice to the terms of this Agreement, the Bank shall prevent the Premises from becoming a refuge for fugitives from justice, or for persons subject to extradition, or persons avoiding service of legal process or judicial proceedings under the laws of South Africa.

Article 8
Protection of the Premises
The Government shall exercise due diligence to ensure the safety and tranquility of the Premises. The Government shall accord to it the same protection and provide security to it on the same basis as is provided to other international organizations and diplomatic missions operating in South Africa in accordance with the Vienna Convention on Diplomatic Relations, 1961.

Article 9
Public Utility Services
1.   The Government undertakes to assist the Bank for the purposes of the operation of the Africa Regional Centre, as far as possible, in obtaining and making available, necessary public services, including but not limited to water, electricity, telephone, fax, internet and other facilities at rates or charges not less favorable than those charged to other comparable international organisations, and in the case of interruption or threatened interruption of service, to give, as far as within its powers, the same priority to the needs of the Bank as to other comparable international organisations and shall take appropriate measures to ensure that the operations of the Africa Regional Centre are not prejudiced.

2.   The Africa Regional Centre shall allow duly authorised representatives of public utilities to inspect, repair, maintain, reconstruct, and relocate utilities, conduits, mains and sewers within the Premises in accordance with the procedures established in consultation with the Bank.

Article 10
Facilities in Respect of Communications
1.   The Bank shall enjoy, in respect of their official communications and the transfer of documents, treatment no less favorable than that accorded by the Government to other international organizations or any other Government, including the latter's diplomatic mission, in the matter of priorities, rates and taxes on mail, cablegrams, telephotos, telephone, telegraph, telex, telefax, internet and other modes of communication.

2.   The official communications and correspondence to, from and between the Africa Regional Centre, in whatever form transmitted, shall be inviolable and shall not be subject to any censorship

or any form of interference. For purposes of this Article, communications shall include, but not be limited to, publications, documents, still and moving pictures, films and sound recordings, and electronic and other modes of communication.

3.   The Bank shall have the right to use codes and to dispatch and receive correspondence and other materials by courier or in sealed bags, which shall have the same privileges and immunities as diplomatic couriers and bags.

Article 11
Exemption from Taxation, Customs Duties, Prohibitions on Imports and Exports

1.   With respect to all official activities, operations and transactions, the Bank, its assets, income and property in South Africa shall be:

   (a) exempt from all forms of taxation and from any obligation with respect to the payment, withholding or collection of any tax or duty; it being understood, however, that it will not claim exemption from taxes which are, in fact, no more than charges for public utility services paid by other international organizations in South Africa;

   (b) exempt from all customs duties, prohibitions and restrictions on goods and articles, including motor vehicles and spare parts, publications, films, still and moving pictures, imported or exported for its official purposes. It is understood, however, that articles imported under such exemption will not be sold in South Africa except under conditions agreed to with the Government.

2.   While the Bank will not, as a general rule, claim exemption from excise duties and from taxes on the sale of movable and immovable property which form part of the price to be paid, when the Africa Regional Centre makes important purchases for official use Pi of property on which such duties and taxes have been charged or are chargeable, the E Government will make appropriate administrative arrangements for the remission or return of the amount of duty or tax.

3.   Documentation signed by or on behalf of the President of the Bank or the Director-General: Africa Regional Centre shall be conclusive evidence as to the necessity of any such imports or exports for the official activities of the Africa Regional Centre.

Article 12
Financial Transactions

The Bank may hold and use funds or negotiable instruments of any kind. The Government recognizes the right of the Bank to maintain and operate accounts in any currency and convert any currency held by it into any other currency. The Bank may freely transfer its funds into South Africa and may also at any time freely transfer all or part of the balance thereof out of South Africa through a non-resident bank account which for that purpose may be switched into any foreign currency.

Article 13
Immunities and Privileges of the Director-General: Africa Regional Centre and Staff

1.   The Government shall accord to the Director-General: Africa Regional Centre and members of his or her family, the same privileges and immunities, exceptions and a facilities as accorded to officials of comparable ranks forming part of diplomatic missions.

2.   The Government shall accord to the Staff as applicable:

   (a) immunity from jurisdiction and all forms of legal process in respect of words spoken or written and all acts performed by them in their official capacity, which shall continue after their termination of service;

   (b) immunity from personal arrest or detention for all acts performed by them in; a their official capacity, which shall continue after their termination of service;

   (c) exemption from taxation in respect of salaries and emoluments paid by the Bank;

   (d) immunity, together with members of their family from immigration restrictions and alien registration and from formalities for the purposes of immigration control;

(e) privileges in respect of exchange facilities as well as VAT (value added tax) refunds on the purchase of goods and services procured or chargeable in South Africa will be governed by the Laws of South Africa;

(f) together with members of their family, the same repatriation facilities in time of international crisis as officials of comparable rank of diplomatic missions;

(g) freedom of movement, within or from South Africa to the extent necessary for carrying out their activities and functions for and on behalf of the Bank and for the purpose of their official communications, to use codes and receive papers and correspondence by courier or sealed in bags;

(h) the same immunities and facilities, including immunity from inspection and seizure of their official baggage, as are accorded to officials in diplomatic missions;

(i) the right for personal use, free of duty or other levies, prohibitions and restrictions (i) to import at the time of first taking up their post and within a g period of six (6) months and (ii) to export, upon termination of their services with the Bank, within a period of 1 year:

   a. their furniture and personal effects;

   b. one (1) motor vehicle, and in the case of officials accompanied by a members of their family, two (2) motor vehicles.

3. Articles imported under such exemptions will not be sold in South Africa except under conditions agreed upon with the Government and in any case not being less favorable than those extended to officials of comparable ranks of other international organizations in South Africa.

4. Nationals or permanent residents of South Africa who are appointed as the Director- General: Africa Regional Centre or employed as Staff shall be entitled only to the immunities set out in sub-Article 2 (a), (b), (g) and (h) of this Article and provided that, in implementing the taxation of income of nationals and permanent residents of South Africa appointed or employed by the Bank, the Bank shall not be required to withhold, collect or pay such taxes.

5. The Bank shall communicate to the Government the names of Staff and members of their family to whom the provisions of the present Article are applicable.

6. The Government shall provide the Director-General: Africa Regional Centre, Staff and members of the family older than eighteen (18) years of age with a special identity card which shall serve to identify the holder to the authorities of South Africa and to certify that the holder enjoys the privileges and immunities specified in this Agreement. Upon the termination of employment or reassignment from South Africa, the special identity card shall be returned promptly to the Government for cancellation.

7. The Government shall authorise and facilitate the registration of vehicles utilised by the Director-General: Africa Regional Centre and Staff as vehicles of similar status of comparable international organisations accredited in South Africa, and issue them with license plates.

Article 14
Immunities and Privileges of Governors, Directors and Representatives of Members of the Bank

All Governors, Directors and representatives of Members of the Bank shall have the following privileges and immunities:

1. immunity from legal process with respect to acts performed by them in their official capacity, except when the Bank waives this immunity;

2. when not local nationals, the same immunities from immigration restrictions, alien registration requirements and national service obligations and the same facilities as regards exchange provisions as are accorded by members to the representatives, officials, and employees of comparable rank of other members;

3. the same privileges in respect of traveling facilities as are accorded by members to representatives, officials and employees of comparable rank or other members.

Article 15
Immunities and Privileges of Experts and Consultants

1.   Experts and Consultants performing functions for the Bank who are not nationals or permanent residents of the Republic of South Africa, shall be accorded the following immunities and privileges as are necessary for the independent exercise of their functions during the period of their mission or contract, including time spent on journeys in connection with their functions:

   (a)   immunity from personal arrest or detention for acts in their official capacity;

   (b)   immunity from seizure of their official baggage;

   (c)   in respect of words spoken or written and acts done by them in the course of the performance of their function, immunity from legal process of every kind;

   (d)   the same facilities in respect of currency or exchange restrictions as are accorded to representatives of foreign governments on temporary official missions;

   (e)   the same protection and repatriation facilities with respect to themselves, and members of their families, as are accorded in time of international crisis to persons of comparable rank of diplomatic missions;

   (f)   for the purpose of their communication with the Bank, have the right to use codes and to receive papers or correspondence by courier or in sealed bags; and

   (g)   exemption from taxation in respect of salaries and emoluments paid by the Bank.

2.   Experts and Consultants who are nationals or permanent residents of South Africa, shall be afforded the immunities referred to in sub-Article 1(a), (b) and (c).

Article 16
Employment of Spouses

Employment of spouses of Staff shall be regulated in separate agreements.

Article 17
Waiver of Immunity

1.   Privileges and immunities are conferred under this Agreement in the interest of the Bank and not for the personal benefit of the individuals themselves.

2.   The Bank may waive to such extent and upon such conditions as it may determine, any of the privileges, immunities and exemptions conferred under this Agreement in cases where such action would, in its opinion, be appropriate and in the best interests of the Bank. The President shall have the right and duty to waive any privilege, immunity or exemption in respect of any Staff of the Bank or any Expert or Consultant performing services for the Bank, other than the President or a Vice-President, where, in her or his opinion, the privilege, immunity or exemption would impede the course of justice and can be waived without prejudice to the interests of the Bank. In similar circumstances and under the same conditions, the Board of Directors shall have the right and duty to waive any privilege, immunity or exemption in respect of the President and a Vice President.

3.   The Bank shall co-operate at all times with the Government to facilitate the proper administration of justice, secure the observance of the Laws of South Africa and prevent the occurrence of any abuse in connection with the immunities and privileges granted in this Agreement.

Article 18
Settlement of Disputes

1.   Any dispute between the Bank and the Government arising out of or relating to this Agreement shall be settled amicably by negotiation or other mode of settlement as may be agreed, failing which such dispute shall be submitted to arbitration at the request of either Party

2.   Each Party shall appoint one arbitrator, and the two arbitrators so appointed shall appoint a third, who shall be the Chairperson. If within two (2) months of the request for arbitration either Party has not appointed an arbitrator, or if within two (2) months of the appointment of two arbitrators, the third arbitrator has not been appointed, either Party may request the President of

the International Court of Justice to make the necessary appointments. All decisions of the arbitrators shall require a vote of two of them and shall be binding on the parties.

3.   The arbitrators shall determine the procedure of the arbitration, and expenses of the arbitration shall be borne by the Parties as assessed by the arbitrators. The arbitral award shall contain a statement of the reasons on which it is based and shall be accepted by the Parties as the final adjudication of the dispute.

Article 19
Interpretation

This Agreement shall be interpreted in accordance with the rules of interpretation provided for in the 1969 Vienna Convention on the Law of Treaties. This Agreement shall no or derogate from the provisions of the Agreement on the New Development Bank.

Article 20
Entry into Force, Amendment and Termination

1.   This Agreement may be amended by mutual consent of the Parties. Amendments shall take the form of a written agreement which shall enter into force in the same manner as this Agreement.

2.   The Parties may enter into such supplementary agreements as may be necessary within the scope of this Agreement.

3.   Each Party shall notify the other of the completion of the constitutional formalities required by its laws for the entry into force of this Agreement. This Agreement shall enter into force on the date of the last written notification.

4.   In case of conflict between this Agreement and the Agreement on the New Development Bank, the Agreement on the New Development Bank shall prevail.

5.   Agreement may be terminated by either Party subject to providing at least one (1) year's prior notice or such extended period as may be agreed to by the Parties.

6.   In event of the termination of this Agreement all relevant provisions shall continue to be applicable for a reasonable period, as agreed to by the Parties, required for settlement of the affairs of the Bank and disposal of its property in South Africa.

IN THE WITNESS OF the undersigned, being duly authorized thereto, have on behalf of the Parties signed and sealed this Agreement in duplicate in English language.

Done at _____Pretoria_____ on this __17__ Day of __August__ 2017

FOR THE NEW DEVELOPMENT BANK

FOR THE GOVERNMENT OF THE REPUBLIC OF SOUTH AFRICA

_____

_____

K.V. Kamath

Maita Nkoana-Mashabane

C.   Headquarter/Host Country Agreements – China 2016

AGREEMENT BETWEEN THE NEW DEVELOPMENT BANK AND THE GOVERNMENT OF THE PEOPLE'S REPUBLIC OF CHINA REGARDING THE HEADQUARTERS OF THE NEW DEVELOPMENT BANK IN SHANGHAI, CHINA

The New Development Bank and the Government of the People's Republic of China;

Taking into account the Agreement on the New Development Bank and its Annex between the Governments of the Federative Republic of Brazil, the Russian Federation, the Republic of India, the People's Republic of China and the Republic of South Africa, signed on 15 July 2014;

Recalling that the Governments of the Federative Republic of Brazil, the Russian Federation, the Republic of India, the People's Republic of China and the Republic of South Africa decided that the New Development Bank shall have its headquarters in Shanghai;

Bearing in mind that the New Development Bank has international legal personality and should be enabled to function effectively;

Desiring to conclude an agreement regarding the establishment of the headquarters of the Bank in the territory of the People's Republic of China and to provide for the status, immunities, privileges and facilities to be accorded to the New Development Bank as well as related matters;

HAVE AGREED as follows:

Article 1
Definitions

The following words, unless otherwise specifically provided, shall mean:

(a) "Agreement on the New Development Bank" - Agreement on the New Development Bank and its Annex between the Governments of the Federative Republic of Brazil, the Russian Federation, the Republic of India, the People's Republic of China and the Republic of South Africa, signed on 15 July 2014 at the city of Fortaleza, Brazil and any amendments thereto;

(b) "Archives of the Bank" - records, correspondence, documents, manuscripts, still and moving pictures, films, sound recordings, electronic records including email, computer programs, written materials, video tapes or discs, discs or tapes containing data, and any information contained therein stored in electronic form or any other form whatsoever, belonging to, or held by the Bank;

(c) "Bank" - the New Development Bank and its subsidiary bodies;

(d) "Dependents" - means spouses or domestic partners, parents and children of a person entitled to benefits under this Agreement who are primarily dependent on such person for financial support;

(e) "Directors" - Directors of the Bank and, unless otherwise specified, their Alternates and Temporary Alternates;

(f) "Experts and Consultants" - means persons who, not being staff of the Bank, have been contracted by the Bank for the purpose of providing expertise and performing certain tasks of the Bank

(g) "Government" -the Government of the People's Republic of China;

(h) "Governors" - Governors of the Bank and unless otherwise specified, their Alternates and Temporary Alternates;

(i) "Headquarters Seat" - the land, buildings and parts of buildings, including access facilities, used for the official activities of the Bank;

(j) "Meetings of the Bank - meetings of the Board of Governors, the Board of Directors or any of their Committees or sub-groups or any other meeting convened by the Bank;

(k)"Member" - a member of the Bank as defined in the Agreement on the New Development Bank;

(l) "Members of Household Staff' - persons other than nationals or permanent residents of the People's Republic of China, employed as domestic staff of the President, Vice-Presidents, Staff of the Bank, or, of Experts or Consultants performing missions or services for the Bank based in the People's Republic of China under contract of at least one year;

(m) "Other Representatives of Members" - all accredited officials of delegations of Members;

(n) "Persons Connected with the Bank" – persons defined as Governors, Alternate Governors, Temporary Alternate Governors, other Representatives of Members, Directors, Alternate Directors, Temporary Alternate Directors, President, Vice-Presidents, Staff of the Bank, and Experts and Consultants;

(o) "President" – the President of the Bank and, during his absence or incapacity, the person authorized to act as President;

(p) "Staff of the Bank" or "Staff" – means employees of the Bank, excluding those both recruited locally and assigned to hourly rates of pay.

Article 2
Legal Status

1. The Bank shall possess international legal personality and full juridical personality in the People's Republic of China. In particular, the Bank shall have the capacity to:

(a) contract;

(b) acquire and dispose of immovable and movable property; and

(c) institute legal proceedings.

2. The Bank shall have the independence and freedom of action belonging to an international organization.

3. The Bank shall have the right to display its flag and its emblem on its premises, the residence and vehicle of the President.

Article 3
The Headquarters Seat of the Bank

1. The Government shall arrange to build and furnish a suitable office building to serve as the Headquarters Seat of the Bank and provide such other facilities as required for its operations. Until the permanent building is ready for permanent use and occupancy of the Bank, the Government shall provide the Bank with suitable temporary office accommodation and facilities to enable the Bank to carry out its purpose and functions.

2. The office building housing the headquarters of the Bank shall be suitable for the requirements of the Bank, the details of which are to be determined in consultation with the Bank.

3. The Government shall provide the permanent building and the temporary office accommodation to the Bank in accordance with paragraphs 1 and 2 of this Article, free of charge. The arrangements with regard to said permanent office building and temporary office accommodation shall be agreed and recorded in a memorandum of understanding between Shanghai Municipality and the Bank.

4. The Government shall not dispose of all or any part of the Headquarters Seat without the consent of the Bank.

Article 4
Immunity from Judicial Proceedings

1. The Bank shall enjoy immunity from every form of legal process, except:

(a) to the extent that the Bank shall have expressly waived any such immunity in any particular case or in any written document;

(b) in respect of a civil action arising out of or in connection with its powers to raise funds, through borrowings or other means, to guarantee obligations, or to buy and sell or underwrite the sale of securities;

(c) in respect of a civil action brought by a third party for damages arising from an accident caused by a vehicle belonging to the Bank or operated on its behalf;

(d) in respect of the enforcement of an arbitration award made against the Bank as a result of an express submission to arbitration by or on behalf of the Bank; or

(e) in respect of any counter-claim directly connected with court proceedings initiated by the Bank.

In such cases, the property of the Bank shall be immune from all forms of seizure, attachment or execution except upon the delivery of final judgment against the Bank.

2.   Notwithstanding the provisions of paragraph 1 of this Article, no action shall be brought against the Bank by the Government, or by any of its agencies or instrumentalities or by any entity or person directly or indirectly acting for or deriving claims from the Government or from any of its agencies or instrumentalities.

3.   The Government shall have recourse to such special procedures for the settlement of controversies between the Bank and its Members as may be prescribed in the Agreement on the New Development Bank, in the By-Laws and regulations of the Bank, or in contracts entered into with the Bank.

Article 5
Inviolability of the Headquarters Seat and Archives and Immunity of Property and Assets

1.   The Headquarters Seat shall be inviolable, and shall be under the control and authority of the Bank.

2.   The archives of the Bank and, in general, all documents belonging to it or held by it, shall be inviolable, wherever located and by whomsoever held.

3.   The property and assets of the Bank shall, wherever located and by whomever held, be immune from all forms of seizure, search, requisition, confiscation, expropriation or any other form of taking or foreclosure or interference, whether by executive, administrative, judicial or legislative action. To the extent necessary to carry out the purpose and functions of the Bank and subject to the provisions of this Agreement, all property and other assets of the Bank shall be exempt from restrictions, regulations, controls and moratoria of any nature.

4.   The authorities of the People's Republic of China, except as provided for in the Agreement on the New Development Bank, shall not enter the Headquarters Seat to perform any official duties therein or execute any legal process or perform any ancillary act such as the seizure of private property without the consent of, and under conditions agreed to by the Bank. The Bank and the Government shall agree on the circumstances under which and the manner in which the authorities of the People's Republic of China may enter the Headquarters Seat without prior consent of the Bank in connection with fire prevention, sanitary regulations or emergencies or for service by post.

5.   The Bank shall have the power to make rules and regulations operative within the Headquarters Seat for the full independent exercise of its operations, administration and performance of its functions. Except as otherwise provided in this Agreement, or in the Articles of Agreement on the New Development Bank, the law applicable in the People's Republic of China shall apply within the Headquarters Seat of the Bank.

6.   Without prejudice to the terms of this Agreement, the Bank shall prevent the Headquarters Seat from becoming a refuge for fugitives from justice, or for persons subject to extradition, or persons avoiding service of legal process or a judicial proceeding.

Article 6
Protection of the Headquarters Seat

1.   The Government shall exercise due diligence to ensure the safety and tranquility of the Headquarters Seat. If so requested by the Bank, the Government shall provide a sufficient number of police for the safety and tranquility of the Headquarters Seat, for the preservation of law and order in the Headquarters Seat and for the removal from there of persons as requested, under the authority of the Bank.

Article 7
Public Services in the Headquarters Seat

1.   The appropriate authorities of the People's Republic of China shall, upon the request of the Bank, ensure that to the extent possible the Bank shall be provided, on terms not less favorable than those accorded to its key Government departments and resident diplomatic missions, with the necessary public services, including but not limited to electricity, water, sewerage, gas, post, telephone, internet broadband services, mobile connections, telegraph, local public transportation, drainage, collection of refuse and fire protection. In case of any disruption or threatened disruption of any of the said services such authorities shall consider the needs of the Bank of equal importance to those of key departments of the Government and shall take corresponding measures to ensure that the operations of the Bank are not prejudiced.

2.   The Bank shall allow duly authorized representatives of public utilities to inspect, repair, maintain, reconstruct, and relocate utilities, conduits, mains and sewers within the Headquarters Seat and its facilities.

Article 8
Communications Facilities

1.   The Bank shall enjoy in the People's Republic of China for its official communications and the transfer of its documents treatment not less advantageous to the Bank than the most favorable treatment accorded by the Government to any international organization or to any other government including its diplomatic mission, in the matter of priorities, rates and surcharges on mails, cables, radiograms, telefax, telephone, internet and other electronic telecommunications facilities, and press rates for information to the press and radio.

2.   The Government shall permit and take appropriate measures to protect unrestricted internet access in the Headquarters Seat of the Bank and other forms of communication by the Bank for all its official activities. All official communication to the Bank and all outward official communications of the Bank, by whatever form transmitted, shall be immune from censorship and from any other form of interference.

3.   For purposes of this Article, communications shall include, without limitation, publications, documents, still and moving pictures, films and sound recordings, and electronic and other telecommunications.

4.   The Bank shall have the right to use codes and to dispatch and receive official correspondence and other official communications by courier or in sealed bags which shall have immunities and privileges not less favorable than those accorded to diplomatic couriers and bags.

Article 9
Property of the Bank and Taxation

1.   The Bank, its property and assets, its operations and transactions, and its income, all pursuant to the Articles of Agreement on the New Development Bank, shall be exempt from all present and future taxes, and from any obligation for the payment, withholding or collection of any tax or duty.

2.   The Bank shall be granted relief from all local taxes or fees levied on the Headquarters Seat of the Bank with the exception of the proportion which, as in the case of diplomatic missions, represents a charge for public services. Such local taxes or fees shall in the first instance be paid by

the Government, which shall recover from the Bank the proportion which represents a charge for public service.

3.   The Bank shall be exempt from car tax, including vehicle tax and vehicle purchase tax, on any official vehicles. Refund of any value added tax paid on official vehicles and on any other goods and services for the official activities of the Bank shall be accorded in accordance with relevant regulations of the People's Republic of China.

4.   The Bank shall be exempt from:

  (a)   all customs duties and other levies on imports or exports by the Bank, within a reasonable quantity, for the official activities of the Bank;

  (b)   all customs duties and other levies on the import or export of publications for the official activities of the Bank;

  (c)   all prohibitions and restrictions on such imports and exports for the official activities of the Bank, except for prohibitions and restrictions on imports or exports relating to health and safety; and

  (d)   any obligation for the payment, withholding or collection of any customs duties or other levies.

5.   Imports (other than publications) shall only be sold, given away, hired out or otherwise disposed of in the People's Republic of China when permitted by the Government under relevant regulations.

6.   Documentation signed by or on behalf of the President shall be conclusive evidence as to the necessity of any such imports or exports for the official activities of the Bank.

Article 10
Income Tax

1.   Salaries and emoluments paid by the Bank to Persons Connected with the Bank shall be exempt from the income tax of the People's Republic of China.

2.   Any pensions or annuities paid by the Bank to former staff of the Bank shall similarly be exempt from the income tax of the People's Republic of China.

3.   The Bank shall be exempt from any obligation for the payment, withholding or collection of any tax owed to the Government by any person mentioned in paragraphs 1 and 2 above in respect of any income arising in the People's Republic of China.

Article 11
Financial Facilities

1.   Notwithstanding financial controls, regulations or moratoria of any kind, the Bank may freely:

  (a)   receive, purchase, hold and dispose of any funds, currencies, financial instruments, securities and gold, operate accounts in any currency, engage in financial transactions and conclude financial contracts; and

  (b)   transfer its funds, currencies, financial instruments, securities and gold, to or from the People's Republic of China or within the People's Republic of China, with due regard to regulations on physical transfers of the currency of the People's Republic of China and of gold, and convert any currency held by it into any other currency.

2.   In exercising its rights under this Article, the Bank shall give due regard to representations made by the Government in so far as the Bank considers that effect can be given to such representations without detriment to its interests.

Article 12
Employment and Social Security

1.   The Bank shall not employ as a Staff of the Bank any person who is present in the People's Republic of China at the time of such employment without taking reasonable steps to ascertain that such person is not present in the People's Republic of China in violation of the relevant immigration

laws or is not subject to a prohibition under those laws from taking up employment in the People's Republic of China.

2.   The terms and conditions of the President, Vice-Presidents, Directors when and if they become a resident body and Staff of the Bank and Experts and Consultants performing missions or services for the Bank, and all matters relating to employment relations between such persons and the Bank, shall be governed exclusively by the Bank's own employment rules, policies and procedures adopted by or under the authority of the Bank's Board of Directors, and shall not be subject to the labor laws of the People's Republic of China.

3.   From the time the Bank establishes its social security program, the President, Vice-Presidents, Directors and Staff of the Bank shall be exempt from the provisions of any social security scheme established by the People's Republic of China, with respect to services rendered for the Bank. In the case of individuals who are nationals or permanent residents of the People's Republic of China and voluntarily participate in such a scheme, the Bank shall be exempt from any obligation for the payment, withholding or collection of any social security contributions or benefits to the People's Republic of China.

Article 13
Access and Residence

1.   The Government shall take measures to facilitate as promptly as possible the entry into, residence and freedom of movement in, and departure from the People's Republic of China of the following persons irrespective of nationality, in accordance with rules and regulations applicable to international organisations:

(a) Governors and other representatives of Members;

(b) Directors;

(c) President and Vice-Presidents;

(d) Staff of the Bank;

(e) Dependents;

(f) Experts and Consultants performing missions for the Bank;

(g) Members of the Household Staff ; and

(h) Other persons invited by the Bank and in possession of written evidence and including evidence in digital form of such invitation.

Article 14
Privileges and Immunities of Persons Connected with Bank

1.   Except as provided in this Article, Persons Connected with the Bank shall:

(a) enjoy immunity from jurisdiction and legal process, including detention and arrest, even after termination of their mission or service, in respect of acts performed by them in their official capacity, including words written or spoken by them; this immunity shall not apply, however, to civil liability either in the case of damage from a road traffic accident, or in the case of other personal injury or death, if either is caused by an act of such person in the People's Republic of China;

(b) be accorded inviolability for all their official papers, documents and records;

(c) be exempt, together with their spouse and minor children, from immigration restrictions and alien registration and from registration formalities for the purposes of immigration control;

(d) be exempt, together with their Dependents, from national service obligations;

(e) have exemption in respect of exchange restrictions no less favorable than that accorded to officials of comparable rank of diplomatic missions;

(f) have the same freedom of movement in the territory of the People's Republic of China, subject to its laws and regulations concerning any zones into which entry may be prohibited or regulated for reasons of national security, and the same treatment in respect of travelling facilities as is generally accorded to officials of comparable rank of diplomatic missions; and

(g) be given, together with their Dependents, the same repatriation facilities in times of international crises as officials of comparable rank of diplomatic missions.

2.   Persons Connected with Bank who are nationals or permanent residents of People's Republic of China shall only enjoy immunity and inviolability as provided for in (a), (b) and (f) of this Article.

Article 15
Privileges and Immunities of Governors and Other Representatives of Members, and Directors

1.   In respect of other matters not covered in Article 14 above, Governors, Directors and Other Representatives of Members, shall enjoy such other immunities, exemptions, privileges and facilities as are stated in Article V of the Convention on the Privileges and Immunities of the Specialized Agencies of the United Nations, during their stay in the People's Republic of China.

2.   Upon the Board of Directors of the Bank becoming a resident body, Directors shall enjoy such other immunities, exemption and facilities as are accorded to diplomatic agents as provided under the 1961 Vienna Convention on Diplomatic Relations.

3.   Governors Directors and Representatives of Members who are nationals or permanent residents of the People's Republic of China shall only enjoy immunities and inviolability as provided for in (a), (b) and (f) of Article 14 of this Agreement.

Article 16
Privileges and Immunities of Staff and Experts and Consultants of the Bank

1.   In addition to the privileges, exemptions and immunities mentioned in Article 14 above, staff of the Bank, Experts and Consultants performing missions for the Bank shall be provided the following privileges, exemptions and immunities:

(a) Refund of VAT on purchase of goods and service within the territory of the People's Republic of China, in accordance with relative Chinese laws and stipulations.

(b) The right to import, free of duty (whether of customs or excise) and other levies, taxes and charges (except payments for services), their household furniture and personal effects (including one motor car per household) within a reasonable amount, which are in their ownership or possession and intended for their personal use or for their establishment, within twelve months after first taking up their post in the People's Republic of China.

(c) The right, on the termination of their functions, to transport abroad their household furniture and personal effects (including one motor car per household), free of customs duties and other taxes and charges (except payments for services).

2.   The privileges referred to above shall be subject to the general restrictions applied in the People's Republic of China to all imports and exports, and to the conditions governing the disposal of goods imported into the People's Republic of China free of customs duties.

3.   Staff of the Bank with a tenure less than 12 months, Experts and Consultants performing missions for the Bank under contract less than 12 months, and nationals and permanent residents of the People's Republic of China shall not enjoy immunities and privileges as provided for in this Article.

Article 17
Privileges and Immunities of Directors, President and Vice-President of the Bank

1.   In addition to the privileges and immunities set out in Article 14, the President shall be accorded in respect of himself and his spouse and minor children all the immunities and privileges accorded to a diplomatic envoy and agent under the 1961 Vienna Convention on Diplomatic Relations.

2.   In addition to the privileges and immunities set out in Articles 14, the President, Vice-Presidents and Directors of the Bank pursuant to the Board of Directors of the Bank becoming a resident body shall be accorded in respect of themselves and their spouse and minor children, all the immunities

and privileges accorded to a diplomatic agent under the 1961 Vienna Convention on Diplomatic Relations, including but not limited to:

(a) immunity from personal arrest or detention and from seizure of their personal baggage;

(b) refund of VAT on purchase of goods and service within the territory of the People's Republic of China in accordance with relative Chinese laws and stipulations;

(c) the right to import, free of duty (whether of customs or excise) and other levies, taxes and charges (except payments for services), their household furniture and personal effects (including one motor car per household) within a reasonable amount, which are in their ownership or possession and intended for their personal use or for their establishment, within twelve (12) months after first taking up their post in the People's Republic of China;

(d) the right, on the termination of their functions, to transport abroad their household furniture and personal effects (including one motor car per household), free of customs duties and other taxes and charges (except payments for services).

3.   The privileges referred to above shall be subject to the general restrictions applied in the People's Republic of China to all imports and exports, and to the conditions governing the disposal of goods imported into the People's Republic of China free of customs duties.

4.   Notwithstanding anything contained in this Article, the Directors, President and Vice-Presidents who are nationals or permanent residents of the People's Republic of China shall only be entitled to:

(a) immunities from legal process, including detention and arrest, for words spoken or written and acts performed in their official capacity;

(b) exemption from taxation and charges in respect of salaries and emoluments paid by the Bank.

Article 18
Working Opportunity of Spouse

1.   The Government will take appropriate measures to facilitate employment of the spouse of President, Vice-Presidents, Directors, Staff and Experts and Consultants performing services for the Bank in China.

2.   The spouse of Directors, President, Vice-Presidents, Staff and Experts and Consultants performing services for the Bank more than 12 months shall be provided with work permits and accorded opportunity to:

(a) hold a post in the representative offices of foreign governments, foreign enterprises, foreign individuals, foreign juridical associations, international organizations and international NGOs, foreign invested Chinese enterprises, Chinese private enterprises, and foreign news agencies;

(b) teach at Chinese colleges and universities.

3.   The spouse of the President, Vice-Presidents, Directors, Staff and Experts and Consultants of the Bank who take up full time professional employment in China shall not be entitled to any privileges and immunities.

Article 19
License Plates and Identity Cards

1.   The vehicles of Directors, President, Vice-Presidents, and Staff of the Bank can bear the appropriate license plate. The vehicles are exempted from being searched, expropriated, seized or mandatorily disposed.

2.   All persons enjoying the privileges and immunities specified in this Agreement shall be provided by the Government with a special identity card which shall serve to identify the holder in relation to authorities of the People's Republic of China and to certify that the holder enjoys the privileges and immunities specified in this Agreement.

3.   The Bank shall from time to time communicate to the Government the names of those to whom the provisions of Articles 14 to 17 shall apply.

Article 20
Waiver of Immunities and Prevention of Abuse

1.   The privileges, immunities and exemptions conferred under this Agreement are granted in the interests of the Bank and not for the personal benefit of the individuals themselves. The Board of Directors may waive to such extent and upon such conditions as it may determine any of the privileges, immunities and exemptions conferred under this Agreement in cases where such action would, in its opinion, be appropriate and in the best interests of the Bank. The President shall have the right and duty to waive any privilege, immunity or exemption in respect of any Staff of the Bank or any Expert or Consultant performing services for the Bank, other than the President or a Vice-President, where, in his or her opinion, the privilege, immunity or exemption would impede the course of justice and can be waived without prejudice to the interests of the Bank. In similar circumstances and under the same conditions, the Board of Directors shall have the right and duty to waive any privilege, immunity or exemption in respect of the President and each Vice-President.

2.   Privileges and immunities accorded to other Representatives of Members under Article 15 of this Agreement are provided in order to assure complete independence in the exercise of their functions, and may be waived by the Member concerned.

Article 21
Settlement of Disputes

1.   Any dispute between the Government and the Bank concerning the interpretation or application of this Agreement which is not settled by negotiation or other agreed mode of settlement, shall be submitted to arbitration at the request of either Party.

2.   In the event of such a request for arbitration, one arbitrator is to be appointed by the Government, one is to be appointed by the Bank, and the third, who shall be chairman of the tribunal, is to be chosen by the first two arbitrators. If within two months of the request for arbitration, either Party has not appointed an arbitrator, or if within two months of the appointment of two arbitrators, the third arbitrator has not been appointed, either Party may request the President of the International Court of Justice to appoint an arbitrator. The procedure for the arbitration shall be fixed by the arbitrators, and the expenses for the arbitration shall be borne by the Parties as assessed by the arbitrators. The arbitral award shall contain a statement of the reasons on which it is based and shall be accepted by the Parties as the final adjudication of the dispute.

Article 22
Interpretation

1.   This Agreement shall be interpreted in accordance with the rules of interpretation provided for in the 1969 Vienna Convention on the Law of Treaties.

2.   This Agreement shall be regarded as supplementary to the Agreement on the New Development Bank and shall not modify or derogate from the provisions and in particular Chapter VI thereof.

Article 23
Final Provisions

1.   The Bank and all persons enjoying the immunities, privileges, exemptions and facilities under this Agreement shall co-operate at all times with the appropriate authorities of the People's Republic of China to facilitate the proper administration of justice and secure the observance of the laws of the People's Republic of China.

2.   Wherever this Agreement imposes obligations on appropriate authorities of the People's Republic of China, the Government shall ensure the fulfillment of such obligations by the appropriate Chinese authorities

3. At the request of either Party, consultation shall take place in respect to the modification of this Agreement. Amendments shall be made in the form of a written agreement by the Government and the Bank, and enter into force in the same manner as this Agreement.

4. The Government and the Bank may enter into such supplementary agreements as may be necessary within me scope of this Agreement.

5. Nothing in this Agreement shall be construed to preclude the adoption of appropriate measures for the security of the state as may be determined by the Government. If the Government considers it necessary to take such measures, it shall consult with the Bank on the measures necessary, to protect the interests of the Bank. The Bank shall collaborate to avoid any prejudice to the security of the People's Republic of China.

6. This Agreement shall enter into force upon signature by the Parties hereto on the date indicated below.

7. This Agreement may be terminated by agreement between the Government and the Bank. In such event, this Agreement shall cease to be in force after the period reasonably required for transfer or disposal of the property of the Bank.

IN WITNESS WHEREOF, the respective representatives, duly authorized thereto, have signed this Agreement in duplicate, in both English and Chinese languages, both texts being equally authentic.

DONE at Shanghai, China on the 27th day of February 2016.

FOR THE NEW DEVELOPMENT BANK

FOR THE GOVERNMENT OF THE PEOPLE'S REPUBLIC OF CHINA

_____

_____

K.V. Kamath

Wang Yi

D.   MoU on Cooperation with the New Development Bank: 9 Jul. 2015, Ufa
       (RUS)

MEMORANDUM OF UNDERSTANDING
ON COOPERATION WITH THE NEW DEVELOPMENT BANK
BY
BANCO NACIONAL DE DESENVOLVIMENTO ECONÔMICO E SOCIAL – BNDES,
STATE CORPORATION "BANK FOR DEVELOPMENT AND FOREIGN ECONOMIC
AFFAIRS (VNESHECONOMBANK)",
EXPORT-IMPORT BANK OF INDIA,
CHINA DEVELOPMENT BANK CORPORATION,
DEVELOPMENT BANK OF SOUTHERN AFRICA LIMITED
Ufa, Russia, July 9, 2015

This Memorandum of Understanding (hereinafter, the MoU) is signed on July 2015 in Ufa, Russian Federation by Banco Nacional de Desenvolvimento Econômico e Social – BNDES, a wholly-owned federal government company duly established and validly existing under the laws of the Federative Republic of Brazil ("Brazil"), with its registered head office in Brasilia, Federal District, and principal place of business at 100 Av. República do Chile, the city of Rio de Janeiro, State of Rio de Janeiro, CEP 20031-917;

State Corporation "Bank for Development and Foreign Economic Affairs (Vnesheconombank)", a state corporation established and existing under the law of the Russian Federation ("Russia") in compliance with Federal Law No. 82-FZ "On Bank for Development" dd. 17.05.2007, with its registered head office at 9 Akademika Sakharova Prospekt, Moscow 107996, the Russian Federation;

Export-Import Bank of India, a state-owned corporation duly established under the Act of Parliament of the Republic of India ("India") and having its head office at Floor 21, World Trade Centre Complex, Cuffe Parade, Mumbai-400 005, the Republic of India;

China Development Bank Corporation, a state-owned corporation duly established under the laws of the People's Republic of China ("China"), with its head office at 18 Fuxingmennei Street, Xicheng District, Beijing 100031, the People's Republic of China; and

Development Bank of Southern Africa Limited, a state-owned development finance institution duly established under the laws of the Republic of South Africa ("South Africa"), with its head office at 1258 Lever Road, Headway Hill, Midrand, 1685, the Republic of South Africa; (each party being individually referred to as the Party and collectively as the Parties),

Taking into consideration close economic cooperation between the Federative Republic of Brazil, the Republic of India, the People's Republic of China, the Russian Federation and the Republic of South Africa, as well as the Agreement on the New Development Bank signed by the BRICS governments on July 15, 2014 in Fortaleza, Brazil;

Acknowledging the strategic relevance of such cooperation for sustainable development and inclusive economic growth;

Given high aspiration towards future economic and investment cooperation within BRICS;

Emphasizing the willingness of the Parties to form a dialogue and to explore areas of cooperation with the New Development Bank on matters of mutual interest;

And in furtherance of the agreements on cooperation concluded thus far by the Parties, the Parties hereto agree as follows:

Article 1. Areas of Cooperation

Guided by the existing international banking practices, all applicable laws and regulations, and principles of equality, mutual benefit, responsible financing, partnership and the balance of interest, the Parties intend to cooperate with the New Development Bank, to the extent that it is within their respective mandates, missions, policies and procedures including in the areas of infrastructure and sustainable development projects and any other areas of mutual interest in order to strengthen and enhance trade and economic relations among member countries.

The Parties are ready to explore cooperation in mobilizing resources for infrastructure and sustainable development projects in BRICS and other emerging economies and developing countries.

Article 2. Forms of Cooperation

The Parties agree to promote cooperation with the New Development Bank and to take coordinated steps towards forming a mutually beneficial partnership with this new financial institution. For this the Parties intend to engage in the following forms of interaction with the New Development Bank within the areas of infrastructure and sustainable development as well as other areas of mutual interest:

- agreements, including loan facilities, currency swaps and issuance of bonds;
- joint programs for project finance;
- information sharing on potential projects, and mechanisms for project monitoring;
- guarantees and counter-guarantees to secure obligations, including in respect of securities issued by the Parties;
- investment funds to finance projects in sectors and industries that are of priority for the Parties;
- experience and knowledge sharing through consultations, conferences, round tables, etc.
- regular dialogue and meetings between the Parties and the New Development Bank.

Article 3. Non-binding

In order to avoid any doubts about rights or obligations related to this MoU, it is recognized by the Parties that this is a statement of good faith intent and mutual understanding of the Parties.

It is not an international agreement nor does it create legally binding rights or obligations, financial or otherwise, on the Parties or their officers or employees. This MoU does not bind the Parties to enter into any agreements or projects, nor does it give any preference right for any agreement, project or transaction each Party intends to enter into.

Nothing contained herein except for confidentiality restrictions of Article 4 below shall confer any legal rights or obligations on any Parties. The terms and conditions of any co-financing to be provided by any of the Parties regarding the areas mentioned in Article 2 will be discussed by the Parties separately from this MoU, on each individual project, under specific individual agreements (contracts).

These and any other activities agreed to between the Parties shall be subject to the respective regulatory requirements, internal objectives, credit approval, functions, policies and procedures of the Parties.

Article 4. Confidentiality Restrictions

The Parties herein agree that all information delivered under this MoU is subject to the laws, programs and policies of their respective governments and, specifically, to laws regulating banking secrecy and regulations to which each Party may be subject in their respective countries. Unless otherwise agreed and required to be disclosed by law, regulation or governmental order, all information received by each Party under this MoU shall be subject to the treatment of confidentiality by the recipient Party and may not be disclosed, without the prior written consent of the disclosing Party, to any third parties.

Article 5. Meetings and Costs

In order to accomplish the cooperation described herein regarding the arrangement of meetings and other activities to establish direct contact among them and to exchange information on a regular basis, the Parties shall proceed in accordance with their respective internal rules.

Except as otherwise agreed in writing by the Parties, each Party shall be responsible for its own costs and expenses in connection with undertaking any action contemplated by this MoU, including but not limited to salary, subsistence, travel and lodging and other costs of such Party's employees.

Article 6. Term and Termination

This MoU will become effective upon the signature of the authorized officials of the respective Parties and will remain in effect for two years from the date of its signature, unless it is extended in writing by common consent of the Parties. The extension of this MoU can be for the same term, provided that the total term of this MoU is no longer than sixty (60) months. Either Party may terminate the cooperation hereunder, but such termination shall not result in the termination of other contracts (agreements) concluded between the Parties.

Article 7. Miscellaneous

(a) The Parties may modify the terms of the MoU at any time by written common consent and any amendments and supplements shall be made in written form and signed by duly authorized representatives of each respective Party and shall be an integral part of this MoU.

(b) Any notice, request, report or other communication in respect hereof, including the termination notice, shall be prepared in the English language and may be delivered by hand or internationally recognized courier service, registered airmail or by e-mail, to the other Party or Parties.

The address, including the relevant department or officer for whose attention communication is to be marked, of each of the Parties is set forth below:

For Banco Nacional de Desenvolvimento Econômico e Social – (BNDES):

> Unit: Deputy Director of International Division
>
> Address: Av. República do Chile, 330 / 21º andar – Torre Oeste Centro, Rio de Janeiro – RJ, CEP 20031-917
>
> Telephone: Tel: + 55 21 2172 6893 E-mail: lbf@bndes.gov.br

For State Corporation «Bank for Development and Foreign Economic Affairs (Vnesheconombank):

> Unit: External Relations Department
>
> Address: 9 Akademika Sakharova Prospekt, Moscow, Russia, 107996 Telephone: +7 495 782 9485
>
> E-mail: brics@veb.ru

For Export-Import Bank of India (Exim Bank):

> Unit: Chief General Manager, Research & Analysis
>
> Address: Floor 21, World Trade Centre Complex, Cuffe Parade, Mumbai, India, 400 005
>
> Telephone: +91 22 22160364
>
> E-mail: cprmenon@eximbankindia.in

For China Development Bank Corporation (CDB):

Unit: International Finance Department

Address: No.18Fuxingmennei Street, Xicheng District, Beijing, the People's Republic of China, 100031

Telephone: +86 10 68307342

E-mail: zhouzhenheng@cdb.cn

For Development Bank of Southern Africa Limited (DBSA):

Department: Office of the Chief Executive Officer

Address: 1258 Lever Road, Headway Hill, Midrand, 1685, South Africa

Telephone: +27 (0)11 313 3341 / 3516 E-mail: bricsicm@dbsa.org

(c) All disputes arising from this MoU or in regard hereto shall be resolved by the Parties through negotiations.

This MoU is intended to define general areas of cooperation between the Parties and shall not create any financial obligations on the Parties. Likewise, unless expressly agreed otherwise in writing, nothing contained herein shall be deemed to obligate either Party to deal exclusively with the other Party with respect to any project, transaction or matter arising during the term of this MoU. Each Party recognizes that the cooperation described in this MoU is not exclusive and that each Party may enter into similar cooperation agreements with any other party or parties.

The Parties may publish this MoU in a form acceptable to each of the Parties in accordance with national laws or internal policies.

In witness whereof, Banco Nacional de Desenvolvimento Econômico e Social – BNDES, State Corporation "Bank for Development and Foreign Economic Affairs (Vnesheconombank)", Export-Import Bank of India, China Development Bank Corporation and Development Bank of Southern Africa Limited, each acting through its duly authorized representative, have executed and delivered this Memorandum of Understanding in five (05) original English language and identical counterparts at the City of Ufa, on this day 9th July 2015.

E.   Agreement on the New Development Bank: 15 Jul. 2014, Fortaleza (BRA)

AGREEMENT ON THE NEW DEVELOPMENT BANK

The Governments of the Federative Republic of Brazil, the Russian Federation, the Republic of India, the People's Republic of China and the Republic of South Africa, collectively the BRICS countries,

RECALLING the decision taken in the fourth BRICS Summit in New Delhi in 2012 and subsequently announced in the fifth BRICS Summit in Durban in 2013 to establish a development bank;

RECOGNIZING the work undertaken by the respective finance ministries;

CONVINCED that the establishment of such a Bank would reflect the close relations among the BRICS countries, while providing a powerful instrument for increasing their economic cooperation;

MINDFUL of a context where emerging market economies and developing countries continue to face significant financing constraints to address infrastructure gaps and sustainable development needs;

Have agreed on the establishment of the New Development Bank (NDB), hereinafter referred to as the Bank, which shall operate in accordance with the provisions of the annexed Articles of Agreement, that constitute an integral part of this Agreement.

Article 1
Purpose and Functions

The Bank shall mobilize resources for infrastructure and sustainable development projects in BRICS and other emerging economies and developing countries, complementing the existing efforts of multilateral and regional financial institutions for global growth and development.

To fulfill its purpose, the Bank shall support public or private projects through loans, guarantees, equity participation and other financial instruments. It shall also cooperate with international organizations and other financial entities, and provide technical assistance for projects to be supported by the Bank.

Article 2
Membership, Voting, Capital and Shares

The founding members of the Bank are the Federative Republic of Brazil, the Russian Federation, the Republic of India, the People's Republic of China and the Republic of South Africa.

The membership shall be open to members of the United Nations, in accordance with the provisions of the Articles of Agreement of the New Development Bank. It shall be open to borrowing and non-borrowing members.

The New Development Bank shall have an initial subscribed capital of US$ 50 billion and an initial authorized capital of US$ 100 billion. The initial subscribed capital shall be equally distributed amongst the founding members. The voting power of each member shall equal its subscribed shares in the capital stock of the Bank.

Article 3
Headquarters, Organization and Management

The Bank will have its Headquarters in Shanghai.

The Bank shall have a Board of Governors, a Board of Directors, a President and Vice-Presidents. The President of the Bank shall be elected from one of the founding members on a rotational basis, and there shall be at least one Vice President from each of the other founding members.

The operations of the Bank shall be conducted in accordance with sound banking principles.

Article 4
Entry into force

This Agreement with its Annex shall enter into force when the instruments of acceptance, ratification or approval have been deposited by all BRICS countries, in accordance with the provisions set forth in the Articles of Agreement of the New Development Bank.

Done in the city of Fortaleza, on the 15th of July of 2014, in a single original in the English language.

Annex
Articles of Agreement of the New Development Bank

The Governments of the Federative Republic of Brazil, the Russian Federation, the Republic of India, the People's Republic of China, and the Republic of South Africa (collectively the BRICS countries):

CONSIDERING the importance of closer economic cooperation among the BRICS countries;

RECOGNIZING the importance of providing resources for projects for the promotion of infrastructure and sustainable development in the BRICS countries and other emerging economies and developing countries;

CONVINCED of the necessity of creating a new international financial institution in order to intermediate resources for the above mentioned purposes;

DESIROUS to contribute to an international financial system conducive to economic and social development respectful of the global environment;

HAVE AGREED as follows:

Chapter I- Establishment, Purposes, Functions and Headquarters

Article 1 – Establishment

The New Development Bank (hereinafter "the Bank"), established by this Agreement, shall operate in accordance with the following provisions.

Article 2 – Purposes

The purpose of the Bank shall be to mobilize resources for infrastructure and sustainable development projects in BRICS and other emerging market economies and developing countries to complement the existing efforts of multilateral and regional financial institutions for global growth and development.

Article 3 – Functions

To fulfill its purpose, the Bank is authorized to exercise the following functions:

i.   to utilize resources at its disposal to support infrastructure and sustainable development projects, public or private, in the BRICS and other emerging market economies and developing countries, through the provision of loans, guarantees, equity participation and other financial instruments;

ii. to cooperate as the Bank may deem appropriate, within its mandate, with international organizations, as well as national entities whether public or private, in particular with international financial institutions and national development banks;

iii. to provide technical assistance for the preparation and implementation of infrastructure and sustainable development projects to be supported by the Bank;

iv. to support infrastructure and sustainable development projects involving more than one country;

v.   to establish, or be entrusted with the administration, of Special Funds which are designed to serve its purpose.

Article 4 – Headquarters

a.   The Bank has its headquarters in Shanghai.

b.   The Bank may establish offices necessary for the performance of its functions. The first regional office shall be in Johannesburg.

Chapter II- Membership, Voting, Capital and Shares

Article 5 – Membership

a.   The founding members of the Bank are the Federative Republic of Brazil, the Russian Federation, the Republic of India, the People's Republic of China, and the Republic of South Africa.

b.   Membership shall be open to members of the United Nations at such times and in accordance with such terms and conditions as the Bank shall determine by a special majority at the Board of Governors.

c.   Membership of the Bank shall be open to borrowing and non-borrowing members.

d.   The Bank may accept, as decided by the Board of Governors, International Financial Institutions as observers at the meetings of the Board of Governors. Countries interested in becoming members may also be invited as observers to these meetings.

Article 6 – Voting

a.   The voting power of each member shall be equal to the number of its subscribed shares in the capital stock of the Bank. In the event of any member failing to pay any part of the amount due in respect of its obligations in relation to paid-in shares under Article 7 of this Agreement, such member shall be unable, for so long as such failure continues, to exercise that percentage of its voting power which corresponds to the percentage which the amount due but unpaid bears to the total amount of paid-in shares subscribed to by that member in the capital stock of the Bank.

b.   Except as otherwise specifically provided for in this Agreement, all matters before the Bank shall be decided by a simple majority of the votes cast. Where provided for in this Agreement, a qualified majority shall be understood as an affirmative vote of two thirds of the total voting power of the members. Where provided for in this Agreement, a special majority shall be understood as an affirmative vote of four of the founding members concurrent with an affirmative vote of two thirds of the total voting power of the members.

c.   In voting in the Board of Governors, each governor shall be entitled to cast the votes of the member country which he represents.

d.   In voting in the Board of Directors each director shall be entitled to cast the number of votes that counted toward his election, which votes need not be cast as a unit.

Article 7 – Authorized and Subscribed Capital

a.   The initial authorized capital of the Bank shall be one hundred billion dollars (US$100,000,000,000). The dollar wherever referred to in this Agreement shall be understood as being the official currency of payment of the United States of America.

b.   The initial authorized capital of the Bank shall be divided into 1,000,000 (one million) shares, having a par value of one hundred thousand dollars (US$ 100,000) each, which shall be available for subscription only by members in accordance with the provisions of this Agreement. The value of 1 (one) share, will also be the minimum amount to be subscribed for participation by a single country.

c.   The initial subscribed capital of the Bank shall be fifty billion dollars (US$50,000,000,000). The subscribed capital stock shall be divided into paid-in shares and callable shares. Shares having an aggregate par value of ten billion dollars (US$10,000,000,000) shall be paid-in shares, and shares having an aggregate par value of forty billion dollars (US$40,000,000,000) shall be callable shares.

d.   An increase of the authorized and subscribed capital stock of the Bank, as well as the proportion between the paid in shares and the callable shares may be decided by the Board of Governors at such time and under such terms and conditions as it may deem advisable, by a special majority of the Board of Governors. In such case, each member shall have a reasonable opportunity to subscribe, under the conditions established in Article 8 and under such other conditions as the Board of Governors shall decide. No member, however, shall be obligated to subscribe to any part of such increased capital.

e.   The Board of Governors shall at intervals of not more than 5 (five) years review the capital stock of the Bank.

Article 8 – Subscription of Shares

a.   Each member shall subscribe to shares of the capital stock of the Bank. The number of shares to be initially subscribed by the founding members shall be those set forth in Attachment 1 of this Agreement, which specifies the obligation of each member as to both paid-in and callable capital. The number of shares to be initially subscribed by other members shall be determined by the Board of Governors by special majority on the occasion of the acceptance of their accession.

b.   Shares of stock initially subscribed by founding members shall be issued at par. Other shares shall be issued at par unless the Board of Governors decides in special circumstances to issue them on other terms.

c.   No increase in the subscription of any member to the capital stock shall become effective, and any right to subscribe thereto is hereby waived, which would have the effect of:

i.   reducing the voting power of the founding members below 55 (fifty-five) per cent of the total voting power;

ii.   increasing the voting power of the non-borrowing member countries above 20 (twenty) per cent of the total voting power;

iii. increasing the voting power of a non-founding member country above 7 (seven) per cent of total voting power.

d.   The liability of the members on shares shall be limited to the unpaid portion of their issue price.

e.   No member shall be liable, by reason of its membership, for obligations of the Bank.

f.   Shares shall not be pledged nor encumbered in any manner. They shall be transferable only to the Bank.

Article 9 – Payment of Subscriptions

a.   On entry into force of this Agreement, payment of the amount initially subscribed by each founding member to the paid-in capital stock of the Bank shall be made in dollars in 7 (seven) installments as provided for in Attachment 2. The first installment shall be paid by each member within 6 (six) months after entry into force of this Agreement. The second installment shall become due 18 (eighteen) months from the entry into force of this Agreement. The remaining 5 (five) installments shall each become due successively 1 (one) year from the date on which the preceding installment becomes due.

b.   The Board of Governors shall determine the dates for the payment of amounts subscribed by the members of the Bank to the paid-in capital stock to which the provisions of paragraph (a) of this article do not apply.

c.   Payment of the amounts subscribed to the callable capital stock of the Bank shall be subject to call only as and when required by the Bank to meet its obligations incurred on borrowing of funds for inclusion in its ordinary capital resources or guarantees chargeable to such resources. In the event of such calls, payment may be made at the option of the member concerned in convertible currency or in the currency required to discharge the obligation of the Bank for the purpose of which the call is made.

d.   Calls on unpaid subscriptions shall be uniform in percentage on all callable shares.

Chapter III - Organization and Management
Article 10 – Structure

The Bank shall have a Board of Governors, a Board of Directors, a President, Vice-Presidents as decided by the Board of Governors, and such other officers and staff as may be considered necessary.

Article 11 – Board of Governors: composition and powers

a.   All the powers of the Bank shall be vested in the Board of Governors consisting of one governor and one alternate appointed by each member in such manner as it may determine. Governors shall be at ministerial level, and may be replaced subject to the pleasure of the member appointing him. No alternate may vote except in the absence of his principal. The Board shall on an annual basis select one of the governors as chairperson.

b.   The Board of Governors may delegate to the Directors authority to exercise any powers of the Board, except the power to:

i.   admit new members and determine the conditions of their admission;

ii.   increase or decrease the capital stock;

iii.   suspend a member;

iv.   amend this Agreement;

v.   decide appeals from interpretations of this agreement given by the Directors;

vi.   authorize the conclusion of general agreements for cooperation with other international organizations;

vii.   determine the distribution of the net income of the Bank;

viii.   decide to terminate the operations of the Bank and to distribute its assets;

ix.   decide on the number of additional Vice-Presidents;

x.   elect the President of the Bank;

xi.   approve a proposal by the Board of Directors to call capital;

xii.   approve the General Strategy of the Bank every 5 (five) years.

c.   The Board of Governors shall hold an annual meeting and such other meetings as may be provided for by the Board or called by the Directors. Meetings of the Board shall be called by the Directors whenever requested by members, the number of which shall be determined by the Board of Governors from time to time.

d.   A quorum for any meeting of the Board of Governors shall be a majority of the Governors, exercising not less than two thirds of the total voting power.

e.   The Board of Governors may by regulation establish a procedure whereby the Directors, when they deem such action to be in the best interests of the Bank, may obtain a vote of the Governors on a specific question without calling a meeting of the Board.

f.   The Board of Governors, and the Directors to the extent authorized, may adopt such rules and regulations as may be necessary or appropriate to conduct the business of the Bank.

g.   Governors and alternates shall serve as such without compensation from the Bank.

h.   The Board of Governors shall determine the salary and terms of the contract of service of the President.

i.   The Board of Governors shall retain full power to exercise authority over any matter delegated to the Board of Directors under paragraph (a) of Article 12.

Article 12 – Board of Directors

a. The Board of Directors shall be responsible for the conduct of the general operations of the Bank, and for this purpose, shall exercise all the powers delegated to them by the Board of Governors, and in particular:

i. in conformity with the general directions of the Board of Governors, take decisions concerning business strategies, country strategies, loans, guarantees, equity investments, borrowing by the Bank, setting basic operational procedures and charges, furnishing of technical assistance and other operations of the Bank;

ii. submit the accounts for each financial year for approval of the Board of Governors at each annual meeting; and

iii. approve the budget of the Bank.

b. Each of the founding members shall appoint 1 (one) Director and 1 (one) alternate. The Board of Governors shall establish by special majority the methodology by which additional Directors and alternates shall be elected, so that the total number of Directors shall be no more than 10 (ten).

c. Directors shall serve a term of 2 (two) years and may be re-elected. A Director shall continue in office until his successor has been chosen and qualified. Alternates shall have full power to act for the respective Director when he is not present.

d. The Board of Directors shall appoint a non-executive chairperson from among the Directors for a mandate of 4 (four) years. If the Director does not serve a full mandate or if he is not re-elected for a second term, the Director that replaces him will serve as chairperson for the remainder of the term.

e. The Board of Directors shall approve the basic organization of the Bank upon proposal by the President, including the number and general responsibilities of the chief administrative and professional positions of the staff.

f. The Board of Directors shall appoint a Credit and Investment Committee and may appoint such other committees as it deems advisable. Membership of such committees need not be limited to Governors, Directors, or alternates.

g. The Board of Directors shall function as a non-resident body, which will meet quarterly, unless the Board of Governors decides otherwise by a qualified majority. If the Board of Governors decides to make the Board of Directors a resident body, the President of the Bank will become henceforth the chairperson of the Board of Directors.

h. A quorum for any meeting of the Directors shall be a majority of the Directors, exercising not less than two-thirds of the total voting power.

i. A member of the Bank may send a representative to attend any meeting of the Board of Directors when a matter especially affecting that member is under consideration. Such right of representation shall be regulated by the Board of Governors.

Article 13 – President and Staff

a. The Board of Governors shall elect a President from one of the founding members on a rotational basis, who shall not be a Governor or a Director or an alternate for either. The President shall be a member of the Board of Directors, but shall have no vote except a deciding vote in case of an equal division. The President may participate in meetings of the Board of Governors, but shall not vote at such meetings. Without prejudice to the mandate established in item (d) below, the President shall cease to hold office should the Board of Governors so decide by a special majority.

b. The President shall be chief of the operating staff of the Bank and shall conduct, under the direction of the Directors, the ordinary business of the Bank, and in particular:

i. being, on this, accountable to the Directors, the President shall be responsible for the organization, appointment and dismissal of the officers and staff, and recommendation of admission and dismissal of Vice Presidents to the Board of Governors;

ii. the President shall head the credit and investment committee, composed also by the Vice-Presidents, that will be responsible for decisions on loans, guarantees, equity investments and technical assistance of no more than a limit amount to be established by the Board of Directors, provided that no objection is raised by any member of Board of Directors within 30 (thirty) days since such project is submitted to the Board.

b.   There shall be at least 1 (one) Vice-President from each founding member except the country represented by the President. Vice-Presidents shall be appointed by the Board of Governors on the recommendation of the President. Vice-Presidents shall exercise such authority and perform such functions in the administration of the Bank, as may be determined by the Board of Directors.

c.   The President and each Vice-President shall serve for a 5 (five) year term, non renewable, except for the first term of the first Vice-Presidents, whose mandate shall be for 6 (six) years.

d.   The Bank, its officers and employees shall not interfere in the political affairs of any member, nor shall they be influenced in their decisions by the political character of the member or members concerned. Only economic considerations shall be relevant to their decisions, and these considerations shall be weighed impartially in order to achieve the purpose and functions stated in Articles 2 and 3.

e.   The President, Vice-Presidents, officers and staff of the Bank, in the discharge of their offices, owe their duty entirely to the Bank and to no other authority. Each member of the Bank shall respect the international character of this duty and shall refrain from all attempts to influence any of them in the discharge of their duties.

Article 14- Publication of Reports and Provision of Information

f.   The Bank shall publish an annual report containing an audited statement of the accounts. It shall also transmit quarterly to the members a summary statement of the financial position and a profit-and-loss statement showing the results of its ordinary operations.

g.   The Bank may also publish such other reports as it deems desirable to carry out its purpose and functions.

Article 15- Transparency and Accountability

The Bank shall ensure that its proceedings are transparent and shall elaborate in its own Rules of Procedure specific provisions regarding access to its documents.

Chapter IV - Operations

Article 16 – Use of Resources

The resources and facilities of the Bank shall be used exclusively to implement the purpose and functions set forth respectively in Articles 2 and 3 of this Agreement.

Article 17 – Depositories

Each member shall designate its central bank as a depository in which the Bank may keep its holdings of such member's currency and other assets of the Bank. If a member has no central bank, it shall, in agreement with the Bank, designate another institution for such purpose.

Article 18 – Categories of Operations

a.   The operations of the Bank shall consist of ordinary operations and special operations. Ordinary operations shall be those financed from the ordinary capital resources of the Bank. Special operations shall be those financed from the Special Funds resources.

b.   The ordinary capital of the Bank shall include the following:

   i.   subscribed capital stock of the Bank, including both paid-in and callable shares, except such part thereof as may be set aside into one or more Special Funds;

   ii.   funds raised by borrowings of the Bank by virtue of powers conferred by Chapter 5 of this Agreement, to which the commitment to calls provided for in item (c) of Article 9 is applicable;

   iii.   funds received in repayment of loans or guarantees and proceeds from the disposal of equity investments made with the resources indicated in (i) and (ii) of this paragraph;

    iv. income derived from loans and equity investments made from the aforementioned funds or from guarantees to which the commitment to calls set forth in item (c) of Article 9 of this Agreement is applicable; and

    v. any other funds or income received by the Bank which do not form part of its Special Funds resources.

c.   The ordinary capital resources and the Special Funds resources of the Bank shall at all times and in all respects be held, used, committed, invested or otherwise disposed of entirely separate from each other. The financial statements of the Bank shall show the ordinary operations and special operations separately.

d.   The ordinary capital resources of the Bank shall, under no circumstances, be charged with, or used to discharge, losses or liabilities arising out of special operations or other activities for which Special Fund resources were originally used or committed.

e.   Expenses appertaining directly to ordinary operations shall be charged to the ordinary capital resources of the Bank. Expenses appertaining directly to the special operations shall be charged to Special Funds resources.

Article 19 – Methods of Operation

a.   The Bank may guarantee, participate in, make loans or support through any other financial instrument, public or private projects, including public-private partnerships, in any borrowing member country, as well as invest in the equity, underwrite the equity issue of securities, or facilitate the access of international capital markets of any business, industrial, agricultural or services enterprise with projects in the territories of borrowing member countries.

b.   The Bank may co-finance, guarantee or co-guarantee, together with international financial institutions, commercial banks or other suitable entities, projects within its mandate.

c.   The Bank may provide technical assistance for the preparation and implementation of projects to be supported by the Bank.

d.   The Board of Governors, by special majority, may approve a general policy under which the Bank is authorized to develop the operations described in the previous items of this article in relation to public or private projects in a non-member emerging economy or developing country, subject to the condition that it involves a material interest of a member, as defined by such policy.

e.   The Board of Directors, by special majority, may exceptionally approve a specific public or private project in a non-member emerging economy or developing country involving the operations described in the previous items of this article. Sovereign guaranteed operations in non-members will be priced in full consideration of the sovereign risks involved, given the risk mitigators offered, and any other conditions established as the Board of Directors may decide.

Article 20 – Limitations on Operations

a.   The total amount outstanding in respect of the ordinary operations of the Bank shall not at any time exceed the total amount of its unimpaired subscribed capital, reserves and surplus included in its ordinary capital resources.

b.   The total amount outstanding in respect of the special operations of the Bank relating to any Special Fund shall not at any time exceed the total amount prescribed in the regulations of that Special Fund.

c.   The Bank shall seek to maintain reasonable diversification in its investments in equity capital. It shall not assume responsibility for managing any entity or enterprise in which it has an investment, except where necessary to safeguard its investments.

Article 21 – Operational Principles

The operations of the Bank shall be conducted in accordance with the following principles:

i.   the Bank shall apply sound banking principles to all its operations, ensure adequate remuneration and have in due regard the risks involved;

ii. the Bank shall not finance any undertaking in the territory of a member if that member objects to such financing;

iii. in preparing any country program or strategy, financing any project or by making designation or reference to a particular territory, or geographic area in its documents, the Bank will not deem to have intended to make any judgment as to the legal or other status of any territory or area;

iv. the Bank shall not allow a disproportionate amount of its resources to be used for the benefit of any member. The Bank shall seek to maintain reasonable diversification in all of its investments;

v.   the Bank shall place no restriction upon the procurement of goods and services from any country member from the proceeds of any loan, investment or other financing undertaken in the ordinary or special operations of the Banks, and shall, in all appropriate cases, make its loans and other operations conditional on invitations to all member countries to tender being arranged;

vi. the proceeds of any loan, investment or other financing undertaken in the ordinary operations of the Bank or with Special Funds established by the Bank shall be used only for procurement in member countries of goods and services produced in member countries, except in any case in which the Board of Directors determines to permit procurement in a non-member country of goods and services produced in a non-member country in special circumstances making such procurement appropriate;

vii. the Bank shall take the necessary measures to ensure that the proceeds of any loan made, guaranteed or participated in by the Bank, or any equity investment, are used only for the purposes for which the loan or the equity investment was granted and with due attention to considerations of economy and efficiency.

Article 22 – Terms and Conditions

a.   In the case of loans made, participated in, or guaranteed by the Bank and equity investments, the contract shall establish the terms and conditions for the loan, guarantee or equity investment concerned in accordance with the policies established by the Board of Directors, including, as the case may be, those relating to payment of principal, interest and other fees, charges, commissions, maturities, currency and dates of payment in respect of the loan, guarantee or equity investment, in accordance with the policies of the Bank. In setting such policies, the Board of Directors shall take fully into account the need to safeguard its income.

b.   In underwriting the sale of securities, the Bank shall charge fees under the terms and conditions established in the policies of the Bank.

Article 23 – Special Funds

c.   The establishment and administration of Special Funds by the Bank shall be approved by the Board of Governors by a qualified majority and shall follow the purposes set forth in Article 2 of this Agreement.

d.   Except when the Board of Governors specifies otherwise, the Special Funds shall be accountable and its operations subjected to the Board of Directors.

e.   The Bank may adopt such special rules and regulations as may be required for the establishment, administration and use of each Special Fund.

Article 24 – Provision of Currencies

The Bank in its operations may provide financing in the local currency of the country in which the operation takes place, provided that adequate policies are put in place to avoid significant currency mismatch.

Article 25 – Methods of Meeting the Losses of the Bank

a.   In cases of default on loans made, participated in or guaranteed by the Bank in its ordinary operations, the Bank shall take, firstly, all necessary actions as it deems appropriate in order to recover the loans made and, secondly, it may modify the terms of the loans, other than the currency of repayment.

b.   Losses arising in the Bank's ordinary operation shall be charged:

   i.   first, to the provisions of the Bank;

   ii.   second, to net income;

   iii.   third, against the special reserve;

   iv.   fourth, against the general reserve and surpluses;

   v.   fifth, against the unimpaired paid-in capital, and

   vi.   last, against an appropriate amount of the uncalled subscribed callable capital which shall be called in accordance with the provisions of paragraphs (c) and (d) of Article 9 of these Articles of Agreement.

c.   In deploying its efforts for credit recovery in case of default, the Bank shall seek the assistance of the authorities of the country where the operation takes place.

Chapter V - Borrowing and other Additional Powers

Article 26– General Powers

In addition to the powers specified elsewhere in this Agreement, the Bank shall have the power to:

a.   borrow funds in member countries or elsewhere, and in this connection to furnish such collateral or other security therefore as the Bank shall determine, provided always that:

   i.   before making a sale of its obligations in the territory of a member country, the Bank shall have obtained its approval;

   ii.   where the obligations of the Bank are to be denominated in the currency of a member, the bank shall have obtained its approval;

   iii.   the Bank shall obtain the approval of the countries referred to in sub-paragraphs (i) and (ii) of this paragraph that the proceeds may be exchanged without restriction for other currencies; and

   iv.   before determining to sell its obligations in a particular country, the Bank shall consider the amount of previous borrowing, if any, in that country, the amount of previous borrowing in other countries, and the possible availability of funds in such other countries; and shall give due regard to the general principle that its borrowings should to the greatest extent possible be diversified as to country of borrowing.

b.   buy and sell securities the Bank has issued or guaranteed or in which it has invested, provided always that it shall have obtained the approval of any country in whose territory the securities are to be bought or sold;

c.   guarantee securities in which it has invested in order to facilitate their sale;

d.   underwrite, or participate in the underwriting of, securities issued by any entity or enterprise for purposes consistent with the purpose of the Bank;

e.   invest funds, not needed in its operations, in such obligations as it may determine, and invest funds held by the Bank for pensions or similar purposes in marketable securities. In doing so, the Bank shall give due consideration to invest such funds in the territories of members in obligations of members or nationals thereof;

f.   exercise such other powers and establish such rules and regulations as may be necessary or appropriate in furtherance of its purpose and functions, consistent with the provisions of this Agreement.

Article 27 – Notice to be placed on Securities

Every security issued or guaranteed by the Bank shall bear on its face a conspicuous statement to the effect that it is not an obligation of any Government, unless it is in fact the obligation of a particular Government, in which case it shall so state.

Chapter VI - Status, Immunities and Privileges

Article 28– Purpose of the Chapter

To enable the Bank effectively to fulfill its purpose and carry out the functions entrusted to it, the status, immunities, exemptions and privileges set forth in this Chapter shall be accorded to the Bank in the territory of each member.

Article 29 – Status

a.   The Bank shall possess full international personality.

b.   In the territory of each member the Bank shall possess full juridical personality and, in particular, full capacity to:

    i.   contract;

    ii.   acquire and dispose of immovable and movable property; and

    iii.   institute legal proceedings

Article 30 – Position of the Bank with Regard to Judicial Process

a.   The Bank shall enjoy immunity from every form of legal process, except in cases arising out of or in connection with the exercise of its powers to borrow money, to guarantee obligations, or to buy and sell or underwrite the sale of securities, in which cases actions may be brought against the Bank in a court of competent jurisdiction in the territory of a country in which the Bank has its headquarters or offices, or has appointed an agent for the purpose of accepting service or notice of process, or has issued or guaranteed securities.

b.   Notwithstanding the provisions of paragraph (a) of this Article, no action shall be brought against the Bank by any member, or by any agency or instrumentality of a member, or by any entity or person directly or indirectly acting for or deriving claims from a member or from any agency or instrumentality of a member. Members shall have recourse to such special procedures for the settlement of controversies between the Bank and its members as may be prescribed in this Agreement, in the by-laws and regulations of the Bank, or in contracts entered into with the Bank.

c.   Property and assets of the Bank shall, wheresoever located and by whomsoever held, be immune from all forms of seizure, attachment or execution before the delivery of final judgment against the Bank.

Article 31 – Freedom and Immunity of Assets and Archives

a.   Property and assets of the Bank, wherever located and by whomsoever held, shall be immune from search, requisition, confiscation, expropriation or any other form of taking or foreclosure by executive or legislative action.

b.   The archives of the Bank and, in general, all documents belonging to it or held by it, shall be inviolable, wherever located.

c.   To the extent necessary to carry out the purpose and functions of the Bank and subject to the provisions of this Agreement, all property and other assets of the Bank shall be exempt from restrictions, regulations, controls and moratoria of any nature.

Article 32 – Privilege for Communications

The official communications of the Bank shall be accorded by each member the same treatment that it accords to the official communications of other members.

Article 33 – Personal Immunities and Privileges

All Governors, Directors, alternates, officers, and employees of the Bank shall have the following privileges and immunities:

  i. immunity from legal process with respect to acts performed by them in their official capacity, except when the Bank waives this immunity;

  ii. when not local nationals, the same immunities from immigration restrictions, alien registration requirements and national service obligations and the same facilities as regards exchange provisions as are accorded by members to the representatives, officials, and employees of comparable rank of other members;

  iii. the same privileges in respect of traveling facilities as are accorded by members to representatives, officials, and employees of comparable rank of other members.

Article 34 – Exemption from Taxation

a. The Bank, its property, other assets, income, transfers and the operations and transactions it carries out pursuant to this Agreement, shall be immune from all taxation, from all restrictions and from all customs duties. The Bank shall also be immune from any obligation relating to the payment, withholding or collection of any tax, or duty.

b. No tax shall be levied on or in respect of salaries and emoluments paid by the Bank to Directors, alternates, officers or employees of the Bank, including experts performing missions for the Bank, except where a member, notwithstanding Article 48(d), deposits with its instrument of ratification, acceptance, approval or accession a declaration that such member retains for itself and its political subdivisions the right to tax salaries and emoluments paid by the Bank to citizens or nationals of such member.

c. No tax of any kind shall be levied on any obligation or security issued by the Bank, including any dividend or interest thereon, by whomsoever held:

  i. which discriminates against such obligation or security solely because it is issued by the Bank; or

  ii. if the sole jurisdictional basis for such taxation is the place or currency in which it is issued, made payable or paid, or the location of any office or place of business maintained by the Bank.

d. No tax of any kind shall be levied on any obligation or security guaranteed by the Bank, including any dividend or interest thereon, by whomsoever held:

  i. which discriminates against such obligation or security solely because it is guaranteed by the Bank; or

  ii. if the sole jurisdictional basis for such taxation is the location of any office or place of business maintained by the Bank.

Article 35 – Implementation

Each member, in accordance with its juridical system, shall promptly take such action as is necessary to make effective in its own territory the provisions set forth in the Chapter and shall inform the Bank of the action which it has taken on the matter.

Article 36 – Waiver of Immunities, Privileges and Exemptions

The immunities, privileges and exemptions conferred under this Chapter are granted in the interest of the Bank. The Board of Directors may waive to such extent and upon such conditions as it may determine any of the immunities, privileges and exemptions conferred under this Chapter in cases where such action would, in its opinion, be appropriate in the best interests of the Bank. The President shall have the right and the duty to waive any immunity, privilege or exemption in respect of any officer, employee or expert of the Bank, other than the President and each Vice-President, where, in his or her opinion, the immunity, privilege or exemption would impede the course of justice and can be waived without prejudice to the interests of the Bank. In similar circumstances and under the same conditions, the Board of Directors shall have the right and the duty to waive any immunity, privilege or exemption in respect of the President and each Vice-President.

Chapter VII - Withdrawal and Suspension of Members, Temporary Suspension and Termination of Operations of the Bank

Article 37 – Withdrawal

a.   Any member may withdraw from the Bank by delivering to the Bank at its headquarters written notice of its intention to do so. Such withdrawal shall become finally effective, and the membership shall cease, on the date specified in the notice but in no event less than 6 (six) months after the notice is delivered to the Bank. However, at any time before the withdrawal becomes finally effective, the member may notify the Bank in writing of the cancellation of its notice of intention to withdraw.

b.   After withdrawing, a member shall remain liable for all direct and contingent obligations to the Bank to which it was subject at the date of delivery of the withdrawal notice, including those specified in Article 39. However, if the withdrawal becomes finally effective, the member shall not incur any liability for obligations resulting from operations of the Bank effected after the date on which the withdrawal notice was received by the Bank.

c.   Upon receipt of a notice of withdrawal, the Board of Governors shall adopt procedures for settlement of accounts with the withdrawing Member country, no later than the date upon which the withdrawal becomes effective.

Article 38 – Suspension of Membership

a.   If a member fails to fulfill any of its obligations to the Bank, the Bank may suspend its membership by decision of the Board of Governors by special majority.

b.   The member so suspended shall automatically cease to be a member of the Bank 1 (one) year from the date of its suspension unless the Board of Governors decides by the same majority to terminate the suspension.

c.   While under suspension, a member shall not be entitled to exercise any rights under this Agreement, except the right of withdrawal, but shall remain subject to all its obligations.

d.   The Board of Governors shall adopt regulations as may be necessary for the implementation of this article.

Article 39 – Settlement of Accounts

a.   After a country ceases to be a member, it no longer shall share in the profits or losses of the Bank, nor shall it incur any liability with respect to loans and guarantees entered into by the Bank thereafter. However, it shall remain liable for all amounts it owes the Bank and for its contingent liabilities to the Bank so long as any part of the loans or guarantees contracted by the Bank before the date on which the country ceased to be a member remains outstanding.

b.   When a country ceases to be a member, the Bank shall arrange for the repurchase of such country's capital stock as a part of the settlement of accounts pursuant to the provisions of this Article; but the country shall have no other rights under this Agreement except as provided in this Article and in Article 46.

c.   The Bank and the country ceasing to be a member may agree on the repurchase of the capital stock on such terms as are deemed appropriate in the circumstances, without regard to the provisions of the following paragraph. Such agreement may provide, among other things, for a final settlement of all obligations of the country to the Bank.

d.   If the agreement referred to in the preceding paragraph has not been consummated within 6 (six) months after the country ceases to be a member or such other time as the Bank and such country may agree upon, the repurchase price of such country's capital stock shall be its book value, according to the books of the Bank, on the date when the country ceased to be a member. Such repurchase shall be subject to the following conditions:

i.   the payment may be made in such installments, at such times and in such available currencies as the Bank determines, taking into account the financial position of the Bank;

ii.   any amount which the Bank owes the country for the repurchase of its capital stock shall be withheld to the extent that the country or any of its subdivisions or agencies remains liable to the Bank as a result of loan or guarantee operations. The amount withheld may, at the option of the Bank, be applied on any such liability as it matures. However, no amount shall be withheld on account of the country's contingent liability for future calls on its subscription pursuant to Article 9(c);

iii.   if the Bank sustains net losses on any loans or participations, or as a result of any guarantees, outstanding on the date the country ceased to be a member, and the amount of such losses exceeds the amount of the reserves provided therefore on such date, such country shall repay on demand the amount by which the repurchase price of its shares would have been reduced, if the losses had been taken into account when the book value of the shares, according to the books of the Bank, was determined. In addition, the former member shall remain liable on any call pursuant to Article 9(c), to the extent that it would have been required to respond if the impairment of capital had occurred and the call had been made at the time the repurchase price of its shares had been determined.

e.   In no event shall any amount due to a country for its shares under this section be paid until 12 (twelve) months after the date upon which the country ceases to be a member. If within that period the Bank terminates operations, all rights of such country shall be determined by the provisions of Articles 41 to 43, and such country shall be considered still a member of the Bank for the purposes of such articles except that it shall have no voting rights.

Article 40 – Temporary Suspension of Operations

In an emergency, the Board of Directors may suspend temporarily operations in respect of new loans, guarantees, underwriting, technical assistance and equity investments pending an opportunity for further consideration and action by the Board of Governors.

Article 41 – Termination of Operations

The Bank may terminate its operations as decided by the Board of Governors by special majority. Upon such termination of operations the Bank shall forthwith cease all activities, except those incidents to the orderly realization, conservation and preservation of its assets and settlement of its obligations.

Article 42 – Liability of Members and Payment of Claims

a.   The liability of all members arising from the subscriptions to the capital stock of the Bank and in respect to the depreciation of their currencies shall continue until all direct and contingent obligations shall have been discharged.

b.   All creditors holding direct claims shall be paid out of the assets of the Bank and then out of payments to the Bank on unpaid or callable subscriptions. Before making any payments to creditors holding direct claims, the Board of Directors shall make such arrangements as are necessary, in its judgment, to ensure a pro rata distribution among holders of direct and contingent claims.

Article 43 – Distribution of Assets

a.   No distribution of assets shall be made to members on account of their subscriptions to the capital stock of the Bank until all liabilities to creditors chargeable to such capital stock shall have been discharged or provided for. Moreover, such distribution must be approved by a decision of the Board of Governors by special majority.

b.   Any distribution of the assets of the Bank to the members shall be in proportion to capital stock held by each member and shall be effected at such times and under such conditions, as the Bank shall deem fair and equitable. The shares of assets distributed need not be uniform as to type of assets. No member shall be entitled to receive its share in such a distribution of assets until it has settled all of its obligations to the Bank.

c.   Any member receiving assets distributed pursuant to this article shall enjoy the same rights with respect to such assets as the Bank enjoyed prior to their distribution.

Chapter VIII – Amendments, Interpretation and Arbitration

Article 44 – Amendments

a.   This Agreement may be amended only by decision of the Board of Governors by special majority.

b.   Any proposal to introduce modifications in this Agreement, whether emanating from a member, a Governor or the Board of Directors, shall be communicated to the chairperson of the Board of Governors who shall bring the proposal before the Board. If the proposed amendment is approved by the Board, the Bank shall ask all members whether they accept the proposed amendment. When the amendment is accepted, ratified or approved by 2/3 (two thirds) of the members, the Bank shall certify the fact by formal communication addressed to all members.

c.   The amendments shall enter into force for all members 3 (three) months after the date of the formal communication provided for in paragraph (b) of this article, unless the Board of Governors specify a different period.

Article 45 – Interpretation

a.   Any question of interpretation of the provisions of this Agreement arising between any member and the Bank or between any members of the Bank shall be submitted to the Board of Directors for decision.

b.   Members especially affected by the question under consideration shall be entitled to direct representation before the Board of Directors as provided in Article 12(i).

c.   In any case where the Board of Directors has given a decision under (a) above, any member may require that the question be submitted to the Board of Governors, whose decision shall be final. Pending the decision of the Board of Governors, the Bank may, so far as it deems it necessary, act on the basis of the decision of the Board of Directors.

Article 46 – Arbitration

a.   If a disagreement should arise between the Bank and a country which has ceased to be a member, or between the Bank and any member after adoption of a decision to terminate the operation of the Bank, such disagreement shall be submitted to arbitration by a tribunal of 3 (three) arbitrators. One of the arbitrators shall be appointed by the Bank, another by the country concerned, and the third, unless the parties otherwise agree, by an authority as may approved by the Board of Governors. If all efforts to reach a unanimous agreement fail, decisions shall be made by a majority vote of the 3 (three) arbitrators.

b.   The third arbitrator shall be empowered to settle all questions of procedure in any case where the parties are in disagreement with respect thereto.

c.   Any disagreement concerning a contract between the Bank and a borrowing country shall be settled according to the respective contract.

Article 47 – Approval deemed given

Whenever the approval of any member is required before any act may be done by the Bank, approval shall be deemed to have been given unless the member presents an objection within such reasonable period as the Bank may fix in notifying the member of the proposed act.

Chapter IX – Final Provisions

Article 48 –Acceptance

a.   Each signatory country shall deposit with the government of the Federative Republic of Brazil an instrument setting forth that it has accepted, ratified or approved this Agreement in accordance with its own laws.

b.   The Government of the Federative Republic of Brazil shall send certified copies of this Agreement to the signatories and duly notify them of each deposit of the instrument of acceptance, ratification or approval made pursuant to the foregoing paragraph, as well as the date thereof.

c.   After the date on which the Bank commences operations, the Government of the Federative Republic of Brazil may receive the instrument of accession to this Agreement from any country whose membership has been approved in accordance with Article 5(b).

d.   The acceptance, ratification or approval of the Agreement, or the accession thereto, shall not contain any objection or reservation.

Article 49 – Entry into Force

d.   This Agreement shall enter into force when instruments of acceptance, ratification or approval have been deposited, in accordance with Article 48 by all BRICS countries.

e.   BRICS countries whose instruments of acceptance, ratification or approval were deposited prior to the date on which the Agreement entered into force shall become members on the date it enters into force. Other countries shall become members on the dates on which their instruments of accession are deposited.

Article 50 – Commencement of Operations

The chair of the BRICS countries shall call the first meeting of the Board of Governors as soon as this Agreement enters into force under Article 49 of this Chapter, in order to take the necessary decisions for the initial operation of the Bank.

Attachment 1

Shares of Initial Subscribed Capital Stock of Founding Members

Each founding member shall initially subscribe 100,000 (one hundred thousand) shares, in a total of ten billion dollars (US$10,000,000,000), of which 20,000 (twenty thousand) shares correspond to paid in capital, in a total of two billion dollars (US$2,000,000,000) and 80,000 (eighty thousand) shares correspond to callable capital, in a total of eight billion dollars (US$8,000,000,000).

Attachment 2

Payment of Initial Subscriptions to the Paid in Capital by the Founding Members

Installment	Paid in capital per country in million dollars
1	150
2	250
3	300
4	300
5	300
6	350
7	350

F.   Establishment of the BRICS-Led Development Bank: 27 Mar. 2013, Durban (ZAF)

STATEMENT BY BRICS LEADERS
ON THE ESTABLISHMENT OF THE BRICS-LED DEVELOPMENT BANK
Durban, South Africa, March 27, 2013

1.   We, the Leaders of Brazil, Russia, India, China and South Africa met on the occasion of the Fifth BRICS Summit on 27 March 2013 in eThekwini, KwaZulu-Natal.

2.   We considered that developing countries face challenges of infrastructure development due to insufficient long-term financing and foreign direct investment, especially investment in capital stock.

3.   This constrains global aggregate demand. BRICS cooperation towards more productive use of global financial resources can make a positive contribution to addressing this problem.

4.   In March 2012 we directed our Finance Ministers to examine the feasibility and viability of setting up a New Development Bank for mobilising resources for infrastructure and sustainable development projects in BRICS and other emerging economies and developing countries, to supplement the existing efforts of multilateral and regional financial institutions for global growth and development.

5.   Following the report from our Finance Ministers, we are satisfied that the establishment of a New Development Bank is feasible and viable.

6.   We have agreed to establish the New Development Bank. The initial capital contribution to the bank should be substantial and sufficient for the bank to be effective in financing infrastructure.

7.   In June 2012, in our meeting in Los Cabos, we tasked our Finance Ministers and Central Bank Governors to explore the construction of a financial safety net through the creation of a Contingent Reserve Arrangement (CRA) amongst BRICS countries. They have concluded that the establishment of a self-managed contingent reserve arrangement would have a positive precautionary effect, help BRICS countries forestall short-term liquidity pressures, provide mutual support and further strengthen financial stability. It would also contribute to strengthening the global financial safety net and complement existing international arrangements as an additional line of defence. We are of the view that the establishment of the CRA with an initial size of US$ 100 billion is feasible and desirable, subject to internal legal frameworks and appropriate safeguards. We direct our Finance Ministers and Central Bank Governors to continue working towards its establishment.

8.   We are grateful to our Finance Ministers and Central Bank Governors for the work undertaken on the New Development Bank and the Contingent Reserve Arrangement and direct them to negotiate and conclude the agreements which will establish them. We will review progress made in these two initiatives at our next meeting in September 2013.

9.   I thank you.

G.   Agreements between BRICS Development Banks: 29 Mar. 2012, New Delhi (IND)

AGREEMENTS BETWEEN BRICS DEVELOMENT BANKS
New Delhi, March 29, 2012

1.   Development banks of BRICS (Brazil, Russia, India, China, and South Africa) have today signed two Agreements - i) Master Agreement on Extending Credit Facility in Local Currency; and ii) BRICS Multilateral Letter of Credit Confirmation Facility Agreement - in the presence of Heads of States/Governments of the BRICS countries. The five participating banks are Banco Nacional de Desenvolvimento Economico e Social - BNDES, Brazil; State Corporation Bank for Development and Foreign Economic Affairs - Vnesheconombank of Russia; Export-Import Bank of India; China Development Bank Corporation, and Development Bank of Southern Africa.

2.   The Master Agreement on Extending Credit Facility in Local Currency is intended to reduce the demand for fully convertible currencies for transactions among BRICS nations, and thereby help reduce the transaction costs of intra-BRICS trade.

3.   The Multilateral Letter of Credit Confirmation Facility Agreement envisages confirmation of L/Cs, upon receipt of a request from the Exporter or the Exporter's Bank or the Indemnifying Party or the Importer's Bank. This arrangement would help reduce transaction costs, besides promoting trade intra-BRICS trade.

4.   These two Agreements are expected to enhance cooperation among the BRICS development banks and to significantly promote intra-BRICS trade.

I.2.   The Contingent Reserve Arrangement (CRA): 15 Jul. 2014, Fortaleza (BRA)

TREATY FOR THE ESTABLISHMENT OF
A BRICS CONTINGENT RESERVE ARRANGEMENT
15 JULY 2014 FORTALEZA (BRAZIL)

This BRICS Contingent Reserve Arrangement ("CRA") is between the Federative Republic of Brazil ("Brazil"), the Russian Federation ("Russia"), the Republic of India ("India"), the People's Republic of China ("China") and the Republic of South Africa ("South Africa") (henceforth referred to, individually, as "Party", and collectively, as the "Parties").

WHEREAS, the Parties agree to establish a self-managed contingent reserve arrangement to forestall short-term balance of payments pressures, provide mutual support and further strengthen financial stability.

WHEREAS, the Parties agree that this contingent reserve arrangement shall contribute to strengthening the global financial safety net and complement existing international monetary and financial arrangements.

THEREFORE, this Treaty sets out the terms and conditions of such contingent reserve arrangement, as follows:

Article 1 - Objective
The CRA is a framework for the provision of support through liquidity and precautionary instruments in response to actual or potential short-term balance of payments pressures.

Article 2 - Size and Individual Commitments
a.   The initial total committed resources of the CRA shall be one hundred billion dollars of the United States of America (USD 100 billion), with individual commitments as follows:

i. China – USD 41 billion

ii. Brazil – USD 18 billion

iii. Russia – USD 18 billion

iv. India – USD 18 billion

v. South Africa – USD 5 billion

b.   The Parties shall be entitled to make a request to access committed resources at any time. Until such time as one of the Parties (the "Requesting Party") makes such a request and that request is acceded to by the other Parties (the "Providing Parties") and effected through a currency swap, each Party shall retain full ownership rights in and possession of the resources that it commits to the CRA. While commitments shall not involve outright transfers of funds, committed resources shall be made available for any eligible request.

Article 3 - Governance and Decision-Making
a.   Governance of the CRA shall be constituted by a Council of CRA Governors (the "Governing Council") and a Standing Committee.

b.   The Governing Council shall comprise one Governor and one Alternate Governor appointed by each Party. Governors must be a Finance Minister, Central Bank Governor, or hold an equivalent post. The Governing Council shall take decisions by consensus and shall be responsible for high level and strategic decisions of the CRA. It is hereby authorized to:

i.   Review and modify the size of the committed resources of the CRA as well as approve changes in the size of individual commitments;

ii. Approve the entry of new countries as Parties to the CRA;

iii. Review and modify the CRA's instruments;

iv. Review and modify the framework for maturities, number of renewals, interest rates, spreads, and fees;

v. Review and modify the preconditions for drawings and renewals;

vi. Review and modify the provisions concerning default and sanctions;

vii. Review and modify the provisions concerning access limits and multipliers;

viii. Review and modify the percentage of access de-linked from IMF arrangements;

ix. Decide upon the creation of a permanent secretariat or the establishment of a dedicated surveillance unit;

x. Approve its own procedural rules;

xi. Review and modify the rules pertaining to the appointment and functions of the coordinator for the Governing Council and the Standing Committee;

xii. Review and modify voting power and decision rules of the Standing Committee;

xiii. Review and modify the authority and functions of the Standing Committee;

xiv. Approve the procedural rules concerning the functioning of the Standing Committee;

xv. Decide upon any other issues not specifically attributed to the Standing Committee.

c.   The Standing Committee shall be responsible for the executive level and operational decisions of the CRA and shall comprise one Director and one Alternate Director appointed by each Party; these shall be appointed from central bank officials unless decided otherwise by the respective Party. It is hereby authorized to:

i. Prepare and submit to the Governing Council its own procedural rules;

ii. Approve requests for support through the liquidity or precautionary instruments;

iii. Approve requests for renewals of support through the liquidity or precautionary instruments;

iv. Approve operational procedures for the liquidity and precautionary instruments;

v. In exceptional circumstances, determine the waiver of conditions of approval, safeguards and required documents under this Treaty;

vi. Approve a Party's encashment request;

vii. Decide whether to impose sanctions in case of a breach of this Treaty;

viii. Carry out other functions attributed to it by the Governing Council.

d.   As a matter of principle, the Standing Committee shall strive for consensus on all matters. The decisions of the Standing Committee pertaining to items C.ii and C.iii shall be taken by simple majority of weighted voting of Providing Parties. The decisions pertaining to items C.v, C.vi and C.vii shall be taken by consensus of the Providing Parties. All other decisions of the Standing Committee shall be taken by consensus.

e.   Whenever a decision is taken by weighted voting, the weight attributed to each Party's vote shall be determined as follows: (i) 5 percent of total voting power shall be equally distributed among the Parties; and (ii) the remainder shall be distributed among the Parties according to the relative size of individual commitments.

Article 4 - Instruments
The CRA shall include the following instruments:

i. A liquidity instrument to provide support in response to short-term balance of payments pressures.

ii. A precautionary instrument committing to provide support in light of potential short-term balance of payments pressures.

Article 5 - Access Limits and Multipliers

a.   The Parties shall be able to access resources subject to maximum access limits equal to a multiple of each Party's individual commitment set forth as follows:

    i.   China shall have a multiplier of 0.5

    ii.   Brazil shall have a multiplier of 1

    iii. Russia shall have a multiplier of 1

    iv. India shall have a multiplier of 1

    v.   South Africa shall have a multiplier of 2

b.   The total amount available under both the precautionary and the liquidity instruments shall not exceed the maximum access for each Party.

c.   A portion (the "De-linked portion"), equal to 30 percent of the maximum access for each Party, shall be available subject only to the agreement of the Providing Parties, which shall be granted whenever the Requesting Party meets the conditions stipulated in Article 14 of this Treaty.

d.   A portion (the "IMF-linked portion"), consisting of the remaining 70 percent of the maximum access, shall be available to the Requesting Party, subject to both:

    i.   The agreement of the Providing Parties, which shall be granted whenever the Requesting Party meets the conditions stipulated in Article 14, and;

    ii.   Evidence of the existence of an on-track arrangement between the IMF and the Requesting Party that involves a commitment of the IMF to provide financing to the Requesting Party based on conditionality, and the compliance of the Requesting Party with the terms and conditions of the arrangement.

e.   Both instruments defined in Article 4 shall have IMF-linked and De-linked portions.

f.   If a Requesting Party has an on-track arrangement with the IMF, it shall be able to access up to 100 percent of its maximum access limit, subject to the provisions under paragraph (d) above.

Article 6 - Inter-central Bank Agreement

In order to carry out the transactions under the liquidity and precautionary instruments mentioned in Article 1, the Central Bank of Brazil, the Central Bank of the Russian Federation, the Reserve Bank of India, the People's Bank of China and the South African Reserve Bank shall enter into an inter-central bank agreement setting out the required operational procedures and guidelines.

Article 7 - Currency Swaps

A Party may request support through one of the instruments specified in Article 4 according to the procedures established by the Standing Committee in accordance with Article 13 of this Treaty. Provision of USD to the Requesting Party shall be effected through currency swaps carried out between the Parties' central banks on the basis of common operational procedures to be defined by the Standing Committee in accordance with Article 3.C.iv and the inter-central bank agreement, entered into pursuant to Article 6.

Article 8 - Definitions

The following terms shall have the respective meanings specified in this Article:

"Requesting Party Currency" shall mean the currency of the Party that requests to draw funds through a currency swap;

"Swap Transaction" shall mean a transaction between the Requesting Party's central bank and a Providing Party's central bank by which the Requesting Party's central bank purchases US dollars (USD) from the Providing Party's central bank in exchange for the Requesting Party Currency, and repurchases on a later date the Requesting Party Currency in exchange for USD;

"Drawing" shall mean the purchase, at the Value Date (defined below), of USD by the Requesting Party's central bank;

"De-linked Drawing" shall mean a Drawing by the central bank of a Party that is not engaged in an IMF arrangement;

"IMF-linked Drawing" shall mean a Drawing by the central bank of a Party that is engaged in an IMF arrangement;

"Business Day" shall mean any day on which markets are open for business in all financial centers needed for the swap transactions to take place;

"Trade Date" of a Drawing or renewal of Drawing shall mean the date in which the spot market exchange rate for the Drawing or renewal of Drawing is established;

"Value Date" of a Drawing or renewal of Drawing shall mean the date the Requesting and Providing Parties' central banks credit each other's accounts. The Value Date shall be the second Business Day after the Trade Date;

"Maturity Date" of a Drawing or renewal of Drawing shall mean the date on which the Requesting Party's central bank shall repurchase the Requesting Party Currency in exchange for USD. If any such Maturity Date should fall on a day which is not a Business Day, the Maturity Date shall be the next Business Day.

Article 9 - Coordination

a.   The Party that chairs the BRICS shall act as coordinator for the Governing Council and for the Standing Committee.

b.   The coordinator shall: (i) convene and chair meetings of the Governing Council and the Standing Committee; (ii) coordinate voting as needed; (iii) provide secretariat services during its term; and (iv) inform the Parties of the activation or renewal of liquidity or precautionary instruments.

c.   Any Party requesting or receiving support through a liquidity or precautionary instrument – Article 4 – or opting out from participating as a Providing Party or asking for encashment of outstanding claims – Article 15(e) – shall not serve as coordinator. In this case, the next chair of the BRICS shall assume the role of coordinator.

Article 10 - Purchase and Repurchase under a Swap Transaction

a.   The exchange rate that shall apply to each purchase and repurchase under a Swap Transaction shall be based on the prevailing exchange rate (hereinafter referred to as "the Swap Exchange Rate") between the Requesting Party Currency and the USD in the Requesting Party's spot market on the Trade Date.

b.   The Requesting Party's central bank shall sell the Requesting Party Currency to the Providing Parties' central banks and purchase USD from them by means of a spot transaction, with a simultaneous agreement by the Requesting Party's central bank to sell USD and to repurchase the Requesting Party Currency from the Providing Parties' central banks on the maturity date. The same exchange rate (i.e., the rate of the spot leg) shall be applied to both the spot and the forward legs of the Swap Transaction.

c.   On the Maturity Date, the Requesting Party's central bank shall transfer the USD plus interest back to the Providing Parties' central banks in exchange for the Requesting Party Currency. No interest shall be accrued on the Requesting Party Currency.

Article 11 - Interest Rate Determination

a.   The interest rate to be paid by the Requesting Party on the USD purchased from the Providing Parties shall be an internationally accepted benchmark interest rate for the corresponding maturity of the swap transaction plus a spread. The spread shall increase periodically by a certain margin, up to a predetermined limit.

b.   In the case of the precautionary instrument, the amount committed but not drawn shall be subject to a commitment fee, to be specified in the inter-central bank agreement.

Article 12 - Maturities

a.   A De-linked Drawing under the liquidity instrument shall have a Maturity Date six months after the Value Date and may be renewed, in whole or in part, three times at most.

b.   An IMF-linked Drawing under the liquidity instrument shall have a Maturity Date one year after the Value Date and may be renewed, in whole or in part, two times at most.

c.   If the Requesting Party is not engaged in an IMF arrangement, access to the precautionary instrument shall have a tenure of six months and may be renewed, in whole or in part, three times at most.

d.   If the Requesting Party is engaged in an IMF arrangement, access to the precautionary instrument shall have a tenure of one year and may be renewed, in whole or in part, two times at most.

e.   The maturity of a De-linked Drawing under the precautionary instrument shall be of six months and that of an IMF-linked Drawing shall be of one year. The precautionary instrument, once drawn upon, shall not be renewed.

f.   The Requesting Party may repurchase the Requesting Party Currency in exchange for USD at the Swap Exchange Rate before the Maturity Date. In this case, the accrued interest rate shall be calculated on the basis of the actual number of days elapsed from (and including) the Value Date to (but not including) the early repurchase date.

Article 13 - Procedures for Requesting or Renewing Support through the Liquidity or Precautionary Instruments

a.   A Party that wishes to request support through the liquidity or precautionary instruments, or renewal of such support, shall notify the members of the Standing Committee of the type of instrument, the amount requested, and the envisaged starting date.

b.   The Requesting Party shall provide evidence that it complies with the safeguards specified in Article 14 below.

c.   Upon receiving the notification, the CRA coordinator shall convene a Standing Committee meeting to discuss and vote the Requesting Party's request. The Standing Committee shall decide upon the request up to seven days after its submission.

d.   Once a request for support through the liquidity instrument is approved, the Requesting Party's central bank and the Providing Parties' central banks shall activate Swap Transactions promptly, in a timeframe to be specified in the inter-central bank agreement.

e.   Once a request for a Drawing under an approved precautionary instrument is made, the Requesting Party's central bank and the Providing Parties' central banks shall activate Swap Transactions promptly, in a timeframe to be specified in the inter-central bank agreement.

f.   If the Requesting Party wishes to renew support through the liquidity instrument, it shall notify the members of the Standing Committee at least fourteen days before the Maturity Date.

g.   If the Requesting Party wishes to renew support through the precautionary instrument, it shall notify the members of the Standing Committee at least seven days before the expiration of access under such instrument.

Article 14 - Conditions of Approval, Safeguards and Required Documents

a.   When submitting a request for support through the liquidity or precautionary instrument, or renewal of such support, the Requesting Party shall sign and deliver a letter of acknowledgement committing to comply with all obligations and safeguards under this Treaty.

b.   The Requesting Party shall also comply with the following conditions and safeguards:

   (i)   Submit all required documents and economic and financial data, as specified by the Standing Committee, and provide clarification to comments;

(ii) Ensure that its obligations under this Treaty at all times constitute direct, unsubordinated and unsecured obligations ranking at least pari passu in right of payment with all other present or future direct, unsubordinated and unsecured foreign currency-denominated external indebtedness of the Requesting Party;

(iii) Have no arrears with the other Parties or their public financial institutions;

(iv) Have no arrears with multilateral and regional financial institutions, including the New Development Bank (NDB);

(v) Be in compliance with surveillance and provision of information obligations to the IMF as defined, respectively, in Articles IV, Sections 1 and 3, and VIII, Section 5, of the Articles of Agreement of said institution.

Article 15 - Burden Sharing, Opt-out and Encashment Provisions

a.   Providing Parties shall share the disbursement of drawings in proportion to their respective commitments to the CRA, subject to paragraphs (b) and (c) of this Article. In no event shall any Party be required to provide more resources than the amount that it has committed to provide in Article 2(a).

b.   The approval of a request for support through the liquidity or precautionary instruments under this Treaty suspends, for as long as such support is in place, the Requesting Party's commitment to participate as a Providing Party in any subsequent request for support through the liquidity or precautionary instruments.

c.   When a request for support through the liquidity or precautionary instruments, or for renewal of such support is presented, a Party may opt-out from participating as a Providing Party, provided this is justified by its balance of payments and reserve position or by an event of force majeure, such as a war or natural disaster. The Party opting-out shall provide the necessary information to justify its decision. In this case, the other Providing Parties shall provide resources to allow opt-out in proportion to their commitments to the CRA, subject to paragraph (a) of this Article.

d.   A Providing Party may request encashment of outstanding claims provided this is justified by its balance of payments and reserve position or by an event of force majeure, such as a war or natural disaster. The Providing Party applying for encashment shall provide the necessary information to justify its request. If the request is approved, the other Providing Parties shall provide resources to allow encashment in proportion to their commitments to the CRA, subject to paragraph (a) of this Article.

e.   A Party that has opted-out or encashed from an outstanding currency swap or has opted out from an outstanding precautionary instrument shall not serve as a coordinator, as defined in Article 9, for the length of the transaction from which the party has opted-out or encashed.

Article 16 - Breaches of Obligations and Sanctions

a.   Failure by a Requesting Party to fulfill payment obligations on the Maturity Date of a Drawing or a renewal of Drawing, unless corrected within 7 days, shall result in the following:

(i) all outstanding obligations of the Requesting Party to repay the Providing Parties under this Treaty shall be immediately due and payable;

(ii) the Requesting Party's eligibility to further Drawings or renewals of Drawings under this Treaty shall be suspended;

(iii) any undrawn portion of a precautionary instrument of the Requesting Party shall be cancelled; and

(iv) any payments by the Requesting Party of its overdue obligations to the Providing Parties must be made on the same date and in proportion to the amounts due to each Party.

b.   In case of an event of force majeure, the application of the measures above may be suspended.

c.   In case of a persistent and/or unjustified delay in settling overdue payment obligations, a Requesting Party's right to participate in any decisions under this Treaty may be suspended. After 30 days of unfulfilled payment obligations, the Providing Parties should consider whether this action is appropriate.

d.   If, after the expiration of a reasonable period following the decision under paragraph (c), the Requesting Party persists in its failure to settle overdue payment obligations, the Governing Council may require the Requesting Party to withdraw from this Treaty.

e.   The Requesting Party in breach of a payment obligation should agree to take measures that preserve the net present value of its obligations if the Providing Parties collectively decide to exercise this option.

f.   In case the Providing Parties decide by consensus at the Governing Council level, the Requesting Party in breach of a payment obligation should agree to a novation of its obligations under this Treaty, including by issuing marketable debt securities that would not be subject to the Requesting Party's jurisdiction. The Requesting Party should not unreasonably withhold consent to terms and conditions of such debt securities as shall be required by the Providing Parties.

g.   The Requesting Party would be liable to a late fee in addition to the interest rate applied to the swap transaction to which payment is overdue. This late fee should increase periodically by a certain margin, up to a predetermined limit.

h.   In case of a breach of any obligation under this Treaty, other than failure by a Requesting Party to fulfill payment obligations, the following sanctions may apply:

  (i)   all outstanding payment obligations under this Treaty shall be immediately due and payable;
  (ii)   eligibility to further Drawings or renewals of Drawings under this Treaty shall be suspended;
  (iii)   any undrawn portion of a precautionary instrument shall be cancelled;
  (iv)   the right to participate in any decisions under this Treaty may be suspended;
  (v)   after the expiration of a reasonable period following the decision under item (iv), the Governing Council may require the Party to withdraw from this Treaty.

i.   The sanctions applied should be commensurate with the severity of the breach.

Article 17 - Language and Communications

a.   The official language of the CRA shall be English. The English language versions of this Treaty and of any documentation under it shall be the official versions. All written and oral communication between the Parties shall be in English, unless the Parties otherwise agree in writing.

b.   Any notice, request, document or other communication submitted under this Treaty shall be in writing, shall refer to this Treaty, and shall be deemed fully given or sent when delivered in accordance with the contact details that shall be provided separately by each Party.

Article 18 - Representation and Warranties

Each of the Parties hereby warrants and represents that:

a.   It has the full power and authority to enter into and perform its obligations under this Treaty and shall provide evidence of such authority if requested by any other Party;

b.   This Treaty and the performance by it of its obligations under this Treaty do not contravene any law or other restriction binding upon it or any of its property, and there is no legal or regulatory hindrance which could affect the legality, validity or enforceability of this Treaty or of obligations hereunder or have a material adverse effect upon its ability to perform such obligations;

c.   All transactions under this Treaty shall be exempt from any administrative or legal obstacles to their completion;

d.   All payments by it under this Treaty shall be made without withholding or deduction for, or on account of, any present or future taxes, duties, assessments or governmental charges of whatever nature imposed or levied by or on behalf of its country or any authority therein or thereof having power to tax. In the event that the withholding or deduction of such taxes, duties, assessments or governmental charges is required by law, it shall pay such additional amounts as may be necessary in order that the net amounts received by the other Parties after such withholding or deduction shall equal the amounts which would have been received under this Treaty in the absence of such withholding or deduction; and

e.   It shall not assign, transfer, delegate, charge or otherwise deal in its obligations under this Treaty without prior written consent of the other Parties.

Article 19 - Legal Status of the CRA

The CRA does not possess independent international legal personality and cannot enter into agreements, sue or be sued.

Article 20 - Dispute Settlement

a.   Any disputes relating to the interpretation of this Treaty shall be solved by consultations in the Governing Council.

b.   If any dispute, controversy or claim relating to the performance, interpretation, construction, breach, termination or invalidity of any provision in this Treaty shall arise and not be resolved amicably by the Governing Council within a reasonable period, it shall be settled by arbitration in accordance with the Arbitration Rules of the United Nations Commission on International Trade Law (excluding Article 26 thereof) in effect on the date of this Treaty (the "UNCITRAL Arbitration Rules"). In case of resorting to arbitration, the language to be used in the proceedings shall be English and the number of arbitrators shall be three.

c.   The Parties agree that in any such arbitration and in any legal proceedings for the recognition of an award rendered in an arbitration conducted pursuant to this Article, including any proceeding required for the purposes of converting an arbitral award into a judgment, they shall not raise any defense which they could not raise but for the fact that they are sovereign state entities.

Article 21 - Withdrawal from and Termination of the Treaty

a.   A Party may withdraw from this Treaty by giving notice of such intention to the other Parties six months prior to the date of the envisaged withdrawal. However, withdrawal from the Treaty by any Party is not allowed for a period of five years from its entry into force.

b.   During this six-month period, the Party that has given notice of such intention shall provide the other Parties with an opportunity to express views on its intention but does not have the right to request or the obligation to provide resources.

c.   In the event that any obligation under this Treaty, including any obligation for the payment of money, remains outstanding at the time of termination of or withdrawal from this Treaty, all the terms and conditions of this Treaty (except for those entitling the Parties to any Drawing or renewal of a Drawing) shall continue to apply until such obligation has been fulfilled.

Article 22 - Acceptance, Depositary and Amendments

a.   This Treaty shall be subject to acceptance, ratification or approval, according to the respective domestic procedures of the Parties.

b.   The instruments of acceptance, ratification or approval shall be deposited with the Federative Republic of Brazil, which shall be the depositary of this Treaty.

c.   The depositary shall promptly inform all Parties of: (i) the date of deposit of each instrument of acceptance, ratification or approval (ii) the date of the entry into force of this Treaty and of any amendments and changes thereto, and (iii) the date of receipt of a withdrawal notice.

d.   If the Party that acts as depositary decides to withdraw from this Treaty, all the terms and conditions of Article 21 shall apply, with the exception that: (i) the depositary shall give notice of its intention to the other Parties; and (ii) as of the date of receipt of the depositary's withdrawal notice, the role of depositary shall be assumed by one of the other Parties, as agreed upon by them.

e.   This Treaty shall not be subject to unilateral reservations.

f.   Any proposal to amend this Treaty shall be communicated to the Party that acts as coordinator for the Governing Council, which shall then bring the proposal before the Governing Council. If the proposed amendment is approved, the coordinator shall ask all Parties whether they accept the proposed amendment. If a Party, according to its domestic procedures, accepts the proposed amendment, it shall notify the depositary accordingly. The amendment shall become effective on the date of receipt of the last notification. Any decision of the Governing Council related to modifying Article 2 shall be considered an amendment.

Article 23 - Entry into Force

This Treaty shall enter into force 30 (thirty) days after the deposit of the fifth instrument of acceptance, according to each Party's legal requirements.

Done in Fortaleza on the 15th of July of 2014, in five originals in English, one for each.

I.3.   The BRICS Agreement on Culture: 9 Jul. 2015, Ufa (RUS)

AGREEMENT
BETWEEN THE GOVERNMENTS OF THE BRICS STATES
ON COOPERATION IN THE FIELD OF CULTURE

The Governments of the Federative Republic of Brazil, the Russian Federation, the Republic of India, the People's Republic of China and the Republic of South Africa (BRICS), hereinafter referred to as the "Parties",

pursuant to the declarations made during the BRICS Summits in the cities of Sanya, Delhi, Durban, and Fortaleza,

being aware of the importance of broadening and deepening the cooperation in the field of culture,

being convinced that cultural dialogue contributes to the progress of nations and better mutual understanding of cultures, facilitating rapprochement of peoples, being firmly committed to the BRICS values in the spirit of openness, inclusiveness, equality, respect for cultural diversity, and mutual respect and learning,

have agreed as follows:

Article 1

In accordance with this Agreement, and laws and policies of their states, the Parties shall develop and promote cooperation and exchanges in the field of culture, including the art of music and dancing, choreography, theatre, circus, archives, publishing and libraries, museums, cultural heritage, fine, decorative and applied arts, audio-visual works, and in other creative activities provided for by this Agreement.

Article 2

The Parties shall cooperate in the sphere of training and skills upgrading of culture and art professionals and heritage practitioners in specific areas.

The Parties shall facilitate exchanges of scientific and research workers, academics, experts and students in the framework of programmes of interest, and develop joint programmes between institutions of culture, art and training of relevant specialists in the Parties' states.

The competent authorities of the Parties shall exchange information on cultural activities taking place in their states involving exchanges of creative and scientific experience. The Parties also encourage the participation of their representatives in such activities.

Article 3

In accordance with their international obligations and laws and policies of their states, the Parties shall cooperate in preventing illicit import, export and transfer of ownership of cultural property of their states, and exchange relevant information in this regard.

Article 4

The Parties recognise the contribution of cultural heritage to the sustainable development agenda, and shall cooperate on programmes in this regard.

The Parties shall promote enhanced cooperation in such fields as protection, preservation, restoration, return and utilisation of cultural heritage objects.

The Parties shall provide mutual support and assistance in the management of cultural heritage sites and submission of applications for inscription of such sites in the World Heritage List.

The Parties shall also promote enhanced cooperation in the field of safeguarding or protection (as the case may be under the laws and regulations of the Parties' states), and promotion of intangible cultural heritage.

Article 5

The Parties shall promote the development of cooperation in the audio-visual field.

National agencies and organizations of their States are encouraged to:

- have screenings of audio-visual works and participation of audio-visual professionals in international activities as per the rules and regulations of the Parties' states;
- work on joint projects with a view to facilitating co-production and exchanges of audio-visual works.

Article 6

The Parties shall assist in developing and facilitating widest possible cooperation in the field of popular and traditional expressions of culture, including organization of exhibitions, festivals, national culture days, traditional festivities and performances of traditional cultural groups within the framework of activities held in their respective States.

Article 7

The Parties shall have consultations and develop cooperation on matters of common interest in the fields of traditional knowledge and cultural expressions.

Article 8

The Parties shall encourage exchanges of young creative teams and young performers for participation in international youth programmes, creative meetings, open-air and youth festivals of arts.

Article 9

For the purposes of facilitating mutual understanding and intercultural cooperation, the Parties shall encourage the exchange of copies of documents and materials related to the culture, history, social and political development of their States.

Article 10

The Parties shall encourage cooperation and exchanges, including through exhibitions, amongst libraries and museums of their States.

Article 11

The Parties shall encourage exchanges and cooperation in the fields of printing and publishing, participation in international book fairs, translation into the languages of the Parties, and support the exchange of visits by the staff of the government and corporate publishing sectors.

Article 12

The Parties will promote cooperation and exchange of experiences between agencies of cultural and education sectors working in the field of creative industries, as a pillar of sustainable development, especially from the viewpoint of research, monitoring, information systems, business support and creative entrepreneurship, and capacity building and skill development of professional staff.

Article 13

Specific terms (including financial ones) of the activities being organized shall be determined through direct consultations between competent authorities of the Parties concerned.

Article 14

Where necessary, the Parties may develop specific programmes of cooperation in arts, culture and heritage and other related spheres.

Article 15

The present Agreement does not restrict the right of the Parties to engage in bilateral and other multilateral cultural exchange programmes.

Article 16

Any amendment to this Agreement shall be made by agreement of all of the Parties, executed in the form of a separate protocol, which shall enter into force according to the procedure established in Article 21.

Article 17

In case of any disagreement among the Parties as to interpretation and/or implementation of this Agreement, the Parties shall seek an amicable resolution of such disagreement by negotiation and consultation through diplomatic channels.

Article 18

The English language shall be used as a working language for cooperation in the framework of the implementation of this Agreement.

Article 19

This Agreement shall not affect any rights and obligations of each of the Parties under any other international treaties to which they are parties.

Article 20

Unless the Parties agree otherwise, termination of this Agreement shall not affect the implementation of programmes and activities agreed upon before the termination of this Agreement.

Article 21

The Government of the Russian Federation shall be the Depositary of this Agreement.

This Agreement shall be concluded for an indefinite period and shall take effect on the date when the Depositary receives the last written notification of completion by each Party signatory to it of the internal procedures necessary for giving effect.

Any Party may withdraw from this Agreement by written notice sent to the Depositary at least three months before the date of withdrawal. The Depositary shall notify the other Parties of such intention within 30 days of receipt of such notice. Such withdrawal does not affect the implementation of programmes and activities agreed upon before the withdrawal comes into effect. The Agreement shall remain in force for the other Parties. Done in XX on the XXXX, 2015, in one original in the English language. The original copy of this Agreement shall be deposited with the Depositary that shall send a certified copy of this Agreement to each Party.

II.   BRICS SUMMIT MEETINGS BY THE HEADS OF STATE

II.1.   10th BRICS Summit 2018: 27 Jul. 2018, Johannesburg (ZAF)

A.   The Johannesburg Declaration 2018

10TH BRICS SUMMIT
JOHANNESBURG DECLARATION
BRICS in Africa:
Collaboration for Inclusive Growth and Shared Prosperity in the 4th Industrial
Revolution
Johannesburg, South Africa, 25-27 July 2018

Preamble

1.   We, the Heads of State and Government of the Federative Republic of Brazil, the Russian Federation, the Republic of India, the People's Republic of China and the Republic of South Africa, met from 25 - 27 July 2018 in Johannesburg, at the 10th BRICS Summit. The 10th BRICS Summit, as a milestone in the history of BRICS, was held under the theme "BRICS in Africa: Collaboration for Inclusive Growth and Shared Prosperity in the 4th Industrial Revolution".

2.   We are meeting on the occasion of the centenary of the birth of Nelson Mandela and we recognise his values, principles and dedication to the service of humanity and acknowledge his contribution to the struggle for democracy internationally and the promotion of the culture of peace throughout the world.

3.   We commend South Africa for the Johannesburg Summit thrust on development, inclusivity and mutual prosperity in the context of technology driven industrialisation and growth.

4.   We, the Heads of State and Government, express satisfaction regarding the achievements of BRICS over the last ten years as a strong demonstration of BRICS cooperation toward the attainment of peace, harmony and shared development and prosperity, and deliberated on ways to consolidate them further.

5.   We reaffirm our commitment to the principles of mutual respect, sovereign equality, democracy, inclusiveness and strengthened collaboration. As we build upon the successive BRICS Summits, we further commit ourselves to enhancing our strategic partnership for the benefit of our people through the promotion of peace, a fairer international order, sustainable development and inclusive growth, and to strengthening the three-pillar-driven cooperation in the areas of economy, peace and security and people-to-people exchanges.

6.   We recommit ourselves to a world of peace and stability, and support the central role of the United Nations, the purposes and principles enshrined in the UN Charter and respect for international law, promoting democracy and the rule of law. We reinforce our commitment to upholding multilateralism and to working together on the implementation of the 2030 Sustainable Development Goals as we foster a more representative, democratic, equitable, fair and just international political and economic order.

7.   We reiterate our determination to work together to strengthen multilateralism and the rule of law in international relations, and to promote a fair, just, equitable, democratic and representative international order.

8. We recommit our support for multilateralism and the central role of the United Nations in international affairs and uphold fair, just and equitable international order based on the purposes and principles enshrined in the Charter of the United Nations, respect for international law, promoting democracy and the rule of law in international relations, and to address common traditional and non-traditional security challenges.

9. We welcome the hosting of the BRICS-Africa Outreach and second BRICS Plus Cooperation with Emerging Markets and Developing Countries (EMDCs) during the Johannesburg Summit.

10. We express satisfaction at the outcomes of Ministerial Meetings that have been held (Annex 1) and look forward to the remainder of meetings to be held under the 2018 BRICS Calendar of Events.

Strengthening Multilateralism, Reforming Global Governance and Addressing Common Challenges

11. We reaffirm our commitment to the United Nations, as the universal multilateral organisation entrusted with the mandate for maintaining international peace and security, advancing global development and promoting and protecting human rights.

12. We reaffirm our commitment to the purposes and principles enshrined in the Charter of the United Nations, and support for the United Nations as the universal intergovernmental organisation entrusted with the responsibility for maintaining international peace and security, advancing sustainable development as well as ensuring the promotion, and protection of human rights and fundamental freedoms.

13. We reiterate our commitment to the strengthening of multilateral institutions of global governance to ensure that they are able to comprehensively address global challenges.

14. We also recognise the inherent strength of regional initiatives in support of the objectives of the broader multilateral system.

15. We further reaffirm our commitment to the centrality of the universal collective security system enshrined in the UN Charter. We recognize the importance of working towards an international system based on international law, with the UN Charter as its fundamental cornerstone, which fosters cooperation and stability in a multipolar order. We note the long overdue outstanding task of ensuring the adequate representation of African States in the UN, especially in peace and security matters.

16. Faced with international challenges requiring our cooperative efforts, we reiterate our commitment to shaping a more fair, just and representative multipolar international order to the shared benefit of humanity, in which the general prohibition of the use of force is fully upheld and which excludes the imposition of unilateral coercive measures outside the framework of the UN Charter. We emphasise the indivisible nature of peace and security and reiterate that no country should enhance its security at the expense of the security of others.

17. We recall the 2005 World Summit Outcome document and reaffirm the need for a comprehensive reform of the UN, including its Security Council, with a view to making it more representative, effective and efficient, and to increase the representation of the developing countries so that it can adequately respond to global challenges. China and Russia reiterate the importance they attach to the status and role of Brazil, India and South Africa in international affairs and support their aspiration to play a greater role in the UN.

18. We underscore the importance of sustained efforts aimed at making the United Nations more effective and efficient in implementing its mandates. We encourage further collaboration amongst the BRICS countries on a better resourced UN, on its administration and budget, on preserving the UN's Member State-driven character and ensuring better oversight of and strengthening the Organisation.

19. We express our support for continued cooperation of BRICS members in areas of mutual interest including through regular exchanges amongst their multilateral Missions.

20. We reaffirm our commitment to fully implementing the 2030 Agenda for Sustainable Development and the Sustainable Development Goals (SDGs), to provide equitable, inclusive, open, all-round innovation-driven and sustainable development, in its three dimensions – economic, social and environmental - in a balanced and integrated manner, towards the ultimate goal of eradicating poverty by 2030. We pledge our support for the important role of the United Nations, including the High Level Political Forum on Sustainable Development (HLPF), in coordinating and reviewing global implementation of the 2030 Agenda, to reform the UN Development System with a view to enhancing its capability in supporting member States in implementing the 2030 Agenda. We urge developed countries to honour their Official Development Assistance (ODA) commitments fully in time and to provide additional development resources to developing countries.

21. Regarding Climate Change, we welcome the progress towards finalizing the Work Programme under the Paris Agreement and express our willingness to continue working constructively with other Parties to conclude its related negotiations at the United Nations Framework Convention on Climate Change (UNFCCC) towards the 24th Conference of the Parties (UNFCCC COP24) to be held in Katowice, Poland in December 2018. We call upon all countries to fully implement the Paris Agreement adopted under the principles of the UNFCCC including the principles of common but differentiated responsibilities and respective capabilities, and urge developed countries to provide financial, technological and capacity-building support to developing countries to enhance their capability in mitigation and adaptation.

22. We undertake to strengthen BRICS cooperation in energy, especially in transitioning to more environmentally sustainable energy systems supportive of the global sustainable development agenda, balanced economic growth and the collective socio-economic wellbeing of our citizens. We continue to strive toward universal energy access, energy security, energy affordability, reduced pollution and environmental conservation. We reaffirm that the diversification of energy supply sources, including renewable and low carbon energy sources, investments in energy and energy infrastructure, energy industry and market development and intra-BRICS collaboration for access to primary energy sources will continue to underpin our energy security. We recognise the need to accelerate energy transition including in transportation, heating and industry uses.

23. We acknowledge the importance of energy efficiency and the popularisation of an energy efficient life style in virtue of its potential contributions to energy security, industrial competitiveness, emissions reduction, economic growth, job creation and other areas when introduced.

24. We acknowledge that the BRICS Ministers of Energy agreed to establish the BRICS Energy Research Cooperation Platform and to develop its Terms of Reference, and note the ongoing discussions for that purpose.

25. We reaffirm and support the establishment of the BRICS Agricultural Research Platform (ARP) initiated by India in 2016. We appreciate the fundamental importance of research, development and innovation in global sustainability and competitiveness. We endeavour to strengthen the agricultural research collaborative networks among the BRICS countries to enhance the resilience of the collective agricultural and food systems in the face of the changing climate. We recognise the need for follow-up steps in implementing the aims and objectives of the ARP. We commit to step up intra-BRICS collaboration including within the frame of the Agriculture Research Platform and the Basic Agriculture Information Exchange System (BAIES).

26. We acknowledge the outcomes of the 4th BRICS Environment Ministers Meeting which was held under the theme "Strengthening cooperation amongst BRICS on Circular Economy in the context of the Sustainable Consumption and Production (SCP)". We note that the circular economy approach represents enormous potential to reduce waste, to forge more environmentally sustainable processes, diversify our economies whilst contributing to economic growth and job creation.

27. We acknowledge the outcomes of the successive BRICS Environment Ministers' Meetings including the implementation of the Environmentally Friendly Technology Platform, Clean Rivers

Umbrella Programme and the Partnership for Urban Environment Sustainability Initiative. The progress in the establishment of the BRICS Environmentally Sound Technology (BEST) Cooperation Platform is acknowledged, which is intended to be practical and results orientated, and would include partners, science organisations, civil society, private sector and financial institutions.

28. We welcome the commitment to enhance cooperation in the field of water on the basis of sustainable development in an integrated way, addressing the themes of water access flood protection, drought management, water supply and sanitation, water and climate, systematically facilitating water pollution prevention and control, river and lake ecosystem restoration and preservation, ecosystem conservation, and water resources management.

29. We acknowledge the BRICS Meeting of Heads of Disaster Management in Buffalo City, wherein the Action Plan 2018-2020, was adopted and the first meeting of the BRICS Joint Task Force was held to further enhance our cooperation in this field.

30. We reaffirm the intention to enhance cooperation and collaboration amongst BRICS countries in the field of biodiversity conservation, sustainable use and equitable access and benefit sharing of biological resources, and also undertake to promote our cooperation in biodiversity-related international conventions and fora including on endangered species and amongst our National Parks authorities.

31. We recognise the vast potential in cooperation and collaboration in advancing the Oceans Economy amongst BRICS countries, which encompasses multiple sectors, including the strategic areas of maritime transport, shipbuilding, offshore oil and exploration, aquaculture, port development, research and technology, conservation and sustainable use of marine resources, marine and coastal tourism, financial and insurance services, as well as coastal industrial zone development.

32. We remain committed to the continued implementation of the Agenda for BRICS cooperation on population matters 2015-2020, which was agreed to by the Ministers responsible for Population Matters in 2014, because the dynamics of population age structure changes in BRICS countries pose challenges and present opportunities, particularly with regard to gender inequality and women's rights, youth development, employment and the future of work, urbanisation, migration and ageing.

33. We deplore the continued terrorist attacks, including in some BRICS countries. We condemn terrorism in all its forms and manifestations wherever committed and by whomsoever. We urge concerted efforts to counter terrorism under the UN auspices on a firm international legal basis and express our conviction that a comprehensive approach is necessary to ensure an effective fight against terrorism. We recall the responsibility of all States to prevent financing of terrorist networks and terrorist actions from their territories.

34. We call upon the international community to establish a genuinely broad international counter-terrorism coalition and support the UN's central coordinating role in this regard. We stress that the fight against terrorism must be conducted in accordance with international law, including the Charter of the United Nations, international refugee and humanitarian law, human rights and fundamental freedoms. We reaffirm our commitment on increasing the effectiveness of the UN counter-terrorism framework, including in the areas of cooperation and coordination among the relevant UN entities, designation of terrorists and terrorist groups and technical assistance to Members States. We call for expeditious finalisation and adoption of the Comprehensive Convention on International Terrorism (CCIT) by the United Nations General Assembly.

35. To address the threat of chemical and biological terrorism, we support and emphasise the need for launching multilateral negotiations on an international convention for the suppression of acts of chemical and biological terrorism, including at the Conference on Disarmament.

36. We firmly believe that those responsible for committing, organising, or supporting terrorist acts must be held accountable. We call upon all nations to adopt a comprehensive approach in combating

terrorism, which should include countering radicalisation, recruitment, travel of Foreign Terrorist Fighters, blocking sources and channels of terrorist financing including, for instance, through organised crime by means of money-laundering, supply of weapons, drug trafficking and other criminal activities, dismantling terrorist bases, and countering misuse of the Internet by terrorist entities through misuse of the latest Information and Communication Technologies (ICTs).

37. We reaffirm the importance of the elaboration under the UN auspices of rules, norms and principles of responsible behaviour of States in ensuring security in the use of ICTs.

38. We embrace the undeniable benefits and new opportunities brought about by the advances in ICTs, especially in the context of the 4th industrial revolution. However, these advances also bring with them new challenges and threats resultant from the growing misuse of ICTs for criminal activities, the increasing malicious use of ICTs by state and non-state actors. In this regard, we stress the importance of international cooperation against terrorist and criminal use of ICTs and therefore reiterate the need to develop a universal regulatory binding instrument on combatting the criminal use of ICTs within the UN. We acknowledge the progress made in promoting cooperation according to the BRICS Roadmap of Practical Cooperation on Ensuring Security in the Use of ICTs or any other mutually agreed mechanism. We also acknowledge the importance to establish a framework of cooperation among BRICS member States on ensuring security in the Use of ICTs and, in this regard, BRICS member States will work towards consideration and elaboration of a BRICS intergovernmental agreement on cooperation on this matter.

Strengthening and Consolidating BRICS Cooperation in International Peace and Security

39. We reaffirm our commitment to collective efforts for peaceful settlement of disputes through political and diplomatic means, and recognise the role of the UN Security Council as bearing the primary responsibility for maintaining international peace and security.

40. We express our concern over the ongoing conflict and heightened tensions in the Middle-East region and our conviction that there is no place for unlawful resorting to force or external interference in any conflict and that, ultimately, lasting peace can only be established through broad-based, inclusive national dialogue with due respect for the independence, territorial integrity and sovereignty of each of the countries of the region. We agree that, in each of the countries in the region, citizens have legitimate aspirations to fully enjoy civil, political, economic, social and cultural rights and fundamental freedoms, especially with regard to the Israeli-Palestinian situation.

41. We agree that the conflicts elsewhere in the Middle East and North Africa should not be used to delay resolution of long-standing conflicts, in particular the Palestinian-Israeli conflict. We reiterate the need for renewed diplomatic efforts to achieve a just, lasting and comprehensive settlement of the Israeli-Palestinian conflict in order to achieve peace and stability in the Middle East on the basis of relevant United Nations resolutions, the Madrid Principles, the Arab Peace Initiative and previous agreements between the parties, through negotiations with a view to creating an independent, viable, territorially contiguous Palestinian State living side by side in peace and security with Israel. We reiterate that the status of Jerusalem is one of the final status issues to be defined in the context of negotiations between Israel and Palestine. With regard to the situation in Gaza, we reiterate our support to the UN General Assembly Resolution (A/RES/ES-10/20) on the protection of the Palestinian population and call for its full implementation.

42. We reiterate our support for the United Nations Relief and Works Agency for Palestine Refugees in the Near East (UNRWA). We commend its vital role in providing health, education and other basic services for almost 5.3 million Palestinian refugees and underscore its relevance to bringing stability to the region and the need for ensuring a more adequate, sufficient, predictable and sustained funding for the Agency.

43. The ongoing conflict and major humanitarian crisis in the Republic of Yemen are also causes for further concern. We call for unhindered access for the provision of humanitarian assistance to all parts of Yemen and urge the international community to expeditiously provide the necessary

assistance. We urge all parties to fully respect international law, to cease hostilities and to return to the UN brokered peace talks, leading to an inclusive Yemeni-led dialogue towards the achievement of a political solution to the conflict.

44. We also call on all parties directly involved in the current diplomatic crisis in the Gulf region to overcome their dissensions through dialogue and welcome the efforts of Kuwait in this regard.

45. We reaffirm our support for the process of an "Afghan-led, Afghan-owned" national peace and reconciliation process. We express our concern over the deteriorating situation in Afghanistan particularly the increase in the number and intensity of terrorist-related attacks on the Afghan National Security Forces, the Government and civilians. We call on the international community to assist the government and the people of Afghanistan with the objective of working towards the realisation of peace. We also welcome the Parliamentary elections that are scheduled to be held in October 2018 and the Presidential elections in 2019.

46. We reaffirm our commitment for a political resolution of the conflict in Syria, through an inclusive "Syrian-led, Syrian-owned" political process that safeguards the state sovereignty, independence and territorial integrity of Syria, in pursuance of United Nations Security Council Resolution 2254 (2015) and taking into account the result of the Congress of the Syrian National Dialogue in Sochi. We reiterate our support for the Geneva process and the mediation offered by the UN, as well as the Astana process which has been showing signs of positive developments on the ground, and stress the complementarity between the two initiatives. We reaffirm our commitment to a peaceful resolution in Syria and our opposition to measures that run contrary to the UN Charter and the authority of the United Nations Security Council (UNSC) and that do not contribute to advancing the political process. We also highlighted the importance of unity in the fight against terrorist organisations in Syria in full observance of the relevant UNSC Resolutions. We reiterate our strong condemnation of the use of chemical weapons by any party, for any purpose and under any circumstances and renew calls for comprehensive, objective, independent, and transparent investigations of all alleged incidents. We call for enhanced efforts to provide necessary humanitarian assistance to the Syrian people, bearing in mind urgent reconstruction needs.

47. Recalling the Joint Comprehensive Plan of Action (JCPOA) on the Iranian nuclear programme we call upon all parties to fully comply with their obligations and ensure full and effective implementation of the JCPOA to promote international and regional peace and security.

48. We welcome recent developments to achieve the complete denuclearisation of the Korean Peninsula and maintain peace and stability in North East Asia. We reaffirm the commitment for a peaceful, diplomatic and political solution to the situation.

49. We express our serious concern about the possibility of an arms race in outer space and of outer space turning into an arena for military confrontation. We reaffirm that the prevention of an arms race, including of the placement of weapons in outer space, would avert a grave danger for international peace and security. We emphasise the paramount importance of strict compliance with the existing legal regime providing for the peaceful use of outer space. We also reaffirm that there is a need to consolidate and reinforce this regime. We welcome the newly established Group of Governmental Experts to discuss possible elements for a legally binding instrument on the prevention of an arms race in outer space including inter alia, on the prevention of the placement of weapons in outer space. We stress that practical transparency and confidence building measures may also contribute towards non-placement of weapons in outer space. We reiterate that the Conference on Disarmament, as the single multilateral disarmament negotiating forum, has the primary role in the negotiation of a multilateral agreement or agreements, as appropriate, on the prevention of an arms race in outer space in all its aspects.

50. We welcome South Africa's hosting of the Meeting of BRICS Ministers of Foreign Affairs/International Relations in Pretoria on 4 June 2018. The Ministers exchanged views on major global political, security, economic and financial issues of common concern and on strengthening

BRICS cooperation. We look forward to the forthcoming Meeting of the BRICS Ministers of Foreign Affairs/International Relations on the margins of the 73rd Session of the United Nations General Assembly.

51. We welcome the 8 th Meeting of the BRICS High Representatives for Security held on 28 and 29 June 2018 in Durban, and commend them for enriching BRICS' dialogue on the global security environment, counter-terrorism, security in the use of ICTs, major international and regional hotspots, transnational organised crime, peacekeeping, as well as the linkage between national security and development issues.

52. We emphasise the important role of United Nations peacekeeping to international peace and security, and the contribution of BRICS countries in this regard. We recognise the need for BRICS countries to further enhance mutual communication and cooperation on peacekeeping matters at the United Nations and the South African initiative for a BRICS working group on peacekeeping in this regard.

53. We commend the African Union for its efforts aimed at resolving and managing conflicts on the continent and welcome the strengthening of the cooperation between the United Nations Security Council and the African Union Peace and Security Council. We commend the African Union's commitment to the "Silencing of the Guns by 2020" and support efforts to strengthen the African Peace and Security Architecture.

BRICS Partnership for Global Economic Recovery, Reform of Financial and Economic Global Governance Institutions, and the Fourth Industrial Revolution

54. We welcome that the global economy has continued to improve, while noting that growth has been less synchronised and that downside risks still remain. This is reflected in a variety of challenges including rising trade conflicts, geopolitical risks, commodity price volatility, high private and public indebtedness, inequality and not sufficiently inclusive growth. We understand the critical importance of ensuring that the benefits from growth are shared in a more inclusive manner. We further stress the importance of a favourable external environment for sustained growth of global trade.

55. BRICS economies continue to support global economic expansion and outlook. We advocate continued use of fiscal, monetary and structural policies in concert, to forge strong, sustainable, balanced and inclusive growth. We express concern at the spill-over effects of macro-economic policy measures in some major advanced economies that may cause economic and financial volatility in emerging economies and impact their growth prospects adversely. We call on major advanced and emerging market economies to continue policy dialogue and coordination in the context of the G20, FSB and other fora to address these potential risks.

56. Recalling the Johannesburg Summit's focus on the 4th Industrial Revolution and the outcomes of the BRICS Meetings of Science and Technology and Industry Ministers, we commend the establishment of the BRICS Partnership on New Industrial Revolution (PartNIR). To commence the full operationalisation of PartNIR, an Advisory Group will be set up, comprising of respective representatives of BRICS Ministries of Industry, in consultation with appropriate Ministries, to develop, as a first step, the Terms of Reference and a Work Plan aligned with the 4th Industrial Revolution priorities, to be submitted to the BRICS Chair. The PartNIR aims at deepening BRICS cooperation in digitalisation, industrialisation, innovation, inclusiveness and investment, to maximise the opportunities and address the challenges arising from the 4th Industrial Revolution. It should enhance comparative advantages, boost economic growth, promote economic transformation of BRICS countries, strengthen sustainable industrial production capacity, create networks of science parks and technology business incubators, and support small and medium-sized enterprises in technology intensive areas. We believe that the initiative to establish the BRICS Networks of Science Parks, Technology Business Incubators and Small and Medium-sized Enterprises is a promising step in that direction.

57. We recognise the critical and positive role the internet plays globally in promoting economic, social and cultural development. In this regard, we commit to continue to work together through the existing mechanisms to contribute to the secure, open, peaceful, cooperative and orderly use of ICTs on the basis of participation by all states on an equal footing in the evolution and functioning of the internet and its governance, bearing in mind the need to involve the relevant stakeholders in their respective roles and responsibilities.

58. We recognise the importance of BRICS scientific, technical, innovation and entrepreneurship cooperation for sustainable development and to enhance inclusive growth. We welcome the dynamic development of BRICS cooperation in science, technology and innovation and attach special importance to the advancement of our joint work in this area. We affirm the value of implementing coordinated BRICS scientific projects aimed at promoting BRICS science, technology and innovation potential as a contribution to our combined efforts in addressing the challenges of the Fourth Industrial Revolution.

59. We commend the progress of ongoing BRICS IPR cooperation. We recognise the importance of the development and transfer of technologies, including to developing countries, contributing to long-term sustainable and balanced global growth, and in this regard stress the importance of strengthening cooperation in intellectual property rights which contributes to innovation and the advent of new technologies to the benefit of society as a whole.

60. We are convinced that trade and technology are vital sources of inclusive growth, including through economic integration and consolidation of global value chains in sustainable and equitable ways. Technological progress will have wide ranging implications for production of goods and services as well as incomes of people. Appropriate policies and measures need to be taken to ensure that the developing countries benefit from the advantages of technological progress and do not suffer from lack of its early adoption. It is essential to develop effective policies to bridge the digital divides, including through supporting people to learn and by adopting new technologies and ensure effective mechanisms for transfer of relevant technologies.

61. We strongly acknowledge that skills development is critical to addressing the emerging mismatch between the new skills demanded by an increasingly technology- and knowledge-driven global economy and the older skill set of many workers. The pace, scale and scope of present-day economic change make it that more challenging. In this regard, we support measures including policy recommendations proposed in the G20 Initiative to Promote Quality Apprenticeship and the BRICS Action Plan for Poverty Alleviation and Reduction through Skills, to further facilitate vocational training, lifelong learning and the training that is relevant to the fast-changing demand of growing economies and world of work.

62. We reaffirm the centrality of the rules-based, transparent, non-discriminatory, open and inclusive multilateral trading system, as embodied in the World Trade Organisation (WTO), that promotes a predictable trade environment and the centrality of the WTO, and recognise the importance of the development dimension, and will make all efforts to strengthen the multilateral trading system.

63. We recognise that the multilateral trading system is facing unprecedented challenges. We underscore the importance of an open world economy, enabling all countries and peoples to share the benefits of globalisation, which should be inclusive and support sustainable development and prosperity of all countries. We call on all WTO members to abide by WTO rules and honour their commitments in the multilateral trading system.

64. We recall that the WTO Dispute Settlement System is a cornerstone of the multilateral trading system and is designed to enhance security and predictability in international trade. We note with concern the impasse in the selection process for new Appellate Body Members that can paralyse the dispute settlement system and undermine the rights and obligations of all Members. We, therefore, urge all Members to engage constructively to address this challenge as a matter of priority.

65. We acknowledge the need to upkeep WTO's negotiating function. We, therefore, agree to constructively engage in further developing the current legal framework of the multilateral trading system within the WTO, taking into consideration the concerns and interests of all WTO members, including in particular the developing members.

66. We acknowledge the importance of infrastructure development and connectivity in Africa and recognise the strides made by the African Union to identify and address the continent's infrastructure challenges, inter alia, through the New Partnership for Africa's Development (NEPAD) and the Programme for Infrastructure Development in Africa (PIDA). We support the importance of stimulating infrastructure investment on the basis of mutual benefit to support industrial development, job-creation, skills development, food and nutrition security and poverty eradication and sustainable development in Africa. We therefore reaffirm our support for sustainable infrastructure development in Africa, including addressing the infrastructure financing deficit.

67. Keenly aware of the need for Africa's industrialisation and the realisation of the African Union's Agenda 2063, we commend African countries and the African Union on the signing of the African Continental Free Trade Area (AfCFTA). The AfCFTA is an important step to economic integration on the continent and the unlocking of the tremendous potential of intra-African trade and in addressing its socio-economic challenges. In this regard, we reiterate our support for Agenda 2063 and efforts to promote continental integration and development.

68. We advocate for a strong Global Financial Safety Net with an adequately resourced, quota-based International Monetary Fund (IMF) at its centre. To this effect, we reaffirm our commitment to conclude the IMF's 15th General Review of Quotas, including a new quota formula while protecting the voice of the poorest countries by the 2019 Spring Meetings and no later than the 2019 Annual Meetings. Governance reform of the IMF should strengthen the voice and representation of the poorest members of the IMF, including Sub-Saharan Africa.

69. We welcome and congratulate Governor Lesetja Kganyago of the South African Reserve Bank on his appointment as the Chair of the International Monetary and Financial Committee.

70. We note the steps undertaken on strengthening and ensuring the operational readiness of the BRICS Contingent Reserve Arrangement (CRA) and welcome the completion of a successful test run of the de-linked portion of the CRA mechanism. We encourage cooperation between the CRA and the IMF.

71. We note with satisfaction the progress achieved on establishing the BRICS Local Currency Bond Fund, and look forward to starting its operation.

72. We agree to further strengthen cooperation on convergence of accounting standards and auditing oversight of BRICS countries in the area of bond issuance, and to further cooperation in these areas.

73. We welcome the signing of the Memorandum of Understanding on Collaborative Research on Distributed Ledger and Blockchain Technology in the Context of the Development of the Digital Economy. We believe that this work will contribute to our cooperation in adapting to the evolving internet economy.

74. Infrastructure, investment and international development assistance projects are the bedrock for sustainable economic development and growth; boosting productivity and enhancing integration. We stress the significance of infrastructure development and integration to foster closer economic ties.

75. We underscore the role that Multilateral Development Banks (MDBs), in particular, the New Development Bank (NDB), are playing in catalysing private sector financing for public infrastructure and investment.

76. We draw satisfaction from the progress made by the NDB in providing resources to contribute to the social, economic and environmental prospects of our countries and expect the Project Preparation Fund to be put into operation soon. We welcome the upcoming establishment of the Americas Regional Office in São Paulo, Brazil, which, alongside the Africa Regional Centre, will help the NDB consolidate its presence in those continents. We note the NDB's Board of Governors' discussions on Innovative Approaches for Development Finance at its 3rd Annual Meeting on 28-29 May in Shanghai, China, that deliberated on the NDB's future development in the changing global environment.

77. We stress the importance of enhancing BRICS financial cooperation to better serve the real economy and meet the development needs of BRICS countries. In the regard, we reaffirm our commitment to facilitate financial market integration through promoting the network of financial institutions and the coverage of financial services within BRICS countries, subject to each country's existing regulatory framework and WTO GATS obligations, and to ensure greater communication and cooperation between financial sector regulators. We will continue to enhance currency cooperation, consistent with each central bank's legal mandate, and to explore more modalities of the cooperation. We will also further expand green financing, so as to promote sustainable development in BRICS countries.

78. We reaffirm our commitment to support international cooperation in combating illicit financial flows, including cooperation within Financial Actions Task Force (FATF) and World Customs Organisation. In this regard, we underscore the importance of increasing mutual exchanges and data sharing. We emphasise the importance of upholding and supporting the objectives of FATF and to intensify our cooperation to implement and improve its Standards on Combating Money Laundering and the Financing of Terrorism and Proliferation in FATF.

79. Corruption remains a global challenge with long-lasting impact, including the undermining of legal systems of states. It also presents a threat to economic growth by discouraging the necessary local and foreign investment in a country. We reaffirm our commitment to international cooperation as envisaged in Chapter IV of the United Nations Convention against Corruption. In that context, we commit to strengthening international cooperation within the context of the BRICS Working Group on Anticorruption Cooperation. Subject to our domestic legal systems we will cooperate in anti-corruption law enforcement, extradition of fugitives, economic and corruption offenders and repatriation in matters relating to assets recovery and other related criminal and non-criminal matters involving corruption and call on the International community to deny safe haven to corrupt persons and proceeds of corruption. We regard experience sharing and exchange as key to increasing mutual understanding and enhancing BRICS anti-corruption cooperation and will continue our efforts in this aspect as we have done in previous years. We will further offer each other support in the implementation of the UNCAC by creating platforms for exchanging information and exploring convergences in multi-lateral platforms. We commend the African Union on choosing 2018 as the year of combating corruption.

80. In operationalising the Strategy for BRICS Economic Partnership, we welcome the positive outcomes of the 8th BRICS Trade Ministers Meeting as supported by the ongoing activities of the BRICS Contact Group on Economic and Trade Issues (CGETI). We also welcome the good progress made in the implementation of the BRICS Action Agenda on Economic and Trade Cooperation. We encourage measures that support greater participation, value addition and upward mobility in Global Value Chains for our firms, particularly in industry and agriculture, especially Micro, Small and Medium Enterprises (MSMEs), including through the preservation of policy space to promote industrial development. In recognising the importance of increased value-added trade amongst BRICS countries, we commend the Ministers of Trade for reconvening CGETI's Trade Promotion Working Group as well as the BRICS E-Commerce Working Group. We welcome the commissioning of the review of the BRICS Joint Trade Study on promoting intra-BRICS Value Added Trade. We welcome the positive outcomes of the 8th BRICS Trade Ministers Meeting on cooperation on the IPR,

e-commerce, trade in service, and further enhancement of cooperation in E-commerce, on standards and technical regulations, MSMEs and model e-port.

81. We welcome the signing of the BRICS Memorandum of Understanding on Regional Aviation. We believe it is an important milestone in strengthening BRICS cooperation in the fields of connectivity and infrastructure.

82. We appreciate the outcomes of cooperation between BRICS Customs Administrations in implementing the Strategic Framework of BRICS Customs Cooperation, and welcome its long-term objectives, including the early conclusion and entry into force of the BRICS Customs Mutual Administrative Assistance Agreement so that the BRICS Authorised Economic Operator Programme is functional by the end of 2022, including mutual recognition of controls and economic operators. In this regard, we further welcome the BRICS Customs Action Plan, which identifies actions that will be taken collectively by the BRICS Customs Administrations in the short, medium and long term to achieve the stated goals and the establishment of BRICS Custom Training Centres. We recognise the potential of the BRICS Customs Cooperation Committee and call for enhanced intra-BRICS cooperation and at relevant multilateral fora, including in trade facilitation, law enforcement, use of advanced information technologies and capacity building.

83. We acknowledge the continued support provided by the BRICS Revenue Authorities for all the international initiatives towards reaching a globally fair and universally transparent tax system. We will continue our commitment to deal with the implications of the digital economy and, within that context, to ensure the fairness of the international tax system particularly towards the prevention of base erosion and shifting of profits, exchange of tax information, both on request and automatically, and needs-based capacity building for developing countries. We commit to deepen exchanges, sharing of experiences, best practices, mutual learning and exchanges of personnel in taxation matters. We welcome the establishment of the Capacity Building Mechanism between BRICS Revenue Authorities.

84. We acknowledge the contributions of the BRICS Business Council and its 5th Annual Report, as well as of the BRICS Business Forum, to enhancing trade and business cooperation in infrastructure, manufacturing, energy, agribusiness, financial services, regional aviation, alignment of technical standards and skills development. We welcome the establishment of Digital Economy Working Group within the framework of BRICS Business Council.

85. Recognizing tourism's great potential to contribute to sustainable economic and social development, we welcome the initiative to establish a BRICS Working Group on Tourism, to foster greater cooperation between the BRICS countries and increase economic development and people-to-people relations. The BRICS Tourism work stream will exchange knowledge, experience and best practices in the areas of travel trade, air connectivity, tourism infrastructure, culture and medical tourism, barriers to tourism marketing, tourism safety and support - financial, insurance and medical. We note with satisfaction that Intra-BRICS Tourism has grown despite the global economic downturn.

People-to-People Cooperation

86. Emphasising the centrality of people in BRICS and its programmes, we commend the steady progress and exchanges in the fields of sports, youth, films, culture, education and tourism.

87. We reaffirm our commitment to a people-centred approach to development that is inclusive of all sectors of our people.

88. We acknowledge the 8th World Water Forum held in Brasilia, the world's major water-related event, held in the Southern Hemisphere for the first time, which contributed to establishing water as a priority at the global level.

89. We stress the importance for the BRICS countries to cooperate in matters related to outer space and we confirm our support to strengthening current initiatives in this field.

90. We commit to strengthening the coordination and cooperation on vaccine research and development within BRICS countries, and welcome the proposal to establish a BRICS vaccine research and development centre.

91. We welcome the 1st WHO Global Ministerial Conference on Ending Tuberculosis in the Sustainable Development Era: A Multisectoral response, in Moscow in 2017, and the resulting Moscow declaration to End TB and stressed the importance of the upcoming 1st High-Level Meeting of the UN General Assembly on Ending Tuberculosis and the 3rd High-Level Meeting of the UN General Assembly on the Prevention and Control of non-communicable diseases, to be held in September 2018.

92. We recognise the importance and role of culture as one of the drivers of the 4th Industrial Revolution and acknowledge the economic opportunities that it presents.

93. We commend the organisation of the 3rd BRICS Film Festival and recognise the need to further deepen cooperation in this field. We acknowledge South Africa's proposal regarding a draft BRICS Treaty on Co-Production of Films to further promote cooperation in this sphere and to showcase the diversity of BRICS cultures.

94. We emphasise the guiding role of the Action Plan for the Implementation of the Agreement between the Governments of the BRICS States on Cooperation in the Field of Culture (2017- 2021) for creative and sustainable cultural cooperation, and we note the various ongoing activities and initiatives of the BRICS culture experts.

95. We acknowledge the 2nd BRICS Seminar on Governance 2018 in Johannesburg, while recognising the intention of Brazil to hold the 3rd meeting in 2019 with greater and more diverse participation of academia and thinktanks of all BRICS countries

96. We acknowledge with satisfaction the progress made towards strengthening cooperation and interaction amongst our people, through exchanges including the Think-Tank Council, the Academic Forum, the Civil BRICS Forum, the Young Diplomats Forum, the Youth Summit and the Young Scientists Forum.

97. We acknowledge the South African initiative regarding a BRICS Foreign Affairs Spokespersons Engagement.

98. We welcome the successful hosting of the 3rd BRICS Games by South Africa and we further note the progress that has been made in establishing the BRICS Sports Council.

99. Emphasising the importance of BRICS parliamentary exchanges, including of Women Parliamentarians, we look forward to further strengthening of BRICS exchanges in this regard.

100.Emphasising the role played by women in promoting inclusive development, we note the work being done to consider the establishment of the BRICS Women's Forum and the BRICS Women's Business Alliance.

101.Brazil, Russia, India, and China commend South Africa's BRICS Chairship in 2018 and express their sincere gratitude to the Government and people of South Africa for hosting the 10th BRICS Summit in Johannesburg.

102.Russia, India, China and South Africa extend full support to Brazil for its BRICS Chairship in 2019 and the hosting of the 11th BRICS Summit.

B.   The Johannesburg Action Plan

ANNEX 1: JOHANNESBURG PLAN OF ACTION
The 10th BRICS Summit – 25 to 27 July (Johannesburg)

We take note of the outcomes of the following meetings held under South Africa's BRICS Chairship leading up to the Johannesburg Summit:

Ministerial Meetings

- Meeting of BRICS Finance Deputies – 17 to 20 March (Buenos Aires)
- Meeting of the BRICS Finance Ministers and Central Bank Governors – 18 to 20 April (Washington, DC)
- Meeting of BRICS Finance Deputies – 18 to 20 April (Washington, DC)
- Meeting of the BRICS Ministers of Environmental Affairs – 18 May (Durban)
- Meeting of the BRICS Ministers of Foreign Affairs/International Relations – 4 June (Pretoria)
- Meeting of BRICS Head of Revenue Authorities – 18 to 21 June 2018 (Johannesburg)
- 8th Meeting of the BRICS Ministers of Agriculture and Agrarian Development – 19 to 22 June (Mpumalanga)
- 8th Meeting of National Security Advisors - 28 to 29 June 2018 (Durban)
- BRICS Energy Ministers - 28 to 29 June (Gauteng)
- Meeting of BRICS Ministers of Disaster Management - 29 June to 1 July (East London)
- 6th Meeting of BRICS Ministers of Science, Technology and Innovation - 3 July (Durban)
- 3rd Meeting of BRICS Industry Ministers - 4 July (Gauteng)
- 8th Meeting of BRICS Trade Ministers - 5 July (Magaliesburg)
- Meeting of BRICS Ministers of Education - 10 July (Cape Town)
- Meeting of BRICS Ministers of Finance and Central Bank Governors – 19 to 22 July (Argentina)
- 8th Meeting of BRICS Ministers of Health - 20 July (Durban)

Senior Official and Sectoral Meetings

- First Meeting of the BRICS Sherpas and Sous-Sherpas – 4 to 6 February (Cape Town)
- First Meeting of the BRICS Anti-Corruption Working Group - 26 February (Buenos Aires, Argentina)
- 17th Meeting of the Contact Group on Economic and Trade Issues (CGETI) – 28 February to 2 March (Johannesburg)
- 9th Technical National Statistics Offices of the BRICS Offices – 13 to 15 March (Pretoria)
- Meeting of BRICS Bond Fund (BBF) Working Group – 17 to 20 March (Buenos Aires)
- Meeting of Customs Experts – 16 to 17 April (Durban)
- 2nd Meeting of the Customs Cooperation Committee – 18 to 19 April (Durban)
- Meeting of BBF Working Group and BRICS CRA Standing Committee – 18 to 20 April (Washington, DC USA)
- Counter-Terrorism Working Group – 19 to 20 April (White River, Nelspruit)

- Second Meeting of the BRICS Sherpas/Sous-Sherpas – 24 to 26 April (Bela Bela, Limpopo)
- First Labour & Employment Working Group (EWG) Meeting – 7 to 10 May (Mpumalanga)
- Second Meeting of the BRICS Intellectual Property Rights Cooperation Mechanism – 10 May (East London)
- Second Meeting of the BRICS E-commerce Working Group – 10 May (East London)
- First Meeting of the BRICS Trade Promotion Working Group – 10 May (East London)
- Meeting of Technical Experts in Technical Regulations, Standards, Conformity Assessment, Metrology and Accreditation – 10 May (East London)
- Workshop on Trade in Services Statistics – 10 May (East London)
- 18th Meeting of the Contact Group on Economic and Trade Issues (CGETI) – 11 to 12 May (East London)
- Meeting of the BRICS Environmental Affairs Working Group Meeting – 14 to 16 May (Pretoria)
- Security in the use of ICTs Working Group – 16 to 17 May (Cape Town)
- Meeting of the BRICS Senior Officials Environmental Affairs – 17 May (Durban)
- Meeting of BRICS Energy Efficiency & Energy Saving Working Group – 17 to 18 May (Cape Town)
- Meeting of the BRICS Think-Tank Council (BTTC) - 28 May (Parktown)
- BRICS Academic Forum – 28 to 31 May (Johannesburg)
- Meeting of the Quality Infrastructure (Standards, Accreditation and Metrology bodies) - 16 May (Gauteng)
- BRICS Meeting on Health on the margins of World Health Assembly – May (Geneva, Switzerland)
- 3rd BRICS Sherpa/Sous-Sherpa Meeting – 2 to 3 June (Pretoria)
- Meeting of Experts on Tax Matters – 18 to 19 June (Cape Town)
- 4th Meeting of Senior Officials/Experts on the Middle East and North Africa (MENA) – 19 June (Pretoria)
- 8th Meeting of the Agriculture Cooperation Working Group – 20 June (Nelspruit)
- Agricultural Field Visits – 22 June
- Meeting of Civil Society Organisations (CSOs) – 25 to 26 June (Johannesburg)
- Civil BRICS – 25 to 27 June (Parktown, Johannesburg)
- 3rd Meeting of the Customs Cooperation Committee – 26 June (Brussels, Belgium)
- 2nd Meeting of the BRICS Anti-Corruption Working Group – 26 June (Paris, France)
- 4th Young Diplomats Forum – 25 to 29 June (Pretoria)
- 3rd BRICS Young Scientists Forum – 25 to 29 June (Durban ICC)
- BRICS Friendship Cities and Local Government Cooperation Forum – 28 to 29 June (East London)
- 4th BRICS STI Working Group Meeting of Funding Parties – 30 June (Durban)
- 8th BRICS Science, Technology and Innovation (STI) - 2 July (Durban)
- 3rd Meeting of Industry Experts - 3 July (Magaliesburg)
- 2nd BRICS Seminar on Governance, 3 to 4 July (Johannesburg)
- 19th Meeting of the Contact Group on Economic and Trade Issues (CGETI) – 2 to 4 July (Gauteng)
- BRICS Network University Conference – 5 to 7 July (Stellenbosch)
- Meeting of BRICS Senior Officials on Education – 9 July (Cape Town)

- ICTI – International Conference on Transport Infrastructure – 9 to 10 July (Pretoria)
- 4th BRICS Youth Summit – 16 to 21 July (Bloemfontein, Free State)
- 3rd BRICS Games – 17 to 22 July (Johannesburg)
- Meeting of the BRICS Health Senior Officials – 18 to 19 July (Durban)
- BBF Working Group Meeting and BRICS CRA Standing Committee Meeting – 19 to 22 July (Argentina)
- Annual Meeting of the BRICS Business Council – 22 to 23 July Durban
- 3rd BRICS Film Festival 2018 – 22 to 28 July (Durban)
- 4th BRICS Sherpa/Sous-Sherpa Meeting – 20 to 24 July (Johannesburg)
- BRICS Business Council Energy Forum – 24 July (Johannesburg)
- BRICS Business Forum - 25 July (Sandton)
- Annual Meeting of the BRICS ICM Chairmen – 25 to 26 July (Cape Town)
- BRICS Financial Forum – 25 to 26 July (Cape Town)

Activities for the Remainder of South Africa's BRICS Chairship 2018

Informal Meeting of the BRICS Leaders (Buenos Aires, Argentina)

Ministerial Meetings
- BRICS Sports Council of Ministers Meeting
- Meeting for BRICS Ministers for Labour & Employment (LEMM) (Durban)
- 4th BRICS Ministers of Communications Meeting (Durban)
- Meeting of the BRICS Ministers of Foreign Affairs/International Relations (New York, USA)
- Meeting of BRICS Finance Ministers and Central Bank Governors
- BRICS Tourism Senior Officials meeting (Gauteng)

Senior Official and Sectoral Meetings
- Second Labour & Employment Working Group (EWG) Meeting (Durban)
- BRICS TB Research Network (Durban)
- 3rd BRICS Media Forum
- 3rd BRICS Working Group on Cooperation in ICT
- BRICS Science, Technology and Innovation Women's Forum (Pretoria)
- Agri-business Roadshow
- BRICS Conference on Development Finance in Africa (Nelson Mandela University, Port Elizabeth)
- BRICS Legal Forum (Cape Town)
- Meeting of the BRICS Culture Senior Officials
- BRICS Cultural Festival (Various Cities)
- Meetings of the BRICS Working Groups (Competition)
- Meeting of Heads of Competition Authorities (Pretoria)
- 3rd BRICS SoE Forum on Governance and Reform (Durban)
- 4th Business to Business (Industry Dialogue) Meeting (Durban)

- 3rd Working Group on ICT Cooperation (Senior Officials) Meeting (Durban)
- 5th Meeting of BRICS Sherpas/Sous Sherpas (New York, USA)
- 2nd BRICS Skills Competition (Johannesburg)
- BRICS CRA Governing Council Meeting and BRICS BF Working Group Meeting (Bali, Indonesia)
- 2nd BRICS STI Working Group Meeting on Biomed and Biotechnology (Cape Town)
- 3rd BRICS Ministers of Culture Meeting 2018 (Durban)
- 4th Round of the BRICS Policy Planning Consultations
- 3rd Meeting of the BRICS Working Group on Geospatial Sciences and its Applications (Pretoria)
- 3rd Meeting of the BRICS Working Group on Prevention and Monitoring of Natural Disasters (Pretoria)
- BRICS National Statistical Office Meeting
- BRICS Space Agencies Forum (Pretoria)
- BRICS Astronomy Conference (Sutherland: SALT – Southern African Large Telescope)
- 6th Meeting of BRICS Sherpas/Sous-Sherpas (Buenos Aires, Argentina)
- BRICS STI Brokerage Event
- BRICS Science Academies Dialogue (Johannesburg)
- 3rd BRICS Water Forum (Pretoria)
- BRICS STI Advisory Councils Roundtable (Pretoria)
- BRICS STI Technology Transfer and SMME Forum (Pretoria)
- 7th Meeting of BRICS Sherpas/Sous-Sherpas
- BRICS Meeting of Officials and Experts on Population Matters (Pilanesberg, Rustenburg)

II.2.   9th BRICS Summit 2017: 4 Sep. 2017, Xiamen (CHN)

A.   The Xiamen Declaration 2017

BRICS LEADERS XIAMEN DECLARATION
Xiamen, China, 4 September 2017

1.   We, the Leaders of the Federative Republic of Brazil, the Russian Federation, the Republic of India, the People's Republic of China and the Republic of South Africa, met on 4 September 2017 in Xiamen, China, at the Ninth BRICS Summit. Under the theme "BRICS: Stronger Partnership for a Brighter Future", we endeavor to build on our achievements already made with a shared vision for future development of BRICS. We also discussed international and regional issues of common concern and adopted the Xiamen Declaration by consensus.

2.   We reiterate that it is the overarching objective and our desire for peace, security, development and cooperation that brought us together 10 years ago. BRICS countries have since traversed a remarkable journey together on their respective development paths tailored to their national circumstances, devoted to growing their economies and improving people's livelihoods. Our committed and concerted efforts have generated a momentum of all-dimensional and multi-layered cooperation fostered by the previous Leaders' Summits. Upholding development and multilateralism, we are working together for a more just, equitable, fair, democratic and representative international political and economic order.

3.   Our cooperation since 2006 has fostered the BRICS spirit featuring mutual respect and understanding, equality, solidarity, openness, inclusiveness and mutually beneficial cooperation, which is our valuable asset and an inexhaustible source of strength for BRICS cooperation. We have shown respect for the development paths of our respective choices, and rendered understanding and support to each other's interests. We have upheld equality and solidarity. We have also embraced openness and inclusiveness, dedicated to forging an open world economy. We have furthered our cooperation with emerging markets and developing countries (EMDCs). We have worked together for mutually beneficial outcomes and common development, constantly deepening BRICS practical cooperation which benefits the world at large.

4.   We draw satisfaction from the many fruitful results of our cooperation, including establishing the New Development Bank (NDB) and the Contingent Reserve Arrangement (CRA), formulating the Strategy for BRICS Economic Partnership, strengthening political and security cooperation including through Meetings of BRICS High Representatives for Security Issues and Foreign Ministers Meetings, and deepening the traditional ties of friendship amongst our peoples.

5.   Recalling our Summits in Ufa and Goa, we will work together to further enhance BRICS strategic partnership for the welfare of our peoples. We commit ourselves to build upon the outcomes and consensus of our previous Summits with unwavering conviction, so as to usher in the second golden decade of BRICS cooperation and solidarity.

6.   Believing in the broad development prospects of our countries and the vast potential of our cooperation, we have full confidence in the future of BRICS. We commit to further strengthen our cooperation.

-    We will energize our practical cooperation to boost development of BRICS countries. We will, inter alia, promote exchanges of good practices and experiences on development, and facilitate market inter-linkages as well as infrastructure and financial integration to achieve interconnected development. We shall also strive towards broad partnerships with EMDCs, and in this context, we will pursue equal-footed and flexible practices and initiatives for dialogue and cooperation with non-BRICS countries, including through BRICS Plus cooperation.

-    We will enhance communication and coordination in improving global economic governance to foster a more just and equitable international economic order. We will work towards enhancement of the voice and representation of BRICS countries and EMDCs in global economic governance and promote an open, inclusive and balanced economic globalization, thus contributing towards development of EMDCs and providing strong impetus to redressing North-South development imbalances and promoting global growth.

-    We will emphasize fairness and justice to safeguard international and regional peace and stability. We will stand firm in upholding a fair and equitable international order based on the central role of the United Nations, the purposes and principles enshrined in the Charter of the United Nations and respect for international law, promoting democracy and the rule of law in international relations, and making joint efforts to address common traditional and non-traditional security challenges, so as to build a brighter shared future for the global community.

-    We will embrace cultural diversity and promote people-to-people exchanges to garner more popular support for BRICS cooperation through deepened traditional friendships. We will expand people-to-people exchanges in all dimensions, encourage all fabrics of the society to participate in BRICS cooperation, promote mutual learning between our cultures and civilizations, enhance communication and mutual understanding among our peoples and deepen traditional friendships, thus making BRICS partnership closer to our people's hearts.

BRICS Practical Economic Cooperation

7.   We note that against the backdrop of more solid global economic growth, enhanced resilience and emerging new drivers, BRICS countries continue to play an important role as engines of global growth. Noting the uncertainties and downside risks that persist, we emphasize the need to be vigilant in guarding against inward-looking policies and tendencies that are weighing on global growth prospects and market confidence. We call upon all countries to calibrate and communicate their macroeconomic and structural policies and strengthen policy coordination.

8.   We note that practical economic cooperation has traditionally served as a foundation of BRICS cooperation, notably through implementing the Strategy for BRICS Economic Partnership and initiatives related to its priority areas such as trade and investment, manufacturing and minerals processing, infrastructure connectivity, financial integration, science, technology and innovation, and Information and Communication Technology (ICT) cooperation, among others. We welcome the first report on the implementation of the Strategy for BRICS Economic Partnership, and the broad package of outcomes delivered by the sectoral ministerial meetings. We commit to use all policy tools -fiscal, monetary and structural -and adopt innovation-driven development strategies to enhance resilience and potentials of our economies, so as to contribute to strong, sustainable, balanced and inclusive global growth.

9.   Stressing the role of enhanced trade and investment cooperation in unleashing the potential of BRICS economies, we agree to improve and broaden trade and investment cooperation mechanism and scope, with a view to enhancing BRICS economic complementarity and diversification in BRICS countries. We welcome the positive outcomes of the 7th BRICS Trade Ministers Meeting in terms of the cooperative frameworks, roadmaps and outlines on trade and investment facilitation and connectivity and enhanced policy sharing, information exchange, capacity building, through

enhanced joint efforts on trade and investment facilitation, trade in services, E-commerce, IPR (in synergy with the cooperation activities among BRICS IP authorities), economic and technical cooperation, SMEs and women economic empowerment. We welcome the setting up of the BRICS E-Port Network that will operate on a voluntary basis and the establishment of the BRICS E-commerce Working Group. We also welcome China's initiative to host an International Import Expo in 2018 and encourage our business communities to actively participate in it.

10. We stress the importance of enhancing BRICS financial cooperation to better serve the real economy and meet the development needs of BRICS countries. We note the agreement by the finance ministers and central bank governors on cooperation on Public Private Partnerships (PPP), including through PPP experience exchange and application of the BRICS Good Practices on PPP Frameworks. We acknowledge the establishment of a temporary task force to conduct technical discussion on various ways of cooperation, including utilizing existing facilities of the MDBs based on national experiences, exploring the possibility of establishing a new PPP Project Preparation Fund and other options. We encourage cooperation and coordination by our accounting standards setters and audit regulators and agree to explore convergence of accounting standards and continue discussion on cooperation on auditing oversight in the area of bond issuance, so as to lay the groundwork for bond market connectivity among BRICS countries, with due regard to applicable national legislation and policies. We agree to promote the development of BRICS Local Currency Bond Markets and jointly establish a BRICS Local Currency Bond Fund, as a means of contribution to the capital sustainability of financing in BRICS countries, boosting the development of BRICS domestic and regional bond markets, including by increasing foreign private sector participation, and enhancing financial resilience of BRICS countries.

11. In order to serve the demand arising from rapid growth of trade and investment among the BRICS countries, we agree to facilitate financial market integration through promoting the network of financial institutions and the coverage of financial services within BRICS countries, subject to each country's existing regulatory framework and WTO obligations, and to ensure greater communication and cooperation between financial sector regulators. We agree to take an active part in the efforts to implement and improve International Standards on Combating Money Laundering and the Financing of Terrorism and Proliferation in FATF, including through cooperation among BRICS Heads of Delegation on AML/CFT, also in the context of the work of BRICS CTWG and by using other platforms and to safeguard integrity of national financial systems. We agree to communicate closely to enhance currency cooperation, consistent with each central bank's legal mandate, including through currency swap, local currency settlement, and local currency direct investment, where appropriate, and to explore more modalities of currency cooperation. We encourage the BRICS Interbank Cooperation Mechanism to continue playing an important role in supporting BRICS economic and trade cooperation. We commend the progress in concluding the Memoranda of Understanding among national development banks of BRICS countries on interbank local currency credit line and on interbank cooperation in relation to credit rating.

12. We highlight the importance of innovation as a key driver for mid and long term economic growth and global sustainable development. We commit to promote cooperation on science, technology and innovation (STI) to forge synergy in tapping new growth momentum for our five economies and continue to address the development challenges we face. We commend the selection of BRICS research and development projects under the BRICS STI Framework Program and note the launch of the 2nd call for projects. We welcome the BRICS STI Cooperation MOU and support enhanced cooperation on innovation and entrepreneurship, including by promoting technology transfer and application, cooperation among science and technology parks and enterprises as well as mobility of researchers, entrepreneurs, professionals and students. We encourage increased

participation of the academia, businesses, civil society and other stakeholders in this process, and support the promotion of STI investment and cross-border investment through existing funding, institutions and platforms including the NDB. We agree to continue to work on a cooperation platform for innovation and entrepreneurship and support the implementation of the BRICS Innovation Cooperation Action Plan 2017-2020.

13. We reaffirm our commitment to BRICS industrial cooperation, including on industrial capacities and policies, new industrial infrastructure and standards, and among small, micro and medium-sized enterprises (SMMEs), so as to jointly seize the opportunities brought about by the new industrial revolution and expedite our respective industrialization processes. We encourage exploring the establishment of BRICS Institute of Future networks. We will enhance joint BRICS research, development and innovation in GT including the Internet of Things, Cloud computing, Big Data, Data Analytics, Nanotechnology, Artificial Intelligence and 5G and their innovative applications to elevate the level of ICT infrastructure and connectivity in our countries. We will advocate the establishment of internationally applicable rules for security of ICT infrastructure, data protection and the Internet that can be widely accepted by all parties concerned, and jointly build a network that is safe and secure. We will increase investment of ICT, recognize the need to further increase investment in ICT Research and development, unleash the dynamics of innovation in producing goods and services. We encourage identification and facilitation of partnership between institutes, organizations, enterprises in the implementation of proof of concepts and pilot projects by leveraging complementary strengths in ICT hardware, software and skills through developing next generation of innovative solutions in the areas of smart cities, health care and energy efficient device, etc. We support active collaboration in implementing the BRICS ICT Development Agenda and Action Plan.

14. We reaffirm our commitment to fully implementing the 2030 Agenda for Sustainable Development. We will also advocate equitable, open, all- round, innovation-driven and inclusive development, to achieve sustainable development in its three dimensions -economic, social and environmental-in a balanced and integrated manner. We support the important role of the United Nations, including the High Level Political Forum on Sustainable Development (HLPF), in coordinating and reviewing global implementation of the 2030 Agenda, and support the need to reform the UN Development System with a view to enhancing its capability in supporting Member States in implementing the 2030 Agenda. We urge developed countries to honor their Official Development Assistance commitments in time and in full and provide more development resources to developing countries.

15. Underlining the strategic importance of energy to economic development, we commit to strengthen BRICS cooperation on energy. We recognize that sustainable development, energy access, and energy security are critical to the shared prosperity and future of the planet. We acknowledge that clean and renewable energy needs to be affordable to all. We will work to foster open, flexible and transparent markets for energy commodities and technologies. We will work together to promote most effective use of fossil fuels and wider use of gas, hydro and nuclear power, which will contribute to the transformation toward a low emissions economy, better energy access, and sustainable development. In this regard, we underline the importance of predictability in accessing technology and finance for expansion of civil nuclear energy capacity which would contribute to sustainable development in BRICS countries. We encourage continued dialogue on the establishment of a BRICS Energy Research Cooperation Platform and urge relevant entities to continue to promote joint research on energy cooperation and energy efficiency.

16. We commit to further promote green development and low-carbon economy, in the context of sustainable development and poverty eradication, enhance BRICS cooperation on climate change

and expand green financing. We call upon all countries to fully implement the Paris Agreement adopted under the principles of the United Nations Framework Convention on Climate Change (UNFCCC) including the principles of common but differentiated responsibilities and respective capabilities, and urge developed countries to provide financial, technological and capacity-building support to developing countries to enhance their capability in mitigation and adaptation.

17. Stressing the importance of environmental cooperation to sustainable development of our countries and the well-being of our peoples, we agree to take concrete actions to advance result-oriented cooperation in such areas as prevention of air and water pollution, waste management and biodiversity conservation. We recognize the importance of an environmentally sound technology platform and of improving urban environmental sustainability, and support BRICS joint efforts in this regard. Brazil, Russia, India and South Africa appreciate and support China's hosting of the meeting of the Conference of the Parties to the Convention on Biological Diversity in 2020.

18. Noting the fruitful agricultural cooperation over the past years, we recognize the unique characteristics and complementarity of BRICS countries in agricultural development and vast cooperation potential in this area. In this connection, we agree to deepen cooperation in the five priority areas such as food security and nutrition, adaptation of agriculture to climate change, agricultural technology cooperation and innovation, agricultural trade and investment, and ICT application in agriculture to contribute to stable global agricultural growth and achievement of Sustainable Development Goals. We welcome the establishment in India of the Coordination Center of BRICS Agriculture Research Platform, a virtual network which will facilitate addressing these priority areas.

19. We express concern over the challenges faced by the African continent in achieving independent and sustainable development and in wildlife conservation. We reaffirm our commitment to strengthen cooperation with Africa and help the continent to address illegal wildlife trade, promote employment, food security, infrastructure development and industrialization including through connectivity and developmental initiatives and projects. We reaffirm our strong support for African Union's implementation of its various programs under Agenda 2063 in pursuit of its continental agenda for peace and socio-economic development.

20. Keenly aware of the negative impact of corruption on sustainable development, we support the efforts to enhance BRICS anti-corruption cooperation. We reaffirm our commitment to intensify dialogue and experience sharing and support compiling a compendium on fighting corruption in BRICS countries. We further acknowledge that illegal flow of the proceeds of corruption impairs economic development and financial stability, and support enhanced cooperation in asset recovery. We support the strengthening of international cooperation against corruption, including through the BRICS Anti-Corruption Working Group, as well as on matters related to asset recovery and persons sought for corruption. We acknowledge that corruption including illicit money and financial flows, and ill-gotten wealth stashed in foreign jurisdictions is a global challenge which may impact negatively on economic growth and sustainable development. We will strive to coordinate our approach in this regard and encourage a stronger global commitment to prevent and combat corruption on the basis of the United Nations Convention against Corruption and other relevant international legal instruments.

21. Living in the era of digital economy, we are ready to use opportunities it provides and address challenges it poses for the global growth. We will act on the basis of principles of innovation, partnership, synergy, flexibility, open and favorable business environment, trust and security, protection of consumer rights in order to ensure the conditions for a thriving and dynamic digital economy that will foster global economic development and benefit everyone.

22. We appreciate the efforts and contribution of the BRICS Business Council and Business Forum to strengthening our economic cooperation in infrastructure, manufacturing, energy, agriculture, financial services, e-commerce, alignment of technical standards and skills development. We welcome the establishment of a working group on regional aviation within the framework of the Business Council and in this connection acknowledge the Brazil's proposal on an MOU on regional aviation partnership. We encourage business communities and associations to actively participate in BRICS cooperation, and give full play to their role as trade and investment facilitation institutions in promoting mutually beneficial cooperation.

23. We recognize the importance of transformation that is taking place in the labor market and the opportunities and challenges it brings. We note with satisfaction the progress in BRICS cooperation with regard to human resources, employment and social security, fostering strong labor market information systems and networking of BRICS of Labor Research Institutes and BRICS Social Security Cooperation Framework. We welcome the achievement of a BRICS common position on governance in the future of work and agree to further strengthen exchanges and cooperation in ensuring full employment, promoting decent work, advancing poverty alleviation and reduction through skills development and achieving universal and sustainable social security systems.

24. We recognize the importance of competition protection to ensure the efficient social and economic development of our countries, to stimulate innovative processes and to provide quality products to our consumers. We note the significance of the interaction between the Competition Authorities of our countries, in particular, in identifying and suppressing restrictive business practices that are of a transboundary nature.

25. We note with satisfaction the progress made by Customs Administrations in their cooperation on trade facilitation, security and enforcement, capacity building and other issues of mutual interest, including through such mechanisms as BRICS Customs Cooperation Committee and BRICS Customs Working Group. We encourage broadened cooperation under the guiding principles of mutual sharing of information, mutual recognition of customs control, and mutual assistance in enforcement so as to boost growth and promote people's welfare. In order to strengthen mutual cooperation in customs matters, we reaffirm our commitment to finalize BRICS Customs Mutual Assistance Agreement at the earliest.

26. We adhere to the principle of utilizing outer space for peaceful purposes and emphasize the need to strengthen the international cooperation in space activities in order to use space technologies to respond to global climate change, environmental protection, disaster prevention and relief and other challenges faced by humankind.

27. Recalling the Saint-Petersburg and Udaipur Declarations of BRICS Ministers for Disaster Management and the decision to establish a BRICS Joint Taskforce on Disaster Risk Management, we underline the importance of consistent joint work of emergency services of BRICS countries aimed at building a safer future by reducing existing disaster risks, including exchange of information on best practices concerning disaster risk management and cooperation in the field of forecasting and early warning for effective response to natural and human induced disasters.

28. We note with satisfaction the progress in BRICS cooperation in such fields as audit, statistics and export credit and agree to further advance cooperation in these fields.

Global Economic Governance

29. We resolve to foster a global economic governance architecture that is more effective and reflective of current global economic landscape, increasing the voice and representation of emerging

markets and developing economies. We reaffirm our commitment to conclude the IMF's 15th General Review of Quotas, including a new quota formula, by the 2019 Spring Meetings and no later than the 2019 Annual Meetings. We will continue to promote the implementation of the World Bank Group Shareholding Review.

30. We emphasize the importance of an open and resilient financial system to sustainable growth and development, and agree to better leverage the benefits of capital flows and manage the risks stemming from excessive cross-border capital flows and fluctuation. The BRICS CRA represents a milestone of BRICS financial cooperation and development, which also contributes to global financial stability. We welcome the establishment of the CRA System of Exchange in Macroeconomic Information (SEMI), and the agreement to further strengthen the research capability of the CRA, and to promote closer cooperation between the IMF and the CRA.

31. We welcome the establishment of the NDB Africa Regional Center launched in South Africa, which is the first regional office of the Bank. We welcome the setting up of the Project Preparation Fund and the approval of the 2nd batch of projects. We congratulate the Bank on the ground-breaking of its permanent headquarters building. We stress the significance of infrastructure connectivity to foster closer economic ties and partnerships among countries. We encourage the NDB to fully leverage its role and enhance cooperation with multilateral development institutions including the World Bank and the Asian Infrastructure Investment Bank as well as with the BRICS Business Council, to forge synergy in mobilizing resources and promote infrastructure construction and sustainable development of BRICS countries.

32. We emphasize the importance of an open and inclusive world economy enabling all countries and peoples to share in the benefits of globalization. We remain firmly committed to a rules-based, transparent, non-discriminatory, open and inclusive multilateral trading system as embodied in the WTO. We reaffirm our commitments to ensure full implementation and enforcement of existing WTO rules and are determined to work together to further strengthen the WTO. We call for the acceleration of the implementation of the Bali and Nairobi MCM outcomes and for the WTO ministerial conference to be held this year in Argentina to produce positive outcomes. We will continue to firmly oppose protectionism. We recommit to our existing pledge for both standstill and rollback of protectionist measures and we call upon other countries to join us in that commitment.

33. Valuing the G20's continued role as the premier forum for international economic cooperation, we reiterate our commitments to the implementation of the outcomes of G20 summits, including the Hamburg Summit and the Hangzhou Summit. We call upon the G20 to further enhance macroeconomic policy coordination to minimize negative spillovers and external shocks to EMDEs. We agree to enhance coordination and cooperation under the Argentina Presidency in 2018, with an aim to make the G20 process and outcomes reflect the interests and priorities of EMDEs.

34. We reaffirm our commitment to achieving a fair and modem global tax system and promoting a more equitable, pro-growth and efficient international tax environment, including to deepening cooperation on addressing Base Erosion and Profit Shifting (BEPS), promoting exchange of tax information and improving capacity-building in developing countries. We will strengthen BRICS tax cooperation to increase BRICS contribution to setting international tax rules and provide, according to each country's priorities, effective and sustainable technical assistance to other developing countries.

International Peace and Security

35. Cognizant of the profound changes the world is undergoing and the global security challenges and threats faced by the international community, we commit to enhance communication and cooperation in international fora on issues concerning international peace and security. We reiterate our commitment to safeguarding world peace and security and to upholding the basic norms of the international law, and the purposes and principles of the Charter of the United Nations including sovereign equality and non-interference in other countries' internal affairs.

36. We welcome the 7th Meeting of the BRICS High Representatives for Security Issues held on 27-28 July 2017 in Beijing, and commend the meeting for having discussion and deepening our common understanding on global governance, counter-terrorism, security in the use of ICTs, energy security, major international and regional hotspots as well as national security and development. We note Brazil's proposal to establish a BRICS Intelligence Forum. We welcome Chair's report to us on the proceedings of the Meeting and encourage the succeeding chairpersonships to continue this exercise. We look forward to enhancing practical security cooperation agreed upon in the above areas.

37. We welcome China's hosting of the Meeting of BRICS Ministers of Foreign Affairs/International Relations in Beijing on 18-19 June 2017 at the initiative of China. Ministers exchanged views on major global political, security, economic and financial issues of common concern and on strengthening BRICS cooperation. We look forward to the upcoming meeting of Foreign Ministers on the margins of the UNGA. We welcome South Africa's offer to host the next stand-alone Foreign Ministers Meeting in 2018.

38. We recall that development and security are closely interlinked, mutually reinforcing and key to attaining sustainable peace. We reiterate our view that the establishment of sustainable peace requires a comprehensive, concerted and determined approach, based on mutual trust, mutual benefit, equity and cooperation that addresses the causes of conflicts including their political, economic and social dimensions. We condemn unilateral military interventions, economic sanctions and arbitrary use of unilateral coercive measures in violation of international law and universally recognized norms of international relations. We emphasize that no country should enhance its security at the expense of the security of others.

39. We reaffirm our commitment to the United Nations as the universal multilateral organization entrusted with the mandate for maintaining international peace and security, advance global development and to promote and protect human rights.

40. We recall the 2005 World Summit Outcome document and reaffirm the need for a comprehensive reform of the UN, including its Security Council, with a view to making it more representative, effective and efficient, and to increase the representation of the developing countries so that it can adequately respond to global challenges. China and Russia reiterate the importance they attach to the status and role of Brazil, India and South Africa in international affairs and support their aspiration to play a greater role in the UN.

41. We reiterate that the only lasting solution to the crisis in Syria is through an inclusive "Syrian-led, Syrian-owned" political process which safeguards the sovereignty, independence and territorial integrity of Syria, in pursuance of the United Nations Security Council Resolution 2254(2015), and promotes the legitimate aspirations of the Syrian people. We strongly support the Geneva Peace Talks and the Astana process, and welcome the creation of the de-escalation areas in Syria, which contributed to decrease the levels of violence and generate positive momentum and conditions for meaningful progress in the peace talks under the auspices of the UN. We oppose the use of chemical weapons by anyone, for any purpose and under any circumstance.

42. We reiterate the urgent need for a just, lasting and comprehensive solution of the Israeli-Palestinian conflict in order to achieve peace and stability in the Middle East on the basis of relevant United Nations resolutions, the Madrid Principles, the Arab Peace Initiative and previous agreements between the parties through negotiations with a view to creating an independent, viable, territorially contiguous Palestinian State living side by side in peace and security with Israel. Committed to making greater contribution to such solution, we express readiness to enhance our contribution towards a just and lasting resolution of the Middle East conflict and support international efforts to promote peace and stability in the region.

43. We congratulate the people and Government of Iraq for the recovery of Mosul and for the progress achieved in the fight against terrorism and reaffirm our commitment to Iraq's sovereignty, territorial integrity and political independence and our support for Iraqi government and its people. We express our concern over the situation in Yemen and urge all parties to cease hostilities and to resume negotiations supported by the United Nations. We also call on all parties directly involved in the current diplomatic crisis in the Gulf region to overcome their dissensions through dialogue and welcome the efforts of Kuwaiti mediation in this regard.

44. We strongly deplore the nuclear test conducted by the DPRK. We express deep concern over the ongoing tension and prolonged nuclear issue on the Korean Peninsula, and emphasize that it should only be settled through peaceful means and direct dialogue of all the parties concerned.

45. We firmly support the Joint Comprehensive Plan of Action (JCPOA) on the Iranian nuclear issue and call upon all relevant parties to comply fully with their obligations and ensure full and effective implementation of the JCPOA to promote international and regional peace and stability.

46. We commend the efforts of African countries, the African Union and sub-regional organizations in addressing regional issues and maintaining regional peace and security, and emphasize the importance of collaboration between the United Nations and the African Union in accordance with the Charter of the United Nations. We support efforts towards comprehensively resolving the issues in Democratic Republic of Congo, Libya, South Sudan, Somalia, Central Africa Republic and Western Sahara.

47. We strongly condemn terrorist attacks resulting in death to innocent Afghan nationals. There is a need for immediate cessation of violence. We reaffirm our support to the people of Afghanistan in their efforts to achieve "Afghan-led and Afghan-owned" peace and national reconciliation, to the ongoing international efforts, including the Moscow Format of consultations on Afghanistan and "Heart of Asia-Istanbul Process", as well as multimodal connectivity projects to promote peace and stability, to the fight against terrorism and drug-threat, and to the national reconstruction efforts by Afghanistan. We support the efforts of the Afghan National Defense and Security Forces in fighting terrorist organizations.

48. We, in this regard, express concern on the security situation in the region and violence caused by the Taliban, ISIL/DAISH, Al-Qaida and its affiliates including Eastern Turkistan Islamic Movement, Islamic Movement of Uzbekistan, the Haqqani network, Lashkar-e-Taiba, Jaish-e-Mohammad, TTP and Hizb ut-Tahrir.

49. We deplore all terrorist attacks worldwide, including attacks in BRICS countries, and condemn terrorism in all its forms and manifestations wherever committed and by whomsoever and stress that there can be no justification whatsoever for any act of terrorism. We reaffirm that those responsible for committing, organizing, or supporting terrorist acts must be held accountable. Recalling the primary leading role and responsibility of states in preventing and countering terrorism, we stress the necessity to develop international cooperation, in accordance with the principles of

international law, including that of sovereign equality of states and non-interference in their internal affairs. We reaffirm solidarity and resolve in the fight against terrorism, value the 2nd BRICS Counter-Terrorism Working Group Meeting held in Beijing on 18 May 2017, and agree to strengthen our cooperation.

50. We call upon all nations to adopt a comprehensive approach in combating terrorism, which should include countering radicalization, recruitment, movement of terrorists including Foreign Terrorist Fighters, blocking sources of financing terrorism including, for instance, through organized crime by means of money-laundering, supply of weapons, drug trafficking and other criminal activities, dismantling terrorist bases, and countering misuse of the Internet including social media by terrorist entities through misuse of the latest Information and Communication Technologies (ICTs). We are committed to prevent and counter the growing spread of terrorist narratives, and to tackle all sources, techniques and channels of terrorist financing. We call for swift and effective implementation of relevant UNSC Resolutions and the FATF International Standards worldwide. We seek to intensify our cooperation in FATF and FATF-style regional bodies (FSRBs). We recall the responsibility of all States to prevent financing of terrorist networks and terrorist actions from their territories.

51. We call upon the international community to establish a genuinely broad international counter-terrorism coalition and support the UN's central coordinating role in this regard. We stress that the fight against terrorism must be conducted in accordance with international law, including the Charter of the United Nations, international refugee and humanitarian law, human rights and fundamental freedoms. We reaffirm our commitment on increasing the effectiveness of the UN counter-terrorism framework, including in the areas of cooperation and coordination among the relevant UN entities, designation of terrorists and terrorist groups and technical assistance to Members States. We call for expeditious finalization and adoption of the Comprehensive Convention on International Terrorism (CCIT) by the United Nations General Assembly.

52. We recognize the important contribution of BRICS countries to United Nations peacekeeping operations, and the importance of United Nations peacekeeping operations to international peace and security. We emphasize the need for BRICS countries to further enhance communication on peacekeeping matters.

53. We reiterate our commitment to address the world drug problem based on the United Nations drug control conventions, through an integrated, comprehensive and balanced approach to drug supply and demand reduction strategies. We stress the importance of the outcome document of the 30th Special Session of the United Nations General Assembly on the world drug problem, and call for strengthening of international and regional cooperation and coordination to counter the global threat caused by the illicit production and trafficking of drugs, especially opiates. We note with deep concern the increasing links in some regions of the world between drug trafficking, money laundering and organized crime and terrorism.

54. We reiterate the need for all countries to cooperate in promoting and protecting human rights and fundamental freedoms under the principles of equality and mutual respect. We agree to continue to treat all human rights, including the right to development, in a fair and equal manner, on the same footing and with the same emphasis. We will strengthen cooperation on issues of common interests both within BRICS and in multilateral fora including the United Nations Human Rights Council, taking into account the necessity to promote, protect and fulfill human rights in a non-selective, non-politicized and constructive manner, and without double standards.

55. Keenly aware of the global security challenges faced by the international community in the area of international migration, we emphasize the growing role of effective migration regulation for the benefit of international security and development of the society.

56. We consider the UN has a central role in developing universally accepted norms of responsible state behavior in the use of ICTs to ensure a peaceful, secure, open, cooperative, stable, orderly, accessible and equitable ICT environment. We emphasize the paramount importance of the principles of international law enshrined in the Charter of the United Nations, particularly the state sovereignty, the political independence, territorial integrity and sovereign equality of states, non-interference in internal affairs of other states and respect for human rights and fundamental freedoms. We emphasize the need to enhance international cooperation against terrorist and criminal misuse of ICTs, reaffirm the general approach laid in the eThekwini, Fortaleza, Ufa and Goa declarations in this regard, and recognize the need for a universal regulatory binding instrument on combatting the criminal use of ICTs under the UN auspices as stated in the Ufa Declaration. We note with satisfaction the progress achieved by the Working Group of Experts of the BRICS States on Security in the use of ICTs. We decide to promote cooperation according to the BRICS Roadmap of Practical Cooperation on Ensuring Security in the Use of ICTs or any other mutually agreed mechanism and acknowledge the initiative of the Russian Federation on a BRICS intergovernmental agreement on cooperation in ensuring security in the use of ICTs.

57. We believe that all states should participate on an equal footing in the evolution and functioning of the Internet and its governance, bearing in mind the need to involve relevant stakeholders in their respective roles and responsibilities. The structures that manage and regulate the critical Internet resources need to be made more representative and inclusive. We note with satisfaction the progress made by the BRICS Working Group on ICT Cooperation. We recognize the necessity to strengthen our cooperation in this area. To that end, BRICS will continue to work together through the existing mechanism to contribute to the secure, open, peaceful and cooperative use of ICTs on the basis of equal participation of the international community in its management.

58. We reiterate that outer space shall be free for peaceful exploration and used by all States on the basis of equality in accordance with international law. Reaffirming that outer space shall remain free from any kind of weapons or any use of force, we stress that negotiations for the conclusion of an international agreement or agreements to prevent an arms race in outer space are a priority task of the United Nations Conference on Disarmament, and support the efforts to start substantive work, inter alia, based on the updated draft treaty on the prevention of the placement of weapons in outer space and of the threat or use of force against outer space objects submitted by China and the Russian Federation. We also note an international initiative for a political obligation on the no first placement of weapons in outer space.

59. Priority should be accorded to ensuring the long-term sustainability of outer space activities, as well as ways and means of preserving outer space for future generations. We note that this is an important objective on the current agenda of the UN Committee on the Peaceful Uses of Outer Space (UNCOPUOS). In this respect, we welcome the decision by the UNCOPUOS Scientific and Technical Sub-Committee Working Group on Long-term Sustainability of Outer Space Activities to conclude negotiations and achieve consensus on the full set of guidelines for the long term sustainability of outer space activities by 2018 to coincide with the commemoration of the 50th Anniversary of the first United Nations Conference on the Exploration and Peaceful Uses of Outer Space (UNISPACE + 50).

People-to-People Exchanges

60. We emphasize the importance of people-to-people exchanges to promoting development and enhancing mutual understanding, friendship and cooperation among BRICS peoples. We agree to deepen cooperation in such fields as culture, education, science and technology, sports and health as well as among media organizations and local governments, to strengthen the third pillar of BRICS cooperation and foster a meaningful resonance of the BRICS partnership amongst its peoples.

61. We value cultural diversity as a precious asset of BRICS cooperation. We stress the role of culture and cultural diversity in promoting sustainable development, and encourage BRICS countries to engage in cultural exchanges and mutual learning to cultivate common values on the basis of diversity and sharing. We welcome the formulation of a BRICS action plan to advance practical cultural cooperation and the establishment of the BRICS Alliance of Libraries, Alliance of Museums, Alliance of Art Museums and National Galleries as well as Alliance of Theater for Children and Young People. We look forward to the success of the BRICS Culture Festival to be held later in mid-September 2017 in Xiamen. We will continue our work on the establishment of a BRICS Cultural Council to provide the necessary platform to enhance cultural cooperation among BRICS countries.

62. We stress the importance of education to promoting sustainable economic and social development, and to strengthening BRICS partnership, and commend the positive progress in our education cooperation. We reiterate our support for BRICS University League and BRICS Network University in conducting education and research cooperation, welcome efforts to promote cooperation among educational think tanks, and exchanges among youth including by organizing youth summer camps and offering more scholarship opportunities to BRICS students. We agree to share experience and practices in realizing education-related sustainable development goals.

63. We believe in the importance of sports cooperation to popularizing traditional sports and deepening the friendship among BRICS peoples. Recalling the successful hosting of BRICS U-17 Football Tournament in Goa in 2016, we commend the success of the First BRICS Games, which was a highlight of this year's people-to-people exchanges. We encourage relevant departments to sign an MOU on sports cooperation to provide greater impetus to sports cooperation among our five countries.

64. We agree to enhance BRICS role in global health governance, especially in the context of the World Health Organization and UN agencies, and foster the development and improve the availability of innovative medical products through promotion of research and development and access to affordable, quality, effective and safe drugs, vaccines, diagnostics and other medical products and technologies as well as to medical services through enhanced health systems and health financing. We agree to improve surveillance capacity and medical services to combat infectious diseases, including Ebola, HIV/AIDS, Tuberculosis and Malaria, as well as non-communicable diseases and encourage greater application of ICTs to improve the level of health service provision. We welcome the outcomes of the BRICS Health Ministers Meeting and High-level Meeting on Traditional Medicine, and commend the establishment of a long-term mechanism for traditional medicine exchanges and cooperation, to promote mutual learning of traditional medicines and pass them down to future generations. We welcome the decision to set up the Tuberculosis Research Network, to be presented at the First WHO Global Ministerial Conference Ending Tuberculosis in the Sustainable Development Era: A Multisectoral Response, Moscow, Russian Federation, 16-17 November 2017. We express support for the meeting as well as the First United Nations General Assembly High-Level Meeting on Tuberculosis in 2018. We commit ourselves to enhanced cooperation at international fora on health matters including at G20.

65. We reaffirm our commitment to promote a long-term and balanced demographic development and continue cooperation on population related matters in accordance with the Agenda for BRICS Cooperation on Population Matters for 2015-2020.

66. We note with satisfaction the progress in the exchanges and cooperation in various areas, including governance, film-making, media, think- tank, youth, parliament, local governments and trade union, and agree to further advance such exchanges and cooperation. We commend the first joint film production by BRICS countries and commend the success of the BRICS Film Festival, the Media Forum, Friendship Cities and Local Governments Cooperation Forum, Youth Forum, Young Diplomats Forum and Young Scientists Forum. We appreciate the successful hosting of the BRICS Forum of Political Parties, Think-Tanks and Civil Society Organizations as well as the Seminar on Governance, and will carry these good initiatives forward in the future. In this regard, we note the proposal to establish by China the BRICS Research and Exchange Fund.

67. We appreciate the important progress in BRICS institutional development and reiterate our commitment to further strengthen it to make BRICS cooperation more responsive to the changing situation. We commend China for taking measures during its Chairmanship to enhance the Sherpas' coordination role in BRICS cooperation. We instruct the Sherpas to continue their discussion concerning BRICS institutional development.

68. We recommit our strong support for multilateralism and the central role of the UN in international affairs. We commit to strengthening the coordination and cooperation among BRICS in the areas of mutual and common interests within the UN and other multilateral institutions, including through regular meetings among our permanent representatives in New York, Geneva and Vienna, and further enhance the voice of BRICS in international fora.

69. In continuation of BRICS tradition of outreach since the Durban Summit, we will hold a Dialogue of Emerging Market and Developing Countries on the implementation of the 2030 Agenda for Sustainable Development and the building of broad partnerships for development under the theme of "Strengthening Mutually-Beneficial Cooperation for Common Development" in promotion of BRICS Plus cooperation.

70. South Africa, Brazil, Russia and India commend China's Chairmanship in 2017 and express sincere gratitude to the Government and people of China for hosting the Ninth BRICS Summit in Xiamen.

71. China, Brazil, Russia and India extend full support for South Africa in hosting the Tenth BRICS Summit in 2018.

B. The Xiamen Declaration 2017: BRICS Cooperation Outcome Documents

ANNEX 1: BRICS COOPERATION OUTCOME DOCUMENTS

The following outcome documents have been adopted.

Press Communique of the BRICS Leaders Informal Meeting in Hamburg

Political and Security Cooperation

1. Media Note of the Meeting of BRICS Ministers of Foreign Affairs/International Relations

2. BRICS Roadmap of Practical Cooperation on Ensuring Security in the Use of ICTs

3. Joint Communique on the Meeting of BRICS Special Envoys on Middle East

Economic Cooperation

1. BRICS Action Agenda on Economic and Trade Cooperation

2. Seventh Meeting of the BRICS Trade Ministers Statement

3. BRICS Trade in Services Cooperation Roadmap

4. Framework on Strengthening the Economic and Technical Cooperation for BRICS Countries

5. BRICS E-Commerce Cooperation Initiative

6. Terms of Reference (ToR) of BRICS E-Commerce Working Group

7. Terms of Reference (ToR) of BRICS Model E-Port Network

8. BRICS IPR Cooperation Guidelines

9. Outlines for BRICS Investment Facilitation

10. Agreed Elements of Financial Deliverables of 2017 BRICS Finance Ministers and Central Bank Governors Meeting

11. BRICS Good Practices on PPP Frameworks

12. Action Plan for Deepening Industrial Cooperation Among BRICS Countries

13. Declaration of the Third BRICS Communications Ministers' Meeting

14. Strategic Framework of BRICS Customs Cooperation

15. BRICS Action Plan for Innovation Cooperation (2017-2020)

16. Hangzhou Declaration of the 5th BRICS Science, Technology & Innovation (STI) Ministerial Meeting

17. Action Plan 2017-2018 in the Framework of BRICS 2015-2018 STI Work Plan

18. Communique of BRICS Heads of Tax Authorities Meeting

19. BRICS Memorandum of Cooperation in Respect of Tax Matters

20. Declaration of the 2nd BRICS Energy Ministerial Meeting

21. Tianjin Statement on Environment of the Third Meeting of BRICS Environment Ministers

22. Joint Declaration of the Seventh Meeting of BRICS Ministers of Agriculture

23. Action Plan 2017-2020 for Agricultural Cooperation of BRICS Countries

24. BRICS Labour and Employment Ministers' Declaration

25. The BRICS Action Plan for Poverty Alleviation and Reduction Through Skills

26. Progress Report on the Implementation of the Strategy for BRICS Economic Partnership

27. Interbank Local Currency Credit Line Agreement Under BRICS Interbank Cooperation Mechanism

28. Cooperation Memorandum Relating to Credit Ratings Under BRICS Interbank Cooperation Mechanism

29. BRICS Partnership for Urban Environmental Sustainability Initiative

30. BRICS Joint Statistical Publication 2017

31. Terms of Reference (ToR) of BRICS Research Infrastructure and Mega-Science Projects Working Group

32. Terms of Reference (ToR) of BRICS Working Group on Science, Technology, Innovation and Entrepreneurship Partnership

33. Memorandum of Understanding Between BRICS Export Credit Agencies and the New Development Bank on General Cooperation

34. The BRICS Common Position on Governance in the Future of Work

35. BRICS Network of Labour Research Institutes Terms of Reference

36. BRICS Social Security Cooperation Framework

37. BRICS Agricultural Development Report 2017

38. Joint Statement of BRICS Business Forum 2017

39. Memorandum of Understanding Between the BRICS Business Council and the New Development Bank on Strategic Cooperation

40. Joint Declaration of BRICS Business Council on Regulatory Cooperation on Standards

People-to-People Exchanges

1. Action Plan for the Implementation of the Agreement between the Governments of the BRICS States on Cooperation in the Field of Culture (2017-2021)

2. Letter of Intent for BRICS Alliance of Libraries Cooperation

3. Letter of Intent of the Founding of the BRICS Alliance of Museums

4. Letter of Intent on the Founding of the BRICS Alliance of Art Museums and National Galleries

5. Letter of Intent for Strategic Cooperation of the BRICS Alliance of Theater for Children and Young People

6. Joint Declaration of BRICS Countries on Strengthening Cooperation in Traditional Medicine

7. Tianjin Communique of BRICS Health Ministers Meeting

8. Beijing Declaration on Education of the Fifth Meeting of BRICS Ministers of Education

9. Action Plan of Promoting BRICS Media Cooperation

10. 2017 BRICS Youth Forum Action Plan

11. Chengdu Initiative of 2017 BRICS Friendship Cities and Local Governments Cooperation Forum

12. Quanzhou Consensus of BRICS Seminar on Governance

13. Fuzhou Initiative of the BRICS Political Parties, Think-Tanks and Civil Society Organizations Forum

14. The 9th BRICS Academic Forum Recommendations to the 9th BRICS Summit

15. Chengdu Consensus of the BRICS Film Delegations of the 2nd BRICS Film Festival

16. BRICS Film Collaboration Plan for the Years 2017 to 2021

17. BFA Program for BRICS Film Students and Talents

18. Joint Declaration on Film Traditional Culture Inheritance and Creative Development of Young Talents

19. BRICS Trade Union Forum Declaration

20. Statement by BRICS Trade Unions to the BRICS Labour and Employment Ministers' Meeting

Note is also taken of the ongoing work on the following documents.

Economic Cooperation

1. The Action Plan on BRICS IPR Cooperation

2. Agreement on Cooperation on the BRCS Remote Sensing Satellite Constellation

3. National Accounting Standards Setters of BRICS Countries Joint Statement

4. BRICS Joint Statement on Audit Regulatory Cooperation

People-to-People Exchanges

1. Memorandum of Understanding on the Establishment of the Council of Regions of BRICS States

2. Memorandum of Understanding on BRICS Sports Cooperation

C.   The Xiamen Action Plan

ANNEX 2: XIAMEN ACTION PLAN

We take note of the following meetings and events held under China's BRICS Chairmanship before the Xiamen Summit.

Ministerial Meetings and Relevant Events

1. BRICS Leaders' Informal Meeting (7 July 2017, Hamburg)

2. Meeting of BRICS High Representatives for Security Issues (27-28 July 2017, Beijing)

3. Meeting of BRICS Ministers of Foreign Affairs/International Relations (18-19 June 2017, Beijing)

4. BRICS Sherpa/Sous-Sherpa Meetings (23-24 February 2017, Nanjing; 14-15 June 2017, Qingdao; 4-5 July 2017, Hamburg; September 2017, Xiamen)

5. BRICS Finance Ministers and Central Bank Governors Meetings/Finance and Central Bank Deputies Meeting (17 March 2017, Baden-Baden; 20 April 2017, Washington D.C.; 19 June 2017, Shanghai)

6. BRICS Local Currency Bond Fund Working Group (20 April, Washington DC; 18 June 2017, Shanghai)

7. BRICS Energy Ministerial Meeting (7 June 2017, Beijing)

8. Meeting of BRICS Ministers of Agriculture and Agrarian Development (16-17 June 2017, Nanjing)

9. BRICS Environment Ministers Meeting (22-23 June 2017, Tianjin)

10. Meeting of BRICS Joint Committee on Space Cooperation (2-3 July 2017, Haikou)

11. Meeting of BRICS Ministers of Education (4-5 July 2017, Beijing)

12. Meeting of BRICS Customs Cooperation Committee (5 July 2017, Brussels)

13. Meeting of BRICS Culture Ministers (5-6 July 2017, Tianjin)

14. BRICS Health Ministers Meeting and High-level Meeting on Traditional Medicine (6-7 July 2017, Tianjin)

15. BRICS Meeting of Drug Regulatory Collaboration (13-14 July 2017, Zhengzhou)

16. BRICS Science, Technology & Innovation Ministerial Meeting (18 July 2017, Hangzhou)

17. Meeting of BRICS Labor and Employment Ministers' Meeting (26-27 July 2017, Chongqing)

18. BRICS Communications Ministers' Meeting (27-28 July 2017, Hangzhou)

19. Meeting of BRICS Heads of Tax Authorities (27-28 July 2017, Hangzhou)

20. BRICS Industry Ministers Meeting (29-30 July 2017, Hangzhou)

21. Meeting of the BRICS Trade Ministers (1-2 August 2017, Shanghai)

22. Annual Meeting of the Board of Governors of the New Development Bank (1-2 April 2017, New Delhi)

23. BRICS Business Forum (3-4 September 2017, Xiamen)

Senior Officials/Working Groups/Expert Meetings

1. Meeting of BRICS Senior Officials on Environment (22 June 2017, Tianjin)

2. Meeting of BRICS Senior Officials on Education (4 July 2017, Beijing)

3. Meeting of BRICS Senior Officials on Culture (5 July 2017, Tianjin)

4. BRICS Health Senior Officials Meeting (5 July 2017, Tianjin)

5. Meeting of BRICS Senior Officials on Science, Technology & Innovation (17 July 2017, Hangzhou)

6. BRICS Business Council (31 March 2017, New Delhi; 31 August-2 September 2017, Shanghai & Xiamen)

7. BRICS Anti-Corruption Working Group Meetings (22 January 2017, Berlin; 9 April 2017, Brasilia)

8. BRICS Intellectual Property Examiner Training Seminar (20-24 February 2017, Nagpur)

9. BRICS Intellectual Property Coordination Group Meeting (22-23 February 2017, Nagpur)

10. Meetings of BRICS Contact Group on Economic and Trade Issues (20-21 March 2017, Beijing; 23-25 May 2017, Beijing; 30-31 July 2017, Shanghai)

11. Technical Meeting of BRICS National Statistics Offices (27-29 March 2017, Shanghai)

12. BRICS Working Group Meeting of Customs (29-31 March 2017, Xiamen)

13. Consultation of BRICS Middle East Special Envoys (11-12 April 2017, Visakhapatnam)

14. BRICS Employment Working Group Meetings (19 April 2017, Yuxi; 25 July 2017, Chongqing)

15. BRICS Environmental Working Group Meeting (25-27 April 2017, Tianjin)

16. BRICS Counter Terrorism Working Group Meeting (18 May 2017, Beijing)

17. First Meeting of BRICS Intellectual Property Rights Mechanism (23 May 2017, Beijing)

18. Working Group for the Meeting of BRICS Ministers of Culture (25 May 2017, Beijing)

19. BRICS Science, Technology & Innovation Funding Working Group Meeting (28-31 May 2017, Pretoria)

20. Meeting of BRICS Working Group on Security in the Use of ICTs (1-2 June 2017, Beijing)

21. Working Group Meeting on BRICS Energy Saving and Improvement of Energy Efficiency (5 June 2017, Beijing)

22. Meeting of Heads of BRICS Export Credit Agencies (12-15 June 2017, Hangzhou)

23. BRICS Working Group Meetings on Agricultural Cooperation (15 June 2017, Nanjing)

24. Technical Group Meeting of BRICS Interbank Cooperation Mechanism (28-29 June 2017, Beijing)

25. Working Group Meeting on Interbank Cooperation Mechanism (28-29 June 2017, Beijing)

26. Meeting of BRICS Heads of Delegation on AML (18-23 June 2017, Spain)

27. BRICS Foreign Policy Planning Dialogue (20-21 July 2017, Beijing)

28. BRICS Consultation of Experts on Peace-keeping Affairs (25 July 2017, Beijing)

29. Meeting of BRICS Experts on Tax Matters (25-26 July 2017, Hangzhou)

30. BRICS Working Group Meeting on ICT Cooperation (26 July 2017, Hangzhou)

31. BRICS Anti-Drug Working Group Meeting (16 August 2017, Weihai)

32. Annual Meeting of Interbank Cooperation Mechanism and Financial Forum (31 August-2 September 2017, Beijing)

33. Meeting of BRICS Heads of Intellectual Property Offices (6-7 April 2017, New Delhi)

34. BRICS Working Group on Science, Technology, Innovation and Entrepreneurship Partnership (9 April, Bengaluru)

35. BRICS Working Group on ICT and High Performance Computing (23-26 April, Guangzhou)

36. BRICS Working Group on Research Infrastructure and Mega-science Projects (15-16 May, Dubna)

37. BRICS Working Group on Solid State Lighting (19-24 June 2017, Hangzhou)

People-to-people Exchanges Events and Other Meetings

1. BRICS Young Diplomats Forum (30 May-3 June 2017, Beijing & Linyi)

2. BRICS Media Forum (6-8 June 2017, Beijing)

3. BRICS Think-Tank Council Meeting (10 June 2017, Fuzhou)

4. BRICS Political Parties, Think Tanks and Civil Society Organizations Forum (10-12 June 2017, Fuzhou)

5. BRICS Games (17-21 June 2017, Guangzhou)

6. BRICS Film Festival (23-27 June 2017, Chengdu)

7. BRICS Friendship Cities and Local Governments Cooperation Forum (11-13 July 2017, Chengdu)

8. BRICS Trade Union Forum (24-25 July 2017, Beijing)

9. BRICS Youth Forum (24-28 July 2017, Beijing)

10. BRICS Young Scientist Forum (11-15 July 2017, Hangzhou)

11. BRICS Seminar on Governance (17-18 August 2017, Quanzhou)

12. BRICS Heads of Prosecution Services Meeting (August 2017, Brazil)

13. BRICS Think-Tank Symposiums (22 March 2017, Beijing; 15 May 2017, Guangzhou; 20 May 2017, Chongqing)

14. BRICS International Festival of Theatre Schools (14-21 May 2017, Moscow)

15. Meeting of BRICS Cooperation in the Field of Competition Law (16-20 May 2017, St. Petersburg)

16. Annual Forum "BRICS: Boosting Economic Cooperation" (1-3 June 2017, St. Petersburg)

17. BRICS Supreme Audit Institutions' Technical Cooperation Meeting (June 28-29, 2017, Pretoria)

18. International Congress of Women of SCO and BRICS Countries (2-4 July 2017, Novosibirsk)

We further take note of the upcoming meetings and events under China's BRICS Chaimanship.

1. The Foreign Ministers Meeting on the margins of UNGA

2. The Fifth BRICS Sherpa/Sous-Sherpa Meeting

3. BRICS Parliamentary Forum

4. Meeting of BRICS Heads of National Statistics Offices

5. BRICS Trade Fair

6. BRICS Legal Advisor Consultation

7. BRICS Forum on SOE Reform and Governance

8. Meeting of BRICS Cooperation in the Field of Competition Law

9. Third Forum on Small Business of the SCO and BRICS Regions

10. BRICS International Competition Conference

11. BRICS Working Group on Astronomy (21-22 September, Pune)

12. BRICS Export Credit Agencies Technical Workshop (31 October-3 November, Nanjing)

13. BRICS Working Group on Materials Science and Nanotechnology (26-27 October 2017, Yekaterinburg)

14. Annual International Academic Conference "Foresight and STI Policy" (1-2 November, Moscow)

15. BRICS Working Group on Biotechnology and Biomedicine, including Human Health and Neuroscience (15-16 November, 2017, Moscow)

16. BRICS meeting on Ageing

Proposals to be further explored

1. Ocean Cooperation
2. Establishment of the PPP Project Preparation Fund
3. Establishment of the BRICS Energy Cooperation Platform
4. BRICS Remote Sensing Satellite Constellation
5. Establishment of the BRICS Customs Training Center in Xiamen
6. Establishment of the BRICS Cultural Council
7. Establishment of the BRICS Council of Regions
8. Tourism Cooperation
9. Creation of the Working Group on Regional Aviation

II.3.   8th BRICS Summit 2016: 16 Oct. 2016, Goa (IND)

A.   The Goa Declaration

8th BRICS SUMMIT

GOA DECLARATION

Goa, India, October 16, 2016

1.   We, the Leaders of the Federative Republic of Brazil, the Russian Federation, the Republic of India, the People's Republic of China and the Republic of South Africa, met on 15-16 October 2016 in Goa, India, at the Eighth BRICS Summit, which was held under the theme "Building Responsive, Inclusive and Collective Solutions."

2.   Recalling all our previous declarations, we emphasise the importance of further strengthening BRICS solidarity and cooperation based on our common interests and key priorities to further strengthen our strategic partnership in the spirit of openness, solidarity, equality, mutual understanding, inclusiveness and mutually beneficial cooperation. We agree that emerging challenges to global peace and security and to sustainable development require further enhancing of our collective efforts.

3.   We agree that BRICS countries represent an influential voice on the global stage through our tangible cooperation, which delivers direct benefits to our people. In this context, we note with satisfaction the operationalisation of the New Development Bank (NDB) and of the Contingent Reserve Arrangement (CRA), which contributes greatly to the global economy and the strengthening of the international financial architecture. We welcome the report presented by NDB President on the work of the Bank during the first year of its operations. We are pleased to note the progress in operationalising the Africa Regional Centre (ARC) of the NDB and pledge our full support in this regard. We look forward to developing new BRICS initiatives in a wider range of areas in the years to come.

4.   We note with appreciation the approval of the first set of loans by the New Development Bank (NDB), particularly in the renewable energy projects in BRICS countries. We express satisfaction with NDB's issuance of the first set of green bonds in RMB. We are pleased to note that the operationalisation of BRICS Contingent Reserve Arrangements (CRA) has strengthened the global financial safety net.

5.   In order to reach out and enrich our understanding and engagement with fellow developing and emerging economies, we will hold an Outreach Summit of BRICS Leaders with the Leaders of BIMSTEC member countries - Bay of Bengal Initiative for Multi-Sectoral Technical and Economic Cooperation comprising of Bangladesh, Bhutan, India, Myanmar, Nepal, Sri Lanka and Thailand. The meeting will be an opportunity to renew our friendship with BIMSTEC countries as well as to jointly explore possibilities of expanding trade and commercial ties, and investment cooperation between BRICS and BIMSTEC countries, while advancing our common goals of peace, development, democracy and prosperity.

6.   We reiterate our common vision of ongoing profound shifts in the world as it transitions to a more just, democratic, and multi-polar international order based on the central role of the United Nations, and respect for international law. We reaffirm the need for strengthening coordination of efforts on global issues and practical cooperation in the spirit of solidarity, mutual understanding and trust. We underline the importance of collective efforts in solving international problems, and for peaceful settlement of disputes through political and diplomatic means, and in this regard, we reiterate our commitment to the principles of the Charter of the United Nations.

7.   We note the global character of current security challenges and threats confronting the international community. We reiterate our view that international efforts to address these challenges, the establishment of sustainable peace as well as the transition to a more just, equitable and democratic multi-polar international order requires a comprehensive, concerted and determined approach, based on spirit of solidarity, mutual trust and benefit, equity and cooperation, strong commitment to international law and the central role of the United Nations as the universal multilateral organisation entrusted with the mandate for maintaining international peace and security, advance global development and to promote and protect human rights. We underline the importance of further strengthening coordination of our efforts in this context.

8.   We reaffirm our commitment to contribute to safeguarding a fair and equitable international order based on the purposes and principles of the Charter of the United Nations including through consistent and universal respect and adherence to the principles and rules of international law in their inter-relation and integrity, compliance by all states with their international legal obligations. We express our commitment to resolutely reject the continued attempts to misrepresent the results of World War II. We recall further that development and security are closely interlinked, mutually reinforcing and key to attaining sustainable peace.

9.   We remain confident that resolving international problems require collective efforts for peaceful settlement of disputes through political and diplomatic means. Implementation of principles of good-faith, sovereign equality of States, non-intervention in the internal affairs of States and cooperation excludes imposition of unilateral coercive measures not based on international law. We condemn unilateral military interventions and economic sanctions in violation of international law and universally recognised norms of international relations. Bearing this in mind, we emphasise the unique importance of the indivisible nature of security, and that no State should strengthen its security at the expense of the security of others.

10.   We recall the 2005 World Summit Outcome document. We reaffirm the need for a comprehensive reform of the UN, including its Security Council, with a view to making it more representative, effective and efficient, and to increase the representation of the developing countries so that it can adequately respond to global challenges. China and Russia reiterate the importance they attach to the status and role of Brazil, India and South Africa in international affairs and support their aspiration to play a greater role in the UN.

11.   We welcome the substantive measures undertaken by the UN membership to make the process of selecting and appointing the UN Secretary-General more transparent and inclusive.

12.   We express our gratitude to UN Secretary-General Mr. Ban Ki-moon for his contributions to the United Nations in the past ten years. We congratulate Mr. António Guterres, on his appointment as the Secretary-General of the United Nations and express our support and to work closely with him.

13.   Cognizant of BRICS countries' significant contributions to UN Peacekeeping operations, and recognising the important role of UN Peacekeeping operations in safeguarding international peace and security, we realise the challenges faced by UN Peacekeeping and emphasise the need to further strengthen its role, capacity, effectiveness, accountability and efficiency, while adhering to the basic principles of peacekeeping. We emphasise that UN Peacekeeping operations should perform the duty of protection of civilians in strict accordance with their respective mandates and in respect of the primary responsibility of the host countries in this regard.

14.   We are deeply concerned about the situation in the Middle East and North Africa. We support all efforts for finding ways to the settlement of the crises in accordance with international law and in conformity with the principles of independence, territorial integrity and sovereignty of the countries of the region. On Syria, we call upon all parties involved to work for a comprehensive and peaceful resolution of the conflict taking into account the legitimate aspirations of the people of Syria, through inclusive national dialogue and a Syrian-led political process based on Geneva Communiqué of 30

June 2012 and in pursuance of the UN Security Council Resolution 2254 and 2268 for their full implementation. While continuing the relentless pursuit against terrorist groups so designated by the UN Security Council including ISIL, Jabhat al-Nusra and other terrorist organisations designated by the UN Security Council.

15.   We reiterate also the necessity to implement the two-state solution of the Palestinian-Israeli conflict on the basis of the relevant UNSC resolutions, the Madrid Principles and Arab Peace Initiative, and previous agreements between the two sides, through negotiations aimed at creating an independent, viable, territorially contiguous Palestinian State living side-by-side in peace with Israel, within secure, mutually agreed and internationally recognised borders on the basis of 1967 lines, with East Jerusalem as its capital, as envisaged in the relevant UN Resolutions.

16.   We express deep concern at the persisting security challenges in Afghanistan and significant increase in terrorist activities in Afghanistan. We affirm support to the efforts of the Afghan Government to achieve Afghan-led and Afghan-owned national reconciliation and combat terrorism, and readiness for constructive cooperation in order to facilitate security in Afghanistan, promote its independent political and economic course, becoming free from terrorism and drug trafficking. The Leaders expressed the view that capable and effective Afghan National Security Forces (ANSF) should be the key to the stabilisation of Afghanistan. In this regard, the Leaders emphasised the need for continued commitment of regional countries and wider international community, including the NATO-led Resolute Support Mission, which as the ISAF's heir has a key role in the ANSF capacity-building. The Leaders stressed the importance of multilateral region-led interaction on Afghan issues, primarily by those organisations, which consist of Afghanistan's neighbouring countries and other regional states, such as the Shanghai Cooperation Organisation, Collective Security Treaty Organization, and the Heart of Asia Conference.

17.   We welcome the African Union's (AU) vision, aspirations, goals and priorities for Africa's development enshrined in Agenda 2063, which is complementary with the 2030 Agenda for Sustainable Development. We reaffirm our support for Africa's implementation of its various programmes in pursuit of its continental agenda for peace and socio economic development. We will continue to engage in joint endeavours to advance Africa's solidarity, unity and strength through support measures for regional integration and sustainable development. We further welcome recent elections that have been held in the continent and the peaceful manner in which they were conducted.

18.   We support the AU's efforts to resolving conflicts through its peace and security architecture, in collaboration with the United Nations and the continent's regional organisations, and to contribute towards lasting and sustainable peace and security in Africa.

19.   We welcome the decision of the African Union's Assembly to operationalise its Peace Fund, in order to contribute to financing of its peace and security operations. We support efforts aimed at full operationalisation of the African Standby Force (ASF) and note the progress being made in this regard, including the contributions by the African Capacity for Immediate Responses to Crises (ACIRC).

20.   We express our concern that political and security instability continues to loom in a number of countries that is exacerbated by terrorism and extremism. We call upon the international community through the United Nations, African Union and regional and international partners to continue their support in addressing these challenges, including post-conflict reconstruction and development efforts.

21.   We welcome the adoption of landmark 2030 Agenda for Sustainable Development and its Sustainable Development Goals during the UN Summit on Sustainable Development on 25 September 2015 and the Addis Ababa Action Agenda at the Third International Conference on Financing for Development. We welcome the people-centred and holistic approach to sustainable

development enshrined in the 2030 Agenda and its emphasis on equality, equity and quality-life to all. We welcome the reaffirmation of the guiding principles of the implementation of the 2030 Agenda, including the principle of Common But Differentiated Responsibilities (CBDR).

22.   The 2030 Agenda, with its overarching focus on poverty eradication, lays an equal and balanced emphasis on the economic, social and environmental dimensions of sustainable development. We call upon developed countries to honour their Official Development Assistance commitments to achieve 0.7% of Gross National Income commitment for Official Development Assistance to developing countries. Those commitments play a crucial role in the implementation of the SDGs. We further welcome the establishment of a Technology Facilitation Mechanism within the UN with a mandate to facilitate technology for the implementation of the SDGs.

23.   We commit to lead by example in the implementation of the 2030 Agenda for Sustainable Development in line with national circumstances and development context respecting the national policy space. We welcome the G20 Action Plan on the 2030 Agenda for Sustainable Development adopted during G20 Hangzhou Summit and commit to its implementation by taking bold transformative steps through both collective and individual concrete actions.

24.   We meet at a time when the global economic recovery is progressing, with improved resilience and emergence of new sources of growth. The growth, though is weaker than expected with downside risks to the global economy continuing to persist. This gets reflected in a variety of challenges including commodity price volatility, weak trade, high private and public indebtedness, inequality and lack of inclusiveness of economic growth. Meanwhile, the benefits from growth need to be shared broadly in an inclusive manner. Geopolitical conflicts, terrorism, refugee flows, illicit financial flows and the outcome of UK referendum have further added to the uncertainty in the global economy.

25.   We reiterate our determination to use all policy tools – monetary, fiscal, and structural, individually and collectively, to achieve the goal of strong, sustainable, balanced and inclusive growth. Monetary policy will continue to support economic activity and ensure price stability, consistent with central bank's mandates. Monetary policy alone, though, cannot lead to balanced and sustainable growth. We, in this regard, underscore the essential role of structural reforms. We emphasise that our fiscal policies are equally important to support our common growth objectives. We also take note that the spill-over effects of certain policy measures in some systemically important advanced economies can have adverse impact on growth prospects of emerging economies.

26.   We recognise that innovation is a key driver for mid and long term growth and sustainable development. We stress the importance of industrialisation and measures that promote industrial development as a core pillar of structural transformation.

27.   We highlight the need to use tax policy and public expenditure in a more growth-friendly way taking into account fiscal space available, that promotes inclusiveness, maintains resilience and ensures sustainability of debt as a share of GDP.

28.   We note the dynamic integration processes across the regions of the world, particularly in Asia, Africa and South America. We affirm our belief to promote growth in the context of regional integration on the basis of principles of equality, openness and inclusiveness. We further believe that this will promote economic expansion through enhanced trade, commercial and investment linkages.

29.   We highlight the importance of public and private investments in infrastructure, including connectivity, to ensure sustained long-term growth. We, in this regard, call for approaches to bridge the financing gap in infrastructure including through enhanced involvement of Multilateral Development Banks.

30. We reaffirm our commitment to a strong, quota based and adequately resourced IMF. Borrowed resources by the IMF should be on a temporary basis. We remain strongly committed to support the coordinated effort by the emerging economies to ensure that the Fifteenth General Review of Quotas, including the new quota formula, will be finalised within the agreed timelines so as to ensure that the increased voice of the dynamic emerging and developing economies reflects their relative contributions to the world economy, while protecting the voices of least developed countries (LDCs), poor countries and regions.

31. We welcome the inclusion of the RMB into the Special Drawing Rights (SDR) currency basket on 10 October 2016.

32. We call for the advanced European economies to meet their commitment to cede two chairs on the Executive Board of the IMF. The reform of the IMF should strengthen the voice and representation of the poorest members of the IMF, including Sub-Saharan Africa.

33. We share concerns regarding the challenges of sovereign debt restructurings, and note that timely and successful debt restructuring is key for ensuring access to international capital markets, and hence economic growth, for countries with high debt levels. We welcome the current discussions to improve the debt restructuring process, and on the revised collective action clauses (CACs).

34. We reiterate our support for the multilateral trading system and the centrality of the WTO as the cornerstone of a rule based, open, transparent, non-discriminatory and inclusive multilateral trading system with development at the core of its agenda. We note the increasing number of bilateral, regional, and plurilateral trade agreements, and reiterate that these should be complementary to the multilateral trading system and encourage the parties thereon to align their work in consolidating the multilateral trading system under the WTO in accordance with the principles of transparency, inclusiveness, and compatibility with the WTO rules.

35. We emphasise the importance of implementing the decisions taken at the Bali and Nairobi Ministerial Conferences. We stress the need to advance negotiations on the remaining Doha Development Agenda (DDA) issues as a matter of priority. We call on all WTO members to work together to ensure a strong development oriented outcome for MC11 and beyond.

36. We appreciate the progress in the implementation of the Strategy for BRICS Economic Partnership and emphasise the importance of the BRICS Roadmap for Trade, Economic and Investment Cooperation until 2020. We believe that close cooperation between the sectoral cooperation mechanisms, BRICS Contact Group on Economic and Trade Issues, the BRICS Business Council, New Development Bank and the BRICS Interbank cooperation mechanism is crucial in strengthening the BRICS economic partnership. We welcome, in this context, the continued realisation of the major BRICS economic initiatives such as enhanced cooperation in e-commerce, "single window", IPR cooperation, trade promotion and micro, small and medium enterprises (MSMEs). We recognise non-tariff measures (NTMs), services sector, and standardisation and conformity assessments as possible areas of future cooperation. We note the meeting of BRICS Trade Ministers in New Delhi on 13 October 2016 and welcome its substantive outcomes.

37. In operationalising the Strategy for BRICS Economic Partnership, we encourage measures that support greater participation, value addition and upward mobility in Global Value Chains of our firms including through the preservation of policy space to promote industrial development.

38. We welcome India's initiative to host the first BRICS Trade Fair in New Delhi. This is an important step towards the implementation of Strategy for BRICS Economic Partnership. We believe this will further consolidate trade and commercial partnership among BRICS countries.

39. We noted the Annual Report by the BRICS Business Council, including the various initiatives undertaken by its Working Groups. We further direct the Council to accelerate the development and

realisation of joint projects which, on a mutually beneficial basis, contribute to the economic objectives of BRICS.

40. We agreed that MSMEs provide major employment opportunities, at comparatively lower capital cost, and create self-employment opportunities in rural and underdeveloped areas. MSMEs thus help assure equitable wealth distribution nationally and globally. We commend organisation of BRICS second round-table on MSMEs by India with a focus on technical and business alliances in MSMEs Sector. We agree to work for greater integration of MSMEs in Regional and Global Value Chains.

41. We commend China for the successful hosting of the 11th G20 Leaders' Summit in Hangzhou and its focus on innovation, structural reform and development as drivers of medium and long term economic growth. We recognise the role of G20 as the premier forum for international and financial cooperation and emphasise the importance of the implementation of the outcomes of G20 Hangzhou Summit, that we believe will foster strong, sustainable, balanced and inclusive growth and will contribute to improved global economic governance and enhance the role of developing countries.

42. We stress the importance to foster an innovative, invigorated, interconnected and inclusive world economy. We will enhance our consultations and coordination on the G20 agenda, especially on issues of mutual interest to the BRICS countries, and promote issues of importance for the Emerging Market and Developing Economies (EMDEs). We will continue to work closely with all G20 members to strengthen macroeconomic cooperation, promote innovation, as well as robust and sustainable trade and investment to propel global growth, improve global economic governance, enhance the role of developing countries, strengthen international financial architecture, support for industrialisation in Africa and least developed countries and enhance cooperation on energy access and efficiency. We stress the need for enhanced international cooperation to address illicit cross-border financial flows, tax evasion and trade mis-invoicing.

43. The role of BRICS and its collaborative efforts in the field of economic and financial co-operation are yielding positive results. We emphasise the importance of our cooperation in order to help stabilise the global economy and to resume growth.

44. We welcome experts exploring the possibility of setting up an independent BRICS Rating Agency based on market-oriented principles, in order to further strengthen the global governance architecture.

45. We welcome the reports of BRICS Think Tanks Council and BRICS Academic Forum that have emerged as valuable platforms for our experts to exchange views. They have submitted their valuable suggestions with regard to promoting market research and analysis in BRICS and developing countries and exploring possibilities of carrying this process forward. We believe that BRICS institution-building is critical to our shared vision of transforming the global financial architecture to one based on the principles of fairness and equity.

46. We emphasise the importance of enhancing intra-BRICS cooperation in the industrial sector, including through the BRICS Industry Ministers Meetings, in order to contribute to the accelerated and sustainable economic growth, the strengthening of comprehensive industrial ties, the promotion of innovation as well as job creation, and improvement of the quality of life of people in BRICS countries.

47. We congratulate the United Nations Industrial Development Organization (UNIDO) for the 50th anniversary of its foundation and recall its unique mandate to promote and accelerate inclusive and sustainable industrial development and its contribution in promoting industrialisation in Africa. We note, in this context, the progress achieved so far in the establishment of the UNIDO-BRICS Technology Platform.

48.   We commend our Customs administrations on the establishment of the Customs Cooperation Committee of BRICS, and on exploring means of further enhancing collaboration in the future, including those aimed at creating legal basis for customs cooperation and facilitating procedures of customs control. We note the signing of the Regulations on Customs Cooperation Committee of the BRICS in line with the undertaking in the Strategy for BRICS Economic Partnership to strengthen interaction among Customs Administrations.

49.   We recall the Fortaleza Declaration wherein we recognised the potential for BRICS insurance and reinsurance markets to pool capacities and had directed our relevant authorities to explore avenues for cooperation in this regard. We would like this work to be expedited.

50.   We reaffirm our commitment towards a globally fair and modern tax system and welcome the progress made on effective and widespread implementation of the internationally agreed standards. We support the implementation of the Base Erosion and Profit Shifting Project (BEPS) with due regard to the national realities of the countries. We encourage countries and International Organisations to assist developing economies in building their tax capacity.

51.   We note that aggressive tax planning and tax practices hurt equitable development and economic growth. Base Erosion and Profit Shifting must be effectively tackled. We affirm that profit should be taxed in the jurisdiction where the economic activity is performed and the value is created. We reaffirm our commitment to support international cooperation in this regard, including in the Common Reporting Standard for Automatic Exchange of Tax Information (AEOI).

52.   We note the ongoing discussions on international taxation matters. In this regard, we recall the Addis Ababa Action Agenda on Financing for Development including its emphasis on inclusive cooperation and dialogue among national tax authorities on international tax matters with increased participation of developing countries and reflecting adequate, equitable, geographical distribution, representing different tax systems.

53.   We support the strengthening of international cooperation against corruption, including through the BRICS Anti-Corruption Working Group, as well as on matters related to asset recovery and persons sought for corruption. We acknowledge that corruption including illicit money and financial flows, and ill-gotten wealth stashed in foreign jurisdictions is a global challenge which may impact negatively on economic growth and sustainable development. We will strive to coordinate our approach in this regard and encourage a stronger global commitment to prevent and combat corruption on the basis of the United Nations Convention against Corruption and other relevant international legal instruments.

54.   We recognise that nuclear energy will play a significant role for some of the BRICS countries in meeting their 2015 Paris Climate Change Agreement commitments and for reducing global greenhouse gas emissions in the long term. In this regard, we underline the importance of predictability in accessing technology and finance for expansion of civil nuclear energy capacity which would contribute to the sustainable development of BRICS countries.

55.   We reiterate that outer space shall be free for peaceful exploration and use by all States on the basis of equality in accordance with international law. Reaffirming that outer space shall remain free from any kind of weapons or any use of force, we stress that negotiations for the conclusion of an international agreement or agreements to prevent an arms race in outer space are a priority task of the United Nations Conference on Disarmament, and support the efforts to start substantive work, inter alia, based on the updated draft treaty on the prevention of the placement of weapons in outer space and of the threat or use of force against outer space objects submitted by China and Russian Federation. We also note an international initiative for a political obligation on the no first placement of weapons in outer space.

56.   Priority should be accorded to ensuring the long-term sustainability of outer space activities, as well as ways and means of preserving outer space for future generations. We note that this is an

important objective on the current agenda of the UN Committee on the Peaceful Uses of Outer Space (UNCOPUOS). In this respect, we welcome the recent decision by the UNCOPUOS Scientific and Technical Sub-Committee Working Group on Long-term Sustainability of Outer Space Activities to conclude negotiations and achieve consensus on the full set of guidelines for the long term sustainability of outer space activities by 2018 to coincide with the commemoration of the 50th Anniversary of the first United Nations Conference on the Exploration and Peaceful Uses of Outer Space (UNISPACE + 50).

57.   We strongly condemn the recent several attacks, against some BRICS countries, including that in India. We strongly condemn terrorism in all its forms and manifestations and stressed that there can be no justification whatsoever for any acts of terrorism, whether based upon ideological, religious, political, racial, ethnic or any other reasons. We agreed to strengthen cooperation in combating international terrorism both at the bilateral level and at international fora.

58.   To address the threat of chemical and biological terrorism, we support and emphasise the need for launching multilateral negotiations on an international convention for the suppression of acts of chemical and biological terrorism, including at the Conference on Disarmament. In this context, we welcome India's offer to host a Conference in 2018 aimed at strengthening international resolve in facing the challenge of the WMD-Terrorism nexus.

59.   We call upon all nations to adopt a comprehensive approach in combating terrorism, which should include countering violent extremism as and when conducive to terrorism, radicalisation, recruitment, movement of terrorists including Foreign Terrorist Fighters, blocking sources of financing terrorism, including through organised crime by means of money-laundering, drug trafficking, criminal activities, dismantling terrorist bases, and countering misuse of the Internet including social media by terror entities through misuse of the latest Information and Communication Technologies (ICTs).Successfully combating terrorism requires a holistic approach. All counter-terrorism measures should uphold international law and respect human rights.

60.   We acknowledge the recent meeting of the BRICS High Representatives on National Security and, in this context, welcome the setting up and the first meeting of the BRICS Joint Working Group on Counter-Terrorism on 14 September 2016 in New Delhi. We believe it will further promote dialogue and understanding among BRICS nations on issues of counter terrorism, as well as coordinate efforts to address the scourge of terrorism.

61.   We acknowledge that international terrorism, especially the Islamic State in Iraq and the Levant (ISIL, also known as Daesh) and affiliated terrorist groups and individuals, constitute a global and unprecedented threat to international peace and security. Stressing UN's central role in coordinating multilateral approaches against terrorism, we urge all nations to undertake effective implementation of relevant UN Security Council Resolutions, and reaffirm our commitment on increasing the effectiveness of the UN counter terrorism framework. We call upon all nations to work together to expedite the adoption of the Comprehensive Convention on International Terrorism (CCIT) in the UN General Assembly without any further delay. We recall the responsibility of all States to prevent terrorist actions from their territories.

62.   We reaffirm our commitment to the FATF International Standards on Combating Money Laundering and the Financing of Terrorism and Proliferation and call for swift, effective and universal implementation of FATF Consolidated Strategy on Combating Terrorist Financing, including effective implementation of its operational plan. We seek to intensify our cooperation in FATF and FATF-style regional bodies (FSRBs).

63.   We welcome the outcome document of the Special session of the General Assembly on the world drug problem, held in New York from 19-21 April 2016. We call for strengthening of international and regional cooperation and coordination to counter the global threat caused by the illicit production and trafficking of drugs, especially opiates. We note with deep concern the

increasing links between drug trafficking and terrorism, money laundering and organised crime. We commend the cooperation between BRICS drug control agencies and welcome the deliberations in second Anti-Drug Working Group Meeting held in New Delhi on 8 July 2016.

64.   We reaffirm that ICT expansion is a key enabler for sustainable development, for international peace and security and for human rights. We agree to strengthen joint efforts to enhance security in the use of ICTs, combating the use of ICTs for criminal and terrorist purposes and improving cooperation between our technical, law enforcement, R&D and innovation in the field of ICTs and capacity building institutions. We affirm our commitment to bridging digital and technological divides, in particular between developed and developing countries. We recognise that our approach must be multidimensional and inclusive and contains an evolving understanding of what constitutes access, emphasising the quality of that access.

65.   We reiterate that the use and development of ICTs through international and regional cooperation and on the basis of universally accepted norms and principles of international law, including the Charter of the UN; in particular political independence, territorial integrity and sovereign equality of States, the settlement of disputes by peaceful means, non-interference in internal affairs of other States as well as respect for human rights and fundamental freedoms, including the right to privacy; are of paramount importance in order to ensure a peaceful, secure and open and cooperative use of ICTs.

66.   The increasing misuse of ICTs for terrorist purposes poses a threat to international peace and security. We emphasise the need to enhance international cooperation against terrorist and criminal misuse of ICTs and reaffirm the general approach laid in the eThekwini, Fortaleza and Ufa declarations in this regard. We reaffirm the key role of the UN in addressing the issues related to the security in the use of ICTs. We will continue to work together for the adoption of the rules, norms and principles of responsible behaviour of States including through the process of UNGGE. We recognise that the states have the leading role to ensure stability and security in the use of ICTs.

67.   We advocate also for an open, non-fragmented and secure Internet, and reaffirm that the Internet is a global resource and that States should participate on an equal footing in its evolution and functioning, taking into account the need to involve relevant stakeholders in their respective roles and responsibilities.

68.   We recognise the importance of energy-saving and energy-efficiency for ensuring sustainable economic development and welcome the Memorandum of Understanding which was signed in this regard.

69.   We recognise the challenge of scaling-up power generation and its efficient distribution, as well as the need to scale up low carbon fuels and other clean energy solutions. We further recognise the level of investments needed in renewable energy in this regard. We therefore believe that international cooperation in this field be focused on access to clean energy technology and finance. We further note the significance of clean energy in achieving Sustainable Development Goals. We recognise that sustainable development, energy access, and energy security are critical to the shared prosperity and future of the planet. We acknowledge that clean and renewable energy needs to be affordable to all.

70.   We support a wider use of natural gas as an economically efficient and clean fuel to promote sustainable development as well as to reduce the greenhouse emissions in accordance with the Paris Agreement on climate change.

71.   We note that BRICS countries face challenges of communicable diseases including HIV and Tuberculosis. We, in this regard, note the efforts made by BRICS Health Ministers to achieve the 90–90–90 HIV treatment target by 2020. We underline the imperative to advance cooperation and action on HIV and TB in the BRICS countries, including in the production of quality-assured drugs and diagnostics.

72. We take note of United Nations High Level Meeting on Ending AIDS in June 2016 and forthcoming Global Conference on TB under WHO auspices in Moscow in 2017.

73. Recognising global health challenges we emphasise the importance of cooperation among BRICS countries in promoting research and development of medicines and diagnostic tools to end epidemics and to facilitate access to safe, effective, quality and affordable essential medicines.

74. We agreed to organise a BRICS High Level Meeting on Traditional Medical Knowledge.

75. We welcome the High Level meeting on Anti-Microbial Resistance (AMR) during UNGA-71, which addresses the serious threat that AMR poses to public health, growth and global economic stability. We will seek to identify possibilities for cooperation among our health and/or regulatory authorities, with a view to share best practices and discuss challenges, as well as identifying potential areas for convergence.

76. We reaffirm our commitment to promote a long-term and balanced demographic development and continue cooperation on population related matters in accordance with the Agenda for BRICS Cooperation on Population Matters for 2015-2020.

77. We welcome the outcomes of the meetings of BRICS Labour & Employment Ministers held on 9 June 2016 in Geneva and on 27-28 September 2016 in New Delhi. We take note of the possibility of bilateral Social Security Agreements between BRICS countries, and of the commitment to take steps to establish a network of lead labour research and training institutes, so as to encourage capacity building, information exchange and sharing of best practices amongst BRICS countries. We recognise quality employment, including a Decent Work Agenda, sustaining social protection and enhancing rights at work, are core to inclusive and sustainable development.

78. We welcome the outcomes of the fourth BRICS Education Ministers' meeting held on 30 September 2016 in New Delhi, including the New Delhi Declaration on Education. We stress the importance of education and skills for economic development, and reaffirm the need for universal access to high-quality education. We are satisfied with the progress of the BRICS Network University (BRICSNU) as well as the BRICS University League (BRICSUL), which will commence their programmes in 2017. These two initiatives will facilitate higher education collaboration and partnerships across the BRICS countries.

79. We appreciate the organisation of Young Diplomats' Forum held on 3-6 September 2016 in Kolkata. We also welcome the signing of the Memorandum of Understanding between BRICS Diplomatic Academies to encourage exchange of knowledge and experiences.

80. We welcome the outcomes of the fourth BRICS STI Ministerial Meeting held on 8 October 2016, wherein they adopted the Jaipur Declaration and endorsed the updated Work Plan (2015-2018) aimed at strengthening cooperation in science, technology and innovation, especially leveraging young scientific talent for addressing societal challenges; creating a networking platform for BRICS young scientists; co-generating new knowledge and innovative products, services and processes; and addressing common global and regional socio-economic challenges utilising shared experiences and complementarities.

81. We stress the importance of implementation of the BRICS Research and Innovation Initiative. We welcome the hosting of the first BRICS Young Scientists Conclave in India, instituting of BRICS Innovative Idea Prize for Young Scientists. We note the progress of the first Call for Proposals under the BRICS STI Framework Programme, in ten thematic areas, with funding commitment from the five BRICS STI Ministries and associated funding bodies. We welcome the establishment of the BRICS Working Group on Research Infrastructure, and Mega-Science to reinforce the BRICS Global Research Advanced Infrastructure Network (BRICS-GRAIN).

82. We welcome the outcomes of the Agriculture Ministers' Meeting, held on 23 September 2016, including the Joint Declaration. We emphasise the importance of ensuring food security, and

addressing malnutrition, eliminating hunger, inequality and poverty through increased agricultural production, productivity, sustainable management of natural resources and trade in agriculture among the BRICS countries. As the world's leading producers of agriculture products and home to large populations, we emphasise the importance of BRICS cooperation in agriculture. We recognize the importance of science-based agriculture and of deploying information and communication technology (ICT).

83.   To further intensify cooperation among BRICS countries in agricultural research policy, science and technology, innovation and capacity building, including technologies for small-holder farming in the BRICS countries, we welcome the signing of the MoU for Establishment of the BRICS Agricultural Research Platform.

84.   Considering the dependence of agriculture on water, we call upon the development of infrastructure for irrigation to assist farmers in building resilience during times of drought and welcome sharing of experiences and expertise in these areas.

85.   We affirm that the value of sharing expertise and experiences among BRICS countries with regard to usage of Information and Communication Technology (ICT) in e-governance, financial inclusion, and targeted delivery of benefits, e-commerce, open government, digital content and services and bridging the digital divide. We support efforts aimed at capacity building for effective participation in e-commerce trade to ensure shared benefits.

86.   We welcome the forthcoming BRICS Telecommunication Ministerial Meeting that will further strengthen our cooperation, including on technology trends, standards developments, skill developments, and policy frameworks.

87.   We believe it is necessary to ensure joint efforts towards diversification of the world market of software and IT equipment. We call for developing and strengthening the ICT cooperation in the framework of the BRICS Working Group on ICT Cooperation.

88.   We welcome the outcomes of the meetings of BRICS Ministers responsible for Disaster Management held on 19-20 April 2016 in St. Petersburg and on 22 August 2016 in Udaipur. We also welcome the Udaipur Declaration adopted at the second meeting and applaud the formation of BRICS Joint Task Force on Disaster Risk Management.

89.   We extend our deepest condolences to the people of Haiti and the Caribbean on the tragic loss of lives following hurricane Matthew. We support the efforts of the UN and humanitarian partners in their response to this tragedy.

90.   We welcome the outcomes of the BRICS Ministerial Meeting on Environment held on 15-16 September 2016, in Goa, including the Goa Statement on Environment. We welcome the decision to share technical expertise in the areas of abatement and control of air and water pollution, efficient management of waste and sustainable management of bio-diversity. We recognise the importance of participation by BRICS countries in environmental cooperation initiatives, including developing a platform for sharing environmentally sound technologies.

91.   We welcome the outcome of the 17th Conference of Parties to the Convention on International Trade in Endangered Species of Wild Fauna and Flora (CITES), held in Johannesburg, South Africa, as a landmark advancement of the regulation of international trade in endangered species from 24 September - 4 October 2016.

92.   We welcome the adoption of the Paris Agreement anchored in the United Nations Framework Convention on Climate Change (UNFCCC), and its signing by a large number of countries on 22 April 2016. We emphasise that the comprehensive, balanced and ambitious nature of the Paris Agreement reaffirms the principles of UNFCCC including the principle of equity and common but differentiated responsibilities and respective capabilities, in light of different national circumstances (CBDR & RC).

93. We welcome the Paris Agreement and its imminent entry into force on 4 November 2016. We call on the developed countries to fulfil their responsibility towards providing the necessary financial resources, technology and capacity building assistance to support the developing countries with respect to both mitigation and adaptation for the implementation of the Paris Agreement.

94. We reiterate the commitments to gender equality and empowerment of all women and girls as contained in the 2030 Agenda. We recognise that women play a vital role as agents of development and acknowledge that their equal and inclusive participation and contribution is crucial to making progress across all Sustainable Development Goals and targets. We emphasise the importance of enhancing accountability for the implementation of these commitments.

95. Cognizant of the potential and diversity of youth population in our countries, their needs and aspirations, we welcome the outcomes of the BRICS Youth Summit in Guwahati including, "Guwahati BRICS Youth Summit 2016 Call to Action" that recognise the importance of education, employment, entrepreneurship, and skills training for them to be socially and economically empowered.

96. We welcome the BRICS Convention on Tourism that was organised in Khajuraho, Madhya Pradesh on 1-2 September 2016 as an effective means to promote tourism cooperation among BRICS countries.

97. As home to 43% of the world population and among the fastest urbanising societies, we recognise the multi-dimensional challenges and opportunities of urbanisation. We affirm our engagement in the process that will lead to adoption of a New Urban Agenda by the Conference of the United Nations on Housing and Sustainable Urban Development – Habitat III (Quito, 17-20 October 2016).We welcome the BRICS Urbanisation Forum, BRICS Friendship Cities Conclave, held in Visakhapatnam on 14-16 September 2016, and in Mumbai on 14-16 April 2016, respectively, which contributed to fostering increased engagements between our cities and stakeholders. We call for enhanced cooperation with regard to strengthening urban governance, making our cities safe and inclusive, improving urban transport, financing of urban infrastructure and building sustainable cities.

98. We note India's initiative on the upcoming BRICS Local Bodies Conference to exchange expertise and best-practices, including in local budgeting.

99. Noting the importance of orderly, safe, regular and responsible migration and mobility of people, we welcome the outcomes of first BRICS Migration Ministers Meeting in Sochi, Russian Federation, on 8 October 2015.

100. We recognise the important role of culture in sustainable development and in fostering mutual understanding and closer cooperation among our peoples. We encourage expansion of cultural exchanges between people of BRICS countries. In this context we commend the hosting of the first BRICS Film Festival in New Delhi on 2-6 September 2016.

101. We welcome the forthcoming meeting of the Second BRICS Parliamentary Forum in Geneva on 23 October 2016 under the theme of 'BRICS Parliamentary Cooperation on the implementation of the SDGs'.

102. We appreciate the deliberations of the BRICS Women Parliamentarians' Forum in Jaipur on 20-21 August, 2016 and the adoption of Jaipur Declaration, centred on SDGs, that inter alia emphasises the commitment to strengthen parliamentary strategic partnerships on all the three dimensions of sustainable development, fostering gender equality and women empowerment.

103. We note the deliberations on a BRICS Railways Research Network aimed at promoting research and development in this field to further growth in our economies in a cost effective and sustainable manner.

104. We congratulate India on organising the first BRICS Under-17 Football Tournament in Goa on 5-15 October 2016. We, in this regard, note the initiative towards a BRICS Sports Council to foster exchanges among BRICS countries.

105. We recognise the increasing trade, business and investment between BRICS countries and the important role of BRICS Interbank Cooperation Mechanism and in this regard welcome the initiative of the Export-Import Bank of India of instituting Annual BRICS Economic Research Award to promote advanced research in economics of relevance to BRICS countries.

106. We reiterate our commitment to strengthening our partnerships for common development. To this end, we endorse the Goa Action Plan.

107. China, South Africa, Brazil and Russia appreciate India's BRICS Chairpersonship and the good pace of BRICS cooperation agenda.

108. We emphasise the importance of review and follow up of implementation of outcome documents and decisions of the BRICS Summits. We task our Sherpas to carry this process forward.

109. China, South Africa, Brazil and Russia express their sincere gratitude to the Government and people of India for hosting the Eighth BRICS Summit in Goa.

110. India, South Africa, Brazil and Russia convey their appreciation to China for its offer to host the Ninth BRICS Summit in 2017 and extend full support to that end.

Goa, India

16 October 2016

B.   The Goa Action Plan

GOA ACTION PLAN

We took note of the following events held under India's BRICS Chairpersonship before the Goa Summit.

Meetings of Parliamentarians & Ministers

1.   BRICS Women Parliamentarians' Forum (20-21 August 2016, Jaipur)

2.   Meeting of National Security Advisers (15-16 September 2016, New Delhi)

3.   Meeting of BRICS Agriculture Ministers (23 September 2016, New Delhi)

4.   Meeting of the BRICS Ministers of Disaster Management (22-23 August 2016, Udaipur)

5.   Meeting of BRICS Education Ministers (30 September 2016, New Delhi)

6.   Meeting of BRICS Environment Ministers (16 September 2016, Goa)

7.   Meetings of BRICS Finance Ministers and Central Bank Governors (14 April 2016, Washington; 14 October 2016, Goa)

8.   Meeting of BRICS Ministers of Foreign Affairs/International Relations on the margins of UNGA (20 September 2016, New York)

9.   Luncheon Meeting of BRICS Health Ministers and Heads of Delegation on the margins of 69th World Health Assembly (24 May 2016, Geneva)

10.   Meeting of BRICS Ministers of Labour & Employment (9 June 2016 on the margins of ILO meeting, Geneva; 27-28 September 2016, Agra)

11.   4th BRICS Science, Technology & Innovation Ministerial Meeting (8 October 2016, Jaipur)

12.   Meeting of BRICS Trade Ministers (13 October 2016, New Delhi)

Meetings of Working Groups/Senior Officials/Technical Groups/Experts Groups

13.   Meeting of BRICS Working Group on Agriculture (22 September 2016, New Delhi)

14.   Meetings of Experts for BRICS Agriculture Research Platform (27-28 June 2016, New Delhi; 21 September 2016, New Delhi)

15.   Meeting of BRICS Senior Officials for Anti-Corruption (16 March 2016 on the margins of OECD Anti-Bribery Convention in Paris; 8 June 2016 on the margins of 2nd G20 ACWG meeting in London)

16.   Anti-Drug Working Group Meeting (8 July 2016, New Delhi)

17.   Meeting of BRICS Competition Authorities on the margins of International Legal Forum (19 May 2016, St. Petersburg, Russia)

18.   Meeting of BRICS Contact Group on Economic and Trade Issues (CGETI) (12 April 2016, New Delhi; 29 July 2016, Agra; 12 October 2016, New Delhi)

19.   Meeting of the Working Group on Counter Terrorism (14 September 2016, New Delhi)

20.   Meeting of BRICS Customs Agencies on the margins of Conference of the World Customs Organization (11-16 July 2016, Brussels)

21.   Meeting of BRICS Heads of Customs Administrations (15-16 October 2016, Goa)

22. Meeting of BRICS Development Partnership Administrations (DPAs) and Forum for Indian Development Cooperation (FIDC) (6-7 August 2016, New Delhi)

23. Meeting of BRICS Senior Officials on Education (29 September 2016, New Delhi)

24. 1st Meeting of BRICS Universities League Members (2 April 2016, Beijing)

25. Meeting of Working Group on Energy Saving and Improvement of Energy Efficiency (4-5 July 2016, Visakhapatnam)

26. Employment Working Group Meeting (27-28 July 2016, Hyderabad)

27. Meeting of BRICS Working Group on Environment (15 September 2016, Goa)

28. BRICS Dialogue on Foreign Policy (25-26 July 2016, Patna)

29. Meeting of Heads of Export Credit Agencies (ECAs) (13 October 2016, New Delhi)

30. 6th Informal meeting of BRICS Finance Officials on the margins of FATF (16 February 2016, Paris)

31. 7th Informal meeting of BRICS Finance Officials on the margins of FATF (18-24 June 2016, Busan, RoK)

32. Technical Group Meeting of BRICS Development Banks (10-11 March 2016, Udaipur)

33. Working Group Meeting of BRICS Development Banks (28-29 July 2016, Mumbai)

34. Working Group Meeting of BRICS Development Banks (on Local Currency Financing) (14 October 2016, Goa)

35. Working Group Meeting of BRICS Development Banks (on Innovation Financing) (14 October 2016, Goa)

36. Annual Meeting of BRICS Interbank Cooperation Mechanism (15 October 2016, Goa)

37. Meeting of Heads of BRICS Development Banks with NDB (15-16 October 2016, Goa)

38. 1st Annual Meeting of the Board of Governors of BRICS NDB (20 July 2016, Shanghai)

39. BRICS Contingent Reserve Arrangement Working Group Meeting (25 February 2016, Shanghai)

40. 2nd BRICS Contingent Reserve Arrangement Standing Committee Meeting (26 February 2016, Shanghai)

41. 2nd BRICS Contingent Reserve Arrangement Governing Council Meeting (6 October 2016, Washington)

42. BRICS Working Group on Geospatial Technology and Application (2 March 2016, Noida)

43. 6th Meeting of Heads of Intellectual Property Offices (HIPO) (20-22 June 2016, Moscow)

44. Meeting of BRICS Network University International Governing Board (IGB) (27 September 2016, Mumbai)

45. BRICS Railway Experts' Meeting (29 April 2016, Lucknow; 14-15 July 2016, Secunderabad)

46. 6th Meeting of BRICS Senior Officials on Science, Technology & Innovation (7 October 2016, Jaipur)

47. Meeting of BRICS Science, Technology & Innovation Funding Working Group (6 October 2016, Jaipur)

48. 2nd Meeting of the BRICS Astronomy Working Group (8 September 2016, Ekaterinburg)

49. 1st Photonics Conference of BRICS Countries (30-31 May 2016, Moscow)

50. 2nd Meeting of BRICS Officials within specialized session "Prevention and Mitigation of Natural Disasters" (26 August 2016, Saint-Petersburg)

51. BRICS Sherpas and Sous-Sherpas meeting (29-30 April 2016, Jaipur; 5-6 August 2016, Bhopal; 2-3 September 2016, Hangzhou; 8-10 October 2016, New Delhi; 12-13 October 2016, Goa)

52. Technical Level Meeting of BRICS National Statistical Agencies (24-26 February 2016, New Delhi)

53. Meeting of Heads of BRICS Supreme Audit Institutions (24 June 2016, Beijing)

Seminars & Workshops

54. BRICS Academic Forum (19-22 September 2016, Goa)

55. BRICS Think Tank Council meeting (23 September 2016, New Delhi)

56. BRICS Civil Forum (3-4 October 2016, New Delhi)

57. BRICS Digital Conclave (28-29 April 2016, New Delhi)

58. Workshop on International Arbitration Mechanism (27 August 2016, New Delhi)

59. Seminar on Challenges in Developing the Bond Market in BRICS (27 September 2016, Mumbai)

60. BRICS Economic Forum (13-14 October 2016, Goa)

61. BRICS Financial Forum (15 October 2016, Goa)

62. Workshop on Financial Inclusion for BRICS Nations (19 September 2016, Mumbai)

63. Seminar on Long Term Infrastructure Financing and PPP best practices (22 September 2016, New Delhi)

64. Workshop on Investment Flows (13 October 2016, Mumbai)

65. BRICS Handicraft Artisans Exchange Programme (6-15 September 2016, Jaipur)

66. Workshop on Access to Medicines and Trade Agreements (23 May 2016, Geneva)

67. Workshop on Health Surveillance System (1-2 August 2016, Bengaluru)

68. 1st General Conference on BRICS Network University (7-8 April 2016, Ekaterinburg, Russia)

69. Workshop on Skill Development (25-29 July 2016, Mumbai)

70. Workshop on Export Credit (14 October 2016, Goa)

71. 2nd Round Table on MSMEs and Seminar on Services (28 July 2016, Agra)

72. BRICS Seminars on NTMs and Services (11 April 2016, New Delhi)

73. BRICS Water Forum (29-30 September 2016, Moscow)

74. BRICS Wellness Forum (10-11 September 2016, Bengaluru)

75. 3rd Meeting of the BRICS Urbanization Forum (14-16 September 2016, Visakhapatnam)

76. BRICS Friendship Cities Conclave (14-16 April 2016, Mumbai)

77. BRICS Smart Cities Workshop (17-19 August 2016, Jaipur)

BRICS Business Council & BRICS Business Forum

78. BRICS Business Council (14 October 2016, New Delhi; 15 October 2016, Goa)

79. BRICS Business Council interaction with BRICS Leaders (16 October 2016, Goa)

80. BRICS Business Forum (13 October 2016, New Delhi)

People-to-People & Business Exchanges

81. BRICS Trade Fair (12-14 October 2016, New Delhi)

82. BRICS Film Festival (2-6 September 2016, New Delhi)

83. BRICS Convention of Tourism (1-2 September 2016, Khajuraho)
84. BRICS U-17 Football Tournament (5-15 October 2016, Delhi-Goa)
85. BRICS Young Diplomats' Forum (3-6 September 2016, Kolkata)
86. BRICS Young Scientists' Conclave (26-30 Sept 2016, Bengaluru)
87. BRICS Youth Summit (1-3 July 2016, Guwahati)

We further took note of the upcoming events under India's BRICS Chairpersonship.

88. BRICS Parliamentary Forum (on the margins of IPU)
89. Meeting of BRICS Energy Ministers
90. 6th Meeting of the BRICS Health Ministers
91. Meeting of BRICS Ministers of Telecommunications
92. Meeting of BRICS Senior Officials for Anti-Corruption
93. Meeting of Senior Officials of Health
94. BRICS Consultations of Middle East Envoys
95. BRICS Sherpas and Sous-Sherpas meetings
96. Meeting of the BRICS Heads of National Statistical Agencies
97. Meeting of BRICS Heads of Tax Authorities
98. Meeting of BRICS Experts on Tax Matters
99. Meetings of BRICS Working Group on ICT Cooperation
100. 2nd Technical Workshop among BRICS Exports Credit Agencies
101. Exhibition and B2B Meetings on ICT
102. BRICS Media Forum
103. Workshop on Anti-Microbial Resistance (AMR)
104. Workshop on Drugs and Medical Devices
105. Workshop on Non Communicable Diseases
106. 4th BRICS Seminar on Population matters
107. Workshop on TB/AIDS
108. Foundation Conference of BRICS Centre for Materials Science and Nanotechnology
109. Conference on Foresight and Science, Technology and Innovation Policy of BRICS countries
110. BRICS Forum on State Owned Enterprises Reforms and Governance
111. Workshop on Sustainable Water Development, Conservation and Efficiency
112. BRICS Local Bodies' Conference (Focus: Budgeting)

Key Initiatives During India's BRICS Chairmanship

1. BRICS Agriculture Research Platform
2. BRICS Railway Research Network
3. BRICS Sports Council
4. BRICS Rating Agency

5. BRICS Institute for Economic Research and Analysis
6. MoU on Environmental Cooperation
7. Regulations on BRICS Customs Cooperation Committee
8. MoU on Cooperation between Diplomatic Academies of BRICS Countries
9. MoU on Cooperation among BRICS Development Banks and the NDB
10. BRICS Women Parliamentarians' Forum
11. BRICS Under-17 Football Tournament
12. BRICS Trade Fair
13. BRICS Film Festival
14. BRICS Convention on Tourism
15. BRICS Digital Conclave
16. BRICS Wellness Forum
17. BRICS Friendship Cities Conclave
18. BRICS Smart Cities Workshop
19. 3rd BRICS Urbanisation Forum
20. BRICS Local Bodies Conference
21. BRICS Handicraft Artisans' Exchange Programme
22. BRICS Young Scientist Conclave
23. BRICS Innovative Idea Prize for Young Scientists
24. BRICS Economic Research Award

II.4.   7th BRICS Summit 2015: 9 Jul. 2015, Ufa (RUS)

A.   The Ufa Declaration

VII BRICS SUMMIT
UFA DECLARATION
Ufa, the Russian Federation, 9 July 2015

1.   We, the leaders of the Federative Republic of Brazil, the Russian Federation, the Republic of India, the People's Republic of China and the Republic of South Africa, met on 9 July 2015, in Ufa, Russia, at the Seventh BRICS Summit, which was held under the theme "BRICS Partnership – a Powerful Factor of Global Development". We discussed issues of common interest in respect of the international agenda as well as key priorities in respect of further strengthening and broadening our intra-BRICS cooperation. We emphasized the importance to strengthen BRICS solidarity and cooperation, and decided to further enhance our strategic partnership on the basis of principles of openness, solidarity, equality and mutual understanding, inclusiveness and mutually beneficial cooperation. We agreed to step up coordinated efforts in responding to emerging challenges, ensuring peace and security, promoting development in a sustainable way, addressing poverty eradication, inequality and unemployment for the benefit of our peoples and the international community. We confirmed our intention to further enhance the collective role of our countries in international affairs.

2.   We welcome the substantive progress that was made since the Fortaleza Summit on 15 July 2014 during the Brazilian BRICS Chairship, especially the establishment of BRICS financial institutions: the New Development Bank (NDB) and the Contingent Reserves Arrangement (CRA). The Ufa Summit marks their entry into force. We also broadened our cooperation in the political, economic and social fields and reaffirmed our focus on strengthening our partnership.

3.   With the aim of consolidating our engagement with other countries, particularly developing countries and emerging market economies, as well as with international and regional institutions, we will hold a meeting with the Heads of States and Governments of the countries of the Eurasian Economic Union and the Shanghai Cooperation Organization (SCO), as well as the Heads of observer States of the SCO. Participants in this meeting share various issues of mutual interest. This lays a solid foundation for launching a broader mutually beneficial dialogue. All of us remain committed to upholding the purposes and principles of the UN Charter and international law and we strive to achieve sustainable economic growth through international cooperation and an enhanced use of regional integration mechanisms in order to improve the welfare and prosperity of our people.

4.   At our meeting we emphasized that the year 2015 marks the 70th Anniversary of the Founding of the United Nations. We reaffirmed our strong commitment to the United Nations as a universal multilateral organization entrusted with the mandate of helping the international community maintain international peace and security, advance global development and promote and protect human rights. The UN enjoys universal membership and has a central role in global affairs and multilateralism. We affirmed the need for comprehensive, transparent and efficient multilateral approaches to addressing global challenges, and in this regard underscored the central role of the United Nations in the ongoing efforts to find common solutions to such challenges. We expressed our intention to contribute to safeguarding a fair and equitable international order based on the purposes and principles of the UN Charter and to fully avail ourselves of the potential of the Organization as a forum for an open and honest debate as well as coordination of global politics in order to prevent war and conflicts and promote progress and development of humankind. We recall the 2005 World Summit Outcome Document and reaffirm the need for a comprehensive reform of the United Nations, including its Security Council with a view to making it more representative and

efficient so that it could better respond to global challenges. China and Russia reiterate the importance they attach to the status and role of Brazil, India and South Africa in international affairs and support their aspiration to play a greater role in the UN.

5.   The year 2015 also marks the 70th Anniversary of the end of World War II. We paid tribute to all those who fought against fascism and militarism and for freedom of nations. We are encouraged that the General Assembly adopted by consensus the resolution 69/267 entitled "Seventieth Anniversary of the End of the Second World War". We welcomed that in conformity with this resolution on 5 May 2015 the General Assembly held a special solemn meeting in commemoration of all victims of the war. We express our commitment to resolutely reject the continued attempts to misrepresent the results of World War II. While remembering the scourge of war, we highlight that it is our common duty to build a future of peace and development.

6.   We assert that peaceful coexistence of nations is impossible without universal, scrupulous and consistent application of the generally recognized principles and rules of international law. The violation of its core principles results in creation of situations threatening international peace and security.

We insist that international law provides tools for achieving international justice, based on principles of good faith and sovereign equality. We emphasize the need for universal adherence to principles and rules of international law in their interrelation and integrity, discarding the resort to "double standards" and avoiding placing interests of some countries above others.

We reaffirm our commitment to rigorous compliance with the principles enshrined in the Charter of the United Nations and the Declaration on Principles of International Law concerning Friendly Relations and Cooperation among States in accordance with the Charter of the United Nations of 1970.

We will further enhance cooperation to defend common interests in respecting and upholding international law based on the UN Charter.

7.   We note the global character of current security challenges and threats and express our support for international efforts to address these challenges in a way that provides equal and indivisible security for all states, through respect for international law and principles of the UN Charter.

We will continue our joint efforts in coordinating positions on shared interests on global peace and security issues for the common well-being of humanity. We stress our commitment to the sustainable and peaceful settlement of disputes, according to principles and purposes of the UN Charter.

8.   We condemn unilateral military interventions and economic sanctions in violation of international law and universally recognized norms of international relations. Bearing this in mind, we emphasize the unique importance of the indivisible nature of security, and that no State should strengthen its security at the expense of the security of others.

9.   We recall that development and security are closely interlinked, mutually reinforcing and key to attaining sustainable peace. We reiterate our view that the establishment of sustainable peace requires a comprehensive, concerted and determined approach, based on mutual trust, mutual benefit, equity and cooperation.

10. We reaffirm the intention to strengthen the principle of equitable and mutually respectful cooperation of sovereign states as the cornerstone of international activities to promote and protect human rights. We will continue to treat all human rights – civil, political, economic, social and cultural rights, as well as the right to development – on the same footing and to give them equal attention. We will take every effort to bolster constructive and non-politicized human rights dialogue at all relevant international fora, including the United Nations.

Within the UN human rights institutions, including the Human Rights Council and the Third Committee of the UN General Assembly we will strengthen coordination of our positions on the issues of mutual interest. We support the universal periodic review carried out by the UN Human Rights Council and will constructively contribute to its work.

11. The global recovery continues, although growth remains fragile, with considerable divergences across countries and regions. In this context, emerging markets and developing countries (EMDCs) continue to be major drivers of global growth. Structural reforms, domestic adjustment and promotion of innovation are important for sustainable growth and provide a strong and sustainable contribution to the world economy. We note the signs of improving growth prospects in some of the key advanced economies. However, risks to the global economy persist. The challenges are related to high public debt and unemployment, poverty and inequality, lower investment and trade, negative real interest rates along with signs of prolonged low inflation in advanced economies. We remain concerned about potential spillover effects from the unconventional monetary policies of the advanced economies, which could cause disruptive volatility of exchange rates, asset prices and capital flows. We call on major economies to strengthen their policy dialogue and coordination in the context of the G20 to reduce the potential risks. It is important to strengthen the framework of international financial cooperation, including through instruments such as swap-lines, to mitigate the negative impacts of monetary policy divergence in reserve currency issuing countries.

12. We express support for the development of action-oriented economic cooperation and systematic strengthening of economic partnership for the recovery of the global economy, resisting protectionism, promoting high and productive employment, reducing possible international financial market risks and strengthening sustainable growth.

We are convinced that further efforts to coordinate macroeconomic policies between all leading economies remain a major prerequisite for early and sustainable recovery of the global economy. We also strive to facilitate market inter-linkages, robust growth and an inclusive and open world economy characterized by efficient resource distribution, free movement of capital, labour and goods, and fair and efficiently regulated competition.

13. Sound macroeconomic policies, efficiently regulated financial markets and robust levels of reserves have allowed the BRICS economies to better deal with the risks and spillover effects presented by the challenging global economic conditions in the last few years. In this context the BRICS economies are taking the necessary steps to secure economic growth, maintain financial stability and speed up structural reforms. We will also continue to work to intensify our financial and economic cooperation, including within the New Development Bank and the BRICS Contingent Reserve Arrangement to build upon our synergies.

We welcome and support the creation of a platform of joint discussion for trade cooperation amongst BRICS countries through enhanced dialogue between the BRICS Export Credit Agencies (ECAs), namely ABGF, ECGC, ECIC SA, EXIAR and SINOSURE. In specific, the BRICS countries have agreed to the establishment of an annual BRICS ECA meeting with the purpose of exploring opportunities for cooperation and future joint action to promote exports among BRICS and to other countries. The inaugural meeting for this new format took place on the sidelines of the Ufa Summit.

14. We reaffirm the important role played by the BRICS Interbank Cooperation Mechanism in expanding the BRICS countries financial and investment cooperation. We appreciate the efforts made by the member banks to explore the BRICS innovation potential. We welcome the signing of the "MoU on Cooperation with the New Development Bank" between our respective national development banks/institutions.

15. We welcome the entry into force of the Agreement on New Development Bank signed during the VI BRICS Summit in Fortaleza. We also welcome the inaugural meeting of the Board of Governors of the NDB held on the eve of the Ufa Summit and chaired by Russia, as well as the work done by the

Interim Board of Directors and the Pre Management Group aimed at the earliest launch of the Bank. We reiterate that the NDB shall serve as a powerful instrument for financing infrastructure investment and sustainable development projects in the BRICS and other developing countries and emerging market economies and for enhancing economic cooperation between our countries. We expect the NDB to approve its inaugural investment projects in the beginning of 2016. We welcome the proposal for the NDB to cooperate closely with existing and new financing mechanisms including the Asian Infrastructure Investment Bank.

16. We welcome the conclusion of the ratification process of the Treaty Establishing a Contingent Reserve Arrangement of the BRICS and its entry into force. We also welcome the signing of the BRICS Inter-Central Bank Agreement that sets technical parameters of operations within the BRICS CRA. We see the creation of the BRICS CRA, allowing its members to provide mutual financial support, as an important step in the financial cooperation of our countries. Furthermore, this new mechanism is a valuable contribution to the global financial safety net.

17. The Strategy for the BRICS Economic Partnership that we adopted today would be the key guideline for expanding trade and investment, manufacturing and minerals processing, energy, agricultural cooperation, science, technology and innovation, financial cooperation, connectivity and ICT cooperation between our countries. We direct the relevant Ministries and concerned agencies of our States to take practical steps for efficient implementation of this Strategy. We emphasize the important role of the New Development Bank, the BRICS Interbank Cooperation Mechanism, the BRICS Business Council, the BRICS Business Forum, and the BRICS Think Tanks Council in the implementation of this Strategy. We also direct our Ministers/Sherpas to look into the feasibility of developing a BRICS trade, economic and investment cooperation roadmap for the period until 2020.

18. We will continue our consultations and coordination on the G20 agenda, especially on issues of mutual interest to the BRICS countries. We will also continue working to bring greater attention to the issues on the G20 agenda that are prioritized by developing countries and emerging markets, such as macroeconomic policy coordination under the G20 Framework for Strong, Sustainable and Balanced growth, containing spillover effects, supporting economic activity, as well as bridging the gaps caused by cross-border impacts of the global financial regulation reform, adaptation to new rules introduced by the Action Plan on Base Erosion and Profit Shifting (BEPS) and the Common Reporting Standard for Automatic Exchange of Tax Information (AEOI). We will continue to appeal for broader and deepened G20 consultations with low-income countries on G20 policy recommendations that will have an impact on them.

The leaders of Brazil, Russia, India and South Africa welcome and support China's upcoming Presidency of the G20. BRICS will work closely with all members to lift global growth, strengthen International Financial Architecture and consolidate the role of the G20 as the premier forum for international financial and economic cooperation.

19. We remain deeply disappointed with the prolonged failure by the United States to ratify the IMF 2010 reform package, which continues to undermine the credibility, legitimacy and effectiveness of the IMF. This prevents the increase in the institution's quota resources and the revision of quotas and voting power in favour of developing countries and emerging markets as agreed by an overwhelming majority of members, including the United States in 2010. We expect the United States to ratify the 2010 reforms by mid-September 2015 as agreed in the IMF. In the meantime, we are prepared to work on interim steps provided they deliver equivalent results to the levels agreed as a part of the 14th General Quota Review. We reaffirm our commitment to maintaining a strong, well-resourced and quota-based IMF and, in this regard, urge other Members to continue the reform process through the 15th General Quota Review without delay.

20. We share concerns regarding the challenges of sovereign debt restructurings. Debt restructurings have often been too slow and too late, thus failing to re-establish debt sustainability and market access in a durable way. The handling of sovereign debt restructurings should be

improved to the benefit of creditors and debtors alike. We welcome the current discussions in the United Nations to improve sovereign debt restructuring processes, as well as the current work to strengthen the contractual approach in order to ensure more timely and orderly restructuring. We emphasize the importance of addressing these challenges and call all G20 countries as well as IFIs to actively participate in these processes.

21. We join in the celebration of the twentieth anniversary of the World Trade Organization (WTO) and reaffirm our support for working together to strengthen an open, transparent, non-discriminatory, and rules-based multilateral trading system as embodied in the WTO. We welcome Kenya's hosting of the 10th WTO Ministerial Conference (MC10) in Nairobi on 15-18 December 2015.

We stress the centrality of the WTO as the institution that sets multilateral trade rules. We note the importance of bilateral, regional and plurilateral trade agreements and encourage the parties to negotiations thereon to comply with the principles of transparency, inclusiveness and compatibility with WTO rules to ensure that they contribute to strengthening the multilateral trading system.

22. We reaffirm the role of the UN Conference on Trade and Development (UNCTAD) as a UN body with a mandate to consider interconnected issues of trade, investment, finance and technologies as related to development. We call on UNCTAD to fulfill its development mandate through more active implementation of technical cooperation programmes and facilitation of policy dialogue, as well as research and capacity-building. We look forward to a successful outcome of UNCTAD XIV.

23. We applaud the progress in the implementation of BRICS Trade and Investment Cooperation Framework. We welcome the Framework for BRICS E-commerce Cooperation as an instrument to promote current and future initiatives with an aim to build a closer economic partnership in this sphere. We instruct our Ministers to continue to explore ways and means in strengthening our cooperation on E-commerce.

We welcome the Initiative on Strengthening IPR Cooperation among the BRICS Countries. We support the efforts aimed at establishing and enhancing the cooperation mechanisms in such areas as SMEs support, trade promotion, sharing experiences on single window projects, inter alia, and direct officials to identify concrete activities in these areas.

24. We acknowledge the potential for expanding the use of our national currencies in transactions between the BRICS countries. We ask the relevant authorities of the BRICS countries to continue discussion on the feasibility of a wider use of national currencies in mutual trade.

25. We will continue our joint efforts aimed at improving competition policy and enforcement.

As important emerging markets and developing countries, BRICS are faced with many similar problems and challenges in terms of economic development and fair competition. It is of significance to strengthen the coordination and cooperation among the BRICS competition agencies.

Considering this, we attach great importance towards developing a mechanism preferably through a joint MoU among the BRICS countries to study the issues of competition with a special focus on socially important economic sectors. The proposed mechanism may facilitate cooperation in competition law and enforcement.

We welcome our relevant agencies' efforts to create conditions for fair competition in pharmaceutical sector.

26. The BRICS countries reaffirm their commitment to participate in the development of international standards of international taxation and cooperation for countering the erosion of tax base and profit shifting, as well as to strengthen mechanisms for ensuring tax transparency and to exchange information for taxation purposes.

We remain deeply concerned about the negative impact of tax evasion, harmful practices, and aggressive tax planning which cause erosion of tax base. Profits should be taxed where the economic activities driving the profits are performed and value is created. We reaffirm our commitment to continue to cooperate in relevant international fora on issues related to the G20/OECD BEPS Action Plan and AEOI. We are engaged in assisting developing countries to strengthen their tax administration capacity, and to promote a deeper engagement of developing countries in the BEPS project and the exchange of tax information. The BRICS countries will share knowledge and best practices in taxation.

27. We reiterate our strong condemnation of terrorism in all its forms and manifestations and stress that there can be no justification, whatsoever, for any acts of terrorism, whether based upon ideological, religious, political, racial, ethnic, or any other justification.

We are determined to consistently strengthen our cooperation in preventing and countering international terrorism. We stress that the UN has a central role in coordinating international action against terrorism, which must be conducted in accordance with international law, including the UN Charter, international refugee and humanitarian law, human rights and fundamental freedoms.

We believe that terrorist threats can be effectively addressed through a comprehensive implementation by states and the international community of all their commitments and obligations arising from all relevant resolutions of the UN Security Council and the UN Global Counter-Terrorism Strategy. We call upon all states and the international community to adhere to their commitments and obligations and in this regard to resist political approaches and selective application.

The BRICS countries reaffirm their commitment to the Financial Action Task Force (FATF) International Standards on Combating Money Laundering and the Financing of Terrorism & Proliferation.

We seek to intensify our cooperation in FATF and FATF-style regional bodies (FSRBs). We recognize that active international collaboration to counter the spread of violent extremism and its ideologies is a necessary prerequisite in the fight against terrorism. At the same time, we underscore that international cooperation on those tracks should rest upon international law taking into consideration that it is the sovereign governments that bear the primary responsibility for preventing and countering violent extremism-related threats.

28. We express deep concern about the world drug problem, which continues to threaten public health, public and human safety and well-being and undermines social, economic and political stability and sustainable development. We plan to address the problem through an integrated and balanced approach to drug supply and demand reduction strategies, in line with the UN conventions of 1961, 1971 and 1988 and other relevant norms and principles of international law. Taking into account the unprecedented global growth in the production and demand of narcotic drugs, we call for more active measures to address the drug problem and to discuss it at the relevant international fora. We reaffirm our commitment to the implementation of the Political Declaration and Plan of Action on International Cooperation towards an Integrated and Balanced Strategy to Counter the World Drug Problem adopted in 2009 at the 64th session of the UN General Assembly, as well as the Joint Ministerial Statement of the 2014 High- Level Review by the Commission on Narcotic Drugs. These provide a solid basis for an open and inclusive UN General Assembly Special Session on the world drug problem to be held in 2016. We will explore convergences in the preparatory process for UNGASS 2016.

We commend the cooperation among our respective drug control authorities, and welcome decisions adopted at the meeting of the BRICS Heads of anti-drug agencies held in Moscow on 22 April 2015, including those aimed at creating mechanisms of interaction in countering the world drug problem; we also take note of the results of the Second Ministerial Anti-Drug Conference held in Moscow on 23 April 2015.

29. We are convinced that corruption is a global challenge which undermines the legal systems of states, negatively affects their sustainable development and may facilitate other forms of crime. We

are confident that international cooperation plays a pivotal role in countering and preventing corruption. We reaffirm our commitment to make every effort to that end, including mutual legal assistance, in accordance with the UN Convention against Corruption (UNCAC) and multilaterally established principles and norms. In this regard, we look forward to the success of the sixth session of the Conference of State parties to the UNCAC, which will take place in St. Petersburg on 2-6 November 2015.

In that context, we decided to create a BRICS Working Group on Anti- Corruption Cooperation.

30. We intend to intensify efforts undertaken by our States to prevent and combat transnational organized crime.

We will work for the inclusion of crime prevention and criminal justice issues among the long-term priorities of the UN agenda. We support efforts of the Conference of the Parties to the UN Convention against Transnational Organized Crime of 2000 to enhance the effectiveness of its application, including through advancing the negotiating process to establish a mechanism to review the implementation of the Convention provisions and its additional protocols.

We stand for the adoption of an integrated and comprehensive approach to the problem of transnational organized crime, taking due cognizance of the outcomes of the 13th United Nations Congress on Crime Prevention and Criminal Justice held in Doha in April 2015.

We aim to deepen interaction among the BRICS countries on issues related to the prevention and combat of transnational organized crime.

31. Piracy and armed robbery at sea represent a significant threat to the security of international navigation and to the security and development of affected regions. While reiterating that Coastal States have the primary responsibility for counteracting these types of criminal offences, we intend to reinforce our cooperation towards this goal and we call upon all parties concerned to remain engaged in the fight against these phenomena. We also stress the need for a comprehensive response to piracy, in order to tackle its underlying causes. We stress the need for an objective assessment of risks in piracy-prone areas with a view to mitigating negative effects on the economy and security of coastal states.

We commend the efforts made by many nations to safeguard the sea lines of communication, and stress the importance of continued joint efforts by the international community to fight piracy and armed robbery at sea. We believe that legal prosecution of pirates should complement the endeavours by the international community to ensure safe navigation. Accountability is a key element to increase the effectiveness of the anti-piracy coalition, as well as the promotion of long-term development policies on land. We underline that a long-lasting solution to the issue of piracy in affected areas requires improving sustainable development, security and stability, and strengthening local institutions and governance.

32. Reaffirming that the exploration and use of outer space shall be for peaceful purposes, we stress that negotiations for the conclusion of an international agreement or agreements to prevent an arms race in outer space are a priority task of the Conference on Disarmament, and support the efforts to start substantive work, inter alia, based on the updated draft treaty on the prevention of the placement of weapons in outer space and of the threat or use of force against outer space objects submitted by China and the Russian Federation.

We recognize our countries can benefit from opportunities for outer space cooperation in order to promote the application of relevant technologies for peaceful purposes. We will intensify our cooperation in the areas of joint application of space technologies, satellite navigation, including GLONASS and Beidou, and space sciences.

We reiterate that outer space shall be free for peaceful exploration and use by all States on a basis of equality in accordance with international law, and the exploration and use of outer space shall be carried out for the benefit and in the interests of all countries, irrespective of their degree of economic or scientific development. We stress that all States should contribute to promoting international cooperation on peaceful exploration and use of outer space while taking into particular account the needs of developing countries. We oppose unilateral measures which may hinder the international cooperation as well as national space activities of the developing countries.

We are firmly convinced that the international community should consistently undertake efforts to raise the basic levels of safety of space activities and operation and prevent conflict. In this connection, our countries can cooperate in working out common approaches in that area. Priority should be accorded to issues related to the safety of space operations, in the broader context of ensuring the long-term sustainability of outer space activities, as well as ways and means of preserving outer space for peaceful purposes, which are on the agenda of the UN Committee on the Peaceful Uses of Outer Space (UNCOPUOS).

33. ICTs are emerging as an important medium to bridge the gap between developed and developing countries, as well as to foster professional and creative talents of people. We recognize the importance of ICTs as a tool for transition from information to a knowledge society and the fact that it is inseparably connected with human development. We support the inclusion of ICT-related issues in the post-2015 development agenda and greater access to ICTs to empower women as well as vulnerable groups to meet the objectives of the agenda.

We also recognize the potential of developing countries in the ICT ecosystem and acknowledge that they have an important role to play in addressing the ICT-related issues in the post-2015 development agenda.

We recognize the urgent need to further strengthen cooperation in the areas of ICTs, including Internet, which is in the interests of our countries. In that context, we decided to constitute a BRICS working group on ICT cooperation. We reiterate the inadmissibility of using ICTs and the Internet to violate human rights and fundamental freedoms, including the right to privacy, and reaffirm that the same rights that people have offline must also be protected online. A system ensuring confidentiality and protection of users' personal data should be considered.

We consider that the Internet is a global resource and that states should participate on an equal footing in its evolution and functioning, taking into account the need to involve relevant stakeholders in their respective roles and responsibilities. We are in favour of an open, non-fragmented and secure Internet. We uphold the roles and responsibilities of national governments in regard to regulation and security of the network.

We acknowledge the need to promote, among others, the principles of multilateralism, democracy, transparency and mutual trust, and stand for the development of universally agreed rules of conduct with regard to the network. It is necessary to ensure that UN plays a facilitating role in setting up international public policies pertaining to the Internet.

We support the evolution of the Internet governance ecosystem, which should be based on an open and democratic process, free from the influence of any unilateral considerations.

34. Information and communications technologies provide citizens with new tools for the effective functioning of economy, society and state. ICTs enhance opportunities for the establishment of global partnerships for sustainable development, the strengthening of international peace and security and for the promotion and protection of human rights. In addition, we express our concern over the use of ICTs for purposes of transnational organized crime, of developing offensive tools, and conducting acts of terrorism. We agree that the use and development of ICTs through international cooperation and universally accepted norms and principles of international law is of paramount importance in order to ensure a peaceful, secure and open digital and Internet space. We reiterate our condemnation of mass electronic surveillance and data collection of individuals all over the world, as well as violation of the sovereignty of States and of human rights, in particular, the right to privacy.

We recognize that states are not at the same level of development and capacity with regard to ICTs. We commit ourselves to focus on expanding universal access to all forms of digital communication and to improve awareness of people in this regard. We also stress the need to promote cooperation among our countries to combat the use of ICTs for criminal and terrorist purposes. We recognize the need for a universal regulatory binding instrument on combating the criminal use of ICTs under the UN auspices. Furthermore, we are concerned with the potential misuse of ICTs for purposes, which threaten international peace and security. We emphasize the central importance of the principles of international law enshrined in the UN Charter, particularly the political independence, territorial integrity and sovereign equality of states, non-interference in internal affairs of other states and respect for human rights and fundamental freedoms.

We reaffirm the general approach set forth in the eThekwini and Fortaleza Declarations on the importance of security in the use of ICTs and the key role of the UN in addressing these issues. We encourage the international community to focus its efforts on confidence-building measures, capacity-building, the non-use of force, and the prevention of conflicts in the use of ICTs. We will seek to develop practical cooperation with each other in order to address common security challenges in the use of ICTs. We will continue to consider the adoption of the rules, norms and principles of responsible behavior of States in this sphere.

In that context, the Working Group of Experts of the BRICS States on security in the use of ICTs will initiate cooperation in the following areas: sharing of information and best practices relating to security in the use of ICTs; effective coordination against cyber-crime; the establishment of nodal points in member- states; intra-BRICS cooperation using the existing Computer Security Incident Response Teams (CSIRT); joint research and development projects; capacity building; and the development of international norms, principles and standards.

35. Noting that the international community increasingly faces grave natural and human-made disasters, we strongly believe that there is a need to promote cooperation in preventing and developing responses to emergency situations.

In that context, we welcome initiatives by India and other BRICS countries concerning cooperation in the above mentioned field, as well as Russia's initiative to convene a meeting of the BRICS Heads of National Agencies Responsible for Disaster Management in St. Petersburg in 2016.

We also acknowledge the fruitful discussions regarding natural disasters taking place within the context of the BRICS cooperation in Science, Technology and Innovation, which already resulted in a BRICS Workshop in this field, organized by Brazil in May 2014.

36. Respecting the independence, unity, sovereignty and territorial integrity of the Syrian Arab Republic, we express deep concern about the ongoing violence in Syria, the deteriorating humanitarian situation and the growing threat of international terrorism and extremism in the region. There is no alternative to the peaceful settlement of the Syrian conflict, we support the efforts aimed at promoting a political and diplomatic settlement of the crisis in Syria through a wide dialogue between the Syrian parties that reflects the aspirations of all sectors of Syrian society and guarantees the rights of all Syrians regardless of their ethnicity or confession on the basis of the Geneva Final Communiqué of 30 June 2012 without preconditions and external interference.

Condemning terrorism in all its forms and manifestations, we call for consolidation of Syrian society in the face of this dangerous threat, strict implementation by the international community of all provisions of the UN Security Council resolutions 2170, 2178 and 2199, particularly dealing with suppression of financing and other forms of supporting terrorists, as well as for compliance with universally recognized norms of international law related to countering terrorism and extremism, including the principles of respect for the sovereignty of the states.

We reiterate our condemnation of any use of toxic chemicals as a weapon in Syria. We commend the outcome of setting international control over the Syrian arsenals of chemical weapons and transferring toxic substances and their precursors from Syrian territory in accordance with the UNSC resolution 2118 and the obligations of Syria under the Convention on the Prohibition of Chemical Weapons. We emphasize that the success of these efforts was the result of a unity of purpose among the members of the Executive Council of the OPCW and the UNSC and constructive cooperation of the Syrian authorities with the special mission of the OPCW/UN.

We express our deep concern about the deterioration of the humanitarian aspects of the Syrian crisis and strongly condemn human rights violations by all parties to the conflict. We reaffirm the need to ensure safe and unhindered access of humanitarian agencies to affected population in accordance with UNSC resolutions 2139(2014), 2165(2014), 2191(2014) and the UN guiding principles of emergency humanitarian assistance. We welcome practical steps taken by the Syrian parties to fulfill the requirements of these resolutions. We reject the politicization of humanitarian assistance in Syria and note the continuing negative impact of unilateral sanctions on the socio-economic situation in Syria.

We express support for the steps of the Russian Federation aimed at promoting a political settlement in Syria, in particular the organization of two rounds of consultations between the Syrian parties in Moscow in January and April 2015, as well as the efforts by the UN Secretary General, his Special Envoy for Syria Staffan de Mistura, and other international and regional efforts aimed at peaceful resolution of the Syrian conflict.

37. We condemn in the strongest terms terrorism in all its forms and manifestations, the continued, widespread and grave abuses of human rights and violations of international humanitarian law committed by the so-called Islamic State of Iraq and the Levant, Al-Nusrah Front and associated terrorist groups, and in particular the persecution of individuals and communities on the basis of their religion or ethnicity, as well all forms of violence against civilians, particularly women and children.

38. We express concerns about spillover effects of the instability in Iraq and Syria resulting in growing terrorist activities in the region, and urge all parties to address the terrorist threat in a consistent manner. We strongly condemn the inhumane acts of violence perpetrated by terrorist and extremist groups, such as the self-styled ISIL, in the territory of the Republic of Iraq, especially those actions consisting of the killing and forced displacement of innocent civilians; and/or related to targeting victims on religious, cultural or ethnic grounds; and/or resulting in the destruction of Iraqi cultural and historical heritage, such as monuments, mosques, churches, museums, palaces and shrines.

We reaffirm our commitment to the territorial integrity, independence and national sovereignty of the Republic of Iraq and reject all forms of foreign interference that may hamper the consolidation of its national democratic institutions and the harmonious coexistence of the rich social fabric of the Iraqi people. We stress our support to the government of Iraq in its efforts to achieve national reconciliation and underscore the key role of the reconciliation process for the achievement of a lasting peace, security and stability in the Republic of Iraq.

We urge the international community to assist Iraq in its efforts to provide humanitarian assistance to internally displaced persons and refugees in the affected areas of that country.

We remain strongly committed to support the Republic of Iraq in achieving stability, peace, democracy, national reconciliation and unity, which is in the interest of regional and global peace and security.

39. Reaffirming our commitment to contribute to a comprehensive, just and lasting settlement of the Israeli-Palestinian conflict on the basis of a universally recognized international legal framework, including the relevant UN resolutions, the Madrid Principles and the Arab Peace Initiative, we strongly believe that the resolution of the Israeli-Palestinian conflict can contribute both to a positive outcome of other crises in the region and to the promotion of sustainable peace in the Middle East.

Therefore, we call upon Israel and Palestine to resume negotiations leading to a two-state solution with a contiguous and viable Palestinian State existing side by side in peace with Israel within mutually agreed and internationally recognized borders based on 1967 lines with East Jerusalem as its capital. In this regard, we note the respective efforts of the Middle East Quartet. We oppose the continuous Israeli settlement activities in the Occupied Territories, which violate international law and seriously undermine peace efforts and threaten the concept of the two-state solution. We welcome all initiatives aimed at achieving intra-Palestinian unity and urge the parties to this process to facilitate to full extent the implementation of the international obligations assumed by Palestine. We call on the UN Security Council to fully exercise its functions under the UN Charter with regard to the Israeli-Palestinian conflict.

We encourage the states that participated in the 2014 International Donors Conference on Reconstruction of Gaza Strip in Cairo to fulfill their pledges and call on Israeli and Palestinian authorities to create the necessary conditions for channelling international aid to the people of Palestine. We welcome the efforts of the UN Relief and Works Agency in providing assistance and protection for Palestine refugees and encourage the international community to further support the Agency. In this context, we welcome the recent accession of Brazil to UNRWA's Advisory Commission.

40. We support the efforts aimed at ensuring the early establishment in the Middle East of a zone free of nuclear weapons and all other weapons of mass destruction on the basis of agreements freely arrived at among the states of the region. We reiterate the call for convening of a conference on the issue to be attended by all states of the region. We urge the Middle East countries to show political will and pragmatic approach and adopt a constructive position for achieving the noble goal of creating a Middle East free of nuclear weapons and all other weapons of mass destruction.

41. We look forward to an early conclusion of the Joint Comprehensive Plan of Action (JCPA) to be agreed upon between China, Germany, France, the Russian Federation, the United Kingdom, the United States and Iran with the participation of EU. This plan of action is supposed to restore full confidence in the exclusively peaceful nature of Iran's nuclear programme and provide for the comprehensive lifting of sanctions imposed on Iran. The JCPA should enable Iran to fully exercise its right to peaceful uses of nuclear energy, including the right to uranium enrichment, under the NPT, and consistent with its international obligations, under strict international safeguards. It should also provide for the normalization of trade and investment with Iran. We believe that the implementation of JCPA would strongly contribute to the strengthening of international and regional security.

42. We welcome the completion of the election process in Afghanistan in 2014 and the establishment of the National Unity Government led by President Ashraf Ghani and Chief Executive Officer Dr. Abdullah Abdullah. We welcome the international community's confirmation of its obligations to Afghanistan that was reflected in the decisions of the London conference held in December 2014.

We believe that a broad and inclusive national reconciliation in Afghanistan which is Afghan-led and Afghan-owned is the surest path to the lasting peace, stability rehabilitation and reconstruction in Afghanistan. We call on all parties concerned to participate in the reconciliation, and call on the armed opposition to disarm, accept the Constitution of Afghanistan and cut ties with Al-Qaeda, ISIS and other terrorist organizations.

We remain concerned about the security in Afghanistan. We reiterate that terrorism and extremism pose a serious threat to the security and stability of Afghanistan, the region and beyond. The appearance and rapid growth of influence of the ISIL, as well as visible deterioration of the security situation along the border of Afghanistan are of serious anxiety. We support the efforts made in fighting against terrorism and extremism in Afghanistan.

For that purpose we confirm our readiness and call upon the international community to remain engaged in Afghanistan and fulfill its long-term commitments on civilian and security assistance, including strengthening its security forces' capability.

Taking into account unprecedented growth in production of narcotic drugs in Afghanistan for the second consecutive year, we call for more active measures to address the drug problem and to discuss it at all relevant international fora. We stand for further strengthening of the Paris Pact as an important interstate framework for fight against the proliferation of opiates originating from Afghanistan.

The UN has a core role to play in the coordination of the international community efforts to settle the situation in Afghanistan.

43. We reiterate our deep concern about the situation in Ukraine. We emphasize that there is no military solution to the conflict and that the only way to reconciliation is through inclusive political dialogue. In this regard we call on all parties to comply with all the provisions of the Package of Measures for the Implementation of the Minsk Agreements, adopted in February 2015 in Minsk by the Contact Group on Ukraine, supported by the leaders of Russia, Germany, France and Ukraine and endorsed by the UN Security Council in its resolution 2202.

44. We express serious concern about the escalation of the armed conflict in Libya, highlighting its extremely negative consequences for the Middle East, North Africa and the Sahel region. We note that the military intervention in this country in 2011 led to the breakdown of integrated state institutions, effective army and law-enforcement bodies, which in turn contributed to the rise of activities of terrorist and extremist groups. We underline the urgency to safeguard the sovereignty of the country and its territorial integrity, and we reaffirm the need to overcome the dissensions between Libyan political forces and to achieve an agreement on the formation of a National Unity Government as soon as possible. In this context, we express our support for the efforts to foster the inter-Libyan dialogue by the UN Secretary-General and his Special Representative for Libya Bernardino Leon, by the neighboring countries and by the African Union.

45. We express our concern about the dire security and humanitarian crisis in South Sudan. We condemn all ceasefire violations and acts of violence against civilians and humanitarian agencies. We call upon all parties to demonstrate the political will and commitment to end the tragedy in South Sudan and to provide conditions for the safe delivery of humanitarian aid to the population. We express our belief that a long-lasting solution to the crisis is only possible through an inclusive political dialogue aimed at national reconciliation. We support efforts being made by the Intergovernmental Authority on Development (IGAD) and other regional and international actors to mediate a political solution to the crisis based on the formation of a transitional government of national unity as well as parallel efforts towards facilitation of mediation between leaders of the various factions of the ruling party, and regret the failure to reach an agreement on power- sharing arrangements by March 2015. We commend the efforts of the UN Mission in South Sudan to fulfill its mandate. We condemn the attacks on UNMIS posts and IDP shelter sites.

46. We welcome the efforts of the Federal Government of Somalia aimed at establishing capable state authorities, solving acute socio-economic problems and building constructive relations with all the Somali regions. We recognize the tangible achievements of the Somalian army and the units of the peace keeping African Union Mission in Somalia (AMISOM) in fighting the Al-Shabaab extremist group. We express our concern about the growth of the terrorist threat in the countries of Northeast and East Africa. We strongly condemn the inhumane attack by Al Shabaab fighters on the University of Garissa, Kenya on 2 April 2015, which resulted in deplorable casualties. We express our solidarity with the Government and the people of Kenya in their struggle against terrorism. We stress that there can be no justification for terrorism whatsoever.

47. We support the activities of the UN Multidimensional Integrated Stabilization Mission in Mali as a part of the efforts of the international community to settle the Malian crisis. We are committed to a political solution to the conflict which would take into account positions of all the parties; we encourage constructive negotiations aimed at securing the territorial integrity and statehood of Mali. We note the signing of the Agreement on Peace and Reconciliation in Mali and commend the mediation efforts of the Algerian Government and other international and regional actors with a view to obtain a political solution for the crisis. We express grave concern about the attempts by various forces to destabilize the situation and disrupt the peace negotiations.

48. We remain concerned about the security and humanitarian situation in eastern parts of the Democratic Republic of the Congo (DRC); the slow pace of the process of disarmament, demobilization and reintegration of ex-combatants into the Congolese society; the illegal exploitation and exportation of natural resources; the high number of refugees from neighbouring countries and internally displaced persons present in the country. We stress the need to revive the implementation process of the framework agreement for peace, security and cooperation in the DRC and the region and to strengthen its government structures. We support the efforts by the Government of the DRC, supported by MONUSCO/UN to bring peace and stability to the DRC, and we call upon all involved parties to honor their obligations in order to achieve lasting peace and stability in the DRC. We commend the efforts to stabilize the region and protect civilian populations, and underline the importance of directing special attention to the situation of women and children in areas of conflict. We reiterate the need for the urgent and effective neutralization of the Democratic Forces for the Liberation of Rwanda (FDLR) and all other negative forces and armed groups. We believe that long-term stability in the DRC cannot be achieved by military means alone.

49. We are concerned about and closely follow the developments in the Republic of Burundi. We urge all actors involved in the current crisis to exercise restraint and resolve their political differences through inclusive dialogue, so that social peace and stability can be restored. We support regional efforts to find a political solution to this crisis and call upon the international community to remain engaged in supporting the regional facilitation of a political solution, as well as in the future socio-economic development of Burundi.

50. We note that the situation in the Central African Republic (CAR) remains unstable: and that issues pertaining to security continue to cause concerns. We underline in this regard that the primary responsibility for developing mutually acceptable modalities of settlement by the conflicting parties is borne by the Government of the CAR, which should create prerequisites for disarmament, demobilization and reintegration of ex-combatants into the civil society. We believe that a comprehensive national dialogue is the only way to achieve long- term stability in the CAR.

We note proceedings of the recently concluded Bangui Forum for Reconciliation that was held 4-11 May 2015 in the Central African Republic and call upon all stakeholders to effectively implement its recommendations.

51. We also express deep concern about the scourge of terrorism and violent extremism and condemn the terrorist acts perpetrated by Al-Shabaab, Boko Haram and other groups, which pose a serious threat to peace and stability in Africa.

52. We emphasize that, in the context of the unstable global financial and economic system and price volatility in global commodity markets, the development of the real sector of economy becomes particularly relevant.

We recognize that industrial development is a fundamental source of growth for the BRICS countries, which possess ample natural resources and significant labor, intellectual and technical capacities. Increasing production and export of high value-added goods will help BRICS countries enhance their national economies, contribute to their participation in global value chains and improve their competitiveness.

In this connection, we reaffirm the unique mandate of the United Nations Industrial Development Organization (UNIDO) to promote and accelerate inclusive and sustainable industrial development.

We are convinced about the importance of economic growth based on the balanced development of all economic sectors and on the development and introduction of advanced technologies and innovations, the mobilization of resources from financial institutions and the encouragement of private investment.

In this context, we note the potential to boost collaboration in developing technology and innovation in the potential sectors of BRICS economies, such as mining and metal industry, pharmaceuticals, information technology, chemicals and petrochemicals, both in the area of exploration and extraction of natural resources and in their processing, transformation and use, including through the promotion of a favourable investment climate and the implementation of mutually beneficial joint projects.

We stress the importance of intensifying cooperation of industrial production capabilities, establishing industrial parks and clusters, technology parks and engineering centers with a view to developing and introducing cutting-edge technologies, providing training for engineering and technical personnel and managers.

We highlight that encouraging investment in priority areas such as infrastructure, logistics and renewable sources of energy is a strategic goal for the sustainable growth of our economies. We reiterate our interest in joining efforts in order to face the challenge of competitiveness. In this regard, the BRICS countries agree to collaborate for the promotion of investment opportunities in railways, roadways, seaports and airports among our countries.

53. We reiterate our commitment to further develop agricultural cooperation, in particular, related to agricultural technologies and innovations, provision of food for the most vulnerable communities, mitigation of the negative impact of climate change on food security and the adaptation of agriculture to climate change, reducing volatility in agricultural markets, sharing up-to-date market information, enhancing trade and investment, including through participation in exhibitions, fairs, and investment forums. We actively support the UN General Assembly decision to declare 2015 the International Year of Soils, and express our intention to contribute to the implementation of effective policies and activities aimed at ensuring sustainable management and protection of soil resources.

We welcome cooperation of our delegations in international organizations, including in UN Food and Agriculture Organization (FAO). We reinforce the importance of the work of the informal consultative group of BRICS countries in Rome.

54. We confirm that the improvement in safety levels of industrial and energy facilities is one of the priority areas for the BRICS countries. In this regard we welcome cooperation between the relevant regulatory bodies of the BRICS countries aimed at better protection of the public and environment in our countries. We also welcome the initiative of the Russian Federation to host the meeting of the BRICS Heads of Industrial and Energy Safety Authorities.

55. In order to ensure well-coordinated work on the post-2015 sustainable development indicators, we task the BRICS national statistical agencies to pursue collaboration on methodological approaches towards establishing these indicators to ensure their comparability and in this regard to cooperate closely on a regular basis within specialized UN commissions and committees.

56. We recognize the significance of connectivity in enhancing economic ties and fostering closer partnership among BRICS countries. We welcome and support BRICS countries' initiatives in promoting connectivity and infrastructure development.

We affirm that connectivity should be strengthened in a comprehensive, integrated and systematic way in the key areas of policy coordination, facilities connectivity, unimpeded trade and people-to-people connections, while making strenuous joint efforts to enhance policy consultation and coordination among BRICS countries on the basis of mutual benefit and win-win cooperation.

We recognize that enhanced people-to-people connectivity will further stimulate interaction among BRICS countries, people and society. We are committed to create favourable conditions for long-term cooperation in the field of tourism.

57. We note with satisfaction the progress achieved in coordination of efforts with regard to human resources and employment, social welfare and security, as well as social integration policy.

We expect the first meeting of the BRICS Ministers of Labour and Employment, which is to take place in February 2016 and will focus on the creation of decent jobs and information sharing on labour and employment issues, will lay a solid foundation for our long-term cooperation in the sphere of social relations and labour.

58. We welcome the outcomes of the first meeting of the BRICS Ministers responsible for population matters (Brasilia, 12 February 2015) and reaffirm our commitment to further cooperation on population and development-related matters that are of common interest, in accordance with the Agenda for BRICS Cooperation on Population Matters for 2015-2020 and in observance of the guiding principles and objectives of the Action Plan of the International Conference on Population and Development (ICPD) in Cairo, and key actions for its further implementation to promote a long-term and balanced demographic development.

We underscore the relevance of the demographic transition and post- transitional challenges, including population ageing and mortality reduction, as well as the importance to effectively use the demographic dividend to advance economic growth and development and to address social issues, in particular gender inequality, elderly care, women's rights and issues facing young people and people with disabilities. We reiterate our commitment to ensure sexual and reproductive health and reproductive rights for all.

We intend to develop our cooperation on population matters by using such formats as annual seminars of officials and experts and regular meetings of ministers responsible for the indicated issues.

For population matters to be more effectively integrated into our macroeconomic, financial and social policies we instruct our experts to hold in Moscow in November 2015 regular BRICS consultations on population matters dedicated to demographic challenges and to how they are related to the economic development of BRICS countries.

59. We acknowledge the transnational nature of migration, and, hence, the importance of mutual cooperation among BRICS countries in this area, including among the relevant national agencies. In this regard, we note the initiative of the Russian Federation to hold the first BRICS Ministerial migration meeting (Heads of migration authorities) during the Russian Chairship.

We express regret for the large-scale loss of lives of migrants in the Mediterranean. We call upon the international community, in particular the countries concerned, to provide necessary assistance to these migrants, and to intensify collective efforts to address the root causes of the growing unregulated migration and displacement of people.

60. We reaffirm the right of every person, without any distinction, to the highest attainable standard of physical and mental health and to the quality of life that is necessary to maintain his or her own health and well-being and the health and well-being of his or her family.

We are concerned about growing and diversifying global threats posed by communicable and non-communicable diseases. They have a negative impact on economic and social development, especially in developing and in the least developed countries.

In this context, we commend the efforts made by the BRICS countries to contribute to enhanced international cooperation to support the efforts of countries to achieve their health goals, including the implementation of universal and equitable access to health services, and ensure affordable, good-quality service delivery while taking into account different national circumstances, policies, priorities and capabilities. We also seek enhanced partnerships by the international community and other stakeholders from both the public and private sectors, including the civil society and academia to improve health for all.

International community is struggling with increased antimicrobial resistance, which contributes to multiplying health risks. We are also concerned with the continuing spread of major diseases (HIV/AIDS, TB, malaria and others), and with the emergence of infections with a pandemic potential, such as highly pathogenic influenza, novel coronavirus or Ebola.

BRICS countries have significant experience in combating communicable diseases. We are willing to cooperate and coordinate our efforts, including with relevant international organizations, to tackle global health challenges and ensure that BRICS countries jointly contribute to improve global health security. In this regard we will work together in such areas as:

- Management of risks related to emerging infections with pandemic potential;
- Compliance with commitments to stop the spread of, and eradicate, communicable diseases that hamper development (HIV/AIDS, tuberculosis, malaria, "neglected" tropical diseases, poliomyelitis, measles);
- Research, development, production and supply of medicines aimed at providing increased access to prevention and treatment of communicable diseases.

We ask our relevant authorities to consider medium-term steps to be taken in these areas to seek the collective and individual input of BRICS countries to global health security from a public health perspective.

61. We are deeply concerned with the impact of the Ebola virus disease (EVD) in Guinea, Liberia and Sierra Leone, including its grave humanitarian, social and economic consequences for these countries and the potential spread of the disease. We highly commend the contribution and commitment of international health and humanitarian relief workers to immediately react to EVD outbreak and the crucial support and assistance provided by the international community to the affected countries of West Africa.

BRICS members contributed significantly in international response to EVD and in support to affected countries. What is more, unprecedented mobilization of national health systems allowed us to see how prepared we are and forced us to search for ways to improve national and regional response measures.

We fully support the work of the United Nations and other international institutions to stop the outbreak, limit the economic and social impact of the disease and prevent its recrudescence, as well as the efforts to reform systems of international response to public health emergencies to make them more effective in the future.

We confirm our commitment to do what is necessary individually and collectively to support these efforts addressing emergency and longer-term systematic issues and gaps in preparedness and response on national, regional and global level and further assist affected countries in combating the disease, as well as to contribute to the ongoing efforts to strengthen health sectors across the region including through the WHO and other international organizations.

62. We welcome the holding of the Second BRICS Science, Technology and Innovation Ministerial Meeting, which took place in Brasilia in March 2015, and celebrate the signature of the Memorandum of Understanding on Cooperation in Science, Technology and Innovation, which provides a strategic framework for cooperation in this field.

We note with interest the potential of BRICS Young Scientist Forum that has been agreed by the BRICS Ministers for Science, Technology and Innovation with India as coordinating country.

We reaffirm our willingness to strengthen cooperation in science, technology and innovation with the purposes of promoting inclusive and sustainable social and economic development, bridging the scientific and technological gap between the BRICS countries and developed countries, providing a new quality of growth based on economic complementarity, as well as finding solutions to the challenges that the world economy faces today.

Taking note of our countries' efforts to create knowledge economies, whose drivers are science, technology and innovation, we will expand cooperation in joint research, design, development, manufacturing and promotion in the field of high- technology products.

Taking into consideration immense research and technological potential in the BRICS countries and building on the provisions of the Memorandum of Understanding on Cooperation in Science, Technology and Innovations, we reaffirm the importance of the development of a BRICS Research and Innovation Initiative which shall cover actions including:

- cooperation within large research infrastructures, including possible consideration of Megascience projects, to achieve scientific and technological breakthroughs in the key areas of cooperation outlined in the Memorandum;

- coordination of the existing large-scale national programs of the BRICS countries;

- development and implementation of a BRICS Framework Programme for funding multilateral joint research projects for research, technology commercialization and innovation involving science and technology ministries and centers, development institutes and national, as well as, if necessary, regional foundations that sponsor research projects;

- establishment of a joint Research and Innovation Platform.

These activities will be carried out as per BRICS STI Work Plan to be endorsed at the next BRICS Meeting of Ministers for Science, Technology and Innovation.

Based on the Brasília Declaration of BRICS Ministers of Science, Technology and Innovation, we encourage increased participation of business, academia and other relevant stakeholders for science, technology and innovation development among BRICS countries.

63. We note the direct interdependence between investment into education, the development of human capital and the improvement of economic performance. We reaffirm the need for equally accessible, high-quality, and lifelong education for all, in line with post-2015 development agenda.

We support efforts to ensure inclusive and equitable quality education. We recognize the importance of Vocational Education and Training as an instrument of improving employment opportunities, including for young people entering the labour market. We encourage students' mobility among BRICS countries.

We encourage exploring the possibilities of skills development cooperation through implementation of the international best practices, including relevant WorldSkills programmes.

We underscore the primary importance of higher education and research and call for exchanging of experiences in recognition of university diplomas and degrees. We call for working towards cooperation between competent authorities of the BRICS countries for accreditation and recognition. We support the independent initiatives to establish the BRICS Network University and the BRICS University League.

64. Taking into account 1966 UNESCO Declaration of Principles of International Cultural Cooperation and 2001 UNESCO Declaration on Cultural Diversity, acknowledging that cultural diversity is the source of development and convinced that cultural exchanges and cooperation facilitate mutual

understanding, we reiterate the importance of cooperation between the BRICS countries in the cultural sphere. Aiming at strengthening and developing friendly relation between our countries and peoples, we will continue to encourage in every possible way direct co-operation between our countries in the sphere of culture and art.

We welcome the signing of the Agreement between the Governments of the BRICS Member States on Cooperation in the Field of Culture. This Agreement will play an important role in expanding and deepening cooperation in the fields of culture and art, in promoting dialogue between cultures, which will help bring closer the cultures and peoples of our countries.

65. The United Nations will hold the Summit this September to review the progress of the MDGs and adopt the post-2015 development agenda, which will guide international development cooperation in the next 15 years. We attach great importance to the Summit and hope that the Summit will demonstrate the strategic vision of the leaders, the solidarity of all parties and their commitment to address global development issues through cooperation.

We reaffirm our commitment to the ambitious post-2015 development agenda, which is to be approved by the UN Summit. We reiterate that the post- 2015 development agenda should be built on the foundation laid by the Millennium Development Goals, ensure completion of unfinished commitments and respond to new challenges. A post-2015 development agenda should furthermore reinforce the international community's commitment to eradicate poverty achieve sustained, equitable and inclusive economic growth and sustainable development, fully comply with all principles of the UN Conference on Environment and Development held in Rio in 1992, including, in particular, the principle of Common But Differentiated Responsibilities (CBDR). We stress the importance of an integrated approach to the means of implementation of the post- 2015 development agenda.

We consider eradication of poverty as an indispensable requirement for and overarching objective towards the attainment of sustainable development, and stress the need for a coherent approach to attain inclusive and balanced integration of economic, social and environmental components of sustainable development. This approach involves working towards a single framework and set of goals that are universal in nature and applicable to all countries while taking into account differing national circumstances and respecting national policies and priorities. It is therefore imperative that we align and build upon existing agreements and the outcomes of multilateral summits and conferences on development. In this regard, we welcome the report of the Open Working Group of the UN GA on Sustainable Development Goals and emphasize that proposals of the Open Working Group should be the main basis for the integration of sustainable development goals into the post-2015 development agenda.

66. We look forward to the success of the Third International Conference on Financing for Development to be held in Addis Ababa, Ethiopia, on 13-16 July 2015. We call on all parties to engage in a fruitful dialogue with a view to adopting an ambitious and effective strategy for mobilizing resources for sustainable development.

Official Development Assistance plays an important role in financing for development. We urge developed countries to honour their commitments in full and on time in this regard. We recognize that the mobilization of domestic and international resources and an enabling domestic and international environment are key drivers for development and we call for a large-scale mobilization of resources from a variety of sources and for the effective use of financing in order to give strong support to developing countries in their efforts to promote sustainable development.

We are committed to further strengthening and supporting South-South cooperation, while stressing that South-South cooperation is not a substitute for, but rather a complement to North-South cooperation which remains the main channel of international development cooperation.

We intend to strengthen partnerships for advancing international development and to begin interaction through dialogue, cooperation and exchange of experience in advancing international development of mutual interest to our countries. In this connection, we welcome plans for a meeting of senior officials of the BRICS countries in charge of international development cooperation.

67. We express our readiness to address climate change in a global context and at the national level and to achieve a comprehensive, effective and equitable agreement under the United Nations Framework Convention on Climate Change.

We stress the importance of transfer of technology and scientific knowledge to address climate change and its adverse effects and therefore agreed to conduct joint research on the priority issues of common interest.

68. We welcome the first meeting of environment ministers of our countries in Moscow on 22 April 2015 that marked the beginning of a new format of cooperation in the environmental area. We support the establishment of a platform for sharing environmentally sound technologies as a new international mechanism for public-private partnerships that can assist in addressing environmental challenges in our countries.

69. Recognizing the importance of monitoring global trends in the energy sector, including making forecasts regarding energy consumption, providing recommendations for the development of energy markets in order to ensure energy security and economic development we call on our relevant agencies to consider the possibilities of energy cooperation within BRICS.

Taking into consideration the role of the energy sector in ensuring the sustainable economic development of the BRICS countries, we welcome balancing the interests of consumers, producers and transit countries of energy resources, creating the conditions for sustainable and predictable development of the energy markets.

Reaffirming the importance and necessity of advancing international cooperation in the field of energy saving, energy efficiency and developing energy efficient technologies, we welcome the holding of the first official meeting on energy efficiency in May 2015 and look forward to developing intra-BRICS cooperation in this area, as well as the establishment of the relevant platform. We welcome the Russian proposal to hold the first meeting of the BRICS Ministers of energy in the end of this year. We urge businesses of the BRICS countries to jointly develop energy efficient technologies and equipment and we call upon BRICS Business Council to study ways of cooperation in this field.

70. We welcome the development of relations between the parliaments, businesses and civil society institutions of the BRICS countries, aimed at promoting friendship and dialogue between our nations.

71. We welcomed the meeting of the Parliamentary Forum held in Moscow in June 2015 and the intention to strengthen and promote inter-parliamentary cooperation, including consultations on the margins of international parliamentary organizations for coordinating joint initiatives and positions.

72. We welcome fruitful meetings of BRICS Business Forum and BRICS Business Council as well as their efforts in strengthening business ties and promoting projects and initiatives between the BRICS countries.

We aim to create a favorable environment for further development of trade, investment and business cooperation between the BRICS countries, including through removing excessive administrative barriers and trade impediments.

We take note of the recommendation of the Business Council regarding the simplification of visa procedures for business travel between the BRICS countries and we ask our relevant authorities to continue to work towards this end.

73. We welcome activities of BRICS Think Tanks Council (BTTC) and the Long-Term Strategy for BRICS Report as well as the 7th Academic Forum in Moscow for expanding BRICS cooperation. We value this permanent platform for in-depth expert opinion and look forward to further consolidated high quality research, analysis, as well as effective think-tank discussions on issues of mutual interest.

The BTTC should further strive to enhance cooperation in future-oriented research, knowledge sharing, capacity building and policy advice between think tanks in BRICS countries.

74. We welcome the initiative of the Russian Chairship in hosting Civil BRICS Forum, which contributes to a dialogue between civil society organizations, academia, business and governments of the BRICS countries on a wide range of important socio-economic issues. We also welcome holding of the Trade Unions Forums as well as the launch of "youth dimension" of our cooperation under the Russian Chairship.

75. We welcome the signing of the MoU on the Creation of the Joint BRICS Website among our Foreign Ministries. It will serve as a platform for informing people of our countries and the wider international community about BRICS principles, goals and practices. We will explore the possibility of developing the BRICS Website as a virtual secretariat.

76. India, China, South Africa and Brazil express their sincere gratitude to the Government and people of Russia for hosting the Seventh BRICS Summit in Ufa.

77. Russia, China, South Africa and Brazil convey their appreciation to India for its offer to host the Eighth BRICS Summit in 2016 and extend their full support to that end.

B.   The Ufa Action Plan

UFA ACTION PLAN

Looking forward to our next meeting to be held on the margins of the G20 Summit (Antalya, Turkey, 15-16 November 2015), we took note of the following events held under the Russian Chairship before the Ufa Summit:

1. Meeting of the Working Group on the creation of the Multilateral Contingent Reserve Arrangement (Washington, 14-15 April 2015).

2. Meeting of Experts on Customs Issues of the BRICS countries (Moscow, 13-14 April 2015).

3. BRICS expert dialogue on e-commerce (Moscow, 14 April 2015).

4. Meetings of the BRICS Finance Ministers and Central Bank Governors (Washington, 16 April 2015; Moscow, 7 July 2015).

5. Meeting of Experts on combating illicit traffic in narcotic drugs, psychotropic substances and their precursors in BRICS countries (Moscow, 20 April 2015).

6. Meeting of the BRICS Environment Ministers (Moscow, 22 April 2015) preceded by the meeting of experts (Moscow, 21 April 2015).

7. Meeting of the BRICS Heads of Anti-drug Agencies (Moscow, 22 April 2015).

8. Meeting of the Heads of BRICS Competition Authorities on the margins of the International Competition Network Conference (Sydney, 28 April – 1 May 2015).

9. BRICS Dialogue on Foreign Policy (Moscow, 15 May 2015).

10. BRICS Consultations on Security of Outer Space Activities (Moscow, 20 May 2015).

11. BRICS Think Tanks Council meeting (Moscow, 21 May 2015).

12. Meeting of the BRICS Deputy Foreign Ministers on the Situation in the Middle East (West Asia) and North Africa (Moscow, 22 May 2015).

13. BRICS Academic Forum (Moscow, 22-23 May 2015).

14. Meeting of the BRICS National Security Advisors (Moscow, 26 May 2015).

15. Meeting of the BRICS Health Ministers on the margins of the WHA (Geneva, 26 May 2015).

16. Meetings of the High Level Working Group on Strategy of BRICS Economic Partnership (Brasilia, December 2014; March 2015 – Under the Brazilian Chairship; Moscow, 16 April; 4-5 June 2015 – under Russian Chairship).

17. BRICS Parliamentary Forum (Moscow, 8 June 2015).

18. Meeting of the representatives of Customs Agencies of the BRICS countries on the margins of the Conference of the World Customs Organization (Brussels, 11-13 June 2015).

19. Meeting of the BRICS Ministers of Culture (Moscow, 16-17 June 2015).

20. BRICS Working Group on Security in the Use of ICTs (Moscow, 16-18 June 2015).

21. BRICS Business Forum (Saint-Petersburg, 18 June 2015).

22. International Conference "Common threats – joint actions: the response of the BRICS countries to dangerous infectious diseases" (Moscow, 23-24 June 2015).

23. Meetings of Heads of BRICS Delegations to FATF (Paris, 24 February 2015; Moscow, 23-24 April 2015; Brisbane, 24 June 2015).

24. Meeting of the BRICS Working Group on Education (Moscow, 25-26 June 2015).

25. Civil BRICS (Moscow, 29 June – 1 July 2015).

26. Meeting of the BRICS Youth Affairs Ministers / Heads of Agencies (Kazan, 4 July 2015).

27. BRICS Youth Summit (Kazan, 4-7 July 2015).

28. Meetings of the BRICS Contact Group on Economic and Trade Issues (Moscow, 15 April 2015; Moscow, 6 July 2015).

29. Meeting of the Board of Governance of the New Development Bank (Moscow, 7 July 2015).

30. Meeting of the BRICS Trade Ministers (Moscow, 7 July 2015).

31. Meeting of the BRICS Science and Technology Funding Parties (Moscow, 6-7 July 2015).

32. BRICS Business Council (Ufa, 8 July 2015).

33. BRICS Financial Forum (Ufa, 8 July 2015).

34. BRICS Trade Unions (Ufa, 9 July 2015).

35. Annual Meeting of the Heads of Banks of the BRICS Interbank Cooperation Mechanism (Ufa, 8 July 2015).

Events to be held under the Russian Chairship:

1. Meeting of the BRICS Ministers of Foreign Affairs/International Relations on the margins of the UN General Assembly.

2. Financial block meetings:
   - meeting of the BRICS Finance Ministers and Central Bank Governors;
   - meeting of the BRICS Deputy Finance Ministers;
   - meetings of the Board of Governance of the New Development Bank;
   - meetings of the Working Group on the Creation of the Multilateral Contingent Reserve Arrangement;
   - meetings of Experts of the Central Banks of BRICS countries on drafting the agreement on the BRICS Contingent Reserve Arrangement;

3. Meeting of the BRICS Health Ministers.

4. Meeting of the BRICS Labour and Employment Ministers.

5. BRICS Seminar on population matters.

6. Meeting of the BRICS Education Ministers.

7. Meeting of the BRICS Agriculture and Agrarian Development Ministers. Meeting of the Agricultural Cooperation Working Group.

8. Meeting of the BRICS Ministers on Science, Technology and Innovation preceded by the meeting of the BRICS Senior Officials on Science, Technology and Innovation.

9. Meeting of the BRICS Heads of Tax Authorities preceded by preparatory BRICS Expert Meeting of Tax Authorities.

10. Meeting of the BRICS Contact Group on Economic and Trade Issues.

11. Meeting of the BRICS Ministers of Telecommunications.

12. Meeting of the BRICS Heads of National Agencies responsible for disaster management.

13. Meeting of the BRICS Heads of the competition authorities (Durban, November 2015).

14. Meeting of the BRICS Heads responsible for national statistics.

15. Forum on Comprehensive Social Protection Systems of BRICS countries on the margins of the BRICS experts meeting on social and labour issues.

16. Meeting of the BRICS Senior Officials responsible for International Development Assistance.

17. BRICS Sherpas and Sous-Sherpas mid-term meeting.

18. Launch of the Joint BRICS Website.

19. Meeting of the BRICS Senior Officials on Anti-corruption (St. Petersburg, November 2015).

20. Meeting of the BRICS Anti-Drug Working Group.

21. Meeting of the Heads of BRICS Delegations to FATF (establishment of BRICS Council on Anti-Money Laundering and Countering the Financing of Terrorism within the FATF).

22. Consultations amongst BRICS Permanent Missions and/or Embassies, as appropriate, in New York, Rome, Paris, Washington, Nairobi and Geneva, where appropriate.

23. Working group on ICT cooperation.

24. BRICS Young Diplomats Forum.

25. BRICS Young Scientists Forum.

26. BRICS Global Universities Summit. Constituent meetings of the BRICS Network University and the BRICS Universities League.

Other initiatives of the Russian Chairship:

1. Meeting of the BRICS Heads of Migration Authorities preceded by the session of the Preparatory Group.

2. Meeting of the BRICS Ministers of Energy preceded by the meeting of Working Group on Energy and Energy Efficiency.

3. High-level BRICS Meeting on Industrial Issues.

4. Meeting of the BRICS Heads of Industrial and Energy Safety Authorities. International Workshop of Industrial Safety Regulation Bodies of BRICS countries "Effective Regulation of Industrial Safety as an Element Stability of National Economy" in an outreach format.

5. International Contest of Young Scientists of the BRICS countries. International Forum of BRICS Young Scientists and Entrepreneurs.

6. Meeting of authorities responsible for legal cooperation and international law within the Ministries of Foreign Affairs at the margins of relevant multilateral fora.

7. Conference on Modernization of the Treasury Systems of the BRICS countries.

8. International Forum of Young Journalists, Bloggers and Photo Reporters, including those representing the BRICS countries.

Areas of cooperation to be explored

1. BRICS Dialogue on Peacekeeping.

2. Establishment of the BRICS Council of Regions.

3. Cooperation and exchange of experiences among BRICS media professionals.

C.   The Strategy for BRICS Economic Partnership

THE STRATEGY FOR BRICS ECONOMIC PARTNERSHIP

Welfare for everyone, development for all

« We envision a future marked by global peace, economic and social progress and enlightened scientific temper. We stand ready to work with others, developed and developing countries together, on the basis of universally recognized norms of international law and multilateral decision making, to deal with the challenges and the opportunities before the world today. Strengthened representation of emerging and developing countries in the institutions of global governance will enhance their effectiveness in achieving this objective » (Delhi Declaration).

« We are ready to explore new areas towards a comprehensive cooperation and a closer economic partnership to facilitate market inter-linkages, financial integration, infrastructure connectivity as well as people-to-people contacts » (Fortaleza Declaration).

I.   Preamble

BRICS is a dialogue and cooperation platform among Member States (Brazil, Russia, India, China and South Africa) which together account for 30% of global land, 43% of global population and 21% of the world's Gross Domestic Product (GDP), 17.3% of global merchandise trade[1], 12.7% of global

---

[1] From WTO statistics gateway.

commercial services[2] and 45% of world's Agriculture Production[3]. This platform aims to promote peace, security, prosperity and development in multipolar, interconnected and globalized world. The BRICS countries represent Asia, Africa, Europe and Latin America, which gives their cooperation a transcontinental dimension making it especially valuable and significant.

The BRICS plays a vital role in the world economy in terms of total production, receiving investment capital, and expanding potential consumer markets. The BRICS economies have been widely regarded as the engines of the global economic recovery, which underscores the changing role of these economies in the world. At the G20' meetings, the BRICS was influential in shaping macroeconomic policies in the aftermath of the recent financial crisis.

At the Summits in Sanya, Delhi, Durban and Fortaleza the BRICS Leaders agreed to build a partnership, in pursuit of increased stability, growth and development. In view of this, BRICS countries should develop pragmatic economic cooperation and forge closer economic partnership in order to contribute to promoting global economic recovery, reduce potential risks in the international financial markets and increase economic growth among its members.

I.1 Purposes

BRICS cooperation is aimed at complementing and strengthening existing bilateral and multilateral relations between Member States. The Strategy for BRICS Economic Partnership (referred hereinafter as the BRICS Strategy) will contribute to increasing the economic growth and competitiveness of the BRICS economies in the global arena. The purposes of the BRICS Strategy are:

- to enhance market access opportunities and facilitate market inter- linkages;
- to promote mutual trade and investment and create a business-friendly environment for investors and entrepreneurs in all BRICS countries;
- to enhance and diversify trade and investment cooperation that support value addition among the BRICS countries;
- to strengthen macroeconomic policy coordination and build resilience to external economic shocks;
- to strive for inclusive economic growth, in order to eradicate poverty, address unemployment and promote social inclusion;
- to promote information exchange through BRICS Virtual Secretariat and BRICS Economic Exchange Platform, as well as other agreed platforms;
- to consolidate efforts in order to ensure a better quality of growth by fostering innovative economic development based on advanced technologies and skills development with a view to build knowledge economies;
- to seek further interaction and cooperation with non-BRICS countries and international organizations and forums. BRICS members will engage with the business communities in their respective countries to implement the Strategy. They will encourage closer collaboration of BRICS business communities.

I.2 Basic Principles

The BRICS Strategy is based on the following principles:

- full respect for the sovereignty of the Member States;
- commitment to international law and recognition of the central role of the United Nations on peace, security and development;

---

[2] From WTO statistics gateway.
[3] FAO Stat.

- account for national interests, priorities, growth and development strategies of the Member States;
- openness, sharing of information and consensus in decision-making;
- commitment to the rules and principles of the multilateral trading system as embodied in the World Trade Organization (WTO);
- recognition of the multipolar nature of the global economic and financial system;
- support for greater exchanges of best practices in enhancing business environment;
- transparency and predictability in the investment environment in line with national policies and priorities;
- commitment to supporting sustainable development, strong, balanced and inclusive growth, financial stability, and balanced combination of measures ensuring social and economic development and protection of the environment;
- commitment to mutually beneficial cooperation with other countries;
- inadmissibility of unilateral economic sanctions in violation of universally recognized norms of international relations.

II. Priority areas for cooperation

II.1 Trade and investment

To achieve sustainable, inclusive and dynamic growth, the BRICS countries should avail themselves of opportunities provided by international economic cooperation, including deepening of trade and investment ties, both within BRICS and with other members of the international community. More active intra-BRICS trade and investment cooperation will contribute to economic growth, and facilitate the use of existing opportunities of BRICS economic complementarity. It will also strengthen the positions of the Member States in the global economy and contribute to addressing domestic economic and social challenges, including job creation and promotion of social inclusion.

BRICS cooperation should be commensurate with the potential and make ample use of the capabilities of its Members and contribute to growth and sustainable development of their economies. BRICS cooperation will help to address emerging challenges to trade and investment, against the backdrop of weak global recovery and other potential risks. Of particular importance is the need to promote value-added trade amongst BRICS countries by focusing on the outcomes of Joint Trade Study.

In order to expand trade and investment cooperation the following goals should be pursued:
- enhancing consultations on macroeconomic and trade policies;
- encouraging trade and investment links between BRICS countries with an emphasis on promoting market access on goods and services amongst BRICS countries and supporting industrial complementarities, sustainable development and inclusive growth;
- simplifying and increasing the efficiency of administrative procedures to facilitate and accelerate mutual trade and investment;
- improving the transparency of trade and investment climate in the framework of international obligations and national legislation;
- creating favorable conditions for development of mutual trade and foreign direct investment in the BRICS countries in order to diversify production and exports;
- encouraging increased cooperation and trade in services, considering the positive impact on productivity and efficiency, including in the manufacturing sector;
- exchanging information on policies impacting trade and investment;
- increasing the share of value-added products in the GDP of the BRICS countries; and enhancing their resilience against fluctuations in the world commodity markets;

- promoting complementarity of production factors such as capital, labour, technology and natural resources;
- using extensively human capacity building mechanisms to increase production capacity and exports of the Member States;
- contributing to the creation and development of hi-tech industries in accordance with the respective trends and requirements of economic growth in the 21st century;
- developing cooperation on social, economic and competition policies;
- promoting the exchange of best practices in corporate social responsibility;
- strengthening customs cooperation, including simplification of customs clearance procedures, exchange of information on national customs law, as well as exchange of best practices;
- cooperating on standardization and conformity assessment through exchange of information, consultations and enquiries based on norms, experience and practices of international organizations, and coordination within those organizations;
- attracting investors and exploring implementation of co-financed projects in infrastructure, as well as in processing and mining industries, including regional projects;
- creating conditions for the BRICS companies, in particular for micro-, small and medium (MSMEs), to be better integrated into the global value chains with higher added value;
- promoting cooperation between MSMEs, including consideration of a BRICS MSMEs Cooperation Agreement, exchange of information and best practices on MSMEs regulation and support, facilitation of MSMEs' access to public services, financing, exports and international projects;
- attracting and promoting investment into Special Economic Zones within BRICS countries;
- developing areas of collaboration of start up projects with participation of entrepreneurs of BRICS countries;
- exchanging experience on programmes directed towards the integration of targeted groups (such as youth, women, socially and economically disadvantaged strata and people with disabilities) and rural communities into the mainstream economy;
- promoting business cooperation through appropriate channels, including through the BRICS Business Council, annual business forums, the Exchanges Alliance, the Interbank Cooperation Forum;
- enhancing communication, cooperation and information exchange regarding legal framework, enforcement and other aspects in the area of Intellectual Property Rights (IPRs);
- promoting e-commerce development and cooperation.

To achieve these objectives the BRICS countries should:
- promote dialogue on BRICS countries' domestic investment policy and on approaches to investment agreements;
- strengthen cooperation among organizations responsible for investment facilitation;
- develop public-private partnerships as a mechanism of attracting additional resources; combining the capabilities of public and private sectors in the BRICS countries on implementing technologically advanced projects, including infrastructure projects;
- explore the possibility of implementing co-financed projects, including regional projects aimed at infrastructure development;
- promote cooperation between customs authorities;
- communicate and coordinate cooperation among Port Administration Departments;
- explore opportunities to identify and harness marine and coastal economic activities which are likely to be economically viable, socially acceptable and environmentally sustainable;

- develop information exchange on existing trade and investment opportunities ensuring the availability of information to business community; create infrastructure for distributing information on investment opportunities;
- enhance cooperation amongst national statistical authorities in data sharing, collection and analysis through the appropriate mechanisms, such as BRICS Heads of National Statistical Institutions Meeting;
- establish cooperation among the respective Ministries, agencies and organizations responsible for MSMEs, particularly with a view to promoting their mutual exchanges and cooperation for facilitating innovation, technology transfer, research and development, including organization of joint international seminars, forums, conferences, fairs, etc.;
- encourage the BRICS Business Council to strengthen and build upon the existing MSME portal which bridges the information gap and eases accessibility of support services to MSMEs;
- develop a short-period mobility programme for young entrepreneurs and scientists of BRICS countries, particularly in the areas of technology and innovation;
- coordinate efforts in arranging exhibitions, industry conferences, round tables and business missions on a regular basis with a view to establish partnerships, initiate projects and inform partners on available business opportunities, including exploring possible joint exhibition of BRICS countries in international trade fairs and organizing possible annual BRICS Trade Fairs;
- enhance cooperation on intellectual property rights;
- increase cooperation and trade in key services.

II.2 Manufacturing and minerals processing

BRICS countries consider the manufacturing sector as one of the most important sources of growth, it may change the structure of the economy, create new jobs, raise the quality of labour and living standards. Growth in production and export of value added goods would provide BRICS economies with an opportunity to gain greater benefits from international cooperation and increase their role in global value chains and raise the level of their competitiveness.

Economic growth attributed to the development of industry and mining will facilitate the strengthening of economic ties between the BRICS countries. It will be based on the development of advanced technologies, innovations as well as downstream value addition through the engagement of public and private sectors as appropriate in the implementation of national development programs, as well as international industrial cooperation and partnerships in the BRICS countries.

Interaction among BRICS countries aimed at technological and industrial development should cover:

- promoting dialogue and practical cooperation in the optimal use of value chains;
- cooperation in raising the technological level of traditional industries;
- cooperation in developing new hi-tech engineering industries and innovation;
- cooperation in the development of technologies, capital goods and machinery related to manufacturing and minerals processing, creating favorable conditions for the BRICS countries to enhance mutual supplies of modern equipment necessary for the development of hi-tech industries, including those based on mineral raw materials;
- attracting investments of the BRICS Member States to minerals processing and machinery and equipment manufacturing;
- cooperation on creating and operating BRICS industrial parks and clusters;
- joint development and application of clean and environmentally friendly industrial technologies;
- promotion of beneficiation of minerals and metals at source for use in traditional and new hi tech industries.

To achieve these goals the BRICS countries should:

- broaden cooperation in the field of technical and vocational education and training (TVET), including educational exchange, on-site training, joint programs including in high-tech engineering industries and engineering as well as management to develop a joint expertise on management and technical studies in a multicultural perspective, taking into account the need to transfer trust and competence;
- encourage development of the BRICS Consolidated Technology Platform introduced by UNIDO/BRICS project in order to contribute to sustainable economic development.

II.3 Energy

Promoting sustainable energy production and consumption is crucial for economic development of the BRICS countries. Balance of interests, transparency and predictability of supply and demand are the priority, given the unequal distribution of conventional energy sources and their limited reserves, coupled with the substantial increase in energy consumption in the developing countries.

Given the growing demand for energy sources, energy-efficient, clean, and environmentally friendly technologies, the BRICS countries stress the importance of sharing experience in the areas related to energy planning, production and consumption, and promoting mutual energy cooperation.

In order to enhance their energy security, BRICS countries should address the following priority areas:

- enhancing awareness of the needs of the energy-producing and energy-consuming countries;
- rendering mutual support for diversification of energy supplies;
- developing energy infrastructure;
- promoting universal access to energy;
- increasing energy efficiency, including joint development and sharing of energy efficient and cleaner energy technologies;
- introducing environmentally friendly technologies of energy production, storage and consumption;
- promoting the use of renewable sources of energy;
- improving the utilization of clean energy sources such as natural gas.

To achieve these goals BRICS countries should:

- promote efficient and environmentally friendly use of fossil fuels in the BRICS countries, including through cooperation in exploration and development of technologies aimed at hard-to-recover resources extraction;
- expand long-term energy supplies;
- establish regular energy dialogue between the BRICS countries in order to discuss long-term and medium-term strategies and energy security issues;
- encourage cooperation for the investments in energy projects in BRICS countries, including projects aimed at oil and gas exploration, energy infrastructure development;
- encourage research on practical implementation of sustainable development initiatives in the BRICS countries, taking into account national interests, including through the BRICS Think-Tanks Council and Academic Forum;
- create the conditions and accelerate the development as well as transfer of energy efficient and environmentally friendly technologies and equipment;
- strengthen cooperation between public and private sector to stimulate investment in energy efficient technologies;
- conduct research and development (R&D) and studies on advanced energy technologies in sectors of mutual interest which contribute to increase in energy efficiency;

- broaden cooperation in the field of educational programs, exchange of information on national policies and practices, conducting conferences, exhibitions, workshops and seminars, through collaborative efforts;
- exchange statistical data and forecasts of development of the national energy systems, as well as information on best practices and energy regulatory frameworks.

II.4 Agricultural cooperation

BRICS countries as large agricultural producers play an important role in the global agriculture market. BRICS countries also provide a fundamental contribution to food security and nutrition, given that a sizeable majority of the 209 million people who have been lifted out of food insecurity in the past two decades reside in the BRICS countries.[4]

Cooperation among BRICS countries will strengthen world food security through sustainably increasing agricultural production and raising the level of productivity in agricultural sector, providing better investment conditions and transparency of the markets, promoting better living standards and access to food.

BRICS cooperation in the area of food security and nutrition and agriculture development will include, in its five priority areas:

Development of a general strategy for ensuring access to food for the most vulnerable population

- exchange of experience in public policies and programmes for food security and nutrition and the strengthening of family farming; elaboration of a General Strategy for ensuring access to food for the most vulnerable populations of BRICS and other developing countries, including through an effective public stock holding policy;
- maintain coordination and dialogue on issues discussed by the FAO governing bodies on information systems such as Agricultural Marketing Information System (AMIS) and on cooperation in the humanitarian field of food assistance, as well as on issues discussed at the Committee on World Food Security;
- cooperate on increasing productivity and sustainability of agricultural production;

Trade and investment promotion

- promote trade and investment in the agricultural sector through participation in exhibitions, trade fairs and investment fora;
- support the creation of substantially improved market access, elimination of export subsidies and significant reduction of the level of trade distorting domestic support;
- ensure safety of food products;
- establish cooperation agreements and arrangements among BRICS countries, with a view to facilitate greater access to their agricultural markets;
- strengthening food safety including through exchange of relevant information;
- cooperation among agencies responsible for sanitary and phytosanitary control;
- exchanging views on labelling rules;
- implementation of joint investment projects in agriculture subject to foreign direct investment policy of the Member States;

---

[4] United Nations Food and Agriculture Organization Report "The State of Food Insecurity in the World 2014".

Basic Agricultural Information Exchange System
- work towards the development of a Basic Agricultural Information Exchange System of BRICS countries, bearing in mind its possible linkage with AMIS in order to avoid unnecessary duplications;

Agricultural technology cooperation and innovation
- intensify cooperation in the areas of agricultural science, technology, innovation and capacity building, including technologies for smallholder farming;

Reduction of negative impact of climate change on food security and adaptation of agriculture to climate change
- enhance cooperation and continue exchanging information and sharing experiences on relevant national policies, programs, plans and climate change adaptation and mitigation strategies.

II.5 Science, Technology and Innovation

Science, Technology and Innovation play a central role in promoting inclusive macroeconomics and social policies and in addressing challenges to humankind posed by the need to simultaneously achieve growth, inclusiveness, environmental protection and preservation. BRICS should harness bilateral synergies to accelerate sustainable development of the five members. The central modalities of this cooperation should be sharing and exchanging information on science, technology and innovation policies and strategies; leveraging contacts and programmes aimed at enhancing collaborative innovation projects among BRICS countries; and the formulation of joint long- term problem-focused cooperation programmes. Their cooperation should be based on the principles of voluntary participation, equality, mutual benefit, reciprocity and subject to the availability of resources for collaboration by each country and having in mind the variable geometry of the research and development systems of the BRICS member countries.

BRICS scientific, technological and innovative cooperation will be carried out as per the provisions of the agreed "MoU on Cooperation in Science, Technology and Innovation" and the overarching vision for implementation of this MoU by BRICS STI ministerial meetings.

The main areas of BRICS cooperation in STI should, inter alia, include:
- Exchange of information on policies and programmes and promotion of innovation and technology transfer;
- Food security and sustainable agriculture;
- Natural disasters;
- New and renewable energy, energy efficiency;
- Nanotechnology;
- High performance computing;
- Basic research;
- Space research and exploration, aeronautics, astronomy and earth observation;
- Medicine and biotechnology;
- Biomedicine and life sciences (biomedical engineering, bioinformatics, biomaterials);
- Water resources and pollution treatment;
- High tech zones/science parks and incubators;
- Technology transfer;
- Science popularization;
- Information and communication technology;
- Clean coal technologies;

- Natural gas and non-conventional gases;
- Ocean and polar sciences;
- Geospatial technologies and its applications.

To achieve these goals the BRICS countries should:
- promote research in the areas of common priority for the BRICS members;
- establish a strategic framework for cooperation in science, technology and innovation amongst the BRICS member countries supported by appropriate BRICS country funding mechanisms, instruments and national rules; and dedicate training programmes to support human capital development in science, technology and innovation, including short-term exchanges between scientists, researchers, technical experts and scholars;
- organize science, technology and innovation workshops, seminars and conferences in mutually agreed areas;
- facilitate access to science and technology infrastructure amongst BRICS member countries;
- engage in cooperation between respective national institutions of science, technology and innovation, research and development, and engineering in order to generate new knowledge and innovation industry, innovative products, services and processes in the BRICS member countries;
- exchange information on scientific and technological policy and programs;
- promote the development of environmentally friendly technologies;
- establish a joint Research and Innovation Networking Platform, aimed inter alia at facilitation of research collaboration;
- consider creating BRICS technology transfer network;
- support MSMEs in technology and innovation activities;
- promote the establishment of common technology platforms, innovation and technology clusters; joint development of high-tech zones / science parks and incubators; creating BRICS research and innovation centers;
- create BRICS Young Scientists Forum and promote involvement of youth in Innovation cooperation;
- exchange o experiences and practices in water management, including on rainwater harvesting, re-use and re-cycling of waste water;
- enhance cooperation on technology and innovation for natural disasters reduction among BRICS nations;
- set up a Disaster Management Centre for facilitating information/ data sharing on disasters and prediction techniques.

II.6 Financial cooperation

Financial issues are an important area of cooperation between BRICS countries and most of them are considered in the framework of the BRICS Finance Ministers and Central Bank Governors' process. The areas of cooperation include:
- establishment of the New Development Bank (NDB) to mobilize resources for infrastructure and sustainable development projects in BRICS and other emerging economies and developing countries, to supplement the existing efforts of multilateral and regional financial institutions for global growth and development;
- establishment of the Contingent Reserve Arrangement (CRA) to contribute to strengthening the global financial safety net and complement existing international monetary and financial arrangements;

- exchange of views and sharing perspectives on the main issues on the G20 agenda, including measures to minimize negative spillovers in global economy and promote growth and job creation, investment and infrastructure, strengthening of the financial system and cooperation on tax matters, and etc.;
- advancing the reforms of International Financial Institutions (IFIs), in particular the International Monetary Fund (IMF) and World Bank Group (WBG) reforms;
- discussion on new topics of mutual interest which could include cooperation in the area of payment systems, in particular, oversight of payment systems and financial industry message standards.

In addition, BRICS countries' development banks will cooperate under the framework of Financial Forum.

II.7 Connectivity

Connectivity is an essential prerequisite for enhancing competitiveness. Strengthening connectivity represents a common necessity for all BRICS countries. Initiatives launched by BRICS countries are of significant importance for connectivity. Connectivity should be strengthened in a comprehensive, integrated and systematic way in key areas including policy coordination, infrastructure connection, trade, financial integration and people-to-people contacts.

II.7.1   Institutional connectivity:

Institutional Connectivity will advance regulatory and procedural cooperation and coherence among the BRICS countries through addressing trade facilitation issues and improving the coherence and interoperability of institutions, mechanisms, and processes. BRICS cooperation in this area should focus on:

- strengthening interaction among Customs and Border Administrations;
- exchange of ideas and experiences on the development of a Single Window;
- enhancing supply chain connectivity through identifying bottlenecks in regional supply chains so as to ensure more efficient and timely operation of supply chains;
- promoting greater regulatory coherence and cooperation through coordination across regulatory standards and trade agencies and assessment of the impact of such regulations.

II.7.2   Physical connectivity:

Development of safe, balanced and dynamic transnational transportation and logistics systems is essential for economic growth of the BRICS countries. Efficient operation of the transportation system is crucial for international trade and integration in global production chains. Communication infrastructure, information and telecommunication technologies, as a key instrument of logistics system, also make a considerable contribution to accelerating growth and cost reduction.

The BRICS cooperation in these sectors is aimed at developing transportation and communication infrastructure and supporting mechanisms, including:

- exchange of information on measures and programs concerning transport and logistics policy, adoption of relevant long-term cooperation programs;
- business dialogue aimed at developing mechanisms of cooperation and exchange of best practices;
- support for transport and communication infrastructure development; search for technological, engineering and legal solutions to develop new international transport corridors in BRICS;
- use of innovative technologies to increase efficiency of transportation and logistics systems;
- promotion of energy efficiency and reduction of polluting emissions in the transportation sector;

- promotion of standardized digital data exchange systems in logistics to facilitate multimodal and intermodal transportation in the BRICS countries;
- cooperation and promotion of technologies of traffic safety control, transportation and infrastructure design, operation and monitoring;
- exchange of experience on development and use of innovative communication equipment, especially intelligent transportation systems and satellite navigation systems;
- development of public private partnership mechanisms, including in construction of highways, ports, airports, development of urban transport and railway infrastructure, subject to proper commercial viability and risk assessment;
- engagement of small and medium-sized enterprises into construction, logistics, maintenance of transportation and infrastructure facilities to address social and development challenges;
- harmonization of systems and processes in the transportation and logistics systems to allow seamless transfer of goods and passengers amongst BRICS countries including through use of ICT tools;
- cooperation in skills training for design, construction and operation of infrastructure facilities, implementation of joint research programs in the areas of content and application development, establishment of training centers networks in the area of information and communication technologies;
- exchange of experiences and practices with regard to efficient city transport systems, dynamic traffic control systems, efficient freight movement systems, and passenger-friendly services, etc.

To achieve these goals the BRICS countries should:
- hold meetings of high-ranking officials from public and private sectors when needed with the view to address current and emerging issues relating to BRICS performance in the field of transport infrastructure, logistics and communications, aimed at supply chain optimization;
- encourage cooperation and exchanges among media professionals from BRICS countries;
- encourage cooperation among BRICS countries' air carriers to enhance transportation efficiency and increase the number of direct flights;
- encourage BRICS countries enterprises to participate in competitive bidding, including joint bids, for infrastructure development;
- promote dialogue and information-sharing on increasing efficiency of railways infrastructure;
- exchange perspectives on satisfying urban mobility needs.

II.7.3   People-to-people connectivity:

Enhanced people-to-people connectivity will further stimulate interaction among BRICS countries, people and societies, promote business, labour and academic mobility and tourism, and strengthen mutual understanding and friendship.

Education

Education has a strategic importance for sustainable development and inclusive economic growth. Through the accelerating progress in the educational field, the BRICS countries commit to attain the Post-2015 Development Agenda objectives and targets related to education and education-related Sustainable Development Goals to ensure equitable, inclusive and quality education and lifelong learning. The BRICS countries acknowledge that vocational and technical education addresses the challenge of integrating young people to the labour market and plays a critical role in preparing skilled workforce needed by the modern world.

Being strategic partners in this regard, the BRICS countries should forge close mutual links to improve the education from the earliest to the highest levels.

The main areas of BRICS educational cooperation should include:
- developing joint methodologies for education indicators;
- sharing best practices in terms of assessing learning outcomes;
- sharing concepts, methods and analytical tools to match demands and supply of vocational and technological education;
- developing higher education, with emphasis on mobility in graduate school, and research;
- establishing networks of researchers and developing joint projects in areas of mutual interest;
- establishing a BRICS University League (association of BRICS universities) and a BRICS Network University;
- exchanging experience and best practices in education;
- development of the skilled workforce needed by the BRICS industries;
- enhancing educational cooperation to strengthen regional ties and promote economic development through knowledge and skills transfer;
- promoting academic mobility, including student exchanges, among BRICS countries;
- exchanging of experiences in recognition of degrees and diplomas between BRICS countries;
- strengthening of higher education system and technical and vocational education and training (TVET);
- data sharing for measuring equity, inclusion and quality improvements based primarily on national assessments, administrative data and national household surveys as well as other data;
- development of joint methodologies for education indicators to support decision making in BRICS countries and provide technical support to the National Institutes of Statistics.

To achieve these goals the BRICS countries should:
- conduct joint scientific research and personnel training;
- share best practices in terms of assessing learning outcomes and report them in order to be useful for policy makers, universities and schools;
- share technical expertise, building linkages and identification and collaboration in addressing gaps in the areas of skill development, curriculum development and reform;
- share benchmark assessment, accreditation standards, and certification and training methods;
- share best practices in areas including policies on skills development, credit framework designs, occupational standards and apprenticeship models;
- prepare skilled workforce needed by the labour market, including through the TVET;
- create a working group to develop a report on the state of vocational and technical education and share concepts, methods and instruments of analysis to match demands and supply of TVET in BRICS countries;
- establish the networks of researchers and develop joint projects;
- establish BRICS University League;
- establish BRICS Network University;
- carry out joint activities on teacher training using also ICT, massive open online courses (MOOCs) and other digital initiatives;
- establish long-term cooperation mechanisms on education including BRICS Education Ministers' Meeting;
- explore credit transfer among BRICS universities.

Tourism
- create favorable conditions for long-term cooperation in the field of tourism for the mutual benefit of the BRICS Member States, in accordance with their national laws and regulations;
- engage in initiatives in the field of human resource development and cooperation to develop, upgrade and expand tourism and travel facilities and services between the BRICS countries;
- undertake efforts to create favorable conditions for the public and private sectors to engage more deeply in investments in tourism and travel between the BRICS countries;
- finalize a Memorandum of Understanding on Tourism.

Business and labour mobility
- facilitate the issuance of visas;
- strengthen occupational safety;
- initiate the modernization of enterprises and industries including through introducing new technologies aimed at creating favorable employment opportunities;
- ensure the fulfillment of workers' rights and protection;
- encourage exchanges among BRICS cultural industries;
- promote greater awareness, understanding and appreciation of each other's culture; explore areas of practical cooperation in this regard, including to implement the agreement on cultural cooperation.

II.8 ICT Cooperation

Information and communications technologies (ICTs), in particular the Internet and other media, can be powerful tools to provide instruments to foster sustainable economic progress and social inclusion. BRICS should strengthen cooperation and promote joint activities and initiatives to address common concerns in the field of ICTs. The main areas of BRICS ICT cooperation will include:
- cooperation on digital economy;
- development of contacts between BRICS   IT/ITeS industries, strengthening cooperation among public private entities;
- exploring the full potential of ICTs, including the Internet, in the pursuit of the purposes of cooperation amongst BRICS;
- communication and cooperation of BRICS on emergency response to information security issues;
- cooperation within BRICS and in other relevant international fora on countering the use of ICTs for criminal and terrorist purposes;
- protection of critical ICT infrastructure and personal information;
- joint research on new technologies and services of information security;
- coordination on agreed ICTs and ICT-related security issues within relevant international organizations and fora;
- promotion of dialogue on internet governance;
- promotion of a peaceful, secure, open, trusted and cooperative digital and Internet space;
- cooperation among the BRICS countries through joint development of software and equipment in the IT-sphere, and promotion of projects in this field;
- consideration of incentives to attract investment and production in BRICS countries by global IT manufacturers and to address human resource and technology gaps through the system of international scientific and technological cooperation;

- promotion of innovative telecommunication equipment, development and introduction of new standards and technologies of communication to promote information/digital society and to resist cyber threats;
- development of cooperation to find new ways of reducing voice, internet and broadband cost; exchange of information and expertise, to contribute to cost reduction including policy and regulatory interventions and implementation;
- cooperation in skills training for design, construction and operation of infrastructure facilities, implementation of joint research programs in the areas of content and application development, establishment of training centers networks in the area of information and communication technologies;
- increase opportunities for the uptake and usage of technology through information exchange as well as joint R&D projects to promote growth in IT manufacturing, including through innovation.

To achieve these goals the BRICS countries should:
- constitute a working group on ICT cooperation to consider, inter alia, ways and measures to promote ICT-related issues and enhance regular interactions at the Ministerial and official levels;
- offer training programmes to support human capital development in information technology and innovation;
- exchange of expertise on information society policies and programs, for the equitable distribution of the benefits of the new technologies and services.

III. Interaction with international and regional economic organizations and fora

Development of intra-BRICS cooperation in various international and regional platforms is vital for the promotion of common interests in international trade, investment, industrial, scientific and technological cooperation. BRICS will strive to further strengthen its role in the global arena by communicating assessments on global macroeconomic situations and trade policies, through existing mechanisms, coordinating positions in international and regional organizations, associations and forums and developing outreach formats of interaction. Cooperation in multilateral bodies and organizations will complement bilateral economic ties among BRICS countries.

BRICS countries will continue to develop cooperation within the UN system as well as with other international economic organizations in accordance with the fundamental principles of the UN Charter.

BRICS countries will continue to pursue reform of the global economic governance institutions and safeguard the interests of BRICS countries as well as other emerging and developing economies.

Participation of BRICS countries in the activities of regional organizations will strengthen their role as regional leaders; promote development, sustainable growth in respective regions and cross-regional cooperation.

III.1 BRICS and WTO

BRICS countries recognize the importance of international trade as a key to new jobs, sustained economic recovery as well as balanced growth and development. The BRICS members reaffirm the value, centrality and primacy of the multilateral trading system in world trade regulation and their commitment to strengthen the rules-based, transparent, non-discriminatory, open and inclusive multilateral trading system as embodied in the WTO.

To that end, BRICS countries urge other countries to resist all forms of trade protectionism and disguised restrictions on trade while supporting the work of the WTO and other international organizations.

BRICS countries will strive to enhance their cooperation to create conditions for expansion and diversification of BRICS participation in global trade. They emphasize the need to coordinate and cooperate in the WTO to develop the Post-Bali work program, and express their strong support for the conclusion of the Doha Round.

III.2 BRICS and the G20

BRICS countries are committed to strengthening the G20 as a premier forum for international economic cooperation. They will continue to actively participate in the work of the G20, exchange views with the aim of further strengthening international financial and economic architecture and achieving strong, sustainable, balanced and inclusive growth. BRICS countries will continue to coordinate and hold preparatory meetings ahead of main G-20 events.

IV. Implementation of the BRICS Strategy

The BRICS Strategy is adopted by the BRICS Leaders in 2015 in the city of Ufa, Russian Federation. The Sherpas will review the BRICS Strategy every five years, or earlier if deemed necessary. The Sherpas will annually report on the progress in the implementation of the BRICS Strategy to the BRICS Leaders.

II.5.   6th BRICS Summit 2014: 15 Jul. 2014, Fortaleza (BRA)

A.   The Fortaleza Declaration

VI BRICS SUMMIT

FORTALEZA DECLARATION

July 15, 2014

1. We, the leaders of the Federative Republic of Brazil, the Russian Federation, the Republic of India, the People's Republic of China and the Republic of South Africa, met in Fortaleza, Brazil, on 15 July 2014 at the Sixth BRICS Summit. To inaugurate the second cycle of BRICS Summits, the theme chosen for our discussions was "Inclusive Growth: Sustainable Solutions", in keeping with the inclusive macroeconomic and social policies carried out by our governments and the imperative to address challenges to humankind posed by the need to simultaneously achieve growth, inclusiveness, protection and preservation.

2. In the aftermath of the first cycle of five Summits, hosted by every BRICS member, our coordination is well established in various multilateral and plurilateral initiatives and intra-BRICS cooperation is expanding to encompass new areas. Our shared views and commitment to international law and to multilateralism, with the United Nations at its center and foundation, are widely recognized and constitute a major contribution to global peace, economic stability, social inclusion, equality, sustainable development and mutually beneficial cooperation with all countries.

3. We renew our openness to increasing engagement with other countries, particularly developing countries and emerging market economies, as well as with international and regional organizations, with a view to fostering cooperation and solidarity in our relations with all nations and peoples. To that effect, we will hold a joint session with the leaders of the South American nations, under the theme of the Sixth BRICS Summit, with a view to furthering cooperation between BRICS and South America. We reaffirm our support for the South American integration processes, and recognize in particular the importance of the Union of South American Nations (UNASUR) in promoting peace and democracy in the region, and in achieving sustainable development and poverty eradication. We believe that strengthened dialogue among BRICS and South American countries can play an active role in enhancing multilateralism and international cooperation, for the promotion of peace, security, economic and social progress and sustainable development in an interdependent and increasingly complex, globalizing world.

4. Since its inception the BRICS have been guided by the overarching objectives of peace, security, development and cooperation. In this new cycle, while remaining committed to those objectives, we pledge to deepen our partnership with a renewed vision, based on openness, inclusiveness and mutually beneficial cooperation. In this sense, we are ready to explore new areas towards a comprehensive cooperation and a closer economic partnership to facilitate market inter-linkages, financial integration, infrastructure connectivity as well as people-to- people contacts.

5. The Sixth Summit takes place at a crucial juncture, as the international community assesses how to address the challenges of strong economic recovery from the global financial crises, sustainable development, including climate change, while also formulating the post-2015 Development Agenda. At the same time, we are confronted with persistent political instability and conflict in various global hotspots and non-conventional emerging threats. On the other hand, international governance structures designed within a different power configuration show increasingly evident signs of losing legitimacy and effectiveness, as transitional and ad hoc arrangements become increasingly prevalent, often at the expense of multilateralism. We believe the BRICS are an important force for incremental change and reform of current institutions towards more representative and equitable governance,

capable of generating more inclusive global growth and fostering a stable, peaceful and prosperous world.

6.   During the first cycle of BRICS Summits, collectively our economies have consolidated their position as the main engines for sustaining the pace of the international economy as it recovers from the recent economic and financial global crisis. The BRICS continue to contribute significantly to global growth and to the reduction of poverty in our own and other countries. Our economic growth and social inclusion policies have helped to stabilize global economy, to foster the creation of jobs, to reduce poverty, and to combat inequality, thus contributing to the achievement of the Millennium Development Goals. In this new cycle, besides its contribution in fostering strong, sustainable and balanced growth, BRICS will continue to play a significant role in promoting social development and in contributing to define the international agenda in this area, building on its experience in addressing the challenges of poverty and inequality.

7.   To better reflect the advancement of the social policies of the BRICS and the positive impacts of its economic growth, we instruct our National Institutes of Statistics and the Ministries of Health and Education to work on the development of joint methodologies for social indicators to be incorporated in the BRICS Joint Statistical Publication. We also encourage the BRICS Think Tanks Council to provide technical support in this task. We further request the BRICS National Institutes of Statistics to discuss the viability and feasibility of a platform for the development of such methodologies and to report thereon.

8.   The world economy has strengthened, with signs of improvement in some advanced economies. Significant downside risks to this recovery remain, however. Unemployment and debt levels are worryingly high and growth remains weak in many advanced economies. Emerging market economies and developing countries (EMDCs) continue to contribute significantly to global growth and will do so in the years to come. Even as the global economy strengthens, monetary policy settings in some advanced economies may bring renewed stress and volatility to financial markets and changes in monetary stance need to be carefully calibrated and clearly communicated in order to minimize negative spillovers.

9.   Strong macroeconomic frameworks, well-regulated financial markets and robust levels of reserves have allowed EMDCs in general, and the BRICS in particular, to better deal with the risks and spillovers presented by the challenging economic conditions in the last few years. Nevertheless, further macroeconomic coordination amongst all major economies, in particular in the G20, remains a critical factor for strengthening the prospects for a vigorous and sustainable recovery worldwide. In this context, we reaffirm our strong commitment to continue working among ourselves and with the global community to foster financial stability, support sustainable, stronger and inclusive growth and promote quality jobs. The BRICS stand ready to contribute to the G20 goal of lifting our collective GDP by more than 2 percent above the trajectory implied by current policies over the coming 5 years.

10. We commend Russia for the successful work during its presidency of the G20 in 2013. The institution of the BRICS Summits largely coincided with the beginning of the global crisis, the first G20 Summits and the consolidation of that Group as the premier forum for economic coordination among its members. As a new round of BRICS Summits begins, we remain committed to deliver constructive responses to global economic and financial challenges and to serve as a strong voice for the promotion of sustainable development, inclusive growth, financial stability and of more representative international economic governance. We will continue to pursue our fruitful coordination and to promote our development goals within the international economic system and financial architecture.

11. BRICS, as well as other EMDCs, continue to face significant financing constraints to address infrastructure gaps and sustainable development needs. With this in mind, we are pleased to announce the signing of the Agreement establishing the New Development Bank (NDB), with the purpose of mobilizing resources for infrastructure and sustainable development projects in BRICS

and other emerging and developing economies. We appreciate the work undertaken by our Finance Ministers. Based on sound banking principles, the NDB will strengthen the cooperation among our countries and will supplement the efforts of multilateral and regional financial institutions for global development, thus contributing to our collective commitments for achieving the goal of strong, sustainable and balanced growth.

12. The Bank shall have an initial authorized capital of US$ 100 billion. The initial subscribed capital shall be of US$ 50 billion, equally shared among founding members. The first chair of the Board of Governors shall be from Russia. The first chair of the Board of Directors shall be from Brazil. The first President of the Bank shall be from India. The headquarters of the Bank shall be located in Shanghai. The New Development Bank Africa Regional Center shall be established in South Africa concurrently with the headquarters. We direct our Finance Ministers to work out the modalities for its operationalization.

13. We are pleased to announce the signing of the Treaty for the establishment of the BRICS Contingent Reserve Arrangement (CRA) with an initial size of US$ 100 billion. This arrangement will have a positive precautionary effect, help countries forestall short-term liquidity pressures, promote further BRICS cooperation, strengthen the global financial safety net and complement existing international arrangements. We appreciate the work undertaken by our Finance Ministers and Central Bank Governors. The Agreement is a framework for the provision of liquidity through currency swaps in response to actual or potential short-term balance of payments pressures.

14. We also welcome the signing of the Memorandum of Understanding on Cooperation among BRICS Export Credit and Guarantees Agencies that will improve the support environment for increasing trade opportunities among our nations.

15. We appreciate the progress our Development Banks have made in enhancing and strengthening the financial ties among BRICS countries. Given the importance of adopting innovation initiatives, we welcome the conclusion of the Cooperation Agreement on Innovation within the BRICS Interbank Cooperation Mechanism.

16. We recognize that there is potential for BRICS insurance and reinsurance markets to pool capacities. We direct our relevant authorities to explore avenues of cooperation in this regard.

17. We believe that sustainable development and economic growth will be facilitated by taxation of revenue generated in jurisdictions where economic activity takes place. We express our concern over the harmful impact of tax evasion, transnational fraud and aggressive tax planning on the world economy. We are aware of the challenges brought by aggressive tax avoidance and non-compliance practices. We, therefore, affirm our commitment to continue a cooperative approach on issues related to tax administrations and to enhance cooperation in the international forums targeting tax base erosion and information exchange for tax purposes. We direct our relevant authorities to explore ways of enhancing cooperation in this area. We also direct our relevant authorities to strengthen cooperation in the field of customs.

18. We remain disappointed and seriously concerned with the current non-implementation of the 2010 International Monetary Fund (IMF) reforms, which negatively impacts on the IMF's legitimacy, credibility and effectiveness. The IMF reform process is based on high-level commitments, which already strengthened the Fund's resources and must also lead to the modernization of its governance structure so as to better reflect the increasing weight of EMDCs in the world economy. The Fund must remain a quota-based institution. We call on the membership of the IMF to find ways to implement the 14th General Review of Quotas without further delay. We reiterate our call on the IMF to develop options to move ahead with its reform process, with a view to ensuring increased voice and representation of EMDCs, in case the 2010 reforms are not entered into force by the end of the year. We also call on the membership of the IMF to reach a final agreement on a new quota

formula together with the 15th General Review of Quotas so as not to further jeopardize the postponed deadline of January 2015.

19. We welcome the goals set by the World Bank Group to help countries end extreme poverty and to promote shared prosperity. We recognize the potential of this new strategy in support of the fulfillment of these ambitious goals by the international community. This potential will only be realized, however, if the institution and its membership effectively move towards more democratic governance structures, strengthen the Bank's financial capacity and explore innovative ways to enhance development financing and knowledge sharing while pursuing a strong client orientation that recognizes each country's development needs. We look forward to initiating the work on the next shareholding review at the World Bank as soon as possible in order to meet the agreed deadline of October 2015. In this sense, we call for an international financial architecture that is more conducive to overcoming development challenges. We have been very active in improving the international financial architecture through our multilateral coordination and through our financial cooperation initiatives, which will, in a complementary manner, increase the diversity and availability of resources for promoting development and ensuring stability in the global economy.

20. We are committed to raise our economic cooperation to a qualitatively new level. To achieve this, we emphasize the importance of establishing a road map for intra-BRICS economic cooperation. In this regard, we welcome the proposals for a "BRICS Economic Cooperation Strategy" and a "Framework of BRICS Closer Economic Partnership", which lay down steps to promote intra-BRICS economic, trade and investment cooperation. Based on the documents tabled and informed by the input of the BRICS Think Tanks Council (BTTC), we instruct our Sherpas to advance discussions with a view to submit their proposal for endorsement by the next BRICS Summit.

21. We believe all countries should enjoy due rights, equal opportunities and fair participation in global economic, financial and trade affairs, recognizing that countries have different capacities and are at different levels of development. We strive for an open world economy with efficient allocation of resources, free flow of goods, and fair and orderly competition to the benefit of all. In reaffirming our support for an open, inclusive, non-discriminatory, transparent and rule-based multilateral trading system, we will continue our efforts towards the successful conclusion of the Doha Round of the World Trade Organization (WTO), following the positive results of the Ninth Ministerial Conference (MC9), held in Bali, Indonesia, in December 2013. In this context, we reaffirm our commitment to establish by the end of this year a post-Bali work program for concluding the Doha Round, based on the progress already made and in keeping with the mandate established in the Doha Development Agenda. We affirm that this work program should prioritize the issues where legally binding outcomes could not be achieved at MC9, including Public Stock-Holding for Food Security Purposes. We look forward to the implementation of the Agreement on Trade Facilitation. We call upon international partners to provide support to the poorest, most vulnerable WTO members to enable them to implement this Agreement, which should support their development objectives. We strongly support the WTO dispute settlement system as a cornerstone of the security and predictability of the multilateral trading system and we will enhance our ongoing dialogue on substantive and practical matters relating to it, including in the ongoing negotiations on WTO Dispute Settlement Understanding reform. We recognize the importance of Regional Trade Agreements, which should complement the multilateral trading system, and of keeping them open, inclusive and transparent, as well as refraining from introducing exclusive and discriminatory clauses and standards.

22. We reaffirm the United Nations Conference on Trade and Development's (UNCTAD) mandate as the focal point in the UN system dedicated to consider the interrelated issues of trade, investment, finance and technology from a development perspective. UNCTAD's mandate and work are unique and necessary to deal with the challenges of development and growth in the increasingly interdependent global economy. In congratulating UNCTAD for the 50th anniversary of its foundation in 2014, which is also the anniversary of the establishment of the Group of 77, we further

reaffirm the importance of strengthening UNCTAD's capacity to deliver on its programs of consensus building, policy dialogue, research, technical cooperation and capacity building so that it is better equipped to deliver on its development mandate.

23. We acknowledge the important role that State Owned Companies (SOCs) play in the economy and encourage our SOCs to continue to explore ways of cooperation, exchange of information and best practices. We also recognize the fundamental role played by small and medium-sized enterprises in the economies of our countries as major creators of jobs and wealth. We will enhance cooperation and recognize the need for strengthening intra-BRICS dialogue with a view to promote international exchange and cooperation and to foster innovation, research and development.

24. We underline that 2015 marks the 70th anniversary of the founding of the United Nations (UN) and the end of the Second World War. In this connection, we support the UN to initiate and organize commemorative events to mark and pay tribute to these two historical moments in human history, and reaffirm our commitment to safeguarding a just and fair international order based on the UN Charter, maintaining world peace and security, as well as promoting human progress and development.

25. We reiterate our strong commitment to the UN as the fundamental multilateral organization entrusted with helping the international community maintain international peace and security, protect and foster human rights and promote sustainable development. The UN enjoys universal membership and is at the very center of global governance and multilateralism. We recall the 2005 World Summit Outcome Document. We reaffirm the need for a comprehensive reform of the UN, including its Security Council, with a view to making it more representative, effective and efficient, so that it can adequately respond to global challenges. China and Russia reiterate the importance they attach to Brazil, India and South Africa's status and role in international affairs and support their aspiration to play a greater role in the UN.

26. We recall that development and security are closely interlinked, mutually reinforcing and key to attaining sustainable peace. We reiterate our view that the establishment of sustainable peace requires a comprehensive, concerted and determined approach, based on mutual trust, mutual benefit, equity and cooperation, that address the root causes of conflicts, including their political, economic and social dimensions. In this context, we also stress the close interrelation between peacekeeping and peacebuilding. We also highlight the importance of bringing gender perspectives to conflict prevention and resolution, peacebuilding, peacekeeping, rehabilitation and reconstruction efforts.

27. We will continue our joint efforts in coordinating positions and acting on shared interests on global peace and security issues for the common well-being of humanity. We stress our commitment to the sustainable and peaceful settlement of disputes, according to the principles and purposes of the UN Charter. We condemn unilateral military interventions and economic sanctions in violation of international law and universally recognized norms of international relations. Bearing this in mind, we emphasize the unique importance of the indivisible nature of security, and that no State should strengthen its security at the expense of the security of others.

28. We agree to continue to treat all human rights, including the right to development, in a fair and equal manner, on the same footing and with the same emphasis. We will foster dialogue and cooperation on the basis of equality and mutual respect in the field of human rights, both within BRICS and in multilateral fora – including the United Nations Human Rights Council where all BRICS serve as members in 2014 – taking into account the necessity to promote, protect and fulfill human rights in a non-selective, non-politicized and constructive manner, and without double standards.

29. We commend the efforts made by the United Nations, the African Union (AU), Economic Community of West African States (ECOWAS) and the Community of Portuguese-Speaking Countries (CPLP), among others, in support for the realization of legislative and presidential elections in Guinea

Bissau, paving the way for the return to constitutional democracy in the country. We recognize the importance of promoting long-term political stability in Guinea- Bissau, which necessarily encompasses measures to reduce food insecurity and to advance a comprehensive security sector reform, as proposed by the Guinea-Bissau Configuration of the UN Peacebuilding Commission. Similarly, we also welcome the efforts of the UN, AU and Southern African Development Community (SADC) in support of legislative and presidential elections in Madagascar, assisting in the return of constitutional democracy in the country.

30. We commend the efforts of the international community in addressing instability in Africa through engagement with, and coordination by, the AU and its Peace and Security Council. We express our deep concern at the deterioration of the security and the humanitarian situation in West Africa. We call upon all parties in these conflicts to cease hostilities, exercise restraint and engage in dialogue to ensure return to peace and stability. However, we also note the progress that has been made in areas of the region in addressing political and security challenges.

31. We also express our concern with the plight of the abducted women and children of Chibok and call for an end to the continued terrorist acts perpetrated by Boko Haram.

32. We support the efforts of the UN Multidimensional Integrated Stabilization Mission in Mali (MINUSMA) in its task to help the Government of Mali fully stabilize the country, facilitate national political dialogue, protect civilians, monitor the human rights situation, create conditions for the provision of humanitarian assistance and the return of displaced persons, and extend the State authority in the whole country. We emphasize the importance of an inclusive political process; the immediate implementation of a disarmament, demobilization and reintegration (DDR) process; and political, economic and social development in order for Mali to achieve sustainable peace and stability.

33. We express our concern about the ongoing political and humanitarian crises in South Sudan. We condemn the continuation of violence against civilians and call upon all parties to ensure a safe environment for the delivery of humanitarian assistance. We also condemn the continuation of confrontations despite the successive commitments to the cessation of hostilities and express our belief that a sustainable solution to the crisis is only possible through an inclusive political dialogue aimed at national reconciliation. We support, in this regard, the regional efforts to find a peaceful solution to the crisis, especially the mediation process led by the Intergovernmental Authority on Development (IGAD). We welcome the "Agreement to Resolve the Crisis in South Sudan", signed on May 9, and expect the political leaders of South Sudan to remain committed to the negotiation process and to the completion of dialogue on the formation of a transitional government of national unity within 60 days, as announced by IGAD on June 10. We commend the efforts of the United Nations Mission in South Sudan to fulfill its mandate and express our deep concern about the armed attacks that were led against UN bases in the country.

34. We reiterate our grave concern with the situation in the Central African Republic (CAR). We strongly condemn the abuses and acts of violence against the civilian population, including sectarian violence, and urge all armed groups to cease hostilities immediately. We recognize the efforts of the Economic Community of Central African States and the AU to restore peace and stability in the country. We commend the establishment of the UN Multidimensional Integrated Stabilization Mission in the CAR (MINUSCA). We express our support for a successful transition from the African-led International Support Mission to the CAR (MISCA) to MINUSCA by 15 September 2014. We urge the transitional authorities in the CAR to adhere strictly to the N'Djamena Roadmap. We call upon all parties to allow safe and unhindered humanitarian access to those in need. We reaffirm our readiness to work with the international community to assist the CAR in accelerating the implementation of the political process of the country.

35. We support the efforts by the UN, in particular the UN Organization Stabilization Mission in the Democratic Republic of the Congo (MONUSCO), deployed under UN Security Council resolution 2098,

and the regional and sub-regional organizations to bring peace and stability to the Democratic Republic of the Congo (DRC), and we call upon all involved to honor their obligations in order to achieve lasting peace and stability in the DRC.

36. We welcome the AU Malabo Summit decision to establish an interim African Capacity for Immediate Response to Crises (ACIRC) by October 2014 to respond quickly to crisis situations as they arise. We stress the importance of adequate support to ensure the timely operationalization of the ACIRC, pending the final establishment of the African Stand-by Force.

37. We express deep concern about the ongoing violence and the deterioration of the humanitarian situation in Syria and condemn the increasing violations of human rights by all parties. We reiterate our view that there is no military solution to the conflict, and highlight the need to avoid its further militarization. We call upon all parties to commit immediately to a complete cease-fire, to halt violence and to allow and facilitate immediate, safe, full and unimpeded access for humanitarian organizations and agencies, in compliance with the UN Security Council resolution 2139. We recognize practical steps undertaken by the Syrian parties in implementing its requirements, including the practice of local cease-fire agreements reached between the Syrian authorities and the opposition forces.

We reiterate our condemnation of terrorism in all its forms and manifestations, wherever it occurs. We are gravely concerned at the continued threat of terrorism and extremism in Syria. We call on all Syrian parties to commit to putting an end to terrorist acts perpetrated by Al-Qaeda, its affiliates and other terrorist organizations.

We strongly condemn the use of chemical weapons in any circumstances. We welcome the decision of the Syrian Arab Republic to accede to the Chemical Weapons Convention. In accordance with related Organization for the Proscription of Chemical Weapons (OPCW) Executive Council decisions and UN Security Council resolution 2118, we reiterate the importance of the complete removal and elimination of the Syrian chemical weapons. We commend the progress in that regard and welcome the announcement that the removal of declared chemicals from the Syrian Arab Republic was completed. We call on all Syrian parties and interested external actors with relevant capabilities to work closely together and with the OPCW and the UN to arrange for the security of the monitoring and destruction mission in its final stage.

We support the mediation role played by the UN. We appreciate the contribution made by former Joint UN – Arab League Special Representative for Syria, Mr. Lakhdar Brahimi, and welcome the appointment of Mr. Staffan De Mistura as UN Special Envoy to Syria, and express our hope for his active efforts to promote an early resumption of comprehensive negotiations. We recall that national dialogue and reconciliation are key to the political solution for the Syrian crisis. We take note of the recent Syrian presidential elections. We stress that only an inclusive political process, led by the Syrians, as recommended in the Action Group on Syria Final Communiqué of 2012, will lead to peace, effective protection of civilians, the realization of the legitimate aspirations of the Syrian society for freedom and prosperity and respect for Syrian independence, territorial integrity and sovereignty. We emphasize that a national reconciliation process needs to be launched as early as possible, in the interest of the national unity of Syria. To that end, we urge all parties in Syria to demonstrate political will, enhance mutual understanding, exercise restraint and commit to seeking common ground in accommodating their differences.

38. We reaffirm our commitment to contribute to a comprehensive, just and lasting settlement of the Arab-Israeli conflict on the basis of the universally recognized international legal framework, including the relevant UN resolutions, the Madrid Principles and the Arab Peace Initiative. We believe that the resolution of the Israeli-Palestinian conflict is a fundamental component for building a sustainable peace in the Middle East. We call upon Israel and Palestine to resume negotiations leading to a two-State solution with a contiguous and economically viable Palestinian State existing side by side in peace with Israel, within mutually agreed and internationally recognized borders

based on the 4 June 1967 lines, with East Jerusalem as its capital. We oppose the continuous construction and expansion of settlements in the Occupied Palestinian Territories by the Israeli Government, which violates international law, gravely undermines peace efforts and threatens the viability of the two-State solution. We welcome recent efforts to achieve intra-Palestinian unity, including the formation of a national unity government and steps towards conducting general elections, which is key element to consolidate a democratic and sustainable Palestinian State, and call on the parties to fully commit to the obligations assumed by Palestine. We call on the UN Security Council to fully exercise its functions under the UN Charter with regard to the Israeli-Palestinian conflict. We recall with satisfaction the decision of the UN General Assembly to proclaim 2014 the International Year of Solidarity with the Palestinian People, welcome the efforts of UN Relief and Works Agency (UNRWA) in providing assistance and protection for Palestine refugees and encourage the international community to continue to support the activities of the agency.

39. We express our support for the convening, at the earliest possible date, of the Conference on the establishment of a Middle East zone free of nuclear weapons and all other weapons of mass destruction. We call upon all states of the region to attend the Conference and to engage constructively and in a pragmatic manner with a view to advancing that goal.

40. Noting the open-ended consultations on a draft International Code of Conduct on Outer Space Activities, and the active and constructive engagement of our countries in these consultations, we call for an inclusive and consensus-based multilateral negotiation to be conducted within the framework of the UN without specific deadlines in order to reach a balanced outcome that addresses the needs and reflects the concerns of all participants. Reaffirming our will that the exploration and use of outer space shall be for peaceful purposes, we stress that negotiations for the conclusion of an international agreement or agreements to prevent an arms race in outer space remain a priority task of the Conference on Disarmament, and welcome the introduction by China and Russia of the updated draft Treaty on the Prevention of the Placement of Weapons in Outer Space, the Threat or Use of Force Against Outer Space Objects.

41. While reiterating our view that there is no alternative to a negotiated solution to the Iranian nuclear issue, we reaffirm our support to its resolution through political and diplomatic means and dialogue. In this context, we welcome the positive momentum generated by talks between Iran and the E3+3 and encourage the thorough implementation of the Geneva Joint Plan of Action of 24 November 2013, with a view to achieving a comprehensive and long-lasting solution to this issue. We also encourage Iran and the International Atomic Energy Agency (IAEA) to continue strengthening their cooperation and dialogue on the basis of the Joint Statement signed on 11 November 2013. We recognize Iran's inalienable right to the peaceful use of nuclear energy in a manner consistent with its international obligations.

42. Recognizing that peace, security and development are closely interlinked, we reaffirm that Afghanistan needs time, development assistance and cooperation, preferential access to world markets and foreign investment to attain lasting peace and stability. We support the commitment of the international community to remain engaged in Afghanistan during the transformation decade (2015-2024), as enunciated at the Bonn International Conference in December 2011. We stress that the UN should play an increasingly important role in assisting Afghanistan's national reconciliation, recovery and economic reconstruction. We also reaffirm our commitment to support Afghanistan's emergence as a peaceful, stable and democratic state, free of terrorism and extremism, and underscore the need for more effective regional and international cooperation for the stabilization of Afghanistan, including by combating terrorism. We extend support to the efforts aimed at combating illicit traffic in opiates originating in Afghanistan within the framework of the Paris Pact. We expect a broad-based and inclusive peace process in Afghanistan which is Afghan-led and Afghan-owned. We welcome the second round of the presidential elections in Afghanistan which contribute to the democratic transfer of power in this country. We welcome China's offer to host the Fourth Heart of Asia Ministerial Conference in August 2014.

43. We are deeply concerned by the situation in Iraq. We strongly support the Iraqi government in its effort to overcome the crisis, uphold national sovereignty and territorial integrity. We are concerned about spillover effects of the instability in Iraq resulting from increased terrorist activities in the region, and urge all parties to address the terrorist threat in a consistent manner. We urge all regional and global players to refrain from interference that will further deepen the crisis and to support the Iraqi government and the people of Iraq in their efforts to overcome the crisis, and build a stable, inclusive and united Iraq. We emphasize the importance of national reconciliation and unity in Iraq, taking into consideration the wars and conflicts the Iraqi people have suffered and in this context we commend the peaceful and orderly holding of the latest parliamentary elections.

44. We express our deep concern with the situation in Ukraine. We call for a comprehensive dialogue, the de-escalation of the conflict and restraint from all the actors involved, with a view to finding a peaceful political solution, in full compliance with the UN Charter and universally recognized human rights and fundamental freedoms.

45. We reaffirm our commitment to continue to tackle transnational organized crime, with full respect for human rights, in order to reduce the negative impact it has on individuals and societies. We encourage joint efforts aimed at preventing and combating transnational criminal activities in accordance with national legislations and international legal instruments, especially the UN Convention against Transnational Organized Crime. In this regard, we welcome BRICS cooperation in multilateral fora, highlighting our engagement in the ECOSOC Commission on Crime Prevention and Criminal Justice.

46. Piracy and armed robbery at sea are complex phenomena that must be fought effectively in a comprehensive and integrated manner. We welcome the efforts made by the international community to counter maritime piracy and call upon all stakeholders – civilian and military, public and private – to remain engaged in the fight against this phenomenon. We also highlight the need for a transparent and objective review of the High Risk Areas, with a view to avoiding unnecessary negative effects on the economy and security of coastal states. We commit to strengthen our cooperation on this serious issue.

47. We are deeply concerned by the world drug problem, which continues to threaten public health, safety and well-being and to undermine social, economic and political stability and sustainable development. We are committed to countering the world drug problem, which remains a common and shared responsibility, through an integrated, multidisciplinary, mutually reinforcing and balanced approach to supply and demand reduction strategies, in line with the three UN drug conventions and other relevant norms and principles of international law. We welcome the substantive work done by Russia in preparing and hosting the International Ministers Meeting on 15 May 2014 to discuss the world drug problem. We take note of the proposal for the creation of an Anti-Drug Working Group presented at the Second Meeting of BRICS Heads of Drug Control Agencies.

48. We reiterate our strong condemnation of terrorism in all its forms and manifestations and stress that there can be no justification, whatsoever, for any acts of terrorism, whether based upon ideological, religious, political, racial, ethnic, or any other justification. We call upon all entities to refrain from financing, encouraging, providing training for or otherwise supporting terrorist activities. We believe that the UN has a central role in coordinating international action against terrorism, which must be conducted in accordance with international law, including the UN Charter, and with respect to human rights and fundamental freedoms. In this context, we reaffirm our commitment to the implementation of the UN Global Counter- Terrorism Strategy. We express our concern at the increasing use, in a globalized society, by terrorists and their supporters, of information and communications technologies (ICTs), in particular the Internet and other media, and reiterate that such technologies can be powerful tools in countering the spread of terrorism, including by promoting tolerance and dialogue among peoples. We will continue to work together to conclude as soon as possible negotiations and to adopt in the UN General Assembly the Comprehensive

Convention on International Terrorism. We also stress the need to promote cooperation among our countries in preventing terrorism, especially in the context of major events.

49. We believe that ICTs should provide instruments to foster sustainable economic progress and social inclusion, working together with the ICT industry, civil society and academia in order to realize the ICT-related potential opportunities and benefits for all. We agree that particular attention should be given to young people and to small and medium-sized enterprises, with a view to promoting international exchange and cooperation, as well as to fostering innovation, ICT research and development. We agree that the use and development of ICTs through international cooperation and universally accepted norms and principles of international law is of paramount importance, in order to ensure a peaceful, secure and open digital and Internet space. We strongly condemn acts of mass electronic surveillance and data collection of individuals all over the world, as well as violation of the sovereignty of States and of human rights, in particular the right to privacy. We take note of the Global Multistakeholder Meeting on the Future of Internet, held in São Paulo, on 23-24 April 2014. We thank Brazil for having organized it.

50. We will explore cooperation on combating cybercrimes and we also recommit to the negotiation of a universal legally binding instrument in that field. We consider that the UN has a central role in this matter. We agree it is necessary to preserve ICTs, particularly the Internet, as an instrument of peace and development and to prevent its use as a weapon. Moreover, we commit ourselves to working together in order to identify possibilities of developing joint activities to address common security concerns in the use of ICTs. We reiterate the common approach set forth in the eThekwini Declaration about the importance of security in the use of ICTs. We welcome the decision of the National Security Advisors to establish a group of experts of BRICS member States which will elaborate practical proposals concerning major fields of cooperation and coordinate our positions in international fora. Bearing in mind the significance of these issues, we take note of Russia's proposal of a BRICS agreement on cooperation in this field to be jointly elaborated.

51. We reiterate our commitment to the implementation of the Convention on Biological Diversity and its Protocols, with special attention to the Strategic Plan for Biodiversity 2011- 2020 and the Aichi Targets. We recognize the challenge posed by the agreed targets on conservation of biodiversity and reaffirm the need to implement the decisions on resource mobilization agreed to by all parties in Hyderabad in 2012, and set resource mobilization targets that are ambitious in order to allow for their fulfillment.

52. Acknowledging that climate change is one of the greatest challenges facing humankind, we call on all countries to build upon the decisions adopted in the UN Framework Convention on Climate Change (UNFCCC) with a view to reaching a successful conclusion by 2015, of negotiations on the development of a protocol, another legal instrument or an agreed outcome with legal force under the Convention applicable to all Parties, in accordance with the principles and provisions of UNFCCC, in particular the principle of common but differentiated responsibilities and respective capabilities. In this regard, we reiterate our support to the Presidency of the 20th session of the Conference of the Parties and the 10th session of the Conference of the Parties serving as the Meeting of the Parties to the Kyoto Protocol, to be held in Lima, Peru, in December 2014. We also note the convening of the UN Climate Summit 2014 to be held this September.

53. While bearing in mind that fossil fuel remains one of the major sources of energy, we reiterate our belief that renewable and clean energy, research and development of new technologies and energy efficiency, can constitute an important driver to promote sustainable development, create new economic growth, reduce energy costs and increase the efficiency in the use of natural resources. Considering the dynamic link between renewable and clean energy and sustainable development, we reaffirm the importance of continuing international efforts aimed at promoting the deployment of renewable and clean energy and energy efficiency technologies, taking into account national policies, priorities and resources. We stand for strengthening international cooperation to promote

renewable and clean energy and to universalize energy access, which is of great importance to improving the standard of living of our peoples.

54. We are committed to working towards an inclusive, transparent and participative intergovernmental process for building a universal and integrated development agenda with poverty eradication as the central and overarching objective. The agenda should integrate the economic, social and environmental dimensions of sustainable development in a balanced and comprehensive manner with concise, implementable and measurable goals, taking into account differing national realities and levels of development and respecting national policies and priorities. The Post-2015 Development Agenda must also be based on and fully respect all Rio principles on sustainable development, including the principle of common but differentiated responsibilities. We welcome the outcome document of the UN General Assembly Special

Event on the Millennium Development Goals, which decided to launch an intergovernmental process at the beginning of the 69th Session of the UN General Assembly that will lead to the adoption of the Post-2015 Development Agenda.

55. We reiterate our commitment to the UN General Assembly Open Working Group on Sustainable Development Goals (SDGs) and to working together to achieve a consensual and ambitious proposal on SDGs. We emphasize the importance of the work by the Intergovernmental Committee of Experts on Sustainable Development Financing and highlight the need for an effective sustainable development financing strategy to facilitate the mobilization of resources in achieving sustainable development objectives and supporting developing countries in the implementation efforts, with ODA as a major source of financing. We support the creation of a facilitation mechanism for the development, transfer and dissemination of clean and environmentally sound technologies and call for the establishment of a working group within the UN on this proposal, taking into account the Rio+20 outcome document and the Secretary General's reports on the issue. In this regard, we reaffirm that the outcome of each of these processes can contribute to the formulation of Sustainable Development Goals.

56. We recognize the strategic importance of education for sustainable development and inclusive economic growth. We reaffirm our commitment to accelerating progress in attaining the Education for All goals and education-related Millennium Development Goals by 2015 and stress that the development agenda beyond 2015 should build on these goals to ensure equitable, inclusive and quality education and lifelong learning for all. We are willing to strengthen intra-BRICS cooperation in the area and welcome the meeting of Ministers of Education held in Paris, in November 2013. We intend to continue cooperation with relevant international organizations. We encourage the initiative to establish the BRICS Network University.

57. In March 2014 we agreed to collaborate through dialogue, cooperation, sharing of experiences and capacity building on population related matters of mutual concern to member states. We recognize the vital importance of the demographic dividend that many of us possess to advance our sustainable development as well as the need to integrate population factors into national development plans, and to promote a long-term balanced population and development. The demographic transition and post-transition challenges, including population ageing and mortality reduction are amongst the most important challenges facing the world today. We confirm our strong commitment to address social issues in general and in particular gender inequality, women's rights and issues facing young people and we reaffirm our determination to ensure sexual and reproductive health and reproductive rights for all.

58. We recognize that corruption negatively affects sustainable economic growth, poverty reduction and financial stability. We are committed to combat domestic and foreign bribery, and strengthen international cooperation, including law enforcement cooperation, in accordance with multilaterally established principles and norms, especially the UN Convention Against Corruption.

59. Considering the link between culture and sustainable development, as well as the role of cultural diplomacy as a promoter of understanding between peoples, we will encourage cooperation between BRICS countries in the cultural sector, including on the multilateral basis. Recognizing the contribution and the benefits of cultural exchanges and cooperation in enhancing our mutual understanding and friendship, we will actively promote greater awareness, understanding and appreciation of each other's arts and culture. In this regard, we ask our relevant authorities responsible for culture to explore areas of practical cooperation, including to expedite negotiations on the draft agreement on cultural cooperation.

60. We are pleased with progress in implementing the eThekwini Action Plan, which further enhanced our cooperation and unleashed greater potential for our development. In this regard, we commend South Africa for the full implementation of the eThekwini Action Plan.

61. We are committed to promoting agricultural cooperation and to exchange information regarding strategies for ensuring access to food for the most vulnerable population, reduction of negative impact of climate change on food security and adaptation of agriculture to climate change. We recall with satisfaction the decision of UN General Assembly to declare 2014 the International Year of Family Farming.

62. We take note of the following meetings which were held in preparation for this Summit:

- Third BRICS Think Tanks Council (BTTC);
- Third BRICS Business Council;
- Sixth Academic Forum;
- Fifth Business Forum;
- Fourth Financial Forum.

63. We welcome the outcomes of the meeting of the BRICS Finance Ministers and Central Bank Governors and endorse the Joint Communiqué of the Meeting of the BRICS Trade Ministers held in preparation for the Summit.

64. The 5th edition of the BRICS Business Forum provided an opportunity for match-making and for in-depth discussion of highly relevant issues of the trade and investment agenda. We welcome the meeting of the BRICS Business Council and commend it for its Annual Report 2013/2014. We encourage the respective business communities to follow-up the initiatives proposed and to deepen dialogue and cooperation in the five areas dealt with by the Industry/Sector Working Groups with a view to intensifying trade and investment flows amongst BRICS countries as well as between BRICS and other partners around the world.

65. We reiterate our commitment made during the BRICS Leaders-Africa Retreat at the 5th BRICS Summit to foster and develop BRICS-Africa cooperation in support of the socioeconomic development of Africa, particularly with regard to infrastructure development and industrialization. We welcome the inclusion of these issues in discussions during the BRICS Business Council Meeting, held in Johannesburg in August 2013.

66. We welcome the BTTC Study "Towards a Long-Term Strategy for BRICS: Recommendations by the BTTC". We acknowledge the decision taken by the BTTC, taken at its Rio de Janeiro meeting in March 2014 to focus its work on the five pillars upon which the BRICS long-term strategy for cooperation will rest. The BTTC is encouraged to develop strategic pathways and action plans that will lead to the realization of this long-term strategy.

67. We welcome the holding of the first Meeting of the BRICS Ministers of Science, Technology and Innovation and the Cape Town Declaration, which is aimed at: (i) strengthening cooperation in science, technology and innovation; (ii) addressing common global and regional socio-economic challenges utilizing shared experiences and complementarities; (iii) co- generating new knowledge and innovative products, services and processes utilizing appropriate funding and investment

instruments; and (iv) promoting, where appropriate, joint BRICS partnerships with other strategic actors in the developing world. We instruct the BRICS Ministers of Science and Technology to sign at their next meeting the Memorandum of Understanding on Science, Technology and Innovation, which provides a strategic framework for cooperation in this field.

68. We welcome the establishment of the BRICS Information Sharing and Exchange Platform, which seeks to facilitate trade and investment cooperation.

69. We will continue to improve competition policy and enforcement, undertake actions to address challenges that BRICS Competition Authorities face and further enable competitive environments in order to enhance contributions to economic growth in our economies. We note South Africa's offer to host the 4th Meeting of BRICS Competition Authorities in 2015.

70. We reiterate our commitment to fostering our partnership for common development. To this end, we adopt the Fortaleza Action Plan.

71. Russia, India, China and South Africa extend their warm appreciation to the Government and people of Brazil for hosting the Sixth BRICS Summit in Fortaleza.

72. Brazil, India, China and South Africa convey their appreciation to Russia for its offer to host the Seventh BRICS Summit in 2015 in the city of Ufa and extend their full support to that end.

B. The Fortaleza Action Plan

FORTALEZA ACTION PLAN

1. Meeting of BRICS Ministers of Foreign Affairs / International Relations on the margins of UN General Assembly.

2. Meeting of BRICS National Security Advisors.

3. Mid-term meeting of BRICS Sherpas and Sous-Sherpas.

4. Meetings of BRICS Finance Ministers and Central Bank Governors on the margins of G20 meetings, WB/IMF meetings, as well as stand-alone meetings, as required.

5. Meetings of BRICS Trade Ministers on the margin of multilateral events, or stand-alone meetings, as required.

6. Meeting of BRICS Ministers of Agriculture and Agrarian Development, preceded by the Meeting of BRICS Agricultural Cooperation Working Group.

7. Meeting of BRICS Health Ministers.

8. Meeting of BRICS Ministers of Science, Technology and Innovation.

9. Meeting of BRICS Ministers of Education.

10. Meeting of Ministers or Senior Officials responsible for social security, on the margins of a multilateral meeting.

11. BRICS Seminar of Officials and Experts on Population Matters.

12. Meeting of BRICS Cooperatives (held in Curitiba on 14-16 May 2014).

13. Meetings of financial and fiscal authorities on the margins of WB/IMF meetings as well as stand-alone meetings, as required.

14. Meetings of the BRICS Contact Group on Economic and Trade Issues (CGETI).

15. Meeting of the BRICS Friendship Cities and Local Governments Cooperation Forum.

16. Meeting of the BRICS Urbanization Forum.

17. Meeting of BRICS Competition Authorities in 2015 in South Africa.

18. Meeting of BRICS Heads of National Statistical Institutions.

19. Meeting of Anti-Drug Experts.

20. Meeting of BRICS Experts on Anti-corruption cooperation, on the margins of a multilateral meeting

21. Consultations amongst BRICS Permanent Missions and/or Embassies, as appropriate, in New York, Vienna, Rome, Paris, Washington, Nairobi and Geneva, where appropriate.

22. Consultative meeting of BRICS Senior Officials on the margins of relevant sustainable development, environment and climate related international fora, where appropriate.

23. Sports and Mega Sporting Events.

New areas of cooperation to be explored

-   Mutual recognition of Higher Education Degrees and Diplomas;
-   Labor and Employment, Social Security, Social Inclusion Public Policies;
-   Foreign Policy Planning Dialogue;
-   Insurance and reinsurance;
-   Seminar of Experts on E-commerce.

II.6.   5th BRICS Summit 2013: 25-27 Mar. 2013, Durban (ZAF)

A.   The eThekwini Declaration

FIFTH BRICS SUMMIT

Durban, March 27, 2013

BRICS and Africa:
Partnership for Development, Integration and Industrialisation

ETHEKWINI DECLARATION

1.   We, the leaders of the Federative Republic of Brazil, the Russian Federation, the Republic of India, the People's Republic of China and the Republic of South Africa, met in Durban, South Africa, on 27 March 2013 at the Fifth BRICS Summit. Our discussions took place under the overarching theme, "BRICS and Africa: Partnership for Development, Integration and Industrialisation". The Fifth BRICS Summit concluded the first cycle of BRICS Summits and we reaffirmed our commitment to the promotion of international law, multilateralism and the central role of the United Nations (UN). Our discussions reflected our growing intra-BRICS solidarity as well as our shared goal to contribute positively to global peace, stability, development and cooperation. We also considered our role in the international system as based on an inclusive approach of shared solidarity and cooperation towards all nations and peoples.

2.   We met at a time which requires that we consider issues of mutual interest and systemic importance in order to share concerns and to develop lasting solutions. We aim at progressively developing BRICS into a full-fledged mechanism of current and long-term coordination on a wide range of key issues of the world economy and politics. The prevailing global governance architecture is regulated by institutions which were conceived in circumstances when the international landscape in all its aspects was characterised by very different challenges and opportunities. As the global economy is being reshaped, we are committed to exploring new models and approaches towards more equitable development and inclusive global growth by emphasising complementarities and building on our respective economic strengths.

3.   We are open to increasing our engagement and cooperation with non-BRICS countries, in particular Emerging Market and Developing Countries (EMDCs), and relevant international and regional organisations, as envisioned in the Sanya Declaration. We will hold a Retreat together with African leaders after this Summit, under the theme, "Unlocking Africa's potential: BRICS and Africa Cooperation on Infrastructure". The Retreat is an opportunity for BRICS and African leaders to discuss how to strengthen cooperation between the BRICS countries and the African Continent.

4.   Recognising the importance of regional integration for Africa's sustainable growth, development and poverty eradication, we reaffirm our support for the Continent's integration processes.

5.   Within the framework of the New Partnership for Africa's Development (NEPAD), we support African countries in their industrialisation process through stimulating foreign direct investment, knowledge exchange, capacity-building and diversification of imports from Africa. We acknowledge that infrastructure development in Africa is important and recognise the strides made by the African Union to identify and address the continent's infrastructure challenges through the development of the Programme for Infrastructure Development in Africa (PIDA), the AU NEPAD Africa Action Plan (2010–2015), the NEPAD Presidential Infrastructure Championing Initiative (PICI), as well as the Regional Infrastructure Development Master Plans that have identified priority infrastructure development projects that are critical to promoting regional integration and industrialisation. We

will seek to stimulate infrastructure investment on the basis of mutual benefit to support industrial development, job-creation, skills development, food and nutrition security and poverty eradication and sustainable development in Africa. We therefore, reaffirm our support for sustainable infrastructure development in Africa.

6.   We note policy actions in Europe, the US and Japan aimed at reducing tail-risks in the world economy. Some of these actions produce negative spillover effects on other economies of the world. Significant risks remain and the performance of the global economy still falls behind our expectations. As a result, uncertainty about strength and durability of the recovery and the direction of policy in some major economies remains high. In some key countries unemployment stays unusually elevated, while high levels of private and public indebtedness inhibit growth. In such circumstances, we reaffirm our strong commitment to support growth and foster financial stability. We also underscore the need for appropriate action to be taken by advanced economies in order to rebuild confidence, foster growth and secure a strong recovery.

7.   Central Banks in advanced economies have responded with unconventional monetary policy actions which have increased global liquidity. While this may be consistent with domestic monetary policy mandates, major Central Banks should avoid the unintended consequences of these actions in the form of increased volatility of capital flows, currencies and commodity prices, which may have negative growth effects on other economies, in particular developing countries.

8.   We welcome the core objectives of the Russian Presidency in the G20 in 2013, in particular the efforts to increased financing for investment and ensure public debt sustainability aimed at ensuring strong, sustainable, inclusive and balanced growth and job creation around the world. We will also continue to prioritise the G20 development agenda as a vital element of global economic stability and long-term sustainable growth and job creation.

9.   Developing countries face challenges of infrastructure development due to insufficient long-term financing and foreign direct investment, especially investment in capital stock. This constrains global aggregate demand. BRICS cooperation towards more productive use of global financial resources can make a positive contribution to addressing this problem. In March 2012 we directed our Finance Ministers to examine the feasibility and viability of setting up a New Development Bank for mobilising resources for infrastructure and sustainable development projects in BRICS and other emerging economies and developing countries, to supplement the existing efforts of multilateral and regional financial institutions for global growth and development. Following the report from our Finance Ministers, we are satisfied that the establishment of a New Development Bank is feasible and viable. We have agreed to establish the New Development Bank. The initial contribution to the Bank should be substantial and sufficient for the Bank to be effective in financing infrastructure.

10.   In June 2012, in our meeting in Los Cabos, we tasked our Finance Ministers and Central Bank Governors to explore the construction of a financial safety net through the creation of a Contingent Reserve Arrangement (CRA) amongst BRICS countries. They have concluded that the establishment of a self-managed contingent reserve arrangement would have a positive precautionary effect, help BRICS countries forestall short-term liquidity pressures, provide mutual support and further strengthen financial stability. It would also contribute to strengthening the global financial safety net and complement existing international arrangements as an additional line of defence. We are of the view that the establishment of the CRA with an initial size of US$ 100 billion is feasible and desirable subject to internal legal frameworks and appropriate safeguards. We direct our Finance Ministers and Central Bank Governors to continue working towards its establishment.

11.   We are grateful to our Finance Ministers and Central Bank Governors for the work undertaken on the New Development Bank and the Contingent Reserve Arrangement and direct them to negotiate and conclude the agreements which will establish them. We will review progress made in these two initiatives at our next meeting in September 2013.

12. We welcome the conclusion between our Export-Import Banks (EXIM) and Development Banks, of both the "Multilateral Agreement on Cooperation and Co-financing for Sustainable Development" and, given the steep growth trajectory of the African continent and the significant infrastructure funding requirements directly emanating from this growth path, the "Multilateral Agreement on Infrastructure Co--Financing for Africa".

13. We call for the reform of International Financial Institutions to make them more representative and to reflect the growing weight of BRICS and other developing countries. We remain concerned with the slow pace of the reform of the IMF. We see an urgent need to implement, as agreed, the 2010 International Monetary Fund (IMF) Governance and Quota Reform. We urge all members to take all necessary steps to achieve an agreement on the quota formula and complete the next general quota review by January 2014. The reform of the IMF should strengthen the voice and representation of the poorest members of the IMF, including Sub-Saharan Africa. All options should be explored, with an open mind, to achieve this. We support the reform and improvement of the international monetary system, with a broad-based international reserve currency system providing stability and certainty. We welcome the discussion about the role of the SDR in the existing international monetary system including the composition of SDR's basket of currencies. We support the IMF to make its surveillance framework more integrated and even-handed. The leadership selection of IFIs should be through an open, transparent and merit-based process and truly open to candidates from the emerging market economies and developing countries.

14. We emphasise the importance of ensuring steady, adequate and predictable access to long term finance for developing countries from a variety of sources. We would like to see concerted global effort towards infrastructure financing and investment through the instrumentality of adequately resourced Multilateral Development Banks (MDBs) and Regional Development Banks (RDBs). We urge all parties to work towards an ambitious International Development Association (IDA) 17 replenishment.

15. We reaffirm our support for an open, transparent and rules-based multilateral trading system. We will continue in our efforts for the successful conclusion of the Doha Round, based on the progress made and in keeping with its mandate, while upholding the principles of transparency, inclusiveness and multilateralism. We are committed to ensure that new proposals and approaches to the Doha Round negotiations will reinforce the core principles and the developmental mandate of the Doha Round. We look forward to significant and meaningful deliverables that are balanced and address key development concerns of the poorest and most vulnerable WTO members, at the ninth Ministerial Conference of the WTO in Bali.

16. We note that the process is underway for the selection of a new WTO Director-General in 2013. We concur that the WTO requires a new leader who demonstrates a commitment to multilateralism and to enhancing the effectiveness of the WTO including through a commitment to support efforts that will lead to an expeditious conclusion of the DDA. We consider that the next Director-General of the WTO should be a representative of a developing country.

17. We reaffirm the United Nations Conference on Trade and Development's (UNCTAD) mandate as the focal point in the UN system dedicated to consider the interrelated issues of trade, investment, finance and technology from a development perspective. UNCTAD's mandate and work are unique and necessary to deal with the challenges of development and growth in the increasingly interdependent global economy. We also reaffirm the importance of strengthening UNCTAD's capacity to deliver on its programmes of consensus building, policy dialogue, research, technical cooperation and capacity building, so that it is better equipped to deliver on its development mandate.

18. We acknowledge the important role that State Owned Companies (SOCs) play in the economy and encourage our SOCs to explore ways of cooperation, exchange of information and best practices.

19. We recognise the fundamental role played by Small and Medium-Sized Enterprises (SMEs) in the economies of our countries. SMEs are major creators of jobs and wealth. In this regard, we will explore opportunities for cooperating in the field of SMEs and recognise the need for promoting dialogue among the respective Ministries and Agencies in charge of the theme, particularly with a view to promoting their international exchange and cooperation and fostering innovation, research and development.

20. We reiterate our strong commitment to the United Nations (UN) as the foremost multilateral forum entrusted with bringing about hope, peace, order and sustainable development to the world. The UN enjoys universal membership and is at the centre of global governance and multilateralism. In this regard, we reaffirm the need for a comprehensive reform of the UN, including its Security Council, with a view to making it more representative, effective and efficient, so that it can be more responsive to global challenges. In this regard, China and Russia reiterate the importance they attach to the status of Brazil, India and South Africa in international affairs and support their aspiration to play a greater role in the UN.

21. We underscore our commitment to work together in the UN to continue our cooperation and strengthen multilateral approaches in international relations based on the rule of law and anchored in the Charter of the United Nations.

22. We are committed to building a harmonious world of lasting peace and common prosperity and reaffirm that the 21st century should be marked by peace, security, development, and cooperation. It is the overarching objective and strong shared desire for peace, security, development and cooperation that brought together BRICS countries.

23. We welcome the twentieth Anniversary of the World Conference on Human Rights and of the Vienna Declaration and Programme of Action and agree to explore cooperation in the field of human rights.

24. We commend the efforts of the international community and acknowledge the central role of the African Union (AU) and its Peace and Security Council in conflict resolution in Africa. We call upon the UNSC to enhance cooperation with the African Union, and its Peace and Security Council, pursuant to UNSC resolutions in this regard. We express our deep concern with instability stretching from North Africa, in particular the Sahel, and the Gulf of Guinea. We also remain concerned about reports of deterioration in humanitarian conditions in some countries.

25. We welcome the appointment of the new Chairperson of the AU Commission as an affirmation of the leadership of women.

26. We express our deep concern with the deterioration of the security and humanitarian situation in Syria and condemn the increasing violations of human rights and of international humanitarian law as a result of continued violence. We believe that the Joint Communiqué of the Geneva Action Group provides a basis for resolution of the Syrian crisis and reaffirm our opposition to any further militarization of the conflict. A Syrian-led political process leading to a transition can be achieved only through broad national dialogue that meets the legitimate aspirations of all sections of Syrian society and respect for Syrian independence, territorial integrity and sovereignty as expressed by the Geneva Joint Communiqué and appropriate UNSC resolutions. We support the efforts of the UN-League of Arab States Joint Special Representative. In view of the deterioration of the humanitarian situation in Syria, we call upon all parties to allow and facilitate immediate, safe, full and unimpeded access to humanitarian organisations to all in need of assistance. We urge all parties to ensure the safety of humanitarian workers.

27. We welcome the admission of Palestine as an Observer State to the United Nations. We are concerned at the lack of progress in the Middle East Peace Process and call on the international community to assist both Israel and Palestine to work towards a two-state solution with a contiguous and economically viable Palestinian state, existing side by side in peace with Israel, within

internationally recognized borders, based on those existing on 4 June 1967, with East Jerusalem as its capital. We are deeply concerned about the construction of Israeli settlements in the Occupied Palestinian Territories, which is a violation of international law and harmful to the peace process. In recalling the primary responsibility of the UNSC in maintaining international peace and security, we note the importance that the Quartet reports regularly to the Council about its efforts, which should contribute to concrete progress.

28. We believe there is no alternative to a negotiated solution to the Iranian nuclear issue. We recognise Iran's right to peaceful uses of nuclear energy consistent with its international obligations, and support resolution of the issues involved through political and diplomatic means and dialogue, including between the International Atomic Energy Agency (IAEA) and Iran and in accordance with the provisions of the relevant UN Security Council Resolutions and consistent with Iran's obligations under the Treaty on the Non-Proliferation of Nuclear Weapons (NPT). We are concerned about threats of military action as well as unilateral sanctions. We note the recent talks held in Almaty and hope that all outstanding issues relating to Iran's nuclear programme will be resolved through discussions and diplomatic means.

29. Afghanistan needs time, development assistance and cooperation, preferential access to world markets, foreign investment and a clear end-state strategy to attain lasting peace and stability. We support the global community's commitment to Afghanistan, enunciated at the Bonn International Conference in December 2011, to remain engaged over the transformation decade from 2015-2024. We affirm our commitment to support Afghanistan's emergence as a peaceful, stable and democratic state, free of terrorism and extremism, and underscore the need for more effective regional and international cooperation for the stabilisation of Afghanistan, including by combating terrorism. We extend support to the efforts aimed at combating illicit traffic in opiates originating in Afghanistan within the framework of the Paris Pact.

30. We commend the efforts of the AU, the Economic Community of West African States (ECOWAS) and Mali aimed at restoring sovereignty and territorial integrity of Mali. We support the civilian efforts of the Malian Government and its international community partners in realising the transitional programme leading up to the presidential and legislative elections. We emphasise the importance of political inclusiveness and economic and social development in order for Mali to achieve sustainable peace and stability. We express concern about the reports of the deterioration in humanitarian conditions in Mali and call upon the international community to continue to cooperate with Mali and its neighbouring countries in order to ensure humanitarian assistance to civilian population affected by the armed conflict.

31. We are gravely concerned with the deterioration in the current situation in the Central African Republic (CAR) and deplore the loss of life. We strongly condemn the abuses and acts of violence against the civilian population and urge all parties to the conflict to immediately cease hostilities and return to negotiations. We call upon all parties to allow safe and unhindered humanitarian access. We are ready to work with the international community to assist in this endeavour and facilitate progress to a peaceful resolution of the conflict. Brazil, Russia and China express their sympathy to the South African and Indian governments for the casualties that their citizens suffered in the CAR.

32. We are gravely concerned by the ongoing instability in the Democratic Republic of the Congo (DRC). We welcome the signing in Addis Ababa on 24 February 2013 of the Peace, Security and Cooperation Framework for the Democratic Republic of the Congo and the Region. We support its independence, territorial integrity and sovereignty. We support the efforts of the UN, AU and sub--regional organisations to bring about peace, security and stability in the country.

33. We reiterate our strong condemnation of terrorism in all its forms and manifestations and stress that there can be no justification, whatsoever, for any acts of terrorism. We believe that the UN has a central role in coordinating international action against terrorism within the framework of the UN Charter and in accordance with principles and norms of international law. In this context, we support

the implementation of the UN General Assembly Global Counter-Terrorism Strategy and are determined to strengthen cooperation in countering this global threat. We also reiterate our call for concluding negotiations as soon as possible in the UN General Assembly on the Comprehensive Convention on International Terrorism and its adoption by all Member States and agreed to work together towards this objective.

34. We recognize the critical positive role the Internet plays globally in promoting economic, social and cultural development. We believe it's important to contribute to and participate in a peaceful, secure, and open cyberspace and we emphasise that security in the use of Information and Communication Technologies (ICTs) through universally accepted norms, standards and practices is of paramount importance.

35. We congratulate Brazil on hosting the UN Conference on Sustainable Development (Rio+20) in June 2012 and welcome the outcome as reflected in "The Future we Want", in particular, the reaffirmation of the Rio Principles and political commitment made towards sustainable development and poverty eradication while creating opportunities for BRICS partners to engage and cooperate in the development of the future Sustainable Development Goals.

36. We congratulate India on the outcome of the 11th Conference of the Parties to the United Nations Conference on Biological Diversity (CBD COP11) and the sixth meeting of the Conference of the Parties serving as the Meeting of the Parties to the Cartagena Protocol on Biosafety.

37. While acknowledging that climate change is one of the greatest challenges and threats towards achieving sustainable development, we call on all parties to build on the decisions adopted in COP18/CMP8 in Doha, with a view to reaching a successful conclusion by 2015, of negotiations on the development of a protocol, another legal instrument or an agreed outcome with legal force under the Convention applicable to all Parties, guided by its principles and provisions.

38. We believe that the internationally agreed development goals including the Millennium Development Goals (MDGs) address the needs of developing countries, many of which continue to face developmental challenges, including widespread poverty and inequality. Low Income Countries (LICs) continue to face challenges that threaten the impressive growth performance of recent years. Volatility in food and other commodity prices have made food security an issue as well as constraining their sources of revenue. Progress in rebuilding macro-economic buffers has been relatively slow, partly due to measures adopted to mitigate the social impact of exogenous shocks. Many LICs are currently in a weaker position to deal with exogenous shocks given the more limited fiscal buffers and the constrained aid envelopes, which will affect their ability to sustain progress towards achieving the MDGs. We reiterate that individual countries, especially in Africa and other developing countries of the South, cannot achieve the MDGs on their own and therefore the centrality of Goal 8 on Global Partnerships for Development to achieve the MDGs should remain at the core of the global development discourse for the UN System. Furthermore, this requires the honouring of all commitments made in the outcome documents of previous major international conferences.

39. We reiterate our commitment to work together for accelerated progress in attaining the Millennium Development Goals (MDGs) by the target date of 2015, and we call upon other members of the international community to work towards the same objective. In this regard, we stress that the development agenda beyond 2015 should build on the MDG framework, keeping the focus on poverty eradication and human development, while addressing emerging challenges of development taking into consideration individual national circumstances of developing countries. In this regard the critical issue of the mobilization of means of implementation in assisting developing countries needs to be an overarching goal. It is important to ensure that any discussion on the UN development agenda, including the "Post 2015 Development Agenda" is an inclusive and transparent inter-Governmental process under a UN-wide process which is universal and broad based.

40. We welcome the establishment of the Open Working Group on the Sustainable Development Goals (SDGs), in line with the Rio+20 Outcome Document which reaffirmed the Rio Principles of Sustainable Development as the basis for addressing new and emerging challenges. We are fully committed to a coordinated inter-governmental process for the elaboration of the UN development agenda.

41. We note the following meetings held in the implementation of the Delhi Action Plan:
- Meeting of Ministers of Foreign Affairs on the margins of UNGA.
- Meeting of National Security Advisors in New Delhi.
- Meetings of Finance Ministers, and Central Bank Governors in Washington DC and Tokyo.
- Meeting of Trade Ministers in Puerto Vallarta.
- Meetings of Health Ministers in New Delhi and Geneva.

42. We welcome the establishment of the BRICS Think Tanks Council and the BRICS Business Council and take note of the following meetings which were held in preparation for this Summit:
- Fifth Academic Forum
- Fourth Business Forum
- Third Financial Forum

43. We welcome the outcomes of the meeting of the BRICS Finance Ministers and Central Bank Governors and endorse the Joint Communique of the Third Meeting of the BRICS Trade Ministers held in preparation for the Summit.

44. We are committed to forging a stronger partnership for common development. To this end, we adopt the eThekwini Action Plan.

45. We agree that the next summit cycles will, in principle, follow the sequence of Brazil, Russia, India, China and South Africa.

46. Brazil, Russia, India and China extend their warm appreciation to the Government and people of South Africa for hosting the Fifth BRICS Summit in Durban.

47. Russia, India, China and South Africa convey their appreciation to Brazil for its offer to host the first Summit of the second cycle of BRICS Summits, i.e. the Sixth BRICS Summit in 2014 and convey their full support thereto.

B.   The eThekwini Action Plan

ETHEKWINI ACTION PLAN

1. Meeting of BRICS Ministers of Foreign Affairs on the margins of UNGA.

2. Meeting of BRICS National Security Advisors.

3. Mid-term meeting of Sherpas and Sous-Sherpas.

4. Meetings of Finance Ministers and Central Bank Governors in the margins of G20 meetings, WB/IMF meetings, as well as stand-alone meetings, as required.

5. Meetings of BRICS Trade Ministers on the margins of multilateral events, or stand-alone meetings, as required.

6. Meeting of BRICS Ministers of Agriculture and Agrarian Development, preceded by a preparatory meeting of experts on agro-products and food security issues and the Meeting of Agriculture Expert Working Group.

7. Meeting of BRICS Health Ministers and preparatory meetings.

8. Meeting of BRICS Officials responsible for population on the margins of relevant multilateral events.

9. Meeting of BRICS Ministers of Science and Technology and meeting of BRICS Senior Officials on Science and Technology.

10. Meeting of BRICS Cooperatives.

11. Meetings of financial and fiscal authorities in the margins of WB/IMF meetings as well as stand-alone meetings, as required.

12. Meetings of the BRICS Contact Group on Economic and Trade Issues (CGETI).

13. Meeting of the BRICS Friendship Cities and Local Governments Cooperation Forum.

14. Meeting of the BRICS Urbanisation Forum.

15. Meeting of BRICS Competition Authorities in 2013 in New Delhi.

16. 5th Meeting of BRICS Heads of National Statistical Institutions.

17. Consultations amongst BRICS Permanent Missions and/or Embassies, as appropriate, in New York, Vienna, Rome, Paris, Washington, Nairobi and Geneva, where appropriate.

18. Consultative meeting of BRICS Senior Officials in the margins of relevant sustainable development, environment and climate related international fora, where appropriate.

New areas of cooperation to be explored
- BRICS Public Diplomacy Forum.
- BRICS Anti-Corruption Cooperation.
- BRICS State Owned Companies / State Owned Enterprises.
- National Agencies Responsible for Drug Control.
- BRICS virtual secretariat.
- BRICS Youth Policy Dialogue.
- Tourism.
- Energy.
- Sports and Mega Sporting Events.

II.7.   4ᵗʰ BRICS Summit 2012: 29 Mar. 2012, New Delhi (IND)

A.   The Delhi Declaration

FOURTH BRICS SUMMIT
DELHI DECLARATION
March 29, 2012

1.   We, the leaders of the Federative Republic of Brazil, the Russian Federation, the Republic of India, the People's Republic of China and the Republic of South Africa, met in New Delhi, India, on 29 March 2012 at the Fourth BRICS Summit. Our discussions, under the overarching theme, "BRICS Partnership for Global Stability, Security and Prosperity", were conducted in an atmosphere of cordiality and warmth and inspired by a shared desire to further strengthen our partnership for common development and take our cooperation forward on the basis of openness, solidarity, mutual understanding and trust.

2.   We met against the backdrop of developments and changes of contemporary global and regional importance - a faltering global recovery made more complex by the situation in the euro zone; concerns of sustainable development and climate change which take on greater relevance as we approach the UN Conference on Sustainable Development (Rio+20) and the Conference of Parties to the Convention on Biological Diversity being hosted in Brazil and India respectively later this year; the upcoming G20 Summit in Mexico and the recent 8th WTO Ministerial Conference in Geneva; and the developing political scenario in the Middle East and North Africa that we view with increasing concern. Our deliberations today reflected our consensus to remain engaged with the world community as we address these challenges to global well-being and stability in a responsible and constructive manner.

3.   BRICS is a platform for dialogue and cooperation amongst countries that represent 43% of the world's population, for the promotion of peace, security and development in a multi-polar, inter-dependent and increasingly complex, globalizing world. Coming, as we do, from Asia, Africa, Europe and Latin America, the transcontinental dimension of our interaction adds to its value and significance.

4.   We envision a future marked by global peace, economic and social progress and enlightened scientific temper. We stand ready to work with others, developed and developing countries together, on the basis of universally recognized norms of international law and multilateral decision making, to deal with the challenges and the opportunities before the world today. Strengthened representation of emerging and developing countries in the institutions of global governance will enhance their effectiveness in achieving this objective.

5.   We are concerned over the current global economic situation. While the BRICS recovered relatively quickly from the global crisis, growth prospects worldwide have again got dampened by market instability especially in the euro zone. The build-up of sovereign debt and concerns over medium to long-term fiscal adjustment in advanced countries are creating an uncertain environment for global growth. Further, excessive liquidity from the aggressive policy actions taken by central banks to stabilize their domestic economies have been spilling over into emerging market economies, fostering excessive volatility in capital flows and commodity prices. The immediate priority at hand is to restore market confidence and get global growth back on track. We will work with the international community to ensure international policy coordination to maintain macroeconomic stability conducive to the healthy recovery of the global economy.

6.   We believe that it is critical for advanced economies to adopt responsible macroeconomic and financial policies, avoid creating excessive global liquidity and undertake structural reforms to lift growth that create jobs. We draw attention to the risks of large and volatile cross-border capital flows being faced by the emerging economies. We call for further international financial regulatory oversight and

reform, strengthening policy coordination and financial regulation and supervision cooperation, and promoting the sound development of global financial markets and banking systems.

7. In this context, we believe that the primary role of the G20 as premier forum for international economic cooperation at this juncture is to facilitate enhanced macroeconomic policy coordination, to enable global economic recovery and secure financial stability, including through an improved international monetary and financial architecture. We approach the next G20 Summit in Mexico with a commitment to work with the Presidency, all members and the international community to achieve positive results, consistent with national policy frameworks, to ensure strong, sustainable and balanced growth.

8. We recognize the importance of the global financial architecture in maintaining the stability and integrity of the global monetary and financial system. We therefore call for a more representative international financial architecture, with an increase in the voice and representation of developing countries and the establishment and improvement of a just international monetary system that can serve the interests of all countries and support the development of emerging and developing economies. Moreover, these economies having experienced broad- based growth are now significant contributors to global recovery.

9. We are however concerned at the slow pace of quota and governance reforms in the IMF. We see an urgent need to implement, as agreed, the 2010 Governance and Quota Reform before the 2012 IMF/World Bank Annual Meeting, as well as the comprehensive review of the quota formula to better reflect economic weights and enhance the voice and representation of emerging market and developing countries by January 2013, followed by the completion of the next general quota review by January 2014. This dynamic process of reform is necessary to ensure the legitimacy and effectiveness of the Fund. We stress that the ongoing effort to increase the lending capacity of the IMF will only be successful if there is confidence that the entire membership of the institution is truly committed to implement the 2010 Reform faithfully. We will work with the international community to ensure that sufficient resources can be mobilized to the IMF in a timely manner as the Fund continues its transition to improve governance and legitimacy. We reiterate our support for measures to protect the voice and representation of the IMF's poorest members.

10. We call upon the IMF to make its surveillance framework more integrated and even-handed, noting that IMF proposals for a new integrated decision on surveillance would be considered before the IMF Spring Meeting.

11. In the current global economic environment, we recognise that there is a pressing need for enhancing the flow of development finance to emerging and developing countries. We therefore call upon the World Bank to give greater priority to mobilising resources and meeting the needs of development finance while reducing lending costs and adopting innovative lending tools.

12. We welcome the candidatures from developing world for the position of the President of the World Bank. We reiterate that the Heads of IMF and World Bank be selected through an open and merit-based process. Furthermore, the new World Bank leadership must commit to transform the Bank into a multilateral institution that truly reflects the vision of all its members, including the governance structure that reflects current economic and political reality. Moreover, the nature of the Bank must shift from an institution that essentially mediates North-South cooperation to an institution that promotes equal partnership with all countries as a way to deal with development issues and to overcome an outdated donor- recipient dichotomy.

13. We have considered the possibility of setting up a new Development Bank for mobilizing resources for infrastructure and sustainable development projects in BRICS and other emerging economies and developing countries, to supplement the existing efforts of multilateral and regional financial institutions for global growth and development. We direct our Finance Ministers to examine the

feasibility and viability of such an initiative, set up a joint working group for further study, and report back to us by the next Summit.

14. Brazil, India, China and South Africa look forward to the Russian Presidency of G20 in 2013 and extend their cooperation.

15. Brazil, India, China and South Africa congratulate the Russian Federation on its accession to the WTO. This makes the WTO more representative and strengthens the rule-based multilateral trading system. We commit to working together to safeguard this system and urge other countries to resist all forms of trade protectionism and disguised restrictions on trade.

16. We will continue our efforts for the successful conclusion of the Doha Round, based on the progress made and in keeping with its mandate. Towards this end, we will explore outcomes in specific areas where progress is possible while preserving the centrality of development and within the overall framework of the single undertaking. We do not support plurilateral initiatives that go against the fundamental principles of transparency, inclusiveness and multilateralism. We believe that such initiatives not only distract members from striving for a collective outcome but also fail to address the development deficit inherited from previous negotiating rounds. Once the ratification process is completed, Russia intends to participate in an active and constructive manner for a balanced outcome of the Doha Round that will help strengthen and develop the multilateral trade system.

17. Considering UNCTAD to be the focal point in the UN system for the treatment of trade and development issues, we intend to invest in improving its traditional activities of consensus-building, technical cooperation and research on issues of economic development and trade. We reiterate our willingness to actively contribute to the achievement of a successful UNCTAD XIII, in April 2012.

18. We agree to build upon our synergies and to work together to intensify trade and investment flows among our countries to advance our respective industrial development and employment objectives. We welcome the outcomes of the second Meeting of BRICS Trade Ministers held in New Delhi on 28 March 2012. We support the regular consultations amongst our Trade Ministers and consider taking suitable measures to facilitate further consolidation of our trade and economic ties. We welcome the conclusion of the Master Agreement on Extending Credit Facility in Local Currency under BRICS Interbank Cooperation Mechanism and the Multilateral Letter of Credit Confirmation Facility Agreement between our EXIM/Development Banks. We believe that these Agreements will serve as useful enabling instruments for enhancing intra-BRICS trade in coming years.

19. We recognize the vital importance that stability, peace and security of the Middle East and North Africa holds for all of us, for the international community, and above all for the countries and their citizens themselves whose lives have been affected by the turbulence that has erupted in the region. We wish to see these countries living in peace and regain stability and prosperity as respected members of the global community.

20. We agree that the period of transformation taking place in the Middle East and North Africa should not be used as a pretext to delay resolution of lasting conflicts but rather it should serve as an incentive to settle them, in particular the Arab- Israeli conflict. Resolution of this and other long-standing regional issues would generally improve the situation in the Middle East and North Africa. Thus we confirm our commitment to achieving comprehensive, just and lasting settlement of the Arab-Israeli conflict on the basis of the universally recognized international legal framework including the relevant UN resolutions, the Madrid principles and the Arab Peace Initiative. We encourage the Quartet to intensify its efforts and call for greater involvement of the UN Security Council in search for a resolution of the Israeli-Palestinian conflict. We also underscore the importance of direct negotiations between the parties to reach final settlement. We call upon Palestinians and Israelis to take constructive measures, rebuild mutual trust and create the right conditions for restarting negotiations, while avoiding unilateral steps, in particular settlement activity in the Occupied Palestinian Territories.

21. We express our deep concern at the current situation in Syria and call for an immediate end to all violence and violations of human rights in that country. Global interests would best be served by dealing with the crisis through peaceful means that encourage broad national dialogues that reflect the legitimate aspirations of all sections of Syrian society and respect Syrian independence, territorial integrity and sovereignty. Our objective is to facilitate a Syrian-led inclusive political process, and we welcome the joint efforts of the United Nations and the Arab League to this end. We encourage the Syrian government and all sections of Syrian society to demonstrate the political will to initiate such a process, which alone can create a new environment for peace. We welcome the appointment of Mr. Kofi Annan as the Joint Special Envoy on the Syrian crisis and the progress made so far, and support him in continuing to play a constructive role in bringing about the political resolution of the crisis.

22. The situation concerning Iran cannot be allowed to escalate into conflict, the disastrous consequences of which will be in no one's interest. Iran has a crucial role to play for the peaceful development and prosperity of a region of high political and economic relevance, and we look to it to play its part as a responsible member of the global community. We are concerned about the situation that is emerging around Iran's nuclear issue. We recognize Iran's right to peaceful uses of nuclear energy consistent with its international obligations, and support resolution of the issues involved through political and diplomatic means and dialogue between the parties concerned, including between the IAEA and Iran and in accordance with the provisions of the relevant UN Security Council Resolutions.

23. Afghanistan needs time, development assistance and cooperation, preferential access to world markets, foreign investment and a clear end-state strategy to attain lasting peace and stability. We support the global community's commitment to Afghanistan, enunciated at the Bonn International Conference in December 2011, to remain engaged over the transformation decade from 2015-2024. We affirm our commitment to support Afghanistan's emergence as a peaceful, stable and democratic state, free of terrorism and extremism, and underscore the need for more effective regional and international cooperation for the stabilisation of Afghanistan, including by combating terrorism.

24. We extend support to the efforts aimed at combating illicit traffic in opiates originating in Afghanistan within the framework of the Paris Pact.

25. We reiterate that there can be no justification, whatsoever, for any act of terrorism in any form or manifestation. We reaffirm our determination to strengthen cooperation in countering this menace and believe that the United Nations has a central role in coordinating international action against terrorism, within the framework of the UN Charter and in accordance with principles and norms of international law. We emphasize the need for an early finalization of the draft of the Comprehensive Convention on International Terrorism in the UN General Assembly and its adoption by all Member States to provide a comprehensive legal framework to address this global scourge.

26. We express our strong commitment to multilateral diplomacy with the United Nations playing a central role in dealing with global challenges and threats. In this regard, we reaffirm the need for a comprehensive reform of the UN, including its Security Council, with a view to making it more effective, efficient and representative so that it can deal with today's global challenges more successfully. China and Russia reiterate the importance they attach to the status of Brazil, India and South Africa in international affairs and support their aspiration to play a greater role in the UN.

27. We recall our close coordination in the Security Council during the year 2011, and underscore our commitment to work together in the UN to continue our cooperation and strengthen multilateral approaches on issues pertaining to global peace and security in the years to come.

28. Accelerating growth and sustainable development, along with food, and energy security, are amongst the most important challenges facing the world today, and central to addressing economic development, eradicating poverty, combating hunger and malnutrition in many developing countries. Creating jobs needed to improve people's living standards worldwide is critical. Sustainable

development is also a key element of our agenda for global recovery and investment for future growth. We owe this responsibility to our future generations.

29. We congratulate South Africa on the successful hosting of the 17th Conference of Parties to the United Nations Framework Convention on Climate Change and the 7th Conference of the Parties serving as the meeting of the Parties to the Kyoto Protocol (COP17/CMP7) in December 2011. We welcome the significant outcomes of the Conference and are ready to work with the international community to implement its decisions in accordance with the principles of equity and common but differentiated responsibilities and respective capabilities.

30. We are fully committed to playing our part in the global fight against climate change and will contribute to the global effort in dealing with climate change issues through sustainable and inclusive growth and not by capping development. We emphasize that developed country Parties to the UNFCCC shall provide enhanced financial, technology and capacity building support for the preparation and implementation of nationally appropriate mitigation actions of developing countries.

31. We believe that the UN Conference on Sustainable Development (Rio+20) is a unique opportunity for the international community to renew its high-level political commitment to supporting the overarching sustainable development framework encompassing inclusive economic growth and development, social progress and environment protection in accordance with the principles and provisions of the Rio Declaration on Environment and Development, including the principle of common but differentiated responsibilities, Agenda 21 and the Johannesburg Plan of Implementation.

32. We consider that sustainable development should be the main paradigm in environmental issues, as well as for economic and social strategies. We acknowledge the relevance and focus of the main themes for the Conference namely, Green Economy in the context of Sustainable Development and Poverty Eradication (GESDPE) as well as Institutional Framework for Sustainable Development (IFSD).

33. China, Russia, India and South Africa look forward to working with Brazil as the host of this important Conference in June, for a successful and practical outcome. Brazil, Russia, China and South Africa also pledge their support to working with India as it hosts the 11th meeting of the Conference of Parties to the Convention on Biological Diversity in October 2012 and look forward to a positive outcome. We will continue our efforts for the implementation of the Convention and its Protocols, with special attention to the Nagoya Protocol on Access to Genetic Resources and the Fair and Equitable Sharing of Benefits Arising from their Utilization, Biodiversity Strategic Plan 2011-2020 and the Resource Mobilization Strategy.

34. We affirm that the concept of a 'green economy', still to be defined at Rio+20, must be understood in the larger framework of sustainable development and poverty eradication and is a means to achieve these fundamental and overriding priorities, not an end in itself. National authorities must be given the flexibility and policy space to make their own choices out of a broad menu of options and define their paths towards sustainable development based on the country's stage of development, national strategies, circumstances and priorities. We resist the introduction of trade and investment barriers in any form on the grounds of developing green economy.

35. The Millennium Development Goals remain a fundamental milestone in the development agenda. To enable developing countries to obtain maximal results in attaining their Millennium Development Goals by the agreed time-line of 2015, we must ensure that growth in these countries is not affected. Any slowdown would have serious consequences for the world economy. Attainment of the MDGs is fundamental to ensuring inclusive, equitable and sustainable global growth and would require continued focus on these goals even beyond 2015, entailing enhanced financing support.

36. We attach the highest importance to economic growth that supports development and stability in Africa, as many of these countries have not yet realised their full economic potential. We will take our cooperation forward to support their efforts to accelerate the diversification and modernisation of their economies. This will be through infrastructure development, knowledge exchange and support for

increased access to technology, enhanced capacity building, and investment in human capital, including within the framework of the New Partnership for Africa's Development (NEPAD).

37. We express our commitment to the alleviation of the humanitarian crisis that still affects millions of people in the Horn of Africa and support international efforts to this end.

38. Excessive volatility in commodity prices, particularly those for food and energy, poses additional risks for the recovery of the world economy. Improved regulation of the derivatives market for commodities is essential to avoid destabilizing impacts on food and energy supplies. We believe that increased energy production capacities and strengthened producer-consumer dialogue are important initiatives that would help in arresting such price volatility.

39. Energy based on fossil fuels will continue to dominate the energy mix for the foreseeable future. We will expand sourcing of clean and renewable energy, and use of energy efficient and alternative technologies, to meet the increasing demand of our economies and our people, and respond to climate concerns as well. In this context, we emphasise that international cooperation in the development of safe nuclear energy for peaceful purposes should proceed under conditions of strict observance of relevant safety standards and requirements concerning design, construction and operation of nuclear power plants. We stress IAEA's essential role in the joint efforts of the international community towards enhancing nuclear safety standards with a view to increasing public confidence in nuclear energy as a clean, affordable, safe and secure source of energy, vital to meeting global energy demands.

40. We have taken note of the substantive efforts made in taking intra-BRICS cooperation forward in a number of sectors so far. We are convinced that there is a storehouse of knowledge, know-how, capacities and best practices available in our countries that we can share and on which we can build meaningful cooperation for the benefit of our peoples. We have endorsed an Action Plan for the coming year with this objective.

41. We appreciate the outcomes of the Second Meeting of BRICS Ministers of Agriculture and Agrarian Development at Chengdu, China in October 2011. We direct our Ministers to take this process forward with particular focus on the potential of cooperation amongst the BRICS to contribute effectively to global food security and nutrition through improved agriculture production and productivity, transparency in markets and reducing excessive volatility in commodity prices, thereby making a difference in the quality of lives of the people particularly in the developing world.

42. Most of BRICS countries face a number of similar public health challenges, including universal access to health services, access to health technologies, including medicines, increasing costs and the growing burden of both communicable and non-communicable diseases. We direct that the BRICS Health Ministers meetings, of which the first was held in Beijing in July 2011, should henceforth be institutionalized in order to address these common challenges in the most cost-effective, equitable and sustainable manner.

43. We have taken note of the meeting of S&T Senior Officials in Dalian, China in September 2011, and, in particular, the growing capacities for research and development and innovation in our countries. We encourage this process both in priority areas of food, pharma, health and energy as well as basic research in the emerging inter-disciplinary fields of nanotechnology, biotechnology, advanced materials science, etc. We encourage flow of knowledge amongst our research institutions through joint projects, workshops and exchanges of young scientists.

44. The challenges of rapid urbanization, faced by all developing societies including our own, are multi-dimensional in nature covering a diversity of inter- linked issues. We direct our respective authorities to coordinate efforts and learn from best practices and technologies available that can make a meaningful difference to our societies. We note with appreciation the first meeting of BRICS Friendship Cities held in Sanya in December 2011 and will take this process forward with an Urbanization and Urban Infrastructure Forum along with the Second BRICS Friendship Cities and Local Governments Cooperation Forum.

45. Given our growing needs for renewable energy resources as well as on energy efficient and environmentally friendly technologies, and our complementary strengths in these areas, we agree to exchange knowledge, know-how, technology and best practices in these areas.

46. It gives us pleasure to release the first ever BRICS Report, coordinated by India, with its special focus on the synergies and complementarities in our economies. We welcome the outcomes of the cooperation among the National Statistical Institutions of BRICS and take note that the updated edition of the BRICS Statistical Publication, released today, serves as a useful reference on BRICS countries.

47. We express our satisfaction at the convening of the III BRICS Business Forum and the II Financial Forum and acknowledge their role in stimulating trade relations among our countries. In this context, we welcome the setting up of BRICS Exchange Alliance, a joint initiative by related BRICS securities exchanges.

48. We encourage expanding the channels of communication, exchanges and people-to-people contact amongst the BRICS, including in the areas of youth, education, culture, tourism and sports.

49. Brazil, Russia, China and South Africa extend their warm appreciation and sincere gratitude to the Government and the people of India for hosting the Fourth BRICS Summit in New Delhi.

50. Brazil, Russia, India and China thank South Africa for its offer to host the Fifth BRICS Summit in 2013 and pledge their full support.

B.   The Delhi Action Plan

DELHI ACTION PLAN

1. Meeting of BRICS Foreign Ministers on sidelines of UNGA.

2. Meetings of Finance Ministers and Central Bank Governors on sidelines of G20 meetings/other multilateral (WB/IMF) meetings.

3. Meeting of financial and fiscal authorities on the sidelines of WB/IMF meetings as well as stand-alone meetings, as required.

4. Meetings of BRICS Trade Ministers on the margins of multilateral events, or stand-alone meetings, as required.

5. The Third Meeting of BRICS Ministers of Agriculture, preceded by a preparatory meeting of experts on agro-products and food security issues and the second Meeting of Agriculture Expert Working Group.

6. Meeting of BRICS High Representatives responsible for national security.

7. The Second BRICS Senior Officials' Meeting on S&T.

8. The First meeting of the BRICS Urbanisation Forum and the second BRICS Friendship Cities and Local Governments Cooperation Forum in 2012 in India.

9. The Second Meeting of BRICS Health Ministers.

10. Mid-term meeting of Sous-Sherpas and Sherpas.

11. Mid-term meeting of CGETI (Contact Group on Economic and Trade Issues).

12. The Third Meeting of BRICS Competition Authorities in 2013.

13. Meeting of experts on a new Development Bank.

14. Meeting of financial authorities to follow up on the findings of the BRICS Report.

15. Consultations amongst BRICS Permanent Missions in New York, Vienna and Geneva, as required.

16. Consultative meeting of BRICS Senior Officials on the margins of relevant environment and climate related international fora, as necessary.

17. New Areas of Cooperation to explore:

   • Multilateral energy cooperation within BRICS framework.
   • (ii)   A general academic evaluation and future long-term strategy for BRICS.
   • (iii) BRICS Youth Policy Dialogue.
   • (iv)   Cooperation in Population related issues.

New Delhi

March 29, 2012

II.8.   3rd BRICS Summit 2011: 14 Apr. 2011, Sanya (CHN)

A.   The Sanya Declaration

SANYA DECLARATION

(BRICS Leaders Meeting, Sanya, Hainan, China, 14 April 2011)

1.   We, the Heads of State and Government of the Federative Republic of Brazil, the Russian Federation, the Republic of India, the People's Republic of China and the Republic of South Africa, met in Sanya, Hainan, China for the BRICS Leaders Meeting on 14 April 2011.

2.   The Heads of State and Government of Brazil, Russia, India and China welcome South Africa joining the BRICS and look forward to strengthening dialogue and cooperation with South Africa within the forum.

3.   It is the overarching objective and strong shared desire for peace, security, development and cooperation that brought together BRICS countries with a total population of nearly 3 billion from different continents. BRICS aims at contributing significantly to the development of humanity and establishing a more equitable and fair world.

4.   The 21st century should be marked by peace, harmony, cooperation and scientific development. Under the theme "Broad Vision, Shared Prosperity", we conducted candid and in-depth discussions and reached broad consensus on strengthening BRICS cooperation as well as on promoting coordination on international and regional issues of common interest.

5.   We affirm that the BRICS and other emerging countries have played an important role in contributing to world peace, security and stability, boosting global economic growth, enhancing multilateralism and promoting greater democracy in international relations.

6.   In the economic, financial and development fields, BRICS serves as a major platform for dialogue and cooperation. We are determined to continue strengthening the BRICS partnership for common development and advance BRICS cooperation in a gradual and pragmatic manner, reflecting the principles of openness, solidarity and mutual assistance. We reiterate that such cooperation is inclusive and non-confrontational. We are open to increasing engagement and cooperation with non-BRICS countries, in particular emerging and developing countries, and relevant international and regional organizations.

7.   We share the view that the world is undergoing far-reaching, complex and profound changes, marked by the strengthening of multipolarity, economic globalization and increasing interdependence. While facing the evolving global environment and a multitude of global threats and challenges, the international community should join hands to strengthen cooperation for common development. Based on universally recognized norms of international law and in a spirit of mutual respect and collective decision making, global economic governance should be strengthened, democracy in international relations should be promoted, and the voice of emerging and developing countries in international affairs should be enhanced.

8.   We express our strong commitment to multilateral diplomacy with the United Nations playing the central role in dealing with global challenges and threats. In this respect, we reaffirm the need for a comprehensive reform of the UN, including its Security Council, with a view to making it more effective, efficient and representative, so that it can deal with today's global challenges more successfully. China and Russia reiterate the importance they attach to the status of India, Brazil and South Africa in international affairs, and understand and support their aspiration to play a greater role in the UN.

9. We underscore that the concurrent presence of all five BRICS countries in the Security Council during the year of 2011 is a valuable opportunity to work closely together on issues of peace and security, to strengthen multilateral approaches and to facilitate future coordination on issues under UN Security Council consideration. We are deeply concerned with the turbulence in the Middle East, the North African and West African regions and sincerely wish that the countries affected achieve peace, stability, prosperity and progress and enjoy their due standing and dignity in the world according to legitimate aspirations of their peoples. We share the principle that the use of force should be avoided. We maintain that the independence, sovereignty, unity and territorial integrity of each nation should be respected.

10. We wish to continue our cooperation in the UN Security Council on Libya. We are of the view that all the parties should resolve their differences through peaceful means and dialogue in which the UN and regional organizations should as appropriate play their role. We also express support for the African Union High- Level Panel Initiative on Libya.

11. We reiterate our strong condemnation of terrorism in all its forms and manifestations and stress that there can be no justification, whatsoever, for any acts of terrorism. We believe that the United Nations has a central role in coordinating the international action against terrorism within the framework of the UN Charter and in accordance with principles and norms of the international law. In this context, we urge early conclusion of negotiations in the UN General Assembly of the Comprehensive Convention on International Terrorism and its adoption by all Member States. We are determined to strengthen our cooperation in countering this global threat. We express our commitment to cooperate for strengthening international information security. We will pay special attention to combat cybercrime.

12. We note that the world economy is gradually recovering from the financial crisis, but still faces uncertainties. Major economies should continue to enhance coordination of macro-economic policies and work together to achieve strong, sustainable and balanced growth.

13. We are committed to assure that the BRICS countries will continue to enjoy strong and sustained economic growth supported by our increased cooperation in economic, finance and trade matters, which will contribute to the long-term steady, sound and balanced growth of the world economy.

14. We support the Group of Twenty (G20) in playing a bigger role in global economic governance as the premier forum for international economic cooperation. We expect new positive outcomes in the fields of economy, finance, trade and development from the G20 Cannes Summit in 2011. We support the ongoing efforts of G20 members to stabilize international financial markets, achieve strong, sustainable and balanced growth and support the growth and development of the global economy. Russia offers to host the G20 Summit in 2013. Brazil, India, China and South Africa welcome and appreciate Russia's offer.

15. We call for a quick achievement of the targets for the reform of the International Monetary Fund agreed to at previous G20 Summits and reiterate that the governing structure of the international financial institutions should reflect the changes in the world economy, increasing the voice and representation of emerging economies and developing countries.

16. Recognizing that the international financial crisis has exposed the inadequacies and deficiencies of the existing international monetary and financial system, we support the reform and improvement of the international monetary system, with a broad-based international reserve currency system providing stability and certainty. We welcome the current discussion about the role of the SDR in the existing international monetary system including the composition of SDR's basket of currencies. We call for more attention to the risks of massive cross-border capital flows now faced by the emerging economies. We call for further international financial regulatory oversight and reform, strengthening policy coordination and financial regulation and supervision cooperation, and promoting the sound development of global financial markets and banking systems.

17. Excessive volatility in commodity prices, particularly those for food and energy, poses new risks for the ongoing recovery of the world economy. We support the international community in strengthening cooperation to ensure stability and strong development of physical market by reducing distortion and further regulate financial market. The international community should work together to increase production capacity, strengthen producer-consumer dialogue to balance supply and demand, and increase support to the developing countries in terms of funding and technologies. The regulation of the derivatives market for commodities should be accordingly strengthened to prevent activities capable of destabilizing markets. We also should address the problem of shortage of reliable and timely information on demand and supply at international, regional and national levels. The BRICS will carry out closer cooperation on food security.

18. We support the development and use of renewable energy resources. We recognize the important role of renewable energy as a means to address climate change. We are convinced of the importance of cooperation and information exchange in the field of development of renewable energy resources.

19. Nuclear energy will continue to be an important element in future energy mix of BRICS countries. International cooperation in the development of safe nuclear energy for peaceful purposes should proceed under conditions of strict observance of relevant safety standards and requirements concerning design, construction and operation of nuclear power plants.

20. Accelerating sustainable growth of developing countries is one of the major challenges for the world. We believe that growth and development are central to addressing poverty and to achieving the Millennium Development Goals (MDGs). Eradication of extreme poverty and hunger is a moral, social, political and economic imperative of humankind and one of the greatest global challenges facing the world today, particularly in Least Developed Countries in Africa and elsewhere.

21. We call on the international community to actively implement the outcome document adopted by the High-level Plenary Meeting of the United Nations General Assembly on the MDGs held in September 2010 and achieve the objectives of the MDGs by 2015 as scheduled.

22. Climate change is one of the global threats challenging the livelihood of communities and countries. China, Brazil, Russia and India appreciate and support South Africa's hosting of UNFCCC COP17/CMP7. We support the Cancun Agreements and are ready to make concerted efforts with the rest of the international community to bring a successful conclusion to the negotiations at the Durban Conference applying the mandate of the Bali Roadmap and in line with the principle of equity and common but differentiated responsibilities. We commit ourselves to work towards a comprehensive, balanced and binding outcome to strengthen the implementation of the United Nations Framework Convention on Climate Change and its Kyoto Protocol. The BRICS will intensify cooperation on the Durban conference. We will enhance our practical cooperation in adapting our economy and society to climate change.

23. Sustainable development, as illustrated by the Rio Declaration on Environment and Development, Agenda 21, the Johannesburg Plan of Implementation and multilateral environmental treaties, should be an important vehicle to advance economic growth. China, Russia, India and South Africa appreciate Brazil as the host of the 2012 UN Conference on Sustainable Development and look forward to working with Brazil to reach new political commitment and achieve positive and practical results in areas of economic growth, social development and environmental protection under the framework of sustainable development. Brazil, Russia, China and South Africa appreciate and support India's hosting of the eleventh meeting of the Conference of the Parties to the Convention on Biological Diversity. Brazil, China and South Africa also appreciate and support India's hosting of the sixth meeting of the Conference of the Parties serving as the meeting of the Parties to the Cartagena Protocol on Biosafety to be held in October 2012.

24. We underscore our firm commitment to strengthen dialogue and cooperation in the fields of social protection, decent work, gender equality, youth, and public health, including the fight against HIV/AIDS.

25. We support infrastructure development in Africa and its industrialization within framework of the New Partnership for Africa's Development (NEPAD).

26. We have agreed to continue further expanding and deepening economic, trade and investment cooperation among our countries. We encourage all countries to refrain from resorting to protectionist measures. We welcome the outcomes of the meeting of BRICS Trade Ministers held in Sanya on 13 April 2011. Brazil, China, India and South Africa remain committed and call upon other members to support a strong, open, rule-based multilateral trading system embodied in the World Trade Organization and a successful, comprehensive and balanced conclusion of the Doha Development Round, built on the progress already made and consistent with its development mandate. Brazil, India, China and South Africa extend full support to an early accession of Russia to the World Trade Organization.

27. We reviewed the progress of the BRICS cooperation in various fields and share the view that such cooperation has been enriching and mutually beneficial and that there is a great scope for closer cooperation among the BRICS. We are focused on the consolidation of BRICS cooperation and the further development of its own agenda. We are determined to translate our political vision into concrete actions and endorse the attached Action Plan, which will serve as the foundation for future cooperation. We will review the implementation of the Action Plan during our next Leaders Meeting.

28. We intend to explore cooperation in the sphere of science, technology and innovation, including the peaceful use of space. We congratulate the Russian people and government upon the 50th anniversary of the flight of Yury Gagarin into the space, which ushered in a new era in development of science and technology.

29. We express our confidence in the success of the 2011 Universiade in Shenzhen, the 2013 Universiade in Kazan, the 2014 Youth Olympic Games in Nanjing, the 2014 Winter Olympic and Paralympics Games in Sochi, the FIFA 2014 World Cup in Brazil, the 2016 Olympic and Paralympics Games in Rio de Janeiro and the FIFA 2018 World Cup in Russia.

30. We extend our deepest condolences to the people of Japan with the great loss of life following the disasters that struck the country. We will continue our practical support to Japan in overcoming consequences of these catastrophes.

31. The leaders of Brazil, Russia, India and South Africa extend our warm appreciation to China for hosting the BRICS Leaders Meeting and the Hainan Provincial Government and Sanya Municipal Government and their people for their support to the Meeting.

32. Brazil, Russia, China and South Africa thank India for hosting the BRICS Leaders Meeting in 2012 and offer their full support.

B.   The Sanya Action Plan

ACTION PLAN

We formulated the Action Plan, laying the foundation for the BRICS cooperation, with the purpose to strengthen BRICS cooperation and benefit our peoples.

I.   Enhance existing cooperation programs

1. Hold the third Meeting of High Representatives for Security Issues in the latter half of 2011 in China.

2. Hold the meeting of Ministers of Foreign Affairs during the 66th Session of the United Nations General Assembly.

3. Hold sherpas/sous-sherpas meeting in due time.

4. Representatives to international organizations based in New York and Geneva meet periodically in an informal manner.

5. Ministers of Finance and Governors of Central Banks meet under the G20 framework and during the annual meetings of the World Bank and International Monetary Fund.

6. Hold the Meeting of Agriculture Expert Working Group and the second Meeting of Ministers of Agriculture in 2011 in China, and cooperate in issues including establishment of BRICS System of Agricultural Information and holding a seminar on food security.

7. Hold the Meeting of the heads of the National Statistical Institutions in September 2011 in China.

8. Hold the second BRICS International Competition Conference in September 2011 in China, and explore the possibility of signing an Agreement on Cooperation between Antimonopoly Agencies.

9. Continue to hold the BRICS Think-tank Symposiums, and consider establishing a network of research centers of all BRICS countries.

10. Hold another Business Forum prior to the next BRICS Leaders Meeting.

11. Strengthen financial cooperation among the BRICS Development Banks.

12. Implement the Protocol of Intent among the BRIC Countries' Supreme Courts.

13. Release the Joint Statistical Publication by BRICS Countries.

14. Continue to hold the Meeting of Cooperatives.

II.   New areas of cooperation

1. Host the first BRICS Friendship Cities and Local Governments Cooperation Forum in 2011 in China.

2. Host the Meeting of Ministers of Health in 2011 in China.

3. Engage in joint research on economic and trade issues.

4. Update, as appropriate, the Bibliography on the BRICS countries.

III.   New proposals to explore

1. Cooperate in the cultural field according to the agreement of the BRICS leaders.

2. Encourage cooperation in sports.

3. Explore the feasibility to cooperate in the field of green economy.

4. Hold a meeting of Senior Officials for discussing ways of promoting scientific, technological and innovation cooperation in BRICS format, including by establishment a working group on cooperation in pharmaceutical industry.

5. Establish, at UNESCO, a "BRICS-UNESCO GROUP", aiming at developing common strategies within the mandate of the Organization.

II.9.   2nd BRIC Summit 2010: 15 Apr. 2010, Brasilia (BRA)

A.   The Brasilia Joint Statement

2ND BRIC SUMMIT OF HEADS OF STATE AND GOVERNMENT:
JOINT STATEMENT
Brasília, April 15, 2010

We, the leaders of the Federative Republic of Brazil, the Russian Federation, the Republic of India and the People's Republic of China, met in Brasília on 15 April 2010 to discuss major issues of the international agenda as well as concrete steps to move forward the cooperation and coordination within BRIC.

We have agreed on the following:

Common Vision and Global Governance

1.   We share the perception that the world is undergoing major and swift changes that highlight the need for corresponding transformations in global governance in all relevant areas.

2.   We underline our support for a multipolar, equitable and democratic world order, based on international law, equality, mutual respect, cooperation, coordinated action and collective decision-making of all States.

3.   We stress the central role played by the G-20 in combating the crisis through unprecedented levels of coordinated action. We welcome the fact that the G-20 was confirmed as the premier forum for international economic coordination and cooperation of all its member states. Compared to previous arrangements, the G-20 is broader, more inclusive, diverse, representative and effective. We call upon all its member states to undertake further efforts to implement jointly the decisions adopted at the three G-20 Summits.

We advocate the need for the G-20 to be proactive and formulate a coherent strategy for the post-crisis period. We stand ready to make a joint contribution to this effort.

4.   We express our strong commitment to multilateral diplomacy with the United Nations playing the central role in dealing with global challenges and threats. In this respect, we reaffirm the need for a comprehensive reform of the UN, with a view to making it more effective, efficient and representative, so that it can deal with today's global challenges more effectively. We reiterate the importance we attach to the status of India and Brazil in international affairs, and understand and support their aspirations to play a greater role in the United Nations.

5.   We believe the deepened and broadened dialogue and cooperation of the BRIC countries is conducive not only to serving common interests of emerging market economies and developing countries, but also to building a harmonious world of lasting peace and common prosperity. We have agreed upon steps to promote dialogue and cooperation among our countries in an incremental, proactive, pragmatic, open and transparent way.

International Economic and Financial Issues

6.   The world economic situation has improved since our first meeting in June 2009, in Ekaterinburg. We welcome the resumption of economic growth, in which emerging market economies are playing a very important role. However, we recognize that the foundation of world economic recovery is not yet solid, with uncertainties remaining. We call upon all states to strengthen macroeconomic cooperation, jointly secure world economic recovery and achieve a strong, sustainable and balanced

growth. We reiterate our determination to make positive efforts in maintaining domestic economic recovery and promoting development in our own countries and worldwide.

7.   We underline the importance of maintaining relative stability of major reserve currencies and sustainability of fiscal policies in order to achieve a strong, long- term balanced economic growth.

8.   We are convinced that emerging market economies and developing countries have the potential to play an even larger and active role as engines of economic growth and prosperity, while at the same time commit to work together with other countries towards reducing imbalances in global economic development and fostering social inclusion.

9.   G-20 members, with a significant contribution from BRIC countries, have greatly increased resources available to the IMF. We support the increase of capital, under the principle of fair burden-sharing, of the International Bank for Reconstruction and Development and of the International Finance Corporation, in addition to more robust, flexible and agile client-driven support for developing economies from multilateral development banks.

10.   Despite promising positive signs, much remains to be done. We believe that the world needs today a reformed and more stable financial architecture that will make the global economy less prone and more resilient to future crises, and that there is a greater need for a more stable, predictable and diversified international monetary system.

11.   We will strive to achieve an ambitious conclusion to the ongoing and long overdue reforms of the Bretton Woods institutions. The IMF and the World Bank urgently need to address their legitimacy deficits. Reforming these institutions' governance structures requires first and foremost a substantial shift in voting power in favor of emerging market economies and developing countries to bring their participation in decision making in line with their relative weight in the world economy. We call for the voting power reform of the World Bank to be fulfilled in the upcoming Spring Meetings, and expect the quota reform of the IMF to be concluded by the G-20 Summit in November this year. We do also agree on the need for an open and merit based selection method, irrespective of nationality, for the heading positions of the IMF and the World Bank. Moreover, staff of these institutions needs to better reflect the diversity of their membership. There is a special need to increase participation of developing countries. The international community must deliver a result worthy of the expectations we all share for these institutions within the agreed timeframe or run the risk of seeing them fade into obsolescence.

12.   In the interest of promoting international economic stability, we have asked our Finance Ministers and Central Bank Governors to look into regional monetary arrangements and discuss modalities of cooperation between our countries in this area. In order to facilitate trade and investment, we will study feasibilities of monetary cooperation, including local currency trade settlement arrangement between our countries.

13.   Recent events have shattered the belief about the self-regulating nature of financial markets. Therefore, there is a pressing need to foster and strengthen cooperation regarding the regulation and supervision of all segments, institutions and instruments of financial markets. We remain committed to improve our own national regulations, to push for the reform of the international financial regulatory system and to work closely with international standard setting bodies, including the Financial Stability Board.

International Trade

14.   We stress the importance of the multilateral trading system, embodied in the World Trade Organization, for providing an open, stable, equitable and non discriminatory environment for international trade. In this connection, we commit ourselves and urge all states to resist all forms of trade protectionism and fight disguised restrictions on trade. We concur in the need for a comprehensive and balanced outcome of the Doha Round of multilateral trade talks, in a manner

that fulfills its mandate as a "development round", based on the progress already made, including with regard to modalities. We take note and strongly support Russia's bid for accession to the WTO.

Development

15. We reiterate the importance of the UN Millennium Declaration and the need to achieve the Millennium Development Goals (MDGs). We underscore the importance of preventing a potential setback to the efforts of poor countries aimed at achieving MDGs due to the effects of the economic and financial crisis. We should also make sustained efforts to achieve the MDGs by 2015, including through technical cooperation and financial support to poor countries in implementation of development policies and social protection for their populations. We expect the UN MDG Summit, in September 2010, to promote the implementation of MDGs through policy recommendations. We stress that sustainable development models and paths of developing countries should be fully respected and necessary policy space of developing countries should be guaranteed.

16. The poorest countries have been the hardest hit by the economic and financial crisis. The commitments regarding the aid to the developing states, especially those related to the MDGs, should be fulfilled, and there should be no reduction in development assistance. An inclusive process of growth for the world economy is not only a matter of solidarity but also an issue of strategic importance for global political and economic stability.

Agriculture

17. We express our satisfaction with the Meeting of Ministers of Agriculture and Agrarian Development in Moscow, where they discussed ways of promoting quadripartite cooperation, with particular attention to family farming. We are convinced that this will contribute towards global food production and food security. We welcome their decision to create an agricultural information base system of the BRIC countries, to develop a strategy for ensuring access to food for vulnerable population, to reduce the negative impact of climate change on food security, and to enhance agriculture technology cooperation and innovation.

Fight against poverty

18. We call upon the international community to make all the necessary efforts to fight poverty, social exclusion and inequality bearing in mind the special needs of developing countries, especially LDCs, small islands and African Countries. We support technical and financial cooperation as means to contribute to the achievement of sustainable social development, with social protection, full employment, and decent work policies and programmes, giving special attention to the most vulnerable groups, such as the poor, women, youth, migrants and persons with disabilities.

Energy

19. We recognize that energy is an essential resource for improving the standard of living of our peoples and that access to energy is of paramount importance to economic growth with equity and social inclusion. We will aim to develop cleaner, more affordable and sustainable energy systems, to promote access to energy and energy efficient technologies and practices in all sectors. We will aim to diversify our energy mix by increasing, where appropriate, the contribution of renewable energy sources, and will encourage the cleaner, more efficient use of fossil fuels and other fuels. In this regard, we reiterate our support to the international cooperation in the field of energy efficiency.

20. We recognize the potential of new, emerging, and environmentally friendly technologies for diversifying energy mix and the creation of jobs. In this regard we will encourage, as appropriate, the sustainable development, production and use of biofuels. In accordance with national priorities, we will work together to facilitate the use of renewable energy, through international cooperation and the sharing of experiences on renewable energy, including biofuels technologies and policies.

21. We believe that BRIC member countries can cooperate in training, R&D, Consultancy services and technology transfer, in the energy sector.

Climate Change

22. We acknowledge that climate change is a serious threat which requires strengthened global action. We commit ourselves to promote the 16th Conference of the Parties to the United Nations Framework Convention on Climate Change and the 6th Conference of the Parties serving as the Meeting of the Parties to the Kyoto Protocol, in Mexico, to achieve a comprehensive, balanced and binding result to strengthen the implementation of the Convention and the Protocol. We believe that the Convention and the Protocol provide the framework for international negotiations on climate change. The negotiations in Mexico should be more inclusive, transparent, and should result in outcomes that are fair and effective in addressing the challenge of climate change, while reflecting the principles of the Convention, especially the principle of equity and common but differentiated responsibilities.

Terrorism

23. We condemn terrorist acts in all forms and manifestations. We note that the fight against international terrorism must be undertaken with due respect to the UN Charter, existing international conventions and protocols, the UN General Assembly and Security Council resolutions relating to international terrorism, and that the prevention of terrorist acts is as important as the repression of terrorism and its financing. In this context, we urge early conclusion of negotiations in the UN General Assembly of the Comprehensive Convention on International Terrorism and its adoption by all Member States.

24. Brazil and China express their sympathy and solidarity with the people and Governments of Russia and India which suffered from recent barbaric terrorist attacks. Terrorism cannot be justified by any reason.

Alliance of Civilizations

25. We affirm the importance of encouraging the dialogue among civilizations, cultures, religions and peoples. In this respect, we support the "Alliance of Civilizations", a United Nations' initiative aimed at building bridges, mutual knowledge and understanding around the world. We praise the Brazilian decision to host, in Rio de Janeiro, in May 2010, the 3rd Global Forum and confirm our intention to be present at the event, in appropriate high level.

Haiti

26. We reaffirm our solidarity towards the Haitian people, who have been struggling under dire circumstances since the earthquake of January 12th, and reiterate our commitment to gather efforts with the international community in order to help rebuilding the country, under the guidance of the Haitian government, and according to the priorities established by the Action Plan for National Recovery and Development of Haiti.

Cooperation

27. We welcome the following sectoral initiatives aimed at strengthening cooperation among our countries:
   a) the first Meeting of Ministers of Agriculture and Agrarian Development;
   b) the Meetings of Ministers of Finance and Governors of Central Banks;
   c) the Meetings of High Representatives for Security Issues;
   d) the I Exchange Program for Magistrates and Judges, of BRIC countries, held in March 2010 in Brazil following the signature in 2009 of the Protocol of Intent among the BRIC countries' Supreme Courts;
   e) the first Meeting of Development Banks;
   f) the first Meeting of the Heads of the National Statistical Institutions;
   g) the Conference of Competition Authorities;

h) the first Meeting of Cooperatives;

i) the first Business Forum;

j) the Conference of think tanks.

28. We also endorse other important manifestations of our desire to deepen our relationship, such as:

a) the joint publication by our respective national statistical institutions which is going to be released today;

b) a feasibility study for developing a joint BRIC encyclopedia.

29. We reaffirm our commitment to advance cooperation among BRIC countries in science, culture and sports.

30. We express our confidence in the success of the 2010 World Expo in Shanghai, the 2010 Commonwealth Games in New Delhi, the 2013 World Student Games in Kazan, the 2014 Winter Olympic and Paralympic Games in Sochi, the FIFA 2014 World Cup in Brazil and the 2016 Olympic and Paralympic Games in Rio de Janeiro.

31. We reaffirm the efforts to strengthen our cooperation and assistance for reduction of natural disasters. Russia and India express their condolences and solidarity with the people and Governments of Brazil and China, for the lives lost in the mudslide in Rio de Janeiro, Brazil, and in the earthquake in Yushu, China.

III BRIC Summit

32. Brazil, Russia and India appreciate the offer of China to host the III BRIC Summit in 2011.

33. Russia, India and China express their profound gratitude to the Government and people of Brazil for hosting the II BRIC Summit.

II.10. 1st BRIC Summit 2009: 16 Jun. 2009, Yekaterinburg (RUS)

A.   The Yekaterinburg Joint Statement

JOINT STATEMENT OF THE BRIC COUNTRIES' LEADERS
Yekaterinburg, Russia, June 16, 2009

We, the leaders of the Federative Republic of Brazil, the Russian Federation, the Republic of India and the People's Republic of China, have discussed the current situation in global economy and other pressing issues of global development, and also prospects for further strengthening collaboration within the BRIC, at our meeting in Yekaterinburg on June 16, 2009.

We have arrived at the following conclusions:

1.   We stress the central role played by the G20 Summits in dealing with the financial crisis. They have fostered cooperation, policy coordination and political dialogue regarding international economic and financial matters.

2.   We call upon all states and relevant international bodies to act vigorously to implement the decisions adopted at the G20 Summit in London on April 2, 2009. We shall cooperate closely among ourselves and with other partners to ensure further progress of collective action at the next G20 Summit to be held in Pittsburgh in September 2009. We look forward to a successful outcome of the United Nations Conference on the World Financial and Economic Crisis and its Impact on Development to be held in New York on June 24-26, 2009.

3.   We are committed to advance the reform of international financial institutions, so as to reflect changes in the global economy. The emerging and developing economies must have greater voice and representation in international financial institutions, whose heads and executives should be appointed through an open, transparent, and merit-based selection process. We also believe that there is a strong need for a stable, predictable and more diversified international monetary system.

4.   We are convinced that a reformed financial and economic architecture should be based, *inter alia*, on the following principles:

- democratic and transparent decision-making and implementation process at the international financial organisations;
- solid legal basis;
- compatibility of activities of effective national regulatory institutions and international standard-setting bodies;
- strengthening of risk management and supervisory practices.

5.   We recognise the important role played by international trade and foreign direct investments in the world economic recovery. We call upon all parties to work together to improve the international trade and investment environment. We urge the international community to keep the multilateral trading system stable, curb trade protectionism, and push for comprehensive and balanced results of the WTO's Doha Development Agenda.

6.   The poorest countries have been hit hardest by the financial crisis. The international community needs to step up efforts to provide liquid financial resources for these countries. The international community should also strive to minimise the impact of the crisis on development and ensure the achievement of the Millennium Development Goals. Developed countries should fulfill their commitment of 0.7% of Gross National Income for the Official Development Assistance and make further efforts in increasing assistance, debt relief, market access and technology transfer for developing countries.

7.   The implementation of the concept of sustainable development, comprising, *inter alia*, the Rio Declaration, Agenda for the 21st Century and multilateral environmental agreements, should be a major vector in the change of paradigm of economic development.

8.   We stand for strengthening coordination and cooperation among states in the energy field, including amongst energy producers and consumers and transit states, in an effort to decrease uncertainty and ensure stability and sustainability. We support diversification of energy resources and supply, including renewable energy, security of energy transit routes and creation of new energy investments and infrastructure.

9.   We support international cooperation in the field of energy efficiency. We stand ready for a constructive dialogue on how to deal with climate change based on the principle of common but differentiated responsibility, given the need to combine measures to protect the climate with steps to fulfill our socio-economic development tasks.

10.   We reaffirm to enhance cooperation among our countries in socially vital areas and to strengthen the efforts for the provision of international humanitarian assistance and for the reduction of natural disaster risks. We take note of the statement on global food security issued today as a major contribution of the BRIC countries to the multilateral efforts to set up the sustainable conditions for this goal.

11.   We reaffirm to advance cooperation among our countries in science and education with the aim, *inter alia*, to engage in fundamental research and development of advanced technologies.

12.   We underline our support for a more democratic and just multi-polar world order based on the rule of international law, equality, mutual respect, cooperation, coordinated action and collective decision-making of all states. We reiterate our support for political and diplomatic efforts to peacefully resolve disputes in international relations.

13.   We strongly condemn terrorism in all its forms and manifestations and reiterate that there can be no justification for any act of terrorism anywhere or for whatever reasons. We note that the draft Comprehensive Convention against International Terrorism is currently under the consideration of the UN General Assembly and call for its urgent adoption.

14.   We express our strong commitment to multilateral diplomacy with the United Nations playing the central role in dealing with global challenges and threats. In this respect, we reaffirm the need for a comprehensive reform of the UN with a view to making it more efficient so that it can deal with today's global challenges more effectively. We reiterate the importance we attach to the status of India and Brazil in international affairs, and understand and support their aspirations to play a greater role in the United Nations.

15.   We have agreed upon steps to promote dialogue and cooperation among our countries in an incremental, proactive, pragmatic, open and transparent way. The dialogue and cooperation of the BRIC countries is conducive not only to serving common interests of emerging market economies and developing countries, but also to building a harmonious world of lasting peace and common prosperity.

16.   Russia, India and China welcome the kind invitation of Brazil to the next BRIC summit it will host in 2010.

III.   BRICS MINISTERIAL MEETINGS

III.1.   BRICS Foreign Ministers

A.   BRICS Ministers of Foreign Affairs/IR: 4 Jun. 2018, Pretoria (ZAF)

MEETING OF THE BRICS MINISTERS OF FOREIGN AFFAIRS/INTERNATIONAL
RELATIONS
4 June 2018, Pretoria, South Africa

1.   The Ministers of Foreign Affairs/International Relations of the Federative Republic of Brazil, the Russian Federation, the Republic of India, the People's Republic of China and the Republic of South Africa, met on 4 June 2018 in Pretoria, South Africa.

2.   The Ministers reflected on the importance of this year marking a decade of BRICS Summits, as a testimony to the fortitude of BRICS cooperation and reiterated the commitment to implement the outcomes and consensus of past BRICS Summits. The Ministers welcomed South Africa's Chairship and looked forward to the 10th BRICS Summit to be held under the theme, "BRICS in Africa: Collaboration for Inclusive Growth and Shared Prosperity in the 4th Industrial Revolution" and committed themselves to work together for a fruitful Johannesburg Summit.

3.   The Ministers recalled the BRICS tradition of outreach to extend its cooperation to fellow developing and emerging economies. In this respect, the Ministers welcomed South Africa's two-pronged outreach approach through the BRICS-Africa Dialogue and the BRICS Plus cooperation, to be held during the Summit.

4.   The Ministers expressed their gratitude to South Africa for hosting the Meeting of the BRICS Ministers of Foreign Affairs/International Relations, contributing positively to the BRICS cooperation. The Ministers exchanged views on current issues of global significance in political, security, economic, financial and sustainable development spheres, as well as intra-BRICS cooperation.

5.   The Ministers reaffirmed their commitment to the United Nations, as the universal multilateral organisation entrusted with the mandate for maintaining international peace and security, advancing global development and to promoting and protecting human rights so as to build a brighter shared future for the global community.

6.   They recalled the 2005 World Summit Outcome document and reaffirmed the need for a comprehensive reform of the UN, including its Security Council, with a view to making it more representative, effective and efficient, and to increase the representation of the developing countries so that it can adequately respond to global challenges. China and Russia reiterate the importance they attach to the status and role of Brazil, India and South Africa in international affairs and support their aspiration to play a greater role in the UN.

7.   The Ministers underscored the importance of sustained efforts aimed at making the United Nations more effective and efficient in implementing the mandates conferred upon it. In this regard, they committed to intensifying dialogue amongst the BRICS countries on the administration and budget of the United Nations, with a view to strengthening the Organization and preserving its Member State-driven character.

8.   The Ministers expressed their support for continued cooperation of BRICS members in areas of mutual interest including through regular exchanges amongst their multilateral Missions.

9.   The Ministers also reconfirmed the commitment to fully implement the 2030 Agenda for Sustainable Development to equitable, inclusive, open, all-round innovation-driven and sustainable development, in its three dimensions – economic, social and environmental – in a balanced and integrated manner. The Ministers pledged their support for the important role of the United Nations, including the High Level Political Forum on Sustainable Development (HLPF), in coordinating and reviewing global implementation of the 2030 Agenda, and support the need to reform the UN Development System with a view to enhancing its capability in supporting member States in implementing the 2030 Agenda. They urged developed countries to honor their Official Development Assistance commitments in time and in full and provide more development resources to developing countries.

10.   The Ministers reaffirmed their commitment to tackling climate change. They welcomed the entry into force of the Paris Agreement under the United Nations Framework Convention on Climate Change, which reflects the principles of common but differentiated responsibilities and respective capabilities. They expressed hope to complete the Paris Agreement Work Programme at COP 24. They drew attention to the importance of strengthening cooperation to face the challenges brought by climate change, which requires financial flows and technology transfer. They therefore urged developed countries to fulfil their commitments in this regard.

11.   The Ministers reiterated BRICS commitment to multilateralism and a rules-based international order and in this regard reaffirmed the centrality of UN, WTO and international law. The Ministers pledged their support to efforts towards making global governance more representative with greater participation of emerging markets and developing countries in global decision making.

12.   The Ministers emphasized the importance of an open and inclusive world economy enabling all countries and peoples to share the benefits of globalization. They underlined their firm commitment to free trade, and the centrality of a rules-based, transparent, non-discriminatory, multilateral trading system as embodied in the WTO. They opposed the new wave of protectionism and the systematic impact of unilateral measures that are incompatible with WTO rules, and undermines global trade, and economic growth. In this regard, they reiterated that the WTO Dispute Settlement System is a cornerstone of the MTS as it is designed to enhance security and predictability in international trade.

13.   The Ministers reaffirmed their resolve to foster a global economic governance architecture that is more effective and reflective of current global economic landscape, increasing the voice and representation of emerging markets and developing economies. They reaffirmed their commitment to conclude the IMF's 15th General Review of Quotas, including a new quota formula, by the 2019 Spring Meetings. They will continue to support the implementation of the World Bank Group Shareholding Review. The Ministers welcomed the institutional progress of the New Development Bank (NDB), including the upcoming establishment of the Americas Regional Office in São Paulo, Brazil, which, alongside the Africa Regional Centre (ARC), will help the NDB consolidate its presence in those continents.

14.   The Ministers deplored the continued terrorist attacks, including in some BRICS countries. They condemned terrorism in all its forms and manifestations wherever committed and by whomsoever. They urged concerted efforts to counter terrorism under the UN auspices on a firm international legal basis, and expressed their conviction that a comprehensive approach was necessary to ensure effective fight against terrorism. They recalled the responsibility of all States to prevent financing of terrorist networks and terrorist actions from their territories. The Ministers highly value the 3rd BRICS Counter-Terrorism Working Group Meeting held in Nelspruit on 19 and 20 April 2018. They called upon for an expedited adoption of the Comprehensive Convention on International Terrorism in the UN General Assembly.

15.   The Ministers expressed concern over the ongoing conflict and heightened tensions in the Middle-East region, especially with regard to the Israeli-Palestinian situation. The Ministers reiterate

the need for renewed diplomatic efforts to achieving a just, lasting and comprehensive settlement of the Israeli-Palestinian conflict in order to achieve peace and stability in the Middle East on the basis of relevant United Nations resolutions, the Madrid Principles, the Arab Peace Initiative and previous agreements between the parties through negotiations with a view to create an independent, viable, territorially contiguous Palestinian State living side by side in peace and security with Israel. The Ministers reiterated that the status of Jerusalem is one of the final status issues to be defined in the context of negotiations between Israel and Palestine.

16. The Ministers reiterated their countries' support to the United Nations Relief and Works Agency for Palestine Refugees in the Near East (UNRWA). They commend the vital role it plays in providing health, education and other basic services for almost 5.3 million Palestinian refugees and underscored its relevance to bringing stability to the region and the need for ensuring a more adequate, sufficient, predictable and sustained funding for the Agency.

17. The ongoing conflict in the Republic of Yemen is a further concern, having become a major humanitarian crisis. The Ministers urge all parties to fully respect international law to cease hostilities and to return to the UN brokered peace talks, leading to an inclusive Yemeni-led dialogue towards the achievement of a political solution to the conflict.

18. The Ministers reaffirmed their support to process of 'Afghan-led, Afghan-owned' national reconciliation process. The Ministers expressed their concern over the deteriorating situation in Afghanistan particularly the increase in the number and intensity of terrorist-related attacks on the Afghan National Security Forces, the Government and civilians. The Ministers called on the international community to assist the government and the people of Afghanistan with stabilising the security situation in the country as well as for the return of dialogue with the objective of working towards the realisation of peace in the country and an inclusive political process. The Ministers also welcomed the Parliamentary elections which are scheduled to be held in October 2018 and the Presidential elections in 2019.

19. The Ministers reaffirmed their commitment for a political resolution of the conflict in Syria, through an inclusive "Syrian-led, Syrian-owned" political process which safeguards the state sovereignty, independence and territorial integrity of Syria, in pursuance of United Nations Security Council Resolution 2254 (2015) and taking into account the result of the Congress of the Syrian National Dialogue in Sochi. They reiterated their support for the Geneva process and the mediation offered by the UN, as well as the Astana process, and stressed the complementarity between the two initiatives. They expressed their support to the efforts by Russia to advance the Syrian national dialogue. The Ministers reaffirmed their commitment to a peaceful resolution in Syria. They expressed their opposition to measures that run contrary to the UN Charter and the authority of the United Nations Security Council (UNSC) and do not contribute to advancing the political process. They also highlighted the importance of unity in the fight against terrorist organizations in Syria in full observance of the relevant UNSC Resolutions. The Ministers reiterated their strong condemnation of the use of chemical weapons by any party, for any purpose and under any circumstances and renewed calls for comprehensive, objective, independent, and transparent investigations of all alleged incidents. The Ministers called for enhancing efforts to provide necessary humanitarian assistance to the Syrian people bearing in mind urgent reconstruction needs.

20. The Ministers recalled the importance that all relevant parties of the Joint Comprehensive Plan of Action (JCPOA) on the Iranian nuclear issue fully comply with their obligations and ensure full and effective implementation of the JCPOA to promote international and regional peace and security.

21. The Ministers welcomed the recent developments to achieve the complete denuclearisation of the Korean Peninsula and maintain peace and stability in North East Asia. The Ministers reaffirmed the commitment for peaceful, diplomatic and political solution to the situation.

22. The Ministers reaffirmed the importance of the elaboration under the UN auspices of rules, norms and principles of responsible behaviour of States in ensuring security in the use of ICTs.

23. The Ministers acknowledged the work to promote cooperation according to the BRICS Roadmap of Practical Cooperation on Ensuring Security in the Use of ICTs or any other mutually agreed mechanism. Ministers acknowledge the initiative of the Russian Federation on a BRICS intergovernmental agreement on cooperation in ensuring security in the use of ICTs and look forward to its consideration at the upcoming meeting of the National Security Advisors/High Representatives in Durban.

24. The Ministers commended African countries and the African Union on the signing of the African Continental Free Trade Area (AfCFTA) as an important step to economic integration on the continent and the unlocking of the tremendous potential of intra-African trade and addressing the socio-economic challenges. In this regard the Ministers reiterated their support for Agenda 2063 and efforts to promote continental integration and development.

25. The Ministers underlined the importance of the upcoming meeting of the National Security Advisors/High Representatives in Durban. They also highlighted their support for the meeting of BRICS Deputy Ministers/Special Envoys on the Middle East and North Africa, in taking BRICS dialogue further.

26. The Ministers look forward to the next meeting on the margins of the 73rd Session of the United Nations General Assembly.

B.   BRICS Ministers of Foreign Affairs/IR: 21 Sep. 2017, New York (USA)

MEETING OF BRICS MINISTERS OF FOREIGN AFFAIRS/INTERNATIONAL RELATIONS
21 September 2017, New York, United States

The BRICS Ministers of Foreign Affairs/International Relations held their annual meeting on the margins of the 72nd session of the United Nations General Assembly (UNGA72) on 21 September 2017. The meeting was chaired by the Minister of International Relations and Cooperation of South Africa in the country's capacity as the incoming BRICS Chair for 2018.

The Ministers expressed their warm appreciation to China for the success of the 9th BRICS Summit held from 4-5 September 2017 in Xiamen. They welcomed the substantive outcomes of the Summit and reaffirmed the commitment for their full implementation of the Xiamen Declaration, as well as the outcomes of the past Summits as adopted by the BRICS Leaders.

The Ministers reaffirmed their strong commitment to uphold development and multilateralism, and to that effect they stressed the need to strengthen coordination and cooperation among BRICS in the areas of mutual and common interests within the United Nations and other multilateral institutions, including through regular meetings among our permanent representatives in New York, Geneva and Vienna, and further enhance the voice of BRICS in international fora.

The Ministers underlined the progress achieved by BRICS since 2006 that has generated a momentum for multi-dimensional cooperation fostered by the Leaders' Summits. They expressed satisfaction from the many fruitful results of BRICS cooperation, in particular the establishment of the New Development Bank (NDB), including its first Africa Regional Centre in Johannesburg, South Africa, and the Contingent Reserve Arrangement (CRA), the formulation of the Strategy for BRICS Economic Partnership, the strengthening of the political and security cooperation including through Meetings of BRICS High Representatives for Security Issues and Foreign Ministers Meetings, and the deepening of the traditional ties of friendship amongst peoples of BRICS countries.

They further pledged to continue working together to uphold mutual respect, equality, solidarity, openness and inclusiveness, to further strengthen strategic partnership cooperation for mutual benefit by constantly deepening BRICS practical cooperation so as to usher in and provide practical content to the second golden decade of BRICS cooperation and solidarity.

The Ministers exchanged views on global and regional issues in the economic and political spheres and recognized that global economic recovery is gaining momentum though uncertainties and downside risks persist globally. They noted that BRICS countries continue to play an important role as engines of global growth. They further reiterated the need to boost world economic growth including through macro-economic policy coordination and improving global economic governance.

The Ministers reaffirmed their commitment to the United Nations as the universal multilateral organization entrusted with the mandate for maintaining international peace and security, advance global development and to promote and protect human rights so as to build a brighter shared future for the global community.

They recalled the 2005 World Summit Outcome document and reaffirm the need for a comprehensive reform of the UN, including its Security Council, with a view to making it more representative, effective and efficient, and to increase the representation of the developing countries so that it can adequately respond to global challenges. China and Russia reiterate the importance they attach to the status and role of Brazil, India and South Africa in international affairs and support their aspiration to play a greater role in the UN.

The Ministers also reconfirmed the commitment to fully implement the 2030 Agenda for Sustainable Development to equitable, inclusive, open, all-round innovation-driven and sustainable development, in its three dimensions – economic, social and environmental – in a balanced and integrated manner. The Ministers pledged their support for the important role of the United Nations, including the High Level Political Forum on Sustainable Development (HLPF), in coordinating and reviewing global implementation of the 2030 Agenda, and support the need to reform the UN Development System with a view to enhancing its capability in supporting member States in implementing the 2030 Agenda.

The Ministers reiterated their strong condemnation of terrorism in all its forms and manifestations. They urged concerted efforts to counter terrorism on a firm international legal basis, under the UN auspices, and expressed their conviction that a comprehensive approach was necessary to ensure effective fight against terrorism. They reaffirmed their commitment to an expeditious adoption of a Comprehensive Convention on International Terrorism at the United Nations. The Ministers stressed the role of the BRICS Counter-Terrorism Working Group in further deepening the dialogue on counter-terrorism cooperation.

The Ministers expressed their concern over continued conflicts and situations in several regions which undermine stability and security and provide fertile grounds for terrorist activities and cause refugee and migration waves. They supported political and diplomatic solutions of conflicts and situations, such as in the Israeli-Palestinian conflict, and in Yemen, Syria, Afghanistan, and in Africa, and the Korean Peninsula.

The Ministers stressed the need to strive towards broad partnerships with EMDCs, and in this context, to pursue equal-footed and flexible practices and initiatives for sustainable dialogue and cooperation with non-BRICS countries, regional or sub-region groups, including through BRICS Plus approach.

The Ministers supported the efforts in deepening people-to-people exchanges and cultural cooperation, in particular strengthening the third pillar of BRICS cooperation so as to deepen bonds and ties amongst its peoples.

The Ministers discussed the possibilities for the mutual support of their initiatives at the 72nd session of the UN General Assembly.

The Ministers were also briefed on approaches for South Africa's incoming BRICS Chairpersonship in 2018. China, Brazil, Russia and India extend full support for South Africa in hosting the Tenth BRICS Summit in 2018. The Ministers also look forward to the Stand-alone Meeting of BRICS Ministers of Foreign Affairs/International Relations in South Africa in 2018.

C.   BRICS Ministers of Foreign Affairs/IR: 18-19 Jun. 2017, Beijing (CHN)

MEETING OF THE BRICS MINISTERS OF FOREIGN AFFAIRS/INTERNATIONAL RELATIONS
18-19 June 2017, Beijing (CHINA)

1.   The Ministers of Foreign Affairs/International Relations of the Federative Republic of Brazil, the Russian Federation, the Republic of India, the People's Republic of China and the Republic of South Africa, met on 18-19 June 2017 in Beijing, China.

2.   The Ministers commend the fruitful cooperation forged in the past and look forward to continued and positive cooperation among BRICS countries. They appreciate China's BRICS Chairship for 2017. They reiterate their commitment to the success of the Ninth BRICS Summit under the theme of "BRICS: Stronger Partnership for a Brighter Future". Recalling the BRICS tradition of outreach activities, they welcome the dialogue to be held during the BRICS Summit in Xiamen with emerging markets and developing countries.

3.   The Ministers exchanged views on a wide range of global political, security, economic and financial issues of importance and mutual concern, as well as cooperation within BRICS. They fully support China's hosting of the 7th Meeting of the BRICS National Security Advisors/High Representatives in July 2017.

4.   The Ministers reaffirm their commitment to safeguarding the purposes and principles of the Charter of the United Nations as well as a fair and just international order, upholding the basic norms of international law such as equal sovereignty and non-interference in other countries' internal affairs, promoting greater democracy and rule of law in international relations, building a brighter shared future for the global community through mutually beneficial international cooperation. They express their commitment to resolutely reject the continued attempts to misrepresent the results of World War II.

5.   The Ministers recall the 2005 World Summit Outcome document. They reaffirm the need for a comprehensive reform of the UN, including its Security Council, with a view to making it more representative, effective and efficient, and to increase the representation of the developing countries so that it can adequately respond to global challenges. China and Russia reiterate the importance they attach to the status and role of Brazil, India and South Africa in international affairs and support their aspiration to play a greater role in the UN.

6.   The Ministers recommit their strong support to multilateralism and the central role of United Nations in international affairs. They commit to strengthening the coordination and cooperation among BRICS in the areas of mutual and common interest within the United Nations and other multilateral institutions, including through regular meetings among their permanent representatives in New York, Geneva and Vienna and further enhance the voice of BRICS in international fora.

7.   The Ministers underscore the importance of the full implementation of the 2030 Agenda for Sustainable Development within the framework of revitalized global partnership for sustainable development. They urge the developed countries to honor their Official Development Assistance commitments. The Ministers reiterate their support for more balanced economic globalization, reject protectionism, and renew their commitment to the promotion of global trade and investment which is conducive to an equitable, inclusive innovative, invigorated and interconnected world economy.

8.   The Ministers welcome the entry into force of the Paris Agreement on climate change on 4 November 2016 and urge all countries to implement the Paris Agreement under the principles of the United Nations Framework Convention on Climate Change including the principles of equity and common but differentiated responsibilities and respective capabilities. They further call upon developed countries to fulfil their commitment to provide necessary financing, technology transfer and capacity building support to developing countries.

9. The Ministers deplore the continued terrorist attacks, including in some BRICS countries. They condemn terrorism in all its forms and manifestations wherever committed and by whomsoever. They reaffirm solidarity and resolve in the fight against terrorism, call upon the international community to establish a genuinely broad international counter-terrorism coalition and support the United Nations' central coordinating role in the international counter-terrorism cooperation. They recall the responsibility of all States to prevent financing of terrorist networks and terrorist actions from their territories. The Ministers highly value the 2nd BRICS Counter-Terrorism Working Group Meeting held in Beijing on 18 May 2017. They call upon an expedited adoption of the Comprehensive Convention on International Terrorism in the UN General Assembly.

10. The Ministers welcome the 2nd BRICS Consultation on UN Peacekeeping Affairs to be held in Beijing in July 2017.

11. The Ministers agree to enhance coordination and cooperation among BRICS on international and regional issues, safeguard justice at the United Nations and other international fora. They support political and diplomatic solution of conflicts, such as Libya and the Korean Peninsula, and promote preventive diplomacy in a consensus-based manner. They condemn unilateral military intervention or economic sanctions in violation of international law and universally recognised norms of international relations.

12. The Ministers reiterate that the only lasting solution to the Syria crisis is an inclusive "Syrian-led, Syrian-owned" political process which safeguard the state sovereignty, independence and territorial integrity of Syria, in pursuance of the United Nations Security Council Resolution 2254(2015). The Ministers strongly support the Geneva Peace Talks and the Astana process, and welcome the creation of the de-escalation areas in Syria. They oppose the use of chemical weapons by anyone, for any purpose and under any circumstance.

13. The Ministers reaffirm their support to the process of "Afghan-led and Afghan-owned" national reconciliation, the ongoing international efforts in support of achieving practical results in that regard, combating terrorism and drug-threat, and support the national reconstruction efforts. The Ministers support the efforts of the Afghan National Defense and Security Forces in fighting against terrorist organizations.

14. The Ministers reiterate the need for a just, lasting and comprehensive settlement of the Israeli-Palestinian conflict in order to achieve peace and stability in the Middle East on the basis of relevant United Nations resolutions, the Madrid Principles, the Arab Peace Initiative and previous agreements between the parties through negotiations with a view to create an independent, viable, territorially contiguous Palestinian State living side by side in peace and security with Israel.

15. The Ministers commend the efforts of African countries, the African Union and sub-regional organisations in addressing regional issues and maintaining regional peace and stability, and emphasize the importance of collaboration between the United Nations and the African Union in accordance with the Charter of the United Nations. They reaffirm their support for African Union's implementation of its various programs including Agenda 2063 in pursuit of its continental agenda for peace and socio-economic development.

16. The Ministers are concerned by the threats and challenges posed by the use of ICTS for criminal and terrorist purposes and the weaponization of outer space and arms race there. They underscore the role of collaborative efforts to address these challenges. They note with satisfaction the work of the Working Group of Experts of the BRICS countries on Security in the Use of ICTs and by the BRICS Anti-corruption Working Group.

17. The Ministers look forward to their meeting on the margins of the 72nd Session of the United Nations General Assembly, and welcome South Africa's offer to host the next stand-alone meeting in 2018.

D.   BRICS Ministers of Foreign Affairs: 20 Sep. 2016, New York (USA)

MEETING OF BRICS MINISTERS OF FOREIGN AFFAIRS
20 September 2016, New York, United States

1.   The BRICS Ministers of Foreign Affairs held their regular meeting on 20 September 2016 on the margins of the 71st session of the United Nations General Assembly.

2.   The Ministers underlined the marked progress achieved since the first Meeting of Foreign Ministers on the margins of the 61st session of the United Nations General Assembly in September 2006, in deepening the BRICS strategic partnership based on the principles of openness, solidarity, equality and mutual understanding, inclusiveness and mutually beneficial cooperation.

3.   The Ministers reiterated their intention to contribute to safeguarding a fair and equitable international order based on the purposes and principles of the UN Charter. They recalled 2005 World Summit Outcome Document. They reaffirmed the need for a comprehensive reform of the United Nations including its Security Council with a view to making it more representative and efficient.

4.   The Ministers reiterated their strong condemnation of terrorism in all its forms and manifestations. They strongly condemned the recent several attacks, against some BRICS countries, including that in India. They urged concerted efforts to counter terrorism on a firm international legal basis, under the UN auspices, and expressed their conviction that a comprehensive approach was necessary to ensure effective fight against terrorism. In this regard, they called for an early conclusion of the negotiations on the Comprehensive Convention against Terrorism.

5.   The Ministers noted the convening of the BRICS National Security Advisors Meeting as well as the constitution of BRICS Working Group on Counter Terrorism and its first meeting in New Delhi.

6.   The Ministers recalled exchanged views on global and regional issues in the economic and political spheres. They are determined to continue to contribute positively to the maintenance of peace, security and stability, including by upholding multilateralism. They also recalled the contribution of BRICS countries in promoting global economic growth.

7.   The Ministers recalled the wide range of cooperation in BRICS, and noted with satisfaction, the progress made by the New Development Bank, the Contingent Reserve Arrangement, and called for the implementation of the Strategy for BRICS Economic Partnership.

8.   The Ministers appreciated India's BRICS Chairpersonship for the year 2016 and the expansion in range of activities organized to date. They expressed their commitment to ensure the success of the forthcoming 8th BRICS Summit in Goa on 15-16 October 2016.

9.   The Ministers reiterated that BRICS countries will continue with their outreach and expand their cooperation with developing countries and emerging market economies in a spirit of solidarity, inclusiveness, and openness.

10. The Ministers welcomed China's incoming BRICS Chairpersonship in 2017 and expressed confidence that intra-BRICS cooperation will be further strengthened.

11. The Ministers welcomed the fruitful discussion by BRICS Leaders at their Informal Meeting on the margins of the G20 Hangzhou Summit.

12. The Ministers warmly congratulated China for the successful hosting of the G20 Hangzhou Summit. They acknowledged the significant outcomes of the G20 Summit, and called for their full

implementation, including in the areas of sustainable development goals, climate change, and on innovation and structural reform as drivers of future economic growth.

13. The Ministers discussed the current state of the global economy, and recognized that global economic recovery continues to be weak and uneven. They reiterated the need to boost world economic growth, macroeconomic policy coordination, improving global economic governance, promoting international trade and investment, addressing income inequality and achieving sustainable development. They called for collective action in this regard.

14. As the Ministers recalled the 2030 Agenda for Sustainable Development, they reaffirmed that poverty eradication is the greatest global challenge and committed to continue to work towards the full implementation of the 17 Sustainable Development Goals. They called upon the international community, especially the developed countries, to fulfil their commitments and provide strong support for developing countries. In this regard they recalled the G20 Action Plan on the 2030 Agenda for Sustainable Development and G20 Initiative on Supporting Industrialization in Africa and LDCs.

15. The Ministers emphasized the need for concerted action in addressing global health challenges. In particular they recalled the importance of a common and inclusive approach to development of medicines, research and diagnostic tools to end epidemics and to facilitate the access to safe, effective, quality and affordable essential medicines.

16. The Ministers welcomed the adoption of the Paris Agreement on climate change and committed to work towards its entry into force with completion of due domestic procedures and its full implementation. They reiterated the principles of UNFCCC including the principle of equity and Common but Differentiated Responsibilities and respective capabilities. They emphasized that developed countries shall continue to provide financial, technical and capacity building support to developing countries with respect to both mitigation and adaptation for the implementation of the Paris Agreement.

17. The Ministers expressed their concern over continued conflicts in several regions which undermine stability and security and provide fertile grounds for terrorist activities and cause refugee and migration waves.

18. The Ministers expressed concern over the situation in the Middle East, and stressed that the international community should work together to pave the way for the political settlement of conflicts through dialogue and negotiations. They recognized the efforts of BRICS countries, in particular that of the Russian Federation aimed at achieving a political solution to the international crisis in Syria including Russia-US arrangements agreed upon in Geneva on September 9, 2016.

19. The Ministers underlined the need to enhance further the efforts to resolve conflicts in Africa led by Africa in collaboration with the UN and the international community. They reiterated that the African Stand-by Force and the African Capacity for Immediate Response to Crisis that are being operationalized within the framework of the African Peace and Security Architecture can contribute significantly to the maintenance of peace and stability on the African continent.

20. The Ministers discussed the possibilities for the mutual support of their initiatives at the 71st session of the UN General Assembly.

E.   BRICS Ministers of Foreign Affairs: 29 Sep. 2015, New York (USA)

MEETING OF BRICS MINISTERS OF FOREIGN AFFAIRS
29 September 2015, New York, United States

The BRICS Ministers of Foreign Affairs held their regular meeting on September 29, 2015, in New York on the margins of this annual session of the United Nations General Assembly which marks the 70th Anniversary of the founding of the United Nations and the end of the Second World War.

The Ministers paid tribute to all those who fought against fascism and militarism and for freedom of nations.

The BRICS Ministers reiterated their intention to contribute to safeguarding a fair and equitable international order based on the purposes and principles of the UN Charter, as stated in the Ufa Summit declaration. They recalled 2005 World Summit Outcome Document. They reaffirmed the need for a comprehensive reform of the United Nations including its Security Council with a view to making it more representative and efficient.

The Ministers discussed the current state of global economy and finances. They recognize the significant contribution of BRICS to the global economy and express full confidence in their economic prospects. They also highlighted the importance of decisive and effective actions to accelerate global growth. They reiterated the urgency of unblocking the IMF reform as a measure to reform global economic governance consistent with the interests and needs of the developing countries.

The Ministers stressed the importance of closer economic, financial and trade cooperation, particularly through policy coordination, timely implementation of the Strategy for BRICS Economic Partnership, and the full functioning of the New Development Bank and its African Regional Centre.

The Ministers expressed their full support for a successful outcome at the COP21 later this year. They called for a comprehensive, balanced and equitable agreement with legal force for the post-2020 period that is in conformity with the principles and provisions of UNFCCC to be attained in an open, transparent, inclusive negotiating process.

The Ministers expressed their concern over continued conflicts in various regions which undermine stability and security and provide fertile grounds for terrorist activities and cause migration waves.

They noted that terrorist activities of the extremist organizations which control large parts of territory of the Republic of Iraq and the Syrian Arab Republic pose a direct threat not only to all the countries of the Middle East, but to the whole international community.

The Ministers reiterated their strong condemnation of terrorism in all its forms and manifestations and expressed their conviction that a comprehensive approach was necessary to ensure an effective fight against terrorism.

The Ministers urged concerted efforts to counter terrorism on a firm international legal basis, under the UN auspices.

The Ministers stressed the need to continue support to the process of political settlement of the conflict in Syria on the basis of the Geneva communique of June 30, 2012.

The Ministers welcomed the efforts to resolve conflicts in Africa led by Africa. They believe that the African Stand-by Force and the African Capacity for Immediate Response to Crises that are being operationalized in the framework of the African Peace and Security Architecture have a significant potential in the maintenance of peace and stability on the African continent.

The Ministers reiterated their deep concern about the situation in Ukraine. They emphasized that there is no military solution to the conflict and that the only way to reconciliation is through inclusive political dialogue. The Ministers called on all parties to comply with all provisions of the Minsk Agreements adopted in February 2015. They urged the parties to observe the achieved ceasefire and make it sustainable.

The Parties discussed the possibilities for the mutual support of each other's initiatives at the 70th session of the UN General Assembly.

The Ministers commended Russia for hosting the VII BRICS Summit in Ufa and expressed their satisfaction with the progress achieved in the implementation of the Ufa Action Plan.

The Minister of Foreign Affairs of India informed the partners of the preparations for the VIII BRICS Summit.

F.   BRICS Deputy Foreign Ministers: 22 May 2015, Moscow (RUS)

JOINT COMMUNIQUÉ
ON THE OUTCOME OF THE MEETING OF BRICS DEPUTY FOREIGN MINISTERS ON
THE SITUATION IN THE MIDDLE EAST (WEST ASIA) AND NORTH AFRICA
22 May 2015, Moscow, Russia

The participants of the meeting expressed their concern about internal crises that have emerged in a number of states in the region in recent years. They firmly advocated that these crises should be resolved in accordance with the international law and only through peaceful means, without resorting to force and external interference and through establishing broad national dialogue with due respect for independence, territorial integrity and sovereignty of the countries of the region. The participants emphasized the legitimacy of the aspirations of the peoples of the region to enjoy full political and social freedoms and for respect to human rights.

BRICS members stand for consolidating international efforts to combat the global threats of violent extremism and terrorism. They stressed that counter-terrorism measures should be undertaken on the firm basis of international law under the aegis of the UN and its Security Council. The participants of the meeting supported the Russian initiative of conducting at the UNSC a comprehensive analysis of causes that have led to the outburst of terrorist activity in the Middle East (West Asia) and North Africa.

In the course of the meeting the role of the UN Security Council as the international body bearing the main responsibility for maintaining international peace and security was underlined. It was also stressed that military interventions that have not been authorized by the Security Council are incompatible with the UN Charter and unacceptable.

Deputy Ministers of Foreign Affairs of BRICS states expressed their deep concern with regard to the continuing violence in Syria, deterioration of humanitarian situation and growing threat of international terrorism and extremism in that country.

The participants confirmed their solid support for the sovereignty and territorial integrity of the Syria and the need for a peaceful solution, led by the Syrians, to the conflict. They also called for renewed efforts towards a political and diplomatic solution in Syria through a broad dialogue on the basis of the Geneva Communiqué of June 30, 2012 without preconditions. In this regard they positively assessed the inter-Syrian consultations with the participation of delegations from the Government of Syria and opposition groups, held in Moscow in January and April 2015 as well as the efforts of the Special Envoy of the UN Secretary General Staffan de Mistura aimed at the resumption of Geneva process.

While condemning terrorism in all its forms and manifestations, the BRICS members called upon all Syrians to join ranks in the face of this dangerous threat and urged the international community to strictly abide by all the obligations pursuant to UNSC resolutions 2170 (2014), 2178 (2014) and 2199 (2015).

While condemning the use of chemical weapons by anyone under any circumstances, BRICS countries called upon the international community to remain united while addressing any allegations on the use of chlorine gas as a weapon in Syria and stressed the importance of continued cooperation between OPCW Technical Secretariat and Syrian authorities.

The BRICS states expressed serious concern about the escalation of the armed conflict in Libya, highlighting its extremely negative consequences for the Middle East (West Asia) and North Africa and the Sahel region. It was noted that the military intervention into this country in 2011 led to the breakdown of integrated state institutes, effective army and law-enforcement bodies, which in turn resulted in the rise of activities of terrorist and extremist groups. The participants expressed their support for the steps undertaken by legitimate Libyan authorities in combating the terrorist threat.

Underlining the urgency to safeguard the sovereignty of the country and its territorial integrity, they reaffirmed the need to overcome the dissensions between Libyan political forces and to achieve an agreement on the formation of a National Unity Government as soon as possible. In this context, they expressed their support for the efforts to foster the interLibyan dialogue by the Special Representative of the UN Secretary General for Libya Bernardino Leon, by the neighboring countries and by the African Union.

The participants of the meeting expressed their concern over the continuing armed conflict in the Yemen Republic which led to the killing of thousands of civilians, including women and children, and to the destruction of a significant part of vital civilian infrastructure, bringing the situation in Yemen on the verge of a humanitarian catastrophe. The participants welcomed the appointment of a new Special Envoy for Yemen and expressed their hope that Mr. Ismail Ould Cheikh Ahmed's work will be successful in reviving a peaceful and inclusive Yemeni-led political process that meets the legitimate demands and aspirations of the Yemeni people.

In this regard the BRICS states called for the immediate ceasefire in Yemen, urging all parties to the Yemeni conflict to resume the nation-wide dialogue in which representatives of Yemeni political forces and different groups of Yemeni population could participate in discussing the future of their country. The participants supported the UNSC call on the Secretary-General to convene a conference of all Yemeni stakeholders, with the intention of brokering a consensus-based political solution to Yemen's crisis.

The BRICS members declared their readiness to provide relevant humanitarian aid and diplomatic assistance in resolving the situation in Yemen.

The participants in the meeting were unanimous that the period of the fundamental transformations that is taking place in the Middle East (West Asia) and North Africa states should not be used as pretext to delay resolution of long-standing conflicts, in particular the Palestinian-Israeli. In this regard they confirmed their commitment to achieving the comprehensive, just and lasting settlement of the Palestinian-Israeli conflict on the basis of the universally recognized international legal framework including respective UN Security Council resolutions, the Madrid principles and the Arab Peace Initiative.

The BRICS states called for an early resumption of the Palestinian-Israeli negotiations aiming at establishing an independent, viable and territorially contiguous Palestinian State within the borders based on June 4, 1967 lines and with East Jerusalem as its capital. They supported the Russian role in the Middle East Quartet aimed at achieving these ends as soon as possible. The BRICS countries expressed their readiness to contribute on a bigger scale towards a just and lasting resolution of the Middle East conflict.

The participants of the meeting appealed to the Palestinians and Israelis to undertake positive steps towards each other to restore mutual trust and create favorable conditions for restarting talks, avoiding unilateral steps, in particular settlement activity in the Occupied Palestinian Territories. They stood for overcoming the inter-Palestinian split based on the PLO political platform and the Arab Peace Initiative.

The BRICS members welcomed the decisions reached on April 2, 2015 in the course of negotiations between "5+1" and Iran concerning the key parameters of the final settlement of the situation related to the Iranian nuclear program. They confirmed every country's right to peacefully develop its atomic energy under IAEA safeguards and observing the norms of international law.

They dully noted the importance of building a system of relations in the Gulf zone that would guarantee equal and reliable security to all States of the sub-region.

The participants decided to convene consultations at the level of Deputies Foreign Ministers of BRICS countries once every year with a venue to be a country hosting BRICS summit. The next consultations will be held in India in 2016.

The participants of the meeting also agreed on the advisability of holding regular consultations on the Middle East (West Asia) and North Africa topics at various venues, including the UN, and confirmed their support for holding informal meetings of their representatives.

G.   BRICS Ministers of Foreign Affairs (Nuclear Security Summit): 24 Mar. 2014, The Hague (NLD)

MEETING OF BRICS MINISTERS ON THE SIDELINES OF THE NUCLEAR SECURITY SUMMIT
24 March 2014, The Hague, Netherlands

Minister Maite Nkoana-Mashabane convened a BRICS Foreign/International Relations Ministers' meeting on Monday, 24 March 2014, on the margins of the Nuclear Security Summit in The Hague, Netherlands.

The meeting was attended by Minister Sergey Lavrov of the Russian Federation, Minister Salaman Khursid of the Republic of India, Minister Wang Yi of the People's Republic of China and Ambassador Carlos Antonio Paranhos, Under-Secretary General for Political Affairs of the Federative Republic of Brazil.

The Ministers recalled the outcome of the Sanya Declaration adopted at the 3rd BRICS Summit held in China, in April 2011, which articulated the fundamental principles that brought the BRICS countries together, namely:

"the overarching objective and strong-shared desire for peace, security, development and cooperation that brought together BRICS countries with the total population of nearly 3 billion from different continents. BRICS aims at contributing significantly to the development of humanity and establishing a more equitably and fair world."

The Declaration further noted that:

"we affirm that the BRICS and other emerging countries have played an important role in contributing to world peace, security and stability, boosting global economic growth, enhancing multilateralism and promoting greater democracy in international relations."

The BRICS Foreign/International Relations Ministers reflected on the political developments in their regions, as well as reviewed cooperation among BRICS countries following the comprehensive implementation of the eThekwini Action Plan.

The Ministers reflected that the role of governments in contemporary world politics should focus on pertinent areas where leadership is required, notably in finance, security, information and production.

The Ministers noted with concern, the recent media statement on the forthcoming G20 Summit to be held in Brisbane in November 2014. The custodianship of the G20 belongs to all Member States equally and no one Member State can unilaterally determine its nature and character.

They reflected on challenges to peace and security, notably the significant infringements of privacy and related rights in the wake of the cyber threats experienced, for which there is a need to address these implications in respect of national laws as well as in terms of international law.

They agreed that BRICS countries would continue to act as positive catalysts for inclusive change in the transformation process towards a new and more equitable global order. The BRICS agenda is not centered around any specific country or related issue and shares a common vision which drives it to also increasingly identify common areas for cooperation to assist with finding global solutions to global challenges.

BRICS countries agreed that the challenges that exist within the regions of the BRICS countries must be addressed within the fold of the United Nations in a calm and level- headed manner. The escalation of hostile language, sanctions and counter-sanctions, and force does not contribute to a sustainable and peaceful solution, according to international law, including the principles and purposes of the United Nations Charter.

The BRICS Foreign/International Relations Ministers wished the Federative Republic of Brazil well for the successful hosting of the FIFA World Cup and the hosting of the Sixth BRICS Summit.

H.   BRICS Foreign Ministers (68th UNGA): 26 Sep. 2013, New York (USA)

JOINT STATEMENT
ISSUED ON THE OCCASION OF THE BRICS FOREIGN MINISTERS MEETING ON THE SIDELINES OF THE 68TH UN GENERAL ASSEMBLY
26 September 2013, New York, United States

The BRICS Foreign Ministers met on 26 September 2013 on the sidelines of the 68th session of the United Nations General Assembly.

The Ministers congratulated the South African Presidency and appreciated the good pace of implementation of the eThekwini Action Plan.

The Ministers exchanged their points of view on the following issues of the United Nations agenda.

SYRIA

The Ministers expressed deep concern about the ongoing violence and the deterioration of the humanitarian situation in Syria. They called upon all parties to commit immediately to a complete cease-fire, to halt violence and to end all violations of human rights and humanitarian law.

Taking note of the Report of the United Nations Secretary-General, the Ministers strongly condemned the use of such weapons by anyone in any circumstances.

The Ministers expressed satisfaction with recent important developments that bring renewed hope for a peaceful resolution to the Syrian conflict. They welcomed the framework agreement for the elimination of Syrian chemical weapons reached by Russia and the United States. They further welcomed, in particular, the decision of the Government of the Syrian Arab Republic to accede to the Chemical Weapons Convention and the commitment of the Syrian authorities to provisionally apply the Convention prior to its entry into force and the delivery of the initial roster. They recognised the key responsibility of the Organisation for the Prohibition of Chemical Weapons (OPCW) in this regard and look forward to the decisions of the OPCW and the Security Council in support to the Framework Agreement.

The Ministers reiterated that there is no military solution to the conflict and that it is time for diplomacy.

They stressed that the elimination of chemical weapons and the political process aimed at resolving the Syrian conflict should be pursued in parallel. They also reiterated their support for the convening of an international conference on the Syrian situation as early as possible. They stressed that only an inclusive political process, led by the Syrians, as recommended in the Action Group on Syria Communiqué issued in 2012 could lead to peace, to the effective protection of civilians and to the realization of the legitimate aspirations of the Syrian society for freedom and prosperity. They expressed their full support to the efforts of the UN-Arab League Representative Lakhdar Brahimi in helping finding a political solution to the crisis.

MIDDLE-EAST PEACE PROCESS

The Ministers welcomed the announcement of the resumption of negotiations between Palestinians and Israelis as an encouraging development. They reaffirmed that the resolution of the Israeli-Palestinian conflict is a prerequisite for building a sustainable and lasting peace in the Middle East region. They expressed their expectation that this renewed effort will lead to a two-state solution with a contiguous and economically viable Palestinian state, existing side by side in peace with Israel, within internationally recognized borders, based on those existing on 4 June 1967, with East

Jerusalem as its capital. In recalling the primary responsibility of the UNSC in maintaining international peace and security, they noted the importance that the Quartet reports regularly to the Council about its efforts, which should contribute to concrete progress. They expressed concern about the construction of Israeli settlements in the Occupied Palestinian Territories, which constitutes a violation of international law and is harmful to the peace process.

CYBER SECURITY

The Ministers expressed their concern about the reported practices of unauthorized interception of communications and data from citizens, businesses and members of governments, compromising national sovereignty and individual rights. They reiterated that it is important to contribute to and participate in a peaceful, secure, and open cyberspace and emphasized that security in the use of Information and Communication Technologies (ICTs) through universally accepted norms, standards and practices is of paramount importance.

The Ministers thanked Brazil for the briefing on the plans and preparations for the VI BRICS Summit to be held in 2014.

I.   BRICS Deputy Ministers of Foreign Affairs: 24 Nov. 2011, Moscow (RUS)

JOINT STATEMENT
OF THE OCCASION OF THE MEETING OF THE BRICS DEPUTY MINISTERS OF FOREIGN AFFAIRS ON THE SITUATION IN THE MIDDLE EAST AND NORTH AFRICA
24 November 2011, Moscow, Russia

On November 24th, 2011, Deputy Ministers of Foreign Affairs of Brazil, Russia, India, China and South Africa met in the format of BRICS to discuss the situation in the Middle East and North Africa (MENA).

The Participants in the meeting underlined the legitimacy of the aspirations of the peoples of the region for greater political and social rights. They agreed that the transformation processes in the region created the need to search for ways of addressing crises in MENA within the framework of international law and only through peaceful means, without resorting to force, through establishing a broad national dialogue with due respect for independence, territorial integrity and sovereignty of the countries in the region. They rejected violence as a means of achieving political goals. They emphasized the need for full respect of human rights by all sides, especially by the authorities, in protecting unarmed civilians.

The role of the UN Security Council was emphasized, since it bears the primary responsibility for the maintaining international peace and security. It was noted that all parties should strictly implement UNSC decisions. They noted that it was inadmissible to impose solutions on the MENA states through outside intervention in the internal political processes.

The BRICS Deputy Foreign Ministers stressed that the only acceptable way to resolve the internal crisis in Syria is through urgent peaceful negotiations with participation of all parties as provided by the Arab League initiative taking into account the legitimate aspirations of all Syrians. Any external interference in Syria's affairs, not in accordance with the UN Charter, should be excluded. In this context the experience of the international community with regard to developments in Libya needs a thorough review to see if the actions taken were in conformity with the provisions of the relevant resolutions of the UN Security Council.

The Participants expressed their support for the Libyan people's democratic aspirations on the basis of public consensus and through a comprehensive national political dialogue with participation of all segments of Libyan society. They reaffirmed the importance of strengthening the leading role of the United Nations and its Security Council in post-conflict settlement and reconstruction in Libya. In this regard, the Participants emphasized the importance of establishment of the United Nations mission in Libya tasked to support the transition process in the country. They also noted the demand for consolidated efforts by the international community, including those of the African Union, with a view to help overcome the devastating consequences of the civil war and reaffirmed the readiness of the BRICS countries to make meaningful contributions to building a free, democratic and stable Libya that enjoys development.

The BRICS countries welcomed the signing of the GCC initiative concerning the peaceful transition of power in Yemen, which took place in Riyadh on November 23. They highly appreciated the constructive position of the Yemeni parties, which demonstrated their responsibility and concern for the interests of the country and its people. The Participants acknowledged the successful efforts undertaken by the international community, Secretary-General of the GCC Mr. Abdellatif Zayani and representative of the UN Secretary-General Mr. Jamal Benomar. The Participants called on all the political forces of Yemen to now do their utmost to implement the agreement on transition of power peacefully. The Participants considered that the approach adopted for addressing the situation in

Yemen, based on the dialogue between the authorities and the opposition, can be applied to similar situations in the region.

The Participants agreed that the period of fundamental transformation taking place in the states of the Middle East and North Africa should not be used as a pretext to delay resolution of lasting conflicts but rather it should serve as an incentive to settle them, in particular the Arab-Israeli one. Resolution of this and other long-standing regional issues would generally improve the situation in the Middle East and North Africa. Thus, at the meeting, the Participants confirm their commitment to achieving comprehensive, just and lasting settlement of the Arab-Israeli conflict on the basis of the universally recognized international legal framework including the relevant UN resolutions, the Madrid principles and the Arab Peace Initiative.

The BRICS states support the resumption of the Palestinian-Israeli negotiations aiming at the establishment of an independent, viable and territorially contiguous Palestinian State with full sovereignty within the 1967 borders, with agreed-upon territorial swaps and with East Jerusalem as its capital. They also encouraged the Quartet to intensify its efforts towards early realization of these goals.

The Participants support Palestinian efforts to achieve UN membership. They also underscored the importance of direct negotiations between the parties to reach final settlement. They call upon Palestinians and Israelis to take constructive measures, rebuild mutual trust and create the right conditions for restarting negotiations, while avoiding unilateral steps, in particular settlement activity in the Occupied Palestinian Territories. They advocated the earliest reunification of the Palestinians. A united position of the Palestinians based on the PLO principles and the Arab Peace Initiative would contribute to progress towards a Palestinian-Israeli settlement, achieving lasting peace and providing security for all the countries and peoples of the region.

The Participants are highly concerned about security and stability in the Gulf region, call for political dialogue in resolving differences and are against the use and threat of force. They advocate settling the situation concerning Iran's nuclear programme only through political and diplomatic means and establishing dialogue between all the parties concerned, in particular between Iran and P5+1, as well as between Iran and the IAEA, in order to clarify the questions regarding Iran's nuclear programme. It has been emphasized that imposing additional and unilateral sanctions on Iran is counterproductive and would only exacerbate the situation. The BRICS states expressed their hope for the successful holding of the 2012 Conference to be attended by all states of the Middle East, on the establishment of the Middle East free of nuclear weapons and all other weapons of mass destruction, on the basis of arrangements freely arrived at by the states of the region.

The Participants stressed the necessity to build a system of relations in the Gulf region that would guarantee equal and reliable security for all States of the sub-region.

The Participants agreed on the convenience of regular consultations on the Middle East and North Africa issues in different fora, including the UN, and reaffirmed their support for informal meetings among their representatives.

J.   BRICS Ministers of Foreign Relations: 16 May 2008, Yekaterinburg (RUS)

MEETING OF MINISTER OF FOREIGN RELATIONS OF BRAZIL, MINISTER OF FOREIGN AFFAIRS OF THE RUSSIAN FEDERATION, MINISTER OF EXTERNAL AFFAIRS OF THE REPUBLIC OF INDIA, AND MINISTER OF FOREIGN AFFAIRS OF THE PEOPLE'S REPUBLIC OF CHINA

16 May 2008, Yekaterinburg, Russia

The Foreign Ministers of Brazil, Russia, India and China (BRIC) held their meeting in Yekaterinburg (Russia) on May 16, 2008.

1.   They emphasized the prospects of the BRIC dialogue based on mutual trust and respect, common interests, coincidence or similarity of approaches toward the pressing problems of global development.

2.   The Ministers agreed that building a more democratic international system founded on the rule of law and multilateral diplomacy is an imperative of our time. They reaffirmed the commitment of the BRICs to work together and with other states in order to strengthen international security and stability, ensure equal opportunities for development to all countries.

3.   The Ministers reiterated that today's world order should be based on the rule of international law and the strengthening of multilateralism with the United Nations playing the central role. They reaffirmed the need for a comprehensive reform of the UN with a view to make it more efficient so that it can deal with the current global challenges more effectively. The Ministers of Russia and China reiterated that their countries attach importance to the status of India and Brazil in international affairs, and understand and support India's and Brazil's aspirations to play a greater role in the United Nations.

4.   The Ministers noted that sustainable development of global economy in the long-term as well as finding solutions to the acute global problems of our time, such as poverty, hunger and diseases are only possible if due account is taken of the interests of all nations and within a just global economic system. Among other issues they discussed the current global food crisis. The Foreign Ministers of Russia, India and China welcomed the initiative of Brazil to organize a meeting of economy and/or finance ministers of the BRIC countries to discuss global economic and financial issues.

5.   The Ministers expressed their strong commitment to multilateral diplomacy in dealing with common challenges to international security. They reiterated their support for political and diplomatic efforts to peacefully resolve disputes in international relations. A cooperative approach to international security is required that takes into account the concerns of all and addresses them in a spirit of dialogue and understanding. The Ministers emphasized that disarmament and non-proliferation are mutually reinforcing. They also agreed on the need for multilateral efforts to prevent an arms race in outer space.

6.   The Ministers unequivocally condemned terrorism in all its forms and manifestations, committed for whatever purposes. They reiterated their perception that terrorism constitutes one of the most serious threats to international peace and security and that the international community should take the necessary steps to enhance cooperation to prevent and combat terrorism. They particularly highlighted the UN cooperation framework and the need for all member states to implement international conventions of the United Nations and UN Security Council resolutions on fighting terrorism. The Ministers emphasized the importance of the implementation of the UN Global Counter-Terrorism Strategy in all its aspects and expressed their opinion that all member states

should make concerted efforts towards expeditious finalization of a Comprehensive Convention on International Terrorism at the UN.

7.   The Ministers noted a close interconnection between energy security, socio-economic development and environmental protection. They reaffirmed their commitment to the multilateral efforts aimed at reaching an optimum balance of interests between producers, transit states and consumers of energy resources. In this respect the parties emphasized the need for supporting programmes to increase access to energy, energy efficiency as well as the development and use of new and renewable sources of energy, including biofuels, compatible with sustainable development.

8.   The Ministers spoke in favour of strengthening international cooperation to address climate change in the context of the UN Framework Convention on Climate Change and its Kyoto Protocol. They expressed their desire to work closely together in order to carry out the Bali commitments.

9.   The Ministers spoke in favour of intensifying the dialogue to achieve the internationally agreed development goals, primarily the Millennium Development Goals, on the basis of global partnership. They support international efforts to combat hunger and poverty.

10. The Ministers noted that the South-South cooperation is an important element of international efforts in the field of development. It was emphasized that the South-South cooperation does not replace but rather complements the traditional forms of development assistance.

11. The Ministers looked forward to continued cooperation between the Group of Eight and its traditional dialogue partners.

12. The Foreign Ministers of Brazil, Russia and India reaffirmed their countries' support for the 2008 Beijing Olympic Games.

13. The Ministers reached an understanding to hold the next BRIC ministerial meeting on the margins of the 63rd session of the UN General Assembly, in New York, in September 2008. The next standalone BRIC Ministerial will be hosted by India.

III.2. BRICS Trade Ministers

A. 8th Meeting of Trade Ministers: 5 Jul. 2018, Magaliesburg (ZAF)

JOINT COMMUNIQUE

1. The 8th BRICS Trade Ministers met on 5 July 2018 in Magaliesburg, South Africa under the chairmanship of Dr. Rob Davies, Minister of Trade and Industry of South Africa. We met in preparation of the 10th Summit convened under the theme "BRICS in Africa: Collaboration for Inclusive Growth and Shared Prosperity in the 4th Industrial Revolution" and had open and constructive discussions.

Global economic developments

2. We note with satisfaction the global economic recovery, albeit still slow in some parts of the world. Downside risks to the global economy, however, remain.

3. We note, with much concern that the world economy remains unbalanced and there is increasing backlash against globalization. Many countries are becoming more inward looking with some major players in international trade seemingly moving away from multilateralism to focus on bilateral trade arrangements.

4. We note with satisfaction that the intra-BRICS exports have significantly increased in recent years but agree that more should be done to increase trade, specifically value added trade, within BRICS.

Current state of play in the WTO

5. We reaffirm the centrality of the rules-based transparent, non-discriminatory, open and inclusive multilateral trading system (MTS), as embodied in the WTO. The MTS has contributed significantly to economic growth, development and employment over the past seventy years. We agree to make all efforts to strengthen the multilateral trading system and make the WTO more responsive to the needs of its members.

6. We recognise that the multilateral trading system is facing unprecedented challenges. We are deeply concerned with the systemic impact of unilateral measures that are incompatible with World Trade Organisation (WTO) rules and that put the multilateral trading system at risk. Of key concern is the disregard of the multilateral rules and principles that underpin international trade. We are further concerned about the increased trade tension which will without a doubt negatively impact countries, including BRICS.

7. We call on all WTO Members to oppose protectionism and honour their commitments, including those in previous Ministerial decisions, in the WTO.

8. We emphasise that global trade rules should facilitate effective participation of all countries in the multilateral trading system, that development must remain integral in the WTO's work and the need to continue to make positive efforts to ensure that developing country Members, and especially the least-developed country Members, secure a share in the growth of world trade commensurate with the needs of their economic development.

9. We emphasise the importance of a functional and effective dispute settlement mechanism. We express our concern on the impasse to the appointment of Appellate Body members and affirm our commitment to work together with other WTO Members to find a solution.

10. In this regard we endorse the BRICS Statement of support for an inclusive multilateral trading system and the Statement on WTO matters, **annexed as A and B**, respectively.

Strengthening intra-BRICS economic cooperation

11. We note that the Contact Group on Economic and Trade Issues (CGETI) has convened three meetings in 2018, and commend the officials for the outcomes achieved in various areas, as outlined below.

12. We direct the CGETI to continue its work in areas where it is possible to deepen intra-BRICS cooperation in a practical way to implement the consensus reached by the previous Leaders summits, including the Strategy for the BRICS Economic Partnership and the BRICS Action Agenda on Economic and Trade Cooperation, while respecting the tradition of each presidency focusing on selected issues in order to pursue a manageable agenda.

Promoting value-added intra-BRICS trade

13. We commend the CGETI for reconvening the Trade Promotion Working Group. We further welcome the commissioning of the review of the BRICS Joint Trade Study on increased value-added trade, and we endorse the terms of reference for the study **(Annex C)**.

Enhancing cooperation on technical regulations, standards, metrology and conformity assessment procedures

14. We endorse the Working Mechanism on technical regulations, standards, metrology and conformity assessment procedures aimed at enhancing co-operation in the fields of technical regulations, standards, metrology and conformity assessment procedures in order to facilitate and increase trade in goods. **(Annexed as D)**

Deepening intra-BRICS investment cooperation

15. We recognise the importance of investment cooperation especially in key sectors that support industrial and manufacturing output. We re-iterate the need for investment cooperation in new sectors that drive technological change particularly in the Fourth Industrial Revolution to ensure integration in the global knowledge and technology sectors.

16. We applaud South Africa's hosting of the BRICS Business Forum on 25 July 2018. The Business Forum aims to promote greater private sector participation in key sectors that will support inclusive growth and economic development, as well as stimulate intra-BRICS investments and encourage partnerships between BRICS companies to enhance foreign direct investments, promote building and integration of value chains and promote investments into key projects in Africa.

Cooperation in Intellectual Property Rights

17. We acknowledge that the Implementation Framework for Intellectual Property Rights Cooperation Mechanism (IPRCM) aims to strengthen and enhance IPR cooperation amongst the BRICS countries. **(Annex E)**

18. We endorse the IPRCM Action Plan **(Annex F)** which encapsulates specific practical activities. Notwithstanding the action plan, it is noted that each Chair will have the flexibility to pursue specific topics in line with its priorities and based on BRICS consensus.

19. We further endorse the development of the BRICS IPR Guidebook, which will serve as a practical guide for IP owners and users in BRICS countries and endorse the outline for the IPR Guidebook. **(Annexed as G)**

20. We also note cooperation under BRICS Heads of Intellectual Property Offices (HIPO) has been going on successfully for six years, which includes sustained progressive activities of cooperation at international fora and the endeavour to explore future cooperation in new technologies.

BRICS Cooperation on Inclusive E-Commerce Development

21. BRICS Ministers have recognised the importance of electronic commerce; beginning in 2015 with the endorsement of the Framework for BRICS E-commerce Cooperation; followed by the 2016 Trade Ministers' Communiqué, supporting cooperation on ecommerce; and subsequently resulting in the endorsement of the BRICS E-Commerce Cooperation Initiative and the establishment of the BRICS E-Commerce Working Group in 2017.

22. E-commerce is an increasingly important economic activity and is transforming the global economy. We undertake to enhance BRICS cooperation on inclusive e-commerce development.

23. We acknowledge the need to examine the development dimensions and the socioeconomic implications to ensure e-commerce better contributes to sustainable development and inclusive growth. We acknowledge in particular the need to address the digital divide. We take note of the e-commerce elements in the UNCTAD Information Economy Report 2017 on Digitalization, Trade and Development.

24. We acknowledge the commencement of the E-Commerce Working Group and agree to take forward our intensified efforts in promoting cooperation on e-commerce by endorsing the BRICS Cooperation Framework on Inclusive E-Commerce Development **(Annex H)** and continue work on initiatives agreed.

25. We recognise the usefulness of sharing experiences in promoting development through e-commerce as an ongoing activity and will explore the possibility of sharing best practices, including continuing discussions on developing case studies. We note the work done thus far and look forward to more efforts in this regard.

Trade in Services

26. We acknowledge that trade in services is an increasingly important economic activity for BRICS countries, driving global economic and trade growth and creating job opportunities, with BRICS countries' contribution to total global Trade in Services amounting to 12.1% in 2016, up from 8% in 2006 (World Bank, 2017). We recognise that BRICS countries have significant potential to enhance collaboration in services trade to promote mutually beneficial outcomes. In this regard, the 6th Meeting of the BRICS Trade Ministers, in New Delhi, India, endorsed the BRICS Framework for Cooperation on Trade in Services. Subsequently, the 7th Meeting of BRICS Trade Ministers, in Shanghai, China, endorsed the BRICS Trade in Services Cooperation Roadmap to further promote cooperation among members in areas of mutual benefit. We applaud the establishment of the BRICS Focal Points on Trade in Services and the initial exchange of information on international trade in services between BRICS members.

27. We are committed to strengthen cooperation in the field of International Trade in Services Statistics. BRICS countries will initially seek to identify areas in which gains are most realistically achievable. We are committed to promote information sharing and capacity building in Trade in Services by enhancing collaboration amongst organizations responsible for international trade in services statistics and other relevant governmental organisations in BRICS Member countries. Furthermore, we agree to continue the discussion on developing a guidebook on Trade in Services.

Cooperation w.r.t. Small, Medium and Micro Enterprises

28. The BRICS Ministers recognises the critical role that MSMEs and cooperatives continue to play in their contribution to economic growth and employment generation.

29. Furthermore, continued collaboration amongst the BRICS countries is significant in particular by promoting and developing the potential of Micro, Small and Medium Enterprises (MSMEs) and cooperatives in the economy.

30. The 10th BRICS Summit therefore further encourages the strengthening of MSME and Cooperatives in line with the BRICS MSME Cooperation Framework to promote cooperation between MSMEs; exchange of information and best practices on MSMEs regulation and support, facilitation of MSME's access to public services, financing, exports and international projects.

31. The BRICS Ministers mandate the CGETI to establish the institutional arrangement of MSMEs **(Annex I)** through holding dedicated CGETI sessions and establishing Focal Points to give effect to the MSME Cooperation Framework. This will contribute to fostering cooperation on MSME promotion and development amongst the BRICS member countries.

Monitoring mechanism for CGETI activities

32. We endorse the BRICS CGETI Monitoring Mechanism as a living document and commend the CGETI for developing a mechanism to track and monitor initiatives, which can be used by future presidencies when setting their own priorities and outcomes. Updating the mechanism would be the responsibility of each current Chair. **(Annex J)**

Other issues

33. We note various initiatives presented to the CGETI by Russia, namely: a BRICS Business Women Alliance for the purpose of supporting women's entrepreneurship; regulatory impact assessment; and economic development and integration of remote areas.

34. We note that Russia is a candidate for hosting the EXPO-2025 in Yekaterinburg.

35. We note commencement of the work on the BRICS Model E-Port Network initiated by China, including the capacity building initiative, and applaud the further discussions held in this regard. We note discussions guided by the ToR and the Annual Work Plan of the BRICS Model E-Port Network on a voluntary basis, and look forward to the Capacity Building Program to be organized in China in September 2018.

36. China will host China International Import Expo on 5-10 November 2018 in Shanghai and welcome BRICS members to display their products at the Expo. The BRICS members welcome the initiative, and encourage their business community to actively participate in it.

Annexes

A. BRICS Statement of support for an inclusive multilateral trading system

B. Statement on WTO matters

C. Terms of Reference for the review of the BRICS Joint Trade Study

D. Working mechanism on technical regulations, standards, metrology, conformity assessment, and accreditation

E. BRICS IPRCM Implementation Framework

F. BRICS IPR Action Plan

G. Outline for the Guidebook on intellectual property rights in BRICS countries

H. BRICS Cooperation Framework on inclusive e-commerce development

I. Terms of Reference to strengthen institutional arrangements on MSME cooperation J. BRICS CGETI Monitoring Mechanism

ANNEX A
BRICS STATEMENT OF SUPPORT FOR AN INCLUSIVE MULTILATERAL TRADING SYSTEM

The BRICS Trade Ministers emphasise the need for inclusive growth and global trade rules that facilitate the effective participation of all countries in the multilateral trading system. In particular the BRICS Trade Ministers:

Re-affirm their commitment to a rules based, transparent, non-discriminatory, open and inclusive multilateral trading system that promotes a predictable trade environment, the centrality of the WTO and reaffirm their opposition to protectionism.

Emphasise that global trade rules should facilitate effective participation of all countries in the multilateral trading system, that development must remain integral in the WTO's work and the need to continue to make positive efforts to ensure that developing country Members, and especially the least-developed country Members, secure a share in the growth of world trade that commensurates with the needs of their economic development.

Further emphasise that provisions for special and differential treatment, including amongst others in agriculture, remain integral. The BRICS Trade Ministers also stress the importance of preserving the necessary policy space for developing Members, especially least developed members; to pursue their development objectives, including industrialization, in order to promote their effective integration into the global economy.

Emphasise the importance of agriculture to our economies and the increasing need to ensure food security. Agricultural reform remains one of the priorities for the WTO. It is therefore critical to address trade distorting domestic support in agriculture with a view to correct the current systemic imbalances.

Stress that trade should support development and underline the need to strengthen the multilateral trading system so that it provides a strong impetus to inclusive prosperity and welfare for all Members.

Underline the importance of Aid for Trade initiatives and trade-related capacity-building that support projects identified by the recipient governments to overcome supply-side constraints, support infrastructure development, and facilitate the integration of developing economies, in particular LDCs in regional and global trade.

Emphasise the importance of a functional and effective dispute settlement mechanism in supporting a rules-based multilateral trading system and in promoting transparent and predictable trade relations among WTO Members.

ANNEX B
STATEMENT ON WTO MATTERS

We reaffirm the centrality of the rules-based multilateral trading system (MTS), as embodied in the WTO. The MTS has contributed significantly to economic growth, development and employment over the past seventy years. We agree to make all efforts to strengthen the multilateral trading system and make the WTO more responsive to the needs of its members.

The MTS is facing unprecedented challenges. We are deeply concerned with the systemic impact of unilateral measures that are incompatible with WTO rules and that put the MTS at risk. We call on all WTO Members to abide by WTO rules and to honor their commitments in the MTS.

We recall that the WTO dispute settlement system is a cornerstone of the MTS and is designed to enhance security and predictability in international trade. This system has proved to be more effective and reliable as compared to its predecessor in the GATT era. We note with concern the impasse in the selection process for new Appellate Body Members that can paralyze the dispute settlement system and undermine the rights and obligations of all Members. We, therefore, urge all Members to engage constructively to address this challenge as a matter of priority.

We, BRICS Ministers responsible for Trade, call upon WTO Members to work together to strengthen the WTO and to address the serious challenges confronting the Organization.

ANNEX C

TERMS OF REFERENCE FOR THE REVIEW OF THE BRICS JOINT TRADE STUDY OF 2014

BACKGROUND

1.   The first report of the BRICS Joint Trade Study was presented to the BRICS Trade Ministers during the 4th meeting held in Fortaleza, Brazil in July 2014.

2.   The 17th meeting of the BRICS Contact Group on Economic and Trade Issues (CGETI) held on 1-2 March 2018 in Johannesburg, South Africa, agreed to update the 2013/14 study. This draft the terms of reference is intended to guide the work. The reviewed Joint Trade Study will identify opportunities to promote greater intra-BRICS trade in value-added products to be advanced as per each BRICS member country's Revealed Comparative Advantage on its top 20 value- added exports.

3.   The Joint Trade Study review process was further undertaken through the presentation of the draft terms of reference which was agreed during the 1st Meeting of the BRICS Trade Promotion Working Group held on the margins of the 18th CGETI meeting on the 10 May 2018.

4.   The final terms of reference for the review of the BRICS Trade Study will be presented to the BRICS Trade Minister's meeting scheduled to be held on the 5th July 2018 for their endorsement. The trade study will comprise of each BRICS member country's chapters on value-added products with potential for intra- BRICS trade.

5.   The BRICS Trade Promotion Working Group agreed that each BRICS Member country will undertake to appoint a research institution to prepare a revised draft country chapter and submits it to South Africa for consolidation into a study.

METHODOLOGY

1.   **For trade data,** we propose the use of a mutually agreeable source of data to be determined by experts by 31 July 2018

2.   **For defining value-added products,** we propose **categories (c) to (f)** of the UNCTAD classification that distinguishes between products by their technological and skills intensity, or the dominant factor input. Member states may on a voluntary basis explore other products in categories (a) and (b) in particular agriculture and agro-processing products for future analysis.

This nomenclature regroups all HS products into 6 groups at the HS6 or HS4 levels, namely:

		Classification	Example of products
Primary Products	a.	**Mineral fuels**	Coal, petroleum and other energy
	b.	**Non-fuel primary commodities**	Agricultural products, including fish,
Value- Added Products	c.	**Resource-intensive manufactures**	Aluminium, paper, leather, silk and furniture,
	d.	**Low-skill and technology intensive**	Textiles, clothing, iron and steel
	e.	**Medium-skill and technology intensive**	Organic and inorganic chemicals, rubber, machinery, electrical equipment and vehicles
	f.	**High-skill and technology intensive**	Pharmaceuticals and high-tech products

3.   The draft Study will be shared amongst the BRICS member countries by end November 2018.

REPORT OUTLINE

1. Executive summary of the study review with recommendations to the BRICS Trade Ministers
2. Introduction and background to the study review
3. Brazil
4. Russia
5. India
6. China
7. South Africa
8. Recommendations based on the updated chapters to the BRICS Trade Ministers

Proposed methodology for BRICS country chapters (15 pages per country case study)

1. Trade between Member States and BRICS – current and future potential (4 pages)
    — Bilateral trade flows between Member States and BRICS from 2013-2017 (aggregate historical picture of exports, imports, trade balance)
    — Top 20 imports from each BRICS member at HS4 level in 2017
    — Top 20 value-added exports to each BRICS member at HS4 level in 2017
    — Top 20 value-added products for BRICS intra-industry trade in 2017 at HS6 level
2. Tariff and non-tariff barriers affecting value-added exports (3 pages)
    — Tariffs applied to Top 20 value-added exports from each BRICS Member (HS4 level)
    — Non-tariff barriers affecting value-added exports of each BRICS Member
3. Potential trade analysis for value-added products (6 pages)
    — Top 20 high potential value-added products(aggregate and value-added sub-category wise) in BRICS for 2017 using Revealed Comparative Advantage (RCA) methodology at HS4 level
    — High potential value-added exports not fully exploited
    — High potential in the BRICS, realised by exports
    — High potential in the BRICS, export supply constraints

ANNEX D

WORKING MECHANISM ON TECHNICAL REGULATIONS, STANDARDS, METROLOGY AND CONFORMITY ASSESSMENT PROCEDURES[1] FOR COOPERATION TO FACILITATE TRADE AMONG THE GOVERNMENTS OF THE FEDERATIVE REPUBLIC OF BRAZIL, THE RUSSIAN FEDERATION, THE REPUBLIC OF INDIA, THE PEOPLE'S REPUBLIC OF CHINA AND THE REPUBLIC OF SOUTH AFRICA

Preamble

The Governments of the Federative Republic of Brazil, the Russian Federation, the Republic of India, the People's Republic of China and the Republic of South Africa, (hereinafter jointly referred to as the "Parties" and in the singular as a "Party");

NOTING the endorsement by the sixth Meeting of the BRICS Trade Ministers of the "Framework for Cooperation on Standardisation and Conformity Assessment" agreed to by the Contact Group on Economic and Trade Issues (CGETI) to ensure that the cooperation leads to a better understanding of each other's quality infrastructure,

NOTING the BRICS Leaders Xiamen Declaration, of 4 September 2017, paragraph 22, appreciating "the efforts and contribution of the BRICS Business Council and Business Forum to strengthening our economic cooperation in infrastructure, manufacturing, energy, agriculture, financial services, e-commerce, alignment of technical standards and skills development, the BRICS Action Plan on Economic and Trade Cooperation and the Joint Declaration of BRICS Business Council on Regulatory Cooperation on Standards";

RESPECTING the rights and obligations provided for in the World Trade Organisation's Agreement on Technical Barriers to Trade (hereinafter referred to as "WTO TBT Agreement");

RECOGNISING the importance of cooperation in the field of technical regulations, standards, metrology and conformity assessment procedures for identifying, preventing and eliminating technical barriers to trade with a view to increasing mutual trade flows;

RECALLING the objective set forth by the Heads of Government of the BRICS countries to increase intra-BRICS trade;

DESIROUS to conclude a voluntary and non-binding Working Mechanism on technical regulations, standards, metrology and conformity assessment procedures for cooperation to facilitate trade;

HEREBY AGREE as follows:

ARTICLE 1
Objectives

This Working Mechanism is hereby established for the Parties to co-operate in the fields of technical regulations, standards, metrology and conformity assessment procedures in order to facilitate and increase trade in goods, within the terms of the WTO TBT Agreement and the recommendations of the BRICS Contact Group on Economic and Trade Issues. This working mechanism is a non-binding living document taking into account the domestic regulatory regime of BRICS Parties.

---

[1] Conformity assessment procedures include: certification, testing, inspection and accreditation.

ARTICLE 2
Cooperation in Exchange of Information, Experiences and Programmes

The Parties will, in accordance with and subject to the domestic law applicable in their respective countries, exchange information and experiences by means of:

(a) making available information on the existing technical regulations, standards, metrology and conformity assessment procedures on request from the National TBT Enquiry Point of each Party;

(b) sharing experiences on the strengthening of National WTO TBT Enquiry Points[2] and National WTO Notification Points[3];

(c) establishing arrangements for the sharing of expertise intended to enhance technical competence of the relevant technical regulations, standards, metrology and conformity assessment procedures;

(d) compliance with the WTO TBT Principles and provisions concerning:

(i) the use of international standards and parts thereof as a basis for technical regulations and conformity assessment procedures;

(ii) sharing of ideas in Good Regulatory Practices; and

(iii) the implementation of the WTO TBT Agreement Annex 3 Code of Good Practice for the Preparation, Adoption and Application of Standards.

(e) identifying Central Focal Points to share information amongst BRICS within the ambit of this working mechanism as provided for in Annex 1;

ARTICLE 3
Co-operation in Standardisation

The Parties will, in accordance with and subject to the domestic law applicable in their respective countries, build confidence for mutually acceptable solutions, by means of –

(a) Promoting the use of relevant international standards and/or the use of relevant parts thereof in areas of mutual interest;

(b) encouraging standardisation bodies to explore the possibility of formulating a common position and assisting each other in [the (international) standardisation setting] organisations, such as International Organization for Standardization (ISO), International Electro-technical Commission (IEC), Codex Alimentarius Commission (CAC) and International Telecommunication Union(ITU) and other organisations that abide by the recognized 6 principles on standards development as adopted by the WTO TBT Committee on 13 November 2000 ; and

(c) fostering standardization bodies to work on other areas identified in the "Framework for Cooperation on Standardisation and Conformity Assessment" adopted by BRICS Trade Ministers in 2016.

---

[2] Article 10.1 of the WTO TBT Agreement.
[3] Article 10.10 of the WTO TBT Agreement.

ARTICLE 4
Co-operation in Metrology

The Parties will, in accordance with and subject to the domestic law applicable in their respective countries, build confidence for mutually acceptable solutions, by means of –

(a) Promoting collaboration between metrology organisations in experiences with metrological legislation and regulation;

(b) supporting and explore resources for scientific and technical collaborations conducted between national metrology institutes by means of personnel exchange, joint research, technical trainings, and bilateral comparisons, etc.; and

(c) Promoting cooperation and mutual support in international organization viz International Bureau of Weights and Measures (BIPM) and International Organisation of Legal Metrology (OIML).

ARTICLE 5
Co-operation in Conformity Assessment Procedures

The Parties will, in accordance with and subject to the domestic law applicable in their respective countries, build confidence for mutually acceptable solutions, by means of –

(a) Intensifying collaboration, with a view to facilitating access to their respective markets, by increasing the mutual knowledge and understanding of their respective systems in the field of conformity assessment procedures; and

(b) promoting collaboration between organizations responsible for testing, certification and inspection in the appropriate international fora.

ARTICLE 5.1
Co-operation in Accreditation

The Parties will, in accordance with and subject to the domestic law applicable in their respective countries, build confidence for mutually acceptable solutions, by means of –

(a) Intensifying collaboration, with a view to facilitating access to their respective markets, by increasing the mutual knowledge and understanding of their respective systems in the field of accreditation; and

(b) coordinating and consolidating positions, to the extent possible, within international accreditation cooperation structures, such as the International Laboratory Accreditation Cooperation (ILAC) and the International Accreditation Forum (IAF) and consider the possibility of agreeing to collaboratively improve involvement in the international accreditation activities and promoting the use of accredited conformity assessment bodies to both industry and regulators.

ARTICLE 6
Implementation

The Parties will, in accordance with and subject to the domestic law applicable in their respective countries –

(a) Negotiate mutually agreed to work plans for the fulfilment of this Working Mechanism;

(b) involve the representatives of the organisations as provided for in Annex 2 and supported by the Central Focal Point; and

(c) inform the Contact Group on Economic and Trade Issues of cooperation initiatives.

ARTICLE 7
Consultation on Specific Concerns relating to the Implementation of this Working Mechanism

Parties shall strive to resolve any specific concerns arising out of the interpretation and implementation of this Working Mechanism through consultations. These consultations shall be held in good faith and Partles shall, based on mutual consensus have full flexibility in conducting these.

ARTICLE 8
Communication

All communication related to this working mechanism shall be done through the Central Focal Point as provided for in Annex 1.

ANNEX 1
(referred to in Articles 2 and 6)

Illustrative list of entities

Central Focal Points

ANNEX E

BRICS IPRCM IMPLEMENTATION FRAMEWORK

1. BACKGROUND

In 2016 the BRICS Intellectual Property Rights Cooperation Mechanism (IPRCM) was established by the Contact Group on Economic and Trade Issues (CGETI) and subsequently adopted by the BRICS Trade Ministers. BRICS IP Co-operation guidelines were successfully concluded during the meetings of the BRICS CGETI and BRICS Trade Ministers, which took place from 30 July-2 August 2017. The principal aim of the IPRCM is to strengthen and enhance IPR cooperation among the BRICS countries.

Earlier, the BRICS Intellectual Property Offices Cooperation Roadmap was agreed by BRICS intellectual property offices in Magaliesburg, South Africa (SA) on 16 May 2013, and subsequently signed during the same year at the Assemblies of the World Intellectual Property Organisation (WIPO). Since the conclusion of the roadmap, BRICS Heads of Intellectual Property Offices (HIPO) have made significant progress in pursuing IP cooperation.

2. GOALS

During its Chairpersonship, SA prioritised the enhancement of BRICS initiatives and undertook to strengthen cooperation on issues pertaining to IP and public health. This includes, among others, exploring approaches relevant to patent expiry and generics.

In particular, the IPRCM Action Plan incorporates SA's proposals on practical activities on IP and public health.

The IPRCM Action Plan and proposed outline of physical BRICS IPR Guidebook have been finalised.

At the same time, CGETI ensures that IPRCM work is in coordination with HIPO and avoids duplication.

3. COORDINATION BETWEEN IPRCM AND HIPO

3.1 CGETI and HIPO interface

The work of CGETI and HIPO must be mutually supportive. To facilitate an approach that allows CGETI deliberations to be cognisant of HIPO developments, the Chairperson of HIPO may be invited to participate in CGETI meetings ex officio. Further, IPRCM and HIPO will coordinate and explore cooperation in all fields of IP.

3.2 Endorsement

3.2.1 Undertaking capacity building initiatives on IP:

Substantive patent examination is a key feature of an IP system. Effective examination of patents can ensure that IP offices are placed in a position to grant patents to inventions that genuinely comply with national law requirements. This is particularly relevant in the context of IP and public health where various patenting practices can result in sub-patentable subject matter being awarded monopoly protection or stifling of further innovation to the detriment of access.

HIPO has operationalised an examiner exchange program. Since 2016, the respective Chair Offices of HIPO have been organising a BRICS Examiners' Training Program for patent examiners of BRICS IP offices on a yearly basis. IPRCM endorses this exercise.

3.2.2 Exploring cooperation mechanisms to exchange sharing of information:

In the context of public health, numerous studies have shown that the availability of patent information is crucial, particularly in the sphere of health products. This reality has led to the establishment of major international medicines patent databases.

At BRICS level, HIPO established the project entitled "Information Services on IP" in 2016. The project aims to exchange patent information and make IP documentation available to the public.

IPRCM endorses and supports such activities, particularly in the context of IP related to health products.

3.2.3 BRICS IP Internet portal:

An IP BRICS website has been launched under the auspices of HIPO. The IPRCM can take advantage of the content on the IP BRICS website. IPRCM endorses and supports such activities.

3.2.4 New technologies and IP:

HIPO is exploring the possibility of capacity building initiatives incorporating new technologies into the IP sector. IPRCM welcomes cooperation on this matter, in particular, by way of exchange of best practices and information on current projects, as well as by encouraging common approaches to the use of new technologies by the authorities specialised in the IP field.

4. IPRCM ACTIVITIES

In furtherance of the work done in 2017, the following activities have been addressed:

4.1 Action Plan

The joint communique of the 7th BRICS Trade Ministers meeting noted the significant progress made in the draft 'Action Plan'. BRICS countries hereby conclude and endorse the same as a living and non-binding document. Notwithstanding, conclusion of the Action Plan, the Chair country of CGETI has the flexibility to pursue specific topics in line with its priorities based on established BRICS IPR Cooperation principles and mutual consensus.

4.2 Guidebook

With the view to promote trade between BRICS countries, the IPRCM has agreed to cooperate to refine the outline of the proposed BRICS IPR guidebook to make it user friendly and serve as a guide for IP owners and users in BRICS countries.

4.3 Further areas of cooperation

IPRCM undertakes to explore other areas of cooperation in the field of IP subject to further internal discussion and coordination with appropriate authorities within the BRICS countries by consensus. Among other initiatives, the IPRCM is exploring the following:

4.3.1 Enhancement of mutual cooperation at international fora:

There are many common interests and viewpoints among BRICS countries that could lead to joint initiatives and enhanced coordination at international fora such as, among others, the World Health Organisation and the World Trade Organisation. The BRICS forum may canvass its joint view in international policy matters related to IP and thereby increase the degree of influence accorded to the BRICS.

4.3.2 Exchange of views and experiences on competition policy as a tool to prevent the abuse of intellectual property rights:

Poor Substantive Search & Examination systems and the presence of patent thickets can lead to barriers to entry for new competitors. As a result, innovation is stifled rather than encouraged. A well thought-out competition policy goes hand in hand with effective enforcement guidelines to ensure that the IP system fulfils its role in the promotion of innovation, economic growth, and legal certainty. The IPRCM will explore cooperation and information exchange on IP and competition related matters.

4.3.3 Organisation of events of mutual interest such as conferences, seminars, and exchange of experts:

BRICS countries agree to exchange information on events that are relevant to IP and, where possible, to co-organise such gatherings. If required, appropriate coordination with HIPO will be pursued.

ANNEX F

BRICS IPR ACTION PLAN

Proponent	Topic
CHINA	Experts Dialogue under BRICS IPR Cooperation Mechanism Objective: Exchange of information on the latest developments in IPR legislations of BRICS countries.
SOUTH AFRICA	IP and Public Health Objective: Cooperation and information exchange among BRICS countries to use TRIPS consistent means of ensuring that IPRs promote rather than hinder access to health products.
BRAZIL	Innovation and IP Policies Objective: Cooperation between BRICS countries to identify and share knowledge about public IP policies and their relationship to innovation in partner countries. Context: The BRICS countries share the common challenge of stimulating and facilitating innovation as a mechanism for promoting economic development. Intellectual property protection is a determining factor in a country's innovation environment. Recognizing the uniqueness of challenges and solutions relevant to each BRICS member, it would be of mutual interest to exchange experiences in practical IP policy solutions that contribute to the development of innovative technologies. Topics for discussion: Debate on the relationship between innovation and IP in promoting development. The balance between IP protection measures and the diffusion dissemination of innovative technology. Exchange of experiences among the BRICS countries in the design, implementation and coordination of public innovation and IP policies. The role of competition policy in ensuring IP continues to foster and reward innovation. Facilitating the transfer of innovative technology between BRICS partners. Facilitating access to the IP system for small and medium-sized enterprises.
INDIA	TRIPS-CBD Objectives: Dialogue on possible ways to energize multilateral negotiations examine the role regional trading agreements and plurilateral treatises could play in protection of genetic resources, traditional knowledge and folklore.
RUSSIA	(1) Develop mechanism(s) to ensure communication between IPRCM and HIPO on the basis of reciprocity Objective: Development of communication mechanism between IPRCM and HIPO on the basis of reciprocity with a view to facilitate mutual support and coordination of activities between IPRCM and HIPO as two main BRICS platforms for IP cooperation, as well as exclusion of duplication of works carried out by BRICS IPR CM and BRICS HIPO. The participation of HIPO Chair in the IPRCM can be encouraged as was the case during the 17th CGETI. Context: During both 6th and 7th Meetings of the BRICS Trade Ministers at New Delhi and Shanghai the Trade Ministers took note of the positive development of both IPRCM and HIPO mechanisms of BRICS cooperation in the IP field. Consequently, Trade Ministers urged both the HIPO and IPRCM to co- ordinate and avoid duplication of their work. Modalities of implementation: monitoring of activities by IPRCM and HIPO on the basis of reciprocity (e.g. through mutual reporting or authorities involved in both mechanisms); holding consultations (through e-mail exchange or authorities involved in both mechanisms); allowing representatives of the HIPO Chair Office to be invited to participate in CGETI meetings ex officio; developing general principles of interaction with any other possible IPR-related cooperation mechanisms among BRICS countries. (2) Exchange of information and best practices regarding possible way of IPR protection, keeping in mind practical situation.

ANNEX G

OUTLINE FOR THE GUIDEBOOK ON INTELLECTUAL PROPERTY RIGHTS IN BRICS COUNTRIES

Protect your Intellectual Property Rights in BRICS

Volume I: Introduction to Legal System and IPR Regulatory Agencies
— Introduction to the Legislation, Executive and Judicial System
— Introduction to the IPR Regulatory Agencies

Volume II: Copyright
— Introduction to the legal framework of Copyright
— Protect your Copyright in 【 】
— Who can apply for Copyright?
— What is the Copyright administrative authority?
— What is the subject matter to be protected by Copyright?
— What are the conditions of conferring Copyright?
— What are the rights to be conferred on owners of Copyright?
— What are the limitations and permissible exceptions?
— Terms of protection
— What are the remedies available in case of infringement of Copyright?

Volume III: Trademarks
— Introduction to the legal framework of Trademarks
— Protect your Trademarks in 【 】
— Who can apply for Trademark?
— What is the Trademark administrative authority?
— What is the subject matter to be protected?
— What are the conditions for registration?
— What are the rights to be conferred on Trademark owners?
— What are the permissible exceptions?
— Terms of protection
— What are the remedies available in case of infringement or unauthorized use of Trademark?

Volume IV: Geographical Indications (GI) / Appellations of Origin (AO)
— Introduction to the legal framework of GI/AO
— Protect your GI/AO in 【 】
— Who can apply for GI/AOs?
— What is the GI/AO administrative authority?
— What is the subject matter to be protected?
— What are the conditions for getting protection?
— Concept of authorized users and rights granted to them?

- What are the benefits of registration?
- How to register GI/AOs of foreign origin/convention countries?
- What is the difference and interplay between GI/AO and Trademarks?
- Terms of protection
- What are the exemptions and limitations?
- What are the remedies available in case of infringement of GI/AO?

Volume V: Industrial Designs
- Introduction to the legal framework of Industrial Designs
- Protect your Industrial Designs in 【 】
- Who can apply for Industrial Design?
- What is the Industrial Designs administrative authority?
- What is an Industrial Design?
- What is eligible for protection as an Industrial design?
- What are the rights on conferred on Industrial Design owners?
- What are the procedures of applying for Industrial Designs?
- What are the permissible exceptions?
- Terms of protection.
- What are the remedies available in case of infringement of Industrial Designs?

Volume VI: Patents
- Introduction to the legal framework of Patent
- Protect your Patents in 【 】
- Who can apply for Patents?
- What is the Patent administrative authority?
- What is the subject matter to be protected by Patents?
- What are the conditions of grant of Patents?
- What are the rights conferred on patentees?
- What are the procedures of applying for Patents?
- What are the permissible limitations and exceptions?
- Terms of protection.
- Provisions regarding revocation and working of Patents?
- What are the remedies available in case of infringement of Patents?

Volume VII: Layout-Designs of Integrated Circuits
- Introduction to the legal framework of Layout-Designs of Integrated Circuits
- Protect your Layout-Designs of Integrated Circuits in 【 】
- Who can apply for Layout-Designs of Integrated Circuits?
- What is the Layout-Designs of Integrated Circuits administrative authority?
- What is a Layout-Design of Integrated Circuits?
- What is eligible for protection as a Layout-Design of Integrated Circuits?

ANNEX H

BRICS COOPERATION FRAMEWORK ON INCLUSIVE E-COMMERCE DEVELOPMENT[4]

BRICS members have recognised the importance of electronic commerce (e- commerce) in international trade. In 2015, the BRICS leaders endorsed the *Framework for BRICS E-commerce Cooperation* under the Russian Presidency, which aims to better integrate BRICS e-commerce markets. In 2016, the BRICS Trade Ministers' Communiqué emphasized the importance of cooperation on e- commerce and BRICS leaders further committed in the Goa Declaration to strengthen such cooperation. In 2017, under the Chinese BRICS presidency, discussions on e-commerce continued with a view to taking concrete actions to enhance e-commerce cooperation. The BRICS leaders and Ministers endorsed BRICS E-Commerce Cooperation Initiative, and agreed to establish a BRICS E- Commerce Working Group, which would meet when necessary, back to back with the CGETI.

In 2018 BRICS members agreed, within the mandate of the CGETI, to further enhance cooperation through the following:

- Promote cooperation on various aspects of inclusive E-commerce development.

- Exchange views and share experiences on best practices, including case studies, on the development aspects of E-Commerce and efforts to bridge the digital divides in order to maximize benefits and promote equitable and inclusive economic growth and sustainable development.

- Promote information sharing on the legal frameworks that ensure leveraging of e-commerce to promote inclusive growth and sustainable development.

- Share perspectives on policy tools to manage the potentially disruptive effects of e-commerce.

- Work with relevant international organizations to enhance understanding of e-commerce and its implications for economic development, including industrial development, based on agreed terms of reference, in relation to formal studies to be adopted by Members.

- Promote to the extent possible investment and development of ICT infrastructure – in recognition of the importance of adequate, cost-effective and reliable connectivity, which is a basic requirement for people and enterprises to engage successfully in e-commerce.

- Explore ways to ensure mutually beneficial economic development through e- commerce to facilitate a win-win outcome.

- Exchange views and share experiences, where possible, on the interface between data and trade related issues, for example: consumer protection, privacy, competition, trade and industry, etc.

- Build a deeper understanding on the relationship between e-commerce related data flows and economic development, and the implications thereof.

- Share information and explore methodologies, where possible, for the collection of e-commerce statistics.

---

[4] This Framework is a living, non-binding document.

ANNEX I

TERMS OF REFERENCE

TO STRENGTHEN INSTITUTIONAL ARRANGEMENTS ON MSME COOPERATION

MANDATE

In October 2016, BRICS Trade Ministers recognised the importance of the Micro, Small and Medium Enterprises (MSME) to the balanced economic development of the BRICS countries. The Ministers acknowledged the role of MSMEs as the engines of export led growth and employment generation given the highest rate of employment per unit of investment in MSMEs; and their crucial role in addressing regional disparity and poverty alleviation.

The MSME sector in many of the BRICS economies contribute directly or indirectly to nearly half of their exports, manufacturing output and GDP. With a view to ensuring greater business engagement amongst MSMEs in the BRICS region, the Ministers emphasised the importance of developing cooperation among MSMEs in the crucial areas of trade and investment.

The Ministers welcomed the BRICS Micro Small and Medium Enterprises (MSME) Cooperation Framework which encourages MSMEs in BRICS to strengthen mutually beneficial commercial relationships. The Framework sets the agenda of cooperation on MSMEs by the BRICS countries.

Based on the above background, it is therefore proposed that the institutional arrangement of MSMEs will be strengthened through holding dedicated CGETI sessions and establishing Focal Points to give effect to the MSME Cooperation Framework.

OBJECTIVES

The objective is to establish the institutional arrangement of MSMEs through holding dedicated CGETI sessions and establishing Focal Points to give effect to the MSME Cooperation Framework. This will contribute to fostering cooperation on MSME promotion and development amongst the BRICS member countries.

SCOPE OF ACTIVITY

The dedicated CGETI sessions will focus activities on the following specific topics:

i. Exchange information on regulatory framework and institutional structure of MSMEs in the region with a view to eventually creating a compendium.

ii. Consider establishing an association of MSME apex chambers and industry bodies in the BRICS region.

iii. Chalk out an agenda specific to MSMEs and explore participation of MSME stakeholders in any BRICS economic event such as trade fairs, exhibitions, buyer-seller meets, conferences etc.

iv. Build upon existing portals or create a separate BRICS MSME specific portal so as to provide a one point access to relevant information and data for mutual interest of all MSME stakeholders.

v. Exchange views on good regulatory practices (GRPs) by MSMEs in the BRICS region.

vi. Undertake joint studies and research on specific areas of mutual interest related to trade and investment for MSMEs in the BRICS region.

vii. Explore and exchange ideas on critical areas for MSMEs like technology transfer, innovations, access to finance and markets, etc.

viii. Any other MSME specific activity mutually agreed by the BRICS countries.

STRUCTURE AND COORDINATION

The BRICS MSME Focal Points shall consist of representatives from the governments of the BRICS members. Respective member countries will appoint relevant representatives based on the above scope of activities.

The coordination of the BRICS MSME Focal Points will be established by the network of contacts, which will communicate by virtual means, without the need of formal meetings.

The BRICS MSME Focal Points can build work connections with the BRICS MSME Business Council, the New Development Bank and other organizations whenever the Focal Points deem necessary.

MEETINGS

The meetings will be synchronized with those of CGETI. Additional meetings where necessary, could be conducted through electronic means when the CGETI is not in session. The members of the dedicated CGETI sessions may agree to invite international organizations or any other expert to attend the meetings and provide technical support based on their respective mandates, knowledge, expertise and global best practices.

WORKING LANGUAGE

For convenience and efficiency of communication, the working language shall be English.

Terms of Reference will be reviewed on the request of one or more members, particularly if there is a change in situation, with a view to modification or amendment.

ANNEX J
CGETI MONITORING MECHANISM

BRICS CGETI: MONITORING MECHANISM			
FOCUS AREA	SPECIFIC TOPIC	INITIATED	SUMMARY: LATEST STATUS
Trade Promotion	Promoting value-added trade		July 2014: The *Joint Trade Study* was presented to BRICS Trade Ministers. The Study identifies many opportunities to promote greater intra-BRICS trade in value-added products, as well as intra-BRICS investment into these sectors.
Trade Promotion	Virtual Trade Promotion working group	Brazil	October 2016: BRICS Trade Ministers adopted the *Terms of Reference of the Trade Promotion Working Group*. The 2nd BRICS Trade Fair took place from 18 to 21 September 2017 in Xiamen, China.
MSMEs	BRICS MSME dialogue	Russia and India CGETI-9; July 2015	October 2016: BRICS Trade Ministers adopted the *BRICS MSME Cooperation Framework*.
E-commerce	BRICS E-commerce cooperation	Russia and China CGETI-10, December 2015	August 2017: BRICS Trade Ministers endorsed the *BRICS E-commerce Cooperation Initiative* and the *Terms of Reference of the BRICS E-commerce Working Group*. Joint BRICS E-commerce study completed but report not yet processed. May 2018: The E-commerce WG convened the 2nd meeting in East London, South Africa.
Non-tariff measures	BRICS Mechanism on non-tariff measures (NTMs)	India CGETI-11, April 2016	October 2016: The **BRICS Mechanism on non-tariff measures** is still a working document and needs further discussion.
Trade in Services	Cooperation in trade in services	India CGETI-11, April 2016	October 2016: BRICS Trade Ministers adopted the *Framework for Cooperation on Trade in Services*. August 2017: BRICS Trade Ministers endorsed the *BRICS Trade in Services Cooperation Roadmap*.
Intellectual Property Rights	IPR Cooperation Mechanism of BRICS countries	China CGETI-11, April 2016	October 2016: BRICS Trade Ministers adopted the terms of reference of the **BRICS IPR Cooperation Mechanism (IPRCM)**. May 2018: The IPRCM convened the 2nd meeting in East London, South Africa.
Trade facilitation	BRICS Single Window Cooperation	Brazil and Russia CGETI-7, December 2017	October 2016: BRICS Trade Ministers adopted the *Framework for BRICS Single Window Cooperation*.
Non-tariff measures	Framework for Cooperation on Standardization, Metrology and Accreditation of conformity assessment bodies among BRICS countries	India CGETI-12, July 2016	October 2016: The *Framework for Cooperation on Standardization, Metrology and Accreditation of conformity assessment bodies among BRICS countries* was adopted by BRICS Trade Ministers.
Trade facilitation	BRICS Model E-port Network	China CGETI-14, March 2017	August 2017: BRICS Trade Ministers endorsed the *Terms of Reference of the BRICS Model E-Port Network*. March 2018: The E-port Network commenced

			its work with a first meeting in Johannesburg, South Africa.
Economic and Technical cooperation	Economic and Technical cooperation	China CGETI-14, March 2017	August 2017: BRICS Trade Ministers endorsed the *Framework on Strengthening the Economic and Technical Cooperation for BRICS Countries*
Investment	Investment facilitation	China CGETI-15, May 2017	August 2017: BRICS Trade Ministers endorsed the *Outlines for BRICS Investment Facilitation*.
Women empowerment	RICS Public-Private Dialogue "Women and E Economy"	Russia CGETI-14, March 2017	July 2017: The first *BRICS Public-Private Dialogue "Women and Economy"* was held in Novosibirsk (Russia). The event resulted in a decision to establish *BRICS Women's Business Club* September 2017: Russia circulated a concept note regarding BRICS Women's Business Club.
BRICS Economic Partnership	Strategy for BRICS Economic Partnership	Russia 5th Summit, March 2013	July 2015: *Strategy for BRICS Economic Partnership* was adopted by BRICS Leaders at the Ufa Summit September 2017: China and Russia prepared a report on the implementation of the Strategy for 2 years, which was presented at the Xiamen Summit
BRICS Economic Partnership	BRICS Roadmap for Trade, Economic and Investment Cooperation until 2020	Russia 5th Summit, March 2013	July 2015: *BRICS Roadmap for Trade, Economic and Investment Cooperation until 2020* was introduced to BRICS partners by Russia July 2016: By decision of CGETI and BRICS Sherpas and Sous-Sherpas, the issue of Roadmap implementation was transferred to the BRICS Business Council.
Regulatory Impact Assessment	BRICS Expert Discussion on Regulatory Impact Assessment	Russia CGETI-15, May 2017	May 2017: Russia presented an initiative on Regulatory Impact Assessment, which is aimed at carrying out expert public-private events on this topic.
Remote Areas Development	Economic Development and Integration of Remote Areas in BRICS Countries	Russia December 2017	March 2018: Russia presented the concept to CGETI-17. Members agreed that Russia will present the Initiative to Sherpas and Sous Sherpas so that internal discussions can take place and consensus obtained. Russia was requested to identify specific trade related issues to be taken to the CGETI.
Supporting the multilateral trading system	Inclusive multilateralism	South Africa CGETI-17, March 2018	March 2018: South Africa presented the concept, and will circulate a draft Narrative. Members will submit their inputs by 29 March 2018. Thereafter South Africa will consult Members towards a revised draft to be considered in the 18th CGETI.
E-commerce	Integration of electronic trading platforms	CGETI-17, March 2018	March 2018: Russia presented the concept to CGETI-17. Consultations are conducted within the framework of the BRICS Business Council.
Action Agenda	BRICS Action Agenda on Economic and Trade Cooperation	China 9th Summit, September 2017	September 2017: *BRICS Action Agenda on Economic and Trade Cooperation* was signed by Trade Ministers in the witness of BRICS Leaders at the Xiamen Summit

B.   7th Meeting of Trade Ministers: 31 Aug. 2017, Shanghai (CHN)

THE 7TH MEETING OF THE BRICS TRADE MINISTERS STATEMENT

1.   The 7th Meeting of the BRICS Trade Ministers was held on 1-2 August 2017 in Shanghai, China under the chairmanship of H.E. Zhong Shan, Minister of Commerce of the People's Republic of China. We reviewed the progress made in economic, trade and investment cooperation, exchanged views on cooperation in key areas, and reached broad consensus on the ways to further enhance BRICS cooperation.

Global Economy and BRICS Trade and Investment Cooperation

2.   We note positive signs in global economic recovery, yet in the meantime, profound challenges remain and there is still lack of robust driving force for global growth. Globalization has encountered significant setbacks and protectionism is on the rise. World economic growth is still on a winding road with uncertainties and destabilizing factors.

3.   We recognize that since the First Meeting of the BRICS Trade Ministers held in 2011, with the joint efforts of all BRICS countries, the economic and trade cooperation mechanism among BRICS countries has improved and pragmatic cooperation has deepened. We agree that, against the current global background, BRICS countries should further strengthen economic and trade cooperation, improve and broaden cooperation mechanism and scope, promote industrial and technical upgrading with a view to enhance economic complementarities and diversification in BRICS countries. Meanwhile, we should jointly tackle the challenges of economic globalization, promote open and equitable world economy, and uphold the common interests of the emerging markets and developing countries with a view to promoting strong, sustainable, balanced and inclusive growth.

Enhancing Trade Facilitation

4.   We welcome the entry into force and the implementation of the WTO Trade Facilitation Agreement. We believe that trade facilitation promotes the development of global trade through reduced trade costs and improved trade efficiency and business environment. To further improve BRICS trade facilitation and strengthen cooperation on the basis of the Framework for BRICS Single Window Cooperation, we endorse the Terms of Reference of the BRICS Model E-Port Network and agree to set up BRICS Model E-Port Network which will operate on a voluntary basis under CGETI. We encourage further information sharing and capacity building on E-Ports construction and operation to improve connectivity, through activities such as expert dialogues and workshops, and build a sound business environment. To further enhance trade facilitation among BRICS countries, we agree to strengthen cooperation in the area of standardization based on operationalization of the Framework for Cooperation on standardization among BRICS countries.

Cultivating an Enabling Investment Environment

5.   Investment facilitation can assist with promoting investment and also help stimulate the process of industrialization and structural transformation of host economies if aligned to national development strategies and objectives. We recognize the role of investment as an important engine of inclusive economic growth and sustainable development.

6.   Building on the existing BRICS outcomes on investment, and with a view to establishing a collaborative mechanism to tap the significant potential to boost intra-BRICS investment and enhance intra-BRICS investment cooperation, we agree to endorse the Outlines for BRICS Investment Facilitation. Recognizing that there are different ways of facilitating investment, the Outlines identify some of the existing good practices of various BRICS countries with regard to enhancing transparency, improving efficiency and promoting cooperation for consideration on a voluntary basis by members for information sharing, discussions and exploration, in line with their domestic legislation and regulations, specific circumstances, priorities and capabilities. BRICS countries fully preserve the right

to regulate, national policy space, policy making and approaches to investment in other bilateral, plurilateral and multilateral frameworks and processes.

7.   We call on BRICS countries to work together to enhance intra-BRICS investment, and to improve the countries' ability to attract investment through, with the support of UNCTAD, technical assistance and capacity building, thus maximizing the beneficial impact of investment.

Expanding Cooperation on Trade in Services

8.   Trade in services is driving global economic and trade growth and creating job opportunities. BRICS countries have significant potential in enhancing collaboration in services trade, which will inject new impetus for trade and economic cooperation. We agree to endorse the BRICS Trade in Services Cooperation Roadmap to further promote cooperation among members in areas of potential mutual benefits. We are committed to strengthening cooperation on information sharing, coordination and promotion, as well as capacity building. The Roadmap will endeavor to enhance cooperation, including exchange of information and promote and facilitate trade in services cooperation among BRICS countries. These efforts could be based on previous cooperation, and in accordance with consultations towards consensus-building. Pragmatic cooperation on certain fundamental service areas will be advanced step by step to expand collaboration. We welcome the progress in developing the ITC Report on BRICS Trade in Services.

Promoting Cooperation on E-commerce

9.   E-commerce has become one of the world's most dynamic and constantly evolving business activities, which is playing an increasingly important role in promoting trade growth, industry transformation and job creation, and has the potential to enable developing countries and SMEs to better participate in and benefit from global value chains and international trade. We duly acknowledge the challenges that digital divide imposes on many developing countries and emphasize the need to bridge the digital divide and address its socio-economic implications to ensure a-commerce better contributes to industrial development and inclusive growth. Recognizing the importance of promoting a-commerce development and cooperation, we agree to take further concrete actions to enhance a-commerce cooperation. We endorse the BRICS E-commerce Cooperation Initiative to jointly enhance cooperation on policy sharing, information exchange including on best practices, and capacity building in order to optimize a-commerce development environment and better leverage thee-commerce opportunities. We agree to establish the BRICS E-commerce Working Group and instruct officials to advance the cooperation guided by the adopted Terms of Reference. We will enhance interaction with business sectors and other stakeholders on a-commerce. We welcome the progress in developing the UNIDO-ITC Report on E-commerce Development, with special thanks to the IOs for their contribution.

Deepening the Cooperation on Intellectual Property Rights

10. As an important factor for economic growth, intellectual property rights (IPR) are closely linked to international trade development Recognizing that BRICS countries face many common challenges in the field of IPR, we note the positive progress made in the establishment of the Intellectual Property Rights Cooperation Mechanism among BRICS (BRICS IPRCM), and we congratulate the successful First Meeting of BRICS IPRCM held on May 23th 2017 in Beijing. We also note the progress made in the IP area at the BRICS HIPO (Heads of IP Offices) level.

In order to advance cooperation in this area in a coordinated manner, we endorse the BRICS IPR Cooperation Guidelines and welcome the progress made on the development of the Action Plan on BRICS IPR Cooperation, and will take concrete actions to promote information exchange, coordination and capacity building on IP, in particular with a view to improve public IP awareness and promote economic and trade cooperation among BRICS countries.

Supporting the Multilateral Trading System

11. We reaffirm the central role of the WTO in today's global economy. The WTO provides the multilateral framework of rules governing international trade relations, an essential mechanism for preventing and resolving trade disputes, and a forum for addressing trade related issues that affect

all WTO members. We remain firmly committed to a rules-based, transparent, non-discriminatory, open and inclusive multilateral trading system as embodied in the WTO. We reaffirm our commitments to ensure full implementation and enforcement of existing WTO rules and are determined to work together to further strengthen the WTO. We call for the acceleration of the implementation of the Bali and Nairobi MCM outcomes and for the WTO Ministerial Conference to be held this year in Argentina to produce positive outcomes.

12. We note with concern the sluggish global trade growth and the rise of protectionist measures. We will continue to firmly oppose trade and investment protectionism and support the ongoing work of the WTO and other International Organizations in monitoring protectionism. We recommit to our existing pledge for both standstill and rollback of protectionist measures and we call upon other countries to join us in that commitment.

13. We call upon the countries that have not joined the WTO to accede as early as possible and note the need for increased efforts to facilitate accessions, especially the need for flexibilities to be shown by Members for accession of least developed countries.

Strengthening Economic and Technical Cooperation

14. We recognize the importance of strengthening economic and technical cooperation and capacity building in the area of trade and investment, including initiatives to promote structural transformation to foster economic development and inclusive growth. We endorse the Framework on Strengthening the Economic and Technical Cooperation for BRICS Countries to conduct economic and technical cooperation and capacity building in areas of trade, investment facilitation, a-commerce, intellectual property rights, trade in services, and other related areas. These should be based on the willingness and actual demands of all BRICS countries. We are willing to make concerted efforts to mobilize more resources to support capacity building programs and encourage BRICS countries to take individual and collective actions, on a voluntary basis, to provide assistance and contribution. We welcome IOs and other stakeholders to facilitate and contribute to this process.

15. China announced it will host International Import Expo next year and welcome BRICS members to display their products at the Expo. The BRICS members welcome the initiative, and encourage their business community to actively participate in it.

16. We welcome the work done by the BRICS Business Council (BBC) and we will continue to work with the BBC and take heed of the opinions and suggestions from the business circle. We thank the WTO, UNCTAD, UNIDO and the ITC for their support to BRICS economic and trade cooperation, and welcome the continuous active participation of relevant IOs in the BRICS cooperation.

Other Issues

17. We welcome the First BRICS Public-Private Dialogue "Women and Economy" held in July 2017, and value its role in establishing the public-private partnership aimed at increasing women's participation in the economy.

18. We take note of the initiative to promote efforts aimed at sharing best practices regarding the implementation of the regulatory impact assessment system.

Annex:

I. Terms of Reference of BRICS Model E-Port Network

II. Outlines for BRICS Investment Facilitation

III. BRICS Trade in Services Cooperation Roadmap

IV. BRICS E-commerce Cooperation Initiative

V. BRICS IPR Cooperation Guidelines

VI. Framework on Strengthening the Economic and Technical Cooperation for BRICS Countries

Annex I: Terms of Reference (ToR) of BRICS Model E-Port Network

Background

1.   In 2015, the Strategy for BRICS Economic Partnership was approved by BRICS leaders, in which exchange of ideas and experiences on the development of a Single Window was highlighted. In 2016, the BRICS trade ministers endorsed the Framework for BRICS Single Window Cooperation. With the development of Information and Communication Technologies (the "ICT"), E-port emerges as particular form of an integrated electronic platform to process and monitor cross-border movement of merchandise and transportation vessels at a port level. This form of Single Window requires a closer co-operation among all relevant trade-related governmental authorities and agencies in relation to ports. In this context, as a step to implement the aforesaid documents and to realize and strengthen single window collaboration, one of the focus areas will be to develop a common understanding of Model E-port Network, promote cooperation and knowledge sharing network on E-ports among BRICS members becomes an avenue for exploring supply chain connectivity, information communication and technology sharing.

Objectives

2.   The objectives of BRICS Model E-Port Network is to explore a mechanism for improving supply chain connectivity and trade facilitation among

3.   BRICS members through the following means:

4.   Promoting further discussions among BRICS members with a view to building an understanding on the concept of the Model E-port Network including implications of the supply chain and trade facilitation in line with the objective of the BRICS countries and respective domestic legal frameworks of what E-port and Single Window are, how they could benefit BRICS supply chain and trade facilitation work, and how they could help BRICS countries accomplish their domestic objectives. Exploring the possibility and modalities of exchanging trade related information, while ensuring data security, and accuracy of the transmitted and processed information.

5.   Exchange information and identify possible areas for knowledge and capacity building in aspect of National Single Window best practice and E-ports modelling, development, operation and control.

6.   Strengthen cooperation in the field of ICT through the exchange of information on the introduction of advanced IT systems to enhance port management, logistics and trade facilitation.

7.   Exchange views and information on best practices for E-port and National Single Window Systems.

Activities

8.   Conduct expert level dialogue to exchange experience and share best practical solutions.

9.   Hold workshops and promote exchange of information on best practices and success cases in regard to specific issues which could include, among others, Single Window and Operational Center and explore the possibility of undertaking cooperative activities within the BRICS Model E- port Network in accordance with recommendation that might be agreed by the CGETI, if needed.

10. Hold workshops targeted at specific issues on a regular basis.

11. Deplore possible capacity building activities and pilot projects based on dialogues and workshops.

12. Strengthen collaboration with the BRICS Customs structures, such as the BRICS Customs Cooperation Committee and the Customs Working

13. Group on related cooperation activities, including holding joint meetings. The cooperation activities under this Network will be conducted on a voluntary and consensus basis, recognising that the BRICS countries are at different stages of development as regards the implementation of electronic trade processing platforms such as National Single Windows or E-Ports.

14. Structure

15. The Overseeing Body

16. The CGETI, in close collaboration with the BRICS Customs Working structure, is the overseeing body of the activities envisaged above.

17. Participation

18. The BRICS Model E-Port Network is an open mechanism established under CGETI. Participating bodies will be nominated by the members to join the network on a voluntary basis.

19. The Terms of Reference will be reviewed and modified upon the request of one or more members.

ANNEX II: OUTLINES FOR BRICS INVESTMENT FACILITATION

1. Investment and investment facilitation has been an important area of cooperation in BRICS. Trade Ministers endorsed BRICS Trade and Investment Cooperation Framework in 2013 and BRICS Trade and Investment Facilitation Action Plan in 2014. The leaders adopted the Strategy for the BRICS Economic Partnership in 2015 as the key guideline for expanding trade and investment within BRICS, and instructed that practical steps be taken for its efficient implementation. The 2016 Trade Ministers Communique also instructed that initiatives and proposals be put forth towards that objective.

2. Investment can promote sustainable development and inclusive growth. Investment facilitation can assist with promoting investment and also help stimulate the process of industrialization and structural transformation of host economies if aligned to national development strategies and objectives. There remains significant potential to boost investment within BRICS as well as enhance intra-BRICS investment cooperation. There are, however, no collaborative mechanisms in place to date to realize this potential.

3. In this light, with a view to establishing a collaborative mechanism to promote intra-BRICS investment and recognising that there are different ways of facilitating investment, including by targeting investments in specific areas to support industrial development priorities, some existing good practices of various BRICS countries to enhance transparency, improve efficiency and promote cooperation are outlined below. These can be considered for information sharing, discussions and exploration by BRICS Countries, including national Investment Promotion Agencies, in line with BRICS countries' domestic legislation and regulations, specific circumstances, priorities and capabilities:

4. Enhancing Transparency. Efforts towards greater transparency of investment laws, regulations and policy measures, such as making publicly available, including through electronic means, such laws, regulations and policy measures and their amendments in a timely manner; exploring the possibility of establishing or designating an Ombudsman or a National Focal Point to handle enquiries and provide information related to investment; and to the extent practicable providing opportunities for stakeholders to comment on investment draft legislations.

5. Improving Efficiency. Efforts to enhance the efficiency of investment screening and approval and give timely decision notification to the applicants; to enable the provision of additional information required for investment application; to foster to the extent possible cooperation and coordination among respective domestic authorities for procedural streamlining by, for example, establishing a

document-collecting "single window"; to lower the costs incurred in investment screening and approval to the extent possible and in line with national competency and capabilities; and to develop guidelines on responsibilities for investors on ethical business practices and corporate social responsibility.

6.   Promoting Cooperation. Efforts for an effective dialogue with the private sector and other relevant stakeholders, and exploration to address issues of interest on investment; for consultations among BRICS countries' competent investment authorities over cooperation areas and issues of common interest, as well as experience sharing; for enhanced exchanges among governments, investment facilitation agencies, industries, academic bodies and research institutions; for organization of investment-related activities on the margins of BRICS Summits to promote intra-BRICS investments; for exploration of the means to create a facilitative environment for investment and investors, including their strategic, technical and capital needs towards final realization of investment projects and for improving, through technical assistance and capacity building, the countries' ability to attract foreign investment.

7.   The above outlines will be considered on a voluntary basis. BRICS countries fully preserve the right to regulate, national policy space, policy making and approaches to investment in other bilateral, plurilateral and multilateral frameworks and processes.

Annex III: BRICS Trade in Services Cooperation Roadmap

Background

1.1   For all BRICS members, services industry contributes to more than half of the GDP, and services trade is becoming an increasingly important part of their foreign trade. According to the WTO statistics, in 2015, the BRICS' service exports totalled $ 0.54 trillion US dollars, accounting for

11.3% of global service exports. In terms of overall services trade, the aggregate of BRICS countries reached nearly $1.3 trillion which is 13.9% of the global commercial services trade. The BRICS members have a strong willingness to strengthen cooperation in the field of services and services trade, and have taken joint efforts to advance cooperation. In 2015, the Strategy for BRICS Economic Partnership was approved by BRICS leaders, in which the services sector was identified as a priority area for future collaboration, notably through further encouraging cooperation in service industry and trade in services, and enhancing the productivity and efficiency of manufacturing sector by developing service industry. In 2016, the BRICS trade ministers highlighted the importance of enhancing cooperation in trade in services and endorsed the Framework for Cooperation on Trade in Services, which identified possible areas of cooperation such as tourism, health, audio visual, professional, computer and related services, research and development, telecommunication and financial services. In Goa, the services industry was identified as a key area of BRICS members' future collaboration in BRICS leaders' speeches.

1.2   Based on previous discussions, BRICS members reaffirm their commitment to further enhance cooperation on services and services trade, in order to add driving force to BRICS economy as well as to create conducive environment for development.

Vision and Principles

2.1   Vision

This roadmap aims at further enhancing BRICS cooperation in order to achieve the following mid-term and long-term visions, while accepting the diverse perspectives of BRICS members on the subject.

2.1.1 Increased competitiveness of the BRICS members' services sector at the regional and global level and enhanced capacity to achieve sustainable development through services sector development and services trade.

2.1.2 Enhanced effectiveness of cooperation among BRICS members on services trade, leading to the increased impact of the BRICS in global services trade.

2.1.3 Increased participation of BRICS members' micro, small and medium-sized enterprises (MSMEs) in services sectors in regional and global value chains, leading to greater contribution to local economic development and job creation.

2.1.4 Enhanced supply capacity to meet BRICS members' increasing demand for more efficient, diversified and innovative services, through knowledge and skills development.

2.2   Principles

To achieve the above goals, BRICS members are encouraged to cooperate on the basis of the following principles:

2.2.1 Recognizing and respecting differences

BRICS members agree to pursue the vision of this roadmap taking into account the diverse perspectives and varying levels of liberalization, while at the same time recognizing and respecting social and cultural differences.

2.2.2 Sharing Opportunities

BRICS members recognize the value of information sharing with a view to develop trade in services, and will seek to work together amongst each other and/or collectively.

2.2.3 Improving trade relations

Bearing in mind the possible complementarities as well as social, cultural and economic differences between BRICS members, a pragmatic approach to enhance services trade cooperation and dialogue shall be adopted, and priority given to key sectors that offer the greatest opportunity for mutual benefit.

2.2.4 Win-win cooperation

Bilateral, plurilateral and collective cooperations are encouraged among BRICS members to achieve win-win and all-win. Whenever possible, cooperation in capacity building for services trade among BRICS members should be strengthened.

Areas of Cooperation, Information Exchanges and Capacity Building

3.1   Areas of Cooperation

3.1.1 BRICS members agree to seek to identify, in accordance with the Framework for Cooperation on Trade in Services, sectors to initiate exploration and dialogue on possible ways to cooperate, among others:

- Tourism and travel related services
- Healthcare services
- Audio-visual Services
- Professional services
- Computer and related services
- Research and development services
- Other business services
- Telecommunication services
- Financial services
- Construction and related engineering services
- Distribution services
- Educational services, including skill development

3.1.2 The roadmap endeavors to enhance cooperation including exchange of information and promote and facilitate trade in services cooperation among BRICS countries.

3.2   Information Exchange

3.2.1 Conduct joint research on the basis of consensus in services trade, exchange views on a regular or ad hoc basis and identify areas for cooperation. For all research projects, members will review the relevant Terms of Reference (ToR) to be proposed by the presidency or any other member and determine the entity or organization to which it will be committed.

3.2.2 Encourage the exchange of experience and expertise regarding the services trade sections in FTA agreements, cooperation protocols, MOUs and other projects which are signed or implemented in BRICS members.

3.3   Cooperation in Statistics

3.3.1 Support BRICS members' statistics agencies to carry out data reconciliation, analysis and information exchange, as well as regular exchanges on best practices related to methodologies for the collection and compilation of services trade data.

3.3.2 Encourage collaboration of statistical organizations in the BRICS member countries for capacity development in capturing services sector data. Explore exchanging trade data with partner countries to reduce the burden of data collection.

3.4   Capacity Building

3.4.1 To encourage and support the strengthening of BRICS members' capacity in services trade management, promotion, statistics, negotiation and international collaboration, through measures including but not limited to training and joint research. The beneficiaries include government agencies, research institutions, non-governmental organizations, enterprises etc.

3.4.2 To support research institutions and associations in their work regarding frontier technology, new business models and cutting-edge industries in services trade. To promote cooperation and, where feasible, a shared understanding, amongst BRICS members on emerging areas, including new services.

3.5   Coordination

3.5.1 Strengthen the regulatory dialogue: The BRICS members agree to exchange experiences and information on services regulations, and, where possible, to explore possibilities for mutual recognition of regulatory standards in line with international standards.

3.5.2 Regulatory transparency: All BRICS members are encouraged to publish all relevant rules, regulations and laws relating to trade in services, preferably in one of the official languages of the WTO.

3.6   Promotion activities

3.6.1 Facilitate the promotion of activities for exchanges between governments, enterprises and associations, in order to encourage cooperation.

3.6.2 Encourage participation in exhibitions and trade fairs related to services sectors in BRICS members. Encourage setting up a section for services trade among BRICS members in their existing and planned state-level economic and trade fairs.

3.7   BRICS members agreed that this roadmap shall be concluded and implemented without prejudice to existing or future services trade agreements.

Communication and Implementation

Establish a liaison mechanism in BRICS members by the existing focal points of the Framework for Cooperation on Trade in Services. Issues regarding implementation of the roadmap should be reported and consulted through the liaison mechanism. BRICS will hold annual meetings back to back with CGETI meetings to review progress, assess the effectiveness and implementation of this Roadmap, identify specific areas of future cooperation.

ANNEX IV: BRICS E-COMMERCE COOPERATION INITIATIVE

Overview

1.   During the last decade, along with the rapid development and widespread application of information and telecommunication technology, e- commerce has maintained high-speed growth, and become one of the world's most dynamic business activities. E-commerce is playing an increasingly important role in promoting the growth of trade, industry transformation and job creation, and has the potential to enable developing countries and MSMEs to better participate in and benefit from global value chains. E-commerce brings overall strategic opportunities for the economic and social development and also profound challenges. BRICS members duly acknowledge the challenges that digital divide imposes on many developing countries and emphasize the need to bridge the digital divide and address its socio-economic implications to ensure a- commerce better contributes to inclusive growth.

2.   After ten years of development, BRICS cooperation is entering a new era. BRICS fully recognized the importance of promoting a-commerce development and cooperation. In 2015, the BRICS leaders endorsed the Framework for BRICS E-commerce Cooperation, which aims to better integrate BRICS a-commerce markets. In 2016, the BRICS Trade Ministers' Communique emphasized the importance of cooperation on e-commerce and BRICS leaders further committed in Goa Declaration to strengthen such cooperation.

3.   In 2017, based on the previous discussions and cooperation, BRICS will take further concrete actions to enhance a-commerce cooperation. According to the related guiding principles, objectives and priorities for cooperation, we will further implement the Framework, and jointly enhance enterprise cooperation, information exchange and capacity building, in order to optimize a-commerce development environment, leverage the a- commerce opportunities for development, including industrial development, generate employment, and inject new impetus into BRICS cooperation.

Actions

1.   Establish the BRICS E-commerce Working Group

To promote the BRICS cooperation on a-commerce, we agree to establish a BRICS E-commerce Working Group which could serve as a body to coordinate inter-government cooperation on a-commerce in agreed areas, including on the basis of outcomes from research and joint studies. The Working Group will periodically meet back to back with the CGETI and conduct activities such as exchanging information including on policy and best practices, providing guidance to the members on enhancing cooperation, and exploring a roadmap for cooperation.

2.   Enhance interaction with the BRICS stakeholders on E-commerce

To boost business cooperation among members, promote information and technology sharing, and strengthen capacity-building, we will enhance interaction with business sectors and other stakeholders on e-commerce.

3.   Undertake research on BRICS E-commerce

To undertake research and joint studies that can cover, based on consensus, among others the following areas: global trends, current status of a-commerce in BRICS, measuring dynamism in a-commerce, regulatory and legal frameworks in BRICS related to a-commerce, participation of MSMEs, existing barriers to cross-border a-commerce among BRICS, the development aspects of a-commerce and recommendations for strengthening a-commerce cooperation within BRICS. For all research projects, members will review the relevant Terms of Reference (ToR) to be proposed by the presidency or any other member and determine the entity or organization to which it will be committed. It is proposed that international organizations provide technical support to this work and share any relevant research.

ANNEX V: BRICS IPR COOPERATION GUIDELINES

Recalling the decisions of the BRICS Trade Ministers to enhance cooperation among BRICS countries on Intellectual Property (IP);

With the aim of strengthening and enhancing Intellectual Property (IP) Cooperation, BRICS countries hereby establish the following general guidelines for implementing BRICS IPRCM:

1.   Sharing and exchanging information on IP legislation and enforcement as well as recent developments, in order to improve the transparency and understanding of IP systems and policies;

2.   Studying the trade-related IP issues with a view to promote international trade, sustainable development and inclusive growth;

3.   Exploring topics that emerge from global IP development trends and strategies (including topics arising from regional trade agreements), and exchanging opinions over such topics that correspond to the development needs of BRICS;

4.   Promoting involvement of IP stakeholders (including legislative, executive and judicial authorities, as well as academia and business community) in IP cooperation, with a view to improve public IP awareness;

5.   Strengthening communication and coordination on IP-related developments within the relevant international organizations with a focus on trade-related aspects as well as other IP issues subject to consensus;

6.   Welcoming technical assistance and support from relevant international organizations for the IP cooperation among BRICS;

7.   Ensuring coordination and synergy as well as avoiding duplication with other IP-related cooperation activities among BRICS countries, in particular with the existing cooperation at the level of BRICS Intellectual Property Offices (HIPO); and

8.   Working on relevant IP issues based on consensus and in line with mutual interests.

ANNEX VI: FRAMEWORK ON STRENGTHENING THE ECONOMIC AND TECHNICAL COOPERATION FOR BRICS COUNTRIES

Background

1.   The new trends in globalization and rapid technology revolution provide unprecedented opportunities for economic growth and employment. While adapting to the fast-changing economic environment, BRICS, which are composed of emerging market economics and developing countries, also face new challenges. As a necessary supplement to trade and investment cooperation, economic and technical cooperation can facilitate participation of BRICS in global trade and help them benefit from it, as well as ensure that free trade can promote sustainable growth and inclusive development, narrow income gaps and improve economic and social welfare.

2.   The 2016 Goa Declaration of the 8th BRICS Summit encouraged capacity building and information exchange amongst BRICS countries in information telecommunication, labor quality and agricultural technology, and encouraged economic and technical cooperation. BRICS are capable and determined to conduct capacity building cooperation based on the specific needs of members. Meanwhile, it is necessary to better integrate current capacity building resources of BRICS in order to meet the demands in a more systematic way. In this regard, the BRICS trade and investment agenda can also contribute to development issues.

Goals

3.   Enhanced efforts on economic and technical cooperation among BRICS members will contribute to the following goals: 1. To promote global and regional value chain integration for BRICS and their MSMEs by systematic measures including the promotion of resource mobilization and provision of tailored capacity building programs; 2. To enhance the capacity of BRICS and their MSMEs to participate in the global market and to improve their access to information, finance and services, and to share good practices in national policies and standards with the view to create a more favorable trade and investment environment; 3. To help BRICS and their MSMEs benefit from global cooperation and competition, and to improve their negotiation capacity on trade and investment related rules.

Actions

4.   The specific actions should be based on the current cooperation mechanism and the actual needs of BRICS members for capacity building in order to guarantee the most efficient utilization of resources.

5.   BRICS agree to conduct capacity building activities within the framework of joint initiative and cooperation mechanism, based on the cooperation vision and specific needs. BRICS members will provide domestic and international training programs when appropriate and feasible. It is envisaged that these efforts could improve the abilities of BRICS on consultation planning, policy design and operation management in specific areas, as well as share the experiences and best practices of members' economy development model and promote technical cooperation to foster economic development and inclusive growth.

6.   Mobilize more resources to support the capacity building programs. Encourage members to take individual and collective actions, on a voluntary basis, to provide any forms of assistance and contributions. And encourage international organizations and other stakeholders to facilitate and contribute to this process.

7.   Share the best practices and successful experience of international organizations and multilateral cooperation mechanisms. Organize seminars and undertake studies, discuss and display successful cases and experiences, develop and implement possible high-level activities. Proposed actions or activities under this framework are to be reported to the CGETI.

Cooperation Areas

8.   BRICS will conduct economic and technical cooperation and capacity building in areas such as trade, promotion and facilitation of investment, e- commerce, intellectual property rights and trade in services which are based on the current CGETI agenda and the actual demands of all members. Areas listed in Strategy for BRICS Economic Partnership and relevant cooperation frameworks will also be considered as priorities. These areas serve as a reference for members engaged in specific activities, and are subject to adjustment according to future cooperation needs.

C.   6th Meeting of Trade Ministers: 13 Oct. 2016, New Delhi (IND)

TRADE MINISTERS COMMUNIQUE

1.   The 6th meeting of the BRICS Trade Ministers was held on 13 October, 2016 in New Delhi on the threshold of the 8th BRICS Summit on 15-16 October, 2016 in Goa, India. The Meeting was preceded by the 13th meeting of the BRICS Contact Group on Economic and Trade Issues (CGETI) which was held from 11-12 October, 2016. The Trade Ministers meeting made an assessment of the BRICS economic scenario in relation to areas of cooperation on trade and investment. The Ministers appreciated the work carried out by BRICS Members during 2016 and urged that this momentum be sustained.

Global Economic Development

2.   The global economic order in 2016 has been shaped by a number of key economic developments such as continued slowdown in global growth and depressed global demand, low commodity and oil prices; new shocks to the global economy, including BREXIT; volatility in the equity and currency markets; strains on the banking sector; political turmoil in some parts of the globe etc. Given this scenario, the Ministers noted that the October, 2016 World Economic Outlook Update of the International Monetary Fund projected the global economic growth forecasts for 2016 and 2017 at 3.1% and 3.4% respectively. The Ministers are of the view that the projected growth rates for 2017 in the Outlook for BRICS countries augurs well when compared with 2016.

3.   Ministers recognized the importance of preserving policy space to promote industrialization, industrial upgrading and value addition as a core pillar for structural transformation and sustainable development and BRICS countries integration into the global economy. They agreed to enhance cooperation in this regard.

The Strategy for BRICS Economic Partnership

4.   The Ministers appreciated the progress in the realization of the Strategy for BRICS Economic Partnership. They directed the CGETI to put forth initiatives and proposals towards the implementation of the Trade and Investment section of the Strategy at the earliest. The Ministers agreed that close cooperation among the CGETI, the BRICS Business Council and New Development Bank is useful for implementing and bringing the BRICS Economic Cooperation to a new high quality level.

Micro Small and Medium Enterprises (MSMEs)

5.   The Ministers recognised the importance of the Micro, Small and Medium Enterprises (MSME) to the balanced economic development of the BRICS countries. The Ministers acknowledge the role of MSMEs as the engines of export led growth and employment generation given the highest rate of employment per unit of investment in MSMEs; and their crucial role in addressing regional disparity and poverty alleviation. The MSME sector in many of the BRICS economies contribute directly or indirectly to nearly half of their exports, manufacturing output and GDP.

6.   The Ministers were cognisant of the impediments faced by MSMEs and the need for cooperation among the BRICS countries to effectively address the barriers to trade and investment amongst the MSMEs.

7.   With a view to ensuring greater business engagement amongst MSMEs in the BRICS region, the Ministers emphasised the importance of developing cooperation among MSMEs in the crucial areas of trade and investment. This cooperation can be in the form of exchange of information on the regulatory framework, rules, regulations and good regulatory practises governing MSMEs; interface among the major chambers of commerce and industry of the MSMEs; and participation of MSME stakeholders in BRICS economic events such as trade fairs, conferences, seminars etc.

8. The Ministers welcome continued efforts to foster cooperation and facilitate exchange of experiences between BRICS countries on MSMEs. In this regard, they welcome the "BRICS Micro Small and Medium Enterprises (MSME) Cooperation Framework" which encourages MSMEs in BRICS to strengthen mutually beneficial commercial relationship. The Framework sets the agenda of cooperation on SMEs by the BRICS countries. The Ministers look forward to constructive engagement on the elements of the cooperation framework by all BRICS Members in the future.

BRICS Business Council and economic cooperation

9. BRICS Trade Ministers considered the continuing role of the BRICS Business Council (BBC) and emphasised the need for the Council to focus on the development and realization of joint projects which would on a mutually beneficial basis contribute to the economic development objectives of BRICS Members. To this end, Trade Ministers urged the BBC to speed up the development of the BRICS Roadmap for Trade, Economic and Investment Cooperation while identifying and implementing suitable projects. In addition, the Council is encouraged to advance key projects as presented by all Member countries. In order to coordinate and advance the BRICS agenda on economic issues, regular engagement by the BBC with BRICS Trade Ministers, as well as the Contact Group on Trade and Economic Issues (CGETI) was requested.

Non-tariff measures (NTM)

10. The Ministers emphasized that the increase in NTMs constrain the participation of developing countries in global trade. The Ministers commended the CGETI for developing a working document on BRICS Mechanism for NTM Resolution. The Ministers agreed in principle to the concepts in the Mechanism and urged the CGETI to advance this work including on the issue of scope.

Standards

11. The Ministers endorsed the Framework for Cooperation on Standardisation that was agreed to by the CGETI. The Ministers urged the CGETI to work on the elements of the Framework with a view to ensuring that the cooperation leads to a better understanding of each other standards. The Framework aims to promote a better understanding and an open dialogue among BRICS countries in this area.

Services

12. The Ministers recognised that the Services sector remains important and contributes to more than half of the GDP of many BRICS countries. Since the services sector is of interest for BRICS economies, it is important for the group to cooperate with the aim of promoting complementarities on services trade. The Ministers highlighted the importance of facilitating expansion of trade in services by addressing existing barriers. The Ministers endorsed the Framework for Cooperation on Trade in Services.

Trade Promotion

13. The Ministers expressed their appreciation that India is holding the 1st BRICS Trade Fair from 12-14 October, 2016 in New Delhi. This Fair is an opportunity for stakeholders in the BRICS region to explore and expand business opportunities and networks. The theme of the Fair namely "Building Responsive, Inclusive and Collective Solutions" is apt in ensuring that the BRICS region as a whole benefits from such events. The focus areas and the showcasing of technologies are important in the context of ensuring a commercially meaningful participation in the Fair. The Ministers welcome the idea of CGETI discussing the possibility of holding BRICS Trade Fairs on a regular basis.

14. The Ministers noted that the BRICS Trade Promotion Working Group would create a forum for the Trade Promotion Agencies in the BRICS region to interface towards the promotion of value added trade which would also support integration into global value chains. It is vital that these agencies co-ordinate in other trade and investment events so that the BRICS value added products and services can be showcased more effectively. The Ministers instructed the working group to effectively

coordinate activities so as to ensure that the BRICS stakeholders can benefit from the participation in such events.

Single Window

15. The Ministers noted that Article 10.4 of the WTO Agreement on Trade Facilitation instructs that WTO Members shall endeavour to establish or maintain a single window. They also appreciated the work being carried out in the BRICS countries for development of national single windows. These would facilitate both exporters and importers who would then need a single point interface for all their clearances.

16. The Ministers endorsed the Framework for BRICS Single Window Cooperation and underlined the importance of closer cooperation among the BRICS countries in the development of their national single windows. They emphasised the need for BRICS countries to operationalize the Framework based on the Guiding Principles, Objectives and Priorities for Cooperation.

IPR Cooperation

17. The Ministers highlighted the importance of cooperation on intellectual property rights (IPR) towards the development of a BRICS perspective that will be informed by their national priorities. In this context, they appreciate the formation of and endorse the BRICS IPR Cooperation Mechanism (IPRCM). They also took note of the existing cooperation mechanism at the level of Heads of Intellectual Property Offices (HIPO). The Ministers urge both the HIPO and IPRCM to co-ordinate and avoid duplication of their work. They instruct the IPRCM to commence their work on the terms of reference decided upon and endeavor to advance cooperation in a more systematic and coordinated manner.

E-commerce

18. The Ministers reiterated the importance of strengthening intra-BRICS cooperation on E-commerce and appreciated the progress achieved since the adoption of the Framework for BRICS E-commerce Cooperation in 2015. The Ministers have emphasized the need for cooperation to boost e-commerce development in the BRICS countries, enhance capacity building and promote cooperation on infrastructure.

19. The Ministers emphasized that the development potential of e-commerce is not fully realized and in this regard they directed the CGETI to implement all areas of the Framework and explore cooperation in areas of common interests. The Ministers took note of the proposal to conduct a joint study to promote areas of common interest in e-commerce and stressed the importance of enhancing the BRICS countries understanding on e-commerce.

BRICS cooperation in the WTO

20. The Ministers reiterated the support for the multilateral trading system and the centrality of the WTO in providing a rules based, transparent, non-discriminatory and inclusive global trading system. The Ministers emphasized the importance of implementing the decisions taken at the Bali and Nairobi Ministerial Conferences. They stressed the need to advance negotiations on the remaining DDA issues as a matter of priority. They called on all WTO members to work together with a sense of urgency and solidarity to ensure a strong development oriented outcome for MC 11 and beyond.

BRICS and the G-20

21. The Ministers commended the work done by China in its current Presidency of the G20. They emphasized the importance of BRICS Members' coordination in the G-20. They welcomed the outcomes of G20 Hangzhou Summit and emphasized the importance of continued efforts to implement those outcomes. They also underlined the importance of the G20 Trade and Investment Working Group (TIWG) in addressing various issues confronting the G20 economies and the call for further collaboration under this framework.

D.   5th Meeting of Trade Ministers: 7 Jul. 2015, Moscow (RUS)

JOINT COMMUNIQUE

1.   The BRICS Trade Ministers met for the fifth time in Moscow, Russia on the eve of the Seventh BRICS Summit. The Ministers reviewed the current state of BRICS trade and economic cooperation, assessed the progress made since the First Meeting of the BRICS Trade Ministers in Sanya in 2011, and discussed the way forward for BRICS.

Global economic developments and their impact on trade and investment relations among the BRICS countries

2.   The Ministers welcomed the enhancement of the BRICS economies' role in global trade and economic system as well as the strengthening of cooperation and the development of economic integration.

3.   The Ministers reviewed current trends in the global economy and their influence on intra-BRICS trade and economic activity. They noted that the slow pace of recovery and fragile growth of the global economy hinder trade and investment flows. In this regard, the Ministers reaffirmed their commitment to implement the decisions taken by the BRICS Leaders at the Summits in Sanya, Delhi, Durban and Fortaleza with the aim to build a partnership that will help increase stability, growth and development of the BRICS economies.

4.   In this context, the Ministers agreed to develop pragmatic economic cooperation and forge a closer economic partnership with a view to promoting global economic recovery, reducing potential risks in international financial markets and strengthening sustainable economic growth in the BRICS members. The Ministers instructed the BRICS Contact Group on Economic and Trade Issues (CGETI) to explore possible ways to enhance intra-BRICS trade and the development of value chains including from the perspective of micro, small and medium scale enterprises (MSMEs).

BRICS cooperation in the WTO and Doha Development Agenda

5.   The Ministers joined in the celebration of the twentieth anniversary of the World Trade Organization (WTO) and reaffirmed their intention to work together to strengthen an open, transparent, non-discriminatory, and rules-based multilateral trading system as embodied in the WTO. They welcomed Kenya's hosting of the 10th WTO Ministerial Conference (MC10) in Nairobi on 15-18 December 2015. They stressed the importance of a successful meeting in Nairobi that brings tangible results and meaningful outcomes on the development agenda, including on the issues of interest to LDCs.

6.   The Ministers commended the adoption of the Protocol of Amendment for the Trade Facilitation Agreement (TFA) in 2014 and called on all WTO Members to contribute to the timely entry into force of the TFA, with predictable resources made available to facilitate its implementation. They also welcomed the decision to make concerted efforts to agree and adopt a permanent solution on the issue of public stockholding for food security purposes by the end of 2015 while underlining the importance of implementation of all Bali Package elements, including LDC issues, such as LDC Services Waiver, as an important part of MC10 results.

7. The Ministers emphasized that the successful conclusion of the Doha Round remains central to the objective of promoting the full integration of developing countries into the global trading system. Therefore, they reaffirmed their commitment to coordinate their efforts in the WTO to formulate the Post-Bali Work program as a key stepping-stone to concluding the Doha Round. This work programme should provide for the full achievement of the key objectives of the DDA, acknowledge the special circumstances of countries and accord priority to development issues.

8. Ministers acknowledged that successful conclusion of the Doha Round is the shared responsibility of all WTO Members. Ministers called on all WTO Members to ensure support to these negotiations.

9. Ministers stressed the centrality of the WTO as the institution that sets multilateral trade rules. They noted the importance of bilateral, regional and plurilateral trade agreements and encourage

the parties to those negotiations to comply with the principles of transparency, inclusiveness and compatibility with WTO rules to ensure that they contribute to strengthening the multilateral trading system.

Cooperation in Global and Regional Organizations and Multilateral Fora

10. The Ministers reaffirmed their commitment to develop cooperation in global and regional organizations and multilateral fora, such as the G20, UNCTAD, WIPO, UNDP and UNIDO amongst others.

11. The Ministers welcomed participation of the BRICS countries in regional integration processes as well as in the activities of regional organizations. They underlined that the development of the expanded dialogue on economic and political agenda with the participation of regional organizations such as Eurasian Economic Union (EEU), the Shanghai Cooperation Organization (SCO) and IBSA Dialogue Forum would contribute to strengthening BRICS economic cooperation. It would also enhance the role of the BRICS countries as regional leaders, enhance development, sustainable growth, as well as strengthen inter-regional ties and promote a multipolar global economic system.

Intra-BRICS Cooperation

12. The Ministers agreed that current circumstances required new approaches, models and mechanisms to strengthen intra-BRICS economic cooperation. They emphasized the need to work together to build on the respective advantages and requirements of the BRICS economies. They agreed that it could be achieved by identifying complementarities and synergies, with a particular attention to key growth sectors.

13. The Ministers welcomed the work done by the BRICS High Level Working Group to fulfill the BRICS Leaders' instruction to finalize the draft Strategy for BRICS Economic Partnership by the BRICS Summit in 2015. The Ministers noted the recommendations outlined in the Strategy and committed to provide full support to their implementation.

14. The Ministers noted the BRICS Roadmap on trade, economic and investment cooperation until 2020 suggested by Russia and directed CGETI to initiate a preliminary discussion on it.

15. Considering the necessity for securing balanced and sustainable development of the BRICS economies, the Ministers welcomed the efforts aiming at ensuring balance of interests of consumers and producers of energy resources, creating transparent and predictable conditions for sustainable development of the world energy market and energy security of BRICS countries as set out in the Strategy for BRICS Economic Partnership.

16. The Ministers noted the importance of exchanging best practices on investment climate improvement and suggested that the BRICS export credit and guarantees agencies, in the framework of the cooperation MoU signed at the Fortaleza Summit, exchange experiences on risk analysis, including the use of country ratings in the light of specific aspects of developing markets.

17. The Ministers recognized the importance of the dialogue on BRICS investment policies and international investment rules and instruct officials to explore ways to improve mutual knowledge of investment policies of the member countries.

18. The Ministers highlighted the relevance of measures aimed at increasing the share of value-added goods in production and exports of the BRICS countries and diversifying their mutual trade. They agreed that these measures would enhance the role of the BRICS countries in global value chains and thus, reduce their dependence on the fluctuations in the world economy.

19. The Ministers noted that trade and investment facilitation as well as strengthening cooperation in the areas of standards, technical regulation and conformity assessment procedures would create favourable conditions for enhancing intra-BRICS trade.

20. The Ministers also highlighted the relevance of the new cooperation initiatives in the fields of trade promotion and trade facilitation, including the establishment of the Trade Promotion Working Group and the organization of a seminar on Single Window Systems. They agreed that such measures could enhance intra-BRICS cooperation and create new opportunities for member countries.

21. The Ministers reaffirmed the importance of strengthening BRICS customs cooperation with a view to facilitating trade amongst the BRICS countries.

22. The Ministers noted the existing imbalance in the development of markets for the establishment and development of software and hardware. They agreed to make joint efforts to avoid excessive market dominance in the global market of software, hardware and equipment in the IT-sphere through cooperation on software development. They also agreed to strengthen cooperation and promote joint activities and initiatives to address common concerns in the field of ICTs, including the Internet (software development, cloud computing, big data and internet of things).

23. The Ministers also highlighted the importance of strengthening intra-BRICS cooperation on e-commerce. They welcomed convening and noted the recommendations of the First BRICS Expert Dialogue on E-Commence (14 April 2015, Moscow). They also welcomed the Framework for BRICS E-commerce Cooperation as an instrument to promote current and future initiatives with an aim to build a closer economic partnership in this sphere.

24. The Ministers reaffirmed that intellectual property rights (IPR) provided incentives that encourage creativity and innovation and emphasize the need to share best practices to ensure IPR regime contributes to the development objectives of countries. They renewed their commitment to enhance cooperation among BRICS countries on IPR. In this regard, the Ministers agreed to coordinate positions in international fora on IP related matters. They welcomed the initiative on strengthening IPR cooperation among BRICS countries and instructed officials to develop the Terms of Reference of the IPR Cooperation mechanism under CGETI.

25. The Ministers noted that MSMEs make a vital contribution to jobs creation and promotion of strong, sustainable and balanced growth and development. In this context, they agreed to work towards identifying promising areas of cooperation among BRICS MSMEs.

26. The Ministers highlighted the importance of the development of new initiatives in this area including the creation of the Expert Dialogue on MSMEs. The Ministers emphasized the importance of developing cooperation among organizations responsible for support and development of BRICS MSMEs and exchanging information and best practices on MSMEs regulation and support, facilitation of MSMEs' access to public services, financing, exports and international projects.

27. The Ministers highlighted the potential for establishing business cooperation among BRICS MSMEs with a view to facilitating their participation in international MSMEs conferences, forums, exhibitions and fairs held in the BRICS countries.

28. The Ministers highlighted that "green economy" in the context of sustainable development and poverty eradication as well as environment protection were crucial for achieving sustainable and balanced growth. Therefore, they welcomed strengthening cooperation between public and private sector to stimulate investment in environmentally friendly and energy efficient technologies, which may also contribute to combating climate change, and noted the importance of joint efforts aimed at environmental protection.

29. The Ministers highlighted that increasing connectivity among the BRICS countries would improve the quality of growth and contribute to economic prosperity and resilience of the BRICS economies.

30. The Ministers emphasized the importance of developing youth cooperation among BRICS countries in the sphere of innovation, youth entrepreneurship and collaboration of startup projects with participation of business leaders from BRICS countries.

31. The Ministers welcomed the efficient work undertaken by the BRICS Business Council as outlined in the Annual Report that brought together companies and business associations and helped foster joint projects and initiatives by the BRICS countries. Further to this, the Ministers commended the Council for establishing the Working Groups on Agri-business and Deregulation; two areas that warrant dedicated attention. The Ministers encouraged the BRICS Business Council to work towards more quantitative and clearly defined outcomes through the development of a tangible work programme.

E.   4th Meeting of Trade Ministers: 14 Jul. 2014, Fortaleza (BRA)

JOINT COMMUNIQUÉ

The Ministers responsible for trade of Brazil, Russia, India, China and South Africa met in Fortaleza, Brazil, on 14 July 2014, on the eve of the Sixth BRICS Summit.

Global economic developments and their impact on trade and investment

1.   The BRICS Trade Ministers reviewed the global economic situation and expressed concern at the slow pace of recovery, which continues to hinder trade and investment flows. They noted that the uncertainty regarding economic growth and policy responses in developed countries could lead to increased volatility in financial markets and further affect the international economy. They emphasized that updating international governance structures remains a necessity for better policy coordination and for the promotion of global economic prosperity.

2.   The Ministers expressed their confidence that, in spite of the challenging economic environment, the BRICS countries will continue to contribute to the global economic recovery. They welcomed the expansion of trade and investment among the BRICS countries and vowed to continue to work to further strengthen their economic relations. In this context, they reaffirmed their commitment to refrain from trade protectionist measures that are incompatible with WTO obligations, while respecting the special and differential treatment for developing countries.

Current state of play in the WTO and the way forward

3.   The BRICS Trade Ministers noted the successful outcome of the WTO Ministerial Conference held in Bali in December 2013. They undertook to pursue vigorously the achievement of the objectives and timelines set out in the Bali Ministerial decisions. They reaffirmed the importance of an open and rules-based multilateral trading system and underlined the central role of the WTO in setting rules for global trade.

4.   The Ministers emphasized that the conclusion of the Doha Round on the basis of its development mandate remains central to the objective of promoting the full integration of developing countries into the global trading system.

5.   The Ministers affirmed their commitment to coordinate efforts with a view to ensuring that the efforts to establish a work programme in the WTO will lead to a balanced, transparent, inclusive and development-oriented outcome in all pillars. The Ministers also reaffirmed that the work programme should reflect the centrality of agriculture and of the development dimension and the commitment to prioritise the issues where legally-binding outcomes could not be achieved at the Bali Ministerial Conference. The Ministers also noted the importance of NAMA and services and the need to work on the existing Doha texts.

BRICS cooperation on trade and investment matters

6.   The Ministers noted that trade and investment make a vital contribution to the creation of jobs and to the promotion of strong, sustainable and balanced growth and development.

7.   The Ministers welcomed the Joint Trade Study prepared by the Contact Group for Economic and Trade Issues (CGETI). The Study makes important recommendations for promoting value-added exports among our countries and ensuring that intra-BRICS trade is more sustainable. They have noted the Report and instructed the CGETI to continue working on its recommendations.

8.   The Ministers took note of the discussions in the CGETI on a range of actions to foster economic cooperation and to promote trade and investment between the BRICS.

9. The Ministers endorsed the BRICS Trade and Investment Facilitation Action Plan developed by the CGETI. They noted that it built upon the BRICS Trade and Investment Cooperation Framework and encouraged BRICS members to implement it on a voluntary basis.

10. The Ministers reaffirmed the importance of a continued dialogue on international investment agreements. They noted the principles outlined in the document "A BRICS Perspective on International Investment Agreements" as a voluntary reference for countries to advance a more balanced approach to investment treaties.

11. The Ministers emphasized the importance of strengthening intra-BRICS cooperation in e-commerce, with a view to extending the opportunities for intra-BRICS trade and enhancing closer economic cooperation. They welcomed the proposal to establish a BRICS Expert Dialogue on Electronic Commerce. They instructed the CGETI to elaborate terms of reference for the Expert Dialogue.

12. The Ministers acknowledged the documents "BRICS Economic Cooperation Strategy" and "Framework of BRICS Closer Economic Partnership" and welcomed the efforts to establish guidelines for a coordinated approach to economic cooperation among the BRICS, especially on trade and investment.

13. The Ministers highlighted the potential for forging closer links between the Micro, Small and Medium Enterprises (MSME) of the BRICS. They instructed their officials to explore ways to promote cooperation in this field, such as sharing information on the MSME regulatory framework, promoting business to business contacts and identifying the appropriate institutional framework for MSME cooperation.

F.   3rd Meeting of Trade Ministers: 26 Mar. 2013, Durban (ZAF)

JOINT COMMUNIQUÉ

BRICS Trade Ministers met for the third time in Durban, South Africa on the eve of the Fifth BRICS Summit convened under the theme "BRICS and Africa: Partnership for Development, Integration and Industrialisation". The Ministers held open and constructive discussions under five main headings.

1. Global Economic Developments

The Ministers expressed concern that global growth weakened considerably during 2012, and is expected to remain subdued. They observed that recession, fragile growth and deflationary conditions in some advanced economies are at the root of the global economic slowdown, and that the impact is spilling over through weaker demand, a significant slowdown in international trade growth, and heightened volatility in capital flows and commodity prices.

The Ministers observed that growth in the BRICS and in some other economies, while less robust than before the global downturn, continues to contribute significantly to the global economic recovery. Ministers welcomed the fact that growth in intra-BRICS trade and investment continued apace despite current circumstances, and they expressed their commitment to continue to work to expand and deepen these increasingly vital and mutually beneficial economic relations.

Given the global slowdown, the Ministers reiterated the need to resist protectionist tendencies and to promote international trade as an engine of economic growth and development, while respecting the WTO consistent policy space available to developing countries to pursue their legitimate objectives of growth, development and stability.

2. The WTO and Doha Development Agenda

The Ministers reaffirmed their view of the centrality of the WTO for a transparent and inclusive rules-based multilateral trading system. They emphasized the continued relevance of the development mandate agreed to at Doha in 2001, and reiterated their commitment to a conclusion of the negotiations based on the progress made since then.

While the Ministers indicated a willingness to explore outcomes in specific areas where progress is possible, they insisted on preserving the centrality of the Doha development mandate and the principle of the single undertaking. They expressed concern at initiatives that may undermine the coherence of the Doha Development Agenda and that deviate from the principles of multilateralism.

BRICS Trade Ministers agreed to strengthen their collaboration to ensure that any meaningful deliverables reached by the Ninth WTO Ministerial Conference in December 2013 are balanced and addresses key developmental concerns of the poorest and most vulnerable WTO members. They also proposed that the Ministerial Conference should re-affirm Members' commitment to conclude the Doha Development Agenda on the basis of its development mandate and the single undertaking.

The Ministers noted the process underway for the selection of a new WTO Director- General in 2013. They concurred that the WTO requires a new leader who demonstrates a commitment to multilateralism and to enhancing the credibility and legitimacy of the WTO including through a commitment to support efforts that will lead to an expeditious conclusion of the Doha Development Agenda.

To address all these and other WTO matters, the Ministers instructed their Ambassadors to the WTO to strengthen and deepen their collaboration and coordination on multilateral trade issues discussed in various international fora.

3. Cooperation in other Multilateral Fora

The Ministers reaffirmed their commitment to cooperate in other multilateral fora where trade and investment issues arise, such as the G20, UNCTAD, UNDP, UNIDO and WIPO, amongst others.

The Ministers observed that in the current global context of economic difficulty and the impasse in the Doha Development Agenda negotiations, UNCTAD could play a vital role in promoting cooperation among Governments and relevant stakeholders in a range of areas relevant to trade and investment from a development perspective. The Ministers agreed to support UNCTAD in this role.

The Ministers believed that the impending appointment of a new Secretary General in UNCTAD, coinciding as it will with leadership changes at the WTO, offers the opportunity to strengthen the working relationship between the two organisations. Such cooperation could aim to ensure that the multilateral trading system is better equipped to deal with old and new challenges confronting the international community in the twenty first century.

4. Intra-BRICS Cooperation

The Ministers agreed that current circumstances required new principles, concepts, models and mechanisms to strengthen intra-BRICS cooperation. They emphasized the need to work together to build on the respective strengths of their economies. They agreed this could be achieved by identifying complementarities in key growth sectors and to cooperate to build the industrial capacities of their respective economies. This could be advanced by further exchanges between industries, trade and investment promotion events and enhanced investment and technical cooperation. Ministers also agreed BRICS countries should establish approaches and mechanisms that encourage mutually beneficial negotiated solutions amongst the BRICS countries when trade frictions arise.

The Ministers endorsed the work of the Senior Officials meeting under the Contact Group for Economic and Trade Issues (CGETI) on trade and services data; cooperation on the development of Small and Medium Enterprises; and Investment. They instructed the CGETI to report progress at the next opportunity. They also welcomed the extensive work programme on customs cooperation and trade facilitation initiated under the BRICS framework that could help to boost intra-BRICS trade.

The Ministers also endorsed the BRICS Trade and Investment Cooperation Framework developed by the CGETI and instructed the CGETI to implement the Framework and build on it in future.

The Ministers welcomed the convening of BRICS Business Forum where approximately 600 companies from the BRICS countries were present. The Forum offered a platform for companies and policy makers to interact and network to promote cooperation in infrastructure development, mining value added production, finance, agriculture and green energy.

The Ministers welcomed the launch of the BRICS Business Council that will bring together business associations from each of the BRICS countries and manage engagement between the business communities on an ongoing basis.

5. BRICS Partnership to Support Africa's Development Agenda

The Ministers recognized that Africa's development prospects are vastly improved, that it is a continent of growing economic opportunity, and that it is increasingly a destination of choice for investors. Africa is now the second fastest growing continent in the world with enormous mineral and agricultural resources, growing markets and a young and dynamic population.

Ministers also recognized that to fully realise its potential, Africa will need to pursue structural transformation that shifts its current growth path onto a more sustainable industrial development path. This requires greater effort and support to the regional and continental integration agenda to integrate markets, spur the development of cross border infrastructure and diversify production bases.

While observing the growing cooperation between individual BRICS countries and African countries across the African continent, BRICS Trade Ministers committed to support Africa's development agenda by strengthening their cooperation in the search for synergies for investment in Africa's infrastructure, agriculture and manufacturing sectors.

G.   BRICS Trade and Investment Cooperation Framework: 26 Mar. 2013, Durban (ZAF)

BRICS TRADE AND INVESTMENT COOPERATION FRAMEWORK
26 March 2013, Durban, South Africa

1.   BACKGROUND

1.1   The Contact Group on Economic and Trade Issues (CGETI) is a key platform for BRICS Members to exchange views on a range of economic, trade and investment related issues. The exchange of policy perspectives and priorities lays an essential basis for enhanced coordination and cooperation among the BRICS Members on these issues.

1.2   This Trade and Investment Cooperation Framework is established under the CGETI and its terms of reference. It aims to locate the specific activities of the Group in a longer- term framework for enhanced coordination and possible joint action.

2.   PRINCIPLES

2.1   To achieve mutually beneficial outcomes, this Trade and Investment Cooperation Framework operate according to the principles of equality, transparency, efficiency, mutual understanding and consensus.

2.2   This framework is open-ended and progressive. The cooperation initiatives may be adjusted enriched and will evolve as issues of concern to its BRICS Members develop and change in the future, with the approval of the BRICS Trade Ministers' Meeting and the CGETI.

3.   OBJECTIVES

This cooperation framework is developed and initiated with the aim of:

3.1   Promoting trade, investment and economic cooperation among the BRICS Members;

3.2   Encouraging trade and investment links between BRICS countries with an emphasis on supporting industrial complementarities, sustainable development and inclusive growth;

3.3   Sharing policy practices on trade and investment among the Members;

3.4   Encouraging initiatives among BRICS Members to support institution-building to enhance productive capacity and value addition across various economic sectors; and

3.5   Enhancing communication and coordination.

4.   AREAS OF WORK

4.1   Multilateral cooperation and coordination

4.1.1 Strengthening coordination in the World Trade Organisation's Doha Round, as well as in other multilateral fora where trade and investment matters arise.

4.1.2 Conducting regular meetings among BRICS high-level officials in multilateral and international organisations where trade and investment matters arise.

4.1.3 Identifying areas for possible development cooperation activities of BRICS that could support the development aspirations of developing countries.

4.2   Promoting and Facilitating Trade and Investment

4.2.1 Enhancing information exchange on trade/investment policies and business opportunities through mechanisms including websites for trade/investment information- sharing.

4.2.2 Encouraging their trade/investment promotion agencies to establish stronger relationships, and providing policy support for trade/investment missions amongst the BRICS Members.

4.2.3 Expanding cooperation on trade/investment promotion platforms such as trade fairs and expositions to increase opportunities for BRICS enterprises to meet, communicate and cooperate with each other.

4.2.4 Improving the transparency of the trade/investment environment in line with their respective laws and regulations.

4.2.5 Enhancing communication and cooperation in the areas of standardisation, certification, inspection and quarantine.

4.2.6 Enhancing communication and cooperation between agencies responsible for trade remedies.

4.2.7 Considering the effect that a positive outcome of the work by Ministries of Finance and Central Banks on settlement in local currencies may have as a support to enhanced intra-BRICS trade.

4.3   Innovation Cooperation

4.3.1 Establishing project platforms to promote communication and cooperation in high- technology areas.

4.3.2 Encouraging the expansion of trade and investment in high value-added products.

4.3.3 Advancing dialogue and communications in emerging industries, and promoting trade and investment in industries that are technology-, knowledge-, or capital- intensive.

4.4   SMEs Cooperation

4.4.1 Conducting information exchange on SMEs regulatory and supporting policies, as well as the experiences and practices in this area.

4.4.2 Exploring possibilities of signing a BRICS SMEs Cooperation Agreement.

4.4.3 Encouraging promotion agencies such as SMEs associations and development centres to establish contacts and hold joint activities including trade/investment expos, human resource training, consulting, seminars, etc.

4.5   Cooperation on Intellectual Property Rights (IPR)

4.5.1 Enhancing information exchange on IPR legislation and enforcement through meetings or seminars.

4.5.2 Jointly developing capacity building programmes in the IPR area.

4.5.3 Promoting cooperation among IPR offices.

4.6   Cooperation on Infrastructure and Industrial Development

4.6.1 Sharing and exchanging information and experiences in infrastructure and construction.

4.6.2 Encouraging relevant enterprises to participate in infrastructure development and construction in the BRICS countries, and having mutually beneficial cooperation with each other.

4.6.3 Analysing the prospects for joint bids by BRICS enterprises in international infrastructure and construction projects.

5.   SPECIFIC ACTIVITIES FOR 2013/2014

The following activities will be encouraged or undertaken by the CGETI during 2013/2014 as part of this Framework:

5.1   The development of BRICS information sharing and exchange platforms, such as the platform initiated by the Centre for BRICS Studies, Fudan University, China.

5.2   Work on reconciling merchandise trade data and models for services trade data collection.

5.3   A joint trade study to identify ways of promoting the export of higher value-added products among the BRICS Members.

5.4   BRICS seminar on investment protection agreements (South Africa, June 2013).

5.5   BRICS investment and trade promotion through the China International Fair for Investment and Trade (China, 8-9 September 2013).

5.6   Import Forum to promote the import of high value-added products from BRICS (China, second half of 2013).

5.7   SME promotion through the China International Small and Medium Enterprises Fair (China, September 2013).

5.8   Coordination for the WTO 9th Ministerial Conference in Bali, Indonesia in December 2013.

H. BRICS Trade Ministers Statement: 19 Apr. 2012, Puerto Vallarta (MEX)

BRICS TRADE MINISTERS' STATEMENT

1. Brazil, Russia, India, China and South Africa welcome the initiative taken by Mexico in hosting the first G20 Trade Ministers' Meeting and expect it to achieve positive results, contributing to strengthening the multilateral trading system and ensuring strong, sustainable and balanced growth and development.

2. The BRICS countries take note of the increasing role of global value chains in trade. They note that many sectors, industries and even countries are not participating in global value chains as fully as some others. In order for global value chains to serve as instruments of growth and development, it would be important to develop a deeper understanding of their developmental impact and the conditions under which they can be used to achieve long term socio-economic gains. In addition, attention should be paid to not impose obstacles for the development and effective functioning of global value chains, for protectionist reasons. In this context, it would be useful to have a member-driven process, in the WTO, UNCTAD and other intergovernmental agencies, to examine this issue, including the identification of more accurate statistical methods to assess value addition.

3. The services sector plays an important role in economic growth and development. Nevertheless, experiences of many countries have shown that in order to benefit from liberalization of services and avoid unintended consequences of premature liberalization, opening services markets should be correctly sequenced, progressive and commensurate with a country's level of development, strength in particular sectors and regulatory capacity. All countries, particularly developing ones, should be able to benefit from balanced and equitable services liberalisation, by gaining additional market access opportunities in sectors and modes of supply where they have a competitive edge.

4. Trade Facilitation can have a dynamic effect on competitiveness and economic integration. However, the costs of implementing trade facilitation measures can be a significant challenge for many developing countries, which have to be met through adequate financial and technical assistance. Due attention has also to be paid simultaneously to the development of export-related infrastructure, especially in LDCs, to obtain a win-win result.

5. Trade finance has an important role in promoting trade through access to affordable credit facilities. Trade cannot flourish without a stable international financial environment, on account of the interconnectedness of the financial markets. This calls for better and more effective regulation of financial markets and supervision of the banking system. Regulatory failures in financial markets can lead to financial crises and in turn adversely affect the availability of trade finance. Excessive liquidity in some countries impacts others as well.

6. Trade can create growth opportunities and trade reforms can reinforce an effective development strategy, but trade openness by itself is not sufficient to ensure growth, development and social inclusiveness. Other complementary policies are needed for this purpose such as sound macroeconomic management, efficient trade institutions, investments in human capital and infrastructure, adjustment support, and the rule of law. A level playing field, that addresses the current inequities in global trade, is also essential. In particular, trade rules and market opening should apply to all economic sectors, including agriculture, while incorporating special flexibilities and "policy space" for developing countries.

7. The net employment effects of increased trade may be positive if other country specific factors such as functioning of the labor and product markets, competitiveness of specific sectors and general macroeconomic framework, act in a favourable manner.

8.   Bearing in mind the positive role that trade can play in boosting and sustaining global demand, fostering job creation and increasing the potential for growth and development, we emphasize the need to resist protectionism in all its forms and to promote international trade, while respecting the WTO consistent policy space available to developing countries to pursue their legitimate objectives of growth, development and stability. We encourage the WTO, UNCTAD and other international agencies to complement their on-going monitoring of trade and trade related measures with a deeper analysis of the impacts of these measures on trade flows.

9.   We urge our fellow G20 Trade Ministers to strengthen coordination in promoting a concerted response to current economic uncertainties. "Win-win" trade policies will be central to global recovery. We, therefore, call upon our fellow G-20 Trade Ministers to identify ways to improve the multilateral trading system so that all economies may pursue a sustainable and "development-friendly" integration in global trade, including adjustment strategies for their industries and workforce, as well as the appropriate social and sectoral policies to respond to existing structural vulnerabilities. The conclusion of the Doha Development Round would be a significant step in this direction. The BRICS WTO members will continue their efforts for the successful conclusion of the Doha Round, based on the progress made and in keeping with its mandate, while upholding the principles of transparency, inclusiveness and multilateralism. We encourage all G20 economies to work constructively toward this end in pursuance of the collective decision taken at the 8th WTO Ministerial Conference.

In this context, we also look forward to a successful conclusion of the UNCTAD XIII in Doha which will provide a useful opportunity to highlight the central role of UNCTAD in the area of trade, development and interrelated issues. We reaffirm the need to strengthen UNCTAD's traditional activities of consensus building, policy dialogue, research, technical cooperation and capacity building, so that it can continue to contribute effectively to its development mandate.

I.   2nd Meeting of Trade Ministers: 28 Mar. 2012, New Delhi (IND)

JOINT PRESS RELEASE

Overview of Global Economic Developments and Impact on Trade and Investment

1.   The BRICS Trade and Economic Ministers reviewed the global economic situation and noted with concern the continuing difficulty faced by many countries and underscored the need for greater policy coordination to ensure a stable and thriving global economy. In such a scenario, the Ministers emphasised the need to resist protectionist tendencies and to promote international trade as an engine of economic growth and development, while respecting the WTO consistent policy space available to developing countries to pursue their legitimate objectives of growth, development and stability. The Ministers noted that subsidies in agriculture by some developed countries continue to distort trade and undermine the food security and development prospects of developing countries particularly LDCs, and urge that such form of protectionism be shunned.

Current state of play of the Doha Round and the way forward

2.   The Ministers of BRICS WTO members expressed deep concern at the current impasse in the Doha Development Round, and reiterated that they remain fully committed to an early conclusion of the negotiations based on the progress made in the Round since 2001. Towards this end, the Ministers expressed their willingness to explore outcomes in specific areas where progress is possible while preserving the centrality of development in the Doha mandate and within the overall framework of the single undertaking. It is of utmost importance that negotiations on any components of the Doha Round are consistent with the existing mandates. The Ministers did not support any plurilateral initiatives that go against the fundamental principles of transparency, inclusiveness and multilateralism. The Minister believed that such initiatives not only distract Members from striving for a collective outcome but also fail to address the development deficit inherited from previous negotiating rounds

3.   The Ministers reiterated that they attach great importance to an open and rule-based multilateral trading system, and in this context, they underlined the central role of the WTO in safeguarding and strengthening the rules with specific reference to the concerns of developing countries and in particular LDCs.

4.   The Ministers welcomed Russia's determination to participate in a constructive and active manner in the DDA negotiations once full membership is attained. A balanced DDA outcome will strengthen and further develop the multilateral trading system.

Cooperation in multilateral fora

5.   The Ministers agreed to coordinate their positions at the WTO and in other multilateral fora such as the forthcoming meeting of the G20 Trade Ministers.

6.   BRICS Ministers look forward to UNCTAD XIII next month in Doha. They reaffirmed the important role of UNCTAD in the area of trade, development and interrelated issues and believe that its mandate should be maintained and strengthened. At a time when the global economy is in crisis, the Doha trade round is at an impasse and multilateralism is under challenge, it is vital for UNCTAD to strengthen its role of policy dialogue, consensus building and capacity building for developing countries.

The way forward on BRICS

7.   The Ministers took note of the discussions in the Contact Group on Economic and Trade Issues (CGETI) on Russia's proposal for setting up BRICS Projects Platforms/ technology pool for joint projects development.

8.   The Ministers directed their officials to explore ways and means for enhancing and furthering intra-BRICS cooperation especially in the areas of customs cooperation, exchange of experiences in trade facilitation, investment promotion SME cooperation and trade data collection and harmonisation, e-commerce cooperation and intellectual property rights cooperation.

Ministers also agreed that officials should work together to ensure that BRICS members enhance their trade, including of higher value added manufactured products, to support industrialisation and employment in their countries.

J. 1st Meeting of Trade Ministers: 14 Dec. 2011, Geneva (CHE)

MINISTERIAL DECLARATION OF THE BRICS TRADE MINISTERS

1. We, the Ministers of Brazil, China, India, Russia, and South Africa, have met on 14 December 2011 in Geneva, before the 8th World Trade Organization (WTO) Ministerial Conference.

2. Following up on our previous meeting held in Sanya, China, on 13 April 2011, we are pleased with the recent establishment of a contact group entrusted with the task of proposing an institutional framework and concrete measures to expand economic cooperation both among BRICS countries and between BRICS countries and all developing countries, within a South-South perspective. We notice that the contact group met for the first time on December 2nd, 2011, in Beijing, China, to further its work.

3. We also note that India would be hosting the Fourth BRICS Summit in New Delhi on 29 March 2012 and the first substantive meeting of the BRICS trade ministers would also take place on 28 March 2012. This would provide a good opportunity to review the outcomes of the MC8 and to devise a common approach on the way ahead.

4. We recognise the huge growth potential both in trade flows among developing countries and in cooperation in investments in the coming decades. We believe that the BRICS countries should play a leading role in South-South cooperation. We are accordingly committed to further expanding economic, trade and investment ties among our countries. Deepened and enlarged economic cooperation of the BRICS countries may be conducive not only to serving our shared interests but also to helping promote growth in the global economy. We agree that steps to strengthening economic and trade cooperation among our countries should be taken in an incremental, proactive, and pragmatic manner.

5. We further recall that, in Sanya, we highlighted our commitment to the WTO trade regime and to the Doha Development Agenda (DDA).

6. In this context, the WTO BRICS countries congratulate Russia, the largest economy outside the multilateral trading system, on the successful conclusion of the accession process to the WTO, and look forward to the forthcoming Ministerial Conference to formally endorse Russia as a new member. This will be a crucial step in making the WTO even more representative and legitimate, further strengthening the multilateral trading system.

7. We express satisfaction at the completion of the accession processes of three other new WTO members: Montenegro, Samoa, and Vanuatu. We also welcome the approval of a new set of guidelines for the accession of the Least Developed Countries that will contribute to our shared goal of reaching universality in WTO membership.

8. In this process of buttressing the multilateral trade system, we underscore the pressing need to further develop its rules and structure to address in particular the concerns and interests of developing countries. The WTO must maintain its central role in monitoring the implementation of the multilateral trade disciplines and commitments, including in the key area of dispute settlement. It also serves as a forum for discussion of trade related matters that all members agree to be relevant and pertinent. The negotiating functions of the Organisation must also be preserved and energised.

9. We attach great importance to the role of the WTO in keeping protectionist forces at bay. Under the present global economic conditions, international trade plays an even more critical role in stimulating economic growth and development. We are in full agreement that all forms of protectionism must be resisted. At the same time, we underscore the need for developing countries to retain and use, when necessary, any existing WTO-consistent policy space. We also underline that trade distorting subsidies granted by developed economies, particularly in agriculture, are one of the

most harmful forms of protectionism. These subsidies generate food insecurity and deny the development potential of this key sector in countries that already face formidable challenges to participate in global trade flows.

10. We are particularly concerned with the existing impasse in the Doha Development Round. Despite these circumstances, we will remain fully engaged in negotiations with a view to concluding the single undertaking within the shortest possible timeframe. We emphasise that negotiations on any component of the DDA must be based on the mandates multilaterally agreed since the launching of the Round in 2001 and on the delicate balance of trade-offs achieved over the last 10 years, which are also reflected in the draft modalities texts of December 2008. We remain willing to conclude the Round on the basis of those draft modalities.

11. We agree that the DDA negotiating stalemate should not discourage members from seeking results in specific areas where they agree that progress is possible. We will instruct our negotiators to engage effectively and constructively whenever such agreement exists. These efforts must not lose sight, however, of the centrality of development in the Doha mandate. Any early outcomes must deliver first on elements of interest to the poorest among the membership. Issues of interest to the developing and the least developing countries must be at the forefront, without linkages to other areas. The full implementation of the Hong Kong Ministerial Declaration regarding the duty-free-quota-free initiative, as well as topics like cotton and agriculture, must be given priority and constitute an integral part of any early agreements. These efforts must be wholly consistent with the existing mandates and observe the principles of transparency and inclusiveness. In this context, we will not encourage or support plurilateral approaches, or any other negotiating modality that may compromise or weaken the multilateral nature of the negotiations.

12. We welcome measures taken by our agencies of technical cooperation in areas which are especially relevant to African countries. They complement initiatives undertaken by the WTO and other relevant international organizations. We underline the need to keep pursuing and enhancing aid-for-trade initiatives that benefit our trading partners. The cooperation with the Cotton-4 economies is a landmark in this field and we commit to maintain and intensify it.

13. The Minister of the Russian Federation recalls that her country is expected to start implementing its commitments in the WTO as of mid-2012. She affirms that, with full WTO membership attained, Russia is going to participate in a constructive and active manner in the DDA negotiations in view of the crucial role that a balanced DDA outcome would have in the strengthening and development of the world trade system.

III.3.   BRICS Agriculture Ministers

A.   8th Meeting of Agriculture Ministers: 22 Jun. 2018, Skukuza (ZAF)

JOINT DECLARATION
OF THE 8TH MEETING OF BRICS MINISTERS OF AGRICULTURE AND AGRARIAN
DEVELOPMENT

1.   We, the Ministers of Agriculture of the Federative Republic of Brazil, the Russian Federation, the Republic of India, the People's Republic of China and the Republic of South Africa, met in Skukuza, Mpumalanga Province South Africa, for the 8th Meeting of BRICS Ministers of Agriculture and Agrarian Development on 22nd June 2018 held under the theme "Promoting Climate Smart Approaches and Actions to Enhance Resilience of Agriculture and Food Production Systems" and discussed issues of common interests on BRICS agricultural development and pointed the way forward for our agricultural cooperation.

2.   BRICS countries cover a total land area of approximately 39 million square kilometers, which is 27% of the world's total land surface. By 2017, the combined nominal Gross Domestic Product (GDP) for the BRICS countries was US$18.273 trillion. BRICS will accelerate its role as a major driving force for world economic development. The combined population of BRICS countries was estimated at 3.065 billion during 2017 and this is approximately 41% of the world population. The United Nations (UN) estimates that world population will grow from the current 7.5 billion to nearly 9.8 billion by 2050 and the BRICS countries are expected to make a significant contribution towards this growth. BRICS countries are expected to increase food accessibility to meet the growing demand of the population.

3.   We are cognisant of progress made towards the achievements of the BRICS agricultural cooperative mechanism which was initiated by the First Meeting of BRIC Ministers of Agriculture held by Russia in 2010.

4.   We acknowledge the need to fastrack progress of BRICS Agricultural Ministers proposals in line with the Xiamen Declaration of the 9th BRICS Summit. Noting that this is the second year of BRICS action plan "2017 – 2020", initiatives inclusive of bilateral agreements were concluded as well as the BRICS seminars to share experiences on agricultural resilience and adaptation to natural disasters. We therefore reconfirm our commitment to further strengthen the agricultural cooperation among members. Areas of collaboration include productivity and profitability through strengthening of sustainable agricultural practices, producers support, enhancement of trade balance, leverage on public research, innovation and technology development including value addition and sharing best practices on climate resilience especially for smallholder farmers and adaptive approaches amongst BRICS countries.

5.   We support the global fight against hunger and the implementation of the 2030 Agenda for sustainable development with the emphasis on its Sustainable Development Goal 2. We take efforts to achieve food security and nutrition and promote advanced development of agriculture and adaptation to climate change.

6.   We acknowledge the need for a comprehensive and integrated approach towards sustainable development goals, especially those closely related to agriculture.

Agricultural development to enhance food security and nutrition

7.   We are concerned about the rising food prices, farmers' income drop and agriculture input costs which have a negative impact to the local and global economies. We underline that making markets

function better can contribute to reducing food price volatility and enhance food security. It is critical to continuously improve support of on and off farm infrastructure, as well as support to producers in the form of advisory services, access to markets, creating efficiency of markets, food safety quality certification programmes as well as technology development and transfer, reducing food loss and waste. We commit to quality certifications to the appropriate farmer categories which should be primarily based on official standards and implemented in a manner that does not increase the farmers' costs.

8.   Efforts to entrench the right to food into legislation are of priority for all Member States, as we note increased food insecurity in developing and poor countries. We acknowledge the need for better baseline information on the state of food insecurity for all Member States in order to strengthen actions to reduce food insecurity. We appreciate Brazil's "Zero Hunger Program", Russia's Russian "Federation Food Security Doctrine", India's "National Food Security Mission", China's "Targeted Poverty Alleviation" and South Africa's "Fetsa Tlala Food Production Initiative".

9.   We fully support the global fight against hunger, encourage members to endorse at the highest level of policy framework and call on the international community to scale up assistance and support the United Nations bodies such as the FAO, IFAD and WFP to achieve initiatives in the Action Plan 2017-2020.

Climate change and agricultural resilience to its adverse impacts

10. We recognize that climate change has imposed threats on global food security, sustainable development and poverty eradication. We prioritise and support climate smart approaches with sustainable agricultural intensification to guide farming activities. We will further build and improve the adaptability of agriculture to climate change and support bio-economy. We intend to continuously increase agricultural production, farming income and promote best practices to better control the impact of climate change and related meteorological hazards. We recognize the particular vulnerability of agriculture to the adverse effects of climate change and the potential impacts to food security.

11. We recognize the importance of climate change adaptation towards sustainable agriculture. We will take efforts to develop, share, promote and transfer environment-friendly climate smart and sustainable agricultural intensification technologies, like integration of crops, livestock and forestry systems for developing countries to enhance resilience of agriculture and food production systems. We unequivocally emphasize the need to align practices of agricultural sustainability by encouraging farmers at various levels towards conserving, protecting and preserving natural resources. We appreciate the consensus reached at the 2017 G20 Agriculture Ministers Meeting on sustainable use of water as a natural resource. We encourage farmers to protect water resources and biodiversity through improved integrated production systems. Promoting cooperation and information exchange on climate change will be prioritised to increase the perception among farmers and policy makers regarding the benefits of fostering resilient agronomical practices that reduce risk associated to the adverse impacts of climate change as well as other relevant meteorological hazards.

12. We will, through exchange programmes, jointly implement education, capacity building and communication activities regarding mitigation adaptation and early warning systems. We acknowledge the importance of stronger surveillance and early warning systems to ensure rapid response in counteracting both natural and man-made disasters including introduction of new pests and diseases. We also encourage efforts to disseminate the use of metadata analysis and other analytic tools as strategic elements to support decision making and the implementation of national adaptation plans.

13. We acknowledge efforts by global communities to develop their national plans and domestic actions to implement the Paris Agreement (PA) through their Nationally Determined Contributions (NDCs). We welcome the outcomes of the Twenty-Third Conference of Parties (COP23) on agriculture under the United Nations Framework Convention on Climate Change (UNFCCC). We believe the

decision reached by Parties on Agriculture called "Koronivia Joint Work on Agriculture" will assist developing countries to improve their agronomical practices, enhance adaptation and resilience of agricultural systems. We appreciate Brazil's "ABC Program" and India's "Soil Health Card Scheme" as examples of national polity aiming to preserve the economic value, increase resilience and adaptive capacity as well as better control emission from agriculture.

Strengthening research and innovation for improved agricultural sustainability

14. We reaffirm and support the establishment of the BRICS Agricultural Research Platform (ARP) initiated by India in 2016. We appreciate the fundamental importance of research, development and innovation in global sustainability and competitiveness. We endeavor to strengthen the agricultural research collaborative networks among the BRICS countries to enhance the resilience of the collective agricultural and food systems in the face of the changing climate. We recognise the need for follow-up steps in implementing the aims and objectives of the ARP.

Strengthening, sharing and exchange of information for better ICT application in BRICS agriculture

15. We need to increase the effective results of the current information sharing and exchange programmes and systems as well the exchange mechanisms on agricultural information such as the Basic Agricultural Information Exchange System (BAIES).

16. We will share achievements of technology innovation, strengthen exchanges and mutual learning of innovations on smart agriculture, in areas such as biotechnology and nanotechnology. We underline the importance of better application of information and communication technologies (ICTs) in agriculture.

Trade and agricultural investment

17. We commit to the reform process in agriculture at the multilateral level, in order to realize our long standing country specific priorities including promotion of fair trade aimed at substantially reducing trade-distorting domestic practices.

18. We intend to enhance the rules-based multilateral trading system by supporting the World Trade Organisation (WTO), upholding scientific principles, reinforcing the work of the international standard-setting organizations and their subsidiary bodies (Codex Alimentarius, OIE and IPPC) related to sanitary and phyto-sanitary measures as well as Technical Barriers to Trade.

19. We will promote targeted investment in ensuring the unlocking of BRICS countries' latent agricultural potential stimulating the commerce of agricultural goods among our countries. We are committed to expanding and facilitating trade including value added products. We also welcome suggestions from the business fora to governments in order to enhance trade and improve the investment opportunities among BRICS countries.

20. We commit to pursue further dialogue with a view to reform the Agreement on Agriculture towards open, fair and non-discriminatory, market-oriented agricultural trading systems.

21. We encourage international financial institutions, including the New Development Bank (NDB) to leverage resources and sharing best practices in international development finance, and to contribute to the global agricultural market and the growth of developing countries and emerging markets.

22. We encourage the BRICS New Development Bank to finance sustainable development projects that can promote growth in agriculture, aquaculture, agro-livestock-forestry integrated system, irrigation infrastructure and other value added activities.

23. We acknowledge the achievements of South-South Cooperation, and will continue to enhance agricultural cooperation among BRICS Countries. We also note the progress of Africa's Agenda 2063 in facilitating rapid growth across sectors in Africa, especially in promoting economic diversification,

expediting agricultural transformation, upgrading agro-processing capacity, and achieving self-sufficiency and increasing food security.

24. We recognize the importance of reinforcing BRICS agricultural Ministers' coordination and collaboration under multilateral mechanisms. We will continue to strengthen communication and coordination within major international institutions and cooperative platforms and fora including the G20, the United Nations, the World Bank, the International Monetary Fund and the WTO.

25. We will endeavor to ensure the full implementation of the Action Plan 2017-2020 for Agricultural Cooperation of BRICS Countries.

26. We express our gratitude to the Ministry of Agriculture, Forestry and Fisheries of the Republic of South Africa for organizing and hosting the 8th Meeting of BRICS Ministers of Agriculture, BRICS seminar on climate smart approaches and we pledge our support and encouragement to the Federative Republic of Brazil, which will be hosting the next meeting in 2019.

B.   7th Meeting of Agriculture Ministers: 16 Jun. 2017, Nanjing (CHN)

JOINT DECLARATION
OF THE SEVENTH MEETING OF BRICS MINISTERS OF AGRICULTURE

1.   We, the Ministers of Agriculture of the Federative Republic of Brazil, the Russian Federation, the Republic of India, the People's Republic of China and the Republic of South Africa, met in Nanjing, China, for the Seventh Meeting of BRICS Ministers of Agriculture on 16 June 2017 which was held under the theme of "BRICS: Innovating and Sharing to Power Agriculture", and discussed issues of common interests on BRICS agricultural development and pointed the way forward for our agricultural cooperation.

2.   BRICS countries cover vast territories and have large populations, and our importance for global governance is ever increasing. In the past 10 years, BRICS has become a major driving force for world economic development, with its share in world economy and trade rising from 12% to 23% and from 11% to 16% respectively.

3.   Based on the Goa Declaration of the 8th BRICS Summit, we reiterate our commitment to further strengthen the agriculture cooperation. Joint mechanism of development of improved technologies, innovations and their sharing and enhancement of communication and coordination on major international and regional issues of common interest, such as productivity and profitability enhancement in BRICS countries, international trade, climate change and the 2030 Agenda for Sustainable Development, food security and nutrition are imminent to promote further development of agriculture and safeguard and expand common interest.

4.   We solemnly commit ourselves to implementing the Strategy for BRICS Economic Partnership, and deepening and expanding economic cooperation in agriculture. We are committed to enhancing multilateral coordination and oppose protectionism. In this sense, we aim to strengthen the rules-based multilateral trading system by consolidating the WTO at its core, upholding scientific principles, reinforcing the work of the international standard-setting bodies related to sanitary and phyto-sanitary issues and encouraging dialogue with a view to further reform the Agreement of Agriculture towards an open and non-discriminatory agricultural trade in line with the Doha Development objectives. Furthermore we stress the importance of a successful WTO Eleventh Ministerial Conference in Buenos Aires in December 2017.

5.   We fully acknowledge the achievements of the BRICS agricultural cooperative mechanism which was initiated by the First Meeting of BRIC Ministers of Agriculture held by Russia in 2010. In the past five years, effective actions have been carried out under the Action Plan (2012-2016) for Agricultural Cooperation of BRICS Countries, namely the Meeting of Agricultural Experts Working Group on Agro-Products and Food Security in Brazil, the "Golden Autumn" Agricultural Exhibition in Russia to display farm produce of BRICS, BRICS Agribusiness Forum in Russia, the BRICS Agricultural Research Platform (ARP) initiated by India, the BRICS Agricultural Information Exchange System (BAIES) and the Report on BRICS Agricultural Development (2017) by China, and the BRICS Workshop on Agriculture and Climate Change held by South Africa.

6.   Agriculture has strategic importance for stability. We actively support the global fight against hunger, encourage members to endorse at the highest level of policy framework and call on the international community to scale up assistance and support the United Nations, especially the Committee on World Food Security, in coordinating efforts to prevent crises from further deteriorating.

7.   We emphasize the importance of food security and nutrition for all countries. It is essential to strengthen capacity building for food security and nutrition, particularly to improve access of the most vulnerable to food. We will take efforts to increase labor productivity of farmers, especially that of smallholders, with technology and enhanced education and training, in order to boost food production and reduce food loss and waste.

8. We underline that making markets function better can contribute to reducing food price volatility and enhance food security. We will also improve conditions of food supply by facilitating trade of agricultural products and investment. We highly appreciate Brazil's "Zero Hunger Program", and call for commitment at the global level to reducing food loss and waste and to food production. We believe that sustainable food security needs to be built on support from social, economic and environmental dimensions.

9. We reiterate the importance of agriculture for the safety of food, resources and the ecosystem. We will align production growth with the carrying capacity of resource and environment to jointly strive for global agricultural sustainability. To promote the greening of agriculture of BRICS, we agree that sustainable agriculture should be extended to other countries to generate economic, social and ecological benefits in full, optimize agricultural ecosystems, and enhance the production of quality and affordable agricultural products.

10. We are committed to agricultural product safety and quality through the implementation of international standards developed by international standard-setting bodies in the sanitary and phytosanitary and technical barriers to trade (TBT) issues, such as the Codex Alimentarius, OIE and IPPC.

11. We stress the need to strengthen agricultural sustainability by improving resource efficiency, conserving and protecting natural resources, and enhancing resilience of regions and ecological systems. We believe that greater sustainability in social, economic, agricultural and environmental terms should be achieved at the global, regional and country levels. We welcome the consensus reached at the 2017 G20 Agriculture Ministers Meeting on sustainable use of water resource.

12. We recognize that climate change has imposed threats on global food security, sustainable development and poverty elimination. We endorse climate-smart approaches to guide farming activities, commit to build and improve the adaptability of agriculture to climate change, continuously increase agricultural production and farming income, reduce or prevent greenhouse gas emissions when possible, and cooperate with international organizations in achieving the United Nations Sustainable Development Goals (UN SDGs). We recognize the importance of agriculture to climate change mitigation and sustainable agriculture will depend on the contribution of other sectors to climate change mitigation.

13. We acknowledge the importance of stronger surveillance and early warning systems to prevent and reduce natural and man-made disasters and food crises for agricultural development in all countries.

14. We place great importance on technology innovation and are committed to advancing innovation on the fronts of food security, sustainable agriculture, and resource and environmental improvement. We value agricultural technology innovation as an important approach to ensuring sustainable food security. We will continue to promote research in and application of technologies that can increase production, improve quality and save water, and will develop cutting-edge technologies such as biotechnology and new resilient farming systems. We will share achievements of technology innovation, strengthen exchanges and mutual learning of innovations on smart agriculture, biotechnology and nanotechnology. We will sign agreements of scientific and technological cooperation, explore new modalities of cooperation, and create fresh momentum for agricultural development.

15. We have made much progress in mechanisms of exchange on agricultural information. The Basic Agricultural Information Exchange System (BAIES) and the Agricultural Research Platform (ARP), in particular, has provided new platform for deeper agricultural cooperation and better information sharing between BRICS.

16. We should build on existing information liaison mechanisms to set up stable teams of liaison officers, and identify information technology supporters and members of expert teams. Agriculture-related information will be exchanged annually to update BRICS basic agricultural database, and the online version of the BAIES will be developed to provide online information sharing. The country that chairs will oversee this process.

17. We acknowledge the considerable achievements made and challenges faced by developing countries in poverty alleviation. We will enhance infrastructures and public services, improve working and living conditions in rural areas, and promote distinctive local crops, livestock and processing business in poor areas, to allow for better self-development in poor areas of BRICS. We stand ready to share successful experience and models of poverty alleviation, in a joint effort to tackle the issue of poverty reduction facing other countries.

18. We are committed to expanding the trade of crops, livestock, fisheries and particularly agricultural products with high added value. We will expand agricultural market access in order to boost economic and social benefits to farmers, herdsmen, fishermen, foresters and other rural residents. We will promote further discussions on the particularities of agricultural trade, especially SPS issues. We welcome holding business fora on agriculture aiming at promoting trade and investment and enhancing transnational cooperation between BRICS agro-businesses. We also welcome suggestions from the business fora to governments in order to enhance trade and improve investment environment.

19. We will promote in-depth cooperation in agricultural investment. Recognizing the broad prospects for cooperation in the comprehensive development of agricultural products, farming and transportation infrastructure, and the establishment of agro-trade zones and logistics centers, we will promote in-depth agricultural cooperation between BRICS and other countries. We support efforts to promote mutual agricultural investment, maintain openness and inclusiveness, and seek common agricultural development.

20. We believe that, cooperation in agricultural trade and investment is an important channel for BRICS to achieve mutually beneficial, all-win, sustainable and inclusive growth. Strengthened agricultural cooperation among BRICS is important for ensuring global food security and stable agricultural development, eradicating poverty, and achieving the UN SDGs. We are committed to facilitating investment and trade by various means including exhibitions and forums, and to encouraging and supporting enterprise participation in trade promotion activities held by BRICS members.

21. We invite international financial institutions to provide significant financial support for the agricultural cooperation and sustainable agricultural development of BRICS, and to contribute to the global agricultural market and the agricultural growth of developing countries and emerging markets.

22. Cooperation between BRICS members is inclusive. We will prioritize the development of bioindustry, agro-processing, investment and trade in farm produce, and agricultural service.

23. We acknowledge the achievements of South-South Cooperation, and continue to enhance agricultural cooperation among BRICS Countries.

24. We note the progress of Africa's Agenda 2063 in facilitating rapid growth across sectors in Africa, especially in promoting economic diversification, expediting agricultural transformation, upgrading agro-processing capacity, and realizing self-sufficiency of food.

25. We recognize the importance of reinforcing coordination and collaboration under multilateral mechanisms. We will continue to strengthen communication and coordination within major international institutions and cooperative frameworks including the G20, the United Nations, the World Bank, the International Monetary Fund, and the World Trade Organization.

26. We have reviewed and approved the Action Plan 2017-2020 for Agricultural Cooperation of BRICS Countries which will steer further cooperation among BRICS members with identified priorities and detailed programs.

27. We express our gratitude to the Ministry of Agriculture of the People's Republic of China for organizing and hosting the Seventh Meeting of BRICS Ministers of Agriculture, and we pledge our support and encouragement to the Republic of South Africa, which will be hosting the next meeting in 2018.

C.   Action Plan 2017-2020 for Agricultural Cooperation of BRICS Countries

ACTION PLAN 2017-2020 FOR AGRICULTURAL COOPERATION OF BRICS COUNTRIES

Based on the consensus reached by the Eighth BRICS Summit;

Considering the effects of the Action Plan 2012-2016 for Agricultural Cooperation of BRICS Countries;

Taking into account the Joint Declaration of the Seventh Meeting of BRICS Ministers of Agriculture;

The Action Plan 2017-2020 for Agricultural Cooperation of BRICS Countries is hereby formulated to be submitted to the Seventh Meeting of BRICS Ministers of Agriculture for review and approval;

BRICS countries shall share/arrange/mobilize appropriate resources to accomplish all the cooperation activities below.

Objectives

This Action Plan is developed to achieve the following aims:

Support the United Nations' (the UN) efforts in fighting poverty and hunger at the global level, exchange policies experience in ensuring food security, enhance food supply capacities of BRICS, and contribute to the mitigation of global food crisis;

Implement national programs of the 2030 Agenda for Sustainable Development, exchange productivity enhancement technologies adaptive to climate change under the framework of agricultural sustainability, and strengthen resilience of agricultural production systems and their adaptability to natural and climate disasters;

Strengthen the rules-based multilateral trading system by consolidating the WTO at its core, upholding scientific principles, reinforcing the work of the international standard-setting bodies related to sanitary and phyto-sanitary and technical trade barrier (TBT) issues and encouraging dialogue with a view to further reform the Agreement of Agriculture towards fair agricultural trade in line with the Doha Development objectives.

Leverage technology innovations to ensure agricultural sustainability, and power agricultural development through technological cooperation and sharing of innovation outcomes;

Build on global economic transformation and on BRICS agriculture strength to enhance trade of quality agro-products and transnational investment of BRICS agribusinesses;

Develop the Basic Agricultural Information Exchange System (BAIES) to exchange and share BRICS basic agricultural information, cooperate on application of modern information technology in agriculture and promote agricultural information and communication technologies of BRICS.

Priorities

I.   Accelerating agricultural development to enhance food security and nutrition

1.   BRICS will deepen exchange and cooperation within international organizations, and continue with efforts to establish the mechanism of convening regular BRICS meetings at the Food and Agriculture Organization of the United Nations (the FAO).

2.   BRICS will conduct joint research, together with international organizations, in effective ways to promote food security cooperation, aiming at continuing with experience exchange on capacity building for food security.3. We will encourage investment cooperation on agricultural infrastructures for sustainable food systems and explore tools for food market forecasting in the mid-and-long-term.

3.   BRICS will exchange experiences in policies aiming at improving the participation of smallholders in the global agricultural value chains at the time of economic transformation, and help smallholders of BRICS increase food productivity and improve food security through meetings, technical cooperation, technology demonstration and training.

II.   Promoting cooperation and exchange on climate change for stronger agricultural resilience to natural risks

1.   BRICS will work together to research and develop technologies that can boost agricultural production and adapt to climate change, especially environment-friendly technologies affordable for developing countries. BRICS will hold seminars to share experiences of agricultural resilience and adaptation to natural disasters.

2.   BRICS will work together on surveillance and early warning on meteorological conditions for agriculture, and will jointly undertake education and communication activities regarding mitigation and adaptation of climate change. By issuing timely and accurate early warning, BRICS aim to actively adapt to climate change, reduce food loss, increase farmers' income, and improve smallholders' adaptability to climate change. We will work together to share best practices on climate change mitigation and promote agricultural resilience.

III.   Strengthening technology innovation and demonstration for greater agricultural sustainability

1.   BRICS will jointly implement thematic research programs as agreed under the Agricultural Research Platform (ARP). BRICS will deepen agricultural technology cooperation in the areas of agricultural biotechnology, plant protection, quality standard of agricultural products, resources and environment.

2.   BRICS will cooperate in the sphere of agricultural technology, and utilize the potential of BRICS for innovative modalities of cooperation on agricultural technology, by encouraging cooperation among all stakeholders in agricultural science and technology.

3.   BRICS will promote cooperative research projects, mutual visits and joint graduate programs, so as to contribute to advances in BRICS agricultural technology and development of agricultural businesses.

IV.   Improving safe agricultural trade and expanding agricultural investment

1.   BRICS will strengthen trade dialogues, build platforms for trade policy exchange, improve trade facilitation, and expand scale and scope of trade in agriculture. BRICS will promote the implementation of international sanitary and phytosanitary standards, in order to harmonize accreditation procedures for exporting establishments.

2.   BRICS will explore diverse and stable agro-trade channels, host international agricultural exhibitions, and encourage businesses to participate in trade promotion activities held by members; and, will promote the development of electronic solutions to lower the cost of international trade.

3.   We will convene meetings of business in agriculture aimed at promoting trade and investment and enhancing transnational cooperation between BRICS agro-businesses.

4.   BRICS will encourage a more active role of the international financial institutions including the New Development Bank (NDB) in advancing agricultural investment.

V. Strengthening, sharing and exchange of information for better ICT application in BRICS agriculture

1. BRICS will improve the Agricultural Information Exchange System (BAIES), put together technology expert teams, improve BRICS databases of basic agricultural information, realize ICT-based management of the BAIES, and exchange agriculture-related information on a regular basis.

2. BRICS will strengthen efforts of collecting and releasing basic agricultural information, identify experts to analyze such information on a regular basis, issue a Report on BRICS Agricultural Development every two years, and research and discuss emerging issues in BRICS agricultural development.

3. BRICS will carry out cooperation on the application of modern information technologies in agriculture, develop demonstration projects of ICT-based smart agriculture, and convene workshops on ICT and modern agriculture, with emphasis on ICT application on agricultural data platforms, precision agriculture, and agricultural value chain integration.

Operational mechanism

1. Each priority shall be led by one BRICS member in collaboration with and participated by other members.

2. Annual debriefings shall be organized to review and evaluate progress of implementation of the Action Plan.

3. The debriefing shall be organized by the country holding the BRICS presidency, and shall produce a progress report for the Meeting of BRICS Ministers of Agriculture.

4. Each member shall have a liaison team, which will be in charge of the accountability report for this Action Plan, and communication on cooperation programs.

D.   6th Meeting of Agriculture Ministers: 23 Sep. 2016, New Delhi (IND)

JOINT DECLARATION
OF BRICS MINISTERS OF AGRICULTURE

1.   We, the Ministers of Agriculture of the Federative Republic of Brazil, the Russian Federation, the Republic of India, the People's Republic of China and the Republic of South Africa met in New Delhi, Republic of India for the sixth Meeting of BRICS Ministers of Agriculture on the 23rd September, 2016, and discussed the way ahead for our future initiatives and continued cooperation.

2.   We appreciate the need and progress made amongst the BRICS member countries in enhancing agriculture technology cooperation and innovation through the creation of a basic agricultural information exchange system, in reducing the impact of climate variability and change on food security and adaptation of agriculture to such changes, and in developing a general strategy for ensuring access to food for the most vulnerable populations and for promoting the trade and investment, which were identified as the main areas of cooperation.

3.   We believe that promoting development of agriculture management and conservation of plant genetic resources for food and agriculture, broadening of the genetic base of crops, livestock and fisheries and increase in the range of genetic diversity available to farmers, and raising the farmer's income are central to addressing the problems of rising income inequality, unemployment, and excessive food price volatility. With the constraints on natural resources such as land and water, the group firmly believes that enhancement in agricultural productivity and production, and product quality can only be achieved through strengthened research, technology transfer, and extension services /comprehensive producer support, and reforming social security and markets.

4.   We also note that solving the problem of chronic household food insecurity is essential, and hence support giving differentiated yet coordinated considerations to transient and persistent food insecurity and nutrition in our policies, with a particular focus on providing them long-term food security. Thus, we recognize that the strategy to overcome the challenge of persistent food insecurity mainly lies in interventions to raise smallholders' productivity and the purchasing power of the poor to improve and ensure food access to this vulnerable group. We commit to continue taking initiatives for cutting cost of food production, and strive for research in produce processing technologies and post-harvest management including storage to reduce food loss and waste.

5.   We acknowledge that changing consumption patterns and higher consumption levels require emphasis on higher investments in the whole value chain, and increase in both public and private sector investments in agriculture. We therefore, commit to develop incentives and foster partnerships with both public and private sector for investments in agriculture. We believe that increasing public investment and creating favorable environment for enhanced private sector participation will promote integration of primary, secondary, and tertiary sectors in rural areas, and spur growth in the agriculture sector.

6.   We recognize that small agricultural holdings face grave challenges of viability and profitability in the context of increasingly complex food value chains, pressure on natural resources and climate change. Since these small holdings provide livelihood opportunities, it is necessary for the governments to protect the interest of these smallholder producers. Many of them lack access to resources. Therefore, governments need to prioritize and strengthen support for family farming and small agricultural holdings, provide a better environment for smallholders' collective actions and organization and their market integration, expand smallholders' access to innovation, inputs, capital, technology, and services, on the basis of gender equality and thus making them an asset in the process of economic transformation.

7.   BRICS Members welcome initiatives that seek to address water management in line with investment in infrastructure, taking into account the dependence of agriculture on water. We resolve to invest in water infrastructure for irrigation to assist farmers in building resilience during times of drought. We stress the necessity to ensure the efficient use of water through designing of appropriate irrigation systems, rainwater harvesting, promotion of alternative methods of production, and to share experiences and expertise in this critical area.

8.   We note that promoting agricultural sustainability is a key component of the 2030 Agenda for Sustainable Development. To maintain productivity growth in a sustainable manner, there is a need to move from input intensive approach to innovation and technology driven production systems to attain optimal resource use efficiency. This could be achieved through exchange of best practices, knowledge, information and technology that are conducive to the conservation and proper use of land, forest, and water.

9.   We recognize the importance of deploying information and communication technology (ICT) in agriculture, as it creates an enabling environment to connect the farmers to inputs, technologies, financial services and markets by enhancing the scales of operation at various stages of production and post- production system.

10.   We emphasize the importance of ensuring food security and nutrition, and eliminating hunger and poverty through increased agricultural production on a sustainable basis. We further envision BRICS as an important agriculture cooperation platform for developing and promoting models of sustainable agriculture and sharing them with others at global level with a view of addressing issues of world hunger, malnutrition, poverty, and income inequality.

11.   It is acknowledged that agricultural land is a finite resource, which is subject to continuous population pressure and demand for alternate use impacting agriculture production. We, therefore, agree that the protection and preservation of cultivable land with high agricultural potential remains our priority.

12.   We acknowledge the importance of the multilateral trade system as a means of promoting global trade. In this context, we welcome the outcomes of the WTO Tenth Ministerial Conference at Nairobi held in December 2015, especially as regards the elimination of agricultural export subsidies. We also recognize the importance of the conclusion of the Trade Facilitation Agreement ratification process for perishable food trade.

13.   We are committed to providing safety and predictability to agricultural trade. In this regard, we will work to consolidate the scientific principles in sanitary and phyto-sanitary discussions. Similarly, we will work together to strengthen the global reference organizations relating to sanitary and phyto-sanitary issues: Codex Alimentarius, OIE (World Organization for Animal Health) and IPPC (International Plant Protection Convention).

14.   We recognize that the commitment of the agricultural sector is critical to the success of the worldwide endeavors to conserve biodiversity and to ensure the continued provision of environmental services. Thus, we propose to share experience on policies regarding conservation of existing native vegetation, including that on the river banks with a view to contributing to our biodiversity goals and targets while supporting the implementation of our nationally determined contributions under the Paris Agreement.

15.   We are deeply concerned about the adverse impact of climate change on agriculture affecting vast sections of population in general and vulnerable ones in particular. Hence, we acknowledge the need for cooperative and coordinated response in combating the negative influence of climate change. We shall therefore promote adoption of climate resilient agricultural technologies and enhance adaptive capacity through continuous exchange of information and sharing of experiences with respect to our relevant national policies, plans, programs, and research. We also recognize the efforts made by other countries through their nationally determined contributions following the

adoption of the historic Paris Agreement under the United Nations Framework Convention on Climate Change (UNFCCC).

16. We further welcome the declaration of the year 2016 as the International Year of Pulses by the United Nations General Assembly and endeavour to promote the value of pulses throughout the food system, recognizing their beneficial effect on soil fertility and in ameliorating malnutrition. We will promote production of pulses in the BRICS countries and raise awareness among the people about their importance in dietary nutrition.

17. We commend the work of BRICS Agriculture Cooperation Working Group and express our satisfaction in implementing the 2012-16 Action Plan. Based on the outcome and lessons of the 2012-16 action plan, we have identified priorities for future cooperation.

18. We welcome the outcome of the meeting of the experts from the BRICS countries held at New Delhi, wherein, it was agreed to develop a virtual BRICS Agricultural Research Platform (BRICS-ARP). This Platform aims to promote food security, sustainable agricultural development and poverty alleviation through strategic cooperation in agriculture among the member countries. Towards this end, the BRICS Members shall cooperate in the domains of agricultural research and development, technology transfer, capacity building and information sharing through networks of agriculture and allied disciplines.

19. We express our gratitude to the Republic of India for organizing and hosting the Sixth Meeting of the Ministers of Agriculture of the BRICS countries and we pledge our support to the People's Republic of China, who will be hosting the seventh meeting in the year 2017.

E.   5th Meeting of Agriculture Ministers: 9 Oct. 2015, Moscow (RUS)

JOINT DECLARATION
OF THE 5TH MEETING OF THE BRICS MINISTERS OF AGRICULTURE AND AGRARIAN DEVELOPMENT

1.   We, the Ministers of Agriculture and Agrarian Development of the Federative Republic of Brazil, the Russian Federation, the Republic of India, the People's Republic of China and the Republic of South Africa met in Moscow, Russian Federation for the 5th Meeting of BRICS Ministers of Agriculture and Agrarian Development on 9 October, 2015.

2.   In the spirit of the "Ufa Declaration" of the Seventh BRICS Leaders Summit we reiterate our commitment to further develop agricultural cooperation, in particular, related to enhancing agricultural trade and investment, agricultural research, technologies and innovations, the protection of the right to adequate food, specially for the most vulnerable communities, by strengthening family farming, creation of a basic agricultural, information exchange system of BRICS countries, mitigation of the negative impact of climate change on food security and nutrition and adaptation of agriculture to climate change.

3.   We recognize the achievements of the BRICS to date in strengthening the global food system by adopting comprehensive measures on boosting agricultural production, trade and investment. The BRICS countries have become an important force to deal with the food security challenge and we agree to further intensify our efforts in building a win-win partnership to increase productivity sustainably in order to feed the world population that is expected to exceed nine billion by 2050.

4.   We welcome the outcomes of the United Nations Sustainable Development Summit held on 25-27 September, 2015 and the adoption of the 2030 Agenda for Sustainable Development. We commit to work towards achieving its Sustainable Development Goal 2 aiming to end hunger, achieve food security and improved nutrition and promote sustainable agriculture.

5.   We appreciate the work of the BRICS Agricultural Cooperation Working Group, express our satisfaction with the progress in implementing the 2012-2016 Action Plans and endorse the Annual Calendar of Activities on 2015-2016 for implementation of the Action Plan (Annex I).

6.   We believe that the established mechanism of consultations among Permanent Representatives of the BRICS nations to the Food and Agriculture Organization of the United Nations (FAO) will play a useful role in coordination and give practical impetus to our cooperation in the field of agriculture and agrarian development.

7.   We welcome the progress made on the five pillars of intra-BRICS cooperation in the agricultural sphere:

Trade and investment promotion

8.   We welcome the launch of the BRICS New Development Bank (NDB) that shall serve as a powerful instrument for financing infrastructure and sustainable development projects in agricultural sphere.

9.   We welcome adoption of the Strategy for BRICS Economic Partnership and agree to take practical steps for its effective implementation, one of which will be preparation of the BRICS Roadmap for trade, economic and investment cooperation until 2020.

10. We acknowledge the importance of the multilateral trade system as a means of promoting global trade and ensuring global food security. And in this context we reiterate the importance of a successful WTO Tenth Ministerial Conference at Nairobi in December 2015.

11. We dedicate ourselves to improving investment climate in our countries and reiterate our support to implementation of the voluntary Principles for Responsible Investment in Agriculture and Food Systems endorsed by the Committee on World Food Security (CFS) in 2014. We also underscore the importance of raising investments at all stages of food value chain and increasing engagement with the private sector in these efforts, inter alia, through the mechanism of public-private partnerships.

12. We agree that business investment and trade cooperation can also be intensified through promotion of agricultural exhibitions, trade fairs and investment fora. In this regard we thank the Russian Federation for hosting the Exhibition of Agricultural Investment Projects of BRICS countries and AgroBusinessForum "Development of Mutual Trade and Investments - Basis for Sustainable Development of Agriculture in the BRICS Countries" held in the framework of the Russian Agricultural Exhibition "Golden Autumn" in October 2015 and look forward to the 13-th International China Agricultural Trade Fair in November 2015.

13. We note that strengthening cooperation and coordination in the areas of development and enforcement of sanitary and phytosanitary (SPS) measures, standards, technical regulation and conformity assessment procedures also creates favorable conditions for enhancing intra- BRICS trade. We encourage our continuing technical dialogue in those areas. In this context we will work together with the relevant international SPS standard setting bodies to ensure that standards, guidelines and recommendations are based on scientific principles and that they adhere to the provisions of the SPS agreements.

Development of a general strategy for ensuring access to food for the most vulnerable population

14. We stress that there are still 795 million people undernourished, 98% of which live in developing countries. Extreme poverty and food insecurity are inextricably linked, and we note with great concern that about 3 quarters of the world's poor live in rural areas. Both poverty and food insecurity should be tackled by combination of social safety nets and measures aimed at increasing agricultural production sustainably.

15. Strengthening family farming, inter alia, is an essential precondition for the eradication of poverty and hunger. In this regard we welcome the events held in 2014 - the International Year of Family Farming – as well as High-Level Forum on Connecting Smallholders to Markets organized by the CFS in June 2015.

16. Recognizing that investments in social protection systems have to be considered as critical catalysts for inclusive growth and sustainable development, we will continue efforts considered necessary in promoting the establishment of more comprehensive nutrition- sensitive social protection programs. We will further promote partnership and cooperation among the BRICS countries, aiming to develop a knowledge-sharing network and platform on best practices to enhance South-South Cooperation for improved social protection systems that foster better food security and nutrition. In this regard we welcome the outcomes of the "Global Forum on Nutrition-Sensitive Social Protection Programs: Towards Partnership for Development" held in Moscow in September 2015.

17. We recall that 2016 will mark 10 years of the 2006 International Conference on Agrarian Reform and Rural Development (ICARRD) organized by FAO in Porto Alegre, Brazil. In this respect, we note efforts by countries and international organizations in promoting the implementation of the Voluntary Guidelines on the Responsible Governance of the Tenure of Land, Fisheries and Forests in the Context of National Food Security (VGGT) endorsed by the CFS in 2012.

18. Ensuring access to food remains a central necessity in the fight against poverty. We are informed about the ongoing progress in the development of the BRICS "General strategy for ensuring access to food for the most vulnerable population". We also take note of the relevant discussions within the Expo Milano 2015 held under the theme "Feeding the Planet: Energy for Life".

Enhancing agricultural technology cooperation and innovation

19. We emphasize our commitment to advance agricultural research, science and technology which can play an important role in increasing agricultural production and productivity, farmers' incomes and in reducing the incidence of global hunger. Towards this end various aspects of agricultural research, including extension to the field level will receive our full attention and priority.

20. We acknowledge that BRICS nations are endowed with advantages of rich biodiversity, scientific capacity, high levels of agricultural production, trade and consumption that could lead to mutually beneficial cooperation. We recognize that favorable policy and regulatory environment is necessary to adopt technological innovations. We highlight the need for long- term cooperation and information sharing in the area of successful identification and implementation of policies and institutional mechanisms that contribute to technology advancement.

21. We highlight that research and human resource development is paramount to improve the overall agricultural technological capacity of countries. In this regard we agree to consider the initiative to establish the BRICS Agriculture Research Centre (BARC) proposed by India to intensify cooperation in the areas of agricultural science, technology, innovation and capacity building including technologies for family farming and to increase yields and farmers' incomes. We expect to discuss this further.

Creation of a basic agricultural information exchange system of BRICS countries

22. We recognize that the exchange of agricultural information can facilitate the identification of agricultural development advantages, advance trade and investment cooperation in the field of agriculture and agrarian development, and play an important role in promoting agriculture in the BRICS countries.

23. We note the progress on establishing the Basic Agricultural Information Exchange System (BAIES) of the BRICS countries since our 2nd Meeting. We welcome further efforts to strengthen consultation and coordination with all parties on the basis of the consensus reached regarding BAIES which will provide information for the decision-making by the BRICS agricultural and agrarian development authorities through robust information collection, processing and exchange among the BRICS countries. The BAIES will have its trial run in 2015 and will be officially launched into operation in 2016.

24. We also support the initiatives to prepare the Report on Agricultural Cooperation of the BRICS countries that is one of the outcomes of the work on BAIES on an annual basis and to nominate focal points responsible for collecting and providing the necessary information. The first Report will be developed and presented at the next Meeting of the BRICS Ministers of Agriculture and Agrarian Development in 2016.

Reduction of negative impact of climate change on food security and adaptation of agriculture to climate change

25. We recognize that negative impact of climate change on agriculture and food security is a global problem of enormous economic, environmental and societal significance. We acknowledge that BRICS can provide global leadership in this regard by developing and applying adaptation technologies that enhance resilience of agricultural systems while increasing sustainable and environmentally friendly agricultural production.

26. We agree that sustainable agricultural production and productivity can be achieved through, inter alia, enhancement of farmland irrigation and drainage infrastructure, development and application of yield-promoting technologies, restoration of degraded land, promotion of sustainable use of natural resources, and improvement of soil fertility. In this context we note with appreciation the outcomes of the varied events held in the framework of the International Year of Soils and

appreciate South Africa for hosting the XIV World Forestry Congress (WFC) in Durban in September 2015.

27. We welcome sharing experiences on climate advisory services, monitoring and Early Warning Systems (EWS) as well as other adaptation strategies such as contingency plans for the extreme weather events and their effects. We also agree to support the efforts to increase investment in sound agricultural insurance and risk management tools, especially for small- holder family farmers, and in research on alternative sources of food, fodder, fiber and energy, inter alia, bio-mass energy. In this regard we support the efforts of the United Nations Framework Convention on Climate Change (UNFCCC) and its Green Climate Fund (GCF) to assist developing countries counter climate change and look forward to the successful outcomes of the COP21 in December 2015. We acknowledge the progress and continuous efforts of the BRICS countries on reducing the negative impact of climate change on food security and promoting measures for the adaptation of agriculture to climate change.

28. We express our gratitude to the Russian Federation for organizing and hosting the 5th Meeting of the BRICS Ministers of Agriculture and Agrarian Development and express our support to India, the host of the upcoming Ministerial Meeting.

F.   4th Meeting of Agriculture Ministers: 13 Mar. 2015, Brasilia (BRA)

JOINT DECLARATION
OF THE 4TH MEETING OF THE BRICS MINISTERS OF AGRICULTURE AND AGRARIAN DEVELOPMENT

1.   In accordance with the mandate contained in the Fortaleza Declaration and Action Plan, adopted by the Leaders at the Sixth BRICS Summit, we, the Ministers of Agriculture and Agrarian Development of the BRICS countries, met in Brasilia, Brazil, on 13 March 2015. We reviewed our prolific cooperation and coordination agenda and discussed the way ahead for future initiatives and enhanced continued cooperation.

We, therefore:

2.   Recalled the commitment, expressed by the Leaders at the Fortaleza Summit, in accordance with Action Plan 2012-2016 for Agricultural Cooperation of BRICS, to promote agricultural cooperation and to exchange information on strategies to ensure access to food for the most vulnerable population, reduction of the negative impact of climate change on food security and adaptation of agriculture to climate change. We emphasized the importance and potential of BRICS cooperation in agriculture and agrarian development and underscored that agricultural development of the BRICS countries plays a key role in ensuring both the prosperity of the global economy and global food security.

3.   Noted that BRICS countries have made a fundamental contribution to world food security, given that a sizeable majority of the 209 million women and men who have been lifted out of food insecurity in the past two decades reside in the BRICS countries, as stated by the United Nations Food and Agriculture Organization (FAO) in its report "The State of Food Insecurity in the World 2014". In particular, we recognized the important role of public procurement programs that purchase food from family farmers for food distribution, school feeding and other programs, as policy instruments for achieving food and nutrition security, while providing access to local markets and income generation for national small-scale food producers in the BRICS and other emerging market economies and developing countries.

4.   Commended the work of BRICS Trade Ministers and reiterated the statement made in their 4th meeting in Fortaleza that the World Trade Organization (WTO) work program should reflect the centrality of agriculture and of the development dimension of the Doha Round. We emphasized that agriculture, and rural and agrarian development are areas in which the five countries are confronted with similar challenges and are in a position to take advantage of similar opportunities. We recalled that the five countries are committed to ensuring food and nutrition security, in our own countries and worldwide; are key global players in the production and trade of agricultural goods; and count with cutting-edge technology in many agricultural sectors.

5.   Expressed our satisfaction with the intense coordination and dialogue between BRICS representatives at FAO, the International Fund for Agricultural Development, the World Food Program and in other relevant multilateral fora. We welcomed the creation of an informal consultative group of BRICS countries in Rome to coordinate initiatives on food security and smallholder agriculture as agreed in the 2012-2016 Action Plan. Among areas to be addressed at the FAO, we agreed to maintain coordination and dialogue on issues discussed by the FAO governing bodies, in particular on the follow up activities of the II International Conference on Nutrition and the International Year of Family Farming, on information systems such as the Agricultural Marketing Information System (AMIS) and on cooperation in the humanitarian field of food assistance, as well as on issues discussed at the Committee on World Food Security.

6. Furthermore, in the context of the ongoing activities of the International Year of Soils, we noted our intention to raise awareness among stakeholders about the importance of soil for agriculture, to support effective policies and actions for the sustainable management and protection of soil resources, to promote investment in sustainable use of soil, to develop and maintain healthy soils for different land users and population groups.

7. Agreed that the Group would exchange views amongst themselves and with BRICS representations to the United Nations (UN) in New York, in particular, on the negotiations of Sustainable Development Goals in the context of the Post-2015 Development Agenda, and to other UN instances where matters related to agriculture, agrarian and rural development are being discussed.

8. Expressed our satisfaction with the ongoing implementation of the Action Plan 2012-2016, adopted in Chengdu, China in 2011, and commended the BRICS Agricultural Cooperation Working Group for the efforts being undertaken to that end.

9. Deeply appreciated Brazil for hosting, prior to our meeting, a Seminar on Public Policies for Food and Nutrition Security and the Strengthening of Family Farming, in which experts exchanged information on the complementarities between successful national strategies of the BRICS countries and their respective regions and examined how to advance in attaining these shared priority goals. It was agreed that the results of the seminar would be systematized as part of the elaboration of a General Strategy for ensuring access to food for the most vulnerable populations of BRICS and other developing countries, in line with the Action Plan 2012-2016.

10. Agreed that BRICS countries should seek to promote trade and investment in the agricultural sector through participation in exhibitions, trade fairs and investment fora. We noted that BRICS countries will host important international agricultural fairs and exhibitions, such as the exhibition of agricultural investment projects of BRICS countries and the Agribusiness Forum in Russia, the Agroexpo in China and the Southern African International Trade Exhibition in South Africa, in 2015, and Agri Expo in India, in 2016.

11. Agreed to establish cooperation agreements and arrangements among BRICS countries, with a view to facilitate greater access to their agricultural markets.

12. Recalled the grave distortion caused by agricultural export subsidies on international trade and reiterated our commitment in supporting WTO negotiations for eliminating the use of this policy instrument by countries as stated in the WTO Ministerial Conference Declaration, adopted in Bali, 2013.

13. Agreed that in line with the Bali Ministerial Conference, multilateral negotiations should prioritize efforts to create a level playing field by substantially improving market access, eliminating export subsidies and significantly reducing the level of trade distorting domestic support. We reaffirmed our commitment to work together to negotiate and make all concerted efforts to agree and adopt a permanent solution to the issue of public stockholding for food security purposes by 31st December 2015 in line with the decision adopted by the WTO General Council on 27th November 2014.

14. Welcomed the presentation of a revised draft proposal for the creation of the Basic Agricultural Information Exchange System of BRICS countries, noted with satisfaction the progress in the elaboration of the proposal and called upon our technical experts to continue their joint work with a view to ensure the system's development and to consider its possible linkage with AMIS in order to avoid unnecessary duplications.

15. Reaffirmed our commitment in intensifying BRICS cooperation in the areas of agricultural science, technology, innovation and capacity building, including technologies for smallholder farming.

16. Highlighted the relevance of ensuring the production of safe and healthy food and consumer protection. In this context, we stressed that science must be the foundation of both national and international food standards and control systems. Moreover, we emphasized that BRICS countries should use, as the basis of their measures, the standards, guidelines and recommendations developed by the international standard-setting bodies such as the FAO/WHO Codex Alimentarius Commission and the World Organization for Animal Health, inter alia, as recognized by the WTO Agreement on the Application of Sanitary and Phytosanitary Measures and the Agreement on Technical Barriers to Trade. Our countries should also exchange views on labelling rules.

17. Expressed our grave concern over the negative impact of climate change, especially the risks posed by extreme weather events, on agriculture and food and nutrition security. We agreed that adapting to the impact of climate change and mitigating its negative effects, while increasing agricultural production, requires evidence-based approaches that consider science, technology and innovation as well as traditional knowledge, as appropriate. We agreed to enhance our cooperation and to continue exchanging information and sharing experiences on our relevant national policies, programs, plans and climate change adaptation strategies.

18. Recalled the signing of the agreement establishing the New Development Bank during the Sixth BRICS Summit and its purpose of mobilizing resources for infrastructure and sustainable development projects in BRICS and other emerging and developing economies.

19. Expressed our appreciation to the Federative Republic of Brazil for organizing and hosting the 4th Meeting of the BRICS Ministers of Agriculture and Agrarian Development and expressed our support to the Russian Federation, the host of the upcoming Ministerial, in its efforts to organize it.

G.   3rd Meeting of Agriculture Ministers: 29 Oct. 2013, Pretoria (ZAF)

THIRD MEETING
OF THE BRICS MINISTERS OF AGRICULTURE AND AGRARIAN DEVELOPMENT

We, the Ministers of Agriculture and Agrarian Development of the Federative Republic of Brazil, the Russian Federation, the Republic of India, the People's Republic of China and the Republic of South Africa met in Pretoria, South Africa for the 3rd Meeting of BRICS Ministers of Agriculture and Agrarian Development on October 29, 2013 under the theme: *"The negative effect of climate change on world food security"*. Our cooperation in the sector of agriculture and agrarian development was characterized by in-depth discussions on common interests and challenges with the view of finding lasting solutions. We therefore;

1.   Noted the "eThekwini Declaration" that was adopted at the 5th BRICS Summit held in Durban, South Africa on March 27, 2013, which encourages ongoing agricultural cooperation amongst the BRICS countries.

2.   Noted that the BRICS countries are actively implementing the consensus reached during the 2nd Meeting of BRICS Ministers of Agriculture and Agrarian Development that was held in Chengdu, the People's Republic of China in 2011.

3.   Noted that the BRICS countries conducted pragmatic cooperation and adopted tangible measures to boost domestic agricultural productivity, which has played a positive role in contributing to food security and promoting economic stability.

4.   Recognised that the BRICS countries are an important grouping to deal with the global food crisis, promote global economic recovery and play an important role in global initiatives on food security.

5.   Welcomed and endorsed the outcome and recommendations, as outlined in the Progress Report contained in the Minutes of the 3rd Meeting of BRICS Agriculture Cooperation Working Group held in Pretoria, South Africa on 26-27 August 2013 in preparation of the 3rd BRICS Ministers of Agriculture and Agrarian Development meeting.

6.   Welcomed the exploratory discussions aimed at establishing the Basic Agricultural Information Exchange System of BRICS countries, while noting that such a system should not be a duplication of the Agriculture Marketing Information System (AMIS) created under the G20 and administered by the Food and Agriculture Organisation (FAO) of the United Nations.

7.   Reaffirmed our support for such a system as a platform for sharing information and called upon our technical experts to continue to work together for the timely development of the system.

8.   Acknowledged that climate change is one of the greatest challenges which adversely impacts agriculture and food security in all countries, particularly developing countries. To this effect our experts held a Seminar in South Africa on 23-25 October 2013 on "Agriculture and Climate Change".

9.   Noted that in addressing food insecurity all efforts must be geared towards enhancing agricultural production and adaptability of agricultural systems to climate change, especially for smallholder farmers.

10. Agreed to cooperate in research, development and application of technologies that enable agriculture to adapt to the effects of climate change.

11. Acknowledged that the internationally agreed development goals, such as the Millennium Development Goals (MDGs), address the needs of developing countries, many of which continue to face developmental challenges, like widespread poverty and inequality.

12. Noted that the volatility in the price and supply of food and other commodities as well as constrained financial resources have compounded the food insecurity for developing countries.

13. Reiterated that individual countries, especially in Africa and other developing countries of the South, cannot achieve the MDGs on their own and therefore the centrality of Goal 8 on Global Partnership for Development to achieve the MDGs should remain at the core of the global development discourse for the United Nations (UN) system.

14. Reiterated our openness to increase engagement and co-operation with other countries, in particular developing countries and relevant international and regional organisations in the field of agriculture.

15. Reaffirmed the expectation of the BRICS Leaders' meeting held in St Petersburg on 5 September 2013 that the 9th World Trade Organization's (WTO) Ministerial Conference scheduled for 3-6 December 2013 in Bali, Indonesia will be a stepping stone to the successful and balanced conclusion of the Doha Development Round.

16. Expressed the hope that consensus will be reached on food security, export competition and the key developmental concerns of the poorest and most vulnerable WTO members and would be addressed during the ninth WTO Ministerial meeting. We will therefore cooperate in the work undertaken in the build-up and during the WTO Ministerial meeting.

17. Agreed on sharing information, policies and best practices to address common problems faced by BRICS countries in agricultural development.

18. Resolved that the enhancement of agricultural cooperation among BRICS countries is of great significance for ensuring global food security and agricultural development towards attaining sustainable development, eradicating poverty and achieving the UN MDGs.

19. Reaffirmed our commitment to strengthen areas of cooperation, namely, information exchange, food security, climate change, agricultural innovation and trade and investment and gradually expand the cooperation so as to address the other challenges to food security.

20. Reaffirmed our commitment to assist other developing countries in enhancing agricultural productivity, paying particular attention to smallholder farmers, women and youth to improve world food security.

21. Welcomed the establishment of the "BRICS Strategic Alliance for Agricultural Technology Cooperation", which will combine our efforts in addressing major challenges in agriculture.

22. Agreed to intensify the exchange and cooperation in areas such as agriculture research and development and capacity building.

23. Noted that cooperation in agricultural trade and investment is vital for mutual development. We recognised the need to increase trade and investment in the agricultural sector through activities such as participation in exhibitions, trade fairs and investment fora.

24. Resolved to forge a stronger partnership for common agriculture and agrarian development and endorsed the 2013/14 Calendar of Events for Agriculture Cooperation Working Group of BRICS.

25. Welcomed the United Nations' Declaration of 2014 as the International Year of Family Farming (IYFF) and committed to support the common agenda of events.

26. The Russian Federation, the Republic of India, the People's Republic of China and the Republic of South Africa conveyed their appreciation to the Federative Republic of Brazil for its offer to host the 4th Meeting of the BRICS Ministers of Agriculture and Agrarian Development in 2014 and expressed their full support thereof.

27. Brazil, Russia, India and China expressed their deep appreciation to South Africa for hosting the 3rd BRICS Ministerial meeting.

Done in the English language with five copies, each copy being equally authentic on 29 October 2013.

H.   2nd Meeting of Agriculture Ministers: 30 Oct. 2011, Chengdu (CHN)

JOINT DECLARATION
OF THE SECOND MEETING OF BRICS MINISTERS OF AGRICULTURE AND AGRARIAN
DEVELOPMENT

1.   In the spirit of the "Sanya Declaration" of the Third BRICS Leaders Meeting, we, the Ministers of Agriculture and Agrarian Development of the Federative Republic of Brazil, the Russian Federation, the Republic of India, the People's Republic of China and the Republic of South Africa met in Chengdu of China for the Second Meeting of BRICS Ministers of Agriculture and Agrarian Development on October 30, 2011. Having adopted the theme of "Making Joint Efforts for World Food Security", the Meeting pointed out direction of cooperation through in-depth discussion on issues of common interests and concerns.

2.   BRICS countries have actively implemented the Moscow Declaration signed at the First Meeting of BRIC Ministers of Agriculture and Agrarian Development in 2010, conducted pragmatic cooperation, and adopted tangible measures to boost domestic agricultural productivity, which has played a positive role in promoting food security and maintaining economic stability. BRICS countries have become an important force to deal with financial crisis and promote global economic recovery.

3.   BRICS countries represent 43% of world population and 18% of global trade, commanding significant global influence. We are committed to enhancing the coordination and communication with international and regional organizations, including G20, FAO, WFP, OIE, CGIAR, etc, with the goal of concerted views of the international community on food security, climate change, environmental protection, trade promotion and other hot topics in the field of global food and agriculture, and continuing to make joint efforts for world food security.

4.   Agriculture is a strategic sector with a close bearing on social stability. As emerging economies, we fully understand the concerns of African countries over food security, and sympathize with their afflictions in this respect, particularly the sufferings of the Horn of Africa from the most serious draught and food deficit in the past 6 decades. We actively support the global endeavor to combat hunger, and call on the international community to make all efforts to further enhance aid, and support the United Nations in playing a coordinating role in preventing further deterioration of the crisis, especially through the FAO's Committee on World Food Security (CSF). Meanwhile, we are committed to making best efforts to help African countries improve their food production capacity so as to enhance food security, particularly among smallholder farmers, through technical cooperation, policy dialogue, agricultural technology demonstration and transfer, personnel training, agricultural infrastructure construction and food aid, among others.

5.   We reiterate that the cooperation between BRICS countries is inclusive by nature. We will actively enhance the coordination and cooperation with other countries in the field of agriculture jointly striving for the reduction of poverty-stricken population with a view to realizing the UN MDGs and promoting world stability, prosperity and development.

6.   We focused our discussion on priority areas of future agricultural cooperation and effective ways to assist other developing countries to achieve food security. We hold the view that, despite differences among BRICS countries and varied characteristics of our agricultural sectors, there are complementarities among us. Therefore, the enhancement of agricultural cooperation among BRICS countries is of great significance for ensuring global food security and sustainable agricultural development, eradicating poverty and achieving the UN MDGs.

7.   In recent years, the international market of agricultural products has been mainly affected by natural disasters, use of food for production of biofuel, speculations and price transmission. As a

result, the price of agricultural products fluctuated violently at a high level. The tight supply-demand relation has posed grave threats to food security and social stability of some developing countries, especially the low-income, food-deficit countries. We reiterate our commitment to carry out closer cooperation on food security within BRICS, and will further explore ways to provide more accurate long-term market forecast for food producers and purchasers to reduce excessive speculative activities. We also call for developed countries to phase out trade-distorting subsidies and barriers.

8.   We believe that stable and robust agricultural development of the BRICS countries is of great significance to world food security. We are committed to developing agriculture actively, strengthening coordination and cooperation, as well as helping other developing countries to improve food productivity while ensuring domestic food security and generation of income and jobs in rural areas, paying particular attention to smallholder farmers, women and youth, so as to make joint efforts to improve world food security.

9.   We reiterate that we will strengthen capacity building for food security and, in particular, improve food access for the most vulnerable population. Therefore, we are committed to increasing comprehensive food productivity of farmers including smallholders by relying on scientific research and technology transfer, creating favorable environment for investment and sustainable utilization of agricultural resources, and promoting agricultural products trade to improve food access.

10. As an important source of energy for human beings, bio-energy is environment-friendly and renewable in nature. We agree to develop bio-energy while ensuring food security by giving consideration to the factors of energy demand, environmental protection and sustainable development. We take note of FAO's analytical framework of Bioenergy and Food Security (BEFS), as one of the instruments that may play a role in assisting the development of national bio-energy policy compatible with the national strategies of poverty reduction, rural development, local energy and food security. We acknowledge the importance of R&D on advanced new processes for the production of bio-fuels and the use of new, non-food and other plant raw materials for bio-fuel production as well as energy efficiency.

11. Sustainable agriculture reduces the chemical input by using renewable resources and it protects resources, improves environment and enhances food production and quality while promoting development. We will advance sustainable agriculture in an effort to achieve the sustainable use of natural resources, land, water resources, and bio-diversity in particular.

12. Climate change is exerting increasing impact on eco-system, agriculture, water resource, social and economic development, as well as people's livelihood. We share common concerns over the negative impact of climate change on agriculture, in particular, over the damage to agricultural production by extreme weather events. We note that agriculture faces triple challenges simultaneously in achieving food security, adapting to climate change and reducing greenhouse gas emission, which requires a sustainable way to promote resources utilization efficiency, improve productivity and enhance adaptability of agricultural systems, especially for small-holder farmers. Therefore, we should cooperate in research, development and application of technologies that can adapt to climate change while increasing agricultural production.

13. We recognize the significance and role of bio-mass energy for socio-economic development in rural areas and mitigation of effects of climate change globally. We, therefore, will unleash each others' advantages and strengthen cooperation in utilization of waste to develop bio-mass energy, e.g., biogas, so as to promote a virtuous ecological cycle, alleviate the damage to forest, reduce soil erosion, improve soil fertility through proper use of fertilizer and preserve bio-diversity.

14. We reiterate that the international community should promptly establish effective technology transfer and dissemination mechanism, facilitate technology sharing, and ensure that the developing countries can afford environment friendly technologies in accordance with principle of common but

differentiated responsibilities. We emphasize climate change should be addressed under the framework of sustainable agricultural development.

15. As big agricultural countries, all BRICS countries enjoy a long history and abundant achievements in traditional agricultural techniques. The application of advanced agricultural technologies exemplified by the "green revolution" has substantially driven up food production and led to profound changes in agricultural sector across the world. With the increasingly complicated international agricultural and food situations and climate changes nowadays, it requires the application of modern agricultural technologies to ensure food security across the world. We undertake to intensify the exchange and cooperation in areas including advanced technologies, equipments and technical human resources with social inclusion, to improve the overall agricultural technology capacity of countries.

16. We undertake to learn and introduce advanced technologies from each other and work jointly for agricultural technology innovations. We will intensify our efforts in developing high-quality, high-yield and stress-resistant crops, boost water-saving, farmland protection and clean production, and promote environment-friendly and resource-saving agriculture, stressing the importance of both modern and traditional agriculture for sustainability.

17. We fully recognize the significant role of biotechnology in bolstering sustainable agriculture and food processing industry. When properly combined with other technologies and the traditional knowledge in food and agricultural production, biotechnology can greatly contribute to meeting the demand of the ever growing and urbanized population. Therefore, we shall strengthen exchange and cooperation in the biotechnology sector.

18. We agree to carry out agricultural human resources exchanges in a variety of forms, including establishing research and development centers and joint laboratories, creating cooperation platforms, implementing joint research projects, organizing exchange visits and adopting joint post-graduate programs, through which strengths of every member in agricultural research will be put into best use to facilitate technical exchange and develop human resources that excel in modern agricultural technologies, contributing to technology advances and agricultural development across the world.

19. To strengthen our dialogue and exchange in key areas of agricultural research and technologies, we agree to establish the "BRICS Strategic Alliance for Agricultural Research and Technology Cooperation", which will pool our efforts in addressing major challenges faced by the world in agricultural technologies. The Alliance will receive guidance and support from the agricultural ministries of the countries.

20. Driven by the growing population, excessive volatility of food prices in short terms and climate change, among other factors, food security will demonstrate an increasingly complex picture. We recognize that the sharing of timely and accurate data on agricultural products supply and demand as well as on population growth is an effective approach to addressing food price volatility and mitigating global food security problems. We encourage the sharing of information concerning common problems faced by BRICS countries in agricultural development; the establishment of information sharing mechanism to exchange basic agricultural data on a regular basis; the construction of an agricultural information and digital agriculture platform; and the gradual enrichment and improvement of the food security information system based on transparent principles.

21. We agree to share information on, inter alia, price and output of agricultural products, and constantly improve the reliability, accuracy, timeliness and comparability of the data on production and consumption of agricultural products.

22. We are deeply convinced that cooperation in agricultural trade and investment serves as a vital channel for win-win outcome and common development. We undertake to boost business

investment and trade cooperation by means of, inter alia, exhibition and forum on trade and investment, encourage and support the participation of enterprises in economic and trade promotion events organized by BRICS countries.

23. We are of the view that regulated cooperation can improve not only efficiency but also effectiveness. Therefore, we approved the Working Procedures for Agricultural Cooperation Working Group of BRICS Countries to establish a regulated agricultural cooperation mechanism.

24. For a closer BRICS agricultural cooperation with more clearly defined targets and higher effectiveness, we adopted the Action Plan 2012-2016 for Agricultural Cooperation of BRICS Countries, which identified five priority areas and direction of cooperation Each area will be coordinated by one country respectively.

25. The Federative Republic of Brazil, the Russian Federation, the People's Republic of China, the Republic of South Africa gratefully support the Republic of India to host the next meeting of the BRICS Ministers of Agriculture and Agrarian Development.

26. All parties celebrated the success of the 2nd Meeting of the BRICS Ministers of Agriculture and Agrarian Development, and the other four parties expressed gratitude to China and highly appreciated its efforts for hosting this meeting.

I.   Action Plan 2012-2016 for Agricultural Cooperation of BRICS Countries

ACTION PLAN 2012-2016 FOR AGRICULTURAL COOPERATION OF BRICS COUNTRIES

Ministers of Agriculture and Agrarian Development of the BRIC countries met for the first time in Moscow on March 26th 2010 and reached consensus on the following actions for agricultural cooperation under this mechanism: firstly, creation of agricultural information base system; secondly, development of a general strategy for ensuring access to food for the most vulnerable population; thirdly, reduction of negative impact of climate change on food security and adaptation of agriculture to climate change; and fourthly, enhance agricultural technology cooperation and innovation.

To implement the consensus reached at the First Meeting of BRIC Ministers of Agriculture and Agrarian Development, the First Meeting of BRICS Agricultural Cooperation Working Group was held in Beijing, China in August 2011. The meeting unanimously agreed to formulate the present Action Plan on Agricultural Cooperation of the BRICS countries for the period of 2012-2016, approved at the Second Meeting of BRICS Ministers of Agriculture and Agrarian Development. Furthermore, the countries will establish an annual calendar of activities which will take into consideration the principles adopted at the Action Plan.

BRICS countries shall share/arrange/mobilize financial resources to cover the cost of all the cooperation activities below.

I.   **Creation of basic agricultural information exchange system of BRICS countries (coordinated by China in collaboration with other four countries)**

1)   Each member country shall make commitment to exchange basic agricultural information on a regular basis;

2)   Each member country shall designate an information officer to be responsible for the collection and compilation of the basic agricultural information and its translation into English and disseminate it to other member countries through the focal point of the BRICS Agricultural Cooperation Working Group;

3)   Information exchange shall mainly be carried out by way of internet in the form of e-mail, instant messaging, and video conferencing, etc;

4)   Information to be exchanged shall include:

   a. Agricultural development policies, including agricultural price support policies, rural finance and insurance policies and agricultural management systems;
   b. Agricultural trade data and policies;
   c. Market prices of major agricultural products;
   d. Dynamic information, such as the latest development in agricultural science and technology; and
   e. Legislation, policies and management strategies related to fisheries and aquaculture;

5)   To create a mechanism of exchange of information on challenges and risk assessment, to assess, in the annual meeting of ACWG, challenges and risks faced by BRICS countries in agriculture and their implication upon global agricultural development;

6)   To work out coordination mechanism on Action Plan implementation and agree to prepare regular national reports;

7)   The information base should be linked to AMIS created under the G20 in order not to duplicate;

8)   Information to be exchanged could be adjusted from time to time on an agreed basis according to needs of all member countries;

9)   Information submitted by all members shall only be shared among ministries of agriculture of the BRICS countries;

10) A mechanism for the exchange of information related to agricultural production, consumption and population growth shall be established and discussion and exchange on common issues to agricultural development of the BRICS countries shall be conducted.

II. Development of a general strategy for ensuring access to food for the most vulnerable population (coordinated by Brazil in collaboration with other four countries)

1)   To hold seminars to exchange policies and experience of the members in ensuring food security of the most vulnerable populations;

2)   Strengthen technological and industrial cooperation on livestock, fisheries, especially in the field of seawater and freshwater aquaculture, to enhance the contribution of fisheries to ensuring national food security;

3)   Capacity building and human resource development strategy to ensure food access for the most vulnerable population;

4)   Hold a seminar "Modernization of feeding systems for the most vulnerable population" with focus on national system of food and nutrition security and public food procurement from smallholder farmers;

5)   Hold a seminar on sustainable intensification of agricultural production and productivity of smallholder farmers;

6)   Creation of a BRICS group in FAO, which would act also within the United Nations World Food Program in order to coordinate initiatives to promote food security, projects in the area of food security and school meals, as well as incentivizing mechanisms for purchasing local food of family agriculture.

III. Reduction of negative impact of climate change on food security and adaptation of agriculture to climate change (coordinated by South Africa in collaboration with other four countries)

1)   Jointly conduct R&D on agricultural greenhouse gas emission measurement and climate resilient high-yield agricultural production. Priority shall be given to technology and methodology of agricultural greenhouse gas measurement, integrated farming systems cultivation of new climate resilient high-yielding crop varieties, R&D on managerial technologies for climate resilient high-yield crop and animal production, and technical development for climate resilient high-yield agricultural production. These activities are to be conducted in principle for R&D purposes only;

2)   Hold seminars to exchange views on conservation farming, water-saving agriculture, agronomic improvement, agricultural insurance and other technical or policy measures to cope with climate change and promote sustainable agricultural development;

3)   Jointly carry out consultation and cooperation on adaptation to climate change in the field of agriculture and share technologies and information related to alternate sources of food, fodder, fiber and energy in climate change prone dry regions;

4)   To harmonize activities in using updated technologies for environment protection and monitoring of negative impact of climate;

5)   China plans to sponsor an agriculture seminar in 2012 under the theme of the impact of climate change on agricultural production and response measures; South Africa will be hosting COP 17 and Brazil the Rio plus 20 in 2012.

IV. Enhance agricultural technology cooperation and innovation (coordinated by India in collaboration with other four countries)

1) Establish a strategic cooperation alliance on agricultural science and technology among the BRICS countries, and hold an agricultural technological cooperation forum alternately in the five countries every other year, so as to strength dialogues and exchanges, jointly analyze major challenges in the world agricultural technologies, and discuss how to share scientific and technological resources, promote agricultural technological development and improve the efficiency of scientific research in the BRICS countries;

2) Hold a conference on "agricultural and fishery cooperation among the BRICS countries" alternately in the five countries every other year to exchange views on agriculture, fisheries and aquaculture development trend and research priorities, and discuss the cooperation on management, research and industry in the fields of agriculture, fisheries and aquaculture among the five countries;

3) Strengthen cooperation in resources and environment as well as development of biomass energy, crop residue recycling and conduct discussion and exchange on agricultural development and energy exploitation, and protection of resources and environment;

4) Conduct collaborative research on low-carbon fishery technologies, including technological development and collaborative research of energy saving and emission reduction of fishing vessels, carbon sink function of aquaculture and artificial wetland, and recycling aquaculture system;

5) To promote setting up shared views concerning strategic objectives that are desired to be reached by 2016;

6) To create an Innovation Projects Store;

7) To promote cooperation on technologies with the aim of strengthening traditional forms of production for the maintenance of biodiversity;

8) Conduct dialogue and share research on food dietary regimes with the aim of widening food production diversity;

9) To promote cooperation on TEEB (The Economy of Ecosystems and Biodiversity) in order to strengthen environmental conservation in agriculture;

10) To cooperate on sustainable use of water and fertilizers;

11) To hold seminars on policy on adoption of frontier sciences of biotechnology;

12) To exchange germplasm resources (genetic resources) (subject to national laws), conduct study on the breeding of hybrid rice, hybrid maize, wheat, pulses, oil seeds, horticulture and other crops and demonstrate and promote conservation farming, soil improvement technology, balanced fertilization, new fertilizer sources and other yield-promoting technologies to increase the unit yield and improve quality of crops.

V. Trade and investment promotion (coordinated by Russia in collaboration with other four countries)

1) Trade and investment cooperation shall be promoted. The BRICS member countries shall make commitment to promote trade and investment cooperation between agricultural enterprises by organizing exhibitions, trade and investment forums, or other events, and encourage and assist enterprises of respective countries to participate in the economic and trade promotion activities held by the BRICS member countries;

2) To promote market infrastructure by designing and developing supporting facilities;

3) To explore the possibilities of increasing the value of agricultural trade and investment.

J.   1st Meeting of Agriculture Ministers: 26 Mar. 2010, Moscow (RUS)

BRIC AGRICULTURE MINISTERS DECLARATION

The joint statement of BRIC countries on the global food security, adopted at the Summit in Yekaterinburg (Russia) on June 16th 2009, considered the issue of global food security and resolved to address the problem of food production and hunger without delay in a comprehensive manner through resolute action by governments and relevant international agencies.

We, the Ministers of Agriculture and Agrarian Development of the BRIC countries first met in Moscow (Russian Federation) on March 26th 2010 and agreed on broad contours of quadrilateral cooperation in the agricultural sector with particular attention to family farming, the development of which will not only help long-term interests of the four states but contribute towards global food security.

Reiterating our support to the initiatives taken at international level such as FAO 2009 World Food Summit in Rome, we intend to develop effective and comprehensive measures for development of agriculture in BRIC countries through close cooperation and coordination in the field of agriculture and allied activities.

Realizing the need for ensuring food security at the global level and addressing the challenge of ensuring stable and sufficient production of basic food grains, to raise living standard, to provide steady and inclusive development of rural areas, to increase efficiency of small and medium sized agro-industrial units and productivity of family farms, there is a need for more intensive cooperation among BRIC countries through the exchange of experience, coordinated action and implementation of joint projects wherever possible and in the interest of the four countries.

Ensuring food security requires a well-functioning world market and trade system for food and agriculture based on the principles of fairness and non-discrimination. In this regard, it is of paramount importance to accelerate the Doha round of talks at the World Trade Organization (WTO).

In order to realize the broad objectives mentioned above the following areas of cooperation are to be considered as priorities.

1.   Creation of agricultural information base system of the BRIC countries

Having a general information based on balances of production and consumption of agricultural products, population growth will facilitate a comprehensive analysis of the condition of food security in the BRIC countries which is considered very important for the solution of problem of food security and help in coordinated approach on formation of national grain reserves taking into account a global picture of food supply.

2.   Development of a general strategy for ensuring access to food for the most vulnerable population

42% of world's population is living in BRIC countries. A substantial percentage of this population belongs to vulnerable groups that require State support for ensuring food security. Therefore, development of a strategy by BRIC countries in the area of food security for vulnerable population assumes great importance. Exchange of experience in the area of food producing and public purchasing systems for distribution and food assistance to vulnerable population and victims of natural calamities becomes important and imperative.

3. Reduction of negative impact of climate change on food security and adaptation of agriculture to climatic changes

Of all the sectors of economy the agrarian sector is the most vulnerable to climatic changes. In order to counter this negative impact, there is a need to develop cooperation through comprehensive adaptive measures, including exchange of experience, best practices and public policies.

At the same time, we urge the international community to promptly establish effective technology transfer and dissemination mechanism, facilitate technology sharing, and ensure that the developing countries can afford environment friendly technologies in accordance with principle of common but differentiated responsibilities. In this context we call upon the developed countries to offer technical and financial assistance on climate change to developing countries, while developing countries to actively take all measures to promote sustainable growth and make their due contribution to counter climate change.

4. Enhance agricultural technology cooperation and innovation

Advancing agricultural research and technology constitute an important way to ensure food security. BRIC countries are distinct from yet complementary with each other in agricultural research and development. We shall take active measures to establish stable, long-term, efficient and effective cooperation and exchange mechanism on agricultural research.

For implementation of measures collectively agreed we have decided to set up a standing Expert working group, which will meet on regular basis, including through video conference.

The Expert working group will prepare specific proposals and report to BRIC Agricultural and Agrarian Development Ministers on implementation of issues outlined in this declaration.

The next meeting of the Ministers of Agriculture and Agrarian Development of the BRIC countries to be organized in 2011.

K.   BRIC Joint Statement on Global Food Safety: 17 Jun. 2009, Yekaterinburg (RUS)

BRIC's Joint Statement on Global Food Security

The fluctuations of global food prices coupled with the global financial crisis are threatening global food security. As a result, the number of people suffering from hunger and malnutrition grows and the progress towards the achievement of the Millennium Development Goals may be reversed. This challenge should be addressed without delay in a comprehensive manner through resolute action by all governments and the relevant international agencies.

The developed and developing countries should address the food security issue according to the principle of common but differentiated responsibility. The developed countries should provide financial and technology support for developing countries in the field of food production capacity. The BRIC countries welcome various initiatives in this field by the UN and its special agencies. The BRIC countries renew their commitment to contribute to the efforts to overcome the global food crisis.

Countering effectively the global food crisis is impossible without a clear and full understanding of its causes. Attempts to explain food price hikes by an increase in consumption in developing countries obscure the true causes which have a complex and multifaceted nature.

Global climate change and natural disasters have direct implications on food security through changes in agro-ecological conditions. Current global economic and financial crisis also has negative impact on food security through shrinking financial resources available to agriculture sector. Restricted market access and trade-distorting subsidies in developed countries have also hampered the development of food production capacity in developing countries over the last thirty years. Further, global market conditions have not created adequate incentives for the expansion of agricultural production in developing and least developed countries that have become main importers of food products.

It is also important to assess the challenges and opportunities posed by the biofuels production and use in view not only of the world's food security, but also of the energy security and sustainable development needs. An international cooperation mechanism needs to be established to review and reevaluate the long-term implications of the development of biomass energy, and develop relevant policy guidance accordingly.

The BRIC countries welcome, therefore, the exchange of experiences in biofuels technologies, norms and regulations, in order to ensure that production and use of biofuels is sustainable, in accordance with the three pillars of sustainable development — social, economic and environmental — and that it takes into account the need to achieve and maintain global food security. Sustainable biofuels can constitute a driving force for social inclusion and income distribution mainly in the impoverished rural areas of developing and least developed countries, where most of the world's famine problems are located.

Tackling effectively the food crisis requires a fully coordinated international response and should include both short-term and long-term measures. The international community needs to work out and consistently implement a comprehensive strategy to resolve this global problem. In this respect, the BRIC countries welcome the outcomes of relevant international fora, including the Food and Agriculture Organization (FAO) High-Level Conference on World Food Security in Rome.

The BRIC countries also welcome the results of the World Grain Forum which was held in Saint Petersburg and call on all interested states and international organisations to take necessary steps to implement the measures agreed upon at the Forum.

Ensuring food security requires a well-functioning world market and trade system for food and agriculture based on the principles of fairness and non-discrimination. In this regard, it is of paramount importance to accelerate the Doha round of talks at the World Trade Organization (WTO) in order to find compromise solutions for radical reductions of multibillion subsidies in the agricultural sector, which distort terms of trade and prevent developing countries from increasing their agricultural production. We are committed to opposing protectionism, establishing a just and reasonable international trade regime for agricultural products, and giving farmers from developing countries incentives to engage in agricultural production.

The BRIC countries support the adoption of a wide range of mid- to long-term measures in order to provide for a solution to the issue of food security. Such measures may include:

a) rendering additional resources and assistance to the agricultural sector through the channels of respective national budgets and international development institutions, mainly to household agriculture, which is the main source for food production;

b) joint technological innovations and international cooperation to introduce advanced technologies in the agricultural sector of developing countries to significantly increase agricultural productivity. Intellectual property rights in the agricultural domain should strike a balance between the common good of humankind and incentives to innovation;

c) upgrading agricultural infrastructure, including irrigation, transportation, supply, storage and distribution systems and promoting technical assistance, access to credit and crop insurance policies. In this context public-private partnerships could play a significant role;

d) improving the exchange of knowledge and commercialisation of sustainable biofuels;

e) ensuring wider food access at the national and international levels through appropriate policies and well-functioning distribution systems especially for the poor and most vulnerable people in developing countries;

f) sharing the best practices of operating successful public distribution programmes; and

g) equipping developing countries with financial and technological means to fully implement adaptation measures to minimize the adverse impacts of climate change on food security.

III.4.   BRICS Science, Technology and Innovation (STI) Ministers

A.   6th Meeting of BRICS STI Ministers: 3 Jul. 2018, Durban (ZAF)

SIXTH BRICS SCIENCE, TECHNOLOGY AND INNOVATION (STI) MINISTERIAL MEETING

DURBAN DECLARATION

Theme: Leveraging BRICS Science, Technology and Innovation to Enhance Inclusive
Growth and Development

Durban, South Africa, 3 July 2018

1.   In preparation for the 10th BRICS Summit in South Africa, and in line with the proposed Johannesburg Declaration and Action Plan to be adopted on 25-27 July 2018 in Johannesburg, South Africa, we the BRICS Ministers for Science, Technology and Innovation met in Durban, South Africa on 3 July 2018, for the 6th BRICS STI Ministerial Meeting.

2.   Noting the proposed theme of the 10th BRICS Summit "BRICS in Africa: Cooperation for Inclusive Growth and Shared Prosperity in the 4th Industrial Revolution", we re-emphasise the importance of the Strategy for BRICS Economic Partnership which underscores the fundamental role of science, technology and innovation as key socio-economic change agents for global and regional progress, growth and stability.

3.   We welcome the proposal to establish a BRICS Vaccine Research and Development Centre, that creates synergies between the BRICS STI and BRICS Health sectoral tracts and agree to investigate the possibility of contributing to its establishment from a science, technology and innovation perspective.

4.   We welcome the establishment of the BRICS Partnership on New Industrial Revolution (PartNIR) with thrusts on innovation. We will explore mobilising STI resources in support of this initiative.

5.   Underlining the theme of the 6th BRICS STI Ministerial Meeting "Leveraging BRICS Science, Technology and Innovation to Enhance Inclusive Growth and Development", we reaffirm our vision to promote science, technology and innovation for human development utilising people-centred and public-good driven policy and implementation frameworks.

6.   Based on the BRICS STI Work Plan 2015-2018, we recognise the progress of STI cooperation since 2015 and in particular the bold efforts of the member countries under the present 2017-2018 BRICS STI Action Plan.

7.   We welcome the hosting the 4th BRICS STI Funding Working Group Meeting in South Africa on 30 June 2018 and welcome the outcomes of the 2nd Call of the BRICS STI Framework Programme and related funding principles, which reaffirms the strategic value of this instrument as a mechanism for promoting BRICS research and technology development. We look forward to launch the 3rd Call for proposals of the BRICS STI Framework Programme in the fourth quarter of 2018 in the following thematic areas: prevention and mitigation of natural disasters; water resources and pollution treatment; geospatial technology and its applications; new and renewable energy, and energy efficiency, including solid state lighting; astronomy; biotechnology and biomedicine including human health and neuroscience; information technologies and high performance computing; ocean and polar science and technology; material science, including nanotechnology; photonics; research infrastructures, including mega-science projects; Science, Technology, Innovation and Entrepreneurship Partnership (STIEP); and aeronautics, with the Russian Federation continuing as

the Call Secretariat. We restate the support of our Ministries and Funding Agencies to continue joint funding of the BRICS STI Framework Programme.

8.   We welcome the successful convening of the 3rd BRICS Young Scientist Forum (YSF) in Durban, South Africa which included a number of new elements such as the BRICS Young Women in Science Dialogue, the BRICS Young Innovator Prize, the BRICS Youth Innovation and Entrepreneurship Workshop, and the BRICS Seminar on Science Diplomacy, Advice and Communication. We strongly recommend that these activities should become permanent features of the BRICS Young Scientist Forum going forward. We support the proposal to establish the BRICS YSF coordinating committee and thank India for agreeing to coordinate and provide a leadership role in this regard. We thank Brazil for offering to host the 4th BRICS Young Scientist Forum in the lead up to the 7th BRICS STI Ministerial Meeting in Brazil in 2019.

9.   We welcome the successful convening of the 2nd Meeting of the BRICS Working Group on Research Infrastructures (RI) in Campinas, Brazil in March 2018 and support the main outcomes of this meeting, in particular, the establishment of a web portal to facilitate cooperation between the BRICS countries in the domain RI and mega-science projects. We view this as an important first step: towards streamlining and strengthening cooperation; to forge closer cooperation on existing major and megascience projects in the BRICS member states; and to plan the possible establishment of future BRICS RI. We thank the Russian Federation for initiating the work on the web portal and agreeing to lead further discussions on the modalities to establish a coordinating mechanism for BRICS RI.

10.   We welcome Russia hosting the 1st BRICS Meeting on Foresight and S&T Priority Setting and the 1st Meeting of the BRICS Working Group on Biotechnology and Biomedicine, including Human Health and Neuroscience (WG Biomed) in November 2017, which approved its Terms of Reference and discussed two main areas for cooperation: Antimicrobial Resistance and Cognitive Disorders. We welcome the hosting of the 1st Meeting of the BRICS Working Group on Nanotechnology and Material Science in October 2017, and note for further discussion the proposal to establish the BRICS Charter of the Network Centre for Material Sciences and Nanotechnologies. We further welcome Russia hosting the 1st Meeting of the Working Group on Photonics in March 2018 and the initiative to create a BRICS Virtual Institute of Photonics (VIP).

11.   We welcome the hosting of the third BRICS Astronomy Working Group meeting in Pune, India in September 2017. We also welcome the hosting of the 2nd Meeting of the BRICS Working Group on Information and Communication Technology and High Performance Computing in May 2018 in India, and support the need for a dedicated Call for Proposals on flagship BRICS R&D projects in disruptive technologies that strategically positions the BRICS partners for leadership in the Fourth Industrial Revolution. We welcome the proposal of the Working group to establish a BRICS Virtual Centre on ICT and HPC. We further welcome the establishment of An Integrated Hub for BRICS Innovation Collaboration on ICT and HPC and thank China, South Africa and India for agreeing to assume a coordinating role in this process.

12.   Pursuant to the BRICS Action Plan for Innovation Cooperation adopted in Hangzhou, China in July 2017, we welcome Brazil's proposal to establish the BRICS networks of science parks, technology business incubators and SMEs, and China's proposal to establish a BRICS Technology Transfer Center under the direction of the BRICS Science, Technology, Innovation and Entrepreneurship Partnership (STIEP) Working Group. We take note of China's proposal in consultation with India to host the 2nd Meeting of the STIEP Working Group, in mid-September of 2018 to give further impetus to this strategic area of cooperation.

13.   Recognising the need to establish inter-BRICS investment instruments for STI, we endorse the initiative to explore possible avenues of assistance for BRICS STI cooperation on innovation and entrepreneurship from the New Development Bank (NDB) and other development financing

platforms and support the proposal to establish a task team to pursue comprehensive discussions with these organisations. We thank South Africa for agreeing to coordinate this engagement.

14. Cognisant of the achievements of BRICS STI since the adoption of the Memorandum of Understanding on Cooperation in Science, Technology and Innovation in March 2015, we note however, that the organization of these activities, which increases in scope and complexity with each passing year, remains ad-hoc in nature. In this regard, we endorse the initiative to investigate the feasibility of establishing a permanent mechanism to manage and coordinate BRICS STI activities and thank South Africa and Russia for offering to lead this process.

15. We endorse the BRICS STI Action Plan 2018-2019 and task our officials under the leadership of Brazil to start in earnest the drafting of the new BRICS Work Plan 2019- 2022 in order for it to be ready for adoption at the 7th BRICS STI Ministerial Meeting in Brazil in 2019.

16. Brazil, Russia, India and China extend their warm appreciation to the Department of Science and Technology of the Republic of South Africa for hosting the 6th BRICS STI Ministerial Meeting and the 8th BRICS STI Senior Officials Meeting.

17. Russia, India, China and South Africa convey their appreciation to Brazil for its offer to host the 7th BRICS STI Ministerial Meeting and the 9th BRICS STI Senior Officials Meeting in 2019 and extend their full support to that end.

Done at Durban, South Africa on 3 July 2018

B.   5ᵗʰ Meeting of BRICS STI Ministers: 18 Jul. 2017, Hangzhou (CHN)

THE 5ᵀᴴ BRICS SCIENCE, TECHNOLOGY & INNOVATION (STI) MINISTERIAL MEETING

HANGZHOU DECLARATION

Theme: Leading through Innovation & Deepening Cooperation

Hangzhou, China, July 18, 2017

1.   In line with the BRICS Memorandum of Understanding on Cooperation in Science, Technology and Innovation signed in March 2015 and the Goa Declaration adopted at the BRICS Summit held in India on October 16, 2016, we, the Ministers for Science, Technology and Innovation of the Federative Republic of Brazil, the Russian Federation, the Republic of India, the People's Republic of China and the Republic of South Africa met in Hangzhou, China, on 18 July, 2017, for the 5th BRICS Science, Technology & Innovation (STI) Ministerial Meeting.

2.   Recalling the theme of the BRICS Xiamen Summit "BRICS: Stronger Partnership for a Brighter Future", we will continue to strengthen pragmatic cooperation in science, technology and innovation (STI) among the BRICS countries, create new cooperation opportunities, expand partnerships, and jointly tackle global challenges.

3.   Based on the theme of the 5th BRICS Science, Technology & Innovation Ministerial Meeting "Leading through Innovation & Deepening Cooperation", we reaffirm the importance of innovation dialogues leading to outcomes and STI cooperation for promoting innovation-driven development and supporting the robust and sustainable growth of the world economy. We will continue to strengthen STI cooperation and implement relevant BRICS research and innovation initiatives mainly by means of exchanges in innovation policies and strategies and drafting of long-term cooperation plans to address common developmental challenges faced by all BRICS countries.

4.   In order to promote innovation and leverage the central role of science and technology in enhancing socio-economic development and driving global sustainable development, we agree to adopt the BRICS Action Plan for Innovation Cooperation. We agree to promote entrepreneurship and build platforms in BRICS countries and mainly collaborate in technology cooperation, technology transfer and translation, science and technology parks, youth innovation and entrepreneurship and in fostering strategic and long term university-industry partnerships so as to build sound ecosystems for innovation and entrepreneurship.

5.   Building on the positive experience and spin-off of the 1st BRICS Young Scientist Conclave under the framework of the BRICS Young Scientist Forum held in India last year, we welcome the convening of the 2nd BRICS Young Scientist Forum in Hangzhou, China. We recognize the potential of the Young Scientist Forum to develop into a powerful networking platform for BRICS young scientists and entrepreneurs and become an important arena to stimulate new academic ideas and train young professionals for the BRICS. We therefore fully support South Africa's decision to host the 3rd Young Scientist Forum in the lead up to the 6th BRICS STI Ministerial Meeting in South Africa in 2018. We encourage representatives of the BRICS thematic working groups to support participation of youth and invite themes for BRICS Young Scientist Forum.

6.   We welcome the approval of the first set of BRICS R&D projects in priority areas. We recognize the importance of the BRICS STI Framework Programme as a mechanism for pooling innovation resources and strengths, and driving development in major areas and key technologies. We welcome the decision to launch the 2nd BRICS STI Call 2017 in six priority areas with Russia continuing as the Call Secretariat. We support the restated commitment of BRICS Science and Technology Ministries and their relevant funding agencies to continue jointly funding such multilateral R&D projects.

7.   Acknowledging the importance of supporting cutting-edge high-impact research, we will encourage researchers from BRICS countries to publish the results of their research in international high-impact journals and participate as external foreign reviewers in the review of research proposals submitted to the funders in other BRICS countries, ensuring the quality of scientific review system within BRICS.

8.   Recognizing the need for setting concerted priorities for S&T cooperation, we promote to support joint activities on identified priorities for S&T cooperation of BRICS countries based on foresight and monitoring of global S&T development.

9.   We welcome India's initiative to coordinate the 1st meeting of BRICS Science and Technology Driven Entrepreneurship and Innovation Partnership in April 9th, 2017; and endorse the Term of Reference of the BRICS Working Group on Science Technology, Innovation and Entrepreneurship Partnership (STIEP).

10.   We welcome China hosting the 1st Working Group Meeting and Innovation Collaboration Forum on Information and Communication Technology and High Performance Computing in April, 2017 which presented several cooperation proposals including working together in relevant flagship projects.

11.   We welcome Russia hosting the 1st Meeting of the BRICS Working Group on Research Infrastructure and Mega-Science Projects to strengthen cooperation on the BRICS Global Research Advanced Infrastructure Network and mega-science projects.

12.   We welcome the convening of the 3rd BRICS STI Funding Working Group Meeting in South Africa in May, 2017 for discussion and negotiation on the approval of the first set of projects to be funded and the second call for proposals, and the outcomes of various thematic working group meetings or workshops.

13.   Based on the BRICS STI Work Plan 2015-2018, we recognize the progress of BRICS STI cooperation since 2015 and adopt the updated BRICS STI Action Plan.

14.   Acknowledging the importance of supporting STI investment and the need to establish inter-BRICS investment instruments, we support explore the possibilities of driving BRICS cooperation on innovation and entrepreneurship through the National Development Banks, New Development Bank and other existing financing platforms.

15.   Brazil, Russia, India and South Africa extend their warm appreciation to the Ministry of Science and Technology of China for hosting the 5th BRICS STI Ministerial Meeting and the 7th BRICS STI Senior Officials Meeting.

16.   Brazil, Russia, India, and China convey their appreciation to South Africa for its offer to host the 6th BRICS STI Ministerial Meeting and the 8th BRICS STI Senior Officials Meeting and extend their full support to that end.

C.   The BRICS Action Plan for Innovation Cooperation (2017-2020)

THE BRICS ACTION PLAN FOR INNOVATION COOPERATION (2017-2020)

I.   Foreword

We, BRICS countries,

1.   With 42% of the world population, contribute 18% of global GDP, 17% of global R&D investment and 27% of science papers published on international journals, as an important force of international economic cooperation and one of the most dynamic and promising emerging economies, BRICS countries are major representatives of emerging economies in the world. Our collective efforts are to undertake innovation and cooperation and facilitate innovation-driven development for sustainable development of the world economy.

2.   Reaffirm that innovation refers to the embodiment of an idea in a technology, product, or process that is new and creates productive value. An innovation is the implementation of a new or significantly improved product (good or service), or process which derives from creative ideas, technological progress, a new marketing method or a new organizational method in business practices, workplace organization or external relations. Innovation covers a wide range of domains with science, technology and innovation (STI) as the core.

3.   We will actively promote cooperation in STI under bilateral and multilateral frameworks in accordance with the *MoU on Cooperation in STI between the Governments of BRICS Countries, Jaipur Declaration*, and the theme of the 5th BRICS STI Ministerial Meeting, thus drive rapid and sustainable economic growth and social progress in the BRICS countries.

4.   Stress that innovation is one of the key driving forces of global sustainable development, playing a fundamental role in promoting economic growth, supporting job creation, entrepreneurship and structural reform, enhancing productivity and competitiveness, providing better services for the citizens and addressing global challenges. The BRICS countries aim to encourage innovation through practical actions to promote sustainable economic growth today and lay a solid foundation for tomorrow.

II.   Action Plan

BRICS countries are facing new challenges in economic development though our economic prospects and growth momentum remain unchanged. In this context, we are committed to the following steps:

1.   Promoting exchanges and good practices among the BRICS countries on innovation strategies and policies; enhancing mutual understanding, complementarity and coordination for the BRICS cooperation in innovation, and in particular, for the attainment of socio-economic progress driven by scientific, technological and social innovation, for the building of a BRICS community of shared values and common future, and for the realization of sustainable development goals.

2.   Strengthening cooperation in scientific and research activities, enhancing cooperation in innovation based on existing mechanisms and joint research programmes including such cooperation conducted through public-private partnerships; fostering strategic and long term university-industry partnerships to address the needs of industry and contributing directly to economic growth and development; continuing to encourage and support research and development projects in the areas of fundamental and applied research and innovation within bilateral and multilateral frameworks and continuing to carry out joint calls for STI projects; understanding the importance of implementing BRICS initiatives related to research and innovation; promoting open science and the sharing of research infrastructure; developing and initiating international mega science programmes.

3.   Organizing joint activities on identifying priorities for STI cooperation of BRICS countries based

on foresight and monitoring of global STI development.

4.   In view of the importance of science and technology parks for regional economic development, encouraging cooperation among science parks including supporting the transnational establishment of BRICS hi-tech enterprises in S&T parks. We welcome the establishment of exchange mechanisms for science parks, and expanding areas of cooperation in these domains.

5.   Encouraging technology transfer among the BRICS countries, strengthening training of technology transfer professionals, developing platforms for collaboration among businesses and academia, enabling extensive and orderly transfer and translation of innovation achievements in the BRICS countries. Utilizing existing technological network platforms as instruments of search for foreign partners for technological collaboration and initiation of joint STI projects.

6.   Promoting BRICS Partnerships on Youth Innovation and Entrepreneurship to carry out pragmatic cooperation, advocating the entrepreneurial spirit of encouraging innovation and tolerating failure, and to create a favorable ecosystem for innovation and entrepreneurship amongst the younger generation.

7.   Acknowledging the importance of supporting STI investment and the need to establish inter-BRICS investment instruments, we support explore the possibilities of driving BRICS cooperation on innovation and entrepreneurship through the National Development Banks, New Development Bank and other existing financing institutions.

8.   Supporting the mobility of STI human resources, especially exchanges among young scientists and entrepreneurs, supporting efforts to help address the future demand for new skills, sharing best practices on enhancing skills training for innovation and entrepreneurship, including improving access to Science, Technology, Engineering and Mathematics (STEM) education, creating jobs through joint research and collaboration in innovation and entrepreneurship, and stressing the role of youth in innovation. Stressing the role of women in science, technology and innovation activities as one of the key priorities of the BRICS STI Agenda.

III. Implementation

The BRICS Science Technology Innovation and Entrepreneurship Partnership (STIEP) Working Group will be responsible for the development of mechanisms and opportunities to implement the Action Plan, which will in the first period focus on the following deliverables:

1.   Creation of networks of science parks, technology business incubators and SMEs, where the innovation actually happens.

2.   Creation of cross-cultural talent pools for converting ideas into solution in domains of ICT, materials, water, health, energy, natural disaster risk reduction and resilience etc.

D.   4th Meeting of BRICS STI Ministers: 8 Oct. 2016, Jaipur (IND)

JAIPUR DECLARATION
Jaipur, the Republic of India, 8 October 2016

Theme: BRICS Science, Technology and Innovation Partnership – Building Responsive Inclusive Collective Solutions

1.   Preparatory to and in line with the proposed Goa Declaration and Action Plan to be adopted at the Eighth BRICS Summit on 15-16 October 2016 in Goa, India, we, the Ministers and their representatives for Science, Technology and Innovation of the Federative Republic of Brazil, the Russian Federation, the Republic of India, the People's Republic of China and the Republic of South Africa, met in Jaipur, the Republic of India, on the 8th of October 2016, for the 4th BRICS Science, Technology and Innovation Ministerial Meeting to build further collaboration based on the provisions of the BRICS Memorandum of Understanding on Cooperation in Science, Technology and Innovation (MoU).

2.   Taking into consideration the theme of the Eighth BRICS Summit – **Building Responsive Inclusive Collective Solutions**; we reaffirm our commitment to implement the Strategy for BRICS Economic Partnership adopted at the BRICS Ufa Summit which emphasized utilizing Science, Technology and Innovation (STI) as key drivers to address global and regional socio-economic challenges.

3.   Welcoming the collective achievements of BRICS partners in the realization of initiatives established in accordance with the BRICS Science, technology and Innovation Work Plan 2015-2018 (Work Plan 2015-2018) and Moscow Declaration adopted on 28 October 2015, we reaffirm our commitment to implement the Work Plan 2015-2018. We will intensify, diversify and institutionalize STI cooperation as outlined in the BRICS MoU on Cooperation in Science, Technology and Innovation through the mechanism of the BRICS Research and Innovation Initiative.

4.   Welcoming the outcomes of the Second Meeting of the BRICS STI Funding Parties on the Development of the BRICS Research and Innovation Initiative and First Meeting of BRICS STI Funding Working Group held in Beijing on 19-21 January 2016, we welcome the signing of the Arrangement of the BRICS STI Framework Program and the Implementation Plan (hereinafter – BRICS Arrangements). These Arrangements will be instrumental in implementation of BRICS countries' joint initiative on multilateral interdisciplinary research & innovation funding under the BRICS STI Framework Program as evident from the launching of the 1st BRICS Pilot Call 2016 in mutually agreed priority areas. We take note of the huge response of BRICS scientists to work together in the BRICS multilateral research projects.

5.   We take note of the conclusions of the First Photonics Conference of BRICS countries held on May 30-31, 2016, Moscow. We welcome the establishment of a BRICS Working Group on Photonics.

6.   We welcome the establishment of BRICS Geospatial Working Group and its 1st Meeting held in India on 3 March 2016.

7.   We welcome the hosting of 1st BRICS Young Scientist Conclave by India during 26-30 September, 2016 under the framework of the BRICS Young Scientist Forum being coordinated by India, as mandated by BRICS Leaders during 7th BRICS Summit. We take note of the recommendations of the BRICS Scientists Conclave.

8.   We welcome India's proposal to host the BRICS Young Scientist Forum-Conclave on a rotation basis in the BRICS Chair country to keep the momentum for engaging youth of BRICS countries and explore mechanisms for implementation.

9.   We welcome India's proposal to establish the **BRICS Innovative Idea Prize for Young Scientists** within the framework of the BRICS Young Scientist Forum.

10. We welcome the establishment of the BRICS Working Group on Astronomy and its meetings held in South Africa and Russia.

11. We take note of the outcomes of the BRICS thematic session on Prevention and Mitigation of Natural Disasters outlined during 6th Annual Conference of the International Society for Integrated Disaster Risk Management hosted by India in October 2015 in New Delhi; and of the BRICS Special Session on Natural Disaster Risk Prevention and Mitigation in Coastal Areas jointly organized by Russia and Brazil in Saint Petersburg on 26 August, 2016.

12. We take note of the 1st Meeting of the BRICS Working Group on Ocean and Polar Science and Technology held in Beijing on 26-28 September 2016 coordinated by Brazil.

13. We take note of the 2nd BRICS Water Forum hosted by Russia during 29-30 September 2016.

14. We take note of the 2nd Meeting of BRICS Working Group on Solid State Lighting hosted by China in November, 2015.

15. We agree to launch the next BRICS Framework Program call for research and innovation proposals in May 2017.

16. We agree on the speedy establishment of the BRICS Working Group on Research Infrastructure, and Mega-Science to reinforce the BRICS Global Research Advanced Infrastructure Network (BRICS-GRAIN). We recommend exploring the possibility of supporting such initiatives through New Development Bank as well as other similar organizations.

17. We encourage synergies of the BRICS Research and Innovation Initiative with the BRICS Network University.

18. We welcome India's proposal to establish a BRICS Science and Technology driven Entrepreneurship and Innovation Partnership. We agree to start consultations and discussions to implement this initiative.

19. Pursuant to the BRICS Work Plan 2015-2018, we take note of the progress made during 2015-2016 and endorse the Action Plan 2016-2017 as updated.

20. Brazil, Russia, China and South Africa convey their appreciation to India for hosting the 4th BRICS STI Ministerial Meeting and 6th BRICS STI SOM in Jaipur.

21. India, Brazil, Russia and South Africa welcome the offer of China to host the 5th BRICS STI Ministerial Meeting and the 7th BRICS STI SOM in 2017.

Done at Jaipur on October 8, 2016

E.   3rd Meeting of BRICS STI Ministers: 28 Oct. 2015, Moscow (RUS)

III BRICS SCIENCE, TECHNOLOGY AND INNOVATION MINISTERIAL MEETING

Theme: BRICS Science, Technology and Innovation Partnership – a Driver of Global Development

MOSCOW DECLARATION

Moscow, the Russian Federation, 28 October 2015

1.   In line with the Ufa Declaration and Action Plan adopted at the Seventh BRICS Summit on 9 July 2015 held in Russia we, the Ministers and their representatives for Science, Technology and Innovation of the Federative Republic of Brazil, the Russian Federation, the Republic of India, the People's Republic of China and the Republic of South Africa, met in Moscow, the Russian Federation, on the 28th of October 2015, for the III BRICS Science, Technology and Innovation Ministerial Meeting to build further collaboration based on the Memorandum of Understanding on Cooperation in Science, Technology and Innovation (MoU) provisions.

2.   Recalling the theme of the Seventh BRICS Summit "BRICS Partnership - a Powerful factor of Global Development", we affirm our willingness to follow the Strategy for BRICS Economic Partnership in addressing common global and regional socio-economic challenges utilizing such drivers as science, technology and innovation (STI).

3.   Welcoming the outcomes of the First Meeting of the BRICS STI Funding Parties on the establishment of the BRICS Research and Innovation Initiative (hereinafter - BRICS R&I Initiative) held on 6-7 July 2015, Moscow, Russia, and highlighting the immense research and technological potential in the BRICS member countries and importance of the development of BRICS R&I Initiative (paragraph 62 of the Ufa Declaration) we agree on the following mechanisms and levels of collaboration: (i) cooperation within large research infrastructures, including mega-science projects; (ii) coordination of the existing large-scale national programmes of the BRICS countries: (iii) development and implementation of a BRICS Framework Programme for funding multilateral joint research projects, technology commercialization and innovation; (iv) establishment of BRICS Research and Innovation Networking Platform.

4.   We welcome the establishment of the Working Group on BRICS large research infrastructures, the Working Group on BRICS funding multilateral joint research projects, technology commercialization and innovation.

5.   We agree on our commitment to develop and implement the BRICS Framework Programme on multilateral research funding through joint calls. Also we propose to use the possibilities of the New Development Bank (Agreement of the New Development Bank signed during the VI BRICS Summit in Fortaleza) as an additional funding instrument to foster further collaboration.

6.   The cooperation focused on the five thematic leadership areas established previously by each country in the Brasilia Declaration, namely: (a) prevention and mitigation of natural disasters, led by Brazil, (b) water resources and pollution treatment, led by Russia, (c) geospatial technology and its applications, led by India, (d) new and renewable energy, and energy efficiency, led by China, and (e) astronomy, led by South Africa, and the activities within these five areas will be implemented by use of the BRICS Research and Innovation Networking Platform developing direct communication channel between stakeholders.

7.   To address common societal challenges and to advance BRICS leadership and cooperation on a global level we welcome the new initiatives:

- Creation of BRICS Young Scientists Forum (India as coordinating country);
- Cooperation on Biotechnology and Biomedicine including Human Health and Neuroscience (Russia and Brazil as coordinating countries);
- Cooperation on Information Technologies and High Performance Computing (China and South Africa as coordinating countries);
- Cooperation on Ocean and Polar Science and Technology (Brazil and Russia as coordinating countries);
- Cooperation on Material science including Nanotechnology (India and Russia as coordinating countries);
- Cooperation on Photonics (India and Russia as coordinating countries).

8.   Encouraging increased participation of business, academia and other relevant stakeholders for STI development among BRICS countries (paragraph 11, Brasilia Declaration) we acknowledge the independent initiatives to establish the BRICS Network University aimed at developing master's and PhD programmes along with joint research projects in knowledge fields priorities corresponding with the main areas of cooperation stated in the Article 3 0f the MoU and the BRICS University League.

9.   We welcome the creation of a BRICS Young Scientists Forum and establishing the BRICS Young Scientist Forum Secretariat in India coordinated by the Department of Science and Technology with commitment and support from all BRICS countries. We also welcome hosting of the BRICS Young Scientist Conclave in 2016 in India and creation of dedicated website for BRICS Young Scientist Forum

10.   We also support creation of BRICS Research and Innovation Networking Platform.

11.   We take note of the following announcements: India and Brazil host the BRICS thematic Session on Prevention and Mitigation of Natural Disasters during the 6th Annual Conference of the International Society for Integrated Disaster Risk Management in October 2015: China hosts the 2nd Meeting of the BRICS Solid-state lightning (SSL) Working Group in November 2015; South Africa hosts the first meeting of the BRICS Astronomy Working Group in December 2015 at the Science Forum South Africa; India hosts the BRICS Working Group on Geospatial Technology Application for Development in March 2016; Russia initiates 2nd Meeting of the Group of STI Funding Parties in January 2016.

12.   We endorse the BRICS Science, Technology and Innovation Work Plan 2015-2018 and reaffirm our commitment to implement it (annexed).

13.   Brazil, India, China and South Africa convey their appreciation to the Russian Federation for hosting the III BRICS STI Ministerial meeting in Moscow.

14.   Russia, Brazil, China and South Africa convey their appreciation to India for its offer to host the IV BRICS STI Ministerial meeting and the VI BRICS STI SOM in 2016 and extend their full support to that end.

F.   The BRICS STI Work Plan 2015-2018: 27 Oct. 2015, Moscow (RUS)

Adopted on 28 October, 2015
and revised on 18 July, 2017

BRICS SCIENCE, TECHNOLOGY AND INNOVATION WORK PLAN 2015-2018

1.   The Ministers and their representatives for Science, Technology and Innovation of the Federative Republic of Brazil, the Russian Federation, the Republic of India, the People's Republic of China and the Republic of South Africa met in Moscow. on October 28, 2015, to endorse the BRICS Science, Technology and Innovation Work Plan 2015-2018 based on the Memorandum of Understanding on Cooperation in Science, Technology and Innovation between the Governments of the Federative Republic of Brazil, the Russian Federation, the Republic of India, the People's Republic of China and the Republic of South Africa (hereinafter - MoU) and the Strategy for BRICS Economic Partnership (hereinafter - Strategy).

2.   This Work Plan focuses on the main areas of cooperation with reference to Article 3 of the MoU Ensuring further collaboration on the basis of mutual benefit of the BRICS countries the Work Plan also provides new research and innovation initiatives.

3.   The BRICS countries responsible for implementation of the activities focused on the five thematic leadership areas as previously stated in the Brasilia Declaration decided to appoint contact institutions for collaboration within the BRICS Research and Innovation Networking Platform developing direct communication channel between stakeholders:

§ Prevention and Mitigation of Natural Disasters (Monitoring & Early Waning): Brazil (leads through the National Center for Monitoring and Early Warning of Natural Disasters - Cemaden);
§ Water resources and pollution treatment: Russia (leads through the Technology Platform for Sustainable Ecological Development);
§ Geospatial technology and its Application for development: India (leads through the National Spatial Data Infrastructure, DST); development of ICT and geospatial technology based Decision Support Systems (DSSs) for multi-hazard and climate risk management and appropriate resilient development planning for sustainable habitat;
§ New and renewable energy, and energy efficiency (Solid-state lightning as a sub-area (SS)) China (leads through the Ministry of Science and Technology - MOST);
§ Astronomy: South Africa (leads through the National Research Foundation).

3.1 In addition to the five thematic areas the new potential initiatives include

§ Creation of BRICS Young Scientists Forum (India as coordinating country);
§ Cooperation on Biotechnology and Biomedicine including Human Health and Neuroscience (Russia and Brazil as coordinating countries);
§ Cooperation on Information Technologies and High Performance Computing (China and South Africa as coordinating countries);
§ Cooperation on Ocean and Polar Science and Technology (Brazil and Russia as coordinating countries);
§ Cooperation on Material science including Nanotechnology (India and Russia as coordinating countries);
§ Cooperation on Photonics (India and Russia as coordinating countries).

4.   Following the principles of the MoU and the Strategy the coordination of the activities within the main areas of cooperation will be implemented by BRICS Research and Innovation Networking

Platform (BRICS RINP) aimed at facilitation of research collaboration. Establishment of the BRICS RINP will contribute to the increasing participation of business, academia and other relevant stakeholders for BRICS STI development focused on the five thematic leadership areas.

5.   Establishment of the Working Groups (WG): WG on the BRICS STI funding, WG on the BRICS research infrastructures, including mega-science projects. Each WG shall have a designated national focal point from each of the BRICS countries. The lead country is responsible for maintaining regular coordinating meetings of the national focal points to monitor, coordinate and implement activities. WGs shall meet at least once a year under the current BRICS Chair country in order to coordinate activities.

6.   In order to foster STI cooperation the BRICS Research and Innovation Initiative (hereinafter – BRICS R&I Initiative) will be implemented providing the following mechanisms and levels of cooperation:

6.1. Promotion of the coordination within large-scale research infrastructure to support initiatives leading to efficient use and development of mega-science projects. Relevant Working Group should elaborate appropriate mechanisms, such as BRICS Global Research Advanced Infrastructure Network (BRICS GRAIN).

6.2. Coordination of existing large-scale national programmes of the BRICS countries

6.3. Promotion research in the main areas of cooperation through implementation of a BRICS Framework Programme for funding multilateral joint projects for research, technology commercialization and innovation, considering following actions:

§ Establishment of the WG on the BRICS STI funding (includes at least one representative from each participating funding party);
§ Development of the BRICS Framework Programme for funding multilateral joint projects for research, technology commercialization and innovation and the Road Map for its implementation;
§ Launch of multilateral joint STI calls in the main areas of cooperation stated in Article 3 of the MoU with corresponding funding from each partner, including a special focus on cooperation with enterprises and industry, generating new knowledge and innovative products, services and processes in the BRICS countries:
§ Exploring the potential of attracting resources of the New Development Bank as an additional funding mechanism of multilateral joint projects within the BRICS Framework Programme;
§ Development of a special funding tools for researchers' mobility to support human capital in STI and promote involvement of youth.

6.4. Establishment of the BRICS RINP to facilitate research collaboration, BRICS technology transfer: to support MSMEs in technology and innovation activities; to develop innovation and technology clusters, high-tech zones / science parks and incubators; to create the BRICS research and innovation centers.

7.   The realization of the present Work Plan is to be defined in the BRICS Action Plan 2015-2016 The Action Plan accumulates the activities in the defined areas, mechanisms and levels of cooperation.

The Action Plan is to be followed up, reviewed and revised by the BRICS Chair country to monitor and coordinate the activities, and prepare reports to the BRICS STI Ministers' and Senior Official's Meetings.

8.   The BRICS national research institutions are encouraged to consider collaboration under BRICS thematic leadership in Biomedicine and life sciences such as:

§ integrated telemedicine systems in the regions of BRICS;

§ international consortium and center of transfer of technology in the field of Biomedicine (BRICS Biomed);

§ systems of pharmacological consortiums with the aim to resolve the problem of "medicinal safety", anti microbial resistance and response to epidemic and emerging diseases.

9. Funding for any initiative established under this Work Plan shall be pursued by the BRICS countries in accordance with Article 6 of the MoU.

Action Plan 2015-2016

1. Activities in the defined main areas of cooperation:

Appointment of a designated national focal points for WGs from each of the BRICS countries by December 2015:

- Establishment of BRICS Water Forum to exchange experiences and practices in water management and pollution treatment in the context of green economy and post-2015 sustainable development goals (Russia);
- Establishment of BRICS Prevention and Mitigation of Natural Disasters Strategic Plan, which will include short term exchange of scientists, researchers, technical specialists and students, capacity building training programmes, organization of workshops, seminars and conferences. information and database sharing, formulation and implementation of joint research programmes and projects, establishment of joint funding mechanisms for support of research programmes and large scale research infrastructure and facilitation of access to science and technology infrastructure among BRICS countries (Brazil);
- Holding BRICS Working Group on Geospatial Technology Application for Development (March 2016, India);
- Holding the 2nd Meeting of the BRICS SSL Working Group (November 2015, China);
- Holding the first Meeting of the BRICS Astronomy Working Group (December 2015);
- ·Creation of experts' network from BRICS countries to support the development of compatible telemedicine systems in BRICS regions (Russia);
- Holding annual conference "Innovative materials for energy and water saving and environmental protection, new trends in the technological development" (Russia);
- Development of ICT and geospatial technology based Decision Support Systems (DSSs) for multi-hazard and climate risk management and appropriate resilient development planning for sustainable habitat;
- Holding annual BRICS Young Scientists Forum (in 2016 by March), including scientific international workshops for young researchers on the priority topics, including lectures, hands-on tutorial sessions and round-table discussions;
- Holding BRICS Young Scientists Forum driven regional scientific activities, including BRICS Young Scientist Conclave (India, 2016); BRICS Young Scientist Website (2016) and scientific international workshops for young researchers on the priority topics, including lectures, hands-on tutorial sessions and round-table discussions;
- Creating a BRICS Young Scientist Website with an interactive online component to broadcast opportunities and initiative for young STI community in the BRICS Region;
- Holding topical workshops to discuss priority areas for joint collaboration with representatives of BRICS countries involving scientific community, business and other interested parties in order to establish new collaboration partnerships;
- Holding the meeting to discuss potential collaboration between BRICS countries in photonics area;
- Organizing and publishing a bibliography on history of science in BRICS countries.

2.   Implementation of the BRICS R&I Initiative

2.1. Establishment of the WG of the BRICS research infrastructures by January, 2016 co-led by Russia and South Africa until the next STI SOM and Ministerial meetings to:

- Delegate participants from each BRICS country to the established WGs Compile a list of major research infrastructures projects from each BRICS country;
- Develop of an Operation Plan on BRICS research infrastructures including mega-science projects;
- Launch pilot projects within the BRICS framework of global research infrastructures such as NICA and others;
- Attract the resources of the New Development Bank as an additional funding mechanism of projects within the Action Plan of the development of global research infrastructures;
- Organize of a kick-off meeting - first meeting of the WG of the BRICS research infrastructures;
- Create registry centers of collective use and unique research facilities in the main areas of cooperation.

2.2. Holding the joint workshop on BRICS STI policies by mid-2016 and series of short-term training programmes on exchange of STI policies in the BRICS countries in 2016-2017 to support coordination of existing large-scale national programs of the BRICS countries

2.3. Promoting the BRICS Framework Programme for funding multilateral joint projects for research, technology commercialization and innovation by launch of multilateral joint STI calls that includes the following:

- Meeting of the WG on the BRICS STI funding in January 2016;
- Decision of the funding parties from the BRICS countries to launch multilateral joint calls in 2016 in the mutually agreed 5 priority areas with a co-investment of resources including funds available in the respective BRICS countries An indicative allocated budget for the 1st call is $ 2 mln from different sources from each BRICS country. Final commitments of the call will be written in the Memorandum of Understanding;
- The Memorandum of Understanding (MoU) for organization of the BRICS multilateral joint call to be signed till the end of 2015;
- Establishment of the Joint Call Secretariat and other joint call structures, including Panel of Experts.

2.4. Activities to facilitate collaboration within the BRICS Research and Innovation Networking Platform:

- Development of a concept note (White Paper) on the BRICS Research and Innovation Networking Platform;
- Identification of relevant BRICS stakeholders and partners;
- Holding an international workshop "BRICS Research and Innovation Networking Platform" and building a Road map for its development;
- Creation of a BRICS STI Information Exchange System.

G. MoU on Cooperation in Science, Technology and Innovation: 9 Jul. 2015, Ufa (RUS)

MEMORANDUM OF UNDERSTANDING ON
COOPERATION IN
SCIENCE, TECHNOLOGY AND INNOVATION BETWEEN
THE GOVERNMENTS OF
THE FEDERATIVE REPUBLIC OF BRAZIL, THE RUSSIAN FEDERATION,
THE REPUBLIC OF INDIA,
THE PEOPLE'S REPUBLIC OF CHINA
AND
THE REPUBLIC OF SOUTH AFRICA

PREAMBLE

The Government of the Federative Republic of Brazil, The Government of the Russian Federation, The Government of the Republic of India, The Government of the People's Republic of China, and The Government of the Republic of South Africa (hereinafter referred to as the "Parties");

REAFFIRMING the overarching vision embodied in the BRICS Summit Declarations, including the 2011 BRICS Sanya Declaration which identified the need "to explore cooperation in the sphere of science, technology and innovation, including the peaceful use of space";

NOTING the recommendations of the First, Second and Third BRICS Science, Technology and Innovation Senior Officials Meetings, held respectively in Dalian, China, in September 2011, Pretoria, South Africa, in November 2012, and New Delhi, India in December 2013;

HARNESSING potential bilateral synergies and other forms of multi-country frameworks of cooperation amongst Brazil, Russia, India, China and South Africa in science, technology and innovation;

DESIROUS to further strengthen cooperation in the fields of science, technology and innovation for accelerated and sustainable socio-economic development amongst the five countries;

RECOGNIZING the importance of cooperation based on the principles of voluntary participation, equality, mutual benefit, reciprocity and subject to the availability of earmarked resources for collaboration by each country;

RECOGNIZING the variable geometry of the research and development systems of the

BRICS member countries;

HEREBY AGREE as follows:

ARTICLE 1
Competent Authorities

The competent authorities responsible for the implementation of this Memorandum of Understanding will be the following designated organisations:

(a) For the Federative Republic of Brazil, the Ministry of Science, Technology and Innovation (MCTI);

(b) For the Russian Federation, the Ministry of Education and Science (MES);

(c) For the Republic of India, the Department of Science and Technology (DST, India);

(d) For the People's Republic of China, the Ministry of Science and Technology (MOST);

(e) For the Republic of South Africa, the Department of Science and Technology (DST, South Africa).

ARTICLE 2
Objectives

The main objectives of this Memorandum of Understanding are:

(a) To establish a strategic framework for cooperation in science, technology and innovation amongst the BRICS member countries;

(b) To address common global and regional socio-economic challenges in the BRICS member countries utilising shared experiences and complementarities in science, technology and innovation;

(c) To co-generate new knowledge and innovative products, services and processes in the BRICS member countries utilising appropriate funding and investment instruments;

(d) To promote, where appropriate, joint BRICS science, technology and innovation partnerships with other strategic actors in the developing world.

ARTICLE 3
Areas of Cooperation

The main areas of cooperation under this Memorandum of Understanding shall include but not be confined to:

(a) Exchange of information on policies and programmes and promotion of innovation and technology transfer;

(b) Food security and sustainable agriculture;

(c) Natural disasters;

(d) New and renewable energy, energy efficiency;

(e) Nanotechnology;

(f) High performance computing;

(g) Basic research;

(h) Space research and exploration, aeronautics, astronomy and earth observation;

(i) Medicine and biotechnology;

(j) Biomedicine and life sciences (biomedical engineering, bioinformatics, biomaterials);

(k) Water resources and pollution treatment;

(l) High tech zones/science parks and incubators;

(m) Technology transfer;

(n) Science popularization;

(o) Information and communication technology;

(p) Clean coal technologies;

(q) Natural gas and non-conventional gases;

(r) Ocean and polar sciences;

(s) Geospatial technologies and its applications.

ARTICLE 4
Mechanisms and Modalities of Cooperation

The principal mechanism for cooperation shall be this Memorandum of Understanding. The Parties or their designated institutions may enter into sub-agreements which shall be governed by the terms of this Memorandum of Understanding.

The modalities of cooperation under this Memorandum of Understanding and sub- agreements arising there-from between the Parties in the fields of science, technology and innovation shall take the following forms:

(a) Short-term exchange of scientists, researchers, technical experts and scholars;

(b) Dedicated training programmes to support human capital development in science, technology and innovation;

(c) Organization of science, technology and innovation workshops seminars and conferences in areas of mutual interest;

(d) Exchange of science, technology and innovation information;

(e) Formulation and implementation of collaborative research and development programmes and projects;

(f) Establishment of joint funding mechanisms to support BRICS research programmes and large-scale research infrastructure projects;

(g) Facilitated access to science and technology infrastructure among BRICS member countries;

(h) Announcement of simultaneous calls for proposals in BRICS member countries;

(i) Cooperation of national science and engineering academies and research agencies.

ARTICLE 5
Governing Structures

The main structures governing cooperation under this Memorandum of Understanding shall include:

1. BRICS Science, Technology and Innovation Ministerial Meeting

2. BRICS Science, Technology and Innovation Senior Officials Meeting

3. BRICS Science, Technology and Innovation Working Group

1. The BRICS Science, Technology and Innovation Ministerial Meeting (comprising Ministers responsible for science, technology and innovation in Brazil, Russia, India, China and South Africa) shall convene at least once every year during the presidency of a member country. The main responsibilities of the BRICS Science, Technology and Innovation Ministerial Meeting will include:

(a) Providing an overarching vision and advice on institutional and financial frameworks for major BRICS science, technology and innovation programmes and initiatives;

(b) Facilitating linkages between the BRICS science, technology and innovation working group and other BRICS sectoral working groups or BRICS expert groups to ensure the effective implementation and realisation of the objectives of this Memorandum of Understanding;

(c) Setting priorities for cooperation and joint action in science, technology and innovation amongst BRICS member countries for a given period of time, taking into account the priority areas indicated in Article (3) above.

2. The BRICS Science, Technology and Innovation Senior Officials' Meeting will constitute Directors-General (or equivalent) of BRICS member countries as the leaders of delegation, BRICS science, technology and innovation country coordinators, focal points, scientists, experts and other relevant officials.

The BRICS Science, Technology and Innovation Senior Officials' Meeting will meet annually in the country where the BRICS Summit is hosted.

Responsibilities of the BRICS Science, Technology and Innovation Senior Officials' Meeting will include:

(a) Exchanging information on recent science, technology and innovation developments as well as identifying common policy challenges in BRICS member countries;

(b) Supporting the implementation of strategic decisions related to science, technology and innovation taken by the BRICS Summits, as well the high-level decisions emanating from BRICS Science, Technology and Innovation Ministerial Meetings;

(c) Facilitating BRICS science, technology and innovation cooperation mainly through the prioritisation of the thematic areas identified in Article (3) of this Memorandum of Understanding;

(d) Configuring appropriate funding mechanisms and instruments to support BRICS science, technology and innovation cooperation;

(e) Harnessing synergies in respect of science, technology and innovation priority directions at bilateral, multilateral and poly-lateral levels within BRICS;

(f) Approving 3-5 year cycles for BRICS science, technology and innovation initiatives and programmes;

(g) Reviewing periodically progress in terms of implementation with respect to science, technology and innovation cooperation under this Memorandum of Understanding, as well as identifying new areas, activities and cooperation modalities of mutual interest;

(h) Providing recommendations for consideration by the BRICS Science, Technology and Innovation Ministerial Meeting to enhance effective implementation of this Memorandum of Understanding;

(i)   Considering other agenda matters deemed appropriate by the BRICS member countries.

3.   The BRICS Science, Technology and Innovation Working Group will constitute the five BRICS science, technology and innovation country coordinators whose responsibilities will include:

(a) Fulfilling the function of Secretariat for the BRICS Science, Technology and Innovation SOM (developing the agenda and annotations for the BRICS science, technology and innovation SOM; recording proceedings of the SOM etc.);

(b) Convening Science, Technology and Innovation Working Group meetings between sessions of the Science, Technology and Innovation SOM.

ARTICLE 6
Funding Mechanisms and Instruments

Science, technology and innovation cooperation under this Memorandum of Understanding will be supported by appropriate BRICS country funding mechanisms, instruments and national rules.

The key objectives of the BRICS science, technology and innovation funding mechanisms and instruments shall be:

(a) To establish R&D programmes in frontier and priority research areas in support of sustainable development in BRICS member countries;

(b) To promote the co-generation of new knowledge and innovative products, services and processes;

(c) To co-invest in large scale research infrastructure projects;

(d) To facilitate technology and knowledge transfer and implementation;

(e) To facilitate policy development in science, technology and innovation;

(f) To facilitate linkages with various forums dealing with business, academia, research and development centres, government agencies and institutions.

ARTICLE 7
Management of Intellectual Property Rights

1. The parties will ensure adequate and effective protection and fair allocation of intellectual property rights of a proprietary nature that may result from the cooperative activities under this Memorandum of Understanding, according to their respective national laws and regulations and their international obligations.

2. The condition for the acquisition, maintenance and commercial exploitation of intellectual property rights over possible products and/or processes that might be obtained under this Memorandum of Understanding will be defined in the specific programmes, contracts or working plans of the activities of cooperation.

3. The specific programmes, contracts or working plans relating to the activities of cooperation mentioned in Paragraph 2 of this Article will set out the conditions regarding the confidentiality of information whose publication and/or disclosure might jeopardize the acquisition, maintenance and commercial exploitation of intellectual property rights obtained under this Memorandum of Understanding. Such specific programmes, contracts or working plans related to the activities of cooperation will establish, where applicable, the rule and procedures concerning the settlement of disputes on intellectual property matters under this Memorandum of Understanding.

ARTICLE 8
Final Dispositions

1. This Memorandum of Understanding will come into force on the date of signature and will remain valid for five (5) years. Thereafter, this Memorandum of Understanding shall be renewed automatically for successive equal periods, unless one of the Parties notifies the others in writing its intention to terminate this Memorandum of Understanding.

2. The present Memorandum of Understanding may be amended at any time, by mutual consent of the Parties, through diplomatic channels.

3. Any Party may, at any time, notify the others of its intention to terminate the present Memorandum of Understanding. Termination will be effective six (6) months after the date of the notification and will not affect the ongoing activities of cooperation, unless otherwise agreed by the Parties.

4. Any dispute related to the interpretation or implementation of the present Memorandum of Understanding will be settled by direct negotiations between the Parties, through diplomatic channels.

IN WITNESS WHEREOF the undersigned, being duly authorized thereto by their respective Governments, have signed this Memorandum of Understanding in five originals, in Portuguese, Russian, Hindi, Chinese and English languages, all texts being equally authentic. In case of any divergence of interpretation, the English text will prevail.

DONE at...................................on this.............day of...2015

FOR THE GOVERNMENT OF THE FEDERATIVE REPUBLIC OF BRAZIL

FOR THE GOVERNMENT OF THE RUSSIAN FEDERATION

FOR THE GOVERNMENT OF THE REPUBLIC OF INDIA

FOR THE GOVERNMENT OF THE PEOPLE'S REPUBLIC OF CHINA

FOR THE GOVERNMENT OF THE REPUBLIC OF SOUTH AFRICA

H.   2nd Meeting of BRICS STI Ministers: 18 Mar. 2015, Brasilia (BRA)

BRASILIA DECLARATION

1.   In line with the Fortaleza Declaration and the Action Plan adopted at the 6th BRICS Summit, on 15 July, 2014 held in Brazil, we, the Ministers for Science, Technology and Innovation of the Federative Republic of Brazil, the Russian Federation, the Republic of India, the People's Republic of China and the Republic of South Africa, met in Brasília, Brazil, on 18 March, 2015, for the 2nd BRICS Science, Technology and Innovation Ministerial Meeting.

2.   Recalling the theme of the 6th BRICS Summit "Inclusive Growth: Sustainable Solutions", we strongly believe that Science, Technology and Innovation play a central role in promoting inclusive macroeconomics and social policies and in the imperative to address challenges to humankind posed by the need to simultaneously achieve growth, inclusiveness, environmental protection and preservation.

3.   We reaffirm that sharing and exchanging information on science, technology and innovation policies and strategies; leveraging contacts and programmes aimed at enhancing collaborative innovation projects among BRICS countries; and the formulation of joint long-term problem-focused cooperation programmes shall constitute the central modalities of this cooperation. In order to facilitate this, appropriate mechanisms of cooperation shall be elaborated and established within the implementation of the BRICS Science, Technology and Innovation initiatives.

4.   We welcome the outcomes of the 1st BRICS Workshop on Prevention and Mitigation of Natural Disasters, held in Brasília, on 7-8 May 2014; of the BRICS Seminar on National Systems of Innovation, held in Brasília, on 25-27 March 2014; of the Meeting of BRICS Solid State Lighting Working Group, held in Guangzhou, China, on 7-9 November 2014; and of the International Conference on Water Management and Ecology in the Framework of Russian Federation participation in BRICS, held in Moscow, Russia, on 4 June 2014.

5.   Following the instructions of the leaders of BRICS member countries, mentioned in paragraph 67 of the Fortaleza Declaration, we express our satisfaction in signing the Memorandum of Understanding on Cooperation in Science, Technology and Innovation (MoU), which establishes a strategic framework for cooperation in priority areas amongst the BRICS member countries.

6.   In order to foster further collaboration and achieve concrete results from the MoU directives, we agree to develop and negotiate a Work Plan 2015-2018, based on the Brazilian proposal, during the Russian presidency of BRICS, to be approved in the next BRICS STI-SOM and signed at the next BRICS STI Ministerial Meeting. The Work Plan will focus on the five priority areas and leadership established previously by each country, namely: (a) prevention and mitigation of natural disasters, to be led by Brazil, (b) water resources and pollution treatment, to be led by Russia, (c) geospatial technology and its applications, to be led by India, (d) new and renewable energy, and energy efficiency, to be led by China, and (e) astronomy, to be led by South Africa. New initiatives agreed by the BRICS countries will also be included in the Work Plan.

7.   We take note of the following announcements: South Africa will convene the 1st Meeting of the BRICS Working Group on Astronomy shortly after this Ministerial; Russia will host International Scientific and Experimental Conference on Water: Technologies, Materials in Industry and Energy Processes in July 2015, in Ufa; China will host the 2nd Meeting of the BRICS SSL Working Group in November 2015; India will host the BRICS Working Group on Geospatial Technology Application for Development in March 2016. We also welcome the Brazilian-Russian proposal, discussed on the occasion of the 4th STI-SOM, to start negotiations among BRICS countries with a view to establishing biomedicine and life sciences as a new priority area for cooperation.

8.   The Work Plan will ensure the development of science, technology and innovation cooperation through the launch of a BRICS Research and Innovation Initiative, which shall cover actions including: (a) cooperation in the framework of major research infrastructures; (b) coordination of existing large-scale national programmes of BRICS countries; (c) setting up a Framework Programme for funding multilateral joint project for research, technology commercialization and innovation; and (d) establishment of a joint Research and Innovation Networking Platform.

9.   We support the creation of a BRICS Young Scientists Forum proposed by India, which intends to establish a platform for young students of science, engineering and applied disciplines as well as for those pursuing research careers in the age group of 22-35 years to gather for: (a) addressing the needs for advancement of skills, research competencies, career, talent and next generation scientific leadership; (b) sharing scientific research results and experiences; (c) discussing novel ideas in emerging frontline fields of S&T; (d) analyzing trends and features of globally important scientific issues; (e) suggesting measures to enhance trans-continental mobility in their scientific research careers.

10.   To increase the competitiveness of the BRICS economies on the global arena, we commit to supporting the BRICS Economic Partnership Strategy, currently under negotiation, which includes Science, Technology and Innovation as a priority. Long-term cooperation in these areas will help bridge the scientific and technological gap between BRICS and developed economies and provide a new quality of growth based on economic complementarity.

11.   We encourage increased participation of business, academia and other relevant stakeholders for science, technology and innovation development among BRICS countries.

12.   We welcome the holding of the 4th BRICS Science, Technology and Innovation Senior Officials Meeting in Brasília, on 17 March 2015, and instruct the Senior Officials to organize the 5th BRICS STI-SOM prior to the 3rd Ministerial Meeting.

13.   Russia, India, China and South Africa extend their warm appreciation to Brazil for hosting the 2nd BRICS Science, Technology and Innovation Ministerial Meeting and the 4th BRICS Science, Technology and Innovation Senior Officials Meeting.

14.   Brazil, India, China and South Africa convey their appreciation to the Russian Federation for its offer to host the 3rd BRICS Science, Technology and Innovation Ministerial Meeting and the 5th BRICS Science, Technology and Innovation Senior Officials Meeting in 2015 and extend their full support to that end.

I.   1st Meeting of BRICS STI Ministers: 10 Feb. 2014, Cape Town (ZAF)

Theme: BRICS Science, Technology and Innovation Cooperation: A Strategic Partnership
for Equitable Growth and Sustainable Development

FIRST BRICS SCIENCE, TECHNOLOGY AND INNOVATION MINISTERIAL MEETING:

CAPE TOWN DECLARATION

Cape Town, South Africa, 10 February 2014

1.   In line with the mandate of the eThekwini Declaration and Action Plan of March 2013 adopted at the Fifth BRICS Summit held in South Africa, we the Ministers and their representatives for Science, Technology and Innovation of the Federative Republic of Brazil, the Russian Federation, the Republic of India, the People's Republic of China and the Republic of South Africa, met in Cape Town, South Africa for the First BRICS Science, Technology and Innovation Ministerial Meeting on 10 February 2014, to discuss and coordinate positions of mutual interest and identify future directions of institutionalizing cooperation in science, technology and innovation within the framework of BRICS.

2.   We reaffirm the vision to strengthen the BRICS partnership for common development and advance cooperation in a gradual and pragmatic manner, reflecting the principles of openness, solidarity and cultural assistance, and give substance to all the calls expressed at previous BRICS Summits to intensify cooperation in the spheres of science, technology and innovation, including the peaceful use of space.

3.   We stress the paramount importance of science, technology and innovation for human development. Indeed, while recognizing the role and significance of competitiveness in the rapid technologically changing global environment, we agree that people-centred and public-good driven science, technology and innovation, supporting equitable growth and sustainable development, shall form the basis of our cooperation within the framework of BRICS.

4.   In order to support this common vision, we agreed to enter into a BRICS Memorandum of Understanding on Cooperation in Science, Technology and Innovation which shall serve as the strategic intergovernmental framework: (i) to strengthen cooperation in science, technology and innovation; (ii) to address common global and regional socio-economic challenges utilizing shared experiences and complementarities; (iii) to co-generate new knowledge and innovative products, services and processes utilizing appropriate funding and investment instruments; (iv) to promote, where appropriate, joint BRICS partnerships with other strategic actors in the developing world.

5.   We agree with the text of the BRICS Memorandum of Understanding on Cooperation in Science, Technology and Innovation and propose that it be signed on the occasion of the Sixth BRICS Summit in Brazil in 2014.

6.   We agree under this BRICS STI framework the main areas of cooperation shall include: exchange of information on policies and programmes and promotion of innovation and technology transfer; food security and sustainable agriculture; climate change and natural disaster preparedness and mitigation; new and renewable energy, energy efficiency; nanotechnology; high performance computing; basic research; space research and exploration, aeronautics, astronomy and earth observation; medicine and biotechnology; biomedicine and life sciences (biomedical engineering, bioinformatics, biomaterials); water resources and pollution treatment; high tech zones/science parks and incubators; technology transfer; science popularization; information and communication technology; clean coal technologies; natural gas and non-conventional gases; ocean and polar sciences; and geospatial technologies and its applications.

7.   In pursuit of cooperation in the above areas, we agree to build upon existing bilateral synergies and other forms of multi-country frameworks of cooperation amongst the BRICS member countries.

8.   With a view to supporting the immediate implementation of the objectives outlined in the BRICS Memorandum of Understanding on Cooperation in Science, Technology and Innovation, we recognize and endorse, as a first step, the establishment of five thematic areas and leadership, namely: (a) climate change and natural disaster mitigation, led by Brazil; (b) water resources and pollution treatment led by Russia (c) geospatial technology and its applications led by India; (d) new and renewable energy, and energy efficiency led by China; and (e) astronomy led by South Africa.

9.   We recognize the sharing and exchange of information on science, technology and innovation policies and strategies and the formulation of joint long-term problem-focused cooperation programmes will constitute the central modalities of this cooperation.

10. We recognize that specific cooperative activities under the BRICS STI framework may necessitate the provision of organizational, legal, financial and staffing support. This relates primarily to stimulating joint investment in the development of high technologies, creating common technology platforms, and the setting up of applied research and innovation centres and laboratories.

11. We recognize the importance and centrality of knowledge and technology transfer as the means of mutually empowering BRICS member countries. In this regard we support efforts to establish BRICS mechanisms that enhance technology and knowledge transfer amongst the member countries.

12. We support the establishment of a dedicated BRICS STI training programme to address human capital challenges in BRICS member countries.

13. We commit to strengthen and improve the governance mechanisms for BRICS STI cooperation, including meetings of STI Ministers, senior officials meetings, as well as the network of national coordinators for cooperation in the spheres of science, technology and innovation.

14. Brazil, Russia, India and China extend warm appreciation and sincere gratitude to the Department of Science and Technology of the Republic of South Africa for hosting the First BRICS Science, Technology and Innovation Ministerial Meeting in Cape Town on 10 February 2014.

15. Russia, India China, and South Africa wish the Brazilian government well in its preparations for the Sixth BRICS Summit where deliberations relating to science, technology and innovation will form part of the agenda.

Done in the English language in five copies, each copy being equally authentic on 10 February 2014 in Cape Town, South Africa.

III.5.   BRICS Health Ministers

A.   8th Meeting of BRICS Health Ministers: 20 Jul. 2018, Durban (ZAF)

DRAFT JOINT COMMUNIQUÉ

1.   Ministers of Health and heads of delegation from the Republic of South Africa, the Federative Republic of Brazil, the Russian Federation, the Republic of India and the People's Republic of China met on 20th July 2018 in Durban, South Africa, for the 8th BRICS Health Ministers Meeting.

2.   Acknowledged Mandela Centenary highlighting the legacy of Madiba and placing emphasis on the culture of volunteerism and the 18th July 2018 marking the day that Nelson Mandela would have turned 100 years old.

3.   Recalled previous Declarations and Joint Communiqués of BRICS on health issues, in particular the Tianjin Declaration of the 7th BRICS Health Ministers meeting, which reaffirmed the commitment to strengthen intra-BRICS coordination and cooperation to promote public health in accordance with "BRICS Framework for Collaboration on Strategic Projects in Health" as well as the Communiqué of the BRICS Health Ministers on the sidelines of the 71st World Health Assembly, in May 2018.

4.   Reaffirmed their commitment to the 2030 Agenda and the attainment of the Sustainable Development Goals and recognized the centrality of the World Health Organization in advancing the global health agenda and reaffirmed the intergovernmental nature of WHO and the need to preserve WHO as the coordinating and leading authority in global health. They reaffirmed the importance of strengthening WHO's emergency response, while maintaining WHO's excellence in meeting its public health functions and mandates.

5.   Acknowledged the choice for the 2018 World Health Assembly main theme: "Health for All: commitment to Universal Health Coverage", wherein they reiterated the call for global, regional and national efforts towards achieving Universal Health Coverage, in line with SDG 3.8. They reiterated their commitment to ensuring the achievement of specific BRICS Member States commitments towards ensuring the attainment of UHC, as pronounced in the opening plenary of the 71st World Health Assembly, in May 2018. They emphasized the need for continuous monitoring and evaluation of UHC efforts in this area.

6.   Reiterated their commitment to collaborate in key areas, focusing on strengthening health systems; reducing non-communicable diseases (NCDs) risk factors through prevention and health promotion; achieve Universal Health Coverage (UHC); promote use of traditional medicine, strategic health technologies, with a focus on communicable and non-communicable diseases; develop new medical technologies and new medical products including vaccines.

7.   Reiterated the work on the BRICS TB Cooperation Plan, approved in the 6th BRICS Health Ministers Meeting, in New Delhi, in 2016, which called for the creation of the BRICS TB Research Network and collaboration with the WHO and other stakeholders to promote scientific research, development and innovation on diagnosis, vaccines, drug regimens for TB and patient service delivery. They noted progress made thus far by the collaboration arising from the meetings held in Rio de Janeiro, Moscow and Johannesburg. They also recognised the need for establishing a BRICS mechanism for financial support of joint research projects that might contribute to global progress.

8.   Welcomed the 1st WHO Global Ministerial Conference on Ending Tuberculosis in the Sustainable Development Era: A Multisectoral response, that was organised jointly with the government of the Russian Federation held in Moscow on 16 and 17 November 2017, and the resulting Moscow declaration to End TB with commitments and support its implementation.

9.   Stressed the importance and affirmed strong support for the 1st High-Level Meeting of the UN General Assembly on Ending Tuberculosis; and the 3rd High-Level Meeting of the UN General Assembly on the Prevention and Control of non-communicable diseases, to be held in September 2018. They expressed their full support for all resolutions adopted at the 71st World Health Assembly in preparation for these meetings.

10.   Resolved to strengthen efforts to make affordable medicines available, including through enhanced R&D innovative approaches, and reiterated their support for the approval of decision WHA71(8), which calls for the elaboration of a comprehensive roadmap report on access to medicines and vaccines, and their support for the approval of decision WHA71(9) which calls for implementation of the Global Strategy and Plan of Action on Public Health, Innovation and Intellectual Property (GSPA-PHI).

11.   Welcomed the recommendations of the UN High Level Panel on access to medicines and resolved to continue working together to improve the access to affordable, quality, effective and safe drugs, vaccines, diagnostics and other medical products and technologies. They committed to strengthen the coordination and cooperation on vaccine research and development within BRICS countries, and welcomed the proposal to establish a BRICS vaccine research and development center as mentioned in the Declaration of the BRICS Science and Technology and Innovation Ministerial Meeting held on 3rd July 2018.

12.   Resolved to continue strengthening efforts to combat Anti-Microbial Resistance (AMR) through enhanced R&D innovation approaches and multi-sectoral coordinated actions in line with the WHO Global Action Plan on AMR and promoting equity and sustainable access to antibiotics.

13.   Reaffirmed the need to support efforts to strengthen Member States' capacities to deal with health emergencies and implement the WHO International Health Regulations (2005). Reemphasized the important work and role of BRICS countries in addressing health emergencies.

14.   Emphasized that prevention and control of NCDs including Cancer, Cardiovascular diseases, Diabetes, Chronic Obstructive Airway and Pulmonary diseases, as well as mental health are essential to reduce premature mortality, enhance productivity and improve quality of life.

15.   Resolved to collaborate in implementing best practices in creating healthy environment through legislative, regulatory and administrative measures, in promoting healthy lifestyles, improving nutrition and preventing and controlling NCDs and their risk factors.

16.   Reaffirmed their commitment to strengthen collaboration for the full implementation of the WHO Framework Convention on Tobacco Control (FCTC) and recognized the need to build on the results achieved so far. They also called for the further step-up of tobacco control measures during the Eighth Conference of Parties to the WHO FCTC, to be held in Geneva, in October 2018.

17.   Agreed to convene the 9th BRICS Health Ministers and Senior Officials meeting in Brazil, in 2019.

B.   7th Meeting of BRICS Health Ministers: 6 Jul. 2017, Tianjin (CHN)

TIANJIN COMMUNIQUÉ

1. Ministers of Health and heads of delegation from the Federative Republic of Brazil, the Russian Federation, the Republic of India, the People's Republic of China and the Republic of South Africa, met at the 7th BRICS Health Ministers' Meeting on 6 July 2017 in Tianjin, China.

2. Committed to strengthen the intra-BRICS cooperation to protect and to promote people's health and achieve the 2030 Sustainable Development Agenda, reiterated the renewed commitment to health by the BRICS leaders as expressed in the Goa Declaration in October 2016, noted the progress made since the first BRICS Health Ministers Meeting and resolved to continue cooperation in the sphere of health through the Technical Working Groups and the BRICS Framework for Collaboration on Strategic Projects in Health, including the TB Cooperation Plan and other action plans adopted on 16 December 2016 in New Delhi on specific areas of cooperation.

3. Stated that they will offer full support to the ninth BRICS Summit in September 2017 in Xiamen, China.

4. Committed to enhance cooperation with WHO, UNAIDS, UNITAID, the Global Fund to Fight AIDS, Tuberculosis and Malaria, GAVI and other international organizations, to increase the accessibility of affordable, quality, effective and safe drugs, vaccines, diagnostics and other medical products, to improve the health care service and satisfy the public health demands. In this context, welcomed the report and recommendations of the UN High-Level Panel on Access to Medicines and reiterated their resolve to promote access to drugs, vaccines, diagnostics and other medical products including through the full use of TRIPS flexibilities. They agreed to protect their policy space against TRIPS plus provisions and other measures that impede or restrict such access.

5. Committed to support and extensively carry out global cooperation projects on public health, and strengthen the role of BRICS countries in global health governance by supporting the coordination and cooperation with international health organizations and institutions through South-South Cooperation, trilateral cooperation, etc.

6. Agreed to promote dialogue among BRICS countries to jointly assess issues of common interest for convergence participation in multilateral fora, and strengthen the role of BRICS countries in global health governance, especially at the World Health Organization and United Nations Organization.

7. Expressed appreciation to Dr. Margaret Chan for her excellent leadership in the past two terms as Director-General of WHO, welcomed the appointment of Dr. Tedros Adhanom Ghebreyesus, newly-elected Director-General of WHO and expressed trust in his leadership of WHO in the global health arena and in addressing global health challenges. Reiterated the commitment to the inter-governmental nature of WHO and to maintaining the integrity, objectivity supremacy and leadership of WHO in the global health arena.

8. Recognized the value and importance of traditional medicine, reaffirmed the support for the WHA resolution on Traditional Medicine (WHA62.13 and WHA67.18) and the WHO Traditional Medicine Strategy 2014-2023, and supported the traditional medicine development initiative proposed in the Joint Declaration of BRICS Countries on Strengthening Cooperation in Traditional Medicine on 6th, July 2017. They agreed that the traditional medicine shall be gradually integrated into national health system as appropriate with relevant regulations and policies. They also agreed that research expert communication, seminars and traditional medicine course promotion shall be supported to safely and effectively apply traditional medicine.

9. Noted that in order to effectively address the existing global health challenges and achieve the health-related SDGs, BRICS countries held a side event on integrated health care delivery system on May 24, 2017 during the 70th World Health Assembly, wherein BRICS' health representatives shared their helpful experience in promoting health equity, strengthening health system and enhancing quality of health services, and showed their willingness to support the progress towards universal health coverage.

10. Agreed to expand BRICS technical cooperation on health including traditional medicine.

11. Agreed to support the collaboration among BRICS regulatory authorities with a view to improving the regulatory standards, and certification systems for medical products to realize their collective potential for enhancing access to quality medicines and ensuring their affordability.

12. Agreed to jointly promote research and development of innovative medical products (drugs, vaccines diagnostics and medical technologies), including through the creation of a research and development consortium on TB, HIV and Malaria. Agreed to prioritize specific R&D needs of developing countries relating to Type I diseases, while upholding the guiding principle of the de-linkage of the cost of research and development and the price of health products.

13. Agreed to set up the TB research network in the framework of the BRICS TB Cooperation Plan approved in the 6th BRICS Health Ministers Meeting, to be presented at the First WHO Global Ministerial Conference Ending Tuberculosis in the Sustainable Development Era: A Multisectoral Response, Moscow, Russian Federation, 16-17 November 2017.

14. Emphasized the importance of child survival through progressive reduction in the maternal mortality, neo-natal mortality, infant mortality, and under-5 mortality, with the aim of achieving the SDGs. Confirmed the endeavors made in this area and to enhance collaboration through exchange of best practices.

15. Recognized the importance of constantly monitoring the outbreak of diseases and the need to further enhance the cooperation of institutions and networks under the mechanism of Global Outbreak Alert and Response Network (GOARN) in light of the guidance of International Health Regulations (2005), to address global threats from possible epidemic of emerging and re-emerging diseases.

16. Reinforced willingness to strengthen their surveillance capacity and health care services to fight infectious diseases such as HIV/AIDS, Tuberculosis and Malaria and non-communicable diseases addressing their risk factors.

17. Recognized that Antimicrobial Resistance including in diseases such as TB and HIV/AIDS, seriously threatens public health, and economic growth, reiterated to support the suggestions of United Nations high-level meeting on antimicrobial resistance by carrying out extensive collaboration on advocacy and education, monitoring of antimicrobial resistance, infection prevention and control, and best application, development and investment of antibiotics, consistent with the balanced approach to addressing the five objectives of the WHO Global Action Plan on AMR. Also re-iterated the need to address issues of equity, affordability and sustainable access to and rational use of existing and new antimicrobials, as well of mobilizing necessary technical and financial resources for implementation.

18. Noted that while significant progress has been made in the global AIDS response, the epidemic is not over yet and therefore committed to collective actions and sustained leadership to fully implement the 2016 UN Political Declaration to achieve the 90-90-90 targets and Ending AIDS by 2030.

19. Acknowledged the need of greater use of Information and Communications Technology to improve accessibility of health services to promote cost-effective diagnostic approach and treatment as well as achieve better maintenance and use of data for surveillance and policy formulation. Encouraged the sharing of best practices on e-Health, m-health and e-governance among BRICS countries.

20. Reiterated their willingness to deepen coordination, cooperation and consultation among BRICS countries on the important issues related to the global health agenda and Traditional Medicine.

21. Expressed support for the First WHO Global Ministerial Conference Ending Tuberculosis in the Sustainable Development Era: A Multisectoral Response, Moscow, Russian Federation, 16-17 November 2017 and the first United Nations General Assembly High-Level Meeting on Tuberculosis in 2018.

22. Supported the proposal to hold the 8th BRICS Health Ministers Meeting in South Africa in 2018.

C.   BRICS Countries Cooperation in Traditional Medicine: 6 Jul. 2017, Tianjin (CHN)

JOINT DECLARATION OF BRICS COUNTRIES
ON STRENGTHENING COOPERATION IN TRADITIONAL MEDICINE

1.   Participants at the BRICS Ministers Meeting and High Level Meeting on Traditional Medicine, in Tianjin, China, this sixth day of July in the year two thousand and seventeen;

2.   Acknowledging the importance of UN Sustainable Development Goal 3 of ensuring healthy lives and promoting well-being for all at all ages by 2030;

3.   Recalling the Resolution WHO 62.13 and WHO 67.18 affirming the growing importance and value of traditional medicine in the provision of health care nationally and globally;

4.   Noting the adoption of the Beijing Declaration on November 8th, 2008, the Shanghai Declaration on November 21st, 2016, recommendations of the BRICS Wellness Workshop held in Bengaluru September 2016, Goa Declaration, October 2016 and Action Plan adopted in BRICS Health Ministers High Level Meeting in December 2016 at New Delhi;

5.   Recognizing traditional medicine as one of the resources of primary health care, including promotive, preventive and affordable health care and to contribute in improving health outcomes;

6.   Noting the concern in the health sector faced by countries including the spread of diseases caused by unhealthy lifestyle, the global financing constraints to provide health care services and the challenges imposed by the aging process in the global society;

7.   Noting that BRICS countries are located in different regions of the world and have rich heritage, wide experience and application of traditional medicine as precious treasure of health, culture, science and technology resources;

8.   Considering the different background, legislations, regulations and application of traditional medicine in each BRICS country and the scope for knowledge exchange and beneficial collaboration within the BRICS and other countries;

9.   Realizing the significance to promote the inheritance, development, integration and use of traditional medicine in health care services, in accordance with national circumstances, BRICS countries, hereby make the following Declaration:

I.   It is necessary to strengthen the integration of traditional medicine in the national health care systems as a valuable means to promote and encourage practice, education and training, therapies and medicines and practitioners of traditional medicine to improve the quality and outreach of health care services in a systematic manner.

II.   The knowledge of traditional medicine should be respected, protected, promoted and appropriately disseminated for proper understanding in terms of safety, efficacy and quality and the role of traditional medicine for preventive, promotive, curative and rehabilitation health care.

III.   Efforts should be made to regulate traditional medicine products and implement the objectives of the Forum set up during the High Level Meeting on Traditional Medicinal knowledge held in Delhi on 16 December, 2016.

IV.   Knowledge and experience of traditional medicine should be scientifically explored for research, development and innovation of health care solutions.

V. BRICS countries should adopt equitable and harmonized approaches to promote effective communication and exchange of knowledge, experiences and expertise among practitioners of traditional medicine and modern medicine.

In accordance with five above-mentioned basic principles, participants at the BRICS High Level Meeting on Traditional Medicine, hereby propose the following initiatives:

I. WHO is requested to assist BRICS countries in implementing the WHO Traditional Medicine Strategy (2014-2023) and promote cooperation and collaboration among member states for this purpose.

II. Governmental and non-governmental organizations in BRICS countries should be encouraged for continuing cooperation and collaboration in the area of traditional medicine including exchange of knowledge, expertise and scientific experiences, capacity building and R and D activities.

III. Other interested governments of professional institutions are welcome to participate in the BRICS traditional medicine dialogue.

D.   6th Meeting of BRICS Health Ministers: 15-16 Dec. 2016, New Delhi (IND)

FINAL DRAFT DELHI COMMUNIQUÉ

The following is the text of the Delhi Communiqué issued today at the end of the two-day 6th BRICS Health Ministers' meet:

1.   The BRICS countries, represented by the Ministers of Health of the Federative Republic of Brazil, the Russian Federation, Republic of India, People's Republic of China and Republic of South Africa, met in New Delhi on 16 December 2016 at the Sixth BRICS Health Ministers Meeting.

2.   Recalled the previous BRICS Health Ministers declarations and joint communiqués[1] in which they committed to strengthen intra-BRICS cooperation to promote health, acknowledged the renewed commitment to health by the BRICS leaders as expressed in the Goa Declaration of October 2016, noted the progress made since the first BRICS Summit and resolved to continue cooperation in the sphere of health through the Technical Working Groups and the "BRICS Framework for Collaboration on Strategic Projects in Health".

3.   Welcomed the recommendations made in the BRICS workshop on drugs and medical devices in Goa, India in November 2016, including the need for concluding a Memorandum of Understanding on regulatory collaboration with a view to improving the regulatory standards, certification and systems for medical products.

4.   Agreed to constitute a working group, to work on strengthening regulatory systems, sharing of information, appropriate regulatory approaches in case of international and national health emergencies and provide recommendations for the promotion of research and development of innovative medical products (drugs, vaccines and medical technologies). Supported promoting existing IT platform and regulatory capacity building through an institutional development plan for BRICS countries.

5.   Noted that BRICS countries face challenges of communicable diseases including HIV and Tuberculosis and vector borne diseases including Malaria. Noted the efforts made by BRICS countries to achieve the 90–90–90 HIV treatment target by 2020 and agreed to make efforts to enhance access to HIV diagnostics and treatment especially to key populations with increased risk of acquiring HIV and exchange experiences of community-based actions to fight HIV/AIDS. Underlined the imperative to advance cooperation and action on research on HIV, TB and Malaria in the BRICS countries, including in the development and production of quality-assured drugs, diagnostics and vaccines.

6.   Adopted the BRICS TB Cooperation Plan and supported the recommendations made by the BRICS workshop on HIV and Tuberculosis, held in Ahmedabad, India in November 2016, including the need for the suggested political, technical and financial actions to address the public health challenges of TB and HIV among BRICS countries. Agreed to the setting up of a BRICS network on TB Research and creation of a research and development consortium on TB, HIV and Malaria including the possibility of international fund raising. Also agreed to support the Global Ministerial Conference on the fight against TB to be held in Moscow in 2017 and the UN High-Level Meeting on TB at United Nations Headquarters in 2018.

---

[1] Moscow Declaration of the BRICS' Health Ministers meeting in October 2015, Brazilian Communiqué of the BRICS Health Ministers Meetings in Brasilia on 5th December 2014 and Beijing and Delhi Declaration and the Cape Town Communiqué of the BRICS Health Ministers Meetings in 2011 and 2013 and the Joint Communiqué of the BRICS Health Ministers in Geneva on 20th May 2013 on the sidelines of the 66th session of the World Health Assembly and the Joint Communiqués of BRICS Member States on Health issued on the sidelines of the 67th, 68th and 69th World Health Assemblies in May 2014, May 2015 and May 2016 respectively.

7. Emphasized the importance of continued cooperation among BRICS countries in promoting research and development of medicines and diagnostic tools to end epidemics including through promoting innovative and sustainable models for health R&D financing and coordination and to facilitate access to safe, effective, quality and affordable medicines, including generic medicines, biological products, and diagnostics.

8. Noted the current global threat of non-communicable diseases (NCDs), agreed to make collaborative efforts to achieve the target of reduction in premature mortality due to NCDs by one-third by the year 2030 as per SDG Target 3.4 and renewed commitment for an effective response to such threat, including through development of cost-effective diagnostics, medicines, technologies and behavioural change strategies required for management of key NCDs, sharing systems for monitoring, surveillance, evaluation and operational research in NCDs and their risk factors, and sharing training programs for various categories of health care personnel in identified areas for capacity building to diagnose and manage NCDs.

9. Appreciated India for a successful organization of the seventh session of the Conference of the Parties to the WHO Framework Convention on Tobacco Control, in November 2016. Renewed their commitment to the Convention, both as a public health treaty and as a Goal under Agenda 2030 for Sustainable Development, particularly Goal 3, to ensure healthy lives and promote well-being for all at all ages. To promote better implementation of the Convention, they stressed the importance of continued research and study by WHO and other stakeholders into the social and economic determinants of tobacco use in all its forms and other products promoting tobacco use as well as the strategies for their control.

10. Recognized that an effective health surveillance is key to controlling both communicable and noncommunicable diseases and eliminating immuno-preventable diseases such as measles, rubella and polio, and that the countries may be using different models for surveillance based on different realities and best practices. Welcomed the recommendations of the BRICS Workshop on "Strengthening Health Surveillance: System and Best Practices" held at Bengaluru, India in August 2016. Expressed commitment to strengthen cooperation in the mechanisms for planning, monitoring and evaluating disease prevention and control activities and capacity-building through surveillance workshops on epidemic prone diseases, NCDs, including cardiovascular diseases and diabetes mellitus, mental health disorders, injury prevention, disaster management (including post disaster surveillance), environmental health and occupational health, as well as HIV/AIDS and TB.

11. Acknowledged that Anti-Microbial Resistance (AMR) is a serious global public health issue and emphasized the need to implement the WHO's Global Action Plan on AMR and National Plans in this regard, addressing issues of equity, affordability and sustainable access to existing and new antimicrobials, as well of mobilizing necessary technical and financial resources for implementation. Welcomed the recommendations from the High Level meeting on Anti-Microbial Resistance (AMR) during UNGA-71, which addresses the serious challenge that AMR poses to public health. Agreed to cooperate through the AMR focal points, regulatory authorities and relevant cross sectors, with a view to share best practices and discuss challenges, as well as identifying potential areas for convergence, such as surveillance, strategies for rational use of antibiotics, strategies to address shortages of first line antibiotics and vaccines, infection prevention and control, strategies for preventing inappropriate use of antibiotics in agricultural sector based on scientific evidence, strengthening research collaboration across sectors and disciplines in the field of AMR as well as enhancing lab activities for quick testing of drug resistance for different pathogens.

12. Noted the successful organization of BRICS Wellness Workshop by Government of India during 10-11 September, 2016 at Bengaluru and the fruitful discussions for cooperation in the area of Traditional medicines. Agreed to convene the BRICS High-level Forum on Traditional Medicine in China in 2017.

13. Acknowledged the value and importance of traditional and alternative systems of medicine as a means of achieving holistic healthcare, and the need of experience and knowledge-sharing for securing public health needs in this regard.

14. Recognized that promoting access to medicines and vaccines, in particular essential medicines, that are affordable, safe, efficacious, and of quality, is imperative for the right of everyone to the enjoyment of the highest attainable standard of physical and mental health. In this context, welcomed the report of the UN High-Level Panel on Access to Medicines, to review and assess proposals and recommended solutions for remedying the policy incoherence between the justifiable rights of inventors, international human rights law, trade rules and public health in the context of health technologies, while looking forward to discussions and follow-up of the Panel's report, through WHO and other relevant UN agencies and international organizations.

15. Reiterated their resolve to promote access to medicines including through the full use of TRIPS flexibilities and to promote these in the bilateral and regional trade agreements in order to protect public health interest. Agreed to work cooperatively in international fora to protect their policy space against TRIPS plus provisions and other measures that impede access to medicines and share these experiences with other developing countries.

16. Emphasized the importance of child survival and development through progressive reduction in the maternal mortality, infant mortality, neo-natal mortality, under-5 mortality and congenital disorders as well as their consequences for child development with the aim of achieving the unfinished agenda of the Millennium Development Goals and the relevant Sustainable Development Goals. Confirmed their commitment to a renewed effort in this area and to enhance collaboration through exchange of best practices.

17. Acknowledged the need of greater use of Information and Communications Technology in Health services to promote cost-effective treatment as well as better maintenance and use of data for surveillance and policy formulation. They encouraged to strengthen cooperation amongst the BRICS countries to share experiences in ICT projects for health including mHealth.

18. Welcomed the recent agreement in the WHO Member State Mechanism in relation to the Working Definitions on SSFFC medical products, in particular, to the consensus on deleting the word 'counterfeit' as it usually refers to IP violations, and excluding any consideration of patents/trade mark or other IP issues while defining 'falsified' medical products.

19. Reiterated their support for the further development of a fully functional WHO Global Observatory on Health R&D and for the implementation and financing of all the selected demonstration projects. They also underscored that the priority setting mechanism and financing mechanism on health R&D should cover the full scope of diseases mentioned in the CEWG report including all Type II and III diseases and specific R&D needs of developing countries relating to Type I diseases, while upholding the guiding principle of the de-linkage of the cost of research and development and the price of health products.

20. Agreed to cooperate for combating mental disorders, including autism and neuro-development disorders, through a multi-pronged approach encompassing a mental health policy, a life cycle approach to address the needs of such individuals throughout life, sharing of innovations in the field of mental health promotion, diagnosis and management and exchange of best practices and experiences.

21. Agreed to enhance cooperation amongst the BRICS countries for capacity development of human resources in public health and clinical medicine. Welcomed the recommendations of the UN High Level Commission on Health Employment and Economic Growth, and looked forward to development of an implementation plan, to amplify gains across the 2030 Agenda for Sustainable Development and with a view to delivering Universal Health Coverage.

22. Agreed to establish platforms for collaboration within BRICS framework and with other countries and international partners with a view to realizing the goals and objectives outlined in this as well as in the past Declarations and Joint Communiques.

23. Adopted the action plans on specific areas of cooperation*·as recommended by the Senior Health Officials meeting held on 15-16 December 2016 in New Delhi.

24. Resolved to continue cooperation in building, responsive, inclusive and collective solutions for sustainable development including in the sphere of health.

25. Thanked India for successfully hosting the 6th BRICS Health Ministers meeting and agreed to convene the 7th BRICS Health Ministers meeting and Meeting of Senior Health Officials in China in 2017.

New Delhi, 16 December, 2016

---

* Action Plans on Strengthening surveillance systems, AMR, NCDs, Regulatory collaboration, Drug Discovery & Development, Research collaboration for TB, HIV and Malaria and Information and Communications Technology in healthcare.

E.   Joint Communiqué of the BRICS Member States on Health: 24 May 2016, Geneva (CHE)

JOINT COMMUNIQUÉ OF THE BRICS MEMBER STATES ON HEALTH
ON THE SIDELINES OF THE 69TH WORLD HEALTH ASSEMBLY

1.   The BRICS countries, represented by the Heads of Delegation of Brazil, China, India, Russia and South Africa, met on 24th May 2016 on the margins of the 69th session of the World Health Assembly in Geneva, Switzerland.

2.   Recalled the Moscow Declaration of the 5th BRICS' Health Ministers meeting in October 2015 and all previous BRICS' Health Ministers declarations and joint communiqués[1] in which they committed to strengthen intra-BRICS cooperation to promote health. Resolved to continue cooperation in the sphere of health through the Technical Working Groups and the "BRICS Framework for Collaboration on Strategic Projects in Health".

3.   Expressed concern at the severe public health impacts caused by the recent Ebola, Zika and Yellow fever outbreaks and emphasized the urgency for international collaboration to strengthen national efforts in building resilient and integrated health systems including IHR (2005) core capacities as well as improving availability to existing medicines and vaccines accelerating R&D efforts for developing new medicines, vaccines and diagnostics for emerging infectious pathogens

4.   Recognized the swift response to the Zika virus outbreak by initially affected countries, PAHO and WHO, while emphasizing the need to sustain efforts in vector control, R&D for vaccine and follow-up and support to affected newborns and their families.

5.   Reaffirmed their commitment the Agenda 2030 for Sustainable Development, particularly Goal 3, to ensure healthy lives and promote well-being for all at all ages, and other interlinked Goals and Targets, taking into account different levels of national development and capacities. Emphasized the importance of addressing the unfinished business of the Millennium Development Goals and achieving Universal Health Coverage and Access, including through the development of affordable health care platforms and addressing human resources for health, including community health workers, which are essential for the fulfillment of the right to health and wellbeing for all. Welcomed the appointment of the United Nations Secretary-General's High-Level Commission on Health Employment and Economic Growth.

6.   Emphasized the importance and need of technology transfer as a means to empower developing countries. Underlined the importance of ensuring access to affordable, quality, efficacious and safe medical products, including generic medicines, biological products, and diagnostics, through the use of TRIPS flexibilities, for the realization of the right to health. They also renewed commitment to strengthening international cooperation in health, and South-South cooperation in particular, with a view to supporting efforts in developing countries to promote health for all.

7.   Emphasized the public health challenge of communicable diseases including vector borne diseases, TB, HIV/AIDS, Hepatitis B and C and the need for making available vaccines, diagnostics and medicines to contain and eventually eliminate these diseases.

---

[1] Brazilian Communiqué of the BRICS Health Ministers Meetings in Brasilia on 5th December 2014 and Beijing and Delhi Declaration and the Cape Town Communiqué of the BRICS Health Ministers Meetings in 2011 and 2013 and the Joint Communiqué of the BRICS Health Ministers in Geneva on 20th May 2013 on the sidelines of the 66th session of the World Health Assembly and the Joint Communiqués of BRICS Member States on Health issued on the sidelines of the 67th and 68th World Health Assemblies in May 2014 and May 2015 respectively.

8. Resolved to continue collaboration on the goal of TB elimination in consonance with the WHO End TB Strategy and share best practices and plans to achieve its ambitious targets including through collaboration on research and development in new TB diagnostics, drugs and vaccines. Also recognized the emerging challenge of MDR-TB and the special efforts required for addressing the same. Reiterated that the work on TB cooperation plan, as agreed at the 4th meeting of BRICS Health Ministers in Brazil, should be continued with the aim to adopt the plan preferably at the next BRICS Health Ministers meeting in late 2016.

9. Acknowledged that Anti-Microbial Resistance (AMR) is a serious global public health issue that could undermine decades of progress in combating infectious diseases and emphasized the need to implement the WHO's Global Action Plan on AMR addressing issues of equity, affordability and sustainable access to medicines, the different capacities of Member States and the adoption of science-based risk analysis as grounds for measures. Called on all countries to recognize and address AMR as a development issue, including at the UN General Assembly High Level Meeting on AMR to be convened in September 2016 in New York and to focus on mobilizing necessary technical and financial resources for the implementation of the WHO Global Action Plan on AMR by all countries.

10. Emphasized that prevention and control of NCDs including Cancer, Cardio-vascular diseases, Diabetes, Chronic Obstructive Airway and Pulmonary diseases, as well as mental health are essential to reduce premature mortality, enhance productivity and improve quality of life. Agreed to strengthen collaboration to address the prevention and control of NCDs and their risk factors and in this context looked forward to the BRICS high-level panel discussion on health promotion to be organized at the 9th Global Conference on Health Promotion in 2016 in Shanghai.

11. Recognized the potential of synergies between Traditional and Complementary Systems of Medicine including Yoga with modern system of medicine, as appropriate to national contexts, and the objective of holistic approach to health care and well-being.

12. Reaffirmed their commitments to strengthen collaboration for the full implementation of the WHO Framework Convention on Tobacco Control (FCTC) and recognized the need to build on the results achieved so far and further step up tobacco control measures at the Seventh Conference of Parties to the WHO FCTC to be hosted by India in November 2016.

13. Acknowledged the unique role of WHO in advancing the global health agenda. Reaffirmed the intergovernmental nature of WHO and the need to preserve WHO as the coordinating and leading authority in global health. Reiterated the need to thoroughly examine the current WHO reform process aimed at improving strategic decision-making of its governing bodies, enhancing transparency and accountability, and strengthening WHO's capacities to better respond to global health challenges including health emergencies. Reaffirmed the importance of strengthening WHO's emergency response, while maintaining WHO's excellence in meeting its public health functions and mandates.

14. Reiterated their support to the full and effective implementation of WHO Global Strategy and Plan of Action on Public Health, Innovation and Intellectual Property and welcomed the extension of the timeframe of the global plan of action from 2015 to 2022. They appreciated the follow-up discussions on the report of the Consultative Expert Working Group on Research and Development: Financing and Coordination, held pursuant to WHA resolution 66.22, and reiterated their support for the further development of a fully functional Global Observatory on Health R&D and for the implementation of all the 6 selected demonstration projects. They also underscored that the priority setting mechanism and financing mechanism on health R&D should cover the full scope of diseases mentioned in the CEWG report including all Type II and III diseases and specific R&D needs of developing countries relating to Type I diseases, should be transparent and should foster innovative and sustainable financing models.

15. Welcomed the convening of the UN Secretary General's High Level Panel on Access to Medicines and acknowledged the need for strengthening policy coherence in relation to international human rights, trade rules and public health to promote access to health technologies including access to medicines, vaccines and diagnostics for all.

16. Appreciated India for hosting an official BRICS side-event on Access to Medicines and Trade Agreements on the margins of the 69th World Health Assembly and make TRIPS flexibilities fully available for use by countries to promote access to medicines, foster innovation and defend their policy space against TRIPS plus provisions and other measures that impede access to medicines and share these experiences with other developing countries.

17. Looked forward to the Rio 2016 Olympic and Paralympic Games and expressed appreciation for all measures taken by the Government of Brazil to ensure the safety of the Olympic family and visitors.

18. Resolved to continue cooperation in building responsive, inclusive and collective solutions for sustainable development including in the sphere of health.

F.   5th Meeting of BRICS Health Ministers: 30 Oct. 2015, Moscow (RUS)

MOSCOW DECLARATION

1.   The BRICS Health Ministers met in Moscow, Russia on October 30, 2015, at the 5thBRICS Health Ministers' meeting.

2.   The Ministers recalled all previous declarations in which they committed to strengthen intra-BRICS cooperation to promote health. They noted the progress made since the first BRICS Summit and acknowledged the renewed commitment to health by the BRICS leaders as expressed in the Ufa Declaration, 2015.

3.   The Ministers highlighted the interdependence between public health and socio- economic development and reiterated the impact of foreign policy on health outcomes which should be reflected accordingly in national and international priorities. The BRICS Health Ministers agreed to have a panel discussion on health promotion during the 9th Global Conference on Health Promotion in 2016 in Shanghai.

4.   The Ministers reaffirmed their commitment to ensure healthy lives and promote well-being for all at all ages as expressed in Goal 3 of Sustainable Development Goals[1] adopted by the UN General Assembly in September, 2015.They also recognized the importance of other Goals which contribute to and impact public health.

5.   The Ministers recognized that BRICS countries continue to face formidable challenges of communicable diseases, which can be addressed, inter alia, through appropriate health security measures in line with International Health Regulations, surveillance systems, innovation in diagnostics and treatment. Promotion of BRICS consortia of researchers to collaborate on clinical trials should be taken forward. The Ministers also recognized that action should be synergized and accelerated to strengthen access to affordable, quality, efficacious and safe drugs, vaccines and delivery of quality health care.

6.   The Ministers resolved to continue collaboration on the goal of TB elimination in consonance with the WHO post 2015 Global TB strategy and Communique of the 4th BRICS Health Ministers' meeting, in which TB vaccine, medicines and diagnostics research are important areas of cooperation. All stakeholders including the private sector should be involved for TB prevention, control and care. The Ministers reiterated that the work on TB cooperation plan should be continued and the plan be adopted preferably at the next BRICS Health Ministers meeting.

7.   The Ministers recalled the Communique of the 4th BRICS Health Ministers' meeting and recommitted their endeavor to achieve the 90-90-90 targets for HIV/AIDS, which is to rapidly reduce new infections and related deaths from HIV, and place BRICS countries on the Fast Track for ending AIDS epidemic by 2030.

8.   The Ministers welcomed the publication of the WHO third report on Neglected Tropical Diseases (NTD) - "Investing to Overcome the Global Impact of Neglected Tropical Diseases". They resolved to strive for achieving the Global 2020 NTD control and elimination goals, for universal coverage of everyone in need by 2030.

9.   The Ministers emphasized that prevention and control of NCDs, such as Cancer, Cardio-vascular diseases, Diabetes, Chronic Obstructive Airway and Pulmonary diseases, among others were essential to reduce premature mortality, enhance productivity and improve quality of life. They appreciated the adoption of non- communicable diseases Action Plan and Monitoring Framework by

---

[1] Transforming our world by 2030: a new agenda for global action. UN Document A/70/L.1.

member states in the World Health Assembly in May, 2013, as well as the inclusion of the prevention and treatment of NCDs in the SDG targets, and agreed to strengthen collaboration to address the prevention and control of NCDs and their risk factors, and to provide affordable and accessible treatment and care.

10. The Ministers agreed that mental health is an extremely important public health issue and that mental well-being is fundamental to a good quality of life and the productivity of individuals, families and communities. The Ministers resolved to collaborate in promoting mental health and well-being in order to bring better health and socio-economic benefits.

11. The Ministers committed to strengthen collaboration on tobacco control with a view to achieving the global voluntary target of 30% relative reduction in the prevalence of current tobacco use in persons aged 15 years and over by the year 2025, through fully implementing the WHO Framework Convention on Tobacco Control and promoting the ratification of the Protocol to Eliminate Illicit Trade in Tobacco Products. The Ministers stressed the importance of monitoring the strategies of the tobacco industry, new forms of tobacco products and nicotine use, and take steps to minimize the introduction and proliferation of such products.

12. The Ministers reaffirmed the importance of addressing global road safety issues through international cooperation, in line with the commitments undertaken in the context of the Global Plan for the Decade of Action for Road Safety 2011-2020. They also welcomed the invitation of Brazil for the Second Global High-Level Conference on Road Safety on 18 and 19 November, 2015.

13. The Ministers agreed to accelerate collaboration through Working Groups, which must discuss specific issues of public health and document and replicate good practices.

14. The Ministers reiterated their commitment for achieving the goal of Universal Health Coverage and noted that in order to measure progress towards this goal, monitoring tools are essential and should be formulated by the BRICS countries. These monitoring tools should be aligned to those of the UN SDGs. They emphasized the need for continued focus on equitable access to healthcare.

15. The Ministers reaffirmed their commitment to coordinate, cooperate and consult on key issues pertaining to the global health agenda. The Ministers recalled the important role the BRICS countries have played in the development of the Global Strategy and Plan of Action on Public Health, Innovation and Intellectual Property and reiterated their commitment to support the full implementation of its provisions.

16. The Ministers of Health of Brazil, China, Russia and South Africa conveyed their appreciation to India for hosting the next Meeting of the Ministers of Health of the BRICS in 2016 and offered their full support.

G.   Joint Communiqué of the BRICS Member States on Health: 19 May 2015, Geneva (CHE)

JOINT COMMUNIQUÉ OF THE BRICS MEMBER STATES ON HEALTH
ON THE SIDELINES OF THE 68TH WORLD HEALTH ASSEMBLY

1.   The BRICS countnes, represented by the Heads of Delegation of Brazil, Russia, India, China and South Africa, met on 19th May 2015 On the sidelines of the 68th session of the World Health Assembly in Geneva, Switzerland.

2.   Recalled the Communique of the BRICS Health Ministers Meetings in Brasilia on 5th December 2014 and Beijing and Delhi Declaration and the Cape Town Communique of the BRICS Health Ministers Meetings in 2011 and 2013 and the Joint Communique of the BRICS Health Ministers in Geneva on 20th May 2013 on the sidelines of the 66th session of the World Health Assembly, in which they committed to strengthen intra-BRICS cooperation for promoting health of the BRICS population. They resolved to continue cooperation in the sphere of health through the Technical Working Groups and the "BRICS Framework for Collaboration on Strategic Projects in Health".

3.   Expressed grave concen about the impact of the Ebola outbreak in West African countries and their sadness at the loss of lives and the suffering it had inflicted. In addition, expressed deep condolences for the people and govemment of Nepal for the lives lost in the recent earthquake.

4.   Reiterated their commitment to collaborate in key thematic areas focusing on strengthening health surveillance systems; reducing Non-Communicable disease (NCD) risk factors through prevention and health promotion; access and Universal Health Coverage (UHC); strategic health technologies, with a focus on communicable and non-communicable diseases; medical technologies; and drug discovery and development.

5.   Noted the significance and relevance of the Millennium Development Goals (MDGs), in particular the health-related MDGs. They called upon UN Member States to give due consideration to health as an important issue in the discussions of the post-2015 development agenda. Emphasized that discussions on access and Universal Health Coverage must encompass strengthening national health systems, including the development of affordable health care platforms and addressing human resources for health, which are essential for the fulfillment of the right to health and wellbeing for all.

6.   Noted the significance of reaching the health-related MDGs, through their inclusion in the Sustainable Development Goals together with injuries and non-communicable diseases, by strengthening public health emergency response system.

7.   Emphasized the importance and need of technology transfer as a means to empower developing countries. They underlined the importance of ensuring access to affordable, quality, efficacious and safe medical products, including generic medicines, biological products, and diagnostics, through the use of TRIPS flexibilities, for the realization of the right to health. They also renewed commitment to strengthening intemational cooperation in health, and South-South cooperation in particular, with a view to supporting efforts in developing countries to promote health for all.

8.   Reiterated their support for the development of a cooperation plan for tuberculosis and welcomed the discussions to develop the operational framework of the aforementioned plan in 2015 as discussed and agreed at the 4th meeting of Ministers of Health of the BRICS in Brazil.

9.   Acknowledged the unique role of WHO in advancing the global health agenda. They reiterated their support to current discussions on the process of reform of WHO so as to better respond to global challenges in programmatic, organizational and operational terms. They reaffirmed the

intergovernmental nature of WHO, and reiterated their commitment to preserve WHO as the coordinating and leading authority in global health.

10. Reiterated their support to the full implementation of WHO Global Strategy and Plan of Action on Public Health, Innovation and Intellectual Property, which gave rise to the Consultative Expert Working Group on Research and Development, and, in this context, drew attention to WHA Resolutions WHA66.22 and WHA65.24 with specific reference to demonstration projects. They further welcomed the implementation of 7 R&D demonstration projects to address identified health gaps that disproportionately affect developing countries, particularly the poor, for which immediate action can be taken, as well as theestablishment of a Global health and Development Observatory within WHO. They also underscored that the discussion of mechanisms for financial contributions to health research and development should be fully transparent and inclusive, with broad engagement of all relevant stakeholders.

11. They also expressed their support for the extension of the timeframes of the global plan of action on public health, innovation and intellectual property adopted by resolution WHA62.16, from 2015 to 2022, as well as to the comprehensive evaluation and overall programme review of the document by experts appointed by Member States.

12. Reiterated their commitment to use TRIPS flexibilities to promote access to medicines, foster innovation and share these experiences with other developing countries.

13. Resolved to continue cooperation in the sphere of health through the "BRICS Framework for Collaboration on Strategic Projects in Health" and support the finalization of the BRICS Monitoring and Evaluation Tool for Access and Universal Health Coverage.

H.   4th Meeting of BRICS Health Ministers: 5 Dec. 2014, Brasilia (BRA)

COMMUNIQUÉ OF THE BRICS HEALTH MINISTERS

The BRICS Health Ministers met in Brasilia on December 5, 2014, at the Fourth Meeting of Ministers of Health of the BRICS.

2.   The Ministers underscored that the Declaration of Fortaleza and its Action Plan, adopted at the Sixth BRICS Summit, inaugurated a new cycle of BRICS coordination. The focus on social inclusion and sustainable development will contribute to the strengthening of intra-BRICS partnership, including cooperation in health.

3.   Considering the impact of tuberculosis in the BRICS countries and in many developing countries, the Ministers approved the development of a cooperation plan that includes a common approach to:

- universal access to first line anti-tuberculosis medicines for all patients with TB in BRICS countries, as well as in low- and middle- income countries;
- scientific research and innovations on diagnostics, treatment including drug resistance and service delivery of TB;
- sharing technologies, identifying manufacturing capacities and means of financing;
- to aspire towards a 90-90-90 TB target (90% of vulnerable groups screened, 90% diagnosed and started on treatment with 90% treatment success);
- and other issues of common interest.

In this context, the Ministers approved the setting up of a working group to develop the operational framework of the aforementioned plan, in the first half of 2015.

4.   The Ministers expressed grave concern about the impact of the Ebola outbreak in West African countries and their sadness at the loss of lives and the suffering it had inflicted. They called for urgent and comprehensive international support to the efforts coordinated by the UN, and particularly to the actions undertaken by the WHO, to accelerate the response to the Ebola outbreak. The Ministers commended the setting up of the UN Mission For Ebola Emergency Response (UNMEER) and expressed their support for its strategic objectives, namely to stop the outbreak, treat the infected, ensure essential services, preserve stability and prevent outbreaks in countries that are currently unaffected. They committed to continue efforts through bilateral, regional and multilateral channels to help ensure a robust and effective response to the outbreak. In dealing with the ongoing outbreak, they urged other countries, to act in line with recommendations of the World Health Organization, including avoiding imposing general trade and travel restrictions on the affected countries.

5.   The Ministers declared their intention to strengthen cooperation on the prevention and control of the Ebola disease in their territories and neighboring regions, in line with efforts coordinated by the United Nations and the World Health Organization (WHO), in accordance with the International Health Regulations (2005) and with particular emphasis in the areas of surveillance, diagnostic technologies, methods and health solutions and workforce training.

6.   The Ministers recognized the importance of the end of HIV/AIDS as proposed by UNAIDS` targets. They recalled the Joint Communiqué of the BRICS Health Ministers Meeting in Cape Town in November 7, 2013, where the BRICS countries committed to collaborate on the development of medicines and the delivery of quality healthcare. In Brasília, they committed to deepen the discussion thereon. The Ministers endeavor to achieve the 90-90-90 HIV treatment target 2020, which is to rapidly reduce new HIV infection and AIDS related deaths including from tuberculosis and put us on the Fast Track to ending AIDS by 2030.

7.   Concerned with sustainable access to new drugs and their impact on health budgets, especially concerning Hepatitis C, HIV and non-communicable diseases, the Ministers reiterated their support

to the effective implementation of the Global Strategy and Plan of Action on Public Health, Innovation and Intellectual Property and to the demonstration projects selected under the Consultative Expert Working Group on Research and Development: Financing and Coordination (CEWG) of the World Health Organization (WHO). They also reaffirmed their support to initiatives and experiences aimed at overcoming barriers in access to medicines, including the full use of TRIPS flexibilities, by means of promoting local production and using other price-reduction mechanisms, as well as fostering innovative and sustainable models for R&D and transfers of technology.

8.   Considering the Global Plan to Combat Neglected Tropical Diseases 2008-2015, WHA Resolution 66.12, the World Health Organization's 2020 Roadmap for Neglected Tropical Diseases, the Ministers recognized the progress made by their governments regarding the fight against neglected diseases. They highlighted that many of these diseases are related to poverty and to the lack of access to information, and the suffering of millions of people can be prevented by the implementation of simple measures. The Ministers agreed to the promotion of cooperation between countries, including the establishment of intersectoral policies to improve access to medicines.

9.   The Ministers acknowledged that antimicrobial resistance is a severe threat to global health that could undermine decades of progress in combating infectious diseases, in particular those brought about through the health-related Millennium Development Goals. They emphasized that the Global Action Plan on Antimicrobial Resistance should take into account the rational use of antimicrobials and the differences between health systems, cultures, ecologies, epidemiology conditions and economic situations, and that it should also provide guidance on how to implement mitigating actions.

10. Recognizing that 80% of premature deaths associated with chronic non-communicable diseases (NCDs) occur in developing countries and that the disproportionate incidence of these illnesses among the poorest populations highlight the need for a comprehensive response to NCDs, the Ministers reaffirmed the commitments made in the Political Declaration on the Prevention and Control of Non-communicable Diseases and in the General Assembly High-Level Meeting on Non-Communicable Diseases of July 2014. They also reiterated their efforts to implement the WHO Global Action Plan for Prevention and Control of Non-Communicable Diseases 2013-2020, adopt strategies to reduce risk factors (tobacco use, unhealthy diet, physical inactivity and the harmful use of alcohol), to strengthen their health systems and to promote research and development and access to medicines.

11. Recognizing that the rates of overweight, obesity and malnutrition-related chronic diseases have been increasing significantly in our countries, the Ministers expressed their interest in sharing strategies and policies. They reiterated their commitment to implement the Rome Declaration and Plan of Action, both resulting from the II International Conference on Nutrition, and agreed to jointly organize a side event during the 68th World Health Assembly with a view to proposing concrete progress to address this common challenge.

12. Considering the high number of deaths from tobacco-related diseases and the financial burden placed on public healthcare systems, the Ministers reaffirmed the commitments assumed under the Framework Convention on Tobacco Control (FCTC) as fundamental to strengthen tobacco control measures. They further recognized the results achieved during the Sixth Session of the Conference of the Parties to the WHO FCTC and the Moscow Declaration as milestones in this challenging journey.

13. Considering that the WHO reform process is aimed at improving strategic decision-making of its governing bodies and at strengthening WHO leadership in global health, and also considering the Framework of engagement with non-State actors drafted by the WHO Secretariat, the Ministers commended the progress made so far and highlighted the importance of engaging Member States in the reform process.

14. Recognizing that healthcare provides a fundamental contribution to a more inclusive and sustainable development model, and highlighting the importance of ensuring universal access to healthcare, the Ministers welcomed the Report of the Open Working Group on Sustainable Development Goals (OWG-SDG), and expressed their commitment to combine efforts during the Intergovernmental Negotiating Process for the Post-2015 Agenda, to be concluded in September 2015.

15. The Ministers recognized the importance of WHA Resolution 67/20 and congratulated the World Health Organization (WHO) and the Government of Brazil for hosting the 16th International Conference of Drug Regulatory Authorities held in Rio de Janeiro in August 2014, and for offering an opportunity to strengthen ties, discuss trends and share solutions of common interest.

16. They recalled the commitments of the Decade of Action for Road Safety 2011-2020 and commended the inclusion of this subject in the Report of the Open Work Group on Sustainable Development Goals. They also welcomed the invitation to return to Brazil on 18 and 19 November 2015 for the Second Global High-Level Conference on Road Safety, an opportunity to review commitments and to discuss new strategies to mitigate one of the leading causes of death among young people aged 15-29.

17. The Ministers of Health of Brazil, India, China and South Africa convey their appreciation to Russia for its offer to host the next Meeting of the Ministers of Health of the BRICS in 2015 and extend their full support to that end.

I.   Joint Communiqué of the BRICS Member States on Health: 20 May 2014, Geneva (CHE)

JOINT COMMUNIQUÉ OF THE BRICS MEMBER STATES ON HEALTH
ON THE SIDELINES OF THE 67TH WORLD HEALTH ASSEMBLY

1. The BRICS countries, represented by the Heads of Delegation of Brazil, Russia, India, China and South Africa, met on 20th May 2014 on the sidelines of the 67th session of the World Health Assembly in Geneva, Switzerland.

2. Recalled the Beijing and Delhi Declaration and the Cape Town Communiqué of the BRICS Health Ministers Meetings in 2011 and 2013 and the Joint Communiqué of the BRICS Health Ministers in Geneva on 20th May 2013 on the sidelines of the 66th session of the World Health Assembly, in which they committed to strengthen intra-BRICS cooperation for promoting health of the BRICS population. They resolved to continue cooperation in the sphere of health through the Technical Working Groups and the "BRICS Framework for Collaboration on Strategic Projects in Health".

3. Reiterated their commitment to collaborate in key thematic areas focusing on strengthening health surveillance systems; reducing Non-Communicable disease (NCD) risk factors through prevention and health promotion; Universal Health Coverage (UHC); strategic health technologies, with a focus on communicable and non-communicable diseases; medical technologies; and drug discovery and development.

4. Noted the significance and relevance of the Millennium Development Goals (MDGs), in particular the health-related MDGs. They called upon UN Member States to give due consideration to health as an important issue in the discussions of the post-2015 development agenda. Emphasized that discussions on Universal Health Coverage must encompass strengthening national health systems and addressing human resources for health, which are essential for the fulfillment of the right to health and wellbeing for all.

5. Emphasized the importance and need of technology transfer as a means to empower developing countries. They underlined the importance of ensuring access to affordable, quality, efficacious and safe medical products, including generic medicines, biological products, and diagnostics, through the use of TRIPS flexibilities, for the realization of the right to health. They also renewed commitment to strengthening international cooperation in health, and South-South cooperation in particular, with a view to supporting efforts in developing countries to promote health for all.

6. Acknowledged the unique role of WHO in advancing the global health agenda. They reiterated their support to current discussions on the process of reform of WHO so as to better respond to global challenges in programmatic, organizational and operational terms. They reaffirmed the intergovernmental nature of WHO, and reiterated their commitment to preserve WHO as the coordinating and leading authority in global health.

7. Reiterated their support to the full implementation of WHO Global Strategy and Plan of Action on Public Health, Innovation and Intellectual Property, which gave rise to the Consultative Expert Working Group on Research and Development, and, in this context, drew attention to WHA Resolutions WHA66.22 and WHA65.24 with specific reference to demonstration projects. They further welcomed the implementation of 8 R&D demonstration projects to address identified health gaps that disproportionately affect developing countries, particularly the poor, for which immediate action can be taken, as well as the establishment of a Global Health and Development Observatory within WHO. They also underscored that the discussion of mechanisms for financial contributions to health research and development should be fully transparent and inclusive, with broad engagement of all relevant stakeholders.

8. Reiterated their commitment to use TRIPS flexibilities to promote access to medicines, foster innovation and share these experiences with other developing countries.

9. Resolved to continue cooperation in the sphere of health through the "BRICS Framework for Collaboration on Strategic Projects in Health" and support the finalization of the BRICS Monitoring and Evaluation Tool for Universal Health Coverage.

J.   3rd Meeting of BRICS Health Ministers: 7 Nov. 2013, Cape Town (ZAF)

CAPE TOWN COMMUNIQUÉ

1.   Consistent with the mandate of the BRICS Leaders as stated in the Sanya, Delhi and eThekwini Declarations, the BRICS Health Ministers met in Cape Town on 7th November 2013 at the 3rd BRICS Health Ministers' Meeting.

The Ministers:

2.   Recalled the Beijing Declaration and Delhi Communiqué of the BRICS Health Ministers Meetings in 2011 and 2013 and Joint Communiqué of the BRICS Health Ministers in Geneva on 20th of May 2013 on the sidelines of the 66th session of the World Health Assembly respectively, where they committed to strengthen intra-BRICS cooperation for promoting health of the BRICS populations. They reiterated that public health is an essential element for social and economic development and committed to act on economic, social and environmental determinants of health.

3.   Reiterated their commitment to collaborate on key thematic areas focusing on strengthening health surveillance systems; reducing Non-Communicable Disease (NCD) risk factors through prevention and health promotion; Universal Health Coverage (UHC); strategic health technologies, with a focus on communicable and non-communicable diseases; medical technologies; and drug discovery and development.

4.   Reaffirmed their commitment to coordinate, cooperate and consult on key issues pertaining to the agenda of the World Health Organisation (WHO).

5.   Renewed their commitment to the effective control of both communicable and non-communicable diseases through cooperation in sharing of existing resource information, development of risk assessment tools, risk mitigation methods, referral systems, life course approaches, community empowerment, monitoring health impact assessments of all public policies at national, regional and international levels.

6.   Recognised that NCDs are now a global priority that affects low, middle and high income countries. They acknowledged that as NCDs are preventable and impact on development, BRICS countries can partner in reducing the burden of diseases through various collaborative initiatives including research on social and economic determinants that contribute to a high incidence of NCDs.

7.   Recognised that BRICS countries face challenges of communicable diseases including HIV and Tuberculosis. They resolved to collaborate and cooperate in the development of capacity and infrastructure to reduce the prevalence and incidence of TB and combating HIV/AIDS. This can be improved through a surveillance system and innovation for new drugs/vaccines, diagnostics and promotion of consortia of researchers to collaborate on clinical trials of drugs and vaccines as well as strengthening access to affordable, quality, efficacious and safe medicines and delivery of quality health care.

8.   Noted the significance and relevance of the Millennium Development Goals (MDGs), in particular health-related MDGs. They called upon the Member States of the United Nations to give due consideration to health as an important issue in the discussions of the post-2015 development agenda.

9.   Emphasized the importance of maternal and child health as a priority with the aim of achieving the MDGs, through progressive reduction in maternal mortality, neo-natal, infant and under-5 mortality. They reiterated their commitment to further enhance services and capacity building so as to ensure improved maternal and child safety and outcomes, and to strengthen collaboration through exchange of best practices.

10. Recognised that effective health surveillance is key to controlling both communicable and non-communicable diseases and also central to the implementation of the International Health Regulations (2005). Further recognising that the countries use different models for surveillance based on their realities and best practices, they committed to strengthen cooperation in the mechanisms for planning, monitoring and evaluating disease prevention and control activities and capacity-building for effective health surveillance systems.

11. Recognised and expressed appreciation for the momentum built with regard to Universal Health Coverage and expressed support for the leadership role and broad direction of WHO's Action Plan and further emphasized the importance of providing access to, in particular, quality Primary Health Care services for all. They emphasized the importance of monitoring progress towards Universal Health Coverage. To this end, they jointly developed a monitoring framework that would help countries track their progress towards achieving Universal Health Coverage. In this regard, the Ministers recognized the importance of strengthening policies and strategies, as well as international cooperation on human resources for health in order to achieve UHC.

12. Recognised the value and importance of evidence-based health policy. They further recognized the need for long term collaboration amongst the BRICS Countries to share the knowledge and best practices through information exchange in order to strengthen the performance of the health systems.

13. Recalled the Beijing Declaration of the 1st BRICS Health Ministers' Meeting in 2011 emphasizing the importance and need of technology transfer as a means to empower developing countries. In this context, they underlined the importance of ensuring access to affordable, quality, efficacious and safe medical products, including generic medicines, biological products, and diagnostics for the realization of the right to health. They renewed their commitment to strengthening international cooperation in health, South-South cooperation in particular, with a view to supporting efforts in developing countries to promote health for all and resolved to establish the BRICS network of technological cooperation.

14. Reiterated their support for the full implementation of WHO Global Strategy and Plan of Action on Public Health, Innovation and Intellectual Property, which gave rise to the Consultative Expert Working Group on Research and Development, and, in this context, drew attention to WHA Resolutions WHA66.22 and WHA65.24 with specific reference on demonstration projects. Acknowledged the value and need for experience and knowledge sharing. Urged BRICS countries to fully participate in the process of implementation of the identified projects through the establishment of networks and expert committees.

15. Focused on the unique strength of BRICS countries such as capacity for R&D and manufacturing of affordable health products and capability to conduct clinical trials. Called for enhanced cooperation in application of biotechnology for health benefits for the population of BRICS and other developing countries.

16. Acknowledging the unique role of WHO in advancing the global health agenda, they reiterated their support to the continued discussions on the process of reform of WHO to better respond to global challenges in programmatic, organizational and operational terms, including the future financing of WHO. They welcomed the initiation of the financing dialogue based on priorities collectively set by WHO Member States in a structured and transparent process.

17. Taking note of the progress made on the implementation of the decisions taken at the Health Ministers' Meeting in Beijing and Delhi, adopted the "BRICS Framework for Collaboration on Strategic Projects in Health".

K.   Joint Communiqué of BRICS Member States on Health: 20 May 2013, Geneva (CHE)

JOINT COMMUNIQUÉ OF BRICS MEMBER STATES ON HEALTH
ON THE SIDELINES OF THE 66TH WORLD HEALTH ASSEMBLY

1.   The BRICS countries, represented by the Ministers of Health of Brazil, Russia, India, China and South Africa, met on 20th of May 2013 on the sidelines of the 66th session of the World Health Assembly in Geneva, Switzerland.

2.   Recalled the Beijing and Delhi Declarations of the BRICS Health Ministers Meetings in 2011 and 2013 respectively, where they committed to strengthen intra-BRICS cooperation for promoting health of the BRICS population. The BRICS Health Ministers resolved to continue cooperation in the sphere of the health through the Technical Working Groups.

3.   Reiterate their commitment to collaborate on five thematic issues namely: strengthening health surveillance system; reducing NCD risk factors, prevention and health promotion and Universal Health Coverage; strategic health technologies, with a focus on communicable and non-communicable diseases; medical technologies; and drug discovery and development.

4.   Drew attention to the WHO report on Monitoring Achievements of the Millennium Development Goals and acknowledged that despite progress made, much needs to be done if these Goals are to be achieved by 2015 and beyond. They undertook to work collaboratively to shape the debate, fully recognizing that there cannot be development without Health. The symbiotic relationship between health and development has been acknowledged by the Ministers. They reiterate their commitment to support WHO as a coordinating authority in global health.

5.   Recalling the Global Strategy for Women's and Children's Health, they reiterate the importance of child survival strategy through progressive reduction in maternal mortality, infant mortality, neo-natal mortality and under-5 mortality, with the aim of achieving the Millennium Development Goals. With respect to the UN Commission on Life saving Commodities for Women and Children, they further acknowledged the role of the WHO in addressing related regulatory pathways and product quality issues, including prequalification and expanding access to selected essential health products for the world's most vulnerable people. They reiterated their commitment to a renewed effort in this area and to enhance collaboration through exchange of best practices.

6.   Recognized the momentum built with regard to Universal Health Coverage, particularly the report of the WHO/ World Bank Ministerial Roundtable Meeting held in February 2013. They expressed support for the leadership role and broad directions of WHO's action plan and further emphasized the importance of providing access to quality Primary health Care services for all, including strengthening other aspects of the health system.

7.   Agreed on the importance of monitoring progress towards Universal Health Coverage. To this end the BRICS countries agreed to identify their institutions to work with WHO in developing a monitoring framework that would help countries track their progress towards achieving Universal Health Coverage.

8.   Expressed their appreciation for work leading to successfully negotiations the first Standard Material Transfer Agreement 2 (SMTA2) and its signing between WHO and one of the largest vaccine manufacturers as a positive step toward the full implementation of the Framework on Pandemic Influenza Preparedness for Sharing of Influenza Viruses an Access and Other Benefits. They reaffirmed their commitment to work with WHO to ensure that the Framework advance equitable and universal access to Influenza Vaccines in response to future pandemics.

9.   Recognized progress made on the three broad areas of WHO reform, namely: programmes and priority-setting; governance; and management, as well as a high-level implementation plan for WHO Reforms. They further highlighted the need to ensure transparency and inclusive decision-making processes within the organization. They expressed their appreciation of the newly established Financing Dialogue Mechanism, designed to give a clearer picture of funding requirements and funding gaps, as well as to improve the predictability and sustainability of funding for the WHO.

10. Welcomed the WHO report of the Consultative Expert Working Group on Research and Development: Financing and Coordination (CEWG). They also welcomed the proposal to establish a Global Health and Development Observatory within WHO's Secretariat in order to monitor and analyze relevant information on health research and development as important steps towards increasing access to affordable medicines. They further welcomed the implementation of a few health R&D demonstration projects to address identified gaps that disproportionately affect developing countries, particularly the poor, and for which immediate action can be taken. They also underscored that the implementation of demonstration projects should be fully transparent and inclusive, with broad engagement of all relevant stakeholders.

11. Emphasized the importance for technology transfer as a means to empower developing countries. They underlined the need to establish the BRICS network of technological cooperation and jointly promote access to affordable, safe, efficacious and quality medical products, through the use of TRIPS flexibilities.

12. Announce that the Technical Working Groups will implement the plans of action adopted by the Ministers in line with the Delhi Declaration. The report of the Technical Working groups will serve as a preparation for the 3rd BRICS Health Ministers Meeting to take place in South Africa.

L.   2nd Meeting of BRICS Health Ministers: 11 Jan. 2013, New Delhi (IND)

BRICS HEALTH MINISTERS COMMUNIQUÉ

1.   The BRICS countries, represented by the Ministers of Health of the Federative Republic of Brazil, the Russian Federation, India, People's Republic of China and Republic of South Africa, met in New Delhi on 11 January 2013 at the Second BRICS Health Ministers' Meeting.

2.   The meeting recalled the Delhi Declaration of 29 March 2012 during the BRICS leaders' summit and the Joint Communiqué of the BRICS Health Ministers at Geneva of 22 May 2012 including specific areas of work under the BRICS Health Platform for each Member State, focused on the theme "BRICS Partnership for Global Stability, Security and Prosperity" to address emerging health threats.

3.   The Ministers recalled that BRICS is a platform for dialogue and cooperation amongst countries representing 43% of the world's population. The Ministers reiterated their commitment to the Beijing Declaration of July 2011 for strengthened collaboration in the area of access to public health and services in BRICS States including implementation of affordable, equitable and sustainable solutions for common health challenges. The Ministers committed to strengthen intra-BRICS cooperation for promoting health of the BRICS population. The BRICS Health Ministers resolved to continue cooperation in the sphere of health through the Technical Working Group.

4.   The Ministers drew attention to the current global threat of non-communicable diseases and noted that in 2008, around 80% of all NCD deaths occurred in low and middle income countries. The Ministers recognized the significant role of BRICS countries in the global process of prevention and control of NCDs including the Moscow Declaration of April 2011, the WHA Resolution 64.11 of May 2011 and the Political Declaration of the UN General Assembly of September 2011.The Ministers recognized the need for more research into the social and economic determinants leading to occurrence of non-communicable diseases, amongst the BRICS countries. They resolved to collaborate and cooperate to promote access to comprehensive and cost-effective prevention, treatment and care for the integrated management of non-communicable diseases, including access to medicines and diagnostics and other technologies.

5.   The Ministers also recognized the need to combat mental disorders through a multi-pronged approach including the World Health Assembly Resolution 65.4, consideration of a Comprehensive Mental Health Action Plan through sharing of innovations in the field of Mental Health Promotion, diagnosis and management, exchange of best practices and experiences amongst BRICS countries.

6.   The Ministers renewed their commitment to the WHO Framework Convention on Tobacco Control and stressed the importance of research and study by WHO and other stakeholders into the social and economic determinants of tobacco use and its control.

7.   The Ministers recognized that multi-drug resistant tuberculosis is a major public health problem for the BRICS countries due to its high prevalence and incidence mostly on the marginalized and vulnerable sections of society. They resolved to collaborate and cooperate for development of capacity and infrastructure to reduce the prevalence and incidence of tuberculosis through innovation for new drugs/vaccines, diagnostics and promotion of consortia of tuberculosis researchers to collaborate on clinical trials of drugs and vaccines, strengthening access to affordable medicines and delivery of quality care. The Ministers also recognized the need to cooperate for adopting and improving systems for notification of tuberculosis patients, availability of anti-tuberculosis drugs at facilities by improving supplier performance, procurement systems and logistics and management of HIV-associated tuberculosis in the primary health care system.

8.   The Ministers called for renewed efforts to face the continued challenge posed by HIV. They committed to focus on cooperation in combating HIV/AIDS through approaches such as innovative

ways to reach out with prevention services, efficacious drugs and diagnostics, exchange of information on newer treatment regimens, determination of recent infections and HIV-TB co-infections. The Ministers agreed to share experience and expertise in the areas of surveillance, existing and new strategies to prevent the spread of HIV, and in rapid scale up of affordable treatment. They reiterated their commitment to ensure that bilateral and regional trade agreements do not undermine TRIPS flexibilities so as to assure availability of affordable generic ARV drugs to developing countries.

9. The Ministers committed to strengthen cooperation to combat malaria through enhanced diagnostics, research and development and committed to facilitate common access to the technologies developed or under development in the BRICS countries.

10. The Ministers renewed their commitment for effective control of both communicable and non-communicable diseases through cooperation in sharing of existing resource information, development of risk assessment tools, risk mitigation methods, referral systems, life course approaches, community empowerment, monitoring health impact assessments of all public policies at national and international levels.

11. Recognizing that an effective health surveillance, including injury surveillance, is the key strategy for controlling both communicable and non-communicable diseases, that surveillance is also the cornerstone around which the implementation of the International Health Regulations (2005) is based and further recognizing that the countries may be using different models for surveillance based on different realities and best practices, the Ministers committed to strengthen cooperation in the mechanisms for planning, monitoring and evaluating disease prevention and control activities and capacity-building for effective health surveillance systems.

12. The Ministers urged focus on the unique strength of BRICS countries such as capacity for R&D and manufacturing of affordable health products, and capability to conduct clinical trials. The Ministers called for strengthened cooperation in application of bio-technology for health benefits for the population of BRICS countries.

13. The Ministers emphasized the importance of child survival through progressive reduction in the maternal mortality, infant mortality, neo-natal mortality and under-5 mortality, with the aim of achieving the Millennium Development Goals. They confirmed their commitment to a renewed effort in this area and to enhance collaboration through exchange of best practices.

14. The Ministers discussed the recommendations of the Consultative Expert Working Group on Health on coordination and financing of R&D for medical products and welcomed the proposal to establish a Global Health R&D observatory as well as the move on holding regional consultations to set up R&D demonstration projects. The Ministers urged that the entire process, including priority setting, should be driven by WHO Member States and should be based on public health needs, in particular those of developing countries, with the cost of R & D delinked from the final products.

15. The Ministers reiterated their support to the continued discussions on the process of reform of WHO, to better respond to global challenges in programmatic, organizational and operational terms, including the future financing of WHO, and welcomed the proposal to establish a financing dialogue based on priorities collectively set by WHO Member States in a structured and transparent process.

16. The Ministers acknowledged the value and importance of traditional medicine and need of experience and knowledge-sharing for securing public health needs. They urged for cooperation amongst the BRICS countries through visits of experts, organization of symposia to encourage the use of traditional medicine, in all spheres of health.

17. The Ministers confirmed their support for the United Nations General Assembly Resolution on universal health coverage and committed to work nationally, regionally and globally to ensure that universal health coverage is achieved.

18. The Ministers recalled the Beijing Declaration of the 1st BRICS Health Ministers' Meeting in 2011, emphasizing the importance and need of technology transfer as a means to empower developing countries. In this context, they underlined the important role of generic medicines in the realization of the right to health. The Ministers renewed their commitment to strengthening international cooperation in health, in particular South-South cooperation, with a view to supporting efforts in developing countries to promote health for all and resolve to establish the BRICS network of technological cooperation.

19. The Ministers acknowledged the need of use of ICT in Health services to promote cost-effective treatment in the remote areas. They encouraged to strengthen cooperation amongst the BRICS countries to share their experiences in e-Health including tele-medicine.

20. The Ministers agreed to cooperate in all international fora regarding matters relating to TRIPS flexibilities with a public health perspective.

21. The Ministers agreed to establish platforms for collaboration within BRICS framework and with other countries with a view to realizing the goals and objectives outlined in this Declaration.

M.   Joint Communiqué of BRICS Member States on Health: 22 May 2012, Geneva (CHE)

JOINT COMMUNIQUÉ OF BRICS MEMBER STATES
ON HEALTH ON THE SIDELINES OF THE 65TH WORLD HEALTH ASSEMBLY

1.   The BRICS countries represented by the Ministers of Health of Brazil, China and South Africa, Permanent Representative of the Russian Federation and the Secretary of Health and Family Welfare, Government of India met on 22nd May, 2012 on the sidelines of the 65th session of the World Health Assembly in Geneva.

2.   Recalled the Beijing Declaration of the first BRICS Health Ministers in 2011, emphasizing the importance and the need of technology transfer as a means to empower developing countries; the important role of generic medicines in the realization of the right to health and to establish priorities in research and development as well as cooperation among BRICS countries including support to transfer of technologies and innovation in a sustainable way to foster cooperation among BRICS countries to make available and improve technology.

3.   Bound by the Delhi Declaration of BRICS Summit in 2012 which urged that meetings of BRICS Health Ministers be held in an institutionalized manner so that the countries of BRICS could jointly address common goals such as promoting innovation and universal access to health technologies including medicines, especially in the context of increasing costs and the growing burden of both communicable diseases and non-communicable diseases (NCDs) and to encourage flow of knowledge amongst research institutions through joint projects, workshops and exchange of visits, particularly by young scientists in areas relating to pharmaceuticals and health.

4.   Expressed their appreciation for the work of Dr. Margaret Chan during her first term as Director General of the World Health Organization. They supported the reelection of Dr. Chan, underlining their confidence in her leadership and in her capacity to guide the Organization through the new challenges in global health.

5.   Exchanged views on the areas of cooperation in the health sector amongst BRICS countries and found it useful to share views in areas where cooperation would be beneficial to the people of the BRICS Member States as well as the world at large.

6.   Reiterated their commitment to provide health care, particularly access to medicines for their people and to address the social determinants of health. They commended the outcomes of the World Conference on Social Determinants of Health, held in October 2011 in Rio de Janeiro, and expressed their support for the endorsement of the Rio Political Declaration by the World Health Assembly as well as for the due consideration of social determinants of health in the assessment of global needs for health, including in the WHO reform process and WHO's future work.

7.   Stressed the importance of Universal Health Coverage as an essential instrument for the achievement of the right to health. Welcomed the growing global support for Universal Health Coverage and sustainable development. They supported the WHO in taking leadership role in advocating for Universal Health Coverage.

8.   Reiterated the relevance of the current process of WHO reform and highlighted the need to ensure transparent and inclusive decision making processes within the Organization. In this context, the importance of multilateralism was underscored as a fundamental principle to strengthen and legitimize WHO as the coordinating authority in global health and promote cooperation in health-related issues among states within WHO.

9. Acknowledged the dual burden of communicable and non-communicable diseases afflicting the people which calls for enhanced funding for the health sector and concerted inter-sectoral action.

10. Recognized the momentum built with regard to prevention and control of non-communicable diseases, particularly the Moscow Declaration on NCDs, WHA resolution 64.11 and the political declaration of the UN High-level meeting on NCDs in 2011.

11. Undertook to work collaboratively in identifying evidence based interventions that are aimed at reducing the effects of risk factors associated with NCDs.

12. Acknowledged the growing expertise available in their countries in research institutes and decided to encourage exchange visits by scientists and taking up of joint research projects for the benefit of all Member-States.

13. Further agreed that surveillance is a key strategy for controlling both communicable and non-communicable diseases. Surveillance data is required to plan, monitor and evaluate disease-control activities and to identify the high risk areas of groups and to detect early warning signals to control outbreak in an early phase. To foster technology cooperation among BRICS Member-States, they decided to include disease surveillance, both for communicable and non-communicable diseases, among the list of areas for cooperation.

14. Underscored that the BRICS countries need to act unitedly to ensure that the World Health Organization remains committed to strengthening of the drug regulatory mechanisms and refrains from involvement with issues related to Intellectual Property Rights enforcement.

15. Welcomed the discussions during the Seminar "Sanitary Regulation Challenges in a World without Borders: Improving Cooperation among Drug Regulatory Agencies" held on 18 May, 2012. They highlighted the importance of national regulatory capacities as a crucial element to improving access to medicines and recognized the need for a sustainable cooperation among national regulatory authorities to efficiently address the current complexities in the production and distribution of medical products.

16. Expressed their appreciation for the outcome of the Open-ended Working Group on Substandard/Spurious/Falsely-labeled/ Falsified/Counterfeit (SSFFC) medical products. They supported the establishment of the Member-State mechanism, which is designed to address the prevention and control of SSFFC medical products from a public health perspective.

17. Welcomed the task completed by the Consultative Expert Working Group on Research and Development: Financing and Coordination (CEWG).

18. Expressed concern at the lack of research for drug discovery and development in the field of diseases like TB, malaria and the neglected diseases.

19. Committed to accelerate both individual and collective efforts to pursue the achievement of the health-related Millennium Development Goals (MDGs).

20. Encouraged by the study on medicine organized by UNAIDS and WHO, expressed support for relevant activities such as mapping and analysis of BRICS countries' technical capacities and weaknesses in accessing medicines and other health technologies, and study of the pharmaceutical sectors and areas of improvement and cooperation with an aim to promote concrete measures to strengthen national capacities.

21. Announced that a meeting of the technical working group will be convened within the next months, in line with the Beijing Declaration. The technical working group will discuss a program of work to advance the health related cooperation among BRICS countries, in particular the establishment of the network of technological cooperation. The deliberations of the working group will serve as a preparation for the next meeting of BRICS Health Ministers as referred in the Delhi Declaration.

22. With these areas of cooperation in mind, affirmed that:

    i. Cooperation among BRICS member states in the field of health and medicine is in the interest of all countries.

    ii. Cooperation among BRICS member states will help address common challenges such as universal access to health services.

    iii. It will also help access to health technologies and generic medicines not only among BRICS member states but the world at large.

    iv. Cooperation in the area of drug discovery and development especially TB, malaria, neglected diseases as well as non- communicable diseases will facilitate availability of new drugs to treat these diseases more effectively.

    v. The right of the Member-States to protect public health and, in particular, to promote access to medicines for all as agreed in the Doha Declaration of 2001.

    vi. Following the Delhi Plan of Action, the Second BRICS Health Ministers meeting will be hosted by India in November, 2012.

N.   1st Meeting of BRICS Health Ministers: 11 Jul. 2011, Beijing (CHN)

BRICS HEALTH MINISTERS DECLARATION

1.   Consistent with the mandate of the Sanya Declaration of the BRICS Leaders Meeting, we, the Health Ministers of the Federative Republic of Brazil, the Russian Federation, the Republic of India, the People's Republic of China and the Republic of South Africa, met in Beijing, China, for the First BRICS Health Ministers' Meeting on 11 July 2011, to discuss and coordinate positions on issues of common interest as well as to identify areas for cooperation in public health. The BRICS Ministers of Health issued the following Declaration:

2.   Public health is an essential element for social and economic development and should be reflected accordingly in national and international policies. The impact of foreign policy on health outcomes is being recognized. We call upon the United Nations General Assembly as well as other major international conferences and fora, to integrate public health into their respective agendas, in order to further promote awareness and contribute to build political consensus and generate broad, sustained and concerted action for public health.

3.   The international health architecture comprises an increasing number of international agencies and organizations, each of them playing a significant role, in their respective areas, to promote public health. In this increasingly complex environment, we are determined to strengthen public health at the global level and to improve the leading and coordinating role of the World Health Organization (WHO) in international health cooperation. We acknowledge that challenges related to food security, climate change, environment, trade and other global issues have an impact on public health. We are committed to support and undertake inclusive global public health cooperation projects, including through South-South and triangular cooperation. We support greater coordination and cooperation among international health and development agencies and organizations, so as to optimize the use of resources and to integrate, in a coherent manner, global health policies.

4.   In view of the financial challenges and growing demands faced by WHO in the aftermath of the economic crisis, we urge Member States, in particular developed countries, to continue to support the Organization with the required resources for the fulfillment of its mandate. In this context, we support innovative financing mechanisms for health as possible means to mobilize additional resources.

5.   We also stress the need and importance of the reform of WHO. We are confident that proposed reform measures which include, among others, focusing on core business, strengthening financing, resource mobilization and strategic communication, strengthening the Organization's role in global health governance, will lead to the improvement of the Organization's transparency, efficiency and accountability. We welcome the decision taken by the WHO Executive Board to establish a transparent, Member State driven and inclusive reform process.

6.   The strengthening of health systems and health financing in developing countries in all regions must be the central goal of the global health community. In our view, WHO has a major role to play in the promotion of access to medication, technology transfer and capacity-building with a view to bring more equity to the health sector worldwide. Success in health outcomes in one country represents success to many others.

7.   Despite our diversity, the BRICS nations face a number of similar public health challenges, including inequitable access to health services and medicines, growing health costs, infectious diseases such as HIV and tuberculosis (TB), while also facing growing rates of non-communicable diseases. The major challenge facing us is how to provide health care to millions of people, in particular among the most vulnerable segments of our populations.

8.   We are committed to continue to collaborate in order to advance access to public health services and goods in our own countries and deliver more cost-effective, equitable and sustainable solutions for common health challenges. We are also committed to support other countries in their efforts to promote health for all.

9.   With those aims in mind, we reaffirm our commitment to promote BRICS as a forum of coordination, cooperation and consultation on relevant matters related to global public health. Therefore, we agree to institutionalize, on a permanent basis, the dialogue among Ministers of Health, as well as among Permanent Representatives in Geneva, to follow-up and implement the health related outcome of the BRICS summit.

10. In light of the theme of the meeting "Global Health- Access to Medicine", which aims to promote innovation and access to affordable medicines, vaccines and other health technologies of assured quality, in support of reaching MDGs 4, 5, 6 and 8 and other public health challenges, we have identified the following priority areas:

    I.   Collaboration to strengthen health systems and overcome barriers to access to affordable, quality, efficacious, safe medical products, vaccines and other health technologies for HIV/AIDS, tuberculosis, viral hepatitis, malaria and other infectious diseases and non-communicable diseases.

    II. Collaboration to explore and promote, where feasible, effective transfer of technology to strengthen innovation capacity to benefit public health in developing countries.

    III. Collaboration with and support of international organizations, including WHO and UNAIDS, the Global Fund to Fight AIDS, Tuberculosis and Malaria and the GAVI alliance, to increase access to affordable, quality, efficacious and safe medicines, vaccines and other medical products that serve public health needs.

11. We agree to establish and encourage a global health agenda for universal access to affordable medicines and health commodities.

12. To accelerate progress towards universal access to HIV prevention, treatment, care and support, we encourage increased access to new and innovative antiretroviral therapies (ART). We are determined to make efforts to simplify treatment regimens, including for second and third line therapy as the incidence of resistance increases. As far as TB and malaria are concerned, we encourage increased innovation, notably in the development of additional diagnostic tools and treatment for the resistant strains of the diseases. We encourage the access to diagnosis and treatment for viral hepatitis.

13. With the increasing need for the WHO Prequalification of Medicines Programme to ensure quality of HIV, TB and malaria medicines as well as vaccines produced by BRICS countries, we call upon the WHO to facilitate prequalification process, the strengthening of national regulatory authorities and the enhancement of exportability of medical products produced in BRICS countries, especially priority vaccines and medicines for HIV/AIDS, TB and malaria.

14. We commend the Moscow Declaration of the First Global Ministerial Meeting on Healthy Lifestyle and Non-communicable Diseases, support the High-level Meeting of the UN General Assembly on Non- communicable Diseases and commit to collectively explore ways to implement the agreements to be reached by September 2011. We welcome the holding, in Rio de Janeiro, next October, of the World Conference on the Social Determinants of Health.

15. We are committed to the full implementation of agreements reached at the High Level Meeting on HIV/AIDS of the United Nations General Assembly (8-10 June, 2011).

16. We emphasize the importance and the need of technology transfer as a means to empower developing countries and enable them to establish efficient health systems. In this context, we underlined the important role of generic medicines in the realization of the right to health.

17. We acknowledge the need to establish priorities in research and development as well as cooperation among BRICS countries, including between stakeholders from the public and private sector, in order to support the transfer of technologies and innovation in a sustainable way.

18. We recall the important role the BRICS countries have played in the development of the Global Strategy and Plan of Action on Public Health, Innovation and Intellectual Property and reiterate our commitment to support the full implementation of its provisions.

19. We welcome the establishment of innovative mechanisms to promote transfer of and access to key health-related technologies where feasible to enhance the availability of affordable medicines in developing countries.

20. Aiming to ensure access to affordable, safe and effective technologies and to expand health benefits, we will foster cooperation among our countries to make available and improve health technology.

21. We are exploring new opportunities for BRICS countries to support the work of health-related international organizations and to benefit from such collaboration. We reiterate our support to UN agencies and programs in this regard, as well as our commitment to further explore bilateral technical cooperation initiatives with developing countries in partnership with WHO, UNAIDS and other UN agencies, as well as global health programs such as the Global Fund to Fight AIDS, Tuberculosis and Malaria, GAVI alliance and the UNITAID.

22. We are determined to ensure that bilateral and regional trade agreements do not undermine TRIPS flexibilities. We support the TRIPS safeguards and are committed to work together with other developing countries to preserve and promote, to the full, the provisions contained in the Doha Declaration on TRIPS and Public Health and of the Global Strategy and Plan of Action on Public Health, Innovation and Intellectual Property. We also support the full implementation of Human Rights Council Resolution 12/24 on access to medicine in the context of the right of everyone to the enjoyment of the highest attainable standard of physical and mental health. In addition, we support the development of innovative mechanisms of transfer of intellectual property rights for priority technologies, to open avenues for BRICS countries to supply these medicines to low and middle income countries.

23. We agree to establish a technical working group to discuss specific proposals, including the idea of setting up a BRICS network of technological cooperation, taking into account of a possible BRICS Health Ministers' Meeting in September, 2011, in conjunction with the UN High Level Meeting on Non-communicable Diseases.

III.6.   BRICS Environment Ministers

A.   BRICS Environment Ministers: 18 May 2018, Zimbali, Durban (ZAF)

JOINT STATEMENT FOR THE FOURTH BRICS MINISTERS OF ENVIRONMENT MEETING

Zimbali, Durban, South Africa, May 18, 2018

We, the Ministers of Environment and Heads of Delegation of the Federative Republic of Brazil, the Russian Federation, the Republic of India, the People's Republic of China and the Republic of South Africa, held the fourth BRICS Environmental Ministers' Meeting in Durban on 18 May 2018.

We reiterate our commitment to the importance of 2030 Agenda for Sustainable Development and the Sustainable Development Goals (SDGs), which clearly articulate international development priorities and global development cooperation towards the ultimate goal of eradicating poverty by 2030.

Through adopting the SDGs, the global community has undertaken significant commitments towards sustainability, development, and prosperity that is shared and equitable, leaving no one behind. The means and mechanisms are of critical importance in the implementation of SDGs and the BRICS countries hereby call for early implementation of the Global commitments towards Technology Facilitation Mechanism and Financing for Development.

We welcome various partnerships for the implementation of the 2030 Agenda for Sustainable Development and call for good governance to enhance implementation actions to integrate sustainable development at the heart of social and economic development policies in relation to Sustainable Consumption and Production (SCP).

With respect to Climate Change, BRICS countries welcome the progress towards finalizing the Work Programme under the Paris Agreement and express our willingness to continue working constructively with other Parties to conclude its related negotiations at the UN Climate Change Conference (UNFCCC) Katowice in December 2018. We reaffirm our commitments to the Paris Agreement and urge developed countries to continue taking the lead and support developing countries, including the transfer of needed technology, which is one of the most critical enablers for climate action.

We reiterate the call to enhance cooperation and collaboration amongst BRICS countries in the field of biodiversity conservation, sustainable use and equitable access and benefit sharing of biological resources, and also undertake to promote cooperation in biodiversity-related international conventions and fora including on endangered species.

We will continue to collaborate on these issues to ensure the success of the Convention on Biological Diversity (COP14) to be held in Egypt in November 2018, and 70th meeting of the Convention on International Trade In Endangered Species of Wild Fauna and Flora (CITES) Standing Committee in Russia in October 2018. BRICS countries committed to fully support the efforts of China in hosting the COP15 of CBD to be held in 2020. Furthermore, we noted with appreciation Brazil's invitation to BRICS countries to attend and fully participate in the 67th International Whaling Commission (IWC) conference to be held in Brazil from 4 to 14 September 2018.

We reviewed and acknowledged the progress made on the key outcomes of the First, Second and Third BRICS Environment Ministers' Meetings hosted by Russia, India and China respectively. These outcomes included progress with implementation of the Environmentally Friendly Technology Platform, Clean Rivers Umbrella Programme and the Partnership for Urban Environment Sustainability Initiative and undertook to continue to implement these initiatives.

We acknowledge the progress in the establishment of the BRICS Environmentally Sound Technology (BEST) Cooperation Platform. The BEST Platform is intended to be a practical and results orientated, which would include partners, science and international organisations, civil society, private sector and financial institutions, including the New Development Bank (NDB). We will use this BEST Platform as a coordinating mechanism for the implementation of agreed upon projects and programmes under the BRICS Environment Memorandum of Understanding.

We welcome the promotion of cooperation within BRICS in the area of waste management and pollution prevention, in particular the theme of the 4th BRICS Environment Minister's meeting of "Strengthening cooperation amongst BRICS on Circular Economy in the context of the Sustainable Consumption and Production (SCP)".

We reaffirm that the promotion of circular approach to Waste Management contributes significantly to the achievement of the SCP Goal as outline in SDG12 of the 2030 Agenda for Sustainable Development, as well as the United Nations Environment Assembly (UNEA) "Towards a Pollution Free Planet" theme.

We acknowledge that the circular economy approach in the context of SCP aims to keep resources in use for as long as possible, extract the maximum value from them whilst in use, then recover and regenerate products and materials at the end of each service life.

We welcome the vast potential in cooperation and collaboration in advancing the Oceans Economy amongst BRICS countries, which encompasses multiple sectors. We will explore enhancing our cooperation on Marine protection and ocean governance taking into account that the scope for cooperation may be limited to the programmes of environmental ministries, although the BRICS Ocean Economy cooperation will seek to influence and cooperate with all sectors of the oceans economy. We undertake to pursue this with the relevant government agencies and stakeholders, including the private sector.

We express our intention to enhance cooperation in the fields of water on the basis of sustainable development in an integrated way, addressing the themes of water security, flood protection, water supply and sanitation, water and climate and systematically facilitating water pollution prevention and control, aquatic ecosystem conservation and water resources management.

We underscore our collective interest in improving our national water infrastructure to secure and manage our natural water sources while considering the traditional knowledge of our indigenous and/or local communities related to water resources and the sustenance thereof.

We welcome the progress in the development on the Memorandum of Understanding (MoU) on Environmental Cooperation and look forward to signing it during the Chairship of South Africa of BRICS.

We also welcome the participation of UN Environment Programme and United Nations Industrial Development Organisation (UNIDO) in BRICS environmental cooperation.

We express our gratitude to the Republic of South Africa for hosting the 3rd Environment Working Group meeting (14-16 May 2018), 4th BRICS Environment Senior Officials and Ministers' Meeting in Zimbali, Durban on 17-18 May 2018.

We welcome the offer of Brazil to host the next BRICS Environment Ministers meeting in 2019.

B.   BRICS Environment Ministers: 23 Jun. 2017, Tianjin (CHN)

THIRD MEETING OF BRICS ENVIRONMENT MINISTERS TIANJIN STATEMENT ON ENVIRONMENT

4th Draft, revised based on discussion on 22 June 2017

Tianjin, China, June 23, 2017

1. We, the Environment Ministers and senior officials of the Federative Republic of Brazil, the Russian Federation, the Republic of India, the People's Republic of China and the Republic of South Africa, held the Third BRICS Environment Ministers' Meeting in Tianjin, China from June 22 to 23, 2017. We reaffirm our commitment to the implementation of the Agenda 2030 for Sustainable Development as well as the Paris Agreement.

2. We reviewed and appreciated the progress made subsequent to the First and Second BRICS Environment Ministers' Meeting hosted by Russia and India at Moscow and Goa respectively.

3. We reaffirmed the importance of BRICS Memorandum of Understanding (MOU) on Environmental Cooperation to be signed at an appropriate time, and expressed the interest of developing a framework agreement on environmental cooperation in the future.

4. We discussed major challenges and opportunities towards achieving sustainable development in its three inter-related and indivisible dimensions: economic, social and environmental at country, regional and global levels.

5. We reiterate our commitment to the principles of the Rio Declaration on Environment and Development of 1992, including equity, dignity and common but differentiated responsibilities.

6. We urge full implementation of the Addis Ababa Action Agenda on financing for sustainable development, including the Technology Facilitation Mechanism. The official development assistance, technology transfer and capacity building remain the key means in addressing global environmental challenges. We reaffirm our call to developed countries to honor their commitments relating to means of implementation and operationalization of Agenda 2030 with a clear roadmap.

7. We underscore the need for means of implementation of Paris Agreement, including transfer of technology from developed to developing countries as one of the most critical enabler for climate actions.

8. We also urge developed countries to honor their commitments and take the lead in providing the financial assistance on climate actions as reflected in UNFCCC Agreements.

9. We appreciate that the conservation and sustainable use of the rich biodiversity of BRICS countries is of special significance for the global environment and to achieve the internationally agreed targets and goals, including SDGs and Aichi targets.

10. We resolve to enhance cooperation in the field of biodiversity conservation, sustainable use and equitable sharing of benefit, and also promote cooperation in biodiversity-related international conventions and fora including on endangered species. We will closely cooperate to ensure the success of COP15 of CBD to be held in China in 2020.

11. We reiterate our intention to promote cooperation within BRICS in the area of pollution prevention, in particular air pollution, which will help achieving Agenda 2030 and is in line with the UNEA 3 theme of "towards a pollution free planet".

12. In our efforts to address the issues raised and in following the guidance given by our leaders, and to provide impetus to fulfilling our commitments in Moscow and Goa Statements with the aim

of developing the Environmentally Friendly Technology Platform, we realized the importance of concrete actions on cooperation, such as the proposals to develop the BRICS Clean Rivers Umbrella Program and the BRICS City Partnership for Environmental Sustainability Initiative.

13. We welcome the hosting by Brazil of the 8th World Water Forum in Brasilia, on 18-23 March 2018, which will promote a timely debate among all stakeholders on the theme "sharing waters".

14. Realizing the global significance of addressing desertification, land degradation and drought, we pledge our full support to the successful COP 13 of the UNCCD taking place in Erdos, Inner Mongolia, the People's Republic of China, on 6-16 September 2017.

15. We welcome the hosting by the Ministry of Environment, Forest and Climate Change and the Ministry of Urban Development, the Government of India of an international workshop on 3R's (Reduce, Reuse and Recycle) in collaboration with UNCRD on 21-24 December 2017.

16. We acknowledge that the Year of Environment was declared by the Russian Federation in 2017 and expect its outcome to contribute to the better state of environment.

17. We also welcome the collaboration of United Nations Environment Programme in the BRICS environmental cooperation.

18. We express our heartfelt appreciation to the government of the People's Republic of China and Tianjin Municipal government and its people for hosting the Third BRICS Environment Ministers' Meeting.

C.   BRICS Environment Ministers: 15-16 Sep. 2016, Goa (IND)

GOA STATEMENT ON ENVIRONMENT:
SECOND MEETING OF BRICS ENVIRONMENT MINISTERS
September 16, 2016, Goa

1.   We, the Environment Ministers and senior officials of the Federative Republic of Brazil, the Russian Federation, the Republic of India, the People's Republic of China and the Republic of South Africa, met in Goa, India on 15 - 16 September 2016 at the Second BRICS Environment Ministers meeting. Our discussions, under the overarching theme "BRICS Partnership for Building Responsive, Inclusive and Collective Solutions", were inspired by a shared desire to strengthen mutual cooperation in the area of environment to achieve equitable, inclusive and sustainable development.

2.   We deeply appreciate the initiative taken by the Russian Federation for hosting the first meeting of BRICS Environment Ministers in Moscow last year and recall the decisions taken during that meeting identifying areas of mutual interest and possibilities of cooperation. We acknowledge the support that we received from our leaders in Ufa declaration of 2015 and the efforts made during the interim period by the countries in fostering cooperation on environmental issues.

3.   We note the emerging global environmental challenges and opportunities that the global community faces today. We recognise that eradication of poverty must be our first priority as it is the poor who bear disproportionate burden of environmental degradation caused by unsustainable and inequitable consumption of resources and emphasize the need for sustainable lifestyles. BRICS countries constitute significant part of world's population, land area and natural resources; thus, the choices that we make have global significance.

4.   We reaffirm our commitment to the Principles of Rio Declaration on Environment and Development, 1992 including Equity, and Common but Differentiated Responsibilities.

      We welcome the adoption of Agenda 2030 for Sustainable Development which is a positive milestone in the global efforts to promote effective sustainable development solutions. We acknowledge that the implementation of Sustainable Development Goals (SDGs) requires transformative leadership that aims to "leave no one behind".

5.   We welcome the adoption of Paris Agreement on Climate Change, and look forward to its ratification by all countries and resolve to work for its full implementation. We emphasize that the countries working on their domestic processes of ratification should continue to be included in the decision making process, in case early entry into force of the Paris Agreement is achieved.

6.   We welcome the Addis Ababa Action Agenda on Financing for Development which reaffirmed strong political commitment to address the challenge of financing and creating an enabling environment at all levels for sustainable development. All sources of finance, technology transfer and capacity building are critical for addressing global environmental issues. We call upon developed countries to honour their commitments relating to means of implementation and facilitate the operationalization of Agenda 2030 with a clear roadmap.

7.   We have agreed on a Memorandum of Understanding and constituted a Joint Working Group on Environment providing impetus to our mutual cooperation on a sustained basis. We have also agreed to meet and convene a meeting of the Joint Working Group annually.

8.   We recognize the importance of abatement and control of air and water pollution. We have agreed to share with each other our technical expertise on air quality and water pollution as well as

conservation and management of water resources and rivers through joint projects and network of our regulatory and technical institutions.

9. We recognize that efficient management of various categories of waste is key for healthy ecosystem and quality of life of our people. We have agreed to enhance our mutual cooperation for efficient management of waste.

10. We acknowledge the rich biodiversity of BRICS countries and its significance for sustainable livelihood and development. We note the considerable experience of our technical institutions and agree to promote closer cooperation among the expert bodies for sustainable management of biodiversity and achieving Sustainable Development Goals. We also take note of China's interest in hosting the CoP-15 of the Convention on Biological Diversity (CBD) in 2020.

11. We welcome South Africa's hosting the 17th Conference of Parties to the Convention on International Trade in Endangered Species of Wild Fauna and Flora (CITES), from 24 September to 5 October 2016 at the Sandton Convention Centre in Johannesburg. In addition, we noted that a Ministerial Lekgotla will be held on the 23 September 2016, which will discuss the nexus between the Agenda 2030 SDGs and CITES with a special focus on how CITES can advance the achievement of the SDGs.

12. We have resolved to develop a platform for sharing environmentally sound technologies as a new international mechanism for public private partnership that can assist in addressing environmental challenges in our countries and promote innovations, knowledge management and capacity building including by means of a common website, a network of technical institutions and to undertake joint projects in areas of mutual interest.

13. We express our gratitude to Government and people of India for hosting the second meeting of the BRICS Environment Ministers and the Government of People's Republic of China for offering to host the next meeting.

D.   BRICS Environment Ministers: 22 Apr. 2015, Moscow (RUS)

STATEMENT: FIRST OFFICIAL MEETING OF BRICS ENVIRONMENT MINISTERS
Moscow, April 22, 2015

We, the BRICS Environment Ministers, assembled for the First official meeting during the Russian Presidency of BRICS in Moscow (the Russian Federation) on 22 April 2015 share the common aspiration that the effective implementation and promotion of an economically, socially and environmentally sustainable future is essential to achieve our overarching priority of poverty eradication.

We recognize that sustainable development should comprehensively address the key challenges of today, in particular, poverty eradication, changing unsustainable and promoting sustainable patterns of consumption and production, protecting and managing the natural resource base of economic and social development and effectively addressing climate change.

We reaffirm our commitment to implement the Rio Declaration, Agenda 21, the Johannesburg Plan of Implementation (JPOI), and the outcomes of the Rio+20 Conference in our respective countries, and through our cooperation within the framework of BRICS in accordance with the Rio principles, including the principle of common but differentiated responsibilities.

We consider that inclusive green economy in the context of sustainable development and poverty eradication is one of the tools available to achieve sustainable development in our countries, in accordance with the national circumstances and priorities.

We acknowledge the progress made on the Millennium Development Goals in the preceding two decades and reaffirm our commitment towards accelerated implementation of the unfinished task. In this context, we look forward to the adoption of ambitious, transformative and equitable Post-2015 development agenda with Sustainable Development Goals at its core. The scale of challenges associated with the implementation of the Post-2015 Development agenda will require shared efforts, strengthened international cooperation and robust means of implementation.

We acknowledge that the increasing number and frequency of the extreme natural phenomena triggered by the human induced climate change are likely to greatly affect societies and economies worldwide.

We will consolidate efforts in our respective countries to develop policies and measures contributing to mitigation efforts and adaptation of the national economies to the adverse impacts of climate change in accordance with the principles of equity, common but differentiated responsibilities and respective capabilities, and other provisions of UNFCCC.

For the realization of our common goals we resolve to:

- Establish a Working group on environment which will identify and discuss the priority areas of cooperation, and decide to convene its first meeting in 2015 in Russia;
- Explore the potential of the BRICS New Development Bank for purposes of funding environmental projects;
- Explore at the Working group level the possibility of establishing a collaborative platform of the BRICS countries intended to share best environmental practices and facilitate the exchange of environmentally sound technologies and know-how with participation of public and private stakeholders, taking into account the existing mechanisms of cooperation;
- Hold regular meetings of Environment Ministers of BRICS.

We deeply appreciate and commend the efforts of the host country, the Russian Federation, in organizing the First Official Meeting of Environment Ministers of BRICS.

III.7. BRICS Labour and Employment Ministers

A.   Meeting of BRICS Labour and Employment Ministers: 3 Aug. 2018, Durban (ZAF)

BRICS LABOUR AND EMPLOYMENT MINISTERS' MEETING
3 August, 2018, Durban, South Africa

Introduction

1.   We, the Ministers of Labour and Employment from the Federative Republic of Brazil, the Russian Federation, the Republic of India, the People's Republic of China and the Republic of South Africa, met in Durban on 2-3 August, for the fourth BRICS Labour and Employment Ministers' Meeting (LEMM). Convening under the theme "Developing countries for inclusive Growth and Shared Prosperity in the New Industrial Revolution", the meeting sought to ensure maximum synergy and continuity for BRICS collaboration within the labour market landscape.

2.   We note that South Africa's Presidency of BRICS comes amid an environment of stabilising global economic growth and employment outlook; however, some labour markets still face diverse challenges with unemployment.

3.   We further take note that the BRICS countries long identified the need for developing pragmatic economic cooperation and forging closer economic and social partnerships in order to increase inclusive economic growth amongst its members. In pursuance of these objectives, the South African Presidency focussed on Youth Employment; Women's participation in the labour market and equal pay for work of equal value; Tripartism and Collective Bargaining; and Social Protection.

4.   We commend the progress and cooperation between our countries in labour and employment issues since the first meeting held in Ufa, Russia, in 2015. The Member Countries continue to share knowledge and also implement joint programmes on matters of labour and employment, social security and social dialogue.

5.   The Ufa Declaration established the Employment Working Group (EWG) which is an important gathering for senior officials and technical experts to deliberate matters of mutual interest. We thus recall that under the Russian Presidency, our countries resolved to formalise their collaboration through the conclusion of a Memorandum of Understanding (MoU) regarding cooperation in the social and labour sphere in order to foster mutual collaboration between Member Countries. We congratulate the South African Presidency for ensuring that this matter has reached its finality as well as the development of a working implementation plan to be handed over to Brazil in 2019.

6.   We further recognise the importance of streamlining the work of the labour and employment working group with other streams as demonstrated by the meeting in Russia, where a joint labour and finance meeting was organised. Coherence and coordination of BRICS EWG with BRICS framework including relevant Working Groups like BRICS finance, education, economic/ trade as well as science, technology and innovation streams are essential.

7.   The 2017 Chongqing Declaration established the BRICS Network of Labour Research Institutes. We re-affirm our support for the BRICS Network and its role in the pursuit of our objectives and broader international frameworks, including the United Nations 2030 Agenda for Sustainable Development.

8.   We welcome the partnership with the International Training Centre of the ILO and call upon them to support the BRICS Network, including on the theme of youth employment in 2018/19. The next step for the BRICS Network, ITC-ILO, ILO and ISSA is the finalisation of the studies of new forms

of employment. The network will also organise more regular face-to- face meetings and will also explore new learning technologies, including virtual network, to deepen cooperation, exchange of information and capacity building.

Youth Employment

9.   Youth employment has become a common denominator in the labour market issue for all Member Countries. We thus commit to developing a comprehensive and coordinated approach, which will promote access to decent work for young women and men. For this to happen, it is essential that we make decent employment creation for youth a policy priority objective which cuts across economic, social and employment policies. Our actions in this regard will include the promotion of stable wage employment, as well as advocating sound pro-employment macroeconomic policies, including employment-intensive investment.

10.   To achieve this cross-cutting ambition, we will facilitate inter-ministerial coordination between relevant Ministries, including those responsible for finance, economic development, trade, industry, education, as well as other Ministries. We also commit to work with other ministries to mobilise necessary resources for mainstreaming youth employment in government policies.

11.   This endeavour will also require sound and effective labour market institutions that should make best use of modern digital technology. We will work towards increasing the effectiveness and impact of labour market information systems, public and private employment services, labour inspections, as well as active labour market policies in order to reach and serve all youth, especially those living in rural areas or engaged in the informal economy.

12.   While we recognise that new forms of employment, such as those in the gig and platform economies, can provide job opportunities for youth, sustained efforts will be needed to ensure that those jobs are decent. More work is also needed to promote skills and training, entrepreneurship and sustainable enterprise development through innovative interventions and solutions in response to new labour market dynamics, both in traditional and emerging sectors.

Social Dialogue

13.   Social dialogue is an essential component of good governance of labour related matters. We acknowledge its contribution in the Member Countries towards inclusive economic development, greater coherence between economic and social policies, and addressing key social challenges such as wage inequalities, regulation of non-standard forms of employment, compliance with labour laws, mitigation of the social costs of market- oriented reforms, and strengthening democracy.

14.   The Member Countries face a number of challenges that affect social dialogue, such as widening inequalities, the changing nature of work and employment relationships, informal employment and an associated lack of workers' protection, and adjustments in public spending. We also note important global developments such as the New Industrial Revolution, which entails increased automation and digitalisation; demographic developments involving migration and refugee crises; as well as climate change that are posing important questions and challenges for the form and organisation of the world of work.

15.   In response, we will work towards the necessary policy reforms to define employment relationships and review laws and regulations in response to the challenges brought by the Future of Work and digitalisation.

16.   We will further explore avenues, in close cooperation with social partners, to improve social dialogue and collective bargaining to be more inclusive and representative of disadvantaged labour market actors such as youth, women, and people with disabilities. To make this possible, we also undertake to explore innovative ways of improving social dialogue and collective bargaining institutions. Furthermore, we will work towards strengthening labour administration systems to support social dialogue more effectively and building the capacity of social partners to participate in

dialogue fora. This will include research on the needs that will emanate from challenges and opportunities from the New Industrial Revolution.

Women's participation in the labour market: Equal pay for work of equal value

17. Attracting and retaining more women in the labour market, and in better- quality jobs, features highly on the development policy agenda. We therefore acknowledge that more and better jobs for women are not just a matter of justice or fairness, but of "smart" economics. In the current context of demographic transitions and structural changes in the organisation of production and work, women can and must contribute to building more sustainable and inclusive economies and societies on conditions of equality with men.

18. The 2030 Agenda for Sustainable Development commits member states to deliver on a number of related and ambitious Sustainable Development Goals (SDGs), such as SDGs 5 and 8, which includes SDG 8.5 that calls upon countries to contribute to achieving equal pay for work of equal value by 2030.

19. Despite some important progress in the past decades, gender gaps in participation by women in the labour market, pay and income, and representation in sectors and occupations remain large and in some instances, are widening. To meet the ambitious goals of the 2030 Sustainable Development Agenda, we commit to put in place policies that will accelerate the pace of progress towards the achievement of gender equality at work.

20. This ambition requires acting simultaneously on various policy fronts: reducing vertical and horizontal occupational segregation and boosting women's entrepreneurship; addressing discrimination in remuneration and valuing women's work fairly; enhancing the quality and safety of working environments, including by protecting women against gender-based violence; making it easier for both women and men to reconcile paid employment with family responsibilities; and increasing women's representation in employers' and workers' organisations.

21. Central to any of these efforts is the fight against discrimination and gender stereotypes. We commit to tackling this issue by adopting a multi-dimensional approach, which may include sound legislative frameworks and their effective enforcement, awareness-campaigns for a wide audience, beginning from primary school, and workplace policies and codes of conduct for gender equality.

22. Due to the inter-relationship among the policy areas mentioned above, coordination among different government agencies is of the essence. Partnerships with workers' and employers' organisations, are also necessary as they will permit an exchange of good practices and learning from each other's experiences, and monitoring and assessing progress, such as the Equal Pay International Coalition (EPIC).

23. We commit to developing and implementing national and workplace policies aimed at improving the quantity and quality of women's participation in the labour force. We also commit to exchanging information and views on latest development on a regular basis with the use of the BRICS Network of Labour Research Institutes.

Social Protection

24. We reaffirm our commitment to universal and sustainable social security systems, including social protection floors, as an integral part of our policies to promote inclusive growth, decent and productive employment, gender equality and social cohesion. Our countries have made significant progress in improving our social security systems, yet more efforts are necessary to close coverage and adequacy gaps, with particular attention to young people and women, the self-employed, workers in rural areas and in the informal economy, also with a view to facilitating their transition from the informal to the formal economy as per ILO Recommendation 204.

25. Ensuring adequate protection for workers across different contractual arrangements is essential for safeguarding their income security and effective access to health care; facilitating the mobility of workers; and for ensuring social justice and economic development. Further efforts to enhance governance and administration, such as by simplifying and streamlining administrative procedures and harnessing digital technologies while protecting personal data, will facilitate compliance and achieve better results.

26. We also recognise the need to safeguard the sustainability and equity of our social security systems through a combination of different instruments, complementing social insurance by non-contributory schemes, and adapting financing mechanisms to changing forms of work and employment.

27. We recognise the essential role of social protection for the 2030 Agenda for Sustainable Development, and for preparing our economies and societies for the future of work. In accelerating progress towards universal and sustainable social security systems, we are guided by international social security standards, particularly Convention No. 102 and Recommendation No. 202. We also acknowledge the value of professional standards for governance and administration, including the ISSA guidelines for social security administration.

28. Building on the previous Declarations of BRICS Summits and the LEMM, as well as the 2030 Agenda for Sustainable Development, we, with the support of the ILO and the ISSA, are committed to deepening social security cooperation among ourselves, and with other countries. In this regard, we will harness the BRICS Social Security Cooperation Framework to tackle current and future challenges, and accelerate progress towards reaching our joint objectives, with specific emphasis on cooperation on the improvement of the social security system, social security agreements, social security administration and promoting international standards and guidelines.

Way Forward

29. We take note of the commitments made at the BRICS Summit held in Johannesburg from 25 to 27 July 2018 with a view to deepening cooperation and coordinating common voice at multilateral arenas between the Member Countries in order to promote development and strengthen global governance to jointly address our common challenges, utilising the BRICS Common Position on Governance in the Future of Work.

30. In this regard, the South African Working Implementation Plan proposal on previous commitments to date is endorsed. Member Countries are called upon to undertake and concretise our efforts by developing practical steps to ensure that the labour and employment stream is beneficial to citizens of our respective countries.

31. We thank our social partners for their valuable contributions in addressing labour and employment challenges, and we commit to strengthening tripartite social dialogue processes for advancing labour market development and improving labour market outcomes.

32. We express gratitude technical partners such as the International Labour Organisation (ILO) and the International Social Security Association (ISSA) for their contributions in supporting BRICS cooperation. We will continue our close cooperation with these and other international organisations.

33. Finally, we would like to show our sincerest appreciation to the South African Presidency for organising the Employment Working Group meeting at Mbombela in May, 2018 and the Labour and Employment Ministers' Meeting at Durban in August, 2018. We look forward to our next meeting under the Presidency of the Federative Republic of Brazil in 2019.

B.   Meeting of BRICS Labour and Employment Ministers: 27 Jul. 2017, Chongqing (CHN)

BRICS LABOUR AND EMPLOYMENT MINISTERS' DECLARATION
27 July 2017, Chongqing, China

Introduction

1.   We, the Ministers of Labour and Employment from the Federative Republic of Brazil, the Russian Federation, the Republic of India, the People's Republic of China and the Republic of South Africa, met in Chongqing on 26-27 July, for the third BRICS Labour and Employment Ministers' Meeting to strengthen intra-BRICS coordination, enhance information sharing, discuss and agree upon specific areas of cooperation in our endeavour to address labour, employment and social security challenges common to the BRICS countries.

2.   The BRICS countries have achieved progress in several labour and social areas while still facing a number of arduous tasks, including improving labour force participation rates, tackling persistent informality, and reducing inequality. At the same time, ongoing structural transformation is leading to strong employment creation in services and increased demand for high-skilled labour, raising both opportunities and challenges for BRICS labour markets.

3.   The 2030 Agenda for Sustainable Development sets ambitious social and labour market goals including ending poverty in all its forms and implementing universal social security systems. We are committed to its implementation collectively and nationally to promote sustained, inclusive and sustainable economic growth, full and productive employment and decent work for all.

4.   We recognize that Labour and Employment Ministers of BRICS countries can collectively play an important role to inject new impetus into deepening the BRICS partnership and opening up a brighter future under the theme and the cooperation priorities of the 2017 BRICS Summit presidency.

5.   In line with the theme of the 2017 BRICS Summit, we focus our discussions on issues of common interest to EWG with respect to governance in the future of work, skills development, social protection, and share best practices.

6.   The BRICS countries continue to focus on and share experiences in the areas of employment generation, skills development, formalization of labour markets and social protection. Following our agreements under the Indian Presidency, we discussed these issues this year, with an emphasis on their implications for the 2030 Agenda for Sustainable Development and the Future of Work.

7.   We recognize that the BRICS Employment Working Group (EWG) established during the Russian Presidency continues to provide an important mechanism for facilitating our joint deliberations on the common policy challenges. We have collaborated successfully in the International Labour Organization (ILO) Governing Body and the International Labour Conference on specific issues of common interest and we pledge to strengthen this collaboration to further promote common objectives in international fora.

Governance in the Future of Work

8.   The world of work has undergone profound transformations over the past several decades bringing opportunities and posing challenges for governance and attainment of decent work for all. We believe that the future of work will offer promising economic opportunities for BRICS, provided that the appropriate policies are harnessed to advance social progress and inclusive development.

9.   We need to proactively promote pro-employment development with innovation and entrepreneurship, establish a more reasonable and effective labour governance system, make

economic development and employment growth mutually reinforcing, continuously improve the employment quality and push forward the achievement of decent work and social justice.

10. The emerging new forms of employment is an important labour market trend calling for actions to address it. We stress the need to improve the governance of work including improving national labour law systems, strengthening labour dispute resolution mechanisms, reinforcing labour law compliance and enforcement systems and adapting social insurance systems to the new situation. We will contribute to the improvement of international labour standards and their implementation in line with the new changes that would affect world of work in future, taking into account the different national conditions of BRICS countries.

11. We recognize the significance of ongoing dialogue initiated by ILO on the future of work, and we have achieved synergy and common positions on these issues (Annex 1 "The BRICS Common Position on Governance in the Future of Work"). We will coordinate our actions in this global endeavour.

Skills for Development

12. We are resolved to achieve the 2030 Sustainable Development Goals on poverty alleviation as a considerable share of the BRICS countries populations remain in poverty. Skills development measures have huge potential in fostering inclusive growth, poverty alleviation and employability of women and men, including young people, older workers, job seekers, those at the risk of lay-offs, and people from poor rural and urban areas.

13. We therefore support measures for better access to vocational training, lifelong learning and the training that is relevant to the fast-changing demand of growing economies. These measures need to be part of comprehensive employment policy approaches that combine skills development with other policy measures. For our coordinated efforts and collective action, we adopt the BRICS Action Plan for Poverty Alleviation and Reduction through Skills (Annex 2).

14. Better quality and more relevant training requires coordination across ministries and sectors as well as systematic solutions for dialogue between the worlds of work and training. In this respect, we recognize the vital importance of demand-driven skills development strategies, based on forward-looking approaches and informed by labour market intelligence. We subscribe to the policy recommendations proposed by the G20 Initiative to Promote Quality Apprenticeship to further facilitate the Enterprise-based quality apprenticeship training and sectoral approaches accompanied by measures that improve the status of vocational training.

15. We also note the importance of fostering strong labour market information systems as a tool to identify priority areas for policy formulation and to enable monitoring of progress for our shared goal of poverty reduction. Ensuring comprehensive, timely and comparable labour market information across BRICS countries is critical in this respect.

Universal and Sustainable Social Security Systems

16. We recognize the important role of universal and sustainable social security systems, including social protection floors, for inclusive growth, decent and productive employment, gender equality and social inclusion. Despite significant progress in our countries, sizeable gaps in coverage and level of benefits as well as sustaining social security systems remain challenges for economic development and social justice. Furthermore these are likely to pose additional challenges in the future due to profound socio-demographic, economic and technological changes. It is particularly important to ensure adequate social security coverage for workers across different contractual arrangements including non-standard forms of employment, supporting the mobility of workers, complementing effective and efficient contributory social insurance schemes with non-contributory schemes, rationally set and adjust the benefit levels while maintaining adequacy of benefits, preserving and further reinforcing the financial basis of the social security systems, including social security funds, and adapting administrative procedures to facilitate compliance.

17. We stay committed to the 2030 Agenda for Sustainable Development through implementing comprehensive social security systems that are effective, equitable, economically sustainable to address the needs of our societies. In doing so, we are guided by international social security standards, which find expression in the ILO Convention No. 102 and Recommendation No. 202. We are also guided by professional standards for governance and administration, including the International Social Security Association (ISSA) guidelines for social security administration.

18. Consistent with the previous Declarations of BRICS Summits and BRICS Labour and Employment Ministers' Meetings, we commit to deepening social security cooperation among ourselves, and with other countries, with the support of the ILO and the ISSA. In this endeavour, we endorse the BRICS Social Security Cooperation Framework (Annex 3) which outlines principles, objectives, areas and methods of our cooperation. We believe the Framework would contribute to the future negotiation process on social security agreements and cooperation on social security administration in the BRICS countries. In relation to paragraph 26 of the Ufa Labour and Employment Ministers Declaration, we reaffirm the commitment to the development of a Memorandum of Understanding between our Ministries regarding cooperation in the social and labour sphere. This Framework will become a part of this Memorandum as soon as it is developed.

The BRICS Labour Research Network

19. Following our agreement during the Indian Presidency, we have taken steps to establish the BRICS Network of Labour Research Institutes, which aims to facilitate capacity building and information exchange, including good practices among BRICS countries. Reaffirming the importance of evidence-based research in social dialogue and policy decisions in our countries, we endorse the BRICS Network of Labour Research Institutes: Terms of Reference (Annex 4), which specify essential details of the Network and request the ILO's support for this.

20. We encourage the BRICS Network of Labour Research Institutes to develop cooperation with Entrepreneurship Research Centre on G20 Economies with a view to exchanging information and sharing best practices, such as promoting entrepreneurship, innovation and skills development.

The way forward

21. We will present this Declaration to the BRICS Summit in Xiamen for our leaders' consideration as they strive to deepen cooperation to promote development and strengthen global governance to jointly address our common challenges.

22. We thank our social partners for their valuable contributions in addressing labour and employment challenges, and we commit to strengthening tripartite social dialogue processes for advancing labour market development and improving labour market outcomes.

23. We thank the ILO, ISSA and national organizations for their contributions in supporting BRICS cooperation. We will continue our close cooperation with these and other international organizations.

24. We thank the Chinese Presidency for organizing the Employment Working Group meeting at Yuxi in April, 2017 and the Labour and Employment Ministers' Meeting at Chongqing in July, 2017. We look forward to our next meeting under the Presidency of South Africa.

Annex 1

The BRICS Common Position on Governance in the Future of Work

New trends such as globalization, technological transformation, demographic and climate changes are profoundly influencing the world of work. With some traditional jobs declining, informal employment continuously expanding and new forms of employment emerging, the BRICS countries need to develop collective plans of governance in the future of work in order to seize new opportunities and address emerging challenges.

With a view to improving the labour law system and international labour governance system, protecting labour rights and interests and making economic growth and decent work mutually reinforcing, the BRICS countries have adopted the following common position on governance in the future of work:

I.   Deal with the future opportunities and challenges in the world of work with employment as the priority objective of economic and social development

1.   Strengthen coordination between employment policy and macroeconomic policy and strive to achieve full and productive employment and decent work.

2.   Take advantage of the deeply integrated global industrialization and digitalisation, seize the opportunity of a new round of technological advances, make innovation as an important driving force for economic development and employment growth, encourage innovation and entrepreneurship and create more quality jobs.

II.   Improve the labour law system and law implementation mechanism in order to deal with the challenges brought by informal employment and new forms of employment

1.   With a focus on new forms of employment including non-standard employment and starting from the perspective of top-level system design and law implementation, make adjustments to labour benchmark systems, labour contract systems, social insurance and other parts of social protection systems.

2.   Continue to push forward the transition from the informal to the formal economy, strengthen policy support and supervision for small and micro enterprises, and provide equal protection for informal workers including but not limited to part-time workers, on-call workers, temporary workers and agency workers.

3.   In response to the new and future changes in the world of work, we commit to optimize the labour dispute resolution mechanism, innovate on the law enforcement concept and practices for labour inspection, adopt holistic approach to ensure full respect of the fundamental principles and rights at work.

III.   Strengthen cooperation among BRICS countries in terms of governance of the world of work and jointly improve the international labour governance system

1.   Take an active part in the ILO Standard Review Mechanism (SRM) process with a view to improve the international labour standards in line with the new changes in the future world of work and the different national conditions of BRICS countries.

2.   Encourage the multilateral and bilateral exchange and cooperation among the labour law implementation agencies in BRICS countries, and explore the establishment of information communication and law enforcement cooperation system.

3.   Utilize the BRICS research institutes network, carry out research cooperation, coordinate positions, and forge new consensus and plans on the governance in the future of work.

Annex 2

The BRICS Action Plan for Poverty Alleviation and Reduction through Skills

The 2030 Agenda for Sustainable Development sets an important target to "end poverty in all its forms everywhere". Today, there are still over 800 million people in the world who are living under the poverty line and there is still a heavy task and a long way to go to reduce poverty around the globe. With large populations and a sizeable share of the world's poor, the BRICS countries have set national priority to eradicate poverty in the near future. Skills development is a critical part of national development strategies to eliminate poverty. The BRICS countries agree to take the following actions to improve the skills level and employability of individuals especially the poor through vocational training in order to achieve poverty reduction and elimination.

I. Policy recommendation

In line with their national situations and priorities, BRICS countries formulate and implement relevant policies and measures to provide assistance for vulnerable groups including people in poor areas, the urban poor and laid-off workers from sunset industries. This is done in order to help them improve their skills and employability in an effective and efficient manner with a view to achieving stable employment in the near future. Policies and measures include but are not limited to the following aspects:

1. Integrate groups including the poor into the overall national plan for vocational training and set up training plans and programs according to the characteristics and needs of various groups.

2. Establish and improve lifelong vocational training and learning system for individuals of varying employment status and different career development stages.

3. Provide vocational training allowances or free training for individuals who participate in vocational training, especially people from poor areas, the urban poor and laid-off workers from sunset industries.

4. Encourage training providers to strengthen research on skill needs of various jobs, develop training courses, enrich training curricula and expand the coverage of vocational training services through new technologies and other innovative services to provide more flexible and convenient training modalities for the general public especially people from poor areas and laid-off workers from sunset industries.

5. Strengthen cooperation between governments, sectors and enterprises to conduct joint research and establish regional and sectoral strategies in order to improve the capacity of the economy to absorb unemployed people. Encourage enterprises especially those with difficulties in the process of restructuring to carry out various forms of skills upgrading training or new skills training in order to promote stable employment or re-employment in new areas.

6. Promote high-quality apprenticeship systems and encourage enterprises to provide training after recruitment and provide sound working conditions for apprentices including proper wages, labour contracts and social security as well as occupational health and safety.

II. Implementation modalities

1. Under the framework of the action plan, each country may, in line with their respective national situations, integrate vocational training into national employment plans, formulate concrete policies and measures and provide progress reports through BRICS Network of Labour Research Institutes.

2. In line with national situations and priorities, strengthen cooperation with stakeholders in the process of implementing the action plan for poverty alleviation and reduction through skills development, including cooperation between relevant government agencies, social partners, vocational training providers, economic sectors and enterprises.

3. Explore and establish the BRICS vocational training providers alliance, carry out mutual visits of trainers and trainees, exchange experiences in terms of curriculum design, teaching methods, cooperation between schools and enterprises.

Annex 3

BRICS Social Security Cooperation Framework

I. Background

1. Promoting universal social security coverage has become an important priority for all national governments. Goal 1.3 of the 2030 Agenda for Sustainable Development requires all countries to "implement nationally appropriate social protection systems and measures for all, including floors, and by 2030 achieve substantial coverage of the poor and the vulnerable". The 2012 Social Protection Floors Recommendation (No. 202) of ILO, along with other Conventions and Recommendations, provides guidance to the member states in building comprehensive social security systems by prioritizing the establishment of social protection floors to guarantee access for all in need to at least a basic level of social security. ISSA has formulated a series of ISSA Guidelines based on internationally recognized standards and good practices in core areas of social security administration which play an important role in facilitating the implementation of various laws and policy measures for ensuring progress towards the realization of national and international objectives.

2. The Declaration of the BRICS Labour and Employment Ministerial Meeting held in Ufa in January 2016 emphasized on the intensification of social protection for vulnerable groups and unemployed people, inclusion of new-type or non-standard workers into the social protection and integration of continuous expansion of basic social protection into the cooperation agenda of the BRICS countries. The Goa BRICS Summit Declaration in October 2016 proposed to explore the possibility of signing bilateral social security agreements among the BRICS countries, encouraging closer cooperation on social security within the group. The

2016 G20 Labour and Employment Ministerial Meeting held in Beijing also put forward a policy recommendation of promoting a fairer and more sustainable social protection system.

3. This cooperation framework is designed to implement the requirements posed by the Declarations of previous BRICS Summits and the commitments of the Declarations of Labour and Employment Ministerial Meetings, which provide guidance for the BRICS countries to deepen coordination and cooperation in the field of social security.

II. Principles

1. In order to achieve mutually beneficial outcomes, this cooperation framework shall operate according to the principles of equality, openness, efficiency, mutual trust and benefit as well as consensus built upon consultation.

2. This cooperation framework is pragmatic, open-ended and progressive. Fields of cooperation and concrete plans may be adjusted and enriched in line with the development situation and change of focus in each country, and determined through discussions in the BRICS Labour and Employment Ministerial Meetings.

III. Objectives

1. Through bilateral and multilateral exchanges and cooperation, promote the reform and improvement of social security systems in the BRICS countries, expand social security coverage and enhance the sustainability of social security so as to adapt to the ever evolving national and international environment.

2. Promote discussion on the signing of bilateral social security agreements between the BRICS countries.

3. Encourage the BRICS countries to establish a liaison mechanism among the social security administrative agencies to carry out case-based assistance and share information and experiences,

so as to promote the improvement of the management and service capacity of administrative agencies and realize good governance and effectively achieve policy objectives.

IV. Fields of Cooperation

1. Cooperation on the improvement of social security system

(i). Leverage the BRICS Network of Labour Research Institutes to carry out joint research on the social security systems of the BRICS countries and exchange on the ways of expanding social security coverage, innovating on management and service modalities and promoting the sustainable development of social security.

(ii). Conduct communication and exchange on the challenges and experiences of the BRICS countries with a view to improve social security systems, expand social security coverage and enhance system sustainability through activities including seminars, mutual visits and personnel training.

2. Cooperation on social security agreements

(i). Carry out exchanges among the BRICS countries on employment and social security for cross-border population flows and, in line with respective work priorities, initiate technical consultation on social security agreements between the BRICS countries and explore the feasibility of launching formal negotiations in this regard.

(ii). Exchange information on practices regarding social security agreements both within and beyond the BRICS countries, and encourage the BRICS countries to initiate consultations on social security agreements in due course.

3. Cooperation on social security administration

(i). Establish a liaison mechanism among the social security administrative agencies in the BRICS countries to be hosted by the ISSA in collaboration with the ILO and identify the liaison agency, contact person and other relevant information in order to facilitate the communication channels.

(ii). Encourage the case-based assistance among social security administrative agencies, especially in terms of social insurance issues.

(iii). Exchange and share the best practices on management and services of administrative agencies through mutual visits and training activities in order to innovate on the modalities of providing services and improve the social security administration capacity.

(iv). Strengthen cooperation among social security training providers in the BRICS countries.

4. Cooperation in promoting international standards and guidelines

(i). In carrying out joint activities under this cooperation framework, give due consideration to promoting the ratification and application of the relevant ILO Conventions and Recommendations on social security as well as the implementation of the ISSA guidelines for social security administration.

(ii). Strengthen cooperation with the ILO and the ISSA, taking into consideration the national situation and the social security development status of the BRICS countries, and push forward the efforts of the BRICS countries through technical consultations, side-events during the International Labour Conferences, BRICS sessions during the World Social Security Forum, seminars and training courses, etc.

5. Implementation Mechanism

Establish a virtual liaison office for social security cooperation among the BRICS countries to be hosted by the ISSA in collaboration with the ILO and this will be a concrete mechanism for implementation of this framework. The virtual liaison office will work under the guidance and management of the BRICS Employment Working Group and will be responsible for drafting, implementing and monitoring the annual action plans. It will be made up of the officers designated by the Ministers in charge of labour, employment and social security affairs in the BRICS countries, as well as representatives from international organizations such as the ILO and ISSA.

Annex 4

BRICS Network of Labour Research Institutes

Terms of Reference

Background

1.   BRICS countries are major emerging economies representing 43% of the world's population and contributing 37% to global GDP and accounting for 17% of world trade.

2.   BRICS Labour and Employment Ministers met in Geneva and New Delhi in June and September of 2016 respectively and discussed issues of inclusive development, including employment creation, social security and formalization, and proposed to establish a Network of Labour Research Institutes. The commitment is aptly captured in the New Delhi Declaration of the BRICS Labour and Employment Ministers.

3.   The establishment of the BRICS Network of Labour Research Institutes aims to realize the outcome of the previous BRICS Labour and Employment Ministers' Meetings. Its main objective is to deepen practical cooperation among BRICS countries, especially focusing on the common challenges of labour and employment faced by BRICS countries and develop possible solutions in order to achieve inclusive growth.

Mandate of the Network

4.   Conduct studies and put forward recommendations to BRICS Employment Working Group on how to address the current and emerging labour, employment and social security issues to accomplish strong, sustainable and inclusive growth.

5.   Carry out research on important issues on the future of work.

6.   Undertake research programmes on decent work goals and identify key strategies to push forward the implementation of the 2030 Agenda for Sustainable Development.

Organization and Structure of the Network

7.   The leading research institute of the BRICS Presidency acts as the rotating coordinator of the BRICS Network of Labour Research Institute.

8.   The leading research institute of BRICS Network of Labour Research Institutes is the major research institute of BRICS countries in the field of labour and employment and is recommended by each BRICS country and invites the participation of relevant universities, research institutes and social partners of the country.

9.   The leading research institutes of BRICS Network of Labour Research Institutes are National Labour Market Observatory of the Ministry of Labour, Brazil, All-Russia Research Institute for Labor of the Ministry of Labor and Social Protection of the Russian Federation, V.V. Giri National Labour Institute of Ministry of Labour & Employment, India, Chinese Academy of Labour and Social Security of Ministry of Human Resources and Social Security, China and the University of Fort Hare, Republic of South Africa. Experts from relevant international organizations would be invited to join the Network. Each country may change the leading research institute during the process of the network operation and inform the rotating coordinator and Employment Working Group accordingly.

10.   The major responsibilities of the rotating coordinator of the network are: proposing the annual research plan or suggested revisions to the research plan; organizing meetings with the participation of all member institutes; drafting and submitting reports to the Ministers' Meeting after consideration by each member and review by the meeting of the working group.

11.   According to the research plan, the leading research institutes are responsible for organizing the relevant institutes in their respective countries to participate in joint research and share research

outcome, participating in the relevant meetings convened by the rotating coordinator, reviewing and improving the reports that are to be submitted to the Ministers' Meeting.

Working mechanism

12. A common virtual platform will be established for communication purposes. Each leading institute appoints a focal contact person and the platform would be maintained by the person appointed by the rotating coordinator.

13. As required by the actual needs of the work to be undertaken, a meeting of the Network of Labour Research Institutes may be convened in parallel with the meeting of the working group for the BRICS Labour and Employment Ministers' Meeting.

14. These Terms of Reference, especially the research priorities may be subject to revisions and such revisions should be submitted to the Employment Working Group for review and adoption.

Research priorities in the near future

15. With respect to the ILO Centenary Initiative on the Future of Work, the research priorities for the year of 2017 are to carry out research on new forms of employment and entrepreneurship, and put forward policy proposals concerning employment and social security in the context of the current status of economy and labour governance systems.

16. In future, one major research field will be defined for each year and proposed by the rotating coordinator and the research will be organized and implemented following the consensus of the EWG meeting. According to the actual situation of BRICS countries, the research priorities for the near future could be as follows:

(1) The mutual recognition of occupational qualification certificates among BRICS countries: the feasibility of mutual recognition and the types of occupational qualification certificates to be mutually recognized.

(2) Bilateral social security agreements: the feasibility of signing bilateral social security agreements among BRICS countries.

(3) The BRICS action plan for poverty alleviation through skills: the outcome of poverty alleviation through skills development of each country and share experiences and best practices including on labour market demand-driven skills development.

(4) Youth employment: the challenges and opportunities of youth employment in BRICS countries and possible policy interventions.

(5) The impact of ageing society on employment and social security: employment and social security in the context of ageing in BRICS.

(6) Assessing and comparing labour market information systems.

(7) Other research priorities proposed by BRICS Labour and Employment Ministers' Meeting and the EWG meeting.

C.   Meeting of BRICS Labour and Employment Ministers: 27-28 Sep. 2016, New Delhi (IND)

BRICS LABOUR AND EMPLOYMENT MINISTERS' DECLARATION
Employment Generation, Social Protection for All and Transition from Informality to Formality
September 2016, New Delhi

Introduction

1.   We, the Ministers of Labour and Employment from the Federative Republic of Brazil, the Russian Federation, the Republic of India, the People's Republic of China and the Republic of South Africa, met at New Delhi, India, on September 27-28, 2016, for the Second BRICS Labour and Employment Ministers' Meeting to strengthen intra-BRICS coordination, enhance information sharing, discuss and agree upon specific areas of cooperation in our endeavor to address labour and employment challenges faced commonly by BRICS member states.

2.   Addressing labour, employment and social issues is imperative for fostering strong, sustainable and inclusive growth. We recognize that the constitution of the BRICS Employment Working Group (BEWG) initiated by the Russian Presidency is an important step for facilitating focused deliberations on BRICS labour and employment issues and achieving the broad objectives of quality and inclusive employment, formalization of labour markets, and exchange of labour market related information.

3.   We have collaborated successfully in the ILO Governing Body and International Labour Conference on specific issues of common interest and we pledge to strengthen this collaboration to further promote common objectives at other international fora.

4.   We recall our meeting hosted by India on the sidelines of the International Labour Conference in June 2016 where we discussed issues of common interest to the group such as employment generation, small and medium enterprises (SMEs), transition to formality, and sharing of good practices.

5.   We acknowledge the importance of global supply chains and its contribution to job creation. We recognize current challenges in addressing labour issues in global supply chains. As a group we will participate in the discussions on global supply chain and endeavour to evolve our approach towards the new policy options.

6.   As key operational areas, the BRICS member states will focus on employment generation, formalization of labour markets and social protection.

Employment Generation

7.   Quality employment plays a central role in ensuring sustainable development and is at the core of the 2030 Development Agenda. In promoting inclusion and greater equality in the labour market, a top priority for BRICS member states is the generation of adequate decent and productive job opportunities, fair wages and adequate social protection systems for all, including floors. This, will in turn help in tackling poverty and lead to sustainable growth.

8.   Technological revolution and structural changes require adequate labour resources. We recognize the importance of addressing labour mobility issues, which can bring potential benefits to our economies. We will focus our analyses at the institutional arrangements and social networks facilitating labour mobility and on forecasting of the labour market needs and the labour force availability.

9.   We resolve to assist each other in sharing best practices in implementing policies and programmes that encourage innovation and entrepreneurship for employment generation. We

intend to strengthen our public employment services to help our labour force, particularly the youth to find employment opportunities. We are also committed to strengthening labour market information systems based on each other's experience.

10. We resolve to improve the employability of our workforce through modernization of skills development systems and life-long learning, which allows workers to remain relevant in the world of work environment that is changing fast due to technological revolution. We believe that expanding and improving education and formal training is of paramount importance to tap the benefits of innovation and to increase productivity, which shall lead to decent jobs.

Formalization of Labour Markets

11. Informality in the labour market remains a big challenge for all BRICS member states. Informality is often linked to low income jobs, lack of social protection and insufficient access to basic services. Recognizing the multiple issues in our national labour markets context, we are committed to tackling both the existing as well as emerging forms of informality. Consistent with the objectives of the ILO Recommendation No.204, we aim at improving the livelihood of workers engaged in the informal economy and facilitating their transition to the formal economy, while at the same time enhancing the productivity and competitiveness of enterprises.

12. We encourage the adoption of measures to enhance employability of workers in the informal economy through expanding social security, skilling and re-skilling of the workforce and adopting amongst others of a regulatory environment, which promotes formalization through easier compliance and adequate safeguards for labour rights.

13. We acknowledge various innovative approaches that have been implemented in BRICS member states aimed at reducing informality and facilitating the transition of workers to formal markets and access to social protection and we pledge to continue our efforts on implementing such actions.

Social Protection

14. We recognize that a crucial way in which governments can positively influence labour market outcomes and reduce exclusion and poverty is by providing social protection to its population. Those who work, and those who are too young or old or unable to work, require protection from idiosyncratic and economy-wide shocks and unanticipated events.

15. We recognize the innovative capacity of our nations in responding to their particular national circumstances and evolving social protection systems that aim to establish the balance between work-incentives, improving human capital and income protection. We resolve to undertake policy measures in a comprehensive manner, with particular attention to including those in the informal economy and outside the scope of the existing schemes.

16. We support designing and implementation of comprehensive social security systems that are effective, equitable, economically sustainable and address the needs of the society. We will encourage bi-lateral social security agreements amongst the BRICS member states and work towards developing a general framework for cooperation.

Way Forward

17. We reiterate our commitment, in line with the Sustainable Development Goals to continue to promote inclusive and sustainable growth, employment and decent work for all with a view to end poverty in all its forms in BRICS member states by 2030. In doing this, we acknowledge all the current initiatives taken including commitment towards ensuring decent work for all, formalization of the informal economy and the extension of social protection.

18. We are committed to take steps to establish a network of lead labour research and training institutions in BRICS member states for undertaking joint research and training activities, capacity

building of various stakeholders and exchange of information in areas of expertise in cooperation with the ILO.

19. We thank our social partners for their inputs in addressing labour and employment challenges. We intend to strengthen our tripartite social dialogue processes for advancing labour market development and promotion of stronger labour market outcomes.

20. We recognise the importance of evidence based research in informing our policy decisions on labour and employment issues and acknowledge the contributions of ILO, the International Social Security Association (ISSA) and national organizations in supporting BRICS co-operation in these areas. We will continue our close cooperation with these and other international organizations.

21. We thank the Indian Presidency for holding the first formal BEWG at Hyderabad, India, on July 27-28, 2016. We further express our appreciation to the Indian leadership in organizing the Labour and Employment Ministerial Meeting at the sidelines of ILC, Geneva in June 2016, and the Second Labour and Employment Ministerial meeting at New Delhi, India. We look forward to our next meeting under the Presidency of the People's Republic of China.

D.   Meeting of BRICS Labour and Employment Ministers: 9 Jun. 2016, Geneva (CHE)

JOINT STATEMENT OF THE BRICS MEMBER STATES ON LABOUR AND EMPLOYMENT
On the sidelines of the 105th International Labour Conference June 9, 2016, Geneva

1.   We the BRICS countries, represented by Labour and Employment Ministers and Heads of Delegation of Brazil, Russia, India, China and South Africa, met on 9th June 2016 on the margins of the 105th session of the International Labour Conference in Geneva, Switzerland.

2.   We reconfirm our conviction that labour and employment policies are critical to foster strong, sustainable and inclusive growth, thus reiterate our commitment to achieve decent work and employment for all as envisaged in the 2030 Agenda for Sustainable Development.

3.   We recall the deliberations in the first BRICS Labour and Employment Ministers' and Social Partner's Meeting under Russian Presidency in Ufa, Russia in January 2016 and firmly believe that strengthening intra-BRICS dialogue and the exchange of experience and information on labour & employment issues is an important step forward in our long-term cooperation for the benefit of our peoples and the international community.

4.   We concur that innovation and job creation, skills development, and social protection constitute the three pillars of inclusive, quality and job rich economic growth. We agree to work on these through an integrated and comprehensive and inclusive policy approach, sharing experiences and developing stakeholders cooperation.

5.   We remain concerned by the existing levels of informality in the labour market and the lack of Decent Work therein. Informality affects segments of workforce, such as women, youth and other vulnerable and marginalised - groups more than others. We reiterate our commitment to strengthen our policy response to the transition from informality to formality taking into account our national contexts and capability.

6.   Meeting new requirements imposed on our labour markets by technological revolution, development of digital economy and innovations, and mitigating their possible negative employment related impacts, facilitating labour skills development and labour mobility are serious challenges for achieving inclusive growth and sustainable development. We reaffirm our commitment to encourage domestic industry and entrepreneurship including Small and Medium Enterprises, to invest in quality job creation and social protection of workers and promote labour mobility.

7.   We recognize the important role of social dialogue and intend to strengthen the cooperation with social partners, in order to achieve stronger labour market outcomes.

8.   We welcome the focus of the World of Work Summit at the 105th International Labour Conference on 'Decent Jobs for Youth' and recognize the need for concerted efforts to impart youth with adequate skills required and necessary for productive jobs.

9.   We believe that informed policy discourse is critical to economic growth and acknowledge the contribution by ILO in enriching our discussions in BRICS.

10. We welcome and support the theme of the G20 Labour and Employment Ministerial Meeting to be held in July 2016 under Chinese Presidency and commit ourselves to strengthen our coordination on issues like promoting Entrepreneurship and Social Security, which are of common interest to us.

11. BRICS countries represent the changing face of labour market. We reiterate our commitment to work more closely in the area of labour and employment and realign our policy tools to the emerging economic & labour market needs.

E.   Meeting of BRICS Labour and Employment Ministers: 26 Jan. 2016, Ufa (RUS)

BRICS LABOUR AND EMPLOYMENT MINISTERS DECLARATION
Quality Jobs and Inclusive Employment Policies

Introduction

1.   We, the Ministers of Labour and Employment from the Federative Republic of Brazil, the Russian Federation, the Republic of India, the People's Republic of China and the Republic of South Africa, met in Ufa, Russian Federation, on 25-26 of January, 2016 at the first BRICS Labour and Employment Ministers meeting to discuss new areas of cooperation in labour and employment, social security and social inclusion, public policies.

2.   Labour and employment policies are of critical importance to foster strong, sustainable and inclusive growth. We consider the expansion of BRICS coordination and cooperation on promotion of quality and inclusive employment, strengthening intra- BRICS dialogue and the exchange of experiences and information on labour and employment issues, social inclusion is an important step forward in our long-term cooperation for the benefit of our peoples and the international community.

3.   We acknowledge the essential role of social dialogue and the importance of collective bargaining, so we welcome the contribution of social partners to the design and implementation of labour and employment policies. We consider the tripartite model of addressing labour and employment issues as efficient and effective as it helps to enrich our engagements and conclusions.

4.   We will further enhance cooperation with international organizations (ILO, World Bank, ISSA and others) to address specific issues of common interest and provide support in working out of coordinated BRICS Strategy to promote decent work.

Quality and inclusive Employment

5.   Quality job creation, based on introduction of new technologies and increasing of labour productivity, skills development, and social protection comprise three pillars, which contribute to inclusiveness of labour market and give vulnerable groups new chances for a decent living. We will strive to achieve the balance between these pillars based on integrative and comprehensive policy approaches, sharing experience, development of stakeholders cooperation, creation of a business friendly environment, and public-private partnerships.

6.   We agree to focus our policies on increasing quality and inclusive employment through facilitation of:
   - Modernization of enterprises and sectors of economy and introduction of new technologies aimed at creating employment opportunities;
   - Development of occupational standards and qualifications;
   - Increasing quality of vocational education and training of workers in line with occupational standards and qualifications that consider current and future requirements of business;
   - Labour mobility;
   - Job search, collection and dissemination of information on job opportunities, especially on modernized productive jobs;
   - Development of regulations covering new or non-standard forms of work that ensures full respect for workers' rights and access to social protection;
   - Strengthening social protection of vulnerable groups and protection of the unemployed looking for job to prevent social exclusion or marginalization from decent work opportunities.

7. We recognize the importance of the implementation of a Decent Work Agenda within the BRICS countries.

Formalization of Labour Markets

8. Formalization of labour markets is a global priority and a priority for BRICS countries. Informality constrains our productivity, potential economic growth and efforts to improve the wellbeing of our people. Strategies to facilitate the transition to formality could include incentivizing employers and supporting workers who seek employment in the formal economy and strengthening labour inspection and enforcement.

9. We acknowledge the efforts made to date and we are determined to put greater emphasis on formalization of our labour markets. We welcome the initiative of the Russian Chairpersonship to develop a well-balanced medium- term Strategy of labour markets formalization as informed by the Recommendation on Transition from the Informal to the Formal Economy (No. 204) adopted by the 104th International Labour Conference in June, 2015.

10. We consider ILO Recommendation No.204 to be an important instrument providing guidance to States on how to help workers and economic units to formalize their activity, as one of the means for promoting decent work and achieving inclusive development.

11. We agree to follow the ILO Recommendation No. 204 to pursue a threefold objective in their policies addressing informality; (1) to facilitate the transition of workers and economic units from the informal to formal economy, while respecting workers' fundamental rights and ensuring opportunities for income security, livelihoods and entrepreneurship; (2) to promote the creation, preservation and sustainability of enterprises and decent jobs in the formal economy and the coherence of macroeconomic, employment, social protection and other social policies; and (3) to prevent the informalization of formal economy.

12. We will use a set of integrated policies that work at both the macroeconomic, financial and labour market levels to reduce labour market informality and create quality jobs in the formal sector of the economy. Integrated approaches offer strong potential dividends for meeting the growth and employment goals of the BRICS.

13. We welcome a special emphasis made on such important elements as inclusion of business-enhancing measures within relevant strategies, strengthening of the capacities of social partners, perfecting of legislation, adaptation of diverse strategies according to national circumstances. We reiterate our commitment to implement policies to promote the creation of quality and productive jobs, including investment incentives, creation of business friendly environment, open access to financial resources. Social dialogue plays an important role in these processes.

14. The introduction of new technologies and increase of job productivity is an important objective. It is necessary to ensure that the new technologies and increased productivity become the basis for job rich growth and contribute to the improvement of people's quality of life and to the respect of decent work.

15. Challenges and opportunities for creating quality jobs in formal sectors and increasing their availability for the job seekers differ by country. Nevertheless, we agree that the following issues constitute the basis for development of high quality formal jobs and increase of formal employment:

- Integration of policies that promote job creation and income generation opportunities in the formal economy
- Creation of formal employment opportunities through enterprise modernization and increase of productivity,
- Development of labour market infrastructure,
- Investing in skills that meet the demands of the formal economy,

- Strengthening of labour inspection,
- Strengthening of occupational safety and health,
- Ensuring the fulfillment of workers rights and protection,
- Extension of adequate social protection to all workers.

16. We see the consolidation of measures aimed at promotion of quality employment with those aimed at formalization of labour markets as a path to create conditions and incentives for the transition to the formal economy and job and income rich growth.

Labour and Employment Information Exchange

17. Information exchange is one of the BRICS priorities. We intend to share labour and employment information related to job creation, transition from informality to formality, labour productivity, youth and women employment, and other topics we may decide.

18. We welcome the inclusion of social- and labour-related Sustainable Development Goals (SDGs) with a range of ambitious targets and results to be achieved by the international community in the social and labour and employment sphere. We strongly support these global goals that reflect the priorities of our governments in the social and labour sphere. We are ready to undertake comprehensive measures to achieve these ambitious targets recognizing that the 2030 Agenda for Sustainable Development is applicable to all, taking into account different national realities, capacities and levels of development and respecting national policies and priorities. The First meeting of BRICS Ministers of Labour and Employment held in Russia in January 2016 further strengthens BRICS cooperation in the Labour and Employment area. Such SDG elements as promoting decent work and employment, extension of universal social protection floors as well as formalization of economy are expected to be considered under the BRICS agenda.

19. We commit to identify a set of labour-related harmonized indicators and work along with the BRICS Statistical Offices, which are engaged in the collection and publications of data, to enable us to track and reflect the progress made in implementing our employment agenda.

20. We will use the BRICS virtual secretariat, available at: http://infobrics.org/, a free resource available in the public domain for coverage of the labour and employment related activities undertaken by BRICS countries.

21. We welcome the initiative of the Russian Chairpersonship on creation of an information resource for social and labour issues of BRICS member-states, which will focus on the development of human resources, including development of modern efficient requirements to skills and qualifications.

Next Steps

22. We will present for the Leaders' consideration our Declaration, and recommend the Leaders to support our commitment to promote quality and inclusive employment, to develop integrated strategies for labour market formalization, informed by the ILO Recommendation 204 and to create a BRICS Labour and Employment information exchange system. We remain committed to implementing effective labour market strategies necessary to strengthen growth and job creation.

23. We agree to continue engaging in dialogue focusing on labour and employment related issues and propose to our Leaders that we convene BRICS labour and employment ministerial meetings on a regular basis.

24. We commit to facilitate the integration of labour market and employment policies with economic, financial, education, and health policies and this could be realized by Joint Inter-Ministerial working group meetings.

25. In recognition of the on-going labour, employment and social inclusion challenges, we recommend that an Employment Working Group be established. The Working Group will explore

and prepare proposals on specific areas of cooperation to address labour market challenges, enhance information sharing and development of labour and employment policies. The Group will report annually to Ministers on progress in tackling these challenges, with an initial focus on promoting coherence among the BRICS policy tracks and developing actions to address issues such as supporting growth, labour markets formalization, labour participation, decreasing unemployment and reducing inequality. We ask the Working Group to focus on preparation of a Strategy of Labour Markets Formalization for our consideration.

26. We welcome the Russian initiative to work out a draft Memorandum of Understanding between our Ministries regarding cooperation in the social and labour sphere as it will serve as a basis for further mutual collaboration of our Ministries.

27. We intend to strengthen our tripartite dialogue format for advancing labour market development and promotion of stronger labour market outcomes. We are grateful for the expertise provided by the ILO, ISSA, World Bank and other international organizations and will continue our cooperation with them.

28. We thank Russia's Chairpersonship for its leadership in organization of the first meeting of the Ministers of Labour and Employment and look forward to our next meeting under the Chairpersonship of the Republic of India.

III.8.   BRICS Education Ministers

A.   6th Meeting of BRICS Education Ministers: 10 Jul. 2018, Cape Town (ZAF)

CAPE TOWN DECLARATION ON EDUCATION AND TRAINING
THE 6TH BRICS EDUCATION MINISTERS MEETING

We, the BRICS Ministers of Education and assigned representatives of the Federative Republic of Brazil, the Russian Federation, the Republic of India, the People's Republic of China, and the Republic of South Africa, having met in Cape Town, the Republic of South Africa on 9 and 10 July 2018 respectively to discuss reforms, development, collaboration and exchanges on education among BRICS countries, hereby:

Recall the roadmap for BRICS education collaboration outlined by the Ministers at their inaugural meeting in November 2013, the Brasilia Declaration of 02 March 2015, the BRICS Moscow Declaration of 18 November 2015, the New Delhi Declaration of 30 September 2016, and the Beijing Declaration of 05 July 2017;

Acknowledge afresh, the significant contribution of education towards the overall development goals of BRICS;

Welcome the initiatives of BRICS Member States to promote a transformative education agenda that actively addresses 21st century challenges and opportunities, especially regarding the technological changes commonly known as the fourth industrial revolution;

Recognise that access to education and training in all BRICS Member States is expanding rapidly, and that all Member States face common challenges in promoting educational equity, fostering quality and inclusive education;

Welcome the sharing of good practices and the promotion of exchange of information among BRICS Member States on the recognition of qualifications, workplace-based learning, technical and vocational education and training, digitisation to improve education and training, as well as on university partnerships; and

To ensure coordination and deeper cooperation among the Member States, hereby declare to:

1.   Reaffirm our commitment to the United Nations Sustainable Development Goal 4 (SDG 4), which aims to "Ensure inclusive and equitable quality education and promote life-long learning opportunities for all" that was set within the 2030 Agenda for Sustainable Development and the SDG 4 - Education 2030 Framework for Action.

2.   Strengthen collaboration in Technical and Vocational Education and Training (TVET) among BRICS Member States through:

2.1. Revitalising the working group on TVET by each Member State identifying a focal point to develop a programme of action for TVET collaboration;

2.2. Facilitating the sharing of information and frameworks about TVET educator development, TVET qualifications and TVET curricula, including the development of open online courses among BRICS Member States;

2.3. Enabling the TVET collaboration, Brazil will:

2.3.1. Host a seminar to showcase innovation among TVET institutions in BRICS Member States; and

2.3.2. Encourage the articulation of joint TVET initiatives with the BRICS Business Council (BRICS Skills Development Working Group) and the BRICS Labour and Employment Ministers Meeting (BRICS Labour Employment Working Group) and the expansion of opportunities for workplace-based learning (WBL).

3. Support the establishment of a coordinating process for the BRICS Network University. Russia has agreed to put together a proposal for the establishment of such a process to be presented at the IGB meeting to be held in October 2018.

4. Support an initiative by South Africa to develop a proposal on a BRICS Network University doctoral programme.

5. Encourage international thematic groups of the BRICS Network University to work upon harmonization of the educational quality standards in the areas of their expertise.

6. Support the establishment of a working group to develop a draft-referencing framework on quality assurance, accreditation and recognition of qualifications, which will enable improved learning and student mobility across BRICS Member States.

7. Share information on existing funding mechanisms within the BRICS Member States that can be used to leverage cooperation.

8. Encourage the BRICS Network University, through the ITGs, to actively pursue research collaboration on the fourth industrial revolution.

9. Encourage the BRICS Network University and BRICS University League to develop proposals on educator and student mobility.

10. Support an initiative by India to develop a proposal on digitisation to improve education and training, as well as policy in this area. This would include a comparative study of digital learning (e-learning) across schools, colleges and universities in BRICS Member States, with a view to, inter alia, learning and applying lessons from good practices.

11. Promote values and ethical practices in education.

12. Jointly explore the possibility of granting BRICS scholarships to students from BRICS Member States to pursue higher studies in each other's countries. This will consolidate BRICS people to people ties and mutual learning.

13. Ensure that the above programmes and projects are coordinated by relevant BRICS senior education officials and focal points assigned by their Ministries.

14. Encourage participation in the fourth general BRICS Network University Conference to be held in Brazil in 2019 and the conference "Education and World Cities" in May 2019 in St. Petersburg, Russia.

The Federative Republic of Brazil, the Russian Federation, the Republic of India, and the People's Republic of China extend their appreciation to the government of the Republic of South Africa for hosting the 6th BRICS Education Ministers Meeting.

The English version of this Declaration has been signed on July 10, 2018 in Cape Town. This Declaration has been executed in five (5) duplicate originals and all originals shall be equally valid.

FEDERATIVE REPUBLIC OF BRAZIL

RUSSIAN FEDERATION

REPUBLIC OF INDIA

PEOPLE'S REPUBLIC OF CHINA

REPUBLIC OF SOUTH AFRICA

B.   5th Meeting of BRICS Education Ministers: 5 Jul. 2017, Beijing (CHN)

BEIJING DECLARATION ON EDUCATION
5TH MEETING OF BRICS MINISTERS OF EDUCATION
Beijing, July 5, 2017

We, the BRICS Ministers of Education and assigned representatives of the Federative Republic of Brazil, the Russian Federation, the Republic of India, the People's Republic of China, and the Republic of South Africa,

Having met in Beijing, the People's Republic of China on July 4th and 5th, 2017 to discuss education reforms, approaches to promoting equity in education and fostering quality education, strengthening BRICS collaboration in the field of education, and exchange of students and scholars and teaching faculty among BRICS Member States;

Recalling Brasilia Declaration on March 2nd, 2015, Moscow Declaration on November 18th, 2015 and New Delhi Declaration on September 30th, 2016;

Committed to the UN Sustainable Development Goal 4 (SDG4)-Education 2030 which aims to "Ensure inclusive and equitable quality education and promote life-long learning opportunities for all" that was set within The 2030 Agenda for Sustainable Development;

Recognizing the significance of collaboration in the field of education for enhancing the overall partnership among BRICS Member States and enhancing people to people exchanges to a higher level;

Realizing that the scale of education development in BRICS Member States is expanding rapidly, and that all Member States face common challenges in promoting educational equity, accessibility and in improving the quality of education;

Considering that higher education contributes to the development of high-level human resources and intellectual support for the economic and social development, studies of BRICS Member States will enhance the mutual understanding between each Member State; and

Recognizing that the mobility of faculty and students, and sharing of information among the Member States is of great importance for the implementation of the consensus arrived at the Meetings of BRICS Ministers of Education;

For ensuring coordinated and deeper cooperation among the Member States, hereby declare to:

1.   Reiterate support for the BRICS Network University (NU) to collaborate in the fields of education, research and innovation. Encourage universities to participate in the BRICS University League.

2.   Increase cultural cooperation through language education and multilingualism to promote mutual understanding of the history and culture of BRICS Member States.

3.   Undertake initiatives to promote professionalization of academics in higher education through the BRICS Network University as a focus of future education development.

4.   Encourage more teachers and educational administrators to learn from experiences of other countries in improving teacher quality and performance, and promoting the development of education through international exchanges.

5.   Strengthen cooperation in the field of Technical and Vocational Education and Training (TVET), share ideas and experiences in the development of vocational educators, and develop projects that are of common interests to BRICS Member States.

6.   Recognize the importance of BRICS Think Tanks Council (BTTC), BRICS Network University as well as other BRICS initiatives, and encourage the streamlining of mechanisms for their closer cooperation to ensure the alignment of their work.

7.   Emphasize the importance of streamlining the cooperation among educational think tanks and education researchers, and welcome China's invitation to host a conference to explore possible cooperation among the various entities in BRICS Member States.

8.   Encourage the organization of "youth winter/summer camps" to reinforce communication and cultural exchanges among the young generation from BRICS Member States.

9.   Encourage Member States to expand the number of scholarship opportunities to students across BRICS Member States.

10. Share the experiences and practices in achieving the SDG4-Education 2030 targets in order to foster a more favorable policy environment, adopt effective practices, and advocate for global educational policies that take into account the common concerns and priorities of the BRICS Member States.

11. Encourage the participation in the 3rd BRICS NU Annual Conference to be held in 2018, in Cape Town, South Africa and in the BRICS Global Business and Innovation Conference to be held in September 2017, in St. Petersburg, Russia.

The Federative Republic of Brazil, the Russian Federation, the Republic of India, and the Republic of South Africa extend their appreciation to the government of the People's Republic of China for hosting the 5thMeeting of BRICS Ministers of Education.

The English version of this Declaration has been signed on July 5th, 2017 in Beijing, People's Republic of China. The Declaration has been executed in five (5) original copies, each copy being equally authentic and valid.

FEDERATIVE REPUBLIC OF BRAZIL

RUSSIAN FEDERATION

REPUBLIC OF INDIA

PEOPLE'S REPUBLIC OF CHINA

REPUBLIC OF SOUTH AFRICA

C.   4th Meeting of BRICS Education Ministers: 30 Sep. 2016, New Delhi (IND)

NEW DELHI DECLARATION ON EDUCATION
30 September 2016, New Delhi

We, the BRICS Ministers of Education and assigned representatives of the Federative Republic of Brazil, the People's Republic of China, the Republic of India, the Russian Federation and the Republic of South Africa,

Having met in New Delhi, the Republic of India on September 30, 2016 to discuss and coordinate areas of mutual interest and develop framework for future cooperation in the field of education,

Following the discussions in the meeting of the BRICS Ministers of Education on November 18, 2015 under the Chair of the Russian Federation and guided by the Moscow Declaration,

Committed to the SDG4 and corresponding targets set within "The 2030 Framework for Action' which serve as the overall guiding framework for the implementation of the Education 2030 agenda,

For ensuring deeper cooperation among the Member States,

Hereby declare to:

1.   Reiterate our commitment to SDG4 which aims to "Ensure inclusive and equitable quality education and promote life-long learning opportunities for all" and the 'Education 2030 Framework for Action', which serve as the overall guiding framework for the implementation of the Education 2030 agenda;

2.   Initiate actions to formulate country–specific targets within the broader scope of the SDG4-related targets with the national and subnational-level education sector development plans/programmes; and build capacity at the national and subnational levels for measuring and monitoring progress towards SDG4 and corresponding targets using the indicators adopted by the UN General Assembly in September 2016;

3.   Reaffirm the need for universal equal access to quality education, including secondary and higher education, technical and vocational education and training, and lifelong learning opportunities for all;

4.   Share the best practise available in BRICS countries on collaboration in education research and innovation through the BRICS Network University.

5.   Organise an annual conference of the BRICS Network University in the country of the current BRICS Chair;

6.   Encourage more universities to participate in the BRICS University League to facilitate student mobility and collaborative research;

7.   Expand technical and vocational education and skills development programmes, for facilitating acquisition of skills and competencies by young people and adults for enhancing their employability and encourage innovation and entrepreneurship;

8.   Strengthen coordination within the BRICS TVET Working Group to: (a) develop national reports, (b) share experiences relating to workforce demands and supply of skilled personnel in BRICS member countries, (c) undertake skill gap analysis in consultation with industry employers for designing TVET programmes, (d) study skill qualification framework in different countries and draft a BRICS TVET qualification framework, and (e) undertake studies to evaluate outcomes of TVET interventions and suggest policy responses. The Working Group will meet at least once a year.

9.   Use information and communication technologies (ICTs) for improving access for education, enhancing the quality of teaching–learning process, teacher development, and strengthening educational planning and management;

10. Identify a nodal institution within each country and create and institutional network to share ICT policies, Open Educational Resources and other e-resources, including e-Libraries, among BRICS member countries;

11. Share information on higher education systems, approval and recognition processes, quality assurance and accreditation and prevalent procedures and practices for evaluation and recognition of qualifications to facilitate academic mobility; may also consider subsequently to constitute and expert group to work towards the development of a framework for mutual recognition of qualifications across BRICS countries;

12. Facilitate mobility of students and scholars, and encourage exchange of teaching faculty, especially those working in the areas relating to the six domains identified for cooperation within the BRICS Network University;

13. Develop and enabling framework to promote research cooperation and knowledge transfer among BRICS countries in collaboration with other BRICS initiatives;

14. Encourage active involvement of the participating universities in the BRICS-UN;

The Federative republic of Brazil, the People's Republic of China, the Russian Federation and the Republic of South Africa extend their appreciation to the Government of India for hosting the 4th meeting of the BRICS Ministers of Education.

Done in the English language, in five copies, each copy being equally authentic, on September 30, 2016, in New Delhi, India.

D.   3rd Meeting of BRICS Education Ministers: 18 Nov. 2015, Moscow (RUS)

DECLARATION OF THE III MEETING OF BRICS MINISTERS OF EDUCATION

We, the Ministers of Education and designated representatives of the BRICS countries, having met in Moscow, the Russian Federation on November 18, 2015 to discuss and coordinate areas of mutual interest and develop the framework for future cooperation in education,

Guided by the Brasilia Declaration encouraging BRICS members to promote strengthening of internationalization of higher education and academic mobility, vocational and technical education as well as to ensure inclusive and equitable quality education and promote lifelong learning opportunities for all,

Supporting UNESCO Education - 2030 Framework for Action on Sustainable Development Goals and enhancing opportunities for collaboration between BRICS and UNESCO,

Committed to building further collaboration in line with the Ufa Declaration and the Strategy for BRICS Economic Partnership,

Reaffirming that the promotion of sustainable development and inclusive growth is the pillar of BRICS educational cooperation, in line with the Post-2015 Development Agenda,

Hereby declare as follows:

In the Field of the Higher Education

1.   Move towards enhanced engagement in education and research in the areas which are of common interest to BRICS member states.

2.   Establish the network of the research-and-education centers of excellence prioritizing the main areas of collaboration in the leading universities of the BRICS countries.

3.   Support joint research projects, encourage more collaborative programmes at post-graduate, doctorate and post-doctorate levels and promote joint-publishing of scientific results by BRICS universities.

4.   Work towards the development of common principles of accreditation and quality assurance.

5.   Promote close collaboration among the BRICS member States for the development of common principles for recognition of diplomas and degrees.

6.   Encourage and support the establishment of the BRICS Universities League;

7.   Constitute the BRICS Network University according to the Memorandum of Understanding on Establishment of the BRICS Network University.

In the Field of the Technical Vocational Education and Training (TVET)

8.   Emphasize the important role of TVET for attracting young people to labour-market

9.   Collaborate to improve the quality of teaching, learning and teachers' education.

10. Develop national reports, share concepts, methods and instruments of analysis matching workforce demand and supply for BRICS member countries.

11. Strengthen initiatives for skills development in BRICS member States through implementation of international best practices, including World Skills.

12. Collaborate on specific projects initiated by the Skills Development Working Group of the BRICS Business Council.

In the Field of the General Education

13. Encourage the comparative studies on the quality of education, including general education, within the BRICS countries to enable benchmarking.

14. Promote lifelong learning and encourage self-education through both formal and informal modes, and strive towards excellence.

15. Provide opportunities for learning of foreign languages and assuring the ability for fluent spoken, written, business and professional communication.

In the Field of Educational Policy Strategy

16. Appoint official representatives of all the BRICS member States to coordinate the programmes and projects of BRICS countries on education.

17. Promote collaborative investment in education for economic growth and development of human resources.

18. Share statistical data and develop methodologies for common education indicators.

19. Work towards harmonization of the statistics in the sphere of education in the BRICS countries taking into account international statistical standards, including ISCED 2011.

20. Ensure information exchanges on national assessment systems, analysis and comparative research, on the instruments of measurement and monitoring of the quality of education.

21. Brazil, India, China and South Africa express their appreciation to Russia for hosting the III BRICS Ministerial Meeting on Education in 2015.

22. Russia, Brazil, China and South Africa convey their appreciation to India for its offer to host the IV BRICS Ministerial Meeting on Education in 2016 and extend their full support to that end.

E.   2nd Meeting of BRICS Education Ministers: 2 Mar. 2015, Brasilia (BRA)

BRASILIA DECLARATION

THE II MEETING OF BRICS MINISTERS OF EDUCATION

1.   In line with the mandate of the Fortaleza Declaration and Action Plan, adopted at the Sixth BRICS Summit held in Fortaleza, Brazil, we, the Ministers of Education and assigned representatives of the Federative Republic of Brazil, the People's Republic of China, the Republic of India, the Russian Federation and the Republic of South Africa, met in Brasilia, Brazil, on March 2nd, 2015, to discuss and coordinate positions in areas of mutual interest and guidelines for future cooperation in education within the framework of BRICS.

2.   We stress the paramount importance of the development of joint methodologies for education indicators to support decision making in BRICS member states and we commit ourselves to collaborate and provide technical support to the National Institutes of Statistics in this task.

3.   We recognize that the indicators for the post-2015 agenda should be based primarily on national assessments, administrative data and national household surveys instead of extension of existing international surveys. We emphasize that all indicators should be capable of measuring equity, inclusion and quality improvements in our education system.

4.   We also recognize the significance of sharing best practices in terms of assessing learning outcomes and how to report them in order to be useful for policy makers, teachers and schools.

5.   We acknowledge that vocational and technical education addresses the challenge of integrating young people to the labour market and plays a critical role in preparing skilled workforce needed by the modern world.

6.   We agree to create a working group to develop a report on the state of vocational and technical education and share concepts, methods and instruments of analysis to match demands and supply of vocational and technical education in each country.

7.   Brazil invites BRICS member states to participate on the 3rd International Forum of Professional Education, to be held in Recife, Brazil, on May 2015.

8.   We consider higher education and research is a priority. Considering that BRICS member states have intensified their internationalization processes of higher education and academic mobility, we put special emphasis on mobility in graduate school, with its capability of establishing networks of researchers and developing joint projects in areas of mutual interest.

9.   We support the initiative of a BRICS University League (association of BRICS universities) and the establishment of a working group to work out the modalities of a BRICS Network University.

10. We agree on the need for further expert discussions and to organize regular meetings of experts, at FAUBAI Conference, Brazil, from April 25th to 29th, 2015, at Saint Petersburg conference, Russian Federation, from May 14th and 15th, and the BRICS Universities Rectors Forum in Beijing, China, in October.

11. We decide that each BRICS member state shall nominate a coordinator for educational matter.

12. In pursuit of cooperation in the abovementioned areas, we agree to build upon existing bilateral synergies and other forms of multi-country frameworks of cooperation amongst the BRICS member states.

13. We recognize the importance of exchanging experience and best practices in education and consider it the pillar of cooperation amongst the Ministries of Education of BRICS member states.

14. We reaffirm the commitment of ensuring inclusive and equitable quality education and promoting lifelong learning opportunities for all, and working towards sustainable development and inclusive growth, in line with the Post-2015 Development Agenda.

15. China, India, Russia and South Africa extend their warm appreciation to the Government of Brazil for hosting the II Meeting of BRICS Ministers of Education.

Done in English language, in five copies, each copy being equally authentic, on March 2nd 2015, in Brasilia, Brazil.

F.   1st Meeting of BRICS Education Ministers: 5 Nov. 2013, Paris (FRA)

BRICS MINISTERS DISCUSS EDUCATION PRESS RELEASE

The South African Minister of Higher Education and Training, Dr B Nzimande hosted the first meeting of the Brazil, Russia, India, China and South Africa (BRICS) Ministers of Education on 05 November 2013, in Paris, France, on the margins of the 37th session of the UNESCO General Conference. The meeting was convened by South Africa as the current Chair of the BRICS grouping. The Minister was supported at this meeting by the Minister of Basic Education, Ms Angie Motshekga and senior officials from both Departments of Basic Education, and Higher Education and Training.

The meeting provided a platform for BRICS Education Minsters to explore areas of collaboration in the fields of education and training between their countries. The meeting also discussed potential areas of cooperation between BRICS and UNESCO in line with the resolution of the 2011 Sanya Summit, held in China. The BRICS Education Ministers meeting sought to underscore the strategic importance of cooperation in education between the BRICS countries, and the need to highlight this at the next BRICS Summit.

Issues such as strengthening collaboration between BRICS universities, partnerships and knowledge exchanges on Technical Vocational Education and Training, portability and transferability of qualifications between BRICS countries were highlighted as important for the cooperation.

Moreover, the Ministers underscored the importance of collaboration with UNESCO in order to accelerate progress towards the achievements of the Education for All (EFA) goals, and also shape discussions on the post 2015 agenda. It was further agreed that Technical Vocational Education and Training should feature strongly on the post 2015 EFA goals.

A meeting with the UNESCO Director General, Ms Irina Bokova took place on 06 November 2013 and agreed that BRICS and UNESCO should work together to assist the least developed countries towards the attainment of global education targets. Amongst issues which were highlighted for cooperation are, the strengthening of data collection systems within BRICS, cooperation and sharing of best practices on Technical Vocational Education and Training. It was further proposed that BRICS and UNESCO should investigate how ICT can be used effectively to improve the quality of learning outcomes.

The BRICS Ministers agreed on the need to establish a mechanism at the highest political and technical level in order to coordinate and implement the identified areas of cooperation which will be coordinated by South Africa as the current Chair of BRICS. The Ministers also agreed that the second meeting of BRICS Education Ministers will be held at the next BRICS Summit of heads of state in 2014.

IV.   ADDITIONAL BRICS SOURCES

IV.1.   Informal BRICS Leaders' Meeting (G20 Summit): 30 Nov. 2018, Buenos Aires (ARG)

MEDIA STATEMENT:

INFORMAL BRICS LEADERS' MEETING ON THE MARGINS OF THE G20 SUMMIT

1.   We, the Heads of State and Government of the Federative Republic of Brazil, the Russian Federation, the Republic of India, the People's Republic of China and the Republic of South Africa, met on 30 November 2018 for the annual Informal BRICS Leaders' Meeting on the margins of the G20 Summit in Buenos Aires, Argentina. We congratulated and supported the Argentine Presidency for G20 in 2018 and expressed our gratitude at the hospitality provided.

2.   We exchanged views on international political, security and global economic-financial issues, as well as challenges facing sustainable development. We recommit ourselves to a world of peace and stability, the central role of the United Nations, the purposes and principles enshrined in the UN Charter, and respect for international law, the promotion of democracy and the rule of law. We reiterate our commitment to working together to strengthen multilateralism and promote a fair, just, equitable, democratic and representative international order.

3.   We deplore continued terrorist attacks, including against some BRICS countries. We condemn terrorism in all forms and manifestations, wherever committed and by whom so ever. We urge concerted efforts to counter terrorism under the UN auspices on a firm international legal basis. We call upon all nations to adopt a comprehensive approach in combating terrorism, including all the elements identified in the Johannesburg Declaration.

4.   We reaffirm our full support for the rules-based multilateral trading system, as embodied in the WTO, to ensure transparent, non-discriminatory, open and inclusive international trade. We express our common readiness to engage in frank and result-oriented discussions with other WTO members with a view to improving the functioning of the WTO.

5.   The spirit and rules of the WTO run counter to unilateral and protectionist measures. We call on all members to oppose such WTO inconsistent measures, stand by their commitments undertaken in the WTO and rollback such measures of a discriminatory and restrictive nature.

6.   We support work towards improvement of the WTO with the view to enhance its relevance and effectiveness to address current and future challenges. In this work the core value and fundamental principles of the WTO should be preserved and interests of all WTO members should be reflected, in particular those of the developing members.

7.   The dispute settlement mechanism of the WTO is essential for its proper functioning. Its effective functioning will give members the required confidence to engage in future negotiating in the WTO. We therefore urge that the Appellate Body selection process be initiated immediately, as an essential prerequisite for the stable and effective functioning of the WTO dispute settlement system.

8.   We reaffirm our commitment to enhance our communication and cooperation and work jointly and collaboratively with other members to enable the WTO to keep up with the changing times, promote inclusive growth and participation of all countries in international trade and play a meaningful role in global economic governance.

9.   We welcome the G20 Argentine Presidency's theme of Building Consensus for Fair and Sustainable Development and its focus on the Future of Work, Infrastructure for Development and Food Security for Sustainable Future.

10.   We recognize the importance of infrastructure for development and commit to contribute to bridging the global infrastructure gap, also by mobilizing resources for sustainable and disaster resilient infrastructure through national and collective initiatives, including the New Development Bank.

11.   We advocate for a strong Global Financial Safety Net with an adequately resourced, quota-based International Monetary Fund (IMF) at its centre. To this effect, we reaffirm our commitment to the conclusion of the IMF's 15th General Review of Quotas, including a new quota formula so as to ensure the increased voice of the dynamic emerging and developing economies to reflect their relative contributions to the world economy while protecting the voices of the least developed counties, by the 2019 Spring Meetings and no later than the 2019 Annual Meetings.

12.   We reinforce our commitment to the implementation of the 2030 Agenda for Sustainable Development and the Sustainable Development Goals that would provide equitable, inclusive, open, all-round innovation-driven and sustainable development, in its three dimensions — economic, social and environmental - in a balanced and integrated manner, towards the ultimate goal of eradicating poverty by 2030. We urge developed countries to honour their ODA commitments fully, in time and to provide additional development resources to developing countries in accordance with the Addis Ababa Action Agenda.

13.   The global economic expansion continues, however, it has been less balanced and downside risks have risen. We are concerned that the negative spill-overs by policy normalization from major advanced economies has been an important source of volatility of some emerging market economies witnessed recently. We call on all economies to strengthen their policy dialogue and coordination in the spirit of partnership at the G20 and other fora to prevent potential risks from spreading.

14.   Regarding Climate Change, we recommit ourselves to the full implementation of the Paris Agreement adopted under the principles of the UNFCCC including the principles of common but differentiated responsibilities and respective capabilities, and urge developed countries to provide financial, technological and capacity-building support to developing countries to enhance their capability in mitigation and adaptation. We call upon all countries to reach a balanced outcome under the Paris Agreement Work Programme during COP-24 that enables operationalization and implementation of the Paris Agreement. We stress the importance and urgency of conducting a successful and ambitious first replenishment process of the Green Climate Fund.

15.   We reiterate our warm appreciation to South Africa for the success of the 10th BRICS Summit, Johannesburg, 25-27 July 2018 and recommit ourselves to enhancing further our strategic partnership for the benefit of our peoples. We express satisfaction with the achievements of BRICS cooperation in the areas of economy, peace and security and people-to-people exchanges under South Africa's Chairship, including the establishment of the BRICS Partnership on New Industrial Revolution (PartNIR), the BRICS Vaccine Research and Development Centre, the BRICS Energy Research Cooperation Platform and the Americas Regional Office of the New Development Bank in São Paulo. We reaffirm our commitment to fully implement the outcomes of the Johannesburg Summit and previous Summits.

16.   We look forward to the 11th BRICS Summit to be hosted by Brazil in 2019 and extend our full support to Brazil as the incoming BRICS Chair.

IV.2.   BRICS Competition Authorities

A.   Joint Statement – Heads of BRICS Competition Authorities: 10 Nov. 2017, Brasilia (BRA)

THE BRASILIA JOINT STATEMENT OF THE HEADS OF
BRICS COMPETITION AUTHORITIES

We, the Heads of Competition Authorities of the Federative Republic of Brazil, the Russian Federation, the Republic of India, the People's Republic of China and the Republic of South Africa, at a meeting on 10 November 2017 during the fifth BRICS International Competition Conference in Brasilia, Brazil which was held under the theme 'Towards a Successful Second Decade of Cooperation':

Recognizing the importance of cooperation amongst BRICS countries in the field of competition policy and law enforcement, based on mutual respect and trust;

Further Recognizing the importance of competition policy and law in fostering inclusive economic growth and broader developmental objectives;

Reaffirming, as set out in the BRICS Leaders Xiamen Declaration of 4 September 2017, our belief in the broad development prospects of our countries and the vast potential of our cooperation, we have full confidence in the future of BRICS;

Agreeing to address the challenges of global economic development including growing inequality and technological transformation through strengthening cooperation in analysis of global markets and innovation landscape for improving merger review and antitrust enforcement in the BRICS countries;

Further Reaffirming our commitment to the activities under the Memorandum of Understanding in the Field of Competition Policy signed at St Petersburg, Russian Federation on 19 May 2016;

Acknowledging the necessity of the continuation of joint work, aimed at enhancing international cooperation in order to develop our respective competition laws as well as to foster our competition enforcement, via consultations, multilateral meetings or any other tools the BRICS Competition Authorities consider appropriate;

Agreeing to continue dedicating efforts towards a general framework for multilateral cooperation aiming at promoting and strengthening cooperation in competition law and policy through exchanges of information and experiences, including capacity building programmes;

Further Acknowledging the necessity of the continuation of discussions on the development of a joint competition resource platform for promoting and enhancing mutually beneficial partnership of the BRICS Competition Authorities.

The Competition Authorities of Brazil, India, China and South Africa support the hosting of the sixth BRICS International Competition Conference during 2019 by the Federal Antimonopoly Service of the Russian Federation.

FOR THE COMPETITION AUTHORITY OF THE FEDERATIVE REPUBLIC OF BRAZIL (CADE)

FOR THE COMPETITION AUTHORITY OF THE RUSSIAN FEDERATION (FAS)

FOR THE COMPETITION AUTHORITY OF THE REPUBLIC OF INDIA (CCI)

FOR THE COMPETITION AUTHORITIES OF THE PEOPLE'S REPUBLIC OF CHINA (NDRC, MOFCOM and SAIC)

FOR THE COMPETITION AUTHORITY OF THE REPUBLIC OF SOUTH AFRICA (CCSA)

B.   MoU between BRICS Competition Authorities: 19 May 2016, Saint-Petersburg (RUS)

MEMORANDUM OF UNDERSTANDING

BETWEEN

THE COMPETITION AUTHORITIES OF

THE FEDERATIVE REPUBLIC OF BRAZIL, THE RUSSIAN FEDERATION, THE REPUBLIC OF INDIA, THE PEOPLE'S REPUBLIC OF CHINA AND THE REPUBLIC OF SOUTH AFRICA

ON

COOPERATION IN THE FIELD OF COMPETITION LAW AND POLICY

Introduction

The Competition Authorities of the Federative Republic of Brazil, the Russian Federation, the Republic of India, the People's Republic of China and the Republic of South Africa (hereinafter jointly referred to as the "Parties" and separately as a "Party");

CONSIDERING their close economic relations;

EXPRESSING the wish to develop and strengthen cooperation in the field of competition law and policy;

RECOGNIZING the need to promote long-term sustainable and rapid development of their respective economies;

BASED on the principles of mutual trust and respect;

NOTING that the firm and effective enforcement of their competition laws are of crucial importance for growth and efficiency in the economy and the protection of consumers;

FURTHER RECOGNIZING that cooperation between the Parties will contribute to improve and strengthen their effectiveness; and

ADDRESSING the assurance of the Parties to give careful consideration to important mutual interests in the application of their competition laws and policies

HAVE REACHED AN UNDERSTANDING as follows:

1. Purpose and Definition

1.1. The purpose of this Memorandum of Understanding is to set up an institutional partnership between the Parties through a general framework for multilateral cooperation. The activities contemplated under this Memorandum of Understanding aim at promoting and strengthening the cooperation in competition law and policy of the Parties through exchanges of information and best practices, as well as through capacity-building activities.

1.2. The term 'Competition Authorities' means:

   1.2.1. For the Federative Republic of Brazil: the Administrative Council for Economic Defense of the Federative Republic of Brazil (CADE)

   1.2.2. For the Russian Federation: the Federal Antimonopoly Service (Russian Federation) (FAS Russia)

   1.2.3. For the Republic of India: the Competition Commission of India (CCI)

1.2.4. For the People's Republic of China: the National Development and Reform Commission of the People's Republic of China (NDRC) , the Ministry of Commerce of the People's Republic of China (MOFCOM), the State Administration for Industry and Commerce of the People's Republic of China (SAIC)

1.2.5. For the Republic of South Africa: the Competition Commission of South Africa (CCSA)

2. Scope of Cooperation

2.1. Subject to available resources, the Parties will cooperate by:

2.1.1 exchanging policies, laws, rules, as well as the progress of legislation, and enforcement in the competition field;

2.1.2 organizing joint studies for the purpose of providing common knowledge on competition issues;

2.1.3 promoting the participation in international conferences, seminars and other relevant events on competition issues organized by the Parties, in particular the BRICS International Competition Conference held once every two years;

2.1.4 cooperating and coordinating with each other if necessary and under reasonable circumstances, subject to their respective laws, in investigations or enforcement proceedings pertaining to violation of competition laws; and

2.1.5 any other means as may be agreed upon in writing by the Parties.

2.2. All communication pursuant to this Memorandum of Understanding will be in writing in the English language and shall be transmitted via e-mail.

2.3. All cooperation pursuant to this Memorandum of Understanding will be subject to the domestic law in force in the territories of the Parties.

2.4. The Parties will notify each other promptly of any changes or amendments to their respective legislation as set out in Annexure A hereto.

3. Liaison Committee

3.1. The Parties will establish a liaison committee in order to ensure adequate communications and consultations among the Parties.

3.2. The liaison committee will consist of one representative of each Party, with the understanding that one representative respectively from the competition authorities of The People's Republic of China will be involved.

3.3. The name and full contact details of each Party's representative to the liaison committee will be circulated to all the Parties.

4. Working Groups

4.1. The Parties may establish working groups to conduct joint studies on matters of common interest.

4.2. A Party may propose, through the Liaison Committee, the establishment of working groups. Each Party may make its own decision whether or not to participate in a working group regard being had to its needs, available resources and any other relevant consideration.

5.   Costs

Each Party will carry its own costs that may result from the implementation of this Memorandum of Understanding.

6.   Confidentiality

6.1. A Party will not be required to communicate information to any of the other Parties if the communication of such information is prohibited by the domestic law of the Party possessing the information or if such communication would be incompatible with the interests of that Party.

6.2. Insofar as confidential information is communicated to a Party, the recipient Party will maintain the confidentiality of any such information communicated to it in confidence.

6.3. Nothing contained in this Memorandum of Understanding will require any Party to take any action or to refrain from taking any action, in a manner inconsistent with its domestic laws, nor will it require any change in such laws.

6.4. The MoU does not restrict the rights of the parties to enter into bilateral and other multilateral MoU's on cooperation in the field of Competition Law and Policy.

7.   Settlement of Disputes

Any dispute between the Parties arising out of the interpretation, application or implementation of this Memorandum of Understanding shall be settled amicably through consultation or negotiation between the Parties.

8.   Entry into Effect, Amendment, Duration and Termination

8.1. This Memorandum of Understanding will come into effect on the date of its signing and shall remain in effect for a period of four (4) years, with the option to renew or extend it further, in such manner and for such periods as agreed by the parties in writing.

8.2. The parties may amend this MOU at any time by mutual written consent.

8.3. A Party may terminate its involvement in this Memorandum of Understanding by giving two (2) months written notice in advance to the other Parties, through its representative on the liaison committee, of its intention to terminate its involvement in this Memorandum of Understanding.

8.4. This Memorandum of Understanding shall not be considered as an international treaty and does not establish any rights or obligations for the Parties, which are regulated by international law.

IN WITNESS WHEREOF the Parties, have signed and sealed this Memorandum of Understanding in seven originals in English.

SIGNED at Saint-Petersburg (Russian Federation) on the 19 of May 2016.

FOR THE COMPETITON AUTHORITY OF THE FEDERATIVE REPUBLIC OF BRAZIL

FOR THE COMPETITON AUTHORITY OF THE RUSSIAN FEDERATION

FOR THE COMPETITON AUTHORITY OF THE REPUBLIC OF INDIA (Competition Commission of India)

FOR THE COMPETITION AUTHORITIES OF THE PEOPLE'S REPUBLIC OF CHINA (NDRC, MOFCOM and SAIC)

FOR THE COMPETITION AUTHORITY OF THE REPUBLIC OF SOUTH AFRICA

ANNEXURE – Competition Legislation of BRICS Member States

Country	Legislation
Brazil	Competition Act – Law No. 12.529/2011
Russia	[PDF] Federal Law No. 135-FZ of 26 July 2006 "On Protection of Competition" (amended 2009).
India	The Competition Act of 2002, 12 of 2003
China	The Law of the People's Republic of China against Unfair Competition (Entering into force on December 1, 1993), the Anti-Monopoly Law of the People's Republic of China (Entering into force on August 1, 2008)
South Africa	Competition Act No. 89 of 1998 as amended

C.   Joint Statement – Heads of BRICS Competition Authorities, 13 Nov. 2015, Durban (ZAF)

JOINT STATEMENT OF THE HEADS OF BRICS COMPETITION AUTHORITIES

We, the Heads of Competition Authorities of the Federative Republic of Brazil, the Russian Federation, the Republic of India, the People's Republic of China and the Republic of South Africa, at a meeting on 13 November 2015 during the 4th BRICS International Competition Conference in Durban, South Africa which was held under the theme "Competition and Inclusive Growth":

Recognising, as set out in the Ufa Declaration of 9 July 2015, that as BRICS countries are emerging markets and developing economies which face similar challenges, it is important to continue in our joint efforts aimed at improving competition law and policy enforcement in order to achieve growth in our economies and the protection of consumers;

Acknowledging that dialogue amongst the BRICS countries in the field of competition policy and enforcement, based on mutual respect and trust, is essential;

Further recognising that effective competition policy enforcement by the BRICS countries requires, in the context of economic globalization, strengthening of the cooperation and coordination between the BRICS competition authorities;

Agreed to conclude the Memorandum of Understanding in the field of competition policy in order to strengthen the cooperation and coordination between the BRICS Competition Authorities;

Agreed to activities under the proposed Memorandum of Understanding to strengthen such cooperation through the sharing of best practices in respect of laws, rules and policies; joint participation in capacity building initiatives such as conferences and seminars; the conduct of joint studies and coordination in enforcement proceedings.

FOR THE COMPETITION AUTHORITY OF THE FEDERATIVE REPUBLIC OF BRAZIL

FOR THE COMPETITION AUTHORITY OF THE RUSSIAN FEDERATION

FOR THE COMPETITION AUTHORITY OF THE REPUBLIC OF INDIA

FOR THE COMPETITION AUTHORITIES OF THE PEOPLE'S REPUBLIC OF CHINA

FOR THE COMPETITION AUTHORITY OF THE REPUBLIC OF SOUTH AFRICA

D.   Joint Statement – Heads of BRICS Competition Authorities, 21 Nov. 2013, New Delhi (IND)

DELHI ACCORD

A Joint Accord signed at the meeting of the Heads of the Competition Authorities of the Federative Republic of Brazil, the Russian Federation, the Republic of India and the People's Republic of China, the Republic of South Africa during the 3rd International Competition Conference held at New Delhi

November 21, 2013 New Delhi INDIA

The Heads of the Competition Authorities of Brazil, Russia, India, China and South Africa (BRICS) held their meeting on November 21, 2013 during the 3rd International Competition Conference jointly organized by them pursuant to the Delhi Declaration and Action Plan adopted at the Fourth and Fifth BRICS Summits.

Recognizing BRICS International Competition Conference as an important platform for dialogue and cooperation on competition policy between the BRICS Competition Authorities, Brazil, Russia, India, China and South Africa decided to carry out the deliberations on 'Competition Enforcement in BRICS: Issues and Challenges' at the conference.

Recognizing the global nature of competition law and its impact on the development of the economy, BRICS Competition Authorities, reflecting the principle of mutual trust and respect, considered the need of establishing good communication between the BRICS Competition Authorities on competition law and policy to further improving and strengthening the relationship between the BRICS Competition Authorities.

BRICS Competition Authorities, while recognizing the benefits of technical cooperation among the competition agencies, in sound and effective enforcement of competition laws expressed their resolve and commitment to exchange views on different aspects of competition policy.

The Heads of the Competition Authorities of BRICS recommended the publication of the material of the 3rd BRICS International Competition Conference on their respective websites for the purpose of competition advocacy.

The Competition Authorities of Brazil, Russia, India and China support the hosting of the Fourth BRICS International Competition Conference during 2015 by the Competition Commission of South Africa.

FOR THE BRAZILIAN COMPETITION POLICY SYSTEM

FOR THE FEDERAL ANTIMONOPOLY SERVICE OF THE RUSSIAN FEDERATION

FOR THE COMPETITION COMMISSION OF INDIA

FOR THE STATE ADMINISTRATION FOR INDUSTRY AND COMMERCE OF THE PEOPLE'S REPUBLIC OF CHINA

FOR THE COMPETITION COMMISSION OF SOUTH AFRICA

IV.3.   MoU on the Creation of the Joint BRICS Website: 9 Jul. 2015, Ufa (RUS)

MOU ON THE CREATION OF THE JOINT BRICS WEBSITE

The Ministry of Foreign Affairs of the Federative Republic of Brazil, the Ministry of Foreign Affairs of the Russian Federation, the Ministry of External Affairs of the Republic of India, the Ministry of Foreign Affairs of the People's Republic of China and the Ministry of International Relations and Cooperation of the Republic of South Africa, hereinafter referred to as the Parties,

Guided by the desire to strengthen comprehensive cooperation between the Member States,

Seeking to develop relations between the foreign policy departments of the Member States,

Driven by the desire to disseminate information on BRICS values, goals and practical activities among the public of our countries as well as the international community,

Seeking to use information and communication technologies to deepen cooperation among Member States and their peoples,

Following the Action Plans adopted at the BRICS Summits in Durban (2013) and in Fortaleza (2014),

The Parties hereby record their understanding to cooperate as follows:

1.   Creation of the Website

The Parties will create a joint website to cover BRICS activities. The website will be a free online public resource.

2.   Objectives of the Website Creation

The website will be created to:

- disseminate information on the activities related to BRICS of a State which currently chairs the BRICS, including its priorities and chairmanship programme, information on previous and upcoming events of the Chairmanship and BRICS-related keynote addresses by the leaders of the Chairing State;
- provide information on the BRICS Member States participation and on the events they hold within the BRICS framework;
- disseminate information on the activity of business and non-governmental organizations aimed at promoting the BRICS objectives;
- disseminate media publications on the BRICS activities;
- inform the public about the history of the BRICS and decisions adopted.

3.   Website Structure

The website will have a modular structure and include:

- module of the incumbent BRICS Chair;
- module of the BRICS Official Documents Archive;
- national modules of the BRICS Member States;
- module of the BRICS News Feed;
- module of Scientific Publications on the BRICS;
- other modules as agreed upon by the Parties.

The module of the incumbent BRICS Chair will be maintained in the national language and in English. The module of the BRICS Official Documents Archive will contain publicly released documents and will be maintained by the Russian Party in Russian, by the Brazilian Party in Portuguese, by the Chinese Party in Chinese, by the Indian Party in Hindi and South African Party in English.

National modules of the BRICS Member States will be maintained by relevant Party.

The module of the BRICS News Feed shall be maintained in the same manner as the national ones.

The module of Scientific Publications on the BRICS will be maintained by the BRICS Think Tanks Council.

There may be other modules as agreed by the Parties.

4. Rights of the Parties

The Parties will have the right to:

- have an easy and full access to information published on the BRICS website, as well as information on the website software;
- participate on an equal footing in resolving issues of the BRICS website management applying the principle of consensus;
- upload relevant information that the Parties consider necessary to the national modules of the BRICS website, and in the period of the BRICS chairmanship – to the module of the incumbent Chair.

5. Responsibilities of the Parties

The Parties will:

- ensure that the Chairmanship module has proper content when the State acts as the BRICS Chair;
- maintain properly their national modules, including their software;
- upload official, public release documents in connection with BRICS events in relevant national languages to the BRICS Official Document Archive;
- take the necessary measures in order to provide for information security for national modules and the website as a whole.

6. Financing of the Website

Each Party intends to provide funding, within existing national resources already assigned to such activity, to support the operation of national module and to posting of all the information in the official language of the State of that Party in each module of the BRICS website.

The Chairmanship module will be financed by the Party whose State chairs the BRICS in the current year. Besides, this Party will provide English translations of all the information posted in that module.

7. Management of the Website

For purposes of managing the site the Party will establish a Board. It will include duly authorized Party's representatives (one from each Party). Functions of the Chair of the Board will be performed by the representative of the incumbent Chair of BRICS. In its work the Board will be guided by the principle of consensus. Its competence will include determining focus areas of the website activities for the long term and resolving issues of its operation. The Board's decisions may be taken by absentee voting. The Board will meet preferably by teleconference or videoconference.

Any Party's representative may be substituted by another duly authorized person. There can be no more than one substitute person. The Board has to be informed in time and in writing about any such arrangements.

8. Final Provisions

The present Memorandum will apply starting from the date of its signature.

The present Memorandum is subject to annual review.

The present Memorandum is concluded for an indefinite period, unless any Party withdraws from it.

The present Memorandum is not an international treaty and does not create rights and obligations regulated by international law.

Signed in on 2015 in five copies in the English language.

IV.4. MoU on Establishment of the BRICS Network University: 2 Mar. 2015, Ufa (RUS)

MOU ON ESTABLISHMENT OF THE BRICS NETWORK UNIVERSITY

We, the undersigned representatives of the BRICS Ministries of Education, plenipotentiary representatives of the BRICS countries Embassies in the Russian Federation and members of the institutions of the BRICS countries; testifying our agreement with the content of the Memorandum of Understanding on Establishment of the BRICS Network University (MoU) for the further amending and definite validation, confirming adherence to the goals of the World Declaration on Higher Education for the Twenty-First Century: Vision and action adopted on 6 0f October 1998, assisting implementation of the UNESCO goal in the development of education as it is stated in the Article I of the UNESCO Constitution: The purpose of the organization is to contribute to peace and security by promoting collaboration among the nations through education, science and culture, guided by the Article 56 0f the Fortaleza Declaration for the initiative to establish the BRICS Network University, following the Brasilia Declaration of the Second Meeting of BRICS Ministers of Education adopted on 2 0f March 2015, which provides for establishment of a working group to work out the modalities of a BRICS Network University (Article 9), taking into account the Principles of the Creation and Functioning of the BRICS Network University declared and adopted by the BRICS Working Group on Education on 26 0f June 2015, guided by the Article 63 0f Ufa Declaration with respect to the support for the establishment of the BRICS Network University and the BRICS University League as independent initiatives, recognizing the strategic importance of education for sustainable development and inclusive economic growth in accordance with the BRICS Economic Partnership Strategy

Have agreed as follows:

Article 1
Definition of BRICS Network University

The BRICS Network University (hereinafter - BRICS NU) is a network of the BRICS member countries' higher education institutions engaged in cooperation and joining the BRICS NU (hereinafter - BRICS NU participants).

BRICS NU is an educational project aimed at developing, preferentially, bilateral/multilateral short-term joint training, master's and PhD programmes along with joint research projects in various knowledge fields according to common standards and quality criteria, given recognition of the learning outcomes by BRICS NU participants as per national criteria.

Article 2
Values and Principles

Activities of the BRICS NU are oriented towards formation of the new generation of highly qualified and motivated professionals, who obtain critical thinking skills, abilities to make and implement innovative decisions concerning the economic and social problems, communication, skills for interactions in a multicultural environment and who are capable of combining traditional knowledge with science and contemporary technologies.

BRICS NU follows these principles:

Openness, which enables various institutions to join to/withdraw from the BRICS NU respecting national criteria and based on the selection procedure.

Focus on educational programmes that can be supplemented by network research and innovation projects.

Equal rights of all participants, meaning that all BRICS NU participants have equal rights in its implementation. The BRICS NU participants are autonomous, independent from each other and relate to each other as equals.

Reciprocity in treatment of all participants involved in joint activities.

Assurance of high quality of the BRICS NU educational programmes, to be ensured through close connections with the research and innovation activity. The BRICS NU participants are committed to the active use of the methods of the problem- and project-based teaching and learning.

Respect for the national regulations, procedures and practices of each BRICS country.

Article 3
Objectives and Goals of the BRICS NU

The BRICS NU is created for:

Providing opportunity of high quality life-long learning through different forms of education, such as traditional academic programmes, short-term programmes, modular courses, etc.;

Facilitating sustainable development of the BRICS countries through creation and dissemination of the knowledge and skills via joint research and educational activities in natural and social sciences, humanities, engineering and other areas in the spirit of pluralism and diversity;

Providing training for the professionals of high qualification for satisfying the needs of the BRICS countries in specific areas by expanding students' access to contemporary methods, forms and education technologies within the frames of the implementation of the BRICS NU educational programmes.

Article 4
The Main Activities of the BRICS NU

The main activities of the BRICS NU are:

Offering in conformity with own laws Masters and Ph.D programmes; short-term training and modular courses;

Development and implementation of joint research projects, innovative activity within the frames of educational programmes;

Organization of the academic mobility of students, the university faculty and staff of the BRICS NU participants.

Article 5
Participants of the BRICS NU

The responsibility for determining the list of the BRICS NU participant institutions rests with the National Ministries of Education of the BRICS countries.

At the stage of the establishment of the BRICS NU the number of the BRICS NU participants does not exceed 12 from each BRICS member country.

Article 6
The BRICS NU Knowledge Field Priorities

Knowledge field priorities of the BRICS NU activity shall correspond to the priorities and main areas of cooperation amongst the BRICS member countries, as they are stated in the Article 3 of the

Memorandum of Understanding on Cooperation in Science, Technology and Innovation between the BRICS member countries, as well as other documents adopted within the frames of the BRICS.

At the stage of the establishment of the BRICS NU the knowledge field priorities include: energy; computer science and information security; BRICS studies; ecology and climate change; water resources and pollution treatment; economics.

In accordance with the decision of the BRICS NU International Governing Board, the grounds for creation and the empowerment of which are described in Article 10 0f the present MoU, other areas of training may be included and other knowledge field priorities may be determined.

Article 7
Formation of the BRICS NU Curricula

The BRICS NU participants will work out the details of: structure and content of educational programmes; mutual recognition of the training outcomes; academic mobility forms as decided by the International Thematic Groups on the knowledge field priorities of the BRICS NU; procedures for admission; principles of educational process arrangement; issues of interim and final certification which are regulated by agreements between BRICS NU participants on joint training of highly qualified personnel.

Article 8
The BRICS NU Education Certificate

Upon completion of the BRICS NU educational programmes, the person who has completed the course of study, passed the relevant examinations and met the requirement of conferment standards or relevant regulations of the graduation institution receives a formal qualification of the institution, in which he or she has enrolled (they may also receive two or more degrees/diplomas/certificates in accordance with the agreements between the BRICS NU participants), as well as the certificate of participation of the BRICS NU.

Article 9
The BRICS NU Governance Structures

The BRICS NU is characterized by transparent administration system aimed at addressing the issues across the network, and at the same time taking into account the priorities of national higher education systems of member countries.

In order to accomplish the objectives and goals of the BRICS NU the following regulatory bodies are created:

- BRICS NU International Governing Board (IGB);
- BRICS NU National Coordination Committee (NCC) or other national governing structure in each of the BRICS countries;
- International Thematic Groups (ITG) on the knowledge field priorities of the BRICS NU.

Article 10
The BRICS NU International Governing Board

The BRICS NU International Governing Board (IGB) is the principal integral body responsible for the activities and development, including outcome assessment of the BRICS NU.

The BRICS NU IGB consists of three representatives of each BRICS country, including:

- plenipotentiary representative of the National Education Ministry for the term appointed by the country in accordance with the national practice but not less than two years;

- representative of the BRICS NU participants from each BRICS NU NCC for the term appointed by the country in accordance with the national practice but not less than three years;

The appointed terms could be extended to another consecutive term.

The BRICS NU IGB arranges in-person meetings upon the request of BRICS NU NCC and ITG or when major decisions need to be made, but at least once a year.

Responsibility for conducting the meetings of the BRICS NU IGB rests on the National Education Ministry from the current BRICS Chairship country whose representative serves as the President of the BRICS NU IGB.

The Vice-President will be appointed from the representatives of the next BRICS Chairship country.

Article 11
The BRICS NU National Coordination Committees
(or other national governing structures)

The BRICS NU National Coordination Committees (NCC) or other national governing structures in each of the BRICS countries:

created by the Ministries of Education of the BRICS countries to ensure operative management of the BRICS NU at the national level;

operate on the basis of the national provision for the establishment of the BRICS NU NCC;

formed in accordance with national guidelines, norms and regulations in each of the BRICS countries;

consist of the BRICS NU participants and of at least two representatives of the National Education Ministries;

may also include scientific community experts in knowledge field priorities of the BRICS NU, representatives of the business community, civil society and international organizations.

Article 12
The BRICS NU International Thematic Groups

International Thematic Groups include representatives of the BRICS NU participants. The members of the ITGs are nominated by the BRICS NU NCCs or other national governing structures in accordance with the national guidelines, norms and regulations in each of the BRICS countries. ITGs are established in line with the BRICS NU knowledge field priorities set out in the Article 6 Of the present MoU. The activities of the ITGs are regulated by the statute for the BRICS NU ITGs approved by the BRICS NU IGB.

The ITGs provide support to the BRICS NU's educational activity in identified knowledge field priorities.

Article 13
The BRICS NU Funding

The BRICS NU activities, concerning each country, will be financed by participating universities' budget, grants, special purpose funds, charitable contributions, etc.

The activities of the national BRICS NU participants and NCCs are financed by each country independently. The financial responsibility for the organization of the meetings of the BRICS NU IGB rests with the current BRICS Chairship country. According to the international practice, international travel fee, board and lodging expenses will be covered by the dispatched party; local transportation, venue rental, etc. will be covered by the current BRICS Chairship country.

Article 14
Other Activities

BRICS NU participants:

Exchange information on BRICS member states' education priorities and national legislation, share documents as well as other information materials in the field of education and science;

Conduct conferences, symposiums, seminars, round tables and other events on topical issues of multilateral cooperation in the field of education;

Arrange short-term network educational programmes: summer and winter schools, graduate seminars, training courses, etc. in knowledge field priorities of the BRICS NU;

Make efforts to launch joint bilateral and multilateral research programmes, as well as contribute to the organization of innovative projects directly related to the BRICS NU educational activities and to jointly own the IPRs that result from such research;

Encourage mutual participation of students belonging to the BRICS NU in various international competitions, festivals, expeditions, as well as sports, tourism, environment etc. related events;

Cooperate in the sphere of education quality assurance;

Exchange information on licensing, certification and accreditation of educational institutions/ organizations of the BRICS countries and their educational programmes.

Article 15
Introduction of Amendments

The present MoU may be amended and supplemented by mutual agreement of the Ministries of Education of the BRICS countries. The amendments and supplements are executed as separate protocols and are considered as integral part hereof.

Article 16
Conflict Resolution

Disagreements between the BRICS NU participants arising from application of the MoU shall be resolved through negotiations and consultations mediated by the BRICS NU IGB.

Article 17
Accession to and Withdrawal from the BRICS NU

The accession to the BRICS NU higher education institutions to the BRICS NU shall be effected on the basis of the application submitted to the BRICS NU NCC or other national governing structure and be approved by a special decision of the BRICS NU IGB, and is executed as a separate protocol which is considered as integral part hereof.

This accession shall be immediately valid and effective for the acceding party from the date of the decision of the BRICS NU IGB.

Any BRICS NU participant higher education institution may withdraw from BRICS NU through a written notice sent to the BRICS NU NCC or other national governing structure not less than 90 days prior to the notice of intention to withdraw. The BRICS NU NCC or other national governing structure shall inform the BRICS NU IGB, which in turn will inform the other BRICS NU participant higher education institutions of this intention to withdraw within thirty days from the date of notification.

In case of the withdrawal of an institution the present MoU's provisions shall remain in force in respect of projects and programmes under implementation until their full completion or with the approval of the BRICS NU NCC or other national governing structure.

Article 18
Duration and Termination of MoU

The present MoU shall be concluded for an indefinite period and shall come into effect upon signature.

The decision on the termination of the present MoU shall be taken by the Ministries of Education of the BRICS countries. All the BRICS NU participant higher education institutions shall be informed of this decision within thirty days from the date of the decision.

In the event of the termination of the present MoU its provisions shall remain in force in respect of ongoing projects and programmes.

Article 19
Other provisions

All other matters not addressed herein shall be resolved by the BRICS NU IGB. Completed in the city of Moscow on 18 November 2015 in 5 copies in the English language.

Completed in the City of Moscow on 18 November 2015 in 5 copies in the English language.

THE FEDERATIVE REPUBLIC OF BRAZIL

THE RUSSIAN FEDERATION

THE REPUBLIC OF INDIA

THE PEOPLE'S REPUBLIC OF CHINA

THE REPUBLIC OF SOUTH AFRICA

IV.5. MoU – BRICS Export Credit Insurance Agencies: 15 Jul. 2014, Fortaleza (BRA)

MEMORANDUM OF UNDERSTANDING

ON COOPERATION

AMONG

BRICS EXPORT CREDIT INSURANCE AGENCIES

Brazilian Guarantees Agency	OJSC «Russian Agency for Export Credit and Investment Insurance»
Export Credit Guarantee Corporation of India Ltd	China Export & Credit Insurance Corporation

Export Credit Insurance
Corporation of South Africa SOC Ltd

Dated July 15, 2014

This **Memorandum of Understanding on Cooperation ("MoU")** is entered into by and among the following export credit insurance agencies of the BRICS countries (the Federative Republic of Brazil, the Russian Federation, Republic of India, People's Republic of China and the Republic of South Africa) respectively:

1. **Brazilian Guarantees Agency (Agência Brasileira Gestora de Fundos Garantidores e Garantias S.A. – "ABGF")**, a state-owned company with the purpose of operating in the guarantee, insurance and reinsurance sectors. ABGF's registered office is at Setor de Autarquia Sul, Quadra 3, Bloco O, 11º andar, Ed. Órgãos Regionais, CEP 70.079-900 – Brasília – DF, Brazil;

2. **OJSC «Russian Agency for Export Credit and Investment Insurance», Russian Federation ("EXIAR")**, fully owned by the State Corporation Bank for Development and Foreign Economic Affairs (Vnesheconombank). EXIAR is a specialized institution playing a strategic role in supporting Russian exports and investments abroad. EXIAR's registered office is at 3, 1st Zachatievsky Pereulok, Bldg. 1, Moscow, 119034;

3. **Export Credit Guarantee Corporation of India Ltd, India ("ECGC")**, an export credit insurance organization fully owned by Government of India. ECGC is established to provide insurance for exporters and banks in India, and to encourage, facilitate and develop trade between India and other countries. ECGC's registered office is at Express Towers, 10th Floor, Nariman Point, Mumbai – 400 021, India;

4. **China Export & Credit Insurance Corporation, P.R. China ("SINOSURE")**, an authorized Chinese export credit insurance institution, fully owned by government. SINOSURE's registered office is at Fortune Times Building, 11 Fenghuiyuan, Xicheng District, Beijing, China; and

5. **Export Credit Insurance Corporation of South Africa Ltd, South Africa ("ECIC")**, an authorized South African export credit insurance company. ECIC is a self-sustained state-owned ECA with its registered office at 349 Witch Hazel Avenue, Highveld Extension 79, Centurion, 0157, South Africa.

hereinafter referred to as "Participant" in singular or collectively as **"the Participants"**.

Whereas the Participants wish to facilitate co-operation between and among them by:

1.   promoting a non-exclusive framework for the development of cooperative efforts between the Participants which will support and encourage trade and investment within the BRICS countries;

2.   promoting a non-exclusive framework of cooperation of joint projects envisaging the supply of goods and services from their respective countries as part of joint projects in third countries, which will internationally promote products and services of BRICS countries;

3.   exchanging experience in export credit and investment insurance; and

4.   exchanging their positions towards international guidelines and regulations on export credits and investment insurance.

THE PARTICIPANTS HAVE REACHED THE FOLLOWING UNDERSTANDING:

ARTICLE 1: CO-OPERATION WITH REGARD TO PROJECTS

a)   The Participants may co-operate in the provision of support for a project in a third country which involves the supply of goods and services from BRICS countries. Each Participant will make its own determination as to whether it will participate in providing support for a project and in accordance with its mandate.

b)   Where the Participants provide support directly for a project in a third country envisaging, the supply of goods and services from BRICS countries to that project:

   i.   ABGF may, under its guarantee and insurance products, support the supply of Brazilian goods and services;

   ii. EXIAR may, under its insurance products, support the supply of Russian goods and services;

   iii. ECGC may, under its insurance products, support the supply of Indian goods and services;

   iv. SINOSURE may, under its guarantee and insurance products, support the Chinese supply of goods and services;

   v.   ECIC may, under its guarantee and insurance products, support the supply of South African goods and services;

   vi. the terms and conditions of support will be subject to the Participants' respective policies and procedures;

   vii. the Participants will, subject to any legal constraints and any requirements for any Participant's consent, provide each other with information on the project and the proposed financing.

c)   In order to provide a single source of export credit support to a project sponsor, each of the Participants, where appropriate, may consider including support for each other's share of a project under its guarantee or, as the case may be, insurance in respect of that project, subject to their respective domestic rules and regulations on the provision of support for foreign content.

d)   Where the Participants contemplate co-operating on a project, they may, during the evaluation, approval, negotiation and documentation stages (and subject to any legal constraints or any requirements for any Participant's consent), share relevant information on the project. Each Party shall use its own documentation and procedures, unless otherwise agreed.

e)   Where the Participants are involved in a project which experiences difficulties after support has been provided, they may make joint efforts to co-operate in order to remedy those difficulties including addressing defaults on payments and debt recovery.

f)   All cooperation on specific projects will be governed by separate agreements entered into by the Participants.

ARTICLE 2: CONSULTATION AND INFORMATION SHARING

a)   In order to support and encourage trade and investments between and among the BRICS countries, the Participants agree to assist each other in obtaining information for risk assessment and claims management with regards to projects in their respective countries.

b)   The Participants may, periodically, share experience on export credit issues and investment insurance in areas of common interest.

c)   The Participants may share views on existing international guidelines and regulations on export credit and investment insurance and may hold discussions on any possible amendments and/or alterations to such guidelines and regulations which will be favourable to the Participants.

ARTICLE 3: CONFIDENTIALITY

a)   "Confidential Information" means any information provided by one Participant ("Disclosing Participant") to another Participant ("Receiving Participant") within the framework of this MoU.

b)   Notwithstanding the foregoing, the following will not constitute Confidential Information for the purposes of this MoU: (i) information which is already in the public domain or lawfully in the possession of the Receiving Party at the time of its disclosure to the Receiving Party by Disclosing Party and is publicly disclosed after the execution of this Memorandum by the Disclosing Party ; (ii) information which was already known to a Receiving Participant on a nonconfidential basis prior to being furnished to it by a Disclosing Participant; or (iii) information which becomes available to a Receiving Participant on a non-confidential basis from a source other than a Disclosing Participant if such source was not subject to any prohibition against transmitting the information to the Receiving Participant.

c)   The Participants are herein expressly authorized to disclose all the Confidential Information to their respective Guardian Authorities (governmental authorities responsible for the Participants), upon a commitment not to transfer such information to governments not involved in the instance in question, and to any auditors assigned by their Guardian Authorities to supervise their activities, to the extent necessary for such supervision. The provisions in this Article will apply regardless of the expiration or termination of this MoU and remain in full force and effect.

ARTICLE 4: OTHER PROVISIONS

a)   This MoU shall take effect on the date it is signed by all the Participants.

b)   This MoU may be reviewed periodically at the request of any of the Participants.

c)   Any Participants may terminate its participation in this MoU by giving a prior written notice of one (1) month to the other participants of its intention to terminate this MOU. Such termination will not affect any commitments assumed prior to such notification.

d)   Any disputes arising from the interpretation or application of this MoU shall be settled through consultations between and among the Participants.

e)   This MoU is only a statement of co-operative intent and sets forth no legal obligations for any Participant.

f)   All written communications required or permitted under the MoU shall be in English and be directed to the following addresses, which may be amended from time to time by the Participants.

FOR ABGF:
Agência Brasileira Gestora de Fundos Garantidores e Garantias S.A.
BRAZIL
ATT: Mr. Marcelo Pinheiro Franco
Fax No: +55 (61) 3412-4004
E-mail: mfranco@abgf.gov.br

FOR EXIAR:
OJSC Russian Agency for Export Credit and Investment Insurance
RUSSIAN FEDERATION
ATT: Mr. Petr M. Fradkov
Chief Executive Officer
Fax No: +7 (495) 783 11 22
Email: Fradkov@exiar.ru

FOR ECGC:
Export Credit Guarantee Corporation of India Limited
INDIA
ATT: Mr. Narayanaswamy Shankar
Chairman-cum-Managing Director
Telephone No: +91 22 66590514
Fax No. -+91 22 66590517
Email: cmd@ecgc.in

FOR SINOSURE:
China Export & Credit Insurance Corporation
CHINA
ATT: Mr. Tan Jian
Fax No. +86 10 6651 2196
Telephone No: +86 10 6658 2316
Email: tanj@sinosure.com.cn

FOR ECIC:
Export Credit Insurance Corporation of South Africa SOC Ltd
SOUTH AFRICA
Kutoane O. Kutoane
Chief Executive Officer
Telephone No: +27 12 471 3800
Email: kkutoane@ecic.co.za

In witness whereof the undersigned being duly authorized thereto by the respective Participants, have signed this MOU done at Fortaleza on the 15th day of July 2014 in five originals in the English language.

For and on behalf of	For and on behalf of
ABGF	**EXIAR**
Signed...................................	Signed...................................
Name: **Marcelo Pinheiro Franco**	Name: **Petr M. Fradkov**
Position: President	Position: Chief Executive Officer
For and on behalf of	For and on behalf of
ECGC	**SINOSURE**
Signed...................................	Signed...................................
Name: **Narayanaswamy Shankar**	Name: **Wang Yi**
Position: Chairman-cum-Managing Director	Position: Chairman

For and on behalf of
ECIC
Signed.................................
Name: **Kutoane Kutoane**
Position: Chief Executive Officer

IV.6.   BRICS Cooperation Agreement on Innovation: 16 Jul. 2014, Fortaleza (BRA)

COOPERATION AGREEMENT ON INNOVATION

Cooperation Agreement on Innovation Between Banco Nacional De Desenvolvimento Economico E Social – BNDES, The Stat Corporation Bank for Development and Forrign Economic Affairs (VNESHECONOMBANK), The Export-Import Bank of India, The China Development Bank Corporation And The Development Bank of South Africa Limited

This BRICS Multilateral Cooperation Agreement on Innovation Is Made In Fortaleza, Brazil, On 16th July, 2014, Amongst:

(1) Banco Nacional de Desenvolvimento Econômico e Social – BNDES ("BNDES"), a wholly-owned federal government company duly established and validly existing under the laws of the Federative Republic of Brazil ("Brazil"), with its registered head office in Brasilia, Federal District, and principal place of business at 100 Av. República do Chile, the city of Rio de Janeiro, State of Rio de Janeiro, CEP 20031-917;

(2) State Corporation «Bank for Development and Foreign Economic Affairs (Vnesheconombank)», a state-owned corporation duly established under the law of the Russian Federation ("Russia"), with its registered head office at 9 Akademika Sakharova Prospekt, Moscow 107996, the Russian Federation;

(3) Export-Import Bank of India ("Exim Bank"), a state-owned corporation duly established under the Act of Parliament of the Republic of India ("India") and having its head office at Floor 21, World Trade Centre Complex, Cuffe Parade, Mumbai-400 005, Republic of India;

(4) China Development Bank Corporation ("CDB"), a state-owned corporation duly established under the laws of the People's Republic of China ("China"), with its head office at No. 18 Fuxingmennei Street, Xicheng District, Beijing, 100031, the People's Republic of China; and

(5) Development Bank of Southern Africa Limited (DBSA), a state-owned development finance institution duly established under the laws of the Republic of South Africa ("South Africa"), with its head office at 1258 Lever Road, Headway Hill, Midrand, 1685, the Republic of South Africa;

(hereinafter individually referred to as a "Party" and collectively referred to as the "Parties") acting in accordance with its respective By-laws:

WHEREAS

A)   On April 15th 2010, BNDES, Vnesheconombank, Exim Bank and CDB executed the Memorandum on Cooperation pursuant to which a cooperation mechanism was established in order to strengthen and develop long-term relationships amongst those institutions. The following year, on April 13th 2011, BNDES, Vnesheconombank, Exim Bank, CDB and DBSA, executed the Protocol of Accession of the DBSA to the Memorandum on Cooperation whereby DBSA became a party to the initiatives set out in the Memorandum on Cooperation mentioned above.

On April 14th 2011, the Parties entered into a Framework Agreement on Financial Cooperation within the BRICS Interbank Cooperation Mechanism ("Framework Agreement"). Under the Framework Agreement the Parties wish to promote and facilitate trade of goods, services, and investment in mutual projects between and among the BRICS Countries.

On March 29th 2012, the Parties concluded the Master Agreement on Extending Credit Facility in Local Currency under BRICS Interbank Cooperation Mechanism, as well as the BRICS Multilateral Letter of Credit Confirmation Facility Agreement. Finally, on March 27th 2013, the Parties signed two new instruments: BRICS Multilateral Cooperation and Co-financing Agreement for Sustainable Development and BRICS Multilateral Infrastructure Co-financing Agreement for Africa.

B)   The Parties wish to further advance the objectives set out in the Framework Agreement and in this instance, more specifically to enhance communication and information sharing among the partner countries in the context of the provisions contained in the Delhi Declaration of the BRICS Leaders.

C)   The Parties have obtained the relevant internal authorization to enter into this Agreement.

NOW, THEREFORE,

Given the increasing necessity of the BRICS Countries in fostering innovation initiatives in the future and in order to facilitate the sharing of information about technological innovation programs within the countries and any other countries within which the Parties may operate and the financing of or investment in such programs, the Parties will endeavor, as the need arises, to enter into multilateral or bilateral agreements ("Multilateral Agreement" or "Bilateral Agreement") aimed at coordinating cooperation, skills transfer and knowledge sharing between and among the Parties. The purposes and intents of this Agreement are to strengthen the relationship between the Parties and establish a framework of cooperation on projects of mutual interest and if necessary the financing of such projects, in accordance with the laws and regulations applicable to each of the Parties. The Parties hereby agree to enter into this BRICS Multilateral Cooperation Agreement on Innovation (hereinafter the "Agreement") as follows:

Clause One
OBJECTIVES /PURPOSE OF THIS COOPERATION AGREEMENT

1.1 Subject to the terms agreed to between the relevant Parties in the Multilateral or Bilateral Agreements, the focus of the relevant Multilateral or Bilateral Agreements may include, but not be limited to, projects and initiatives that foster investments in technological innovation with emphasis on infrastructure and sustainable energy, including process and product innovation in different fields, related to industries, services and agribusiness, such as:

    1.1.1 promoting knowledge sharing initiatives related to best practices, innovative financing, emerging technologies and financing of innovation projects;

    1.1.2 exchanging views, experience and expertise on financing innovation, as and when the Parties mutually deem it to be appropriate;

    1.1.3 conducting dialogues and other forms of knowledge sharing, in accordance with each Party's relevant internal policies and regulations; and

    1.1.4 co-financing initiatives aimed at the technological development of areas of mutual interest to the Parties, consistent with the applicable laws and regulations of their respective countries.

1.2 The Agreement aims to increase the priority given by the Parties in seeking cooperation with each other to increase the flow of funding directed towards innovation projects relevant to the development objectives and mandates of the respective Parties.

1.3 For the purpose of furthering effective cooperation amongst the Parties, consultations may be held from time to time at the request of any of the Parties in order to identify new areas of cooperation, review existing operations and discuss any other matters pertaining to innovation financing. Such consultations may be in the form of meetings or other methods of interaction as agreed between and among the Parties.

Clause Two
MULTILATERAL OR BILATERAL AGREEMENTS

2.1 Whereas this Agreement provides an outline for the cooperation between the Parties, the range of skills, tools, knowledge and technologies shared, together with the exact nature thereof will be limited to those agreed to between and among the Parties to a Multilateral or Bilateral Agreement.

2.2 The execution of any Multilateral or Bilateral Agreement shall be subject to the approval of the relevant regulatory authorities of the Parties to such agreement and to each Party's internal approval processes.

2.3 These and any other activities agreed between and among the Parties shall be subject to the internal objectives, functions, policies and procedures of the respective Parties.

Clause Three
MISCELLANEOUS

3.1 The Parties shall endeavor to share all pertinent information relating to the implementation of this Agreement, except for any information which a Party determines, at its own discretion, to be confidential and which is communicated as being confidential in writing.

3.2 The Parties herein agree that the information delivered under this Agreement is subject to the laws, programs and policies of their respective governments and, specifically, to laws regulating banking confidentiality to which each Party may be subject in their respective countries.

3.3 In order to avoid any doubts about rights or obligations related to this Agreement, it is recognized by the Parties that this Agreement is a statement of good faith, intent and mutual understanding of the Parties. This Agreement does not, nor does it intend to create any rights to, or impose any legal obligations or liabilities, financial or otherwise, on any of the Parties hereto or their officers or employees, nor does it bind the Parties to enter into any agreements, nor gives any preferential right for any agreement each Party intends to enter. Nothing contained herein shall confer any legal rights or obligations on third parties.

3.4 Each Party recognizes that the cooperation described in this Agreement is not exclusive and that each Party may enter into similar cooperation agreements with any other party or parties.

3.5 Any dispute arising out of or in connection with this Agreement shall be resolved through consultation on a cooperative basis between and among the Parties.

3.6 Any communication to be made under or in connection with this Agreement shall be made in writing and may be made by fax, letter, or e-mail.

3.7 Except as otherwise agreed in writing by the Parties, each Party shall be responsible for its own costs and expenses in connection with undertaking any action contemplated by this Agreement, including but not limited to salary, travel and lodging and other costs of such Party's employees.

3.8 The address, including the relevant department or officer for whose attention communication is to be marked, of each of the Parties is set forth below:

Banco Nacional de Desenvolvimento Econômico e Social–BNDES
Unit: International Division
Address:Av. República do Chile 330, 21st floor, Rio de Janeiro, State of Rio de Janeiro, Brazil
Postal Code: CEP 20031-170
Telephone: +55212172-8142
Fax: +55212172-6286
E-mail: lbf@bndes.gov.br

State Corporation «Bank for Development and Foreign Economic Affairs (Vnesheconombank)»

Unit: External Relations Department
Address:9 Akademika Sakharova Prospekt, Moscow, Russia
Postal Code: 107996
Telephone: +7 495 782 9485
Fax: +7 495 604 6183
E-mail: iao@veb.ru

Export-Import Bank of India
Unit: Chief General Manager, Research & Analysis
Address:Floor 21, World Trade Centre Complex, Cuffe Parade, Mumbai, India
Postal Code: 400 005
Telephone: +91-22-22160364
Fax: +91-22-22180743
E-mail: prahalathan@eximbankindia.in

China Development Bank Corporation
Unit: International Finance Department
Address:No. 18 Fuxingmennei Street, Xicheng District, Beijing, People's Republic of China
Postal Code: 100031
Telephone: +861068307342
Fax: +861068306541
E-mail: zhouzhenheng@cdb.cn

Development Bank of Southern Africa Limited
Department:Office of the Chief Executive Officer
Address:1258 Lever Road, Headway Hill, Midrand, 1685, South Africa
Telephone: +27 (0)11 313 3341 / 3516
Fax: +27 (0)11 206 3341 / 3516
E-mail: ernestd@dbsa.org

or any substitute department, address, telephone number, fax number, or e-mail address as any Party may notify to the other Parties.

Clause Four
EFFECTIVENESS

4.1 This Agreement shall be executed in quintuplet with each Party holding one executed copy, and each such copy shall be treated as an original.

4.2 Any amendments and supplements to this Agreement will be made in the written form and signed by duly authorized representative of each respective Party and shall be an integral part of this Agreement.

4.3 This Agreement shall come into effect from the date of its signing by the authorized persons of all the Parties and shall remain in full force and effect for five (5) years from the date thereof. Thereafter, it will be renewable for further successive periods by mutual written consent of the Parties. Any Party may decide to terminate this Agreement with not less than 60 (sixty) days prior written notice to the other Parties (unless earlier termination is required by law). In this case, the other Parties may, jointly, decide to continue this Agreement excluding the Party that has given the termination notice. The termination of this Agreement shall not result in the termination of any other agreements between and among the Parties.

Clause Five
PUBLICITY

5.1 Notwithstanding the obligations under Clause 3.2 (confidentiality restrictions) and in order to comply with internal policies, the Parties may publish a summary of this Agreement. Signed at _____ on 2014 in Five originals in the English language.

Banco Nacional de Desenvolvimento Econômico e Social – BNDES

Signature: _____

Name:

Title:

State Corporation «Bank for Development and Foreign Economic Affairs (Vnesheconombank)»

Signature: _____

Name:

Title:

Export-Import Bank of India

Signature: _____

Name:

Title:

China Development Bank Corporation

Signature: _____

Name:

Title:

Development Bank of Southern Africa Limited

Signature: _____

Name:

Title:

V.   THE BRICS LEGAL FORUM

V.1.   5th BRICS Legal Forum: 24 Aug. 2018, Cape Town (ZAF)

CAPE TOWN SOUTH AFRICA DECLARATION

1.   We, the representatives of the legal communities of BRICS member states, steeped in the values and principles encapsulated in the concept of the Rule of Law and giving highest value to the fundamental guarantees of human dignity, liberty and equality, having met in Cape Town from 23 to 24 August 2018 and deliberated on various legal issues that impact on socio-economic activities, trade and dispute resolution.

2.   Acknowledging and supporting the objectives in the declarations signed by the BRICS heads of states, including the 10th BRICS Summit Johannesburg Declaration under the theme BRICS in Africa: Collaboration for Inclusive Growth and Shared Prosperity in the Fourth Industrial Revolution, we reaffirm our commitment to work towards realisation of these objectives by helping to create legal and policy frameworks having their basis in fairness, equality, inclusion, respect for social and human rights and the rule of law.

3.   We acknowledge Law Society of South Africa for hosting the 5th BRICS Legal Forum in which implementation of our declarations, creation of BRICS Legal Forum institutions and setting up of networks of emerging nations took a center stage.

4.   We considered and reaffirmed our commitment for helping create a rule based, fair, just and equitable democratic international trade and economic order based on principles of multilaterism and the rule of law that provides for sustainable development and inclusive growth and in order to achieve that, help create commercial and investment disputes resolution mechanisms and institutions which are fair, efficient, representative and inclusive in their character and cater to the needs and requirements of BRICS and emerging markets and developing economies.

5.   We will endeavour, wherever possible, to leverage existing dispute resolution institutions in member states and between member states to quickly establish BRICS dispute resolution centres within the shortest reasonable time in order to have institutions ready to handle disputes that may arise, provided such institutions adhere to the Rules and Procedures set by the relevant expert committee of BRICS Legal Forum.

6.   We, endorse in principle the approach paper presented by the Bar Association of India which builds upon the resolution adopted in the Moscow declaration of the Legal Forum to create a network of commercial dispute resolution institutions in the BRICS and emerging markets and developing economies and to build professional capacity and required expertise in the BRICS countries and emerging markets and developing economies by collaborating with existing institutions and dispute resolution centres in the emerging world and to collaborate with new multilateral institutions created by BRICS, i.e. the New Development Bank and those anchored and supported by BRICS member states like the Asia Infrastructure Investment Bank, decided to take further steps to refine and to prepare a road map to implement the initiative through active and collaborative participation of all member states. We resolve to develop and promote effective mechanisms of dispute resolution through the process of commercial mediation.

7.   We recognise the need to setup an ecosystem and networks to advance our objective of developing a just and fair world order in socio-economic activities of emerging economies.

8.   Considering that the BRICS Legal Forum in Cape Town has been included in the official and sectoral meetings mentioned in the X BRICS summit Johannesburg declaration 2018, we will

approach the Governments of our countries with the purpose to seek representation and participation of the BRICS Legal Forum representatives of the BRICS summit meetings.

9. We recognise the importance of enhancing high level professional exchange for further development of the BRICS Legal Forum effectiveness. This will be achieved through discussions and making decision on consensus. Further, we will conduct BRICS Legal Forum activities through various established committees of the BRICS Legal Forum based on rules and procedures adopted.

10. We are aware of the need to establish institutions and capacitating them in order to be able to implement our declarations and promoting annual legal talents program for young lawyers and exchange of students and experts among BRICS member states. We acknowledge the contribution of the Moscow State Institute of International Relations of the Ministry of Foreign Affairs of the Russian Federation and the Association of Lawyers of Russia; for hosting the BRICS Legal Talent program as part of the IV BRICS Legal Forum.

11. Having agreed to set up BRICS Legal Forum institutions and their operating principles and mechanisms, we are poised to build upon and implement more effectively the resolutions passed in each declaration in member state, do hereby resolve to establish the Evaluation and Coordination Committee of the BRICS Legal Forum. A Committee that will promote that the adopted declarations are implemented by all member states. For this purpose, a terms of reference will be developed by a working group to be appointed and later approved by the heads of delegations.

12. We recognise the imperative of sustainable development, conducive trade environment including commercial environment free from corrupt tendencies in carrying out our mandate. Accordingly, we support initiatives aimed at dealing with crimes such as corruption, tax evasion, money laundering and drug trafficking.

13. We resolve to constitute a working group to help develop a mechanism within BRICS to cooperate in anti-corruption and money laundering law enforcement, extradition of fugitives, economic and corruption offenders and repatriation in matters relating to assets recovery and other related criminal and non-criminal matters involving corruption to ensure a robust implementation of the United Nation Convention against Corruption in the BRICS countries.

14. We resolve to constitute working groups:

14.1 to help develop a mechanism within BRICS for effective implementation and enforcement of laws relating to drugs trafficking and drug induced violence and crime.

14.2 to develop legal cooperation and approaches in relation to custody and welfare of children in cross border family disputes and crimes against women and children.

15. We resolve to further strengthen our collaboration to help implementation aspects of Johannesburg declaration having a bearing to our role as lawyers in society and trade, particularly in relation to

(i) Artificial Intelligence and Information and Communication Technology which are integral to the fourth industrial revolution but require constant legal cooperation and development of legal frameworks to prevent cybercrimes and to address security related implications and threats that arise from misuse of ICT and

(ii) For implementation of the UN 2030 Agenda of Sustainable Development and Sustainable Development Goals (SDGs) by helping strengthen the institutions and legal and policy mechanisms that promote and sustain the rule of law in order to pave the way for equitable, inclusive, open, all round innovation driven development, encapsulating concerns of environmental and ecologically balanced economic growth to achieve the ultimate goal of eradication of poverty.

16. We will take steps to achieve better coordination and integration in the BRICS activities framework and to ensure collaboration and interaction with other stakeholders and participation in meetings and events organised by them each year, such as BRICS Business Forum etc.

17. Participants of the V BRICS Legal Forum (South Africa) express gratitude to the host party, the Law Society of South Africa, and highly appreciate its efforts in organising a very high quality Forum both in terms of content and hospitality.

18. We unanimously accept and endorse the proposal of OAB to host the VI Legal Forum in Brazil in 2019 to take forward the spirit and objectives of the BRICS Legal Forum to structure a new world order based on the principles of fairness, justice, equality and inclusiveness and thank them for this gesture.

Signed at Cape Town, South Africa on the 24 August 2018 by the following representatives

Mr. Marcus Vinicus F. Coêlho	Mr. Stanislav Alexandrov
Brazil Bar Association	Association of Lawyers of Russia
Mr. Prashant Kumar	Ms. Pinky Anand
Bar Association of India	Bar Association of India
Mr. Zhang Mingqi	Ms. Lin Yanping
China Law Society	East China University of Political Science and Law
Mr. Etienne Barnard	
Law Society of South Africa	

V.2. 4th BRICS Legal Forum: 1 Dec. 2017, Moscow (RUS)

MOSCOW DECLARATION

WE, representatives of the legal communities of the BRICS member states, having gathered here in Moscow, Russian Federation, on 30 November – 1 December 2017 at the IV BRICS Legal Forum entitled "Interaction between the legal systems of the BRICS member states: towards an equitable global order";

CONSIDERING the provisions of the final documents of the leaders summits of the BRICS member states, including the BRICS Leaders Xiamen Declaration (Xiamen, China, 4 September 2017);

SUPPORTING the objectives to create a more just, equitable, stable, democratic, representative international political and economic order rooted in the core values of social and human rights and the rule of law;

RECOGNISING the need to enhance cooperation within BRICS, based on the principles of equality, respect for sovereignty and mutual benefit;

ATTACHING great importance to the development of mutual understanding and dialogue amongst the legal community of BRICS for the promotion of the rule of law to preserve and promote human dignity and freedom through equitable and inclusive social, economic, political and cultural development;

STRIVING to accomplish the spirit of the 2014 Brasilia Declaration, 2015 Shanghai Declaration and 2016 New Delhi Declaration of BRICS Legal Forum by forming practical structures for implementation and monitoring;

AFFIRMING the importance of strengthening the fruitful cooperation between the BRICS member states in the sphere of law and jurisprudence, as well as the need to establish more effective conditions for exchange at the professional and academic level;

DECLARE hereby as follows:

1. Cooperation in the sphere of law, which encompasses economic, social and other spheres of human enterprise, is integral to the development of BRICS and needs to be acknowledged as an important part of the BRICS initiative;

2. The main objectives of legal cooperation within BRICS are:

   - Exchanging experience between legal communities at the institutional level amongst the judges, lawyers and legal academics in different spheres, in particular regarding to national doctrines and practices for business and international trade;

   - Organisation of an effective communication and exchange of knowledge, students and faculty between law schools of the BRICS member states;

   - Development of professional relationships and business contacts between legal practitioners of the BRICS member states, by providing platforms for collaboration, networking and exchange of knowledge and practices and publishing the outcomes thereof;

   - Establishment of a BRICS Legal Forum "think tank" as a Centre for Legal Policy for BRICS to conduct research and carry out monitoring of legal aspects of BRICS functioning, including those which contribute to the promotion of the rule of law as constitutionally entrenched in each jurisdiction to achieve inclusive human development;

   - Establishment of a Board of Governors for policy direction and a Panel of Arbitrators and common institutional rules to coordinate and fuse the functioning of the BRICS Dispute

Resolution Centers already established at Shanghai and New Delhi and the proposed Centers in Brazil, Russia and South Africa, to create a wider and broader framework of neutrality under the BRICS framework, for disputes arising within and outside of BRICS, and to set in motion a time bound plan of action for implementation. The day-to-day administration and conduct of affairs of these centers will continue to vest in the respective jurisdictions. The concept paper proposed by the Bar Association of India will be fine tuned by January 31, 2018 and adopted as a Road Map by email circulation by the steering committee of the Forum, which is mandated to take further steps in this direction.

3.   We propose the following as further areas of legal cooperation within BRICS:

- Organisation of networking structures aimed at exchanging knowledge, information and best practices between judges, advocates, prosecutors and other representatives of legal professions of the BRICS member states;

- Preparation of analytic reviews of legislation of the BRICS member states within the framework of cooperation in comparative law research (general and/or thematic reviews, such as "Business Law of the BRICS member states");

- Holding international conferences for exchanging experiences and for deepening cooperation in the areas of business laws, dispute resolution, anti-corruption, money laundering, terrorism and to develop common approach and strategy to contribute to the development of international law and conventions and model laws and frameworks at various international fora, including related to the UN and other international bodies active in this area;

- Publication of a research journal on the development of the BRICS legislation (for example, "BRICS Law Review");

- Formation of a working group on development and harmonisation of tax laws in BRICS;

- Formation of a working group on Development of Legal Framework for Digital Economy and Governance and Regulation of Innovations in Artificial Intelligence and Internet of Things;

- Formation of a rules drafting committee for harmonisation and development of common institutional rules of arbitration centers;

- Formation of the Working Group on Study and Harmonisation of Business and Contract Laws.

Member Organisations shall make serious endeavor to nominate at the earliest 3 representatives each to form each working group, composed of established domain experts and practitioners, who will elect the chair and co-chair and will hold constructive meetings before the next Forum in South Africa and circulate draft rules 4 weeks prior to the V Legal Forum. The Working Groups will be empowered to co-opt experts to assist in their functioning.

Assessing the outcomes of the IV (Moscow) BRICS Forum, we, on behalf of its participants – legal communities of the BRICS member states, state the following:

1.   We are conscious that the development of legislation of the BRICS member states on the principles of protecting national sovereignty, democracy, rule of law, human rights and affording political and social guarantees by all the people, living in the BRICS member states, shall lead to sustainable political, social and economic development of these countries and their mutually beneficial cooperation.

Unification of legal regulations and their harmonisation, balanced reception and incorporation shall serve as the basis for interaction of legal systems of the BRICS member states subject to the principles of independence, respect for state sovereignty and national law.

International treaties, model "soft" rule-making, use of progressive global practice are the instruments of modern legal order, in the development of which the BRICS member states should contribute in a collective and collaborative manner and be guided by these instruments in fostering legal cooperation.

2.   We envisage that the legal communities of BRICS shall act in a coherent, balanced and collaborative manner, with commonality of purpose, by forming positions respectful of legal identity and sovereignty of each member state, to develop and adopt uniform legal approaches and standards beneficial not only for BRICS, but to serve as benchmarks for international cooperation per se to achieve the objective of general welfare through sustainable economic growth.

We underline the need of continuing our efforts in the sphere of tax and customs policy, establishment of information transparency and accessibility, countering corruption, money laundering and fair and transparent disclosure of beneficial ownership of business structures.

We believe that approving the multilateral model convention on cross-border tax dispute resolution is an important step towards improving tax relations between the BRICS member states.

3.   We acknowledge the need to continue our efforts to prevent conflicts of national jurisdictions, improve jurisdictional attractiveness of each BRICS member state, which leads to an increase of international attractiveness of BRICS as a whole.

Unification of national substantive and conflict-of-law rules is the most effective way to improve the jurisdictional attractiveness. State security of foreign investment is the key to form sustainable and favorable investment climate. Mutual recognition and enforcement of foreign judgments and arbitral awards determine the enhancement of credibility of the foreign jurisdiction. The BRICS legal communities intend to continue the cooperation on improving arbitral and other forms of cross-border dispute resolution, on lines of the initiative that forms part of the core objective of this declaration above and to further innovate and expand the same.

4.   We emphasise that coordinated efforts to ensure the stability of constitutional order of the BRICS member states, counter global terrorism, corruption, protect the sovereignty, security and territorial integrity of our states shall become one of the most important areas of cooperation between the BRICS legal communities.

Fight against arms, drug trafficking and transnational terrorism are essential elements of joint efforts in the sphere of international security. The BRICS legal communities call to intensify the cooperation in this sphere to increase the joint contribution to face the major global threats.

5.   We recognise the importance of environmental issues in all the BRICS member states and the need to enhance the international legal cooperation for ensuring environmental safety, creating legal mechanisms to prevent catastrophic climate change on our planet, legal basis of using the newest energy- and resource-saving technology, aimed at the protection of the environment.

We will continue our joint researches and exchanging experience of the legal regulation in the sphere of environmental safety and protection from pollution, as well as natural resources management of the BRICS member states, in accordance with national conditions and priorities.

We intend to continue an active exchange of experience relating to the elaboration of sports legislation and management of sports activities. Preventing and combatting doping and corruption in sports are an important area of legal cooperation of the BRICS member states. With particular interest, we explore the possibility of forming an international legal mechanism of realisation and protection of intellectual property (IP) rights of the sportspersons.

We unanimously accept and endorse the proposal of the Law Society of South Africa to host the V Legal Forum in South Africa in 2018 and thank them for this gesture.

Participants of the IV BRICS Legal Forum (Moscow, Russian Federation) express gratitude to the host party, Russian Federation, and highly appreciate its efforts in organising a very high quality Forum both in terms of content and hospitality.

V.3.   3rd BRICS Legal Forum: 12 Sep. 2016, New Delhi (IND)

THE NEW DELHI DECLARATION 2016

WE, the representatives of the legal communities of the BRICS having gathered here in New Delhi, on this 12th day of September, Two Thousand and Sixteen, at the Third BRICS Legal Forum, organized around the theme of Developing Legal Frameworks for Building Responsive, Inclusive and Collective Solutions, not only to benefit the peoples of BRICS but the countries of the entire emerging world.

Committed to take further initiatives launched at Brasilia in December 2014 and Shanghai in October 2015, resolve to deepen our engagement to build further on such initiatives.

Recognizing the core elements of Brasilia and Shanghai declarations are at the heart of the initiatives of the BRICS Legal Forum and will remain so.

Recognizing Brasilia Declaration had inter alia, stipulated that the members of the Legal communities of the BRICS have constituted themselves in BRICS Legal Forum to

Assist in development of a conducive legal and policy framework for the growth of business and trade in the BRICS countries, thereby helping create greater investment, trade and employment opportunities, paying the way for the BRICS countries to realize the harmonious developmental goals to serve the needs, requirements and aspirations of their peoples.

Strive to promote excellence in legal profession and human resources in BRICS region and undertake and encourage legal research on issues of common importance and provide legal-intellectual support for development of policy and legislative frameworks.

Noting that the Shanghai Declaration, adopted on 13th October, 2015 at Shanghai, during the 2nd BRICS Legal Forum, besides recognizing the Brasilia Declaration, recognized the efforts to establish a Steering Committee of BRICS Legal Forum and resolved that the Steering Committee shall meet once a year alongside the BRICS Legal Forum.

Mindful that the Shanghai Declaration had noted that in the context of globalization, an open international environment with fair, reasonable and equitable rules is necessary for the economic transformation and development of emerging markets. We underline the importance of legal diplomacy in promoting greater democratic, more lawful and more balanced international relations, and in advancing reform in global governance. With a focused attention to the latest developments and implementation outcomes of global legal systems and policies, we are willing to coordinate international relations through legal approaches to seek shared interests and common ground while putting aside differences, and to promote communication and collaboration on legal issues in a proactive and practical way by holding regular international conferences for extensive exchange of information and ideas. In this regard, we aim to make contributions to the development of global legal systems and policies.

Conscious that the Shanghai Declaration further noted that "We recognize the fundamental legal, political and constitutional values, concepts, cultures and principles of all countries who are involved in the Forum, with a common aim to promote and protect the Rule of Law and universal human lights. We acknowledge and safeguard the independence and integrity of the legal profession."

Aware that the Shanghai Declaration also supported the initiatives of alliance of BRICS Law Universities and with inauguration of Shanghai Centre for BRICS Dispute Resolution Settlement and its Expert Committee envisaged that concrete measures be taken to enhance the mechanism to set up centres in Russia, Brazil, India and South Africa respectively which will be structured in a manner so as to secure more opportunities and to promote excellence within BRICS. The Shanghai Declaration and Expert Meeting at Ekaterinburgh also "noted the importance of cooperation in intra-BRICS' construction of financial and legal framework.

Now at New Delhi, at the Third BRICS Legal Forum, on this 12th day of September, Two Thousand Sixteen, we, the members of the Legal Communities of BRICS

Recognize and applaud the establishment of International Dispute Resolution Centre for BRICS and Emerging Economies at New Delhi (New Delhi Centre), which will have its own expert committee on lines of the Shanghai Expert Committee and will co-opt members from other BRICS jurisdictions, which will also be establishing similar Centres for Dispute Resolution through arbitration as also Mediation on the lines of the Mediation Centre for BRICS and Developing Countries at Ekaterinburgh (Russia).

Propose to establish Professional Committees for BRICS Dispute Resolution and Mediation to furthering deepen the development of "diversified dispute resolution mechanism" created during the Second BRICS Legal Forum with the objectives to create a platform for experience sharing and to work together to finalize its membership and goals to achieve the objective of creating world class institutions which will emerge as a fora of choice for dispute resolution for not only BRICS countries but for the entire emerging world.

Resolve to develop and sign a Memorandum of Understanding to create BRICS Expert Committee for enhancing capacity building and promoting understanding of Financial and Tax Law in each of the BRICS countries by making suggestions to respective governments in order to take forward the intention of BRICS countries to strengthen financial cooperation and trade announced firstly in the third BRICS Summit in Sanya in 2011 where Sanya Declaration was signed.

Recognize the importance of establishment of BRICS New Development Bank that provides a powerful instrument for increasing BRICS financial cooperation, being mindful of a context where emerging market economies and developing countries continue to face financial constraints and legal barriers to address sustainable development needs and to help achieve those aims by assisting the governments by providing inputs, advice and suggestions for bringing transparency in governance and operational structures of BRICS NDB.

Affirm that the Forum strives to retain and maintain its character as an independent and non-political platform for the legal communities in BRICS, the wider geo-political realities in seeking rebalancing of power in global trade and economic regime remains central to its objectives, which realities impact not just the trade but through subtle crafting of governing instruments, practices, currencies valuation, financial networks and institutions, and other such devices, impact the valuation of economic output of countries, which ultimately has impact on the capacity of these countries to service the basic requirements of their peoples, without which any attribution of basic human rights would remain empty vessels.

Cognizant of the fact that the global regimes being pushed for acceptance and recognition as preconditions for investment in the form of labour standards, environment and intellectual property regimes, may have restrictive propensity, and tend to become discriminatory in operation and can work as devices to pare down cost advantage and render manufacturing uncompetitive, while at the same time pushing demands to open markets, thereby seeking to inhibit the engines of economic growth and reducing the capacity of governments to invest in human capital, skill development and for bringing and enabling more and more people in economic value generation pool.

Resolve to create within BRICS the standards and principles regarding labour standards, environmental standards, intellectual property regimes which are in harmony with the needs and requirements of BRICS countries to serve their vast populations.

Recognize that all these endeavours are rooted in the concept of the Rule of Law which attains its fruition only through substantive equality and economic empowerment and upliftment of standards of life of the entirety of populations by building inclusive systems in contradistinction to the systems that create privileges mainly for those who already are well endowed economically.

Resolve to adhere to and respect the principle of the Rule of Law in order to facilitate certainty in promoting relationships and trade within and amongst BRICS countries.

Deem it an article of faith that any investor entity, foreign or domestic, which makes investment, as a business proposition, to profit from exploitation of natural resources or access to local markets, is solely responsible for being diligent to safeguard its commercial interests, and cannot claim reparation of losses through treaty arbitration or other such devices, from sovereign governments, at the cost of local populations, to serve whom such investment proposals brought in the first place. In this regard the Forum will seek expansion of Universal Declaration of Human Rights, to include a right of local populations and communities against economic exploitation and exclusion from their traditional source of livelihood and way of life, without consent and advance provision for fair compensation and rehabilitation.

Underline our support for a fair, just, inclusive and orderly international financial order and creation of laws and legal frameworks that equally benefit developed and emerging world.

Resolve to create and facilitate networks of lawyers and alliance of law firms in BRICS countries to enable them to grow and compete with the global law firms. To achieve this objective the Forum will canvass with the respective Governments to promote mutual preferential access for BRICS countries legal professionals.

Undertake to appoint and designate a nodal person for each country to facilitate coordination and communication for ongoing deliberations in order to fine tune and establish operational structures for implementation of the Forum agenda and constitute working groups to finalize the cooperation and working frameworks and finalization of MoUs and terms of reference of Committees etc. envisaged in this declaration and share this with other member organizations at the conclusion of the Third Forum.

Authorize and Mandate the Bar Association of India to develop and host bricslegalforum.com website by firstly putting the agreed content in terms of Brasilia, Shanghai and New Delhi Declarations in English, Chinese, Portuguese and Russian, with translated texts to be provided by respective national organizations, and to upload further material on the basis of consensus arrived by communicating through nodal contact for each country.

Resolve that wherever possible and required cooperate with respective Governments and other organizations, will hold meetings and deliberations of legal experts of BRICS in order to present cohesive stand and formulations to international bodies to ensure that global legal and policy frameworks that are being developed are inclusive and amenable to the needs and aspirations of the emerging world and BRICS countries.

Luiz Tarcisio Teixeira Ferreira, Brazil Chair of Co-ordination "BRICS, USA and Italy" the Order of Lawyers of Brazil	Alexey A. Klishin, Russia Chairman of Legal Commission of modern integration process, Association of Lawyers of Russia
K.K. Venugopal, India Co-Chair, Third BRICS Legal Forum	Dr. Pinky Anand, India Amity University, Noida, Uttar Pradesh, India
Chen Jiping, China Executive Vice-President of China Law Society	Lin Yanping, China Vice-President of East China University of Political Science and Law
Mvuso Notyesi, South Africa Co-Chairperson of the Law Society of South Africa	

V.4.   2ⁿᵈ BRICS Legal Forum: 15 Oct. 2015, Shanghai (CHN)

II BRICS Legal Forum SHANGHAI DECLARATION

1.   We, represented by legal communities of BRICS member states, met in Shanghai, China, on 15 October, 2015 at the II BRICS Legal Forum, which was held under the theme "Legal Cooperation: Towards a BRICS Community of Shared Destiny". We discussed legal issues of common interest in respect of rule of law, financial cooperation and dispute settlement mechanisms as well as key priorities in respect of further strengthening and broadening our intra-BRICS legal cooperation. We emphasized the importance to strengthen BRICS solidarity and cooperation, and decided to further enhance our strategic partnership on the basis of principles of openness, solidarity, equality, transparency and mutual understanding, inclusiveness and mutually beneficial cooperation. We agreed to step up coordinated efforts in responding to emerging challenges, ensuring peace and security, promoting development in a sustainable way for the benefit of our peoples and the international community. We confirmed our intention to further enhance the collective role of our countries in international affairs towards development of a more just and fair global economic and social order, based on the principles of equality and the rule of law.

2.   We firmly believe the BRICS Legal Forum plays an important role in upholding rule of law, economic and social development, and to facilitate closer partnership of BRICS member states, in developing a legal framework and normative structure for a new world economic order that caters to the needs of more than half of the population of the world. We recognize the Brasilia Declaration adopted at the I BRICS Legal Forum as the guideline of expanding and deepening the legal exchange and cooperation among our member states, and we are committed to take all such necessary and further steps for effective implementation of the Brasilia Declaration as decided during the I BRICS Forum and reaffirmed and reiterated at Shanghai during the II BRICS Legal Forum.

3.   We note that in the context of globalization, an open international environment with fair, reasonable and equitable rules is necessary for the economic transformation and development of emerging markets. We underline the importance of legal diplomacy in promoting greater democratic, more lawful and more balanced international relations, and in advancing reform in global governance. With a focused attention to the latest developments and implementation outcomes of global legal systems and policies, we are willing to coordinate international relations through legal approaches to seek shared interests and common ground while putting aside differences, and to promote communication and collaboration on legal issues in a proactive and practical way by holding regular international conferences for extensive exchange of information and ideas. In this regard, we aim to make contributions to the development of global legal systems and policies.

4.   We recognize the fundamental legal, political and constitutional values, concepts, cultures and principles of all countries who are involved in the Forum, with a common aim to promote and protect the Rule of Law and universal human rights. We acknowledge and safeguard the independence and integrity of the legal profession.

5.   We speak highly of the formation of the Steering Committee of BRICS Legal Forum during the meeting on 13 October 2015 in Shanghai and are committed to finalize its structure. We believe the Steering Committee has a fundamental role in the development planning, strategy formulation, articulation and synergies that unite the legal communities to put forward the BRICS Legal Forum. We agree that the Steering Committee meet at least once a year called by the host association of BRICS Legal Forum that very year.

6.   We attach a great value of legal research within BRICS countries and the foundation of the BRICS Legal Research Institute in ECUPL, the BRICS Law Institute in Ural State Law University and the research unit within the Centre for Comparative Law in Africa at the University of Cape Town. Such institutes, together with those to be opened in other partner universities, will provide a platform for the BRICS legal academia and professionals to carry out fundamental, systematic and prospective studies in law, centering on the issues arising from legal theories and practice in BRICS cooperation.

7.   We support the initiative of "The Alliance of BRICS Law Universities" put forward by Pontificial Catholic University of Sao Paulo, Ural State Law University, Kutafm Moscow State Law University, Amity Law School, Indian Law Institute, East China University of Political Science and Law and University of Cape Town called, with "equality, collaboration, openness and diversity" as guiding rules, aiming to promote the bilateral and multilateral legal cooperation among the universities of BRICS member states to which the Alliance is opened, and carry out the cooperative education and training program, target to collaboratively cultivate a number of jurists and lawyers with global outlook and understanding of international legal affairs who will be able to provide intellectual support to governments, legal professionals, transnational enterprises of BRICS member states. In this regard, we highly appreciate the establishment of "BRICS Legal Training Base".

8.   We recognize that with the development of the economic relations among BRICS countries, a fair and efficient dispute resolution mechanism with BRICS characteristics within BRICS countries is necessary to resolve increasing cross border disputes. We are pleased to announce the inauguration of Shanghai Center for BRICS Dispute Settlement and its expert committee. We shall promote concrete measures to enhance the mechanism to set up centers in Brazil, Russia, India and South Africa respectively, embodying the principles of the Shanghai Declaration, aiming to provide a comprehensive network for legal professionals of the BRICS countries to cooperate effectively and efficiently in dispute settlement, while satisfying the practical needs of these countries for international collaboration.

9.   We note the importance of strengthening the cooperation intra-BRICS construction of financial legal framework.

10. Legal communities of Brazil, India, Russia, South Africa and China express their sincere gratitude to China Law Society and East China University of Political Science and Law for hosting the II BRICS Legal Forum in Shanghai.

11. Legal communities of Brazil, Russia, China, and South Africa convey their appreciation to India for its offer to host the III BRICS Legal Forum in 2016 and extend their full support to that end.

Signed by:

Luiz Tarcisio Teixeira Ferreira	VIktor BLazheev
Brazilian Bar Association	Association of Lawyers of Russia
K.K. Venugopal	Bao Shaokun
Bar Association of India	China Law Society
Xolani Maxwell Boqwana	Salvatore Mancuso
Law Society of South Africa	University of Cape Town
LIU Xiaohong	CAO Hua
East China University of Political Science and Law	Bureau of International Cooperation, The Supreme People's Procuratorate of the PRC
LIN Guoping	Patrick Lane SC
Shanghai Law Society	Arbitration Foundation of Southern Africa
Luis Fernando Massonetto	LI Xueyao
University of Sao Paulo Professor	Shanghai University of Finance and Economics
Danil Vladimirovich Vinnitskiy	Sh. Rakesh Munjal
Ural State Law University	India Law Institute
CHEN Yundong	Pinky Anand
Yunnan University	Amity University
SHAO Xinlian	TANG Yi
Beijing Law Society	Chongqing Law Society
WEI Jun	QI Kang
Guangxi Law Society	Yunnan Law Society
Patrick Lane SC	Li Zhigang
Africa ADR	Shanghai International Arbitration Center
June Conolly	LV Hongbing
Association of Arbitration (Southern Africa)	Grandall Law Firm
LV Yi	YANG Song
Shanghai Junyue Law Firm	Liaoning University
Claudio Finkelstein	
Pontifical Catholic University of Sao Paolo	

V.5.   1st BRICS Legal Forum: 12 Dec. 2014, Brasilia (BRA)

BRASILIA DECLARATION

WE, represented by legal communities of the BRICS member states having gathered here in Brasilia, on this 12nd day of December Two Thousand and Fourteen.

BELIEVING in the objectives of the BRICS nations as meeting the common interests of emerging market economies and developing countries:

SHARING the common aspirations of our people m the BRICS nations to live in peace, freedom, social justice and economic prosperity.

UNDERLINING our support for a multipolar, equitable and democratic and democratic world order, based on international, law, equality, mutual respect, cooperation, coordinated action and collective decision-making of all States.

CONSCIOUS that in order to realize the said objectives it is necessary to develop co-operation among legal communities oi the BRICS nations.

AWARE of the fact that law and the legal community have a role to play in developing a legal framework and normative structure for a new world economic order that caters to the needs of more than half the population of the world.

DO HEREBY establish jointly the BRICS Legal Forum.

I.   OBJECTIVES

The objectives of the BRICS Legal Forum shall be:

(i)   To promote the legal diplomacy, bring together the legal communities of the BRICS member states for closer cooperation, and promote exchange of legal theory and practice.

(ii)   To use and develop law as an instrument of social change for development as well as for building co-operation among the peoples of the BRICS nations, facilitate BRICS cooperation mechanism, and explore more international space for the development of BRICS nations.

(iii)   To make joint efforts for the reinforcement and strengthening of the rule of law, social, economic and human rights.

(iv)   To cooperate in advancing the status of legal professionals, in developing the legal profession and the scope of its activities and in strengthening the activities of the legal profession and the judiciary in the BRICS countries.

(v)   To interact with international legal associations worldwide for the purpose of advancing the objectives mentioned herein.

II.   Language

Portuguese, Russian, English and Chinese serve as official language of BRICS Legal Forum, however the communications between the Members will be in English.

III.   Vision, Mission and Strategy:

Vision

We shall co-host a high-level forum, thereby promoting the exchanges and cooperation between legal communities, governments and business communities of BRICS member states, and providing legal support for each of our countries in its all-round development.

Mission

To realize the Vision, the Forum will endeavor to

1. Provide a platform for high-level interactions between legal professionals, government functionaries and business leaders, to promote mutual understanding of diverse BRICS legal systems, policy and legal frameworks, and foster a deeper sense of social responsibility among legal organizations within the region, contributing for the promotion of the Rule of Law, social, economic and cultural developments.

2. Assist in development of a conducive legal and policy framework for the growth of business and trade in the BRICS countries, thereby helping create greater investment, trade and employment opportunities, paying the way for the BRICS countries to realize the harmonious developmental goals to serve the needs, requirements and aspirations of their peoples.

3. Strive to promote excellence in legal profession and human resources in BRICS region and undertake and encourage legal research on issues of common importance and provide legal intellectual support for development of policy and legislative frameworks.

Strategy

The Forum will pursue its Mission through the adoption and implementation of appropriate strategies, which will include:

1. Convening conferences, seminars and lectures on a regular basis, to discuss the important emerging legal issues in the area of policy, governance, economic regulation, sustainable development, environment and socio-cultural aspects.

2. Cooperate with the other organizations within this region to promote and strengthen the exchange and cooperation among the legal organizations, education and research institutions, business enterprises, governments and non-government groups in matters of trade, investment, etc.

3. Pursue both independent and collaborative research activities, especially in the areas of legal research, financial cooperation, alternative dispute resolution, legal services and legal professional training, which will contribute to the overall goals of the Forum.

4. Establish a legal think-thank to act as a brains trust to help power the BRICS countries to be at the forefront of world trade and economic order to bring equal opportunities and benefits to half the population of the globe which the BRICS countries together account for.

IV. Founding Organizations and Participating Members

Founding organizations of BRICS Legal Forum include Bar Association of Brazil, Association of Lawyers of Russia, Bar Association of India, China Law Society, Law Society of South Africa, the University of Cape Town and East China University of Political Science and Law.

BRICS Legal Forum is an open platform, and we expect the legal authorities, legal organizations, universities and other legal units to take part in and become the Participating Members of the Forum.

Mr. Luiz Tarcisio Teixeira Ferreira The Brazilian Bar Association	Mr. Alexey A. Klishin Association of Lawyers of Russia
Mr. Prashant Kumar The Bar Association of India	Mr. Bao Shaokun China Law Society
Mr. Mas Boqwana Law Society of South Africa	Professor Salvatore Mancuso University of Cape Town
Professor Du Zhichun East China University of Political Science and Law	

INDEX